MATTER *matters*

MATTER *matters*

End of Life Reflections on Paganism

MICHAEL YORK

CONTENTS

Acknowledgements

There has been just about everyone in my life I would wish to mention and express my gratitude for having known and for having been a part of what seems to me to have been a staggering marvel of engagement and accumulating joy. Some, but only a vast minority, are mentioned in the pages to follow.

Among the foremost who are yet still among the living that I can still thank are my wife Nancy York as well as the others of our San Francisco 'family': Coral Paris (mother of Richard's daughter Iana), Rosanne Donahue, and Anna Quinn Wilson (formerly Nancy Bourgeois). Out of touch is Jan Parisi and lost to us are John Wilson, Warren Lee, Lynne Eggers (the 'saint') and Marlowe Rosin. The 'immediate' London family are Gin Dunscombe, Rix Pyke, Chloe Dunscombe, 'Woody' Pyke, Sylvester Sewell and Cosmos Pyke, but it extends much further.

Among those who moved onto the great unknown, there are just too many, but I miss dearly Peggy Wilson, Robert Pfeiffer, Donald Lipper, Joop Slagter (my first lover), Vassili Lambrinos (my second lover), Alan Bates, Toni Morgan, Stephanie Freydont and Shirley Eastham. Then, too, I wish to mention my parents Otto and Myrth York as well as my grandmother, Gertrude Zeth Brooks, author of *First Ladies of the White House*.

There are many too many more dear friends that could be mentioned with hopefully not offending those who I am not mentioning here. I shall signal my oldest friend from childhood days, Fred Profeta; my first publisher and subsequently dear friend Jay Wilson; Jezznette Wilcox (my cousin); John Walder (college roommate); Bron Taylor (colleague and friend); Barbara McGraw (another colleague and friend); Marie-Laure Legroux (a French love); Meg Sanders (an English love); Vicky Enea (a love); Amy Whitehead (a favourite student); Charles Leslie (Leslie-Lohman Museum of Art); Claire Bellenis (my dear Heathen love); Freeman Gunter (DocHabib); Natacha Dauphin (a 'daughter'); and Jim Clark (artist and steady friend).

There are seven people I would like to thank in particular for the production of this autobiography. Theitic for his original inspiration, feedback and encouragement. Stead Steadman provided me with a detailed commentary and most helpful suggestions. Drew Stevens asked if he could do the type setting and has as a result been amazing to work with. The thanks of the book are primary due to him. My gratitude extends further to Frances Ross for designing the book's beautiful covers. Alexander Nielsen and Helen Copper of Amazon Publishing have been seminally important. It has been a pleasure to work with them both. And finally, my marital partner, Richard Switzler, who has never ceased to entertain and challenge my thought for nearly a half-century and who has been the loving company that has completed my life itself.

CHAPTER ONE

Heathen folkish religion / Haight-Ashbury / Central California Indians / escape to Europe; New Religious Movements and New Age / paganism-Paganism / pagan pluralism / telluric paganism; possible end of civilisation / Brexit / confederacy / America First; childhood encounters with nature / Buffalo, Maplewood and early childhood / Joseph Noble / early altars / early love of music / Ferm's *Encyclopedia of Religion* / Aten & God / high school / end of WWII / New York / graduation / Purdue University / more music / the walkout / Easter break and Brahman / staying awake / Mother / New York University / University of California Santa Barbara-Huxley-peyote in San Francisco; Laredo & peyote / Oslo / Joop Slagter / Trump / European travels / Will Durant / Venice / youth / Grafing / Haight-Ashbury / Anton LaVey / my 30th birthday / fleeing to Europe / Roselle's statement / Amsterdam & the house / Haight-Ashbury / Daesh / the UBI; the dragon / ecology; Wales & the Mabinogion / the 'Draft Pagan Community Statement on the Environment' / my Lotus World / the earth's aura / magic-religion-science; Scotland & American Exceptionalism / Orkney / Populism / world problems / French politicians and imperial Rome / the Dhaka murders / music & health / Giulio Regeni / the underbelly of civilisation / Christianity, Abrahamism & religion / Beirut, Bataclan in Paris, San Bernardino / my 'Bottom Line' response & the Abrahamic 'God' / pluralist society / *je suis Charlie* aftermath / satire / beauty as truth or value / religious violence / humour / the natural flow / art / divine miraculousness / anthropocene or anthropocide / Lucifer the light-bearer / 13.5% of the world's population is hungry / accusations of 'toxicity' / Judaism, Deism, my mantra & co-nature / pantheism & health / Jeremy Corbyn / the British cocoon; marijuana and entheogenic sacraments

The notion of pagan spirituality and practice is something to which I have devoted my life. At heart I perceive paganism as youthful and energetic – particularly attractive to the young. But what is it for the full range of life – including where I find myself at present at the threshold of winter's age if not beyond? I will admit for a start that pagan spirituality is increasingly a conundrum. More and more there appears to be little agreement on what it is, what it possibly should be, or what it could be. It ranges in part from something like Bron Taylor's Dark Green Religion and Mark Green's Atheopaganism to the folkish 'religion' of Heathenism. This last I find horrid in its racist chauvinisms and predominantly small-mindedness;

the former two are admirable but also in some respects deficient. What I wish to do in the following pages is explore how I have encountered pagan spirituality and in contrast to the other competing and established religions such as Christianity, Islam and Hinduism. As I feel more acutely every day that my life, a wonderful life for which I am constantly grateful, is passing into its final days, I wish to consider both the seminal importance of what I still hold to be a sustainable and important outlook and attempt to gage both its validity and meaning in our topsy-turvy world that dances frenetically between advance and regression and a seemingly likely environmental catastrophe.

My musings and examinations will be random. Although I have become an academic, and by hook or by crook I even acquired a professorship, what follows here is not a scholarly work. Much of it will be personal in which I will try to explain who I am and what I have experienced over the long march of time and, consequently, maybe why I think the way that I do. There are of course many places in which I could start, but I wish briefly to sketch my philosophical or educational journey first.

I trace this voyage to some incomparable days in San Francisco. I was in my twenties, and the flower culture of Haight-Ashbury erupted all around me. I was living at the time in the Haight district on the corner of Carl and Cole Streets. These were unique and heady times, and as thrilling as they were, I also sought occasional escape into the rural countryside away from the city. The magnificence of the star-studded skies to be seen when beyond urban light pollution was to me simply overwhelming – reminiscent perhaps of summer camp times in my childhood but now even more intense and, yes, even magical. I became completely intrigued to understand how the indigenous Native Americans appreciated this stellar dazzle among which one felt that being able to grab a handful of stars was more than possible. What stories, what myths, did they have? As I explored Central Californian Indian culture, I discovered ironically that they had next to no stories about or names for the nocturnal lights, but what I did find was a beautiful and harmonious lifestyle shared between a host of different-language-speaking peoples (Pomo, Costanoan, Maidu, Miwok, etc.) that for all practical purposes had come to be obliterated by invading Euro-Americans.

My response to this finding was deep shame. I felt that unless I was willing to live in a teepee and adopt an indigenous way of living, I could not remain in America. The logical option for me was to immigrate to Europe from where my ancestors had come. As these were also the uneasy days of the Nixon administration, flight was doubly encouraged, and I managed to convince about half of our San Francisco-born 'family tribe' to flee with me. And once in Europe, I proceeded to investigate and uncover European ancestry – especially spiritual ancestry – as I had done with indigenous Californian peoples. The upshot of this exploration became my *magnum opus* on the Indo-European-speaking peoples, their myths and their cult. But then to get this work eventually published, at some point I realised that I would be obligated to read for a Ph.D. Eventually, I ended up with Kings College in London, and so my academic career began.

With my scholastic re-engagement, my interest has always been paganism, but at the time I began my Ph.D. studies there was no one who could monitor in the subject. Consequently, I commenced with religious studies and specifically with the area that has been called 'new religious movements' (NRMs). Even more specifically, I focused on the NRM that was becoming known as the New Age Movement. This would have been in the late 1980s – around the time my daughter was born (1989). In time, with some careful manoeuvring and navigation, I was able to extend my doctoral subject from New Age to include Neo-paganism. My project became one of comparing the two movements and discerning how they might be similar and how different. At this point, the New Age metaphor was frequently welcomed by Pagans (Vivianne Crowley, Mike Howard), and to some extent I thought of Neo-paganism as a branch or subgrouping of New Age itself. Much later, however, this has reversed for me, and I now tend to think of New Age as a subdivision of the broader category of Paganism. There is also here the question of small p versus big P, that is, paganism vis-à-vis Paganism. I will address this issue later but will state for now that my preference is for the former in which I approach pagan sentiment as first and foremost a noninstitutionalised spirituality.

It is important, nevertheless, to recognise that there are two types of pagans. The more comprehensive set includes anyone who identifies herself/himself as pagan. This takes into consideration gnostic pagans, folkish heathens and nature-oriented or nature-venerating atheists. In the overall spirit of the contemporary pagan pluralistic affirmation, from this perspective, paganism is inclusive and expressive of great variety. Given that the 'movement', if that is what it could be called, has no established leadership (e.g., a pope, a universally accepted charismatic figure, or adjudicating authority), there is no one who can legitimately say that someone who claims a pagan identity is not a pagan.

The other form of paganism and the expression with which I am principally interested and with which I personally identify I shall term 'telluric paganism'. These are people who not only cherish the earth as sacred in and of herself but also do not consider the material as other than and separate from the spiritual. We derive the term 'telluric' from the Roman name for the earth, the Latin equivalent of the Greek Gaia, who was known as the goddess Tellus. From *tellus* (genitive *telluris*) we derive our English word for something that pertains to or proceeds from the earth. However, the French cognate comes even more fully to the pagan understanding that I hold. *Tellurique* includes the connotation of an emanation that emerges from the earth. A classic application of the French term is suggested when horses rear up and refuse to cross a particular spot in, for instance, a forest journey. Perhaps in addition, the term might be used for something like the volcano, but within the European tradition of spiritual language, the volcano becomes a chief metaphor for what might be considered the anti-divine. Instead, it is probably more appropriate to regard *tellurique* and by extension *telluric* as expressive of the numinousness, such as belonging to the spring or well.

In other words, telluric paganism is a devotion to the earth as both the concrete metaphor of nature and as the chief source (perhaps only source?) of enchantment. It concerns both the natural and what I have come to prefer to speak of as the co-natural (in place of the preternatural and especially the supernatural). It is here where the telluric pagan differs from the secularist or atheist. There is not only a reverence for the earth or nature or both but also an understanding and acceptance of the magical. One of the 'fathers' of sociology, as well as the sociology of religion which appears to be its central and inaugural interest, is Max Weber (along with Emile Durkheim and Karl Marx), and Weber saw a diminishment in the human enterprise with the contemporary increase in bureaucracy and secular rationalization by Western society. Borrowing the term *Entzauberung* from the German poet Friedrich Schiller (*Ode to Joy*), Weber called for the necessity of 're-enchantment'. I think contemporary paganism both in its pluralistic broad sense but especially in its more specific telluric pagan formulations has been reborn in our times precisely out of this need to reintegrate the sacred with the profane. The thrust of the contemporary rebirth of pagan thought is to dissolve the 'iron cage' of disenchanted modernity without regressing into Abrahamic, Dharmic or secular paradigms. If secularism has freed many from the intimidations of Christian and Islamic fear and/or desires for worldly escape, it is paganism that progresses further and away from the purely nonreligious into an understanding and utility of thaumaturgic ecstasy. For me, this is the purpose and *raison d'être* of paganism in our world of today and tomorrow.

But if paganism – and particularly telluric paganism – is a necessary spiritual and cultural reflex, what has happened – or *is* happening – to its development? And what are the obstacles it faces even if and when it might 'get its act together'? This second question is a grim one in itself. According to Matt Taibbi, the recently published *Fire and Fury* foretells for most of the world 'the end of civilization'. Perhaps that is too extreme a consequence, but only perhaps. It certainly looks like radical change is imminent. We have recreated today something akin to the feudal divide of the Middle Ages – now one between the POP or point-one-percenters and the rest of us. The nonequality of wealth at present far exceeds the former Medieval wherewithal between the nobles and the serfs. I do not consider myself a communist – especially a Marxist, but I also have my doubts concerning socialism and in particular as it is being endorsed by Jeremy Corbyn. My sympathies might be libertarian but not in an Ayn Rand or Tea Party sense but instead as tempered by liberal values. I am well aware, however, that both 'liberal' and 'neoliberal' have become negatives. I blame the start of this transformation on presidential candidate Michael Dukakis who, when labelled with the alleged dirty word 'liberal' by Papa Bush and the Republican Party, sought at first to deny that he was and only several months later did what he should have done right from the start, namely, embrace the tradition and say yes, he was proud to be a liberal.

I detest the Conservatives or Tories and the Brexiters in particular. The 'Little England' mentality for me is regressive and pathetic and without any legitimate sense of imagination and adventure. I certainly admit that the European Union is in need of radical reform, but a much wiser course for Britain would appear to be not to rescind its ability to influence EU regulations let alone institutional structures. By leaving the Union, it is no longer in a position to do this. In the United Kingdom itself, my support is first for the Liberal Democrats and secondly for the Greens. In all, I want to consider myself a 'confederate' – uncapitalised since 'Confederate' carries the specific idea of the 'Confederate States of America', and this is not my intention. Rather, I want to support viably working alliances between independent but cooperating states or groups of people.

In the meantime, that is before we can achieve union through agreement or treaty – if ever, I am finding our world as a whole steadily splintering and becoming little more than a hodgepodge of countries that are inwardly focused and regressively concerned with evermore rules and regulations aiming for protection and fortress privacy. The labyrinth that results is one that is not commensurate with the aspirations toward human dignity that I remember being taught as a child. We are instead creating a nightmarish miasma that dwarfs our best potentials and, for the most part, allowing a peep of headless chickens to scramble haphazardly in the role of being our leaders. It would be risible if it were not so pathetic.

Less and less does there appear any genuine international cooperation. With such attitudes as 'America First' and totalitarian imposition in places like the Stans, several countries within Africa (e.g., Eritrea, Sudan) as well as Saudi Arabia, North Korea, presumably both Russia and China, and, I would include, Turkey, Myanmar, Belarus and increasingly even that 'great bastion of democracy', the United States, the planet becomes for evermore an 'every man for himself' divisive dissociation. With our world presently facing such catastrophes as climate change, pollution, overpopulation, poverty and destructive conflict, the need and legitimate aesthetic can only be for us all to work together in the light of global vision and future sustainability. Perhaps this is where paganism becomes progressively important, but the pagan continual marginality and fractured and noncohesive mode of operation makes its necessary contribution all the more unlikely. It is to be granted that assessing a nation as a dictatorship is often a subjective judgment and coloured by bias. It is enough perhaps to recognise that democratic freedom is often a nonexistent for many, many people and that, at the same time, real worldwide problems do exist that are not being adequately addressed. Do we, therefore, remain heedless and hide our heads in an ostrich fashion, or do we wake up and end the nightmare?

But can we wake up? Can we end the horror? Or can we instead simply keep successfully out of sight? Around us is a perpetual oscillation – one between the type of mentality that sponsors renditions (CIA flights from rustic North Carolina) and that of a couple who shackle and malnourish their thirteen children (in California), and simultaneously it is a sell-off from sea to shining sea! For the rest, it is bureaucracy in the most stifling of soul-arrestment along with the plethora of social network preoccupation and online inundation. We must 'pay our fair share', but what is fair and what is reasonable payment? Who truly has the moral and objective authority to say?

We can ask these kinds of questions, or we can ignore them. And ignoring often appears to be the easiest for most of us. But asking them results for the greater part in frustration for the those of us who do. And yet, in all this, I suspect that a pagan orientation – to the degree that it escapes sectarian restriction as well as petty personal rivalries and inflated bids for self-aggrandisement – offers the best navigation and chance for locating viable solutions.

As a child, I enjoyed lying on the ground and looking upward into the leafy canopy of a tree or the patterns of clouds in the sky. I also delighted in the woodlands, brooks, meadows, rivers, matinal bird song and the expanse, waves and salty aroma of the seashore, but whether any of this could be interpreted as paganism, I have my doubts. These were the pleasures most any child would have when given the opportunity. My fortunate circumstances were to have had most of my early years in the suburban reaches of New York City and bordering access to the South Mountain Reservation. I had been born in Buffalo, New York – maybe only days before or after the Second World War began. My father was austere and brilliant. My mother was warm, elegant and beautiful. Gershwin's *Summertime*, 'my daddy's rich and my mama's good looking', could have been written for me. An early memory is that of circling around the block on which we lived with one part encompassed by night; the other in day. But this could not have really happened. I do remember having a hand-puppet of Hitler with a string attached to the nose and with a ring on the other end. The idea was to swing the ring so that it looped over the figure's large nose. I do not think I could ever do it. The war ended, and I was with my grandparents in Manhattan when it did. I remember in Bryant Park passageway tunnels through the mountains of newspapers that had been thrown from windows in celebration – the walls of which towered over my head.

My childhood was reasonably happy. I grew up in suburbia fourteen miles as the crow flies from the centre of Manhattan. My hometown of Maplewood, New Jersey could easily have been the prototype of Peyton Place. My father and I were locked into some kind of competitive relationship from times before I could even remember. My mother was the sunshine and did her best to make the early years for me and my younger brother and sister complete and joyful. We lived an upper middle-class life. Because of its educational system, my parents had chosen Maplewood. It had been ranked the second best in the country at the time. The best was that of Evanston, Illinois, but my mother, perhaps wisely, refused that possibility saying that it was too near to her in-laws. But it was that choice of schools for which I have always been grateful to my parents for having provided.

Much of my earliest years was a fog. I had begun kindergarten in Maplewood where the agony of learning how to tie my shoes was excruciating. For my first-grade year, my parents had moved to a different town and then subsequently returned to Maplewood. But the one school system taught reading by sight whereas in the Maplewood-South Orange school system, we were taught to read phonetically. As a result of being introduced to two different methods at a critical moment, I have always since had difficulty in reading and remain to this day a slow reader. I also cringed with the all-too-frequent spelling tests as well. I could rarely complete them and would stuff the unfinished exams into my desk. There followed one day an embarrassing moment when our teacher came up to my desk with a waste paper basket and had me empty the contents of my desk into it. But this was also thrilling because I was not going to have to finish all those unfinished and unbearable spelling tests. Grade school eventually finished and was succeeded by junior high school, and for some reason with that change, I was able to 'wake up' and transformed from a below-average student to an above-average one. My high school years were some of the happiest of times. I had been given the advice that these were the years of unbounded freedom in which I had no real responsibilities. Those would come later; this was instead the moment to enjoy.

Whether or not my pagan inclination began with my childhood encounters with nature, I remember Joseph Noble displaying to our evening fellowship at our local Methodist church his collection of marvellous Dravidian statues including those of Vishnu, Shiva and Parvati. Mr. Noble was at the time the vice director of operations for the Metropolitan Museum of Art. He subsequently gained renown by discovering that several supposedly ancient terra-cotta Etruscan warriors were forgeries. He was proved to be wrong when later he claimed that a famous Greek horse statue in the Met's collection was also bogus. Still later, he became the director of the Museum of the City of New York.

If my idolatrous adoration began with the presentation of the Hindu *murti* or figures or if it was something that preceded, I can no longer remember, but from an early age I assembled altars and would pray to all gods. I lit candles and incense and viewed my surroundings through the filtering light of a glass of red wine. My parents had a record collection, and my mystical journeyings were accompanied by the likes of Stravinsky's *Firebird Suite, Petrushka* and *Le Sacre du Printemps,* Brahms' *Song of Destiny,* Mendelssohn's *A Midsummer Night's Dream,* Cole Porter's *Night and Day,* Rimsky-Korsakov's *Flight of the Bumble Bee* and Beethoven's *Ninth Symphony.* In time, I discovered Ravel's *Daphnis et Chloe* which has ever since informed a fundamental spirit that for me eventually I understood as pagan.

In my high school years, late teens, I became increasingly active in the Methodist Youth Fellowship of our local church, the Morrow Memorial Church, but this also functioned as a vehicle through which I could study all religions – all of which I found fascinating and offering valuable insights. And the church contained as well a copy of Vergilius Ferm's *An Encyclopedia of Religion* which became an early and lifelong favourite. But I began to wonder, as a Christian, if I should be worshipping all gods and not just the Christian 'God'. So in time, I abandoned the others but continued with both Yahweh and Akhenaten's monotheistic solar figure alone – considering them one-and-the-same.

My high school years for the most part were wonderful. On their eve, having been told that these would be the freest time ever and without the burdens and obligations that are part of adulthood, I should, to the best of my abilities and mindfulness, enjoy this freedom. And I did. My mother was incomparably easy. If and when I did not want to go to school for the day but instead to Manhattan, she would always allow me and then would cover with some excuse for school. I did not take advantage of her laxity and do this overly often, but I have memories of wonderful wanderings in the city, visits to my great-aunt who reminded me of my grandmother, her sister, and to Champlain – a French restaurant with sawdust on the floor and swinging doors to the kitchen through which came the waiters carrying large round trays above a shoulder. And this was where I could order a glass of red wine with my luncheon meal from the age of fourteen. In addition, there was the colourful Washington Market dating from 1812 that occupied a full block in lower Manhattan that also had sawdust-covered floors. This Tribeca marketplace specialised in produce and was occupied primarily by family-run stalls. Both the Champlain and the market are long gone but still in my memory belong to the thrill of the New York I originally knew.

Even earlier, when I was little, I would visit and stay with my grandparents who managed to keep a small apartment in the Harvard Club on 44th Street. The club was for men only, but my grandparents were master finaglers, and that is where they both lived when not in the rural countryside of West Nyack. I remember a dark old-fashioned New York apartment, mysterious and fascinating. There is also the memory repeatedly of falling to sleep with the thrilling sound from the clatter of dishes being washed in the restaurant next door. I must have been with my grandparents when the second World War ended for among my memories are the Bryant Park newspaper tunnels that had formed in celebration.

I can still remember around this time or shortly before it when, in the playground of my New Jersey suburbia grade school, my friend Fred told me that New York was just over the horizon to the east. I could not believe it. The 'capital of the world' is just there? New York City was a legend; how could it be so close and accessible? But it was! This was certainly an early magical revelation. Over the years that ensued, the urban mysteries that I came to treasure included seedy Nassau Street, the uptown Vedanta Society of New York, sultry summer nights in and around Washington Square Park, the Hoboken ferry & PATH tube, elegant bars in Rockefeller Center, the Village, Central Park, Broadway and theatre, 42nd Street, brownstones, high rises, restaurants, delis, 5th Avenue, St. Patrick's Cathedral, New York University, Lincoln Center, the Metropolitan Museum of Art, the Planetarium and Natural History Museum, the Museum of Modern Art, the Frick Museum, the Empire State Building, the Statue of Liberty, the Cloisters, the World Trade Tower Windows on the World, and all the endless diversity and cosmopolitanism of one of the most fascinating places in the world.

But the marvelousness of high school came to an end. I graduated. We all graduated I believe. Columbia High School had a tradition of the junior year students putting on a musical. Since we were fortunate to have Michael Small (*Klute, Marathon Man, The Parallax View*) in our class, we wrote our own musical, and Michael did the music. *Up 'n' At 'Em* became a thrilling and unifying experience. Previously, we were fairly evenly divided between Protestant, Catholic and Jewish and socialised within the community to which we belonged. But during the dress rehearsal, it seemed that everyone suddenly realised we were one. The parents of one gal were away in Miami for vacation, and she offered her house for our cast party. It became the only time my mother ever scolded me because, following the dress rehearsal and the two nights of performance, I did not get home until the wee hours of the morning. But we were one and have continued as such through class reunions ever since. Upon graduation, virtually all of us went to The Shore – for us, the New Jersey Atlantic coast that stretched south from Point Pleasant. A group of us rented a beach house in Chadwick Beach. Since I had not yet begun to drink alcohol – at least like the others, I became the nursemaid and the one who cleaned up after those of us who had become helplessly ill.

College extended both the highs and lows of my Suburbia years. My father insisted I enrol in Purdue University, his alma mater, for the study of chemical engineering. This last was not my forté, and although in high school, maths and science were among the subjects for which I had higher grades, in the college level it became increasingly clear that I do not possess an engineering mind. I had been above average with physics in high school, but this was not the case afterwards. Desperately wanting me to study chemical engineering, my father had said that afterwards I could do philosophy which was my desire. I remember while walking back and forth from classes fantasizing almost incessantly on living in ancient Egypt. This was an obvious escapism from the perpetual grind of subjects that were more ordeal than pleasure. Somehow, I had done fairly well during my first year of college, but I was repeating Quantitative Chemistry in my second. My nemesis seemed to be my lack of skill when using long awkward tongs to transfer a crucible containing something molten from a blazingly and extremely hot furnace to a weighing scale and when even breathing could nullify the imperative accuracy of the measuring process – one which required the highest degree of precision possible. For my sophomore year, I had moved from the Cary Quadrangle to the Sigma Phi Epsilon fraternity house which I have discovered online to have been suspended for four years (until 2020) for 'violations of alcohol, hazing and unregistered functions'. In my day, there was a concerted effort by the fraternity to excel on all fronts and be number one. I am not certain we achieved this, but we were at least close. When I was beginning as a pledge, two frat brothers asked if there was a pledge who would want to share their study room to enjoy and not mind listening to classical music. Expecting a stampede, I rushed afterwards to ask if I could be the one and since no one else had asked at all, I was accepted. One of my roommates became subsequently my 'Big Brother', and he introduced me to Renata Tebaldi through her entry moment in the opera *Madam Butterfly*. The local record store in Lafayette became a favourite hang-out where I discovered the musics of Walter Piston, Ernest Block, Howard Hanson, Maurice Ravel, Claude Debussy, George Enescu, Béla Bartók, Carl Orff, Carlos Chávez, Aram Khachaturian, Gustav Holst and Jacques Ibert. Through the sounds from these composers, my engagement with reverie softened the technical fastidiousness with which I was otherwise involved. And beyond my love of classical music, there is also jazz, and I already knew enough to be shocked when I went to a local concert in which Ella Fitzgerald was only one of the lead-in performers. But this was Indiana as well as the times.

The alcohol infringement that has contributed to my chapter's house present closing sparks recollections of binge episodes from my own time at university. There was a Lafayette bar to which we could go even as freshmen and be served. I had had a 'mother fixation' and often, from high school days on, would 'fall in love' with older women. The waitress in Lafayette was especially endearing, and this seemed to be reciprocal. Gigi always served us even though we were underaged freshmen. And of course, during these early times, I did not know how to drink and remember violently puking once during my freshman year. I had not yet learned what my mother had about not mixing alcohols and got ill once we were back at Cary Hall. At the fraternity, however, I have no recollection of alcohol consumption until our pledge walk-out. We had gone to the Sig Ep house at Miami University in Oxford, Ohio for the weekend during which alcoholic consumption was part of the occasion. What I do remember was drinking a pint of vodka and a half a pint of bourbon in fifteen minutes and then being chased by the others. I fell off a small cliff and yelled back to those trying to catch me to 'Watch out for that bump'. The last thing I do remember was running down a road, perhaps a highway, along the white line. I slept through all the rest – including a night of dry-heaving. When I woke the next morning in the Sig Ep fraternity house, I discovered that my brothers-to-be had been terrified as I had turned green during the night and yet none of us were legally of age to drink. The cook of the house, an African-American, gave me a glass of tomato juice which I immediately lost but still remember the taste of the freshly ground pepper he had added to it. Subsequent to all this, I could not even use aftershave lotion and did not touch strong alcohol again for a good decade.

Back at Purdue, I continued to struggle with chemical engineering.

When the Easter break of my sophomore year arrived, four of us drove to Fort Lauderdale where Bob Pfeiffer's parents lived. It was an incredible week of ecstasy, parties and thousands of university students crossing back and forth from the packed beach on one side of the road to the one-block stretch of packed bars on the other. In between the sun and sand and constant frolicking, I was now reading Will Durant's *The Pleasures of Philosophy*, and this work put the nail into the coffin of my Abrahamic faith – liberating me from the Methodism and Christianity in which I had been raised. I recall at the time looking out to the vacant expanse of lonely ocean from where we were all gathered on the beach and thinking that there was nothing apart from the vast impersonal *brahman* – a constant drone beneath the abandon of the present party time – and that the only valid goal was to achieve liberation through identity and/or fusion of my soul or Atman with this void.

Returning to Indiana, I realised at this point that I had to withdraw from university and my chemical engineering studies if I were to have any kind of decent grade average left. After what had been a wonderful week in Florida, it was back to the nightmare of lab work for Quantitative Chemistry. I do think that had I completed the course this second time, I would have passed, but after discussions with my fraternity brothers, I came to the decision that I should seek to withdraw mid-semester to preserve my overall grade score. My recourse accordingly was to keep myself awake for a week in order to look ill and withdraw on that basis. This became a surreal adventure. The nights were the most difficult. The Sigma Phi Epsilon fraternity pledges at this time adored me because, in order to keep myself awake, I cleaned the house from bottom to top throughout the night – washing and reinstalling the drapes, polishing the floors, setting the tables for upcoming meals and doing whatever I could to keep myself from falling asleep which otherwise would happen as I drank a glass of milk or tried to cross a street. I would even walk into trees. Finally, my appointment with the university's doctor arrived, but with my Florida tan, I did not look in the least bit sick. When the doctor's back was turned toward me, I would hold my breath and blow hard on my thumb in my mouth in hopes that I could make myself faint. But this did not work either. It did turn out that I had contracted histoplasmosis, but the tests had not yet come back from the laboratory, and this infection itself would have qualified me for withdrawal. Fortunately, the doctor, bless him, divined that something was wrong and got me to confess that I detested chemical engineering. He agreed then to give me a medical withdrawal from school if I would agree not to come back to Purdue to resume study in the same subject. I had no difficulty in making this compact.

Suddenly I was free! In quitting my studies, in my mind I was severing myself from my past and my family. I had resolved to hitchhike to New Orleans and find my future there. But first I had to sleep. I had written a noncommital letter to my parents who were able to 'read between the lines', and after an hour of sleeping after a week of not, I was awakened for a phone call from my father. Whatever I did say or was resolved not to say, he felt that he had completely failed with me. My complete lack of being informative or offering any explanation must have been devastating to my father. I do not remember much of our conversation, but the next thing I knew was that my mother was driving out to fetch me. However, in Pennsylvania she hit an ice patch on the road and flipped the car over. When she arrived finally at the fraternity house, she was black-and-blue from head to toe. I had no choice but to accompany her home to New Jersey.

What followed was an interlude of virtual oblivion. I do not remember much of the month or so that followed; my memory at this point is mostly a blank. My parents sent me to a vocational aptitude centre in Hoboken. What I appeared to be best suited for was hotel management, but the psychologist informed my parents that I was on the verge of a nervous breakdown and that it was imperative for me to be allowed to do whatever I wanted. I only knew that I did want to continue my education. The one class I had enjoyed at Purdue was the required one in English. The instructor had commented on the 'musical' way I composed sentences and paragraphs. This observation on his part was among the more encouraging things I had ever been told. What followed from this was a week working for my father at his stall for a chem show in the New York Coliseum formerly at Columbus Circle. And in addition to this was my enrolment into the summer school semesters at New York University. This last was heavenly. I had two semesters of art history and two of philosophy. I learned about Marxism, Positivism and Existentialism. But next to my father's exhibit in the Coliseum had been a delightful young lady who let me know about a university on a beach in California, namely, the University of California Santa Barbara. I had already applied to both the University of California in Berkeley and to the University of Southern California in Los Angeles – California being what seemed to me the furthest feasibly away from home. Hawaii would have been the next choice. My application to UC Berkeley was rejected, and while I had been accepted by the University of Southern California, I reapplied to the Santa Barbara campus and mentioned that my grandmother had taught for the

University of California in Berkeley. It was on the basis of my grandmother's matriculation that I was admitted to UCSB. When I received word of my acceptance, I had only one day to select a major. I skimmed the course listing, and as English sounded to me the most general and least technical available, I chose that and have never since come to regret that choice.

And California too was a dream. I had been there once previously for the Boy Scout Jamboree in 1953. Someone recently has mentioned the traffic lights that used to be on Highway 101, and there was the old Hollister Road that we would drive from Goleta into Santa Barbara. It was a much different California than it is today, and the UCSB campus was only into its second year since its transfer from the city of Santa Barbara itself – with an enrolment of approximately 2,000. My roommate John Walder was the last person successfully to enrol into the seminar that Aldous Huxley was offering, and this hurt, but I did attend every open lecture this hero of mine gave as well as his talk at the Vedanta Temple in Montecito. John mentioned that he had met a schoolteacher in San Francisco, Langston Bowen, and during our first break we went to him and had our initial experience of peyote. I had previously been inspired in this direction after reading Robert Gordon Wasson's 1957 *Life Magazine*'s article 'Seeking the Magic Mushroom'.

My memories of this magical time in the fog of southern San Francisco include Bartok's *Miraculous Mandarin* and Shostakovich's *Tenth Symphony* as well as, over the morning's breakfast pancakes, Bach's *Brandenburg Concertos*. And at this stage in what became the beginning of my shamanic career, I seemed to have been born with a mystical silver spoon in my mouth. Eventually I wandered out into the mysterious and unknown streets of the city, managed to get lost, and found some friendly and helpful San Franciscans who took me by car back to Langston's house. But through this all, new horizons and new worlds opened up to me for the first time. I had come to experience the otherworld.

The college days themselves have become dreamy recollections – of youthful memories, longing attractions, and stimulating education. The critic Hugh Kenner was at the time the chair of the English Department, and it was through him I learned the beauty and intrigue of etymological analysis. Both Aldous Huxley and Christopher Isherwood were Visiting Professors who gave provocative lectures. My orientation these days was with Vedanta, but I descended to the Inferno with Dante, ranged through America with Walt Whitman, and cascaded the supernal with William Butler Yates. And on more purely exploratory levels, there were experiments with datura and jimson weed and with whatever else was available at the time. And after graduation, thanks to Henry James, despite being allegedly only a state of mind, Europe became my destination.

Apparently, the human species is distinguishable in part through its lengthy neotenous condition. When I recollect my own childhood, I recall a prolonged period of murkiness and bewilderment. Much of my earliest memories comprises times of struggle – seeking to understand what was happening and finding a place of surviving within the mystery and confusion. I fantasise constantly upon far-off exotic and ancient times and places. It is clear to me now that I was an escapist dreamer. My earliest times were not especially overly happy ones, but I did thrill over an acceptance of nature spirits, fairies, the magical and wondrous. This hidden but almost visible dimension was thrilling and added to the call of the enigmatic other that was both immediate and faraway, palpable and distant. There were indeed moments, many in fact, of excitement, adventure and discovery. There were circuses, the Manhattan skyscrapers, the Jersey shore, the woods both on South Mountain and in summer camps, incense and candles, books and my parents' record collection that had also included Benny Goodman's Carnegie Hall concert and Bizet's opera *Carmen.*

If and when I reflect now on those earliest of years, much of it is embarrassing to me. I was never ambitious, never it seems now particularly discerning and instead subject much to the buffeting influences of occasion and environment while riveted by shameful lust and unfulfilled longing. I was scarcely ever in control save for when I was 'safely' within the prism of my private fantasies and vague but wished for expectations. My high school years somehow were good ones – not perfect but at least the dawning of sensual mystery and awareness of a freedom beyond further horizons. And all the same, I enjoyed school and learning and friendships.

The campus in Goleta was minute – especially compared to what it is today. I lived the first year in the Anacapa Hall on campus and my second year in Isla Vista. Hugh Kenner, Aldous Huxley and Christopher Isherwood among others were pure delights. For the intervening summer, I attended summer school at the University of California, Berkeley where I lived in a boarding house run by a German *hausfrau* and which subsequently was demolished for the creation of People's Park. And these were all intoxicating days. I adored California which still retained some of the mythic sheen of 1940s Hollywood. And, of course, that initial experience with peyote in San Francisco during our first semester break was momentous. My roommate

John and I continued with related experiments once we were living privately next to the coastal cliffs of Isla Vista. I also frequented the Vedanta Temple in Montecito across Ladera Lane from the residence of the head of the Art Department, Howard Fenton, who became a lifelong friend. When I graduated, my immediate destination was Europe.

In the summer that followed my college graduation, I drove my 1954 Chevrolet convertible from Santa Barbara across the United States – aiming first for Laredo, Texas. I could not find the Smith Cactus Farm and finally asked at the Jones Cactus Farm where it was. Mrs. Jones, a sweet grandmotherly type, asked what was it I wanted. I was reluctant to say but admitted 'Peyote.'

'Oh, I have that,' she replied.

From Laredo, I travelled to my family's home in New Jersey with the top down and the peyote buttons drying in the sun on the back seat of the car. Subsequently, after I had reached home, when I drove the automobile to the road inspection centre, I was stopped by a policeman and given a ticket for not having the required certificate on the windshield. He would not believe me that I was driving the car then and there for her inspection. So eventually I went to court. I could show that the vehicle had been inspected an hour after I had been given the ticket, and my mother attested 'Oh, yes!' when the judge asked if the car had sat on our property and had not been used since I had got her home. I remember zeroing in on the judge's gavel and thinking of Thor's hammer in connection with justice and being convinced that I would win. And I did.

While at home, and with the Mexican psychotropic cactus buttons having dried in the sun, I ground everything in an osterizer and then put it into horse-sized capsules. I sailed on the Norwegian-American line to Oslo. Such were the times, infinitely more amenable and unsuspecting of anything, that I never thought not to travel anywhere with what I was carrying – from Norway where my ship had completed its North Atlantic crossing to Morocco, from London to Istanbul, from Greece and Italy to Spain and Portugal as well as Germany, Switzerland and Austria. Each was an adventure and a constantly fascinating thrill. I was at last in Europe and thoroughly ready to confront the magic of the Continent. From Norway's capital, I hitchhiked first to Stockholm, but this was not easy. Finally, about midway, I noticed a Swedish bakery that had a collection of small foreign flags among the various pastries in its window. Reluctant but even more desperate, I entered the shop and asked if I could purchase their American flag. I think the shopkeepers were completely surprised by my request that they could not say no. With the flag now attached to my backpack, it was indeed much easier to get a ride. People wanted to practice their English.

Copenhagen and Hamburg were as fascinatingly marvellous as had been Oslo and Stockholm. In each as well as in between I soaked in my first impressions of Europe and the excitement of encountering foreign lands and customs. And then it was Amsterdam, and this felt immediately like a new home. I did not know at the time that it would indeed eventually become my first permanent home abroad, but there were post-graduate studies and the hippy counterculture times to come first. But already the canals of Amsterdam were a perpetual intriguing delight and every step revealed some new discovery. I found a hotel on the Weteringschans. It no longer exists, but from there I visited the city as well as the family of one of the Dutch hitchhikers I had met while seeking to find a ride out of Hamburg. I sat next to a man in the restaurant that I had chosen for a meal before a concert in the Oude Kerk. He had not known about this event, and we went together. Afterwards he introduced me to the D.O.K. De Odeon Kring, a postwar basement discotheque, was the first and largest centre of its kind for gay people in Europe. It had no signpost but instead only an inconspicuous locked door and a buzzer to signal for wishing to enter. There was a nominal entrance fee, and upon showing a passport one received a two-week pass. Years later when we had the commune in Amsterdam, the DOK became our second living room. But on my first occasion, I was more than thrilled when Joop, a schoolteacher, came up to me and asked me to dance – thrilled until he began to explain that he had an engagement that he had to attend shortly. I was still only 21 but reacted silently by thinking here is that 'old' come-on leading to nowhere. Had I already had that experience to be able to think as such? But then Joop offered for me to wait for him at his apartment on the Prinsengracht. He wrote the address on a match box cover and drew a picture of the door leading to his basement flat. I was a bit stunned when he then entrusted to me his keys – the bundle seemed close to containing a hundred items, and he laughed and explained that having so many keys made him feel important. I found his one-room basement apartment and, inside, virtually all my favourite musics from Billy Holiday and Ella Fitzgerald to Shostakovich, Ravel and Debussy. Over the years that followed, I have always rejoiced over the similarity between my musical tastes and Joop's. If

I came to discover a new composer whom I liked, almost always Joop was already familiar with and enjoying the same. Consequently, it was only natural on my first night on the Prinsengracht when I already was in heaven, that I asked Joop if he might be interested in trying some of the peyote I had brought with me to Europe and which filled the whole lower half of my knapsack. Since as a teacher he was not free during the week, perhaps the following weekend? Joop's answer was 'Yes'.

Our hallucinogenic excursion that followed became something more magical than I had ever previously experienced. We travelled to the Arcadian fields of ancient Greece and the land of the gods and through mystical dimensions and Xanadus of the cosmos. I knew Pan as well as that glorious mystery that allows one to know how beautiful and joyous it could be for *everyone*. At some point we donned long WWII army jackets and stepped outside into the glistening fog. Each drop of falling water was like a silent but miraculous lightning streak. Nearby was the Lemaire Gallery, and the idols of gods in the shop window became alive and pregnant with depthless inscrutability for us. In all, the venture was a supreme peak, what we referred to as a *moment supreme*, and my only regret was to wonder why this incomparable happening had to occur so early in my life. I could never reach such a height again, and any future prospect would be in some sense downhill. I suppose in some understanding it was the end for me of the unlimited promise of youth.

But it was several months or so later when I was lost on that small alley street in Venice. Yes, I was in Europe – magical Europe! And that 3 o'clock Wednesday moment before the Peggy Guggenheim Museum was as fortuitous as it ever gets. Surrealism remains the art form that for me at least most speaks to the psychedelic experience, and I remember floating for days after this serendipitous encounter in the dream-reality I had earlier come to know in Amsterdam. The crossing of paths is basically akin to the nature of spellbinding. And whether in a museum-temple, concert hall or woods or open space, it is the intersecting with spirit – perhaps through the image reflecting from a work of art or the passing of a warmer segment of air on its way past to somewhere else – that occasionally forms the medium by which we might recall enchantment and the holiness of life.

In recollection, that wonderful time in 1961–1962 was seemingly completely different from the feuds and debates of today: Trump and his Mexican wall and May and her refusal of a second referendum on Britain's exit from the European Union. Even worse, of course, at my current time of writing, are the migration crisis the Continent faces, the ongoing war and starvation in Yemen, and the civil unrest of Syria, Iraq and Afghanistan as well as Africa's calamities and the Mexican drug war let alone the conflicts of Israel-Palestine, Kashmir, Myamar, Libya, Ukraine and the Philippines. Then too we have at present or have recently had such dictatorships as those of Omar al-Bashir in Sudan, Kim Jong-il in North Korea, Alexander Lukashenko in Belarus and Iran's Guardian Council of mullahs. Hardly less frightening are the far-right conservative and/or populist heads of state like Brazil's Jair Bolsonaro, Hungary's Viktor Orbán, Narenda Modi in India, Recep Erdogan of Turkey, Poland's Andrzej Sebastian Duda, and Czechia's Andrej Babiš and Miloš Zeman. And now too, of course, Belarus' Alexander Lukashenko. By contrast, my early time in Europe simply coincided with the Cold War and in between the Bay of Pigs Invasion and the Cuban Missile Crisis. There were also the Vietnam and Portuguese Colonial wars, but these were in different and faraway parts of the world. My political awareness and comprehension of the time appears to me little different than that of my own children today – both still in their late twenties/early thirties.

Instead of the underbelly of corruption and savagery that was doubtlessly no less operative then as now, Europe was a wondrous celebration for the most part – successfully re-emerging from World War II horrors. To shower in the day, we still had to find a public bathhouse, and refrigerators were virtually nonexistent. When I first moved to Europe nearly a decade later, the reduced standards of living were still dominantly operative, though within a mere two years later they had substantially vanished.

But as it still is, Europe at the time was to be seen. So eventually I departed from Amsterdam and hitchhiked first to Brussels – described by the family I stayed with as an island of French in a sea of Flemish. My mother had gone to a reception for returning European exchange students and then sent me a list of possible contacts. I used the addresses. In Belgium, I was feasted by the Spehl family not only with delicious food but with museums, churches, sightseeing and an excursion to Bruges – certainly one of the most charming medieval centres to be found anywhere and into our present times.

But finally, it was time to continue my travels. I was taken to the outskirts of Brussels to the road that led to Paris. There had to be at least thirty others along the highway who were hoping for a ride. I realised it would be impossible as I walked to the end of the queue and began to search a place where I could set up for the coming night. But that American flag did the trick, and while I was looking elsewhere, a car stopped and then took me the whole way to the Gare du Nord. Since I was being driven, I did not have a chance to change money into French francs at the border. So I went immediately to the bureau in the Paris train station to find that it had just closed for the night. I asked where it was possible to exchange and was directed to a hotel opposite the station. But reaching its *bureau de change*, it too had just closed. Here too, I asked the woman at the desk where it was possible to get some francs. '*sais pas, sais pas*!' was all I received indifferently. Welcome to Paris for the first time! With my sleeping bag, I searched for somewhere to spend the night. If there were possibilities such as around a church, they were always inaccessible by formidable fencing. Finally, I located a bush in the Parc de Buttes-Chaumont under which I had my first night in the City of Lights.

Was I yet a pagan at this point? I would need to say no. It was in my little more than three-and-a-half academically depressing semesters at Purdue University studying Chemical Engineering, when I had read Will Durant's *The Pleasures of Philosophy: A Survey of Human Life and Destiny* that, as a result of both my difficulties with my study program and the insight gained from Durant, I lost my belief in the Methodism in which I had been raised (I even had played the part of Charles Wesley in a play while at Purdue). Henceforth, I came to range principally as an atheist to, at best, a profoundly detached acceptance of Hinduism's coldly impersonal Brahman. If I can remember correctly, this would have been my spiritual sentiment during my early days of European vagabonding. Certainly, the corporeal tones and cosmic rainbows of touchable colours I had experienced in San Francisco, Santa Barbara and Amsterdam allowed me a mystical enchantment within the otherwise empty and meaningless universe I had come to accept.

The Amsterdam experience re-impacted at full force once I found myself lost in Venice. Before that, I believe to Paris, my parents had sent me a Eurail Pass. With it, I travelled to Barcelona, Madrid and Lisbon including an excursion to Tangiers and continuing on through the south of France and the entire circumference of Italy and Sicily. The pass allowed unlimited free travel throughout Europe and in those days could only be purchased abroad (hence the need for my parents to purchase and send it) and was only for first class travel. Since it was something new, it was not until I reached the Riviera after Spain that a conductor noticed that my three-month pass had not yet been validated. Consequently, in all, I was able to travel altogether four-and-a-half months with that delightful card which allowed me, among other things to sleep comfortably on the train (instead of in a youth hostel) or in a train station itself.

In any event, wandering through the depthless and fascinating Venetian labyrinth, I came to the end of a street one day to a gate with a very small plaque indicating that it was the Peggy Guggenheim residence and museum open only from 3 to 5 on Wednesdays. I looked at my watch, and it was 3 o'clock – and it was Wednesday! I entered and what I first discovered was the most incredibly attractive staff of beautiful young men and women who welcomed me. Miss Guggenheim was continually on the telephone in the garden for the two hours I was there. There were poodles scampering about and, in the garden, tombstones marking the graves of previous poodles that had preceded the current pets. But what was the most memorable and stunning was the collection of Max Ernst's surrealistic paintings on the walls of the gallery sections – with large pornographic Polynesian statues set into the spaces between them. The museum still exists, but the art work on show is not what I encountered in the early 1960s. But on that occasion when the villa was still the residence of Miss Guggenheim, the experience of this oasis was nothing short of a surprising and spontaneous magical interlude, and it had the effect of transporting me back into the peyote sessions I had had in Amsterdam with Joop. I think I walked on a cloud for several days thereafter. All in all, my various shamanic wanderings have been comfortable not only along Ernst's coral reef beaches but also in the worlds portrayed by Hieronymus Bosch, Debussy, Ravel, Bartok, Shostakovich and Arnold. Along with the vistas and intimacies of painting, landscapes or minutia, those moments through which one can approach musical notes as substantial and touchable are in addition inspiringly antipodal. I am eternally grateful for the privilege of dancing the otherworld along the canals of Amsterdam, the banks of the Kashi Coast and the shores of Rhode Island, California and Tulum, within the Roman Forum, the streets of Manhattan and the cemetery of San Juan, and amid ancient Celtic tombs of Ireland, Nordic pagan sites in the area of Uppsala, the hot spring of Goulimine and the beauties of the Alps. My unexpected visit to La Casa Guggenheim served for me as a confirmation that the route I have chosen, as difficult as it may at times be, was the right one. Coinciding with both nature and art, as well as through them both, I remain convinced that the entheogenic mystical realm provides a dimension, if and when approached judiciously and carefully, to expand human horizons.

I recognise that religion can offer forms of consolation in times of stress or grief, but I am unable to think of it apart from principally bestowing experiences of the ecstatic. These last need not be exclusively whirling-dervish types of abandoned frenzy but can range from the serene to the thrill of discovery to manifestations of pure bliss. It is to be granted that the energies of youth are perhaps the most commensurate for the joyous dimensions of jubilation, and my reminiscence of my early times in Amsterdam, Venice and the Aegean reaffirm for me that splendid combination of being young, open and adventurous.

My first times in Europe continued with my falling off a bus in London, knocking every bit of air out of my lungs in the process, developing subsequently an influenza of the vertebrae as a result, wanting to exchange/end the subsequently unbearable pain by jumping off the steeple of the Ulmer Münster, being miraculously saved and cured in Ulm instead, two months of German language studying with the Goethe-Institut in Grafing, Bavaria, the acquisition of a VW Beetle, and eventual return to America, a brief sojourn in Laguna Beach, a longer one in Los Angeles and my completion of an MA in International Relations at San Francisco State College as the Haight-Ashbury experiment unfolded into an all-engulfing matrix that provided a subcultural event of such unprecedented collective joy that most of us who knew it will still say all these years later that it was a time 'we never would have wanted to miss'. And out of this mad and wondrous embrace, I sailed for a second time to Europe.

One noteworthy experience before that embarkation consisted of the catechism classes I took with Anton LaVey's Church of Satan. At the conclusion, the necessity of swearing eternal fealty to LaVey as the Satanic Pope was something I could not do. An unending LSD nightmare ensued on Strawberry Hill in Golden Gate Park. It was Easter. This served as a pivot in the year of celebrations on that site in which our Strawberry Hill Coven indulged. Whereas we had begun with antichurch Mephistophelian metaphor, belladonna consumption and the employment of a flying ointment while next to an inexplicably undetectable bonfire in the park, we ended the year still naked but in a circle with our feet touching each other's in the centre while chanting the Om syllable.

Mother said on the phone on my birthday, 'Why are you not here'?

'What do you mean? Why should I be'?

'It's your 30th birthday'.

'Yes, I know it is'.

'You come into your trust fund today'.

'I thought he had changed it'!

'I did too, but he found out that he couldn't', Mother replied.

It was not a lot of money but more than I had ever had and enough to raise eyebrows when I asked a teller in my hometown of Maplewood to check my balance for me. And it was enough for me to buy the house in Amsterdam and what I thought could be enough to live on for the rest of my life. It was not, but I was not to realise that until several years later. The group, the Strawberry Hill Coven, we had formed in San Francisco we still refer to as 'the family', and I managed to convince half of us to flee as I was about to do to Europe. The day I departed from San Francisco was that of the Kent State shootings. The Charles Manson murders had also occurred the previous summer more-or-less bringing the curtain down on the hippie phenomenon. Nevertheless, according to *National Geographic* writer William Davenport and his artist wife Roselle, a student of Fernand Léger – the couple being the doyens of the expat community of the area I came in time to settle within in the Provence, it was the Counterculture who were responsible for getting the United States out of the Vietnam War.

When the time came to depart, Amsterdam had been selected as our 'family's' destination. Once there but with winter not far off and me with my surprising bit of funds, I purchased a canal house in the centre of the city. It was one of the most fortuitous moves I have ever made; something I could never do now with today's prices. But our commune had now a home. This all was many years ago from the time I now write. When I first left San Francisco, I was thinking that I would only return in the future to America for funerals. Beside the Kent State shootings, the Kennedys had already been assassinated and Martin Luther King, Jr. as well. Of the core group with whom I had bonded in San Francisco, about half had also left the United States, and it was Amsterdam where we caught up with another. My wife Nancy had left the City by the Bay for Europe twice before I did but only finally reached 'the other side of The Pond' a decade or two later.

Amsterdam at the time of my arrival – along with Richard, Warren, Rosanne, Coral, Iana and Jan – was a heady refuge and ultimately the transplant destination for many of us from the descent of the curtain on the prolonged countercultural party of Haight-Ashbury. Others had withdrawn to the California hinterlands, some retreated to Canada, some to Asia, but for me and my group and a steady stream of others it was Europe. Having arrived in Amsterdam in October and foreseeing the approach of winter and the homelessness of my friends, it was along with the assistance of my first lover, the Friesian poet Johannes 'Joop' Slagter, that I found a lovely canal house for sale by two spinster sisters. They had been born and raised in the house and still lived in it. As they explained to me, four people of their family had died in the building, and eight were born there. An accountant's office occupied the ground floor, and we moved into the three floors above the office as well as the souterrain beneath it. The sisters also explained that around 1915 their family had constructed a bay window inside their living room and in the middle of the night knocked down part of the external wall and extended the construction to the outside of the house's front. Whether this is still the case or not – and doubtfully that it is, in the Netherlands if something became a *fait accompli*, it was allowed by municipal authorities to persist.

In San Francisco, I had referred to two people I knew as my 'co-gurus'. One of these was Jere Franzway who was my 'dealer' and, when I first met him, had organised a commune on Clara Street. In 1969, the English poet Thom Gunn published his poem *The Fair in the Woods, to Jere Franzway*. And what I learned from Jere was the art of giving parties. Consequently, as 'The House' in Amsterdam was filling up and Yule was approaching, we decided to celebrate both the seven-days of the Saturnalia and the twelve-days of Christmas – making altogether a twenty-one day party. And it was an open house.

The daily routine for the 21-day celebration began with rising as early as we could, cleaning the house as best we could and in preparation for others to arrive for the festivities, securing and cooking some sort of fowl for each day – turkey for one, pheasant for another, duck, swan, capon, quail, goose, etc. – always fowl and always different. Opening the doors for the day's banquet between 4 and 8 PM and then partying for most of the night. There were some variations – for instance, for midwinter's itself, a group of the fellows retreated to Lukewierum in Friesland where Joop had lent us his enchanting house. It was a brief and magical oasis moment of repose and quieter shamanic explorations for Warren, Richard, me, our companions and a few others. Then we were back to the seemingly endless foray. Overall, it was an exhausting period of time, and midway I found myself renaming the party 'And They Shoot Horses, Don't They?' after the Jane Fonda film about the dance marathons in the 1930s. We decided to restrict the party until midnight, but many knew that we would continue afterwards and hid behind chairs, under beds, in closets, etc. At one point, we had to 'ship' Coral and her and Richard's three-year-old daughter, Iana, to Morocco – Coral not being able to endure the festivities through to their end. The bathtub in those days was *always* in use, and if you wanted to bathe, one had simply to step in at one end with someone else at the other. It had been a particularly cold winter, and many used our house as a place of refuge to keep warm, etc. We would collect our mail at the American Express office on the Damrak, and the young lady who was handling it for us would tell us that everyone was complaining that because of some enormous party that was occurring in Amsterdam, there was no dope available throughout the city.

On the first day after the party had *finally* concluded I opened the post and read the newspaper. In the paper we learned that Blind Bob and a few others who had become party regulars had been deported after demonstrating nude in front of the American consulate. One of the letters informed me that the house insurance had been cancelled. The insurance representative had come by one morning to ask for my payment, and I – in full party spirit – invited him to come back in the evening. The numbers of people and burning candles throughout every space of the house horrified him. Another letter revealed that my bank account had been totally emptied. In despair at one point, I had signed a blank check to a young German lad which he promptly used to clear everything out of the account. Needing space and quiet, Rosanne and I retreated in my VW Beetle and headed for Africa – but that is another story.

In all, the commune lasted nearly four years. Everyone would contribute ten guilders to 'the pot' for the week, and in those days of the 1970s, we were able to survive with that. The permanent residents fluctuated between thirteen to twenty people, but at other times it was more like forty and sometimes as many as eighty. Much of what we furnished The House with was what we literally found on the street. These became marvellous times of comradery, resourcefulness and riding the crest of the spiritual high that had begun for us all in San Francisco. Retrospectively considering our behaviour at the time, we were naively flamboyant, more than colourful and undoubtedly notorious. Across the canal and one block further, Nicolas and Magdalena Schors had an antiquarian and occult book shop. Becoming acquainted with them, they wondered one day if I might know anyone who could work for them and assist in their business. Returning to The House, I asked, and Warren and his then Dutch girlfriend Jackie both jumped at the opportunity. Over the years, both Nick and his wife became good friends and more than helpful allies. Nick was able to prevent the Dutch police at one point from giving my name to Interpol when I had sublet the house to what turned out to be a group of Irish mercenaries – probably the IRA.

Years later, when Nick was 89, he told me about another earlier occasion in which someone had phoned him from the police department asking about me and informing Nick that he was observing me from a house across the street while holding a rifle. Nick proceeded to speak about my 'sterling' character and that I visited him and his wife frequently. In their conversation, Nick also informed the officer that he himself had once lived in a commune with three women. 'Really?' the man responded aghast. The divide between experimental recklessness and the establishment that we had encountered in California and elsewhere in the United States differed little to what we came to find in Europe.

One of the things that Joop had taught me was the love of the sidewalk café. Here one can enjoy a beverage while gazing leisurely upon the everchanging passersby. As a form of entertainment, open-air tables facing pedestrians is little different from the theatre or concert hall let alone the cinema or sporting venue. There is a focusing audience for each even if the focus varies from one type to the next. But all these distractions are what is needed to counterbalance the otherwise horrendous activity of contemporary society. For myself, I am at my present stage of advancing life increasingly mindful of attempting to loop gentle otherworld streams through the busyness of today's world. This has become more a necessity of survival than simply one for pleasure.

In my younger days, still in my twenties, I settled into an apartment on the corner of Carl and Cole Streets in San Francisco and from there commuted to San Francisco State for my Master's Degree in International Relations. As December approached, my tradition became one of wandering over to Haight Street to a European German bakery for their *Weihnachtstollen*. At that time, the street was a centre of one of the city's many delicatessen districts. But one year, I went for my annual purchase and was shocked to find the bakery gone and replaced by something calling itself the Psychedelic Shop. In time, Peggy opened up a clothing store directly across the street from the bookshop, and the young people who gathered in front of the latter now had another place to move back and forth between. And within six months from that point, the proverbial Haight-Ashbury movement had begun, and the area erupted into the birthplace of hippiedom.

These were the most marvellous of days, and no one I have ever met since will not utter the cliché and say that they would never have wanted to miss them. Instant comradeship was the norm. People were open, sharing and joyous. Perhaps what comes the closest today might be the Burning

Man times in Black Rock, Nevada. The late 60s were a continuous party – experimental to be sure, with communal living, colourful tribal-like events and an unprecedented sense of freedom. Our naivety is certainly not to be denied. We earnestly believed that the world had changed and would not return to the establishment-dominance that had preceded. And, of course, in this we were wrong. Suddenly the writing was on the wall. For me, this occurred when, in 1969, four of us had gone north to retrieve a stolen car that had been recovered in Oregon and then continued further, first to the Sky River Festival and Lighter Than Air Fair in Tenino, Washington, and then to Fritz Perls' Gestalt centre in British Columbia. This last was seminal, and Perl's past immigrations provided for me the insight eventually to convince a number of our group to depart from America for Europe.

And the irony in all this is that America in the approach of the 1970s was terrifying and for me and many of my friends and loved ones a place from which to escape, and now, after five decades and an intervening return on my part to Turtle Island, I am finding myself in full circle and once again rejecting the country with an equal intensity of horror. Unable to sleep as I write this, I have just read Eric Margolis' 'Just Say No' blog condemning the United States' inability to enforce the international status quo that provided the nation formerly with both wealth and power. I have had to grieve for the Yazidis who share in some respects a similar spiritual tradition to my own. I grieve in fact for any minority peoples who are persecuted and displaced if not simply murdered. And yet at the same time as global horror continues to unfurl, and with the weather cooperating, Amsterdam in support of ALS could hold its City Swim marathon in its canals, concluding just around the corner from where I live. When I last witnessed this race, over two million euros had been raised through the effort in a land that, all the same, is not without its own problems and difficulties but nevertheless is one that appears to be balanced, relatively sane and happy.

Our Western civilization has had indeed its imperial aspirations and at present these do not seem to have diminished but rather have increased. There are things we have done wrong and continue to do so, but at the same time, European culture is something I treasure and wish still to champion – not *over* the world's other cultural developments but *alongside* with them. There is indeed a comfort and sense of security that I enjoy in Amsterdam, London, Paris and the Provence, and while the militarisation of the American police continues increasingly to horrify and the absurdity of lax gun control continues to astonish, I expect that for great swathes of that North

American country, the same sense of comfort and security also prevails both daily and immediately. The Islamic State of Daesh, by contrast, exemplifies for me the worst of human development, and while American-led renditions, torturing and random drone bombing would appear to have undeniable affinities with both Jihadist Islam and a human loss of honour, some photos sent to me by my outraged cousin who lives in New Orleans that reveal the most gruesome collection of beheadings in what are currently Iraq and Syria underscore the cancerous depravity of which human nature is most shamefully capable. With my particular pagan sentiment, I will not call this hideousness 'evil', whether jihadist or American, but rather a terrible and ravaging illness born from both arrogant myopia and pitiable ignorance. Understandably, one response to disease is the allopathic desire to cut it out, to eliminate and eradicate it, and the international and regional coalition that is being formed to combat the Islamic State militants falls in line with this response. Our desire is always for the cure, though some treatments are better, more effective and lasting than others. The homeopathic remedy at present, however, seems to be out of the question.

It is declared continuously that jihadism is not representative of Islam more widely, and perhaps the same might be said concerning Dominionism and the like and Christianity as a whole, but for the polycentric future that I envision, the consideration that Abrahamism itself has been the root of the world's difficulties will have won the day. Proton-therapy without collateral damage and casualty is perhaps one way forward, but most important has become the recognition that a healthy organism itself is resistant to disease. Whoever was behind the creation of 'Ground Zero', it nevertheless launched an imbalanced madness – augmented by a lack of mature wisdom, and today's current resurrection of the Crusades is the egregious result with which we all must currently labour.

It is a different world now more than a half-century later from when I moved or escaped to Europe. I treasure that so much of my traveling and psychotropic adventure coincided with my youth. The body no longer responds to either with the same intensity and exuberance. My curiosity and desire for change still propel me on occasional peregrinations, and a commitment toward maintaining shamanic credentials allows me to participate in intermittent mind alteration as well. But these are less now the experience of unbridled discovery and more often interruptions to the process of daily maintenance and the work foci on hand. The museum and theatre are my temples, and a shared meal with friends and loved ones is the sacred epiphany. There is a quiet joyful acceptance and gratitude for all the glorious past times that have been, and these are now the kindling for the wonder of our present world and the possibility of a promising future.

UBI experiments are presently being undertaken in Brazil's beachfront town of Marica as well as in Finland, Scotland, Kenya and The Netherlands. The universal basic income has been a manifesto pledge of French presidential candidate, Benoît Hamon. He expressed his want for an unconditional income for every individual in France. Commitment to the idea is also to be found with the UK's Green and Scottish National Parties. As the economic effects of increasing digitalization and automation reduce the possibilities of employment, the UBI becomes correspondingly more and more a feasible solution to chronic unemployment. A Dutch author during a radio interview concerning the UBI has said that when a person is asked what would he or she do with the extra income the response is almost invariably pragmatic – e.g., secure a roof over one's head, purchase hearing aids, use the extra time afforded toward voluntary work, etc. The writer claimed that the evidence supports this positive employment of the state-given funds. However, when asked what one thought that other people would do with the bonus money, most say that it would be used to purchase alcohol or drugs. One argument for the UBI despite the misperceptions of its negative applications is that it costs the state more when its people are poor and cannot afford the basic necessities that the state in turn must then cover for them.

So let me now switch to the dragon. In the Western tradition, this is the monstrous enemy – one that is finally vanquished by the hero (such as in the stories of Zeus and Typhon, Indra and Vritra, George and the serpent). In the East, by contrast, especially with China, the dragon represents the force of fertility and is considered a positive being. I lived in London during the times that the ecological group known as the Dragon Environmental Network came into being. The dominant ritual upon which we engaged collectively was to invoke the telluric forces inherent in the earth and pictured as a dragon. I realise now that we were incorporating a foreign idea into indigenous practice. Although this may rub me against the grain when exploring atavistic and subliminal perceptions that are integral to the specifics of cultural inheritance, I realise that contemporary paganism has emerged increasingly as something cosmopolitan rather than ethnically compartmentalised and being identifiable as Classical, Celtic, Heathen or Egyptian, etc. This newer development may not be my preferred form, but it is what it is, and I remain with the conviction that earth-loving, nature venerating and locally-centred manifestations of spirituality are in general an important contribution and necessary *modus vivendi* distinct from the Abrahamic hegemony that emerged historically to dominate the West and claim half the world of today but which nonetheless constitutes a retro-orientation for a viable human and planetary progress. Though I was born and raised a Methodist and still retain a respect for the writings of John Wesley, I no longer consider myself a Christian.

'George' derives from Zeus *Geourgos*, that is, Zeus the farmer – literally, the 'earth-worker'. The symbolism here is multiple. The dragon represents the sterility of the primordial chaos. He survives as the Vedic Vritra who withholds the monsoon rains until he is vanquished by the thunder-lord Indra. In the Greek formulation of the mythic prototype, Typhon seeks to overthrow Zeus and, for a while, gets the better of the king of the gods. In the George and the dragon derivative of the earlier tale, the hero frees the maiden of promise who has been captured by the monster. The 'earth-worker' is of course the farmer, and the vanquishing weapon has become the plough that transforms the barren land into the fertile field of produce. This weapon is more often symbolised as the lightning bolt – the natural phenomenon that brings about the fructifying rains. But the bolt or *vajra* is also, metaphorically speaking, the phallus – the male instrument that brings about pregnancy and ultimately burgeoning life. While dragonslaying has emerged in our own times as something essentially non-PC and a supposed remnant of a patriarchal subjugation of women, the heroic motif remains central to mythopoetic imagination – especially for the earliest religious and artistic heritage of the West. With Zeus' victory over Typhon or the Hittite weather-god's defeat of Illuyanka or Indra's destruction of Vritra, divine order is established. And also, in each of these instances, the dragon is male and not female and, if not slain outright, is neutered through castration – because as symbolic of primal sterility, that is what he is from the start – the myth simply transforming an allegory into a narrative: a tale to be told for entertainment and elucidation around the hearth or camp fire of old.

The current defence of the dragon results from the political feminism of our day. The re-affirmation of women not as objects, playthings or second-class persons but as human beings of equal status and worth as any male person is a revolutionary development of our times that has been perhaps long overdue but ultimately imperative to any advance for humanity – especially one that rests upon recognizing the intrinsic worth of the individual. My only objection is one I have toward any self-interest identity – be it gay rights, pagan rights, class rights, etc. What we all truly want are human rights, and when the focus is on the specific rather than the whole, a judicious recognition of boundaries is too often lost and one never knows when to stop with insistent demands. The re-interpretation of the dragon as the victim of patriarchal aggression is a case in point. The dragons I have so far mentioned are male and not embodiments of the suppressed female. And by the same token, just as all men are not evil, not all goddesses are divinely good ones. The negative female dragon of the West derives from the Levant as a representation of the primordial chaos against which an ordered and functional creation has evolved. For the Babylonians, she was known as Tiamat, and her only desire became her wish to stop the 'noise' of humans and return to the original void of stasis. As a prototype of Zeus, the weather-god / lord of thunder Marduk slays Tiamat so that the natural order can flourish and continue. Within the Western tradition, Tiamat's closest affinity is perhaps with the Python of Delphi who is subdued by Apollo, the god of youth and light. Sometimes Python is understood as masculine – perhaps a variant of the cosmic Typhon/Typhoeus, but by some she is considered a *drakaina* or female dragon who is otherwise known as Delphyne.

When asked by a reporter when might the killing and slaughter in Israel end, Netanyahu's brother-in-law points affirmatively to the sky and proclaims defiantly, 'When God in heaven decides!' Desert Abrahamists have come to understand the entity worshipped as transcendent and other than earth and nature, and they have venerated this figure through meteorites as special objects that have fallen to the planet from outer space. This same being or nonbeing was understood by Indo-Europeans and other pagan peoples as the dragon who was subdued or slain by the hero-god in the establishment of order, harmony and civilisation. This dragon is variously personified as male, female or a castrated male. Feminists of our own day tend to revere the dragon as the degraded and suffering female. For the Mesopotamians, the primordial dragon was split into two to become the heaven and earth themselves. The Greek Zeus confined Typhon beneath Mount Aetna where he became the forge of his continuation, the smith-god Hephaestus. In other words, along with the creation myths as emergence, battle or artisan-fashioning, the heroic conflict notion also has the possibility of not simply annihilating the dragon but domesticating it. This is what the Greeks did with Hephaestus. As the blacksmith of the gods, he becomes their metal-worker.

From a pagan perspective, the Abrahamic 'God' is the annihilation-seeking dragon – a personification of the void of primordial chaos and antecedent of emerging Gaia that seeks to obliterate all the 'noise' of creation that ensues from the earth. A different pagan concept is that of the Chinese who see the dragon as an auspicious being responsible for fertility and good fortune. Perhaps we have reached the current impasse of human history in which religious polarity is becoming increasingly deadly and our survival tactic necessitates a reconciliation between the divine and the dragonish. Are we obliged to transform the chaos of entropy and stagnation into one of unlimited potential and fruitfulness? Does this require the changing of chaos into what James Joyce refers to as chaosmos or at least recognising and harnessing to whatever degree possible chaosmos as the liminal membrane between chaos and order?

St. George the dragonslayer descends from Zeus Georgos, the slayer of Typhon. Literally, the god's epithet signifies 'earth' [Gaia] plus 'worker' [*ergon* or *ergazomenos*] which renders Zeus as the farmer. In other words, Zeus the farmer is the husbandman or tiller of the earth who renders the ground fruitful. The phallic implications of this mythogem always remain just beneath the surface. In this case, the agricultural tool is both the lightning bolt and the deity's *membrum virile*. In the depictions of St. George's vanquishing the dragon, it is the maiden that is also present who is being rescued. That is, the male hero, at heart the agriculturalist, fructifies the barren or sterile and non-productive earth into being the fruitful source of produce and nourishment. The dragon represents the former; the liberated damsel in distress is the latter. What this means is that chaos retains the potential for the order of creation – or, if not chaos itself, at least the complexly latent border zone of chaos that is otherwise understood as chaosmos. It is precisely in this liminal threshold of the void where the dragon can be converted into a creative positive from an entropic negative.

If the female serpent is a wantonly and promiscuous sexual creature, in the ancient formulations of the myth, it is no less the sexual potency of the male that is the seminal agent of transformation. But even if the female is willing, in today's recasting of the primary myth, the male's subjugation of the sexual partner is often rejected as rape or coercion. It is no longer accepted, even metaphorically, as a permissible mode of encouraging positive change. The hero as farmer, however, may still be an appropriate narrative for dragon domestication. With, however, the demise of the small-scale farmer and his replacement by large-scale agribusiness, the consequences in relation to an increasing despoliation of the earth return us to a further vile dragonish manifestation. Global warming is the greatest threat to our planet today, and between our ceaseless burning of fossil fuels and the decimation of our rainforests, the lungs of the planet, our very future is in peril and much of the world for our children's children will have been reshaped by our own mishandling of the earth.

The environment is thus the major concern within present-day chaos and any viable likelihood for Collaborative Survival in the Anthropocene- or imagined Lotocene-to-come. The *Accord de Paris* or Paris Agreement on climate change, ratified by representatives of 196 parties to the 21st Conference of the Parties of the United Nations Framework Convention on Climate Change, signed by June 2017 by 195 UNFCCC members and ratified by 148, was an unexpected and hard-won comprehensive global endorsement to curb greenhouse gas emissions. Unlike the legally enforced commitments of the Kyoto Protocol of 1997 which entered into force in 2005, the Paris Agreement is consensual and formulated around voluntary and nationally determined targets. Future sustainable development is to be sought in reducing carbon emission and the use of fossil fuels.

The Paris Agreement is not at all perfect and falls far short of what was wanted and perhaps needed. The city-state world that I portray in my novel for the future is one that has been significantly reshaped by sealevel rise resulting from catastrophic heating of the earth's atmosphere. The Earth Day 2016 accord recognises the need to avert, minimise and address loss and damage resulting from shoreline retreat and increased flooding but does not include mechanisms for compensation or liability. It amounts to being a document of promises but one without secure commitments. Currently, the highest polluters are China and the United States contributing together to over a third of the greenhouse gases worldwide. These are followed in descending order by Russia, India, Japan, Brazil and Germany. Those nations which contribute less than 2% but more than 1% are Canada, South Korea, Mexico, the United Kingdom, Indonesia, Australia, South Africa, France, Iran, Turkey, Italy, Poland and Ukraine.

The fossil fuel contention is compounded over the disagreement voiced by various factions that deny climate change. Denialism appears to be sponsored chiefly by political and industrial interests – such as conservative think tanks and the fossil fuel industry – and is opposed to governmental regulation of CO_2 emissions. Climate change denialism dismisses mainstream scientific opinion concerning the rate, extent or significance of climatic changes to the environment as either caused by humans or their actual impact on nature and human society. While the scientific consensus has been put at 97%, the minority of contrarian scientists argue against anthropogenic global warming by maintaining that there is instead a global cooling and that carbon dioxide in the atmosphere is not increasing. They claim that there is no evidence that warming is impacting the environment, and, even if there were, the role of human activity in the process is negligible. But further, if there is a counterargument that human impact is not negligible, the climate changes are then claimed to be essentially positive. Finally, when and if such changes become harmful, supposedly human ingenuity will successfully intervene when necessary.

What appears to be pseudoscience rather than healthy scientific doubt, what is frequently termed 'climate scepticism', amounts to an *a priori* rejection without objective consideration and one that endeavours to reduce spending on environmental research and funding for carbon dioxide monitoring. The deniers repudiate that there is polar ozone depletion, acid rain, summer droughts, heat waves, storms, floods and loss of biodiversity – alleging that these allegations are disseminated falsely and constitute what they claim to be a global warming conspiracy. The media have not helped in dispelling ammunition for the contrarian scientists through their fostering the misleading impression that climate change itself is still disputed within the scientific community. Explicit denial of global warming is motivated by reacting to any coordinated attempts for alleviation and conservationist regulation as threats to private property, free trade and global capitalism. By contrast, implicit denial is judged to be doing little or nothing even when the need for environmental stewardship is recognised and admitted. The claim that climate change is a myth had, therefore, allowed the United States to succumb to the doubt-raising industry and withdraw from the Paris Agreement. But despite this colossal monkey wrench being thrown into the global community's attempt to curb greenhouse gas emissions and prevent expensive and even fatal alteration to the planet's climate, such parties as China, the European Union, the states of California and New York, cities like Chicago, and even some of the oil industries themselves declared their intention to continue to support the Paris Climate Agreement.

So, there is hope. But along with populist 'revolution', ongoing warfare and looming ecological disaster, life is tough, and none of us – at least in our own day and age – get out of it alive. Indeed, life in its resistance to death has its vagaries, its ups and downs, and some of us appear to be much more fortunate than others. For those without homes, those displaced, those who have been forced into becoming refugees, those without food, those confronting disease, those who are confronted in a purely raw sense with the abrupt loss and devastating injury to self or loved ones, it is precisely these the rest of us must help and help them to help themselves. The options before all of us are not simple or easy ones. Work and sacrifices are required of everyone as well as a liberation from the exclusive 'me and mine' obstinacy. And it is within this effort, the effort that life itself requires, demands and affords, within the toil and disappointment that everyone endures at some point, that it is also imperative to find the occasional oasis and interlude of respite, delight and commemoration. Whether we believe in the gods or not, whether we can use the gods or not, it is the ability to honour the other – whether as nature, humanity, sentience or the awesome – that lies at the core of all celebration, and it is celebration that constitutes our only viable *raison d'être* for life.

Sadly, it is those who have lost access to the celebratory who are the lost souls. It is they among the noncelebrants who have become the cancerous illness that plagues our human ascent – even if and when that launch leads nowhere beyond the pure bliss of being here-and-now. It is that sickness of myopia and destructive greed that is the malignant pall betraying the balanced and healthy organism we might know as the human-in-nature and nature-in-the-human. It is instead the very flourishing of the human from the earth and as the earth, the personification of the earth, that is the divine – divinity in however it is represented, approached, worshipped or understood.

After a nature-psychedelic retreat in northwest Wales, I became even more mindful of the importance of organic balance with recycling and walking gently upon the earth. The sanctuary haven adjacent to a speaking river, woods and slate cliffs also brought home the joy of being with a community of likeminded adventurers and the emotional bonding that develops with an intense duration of relaxed and blissful intimacy. Admittedly, it was in part a question of endurance and hardship – especially for those who have reached the age accumulation I have, but it was doable all the same and emboldened as well by the solicitations of those younger and more able. In all, I was able to learn that the gods of the Mabinogion are alive in the campfire storytelling and the sounds and silences of the embracing forests.

Related further to the pagan ecological concern, I became engaged with other contemporary pagans whose endeavour was to formulate a 'Draft Pagan Community Statement on the Environment'. I had my doubts as to how successful this effort might be. The proverbial comment concerning seeking a working agreement among contemporary pagans considers the attempt to be akin to trying to herd a bunch of cats. But the ecological state of the planet is nevertheless virtually beyond being critical, and as the environment is central to pagan spirituality, the endeavour was as valid as far as it might be taken. Sustaining the well-being of earth may not be as important for someone like myself who is now in the autumn years of life, but it is absolutely essential for our children and their children. As a result, I had made the following suggestion to the drafting working group for whatever it was worth and for however much it was to be considered:

> Paganism is a congeries of spiritual thought and practice that collectively value life and this-world above notions of rewards or punishments in some next world and above attempts to escape from this world as a form of burdensome imprisonment. While it shares affinities with Abrahamic, Dharmic and Secular orientations, it differs respectively from each in approaching the sacred principally as immanent, corporeal and thaumaturgic. This understanding for the pagan is embodied primarily in the natural world, and the pagan-oriented person accordingly seeks to live in harmony with the rhythms of nature – respecting both the technological potentials of human ingenuity and the organic actuality of telluric origins. The crucial balance between both the actual and the potential is sought by the pagan through reverence of the natural world that is accepted as our greater environment. Resulting from its singular valuation of life and the physical world that supports it, paganism/Paganism in all its varieties affirms and celebrates ecological awareness, environmental protection, restoration of planetary health and reformed interaction between the human and our given habitat that are sustainably balanced.

Between our present times and those of my imagined and hoped for future, I suspect that pollution will greatly increase, natural forests and jungles will greatly decrease and global upheaval will be immense. Under the current conditions of national and religious rivalries let alone dominating corporate interests, I remain less than optimistic that the human species will be able to avert the catastrophe that lies ahead, and though I still consider myself essentially to be a 'militant optimist', I reflect that the worst is yet to come before anything better is to be upon us.

In the spring time, I continue to enjoy the profusion of blossoming lilac, wisteria, rhododendron, apple, cherry, damson, plum, magnolia, dogwood, hawthorn, and chestnut trees, while there is nonetheless an ongoing debate over whether contemporary paganism is dying or even deserves to die. The issue seems to be tied up with the institutionalization of religion itself. Institutes require people to set them up and then maintain them. But the people behind organizations themselves require energy and resources to perform the work that is necessary. With paganism today, however, there are few financial resources, and there is also the problem of 'burnout' with the few dedicated individuals there are. Maybe in my 'Lotus World' for a far-off future, people will live much longer lives if not forever, but in today's world even for the energetic souls we have amid us the clock still runs out in time.

For religion, increasingly the culprit appears to be its institutional structures and often with the mainstream religions what is perceived as their authoritative natures. It is probably for this reason that there is a growing sentiment in which an individual declares that she or he is spiritual but not religious. In our celebration of earth, it is science that we want to revere. The Earth Day March for Science worldwide rallies have been a plea to recognise and endorse what science uncovers as causal factors and possible rectifications behind climate change. Science and her methodology are allies and are not to be dismissed for profit motives. We require an awakened politic that can understand and accept this. We do not want or need populist politicians who promote 'alternative facts' and ignore scientific evidence.

The earth's aura is something that largely or essentially escapes empirical categorization. The acceptance of science, however, does not mean we must preclude the gods and/or the sacrality of enchantment. The world of magic may be perceived as a twin to the world of science. Technology itself is designated by a derivative of *techne* – a Greek word for magic. If in the evolutionary explanation of magic being superseded by religion and religion in turn being superseded by science, that is, in a supposed progression from savagery to civilization, religion is presented as a development of thought that intervenes between magic and science. Magic from this perspective is conceived as a product of a ruder and earlier phase of the human mind. Accordingly, it becomes a 'false science' that is allegedly accepted by ignorant peasant folk and uneducated or unassimilated indigenes.

Religion then is often hailed as the liberator from the primordial mentality of humankind. But getting on top invariably means that someone is going to want to get on top of you. If religion superseded magic, science has superseded religion. But could we ignore religion? Without religion – and especially when conceived as a stage of development, we could simply employ magic and science as two *bona fide* co-existing approaches. The one is concerned with the empirical understanding of earth, nature and the social. The other involves and works with what, in a word, we might refer to as the earth's aura, perhaps to be perceived as a sublimation of the physical. Largely if not inalienably invisible to empirical investigation, the auric is met through metaphor or symbol. We may, however, actively experience it through our this-world encounters with deific vehicles and fetishes. The mysterious beyond as it once existed is known and exposed today through televised news, the video and internet. It has become less and less an unknown geographic distance or other. Consequently, in the face of technology's takeover, what is left to be the beyond today is instead the auric world of the preternatural.

Lounging in relative comfort on yon bonnie banks o' Loch Lomond, the beauty of the area alone allows one to forget – almost – the division and recriminations let alone the disgust vis-á-vis the world at large of 'American exceptionalism'. How early it is yet to know how atrocious the 'making America great again' agenda shall prove to be. But following the Bataclan horror in Paris, an alt-right tidal wave appears, however understandable, to be disappointingly rising. The majesty of snow-covered Ben Lomond alit in the sun in the distance from the rain cloud-cover of the loch's west bank antiphonally looms in silence against the cacophony of the Babel of dissension, different arguments, powerlessness and unsurprising shock screaming across the internet and in demonstrations in Los Angeles, New York, Chicago, Portland and elsewhere. The spirit of Scottish independence and the magnificent terrestrial beauty of the land here assuage for the moment the unease that otherwise plagues one's hope and imagination.

On Orkney, the living stones of Stenness and those forming the Ring of Brodgar stand quietly in awesome and challenging mystery. Instead, these upright orthostats are for me to kiss and leave a fleeting trace of my passing in touching such ancient, ancient presences that may yet last at least as long after me as they have already preceded my own duration. Beyond this momentary but blessed solitude, the populist fury has come to engulf a resentful and angry status quo. This last simultaneously is both understandable vis-á-vis the privileges and arrogance of a controlling elite and pathetically sad in its ignorant and ineffectual vision. My sole consolation is to guess that, in the process, a goodly portion of my already lost inheritance has been gratuitously wasted in the support of the neoliberal machine. Any protection of the American Supreme Court has been shown to be a futile cause. The many poignant issues include Roe v. Wade, Citizens United, gun control, student loans, women's equality, LGBTQ rights, affordable health care and safe energy needs, but the single most important focus of all has to be climate change itself. In the face of irrefutable scientific evidence, the global warming of our environment and the impact that it has on us and especially on our future generations can only be denied by those with a wilful ignorance and inability or nondesire to be honestly intelligent. The Paris Agreement may not go nearly far enough for what is required, but at least it is a necessary, important and collective start. It merits to be respected and implemented. Beyond this, as Leonardo DiCaprio presents it, we need to learn to consume differently with what we purchase and eat and how we procure our power, and we demand to vote for leaders who will fight for climate change. This last entails ending fossil fuel subsidies, investing in renewables, leaving nonrenewable fuels in the ground and supporting a price to be placed on carbon. To protect our planet's critical rainforests, we all are required to surrender and pay a voluntary carbon tax.

Consequently, in the irony of our own times, we oscillate between the possibilities of nuclear annihilation, our ever-expanding arsenal of catastrophic weapons, plague and influenza pandemics and the Greenhouse Effect let alone terrorism, war, colossal migration and starvation. Natural possibilities such as asteroid collision of the earth and the eruption of the Yellowstone super volcano could in themselves trigger a massive chain of destructive events, blocking out the sun, plummeting global temperatures, Antarctica ice sheet collapse, rise in global sea levels, desalination of the ocean depths and disruption of the Gulf Stream – many of which consequences we ourselves are increasingly causal factors even without the interventions of nature. Christian Abrahamists of the fundamentalist variety often appear to welcome the possibility of Armageddon – presumably to hasten the Second Coming. But for all the rehabilitation of the anti-divine dragon, the personification of chaos as a worshipped being is still the 'God' behind the Christian Crusades, the Inter Caetera Papal Bull, the French Wars of Religion and Daesh Jihadist-Salafism. The ancients understood the devastating forces of nature if not also the lethally crippling acts of human misbehaviour as symbolised in the anti-cosmos dragon. The taming of such a force is the greatest task faced by god and human alike.

And where to proceed from here – the suspension of Shengen? Or the Isilist danger to the Mosul Dam? The Zika virus threat in Latin America? The coronavirus outbreak in China? The continued collapse of the global price of oil? The dim prospect of any and all Syrian peace talks? The 2016 American elections and unacceptability of Donald Trump, Ted Cruz, Hillary Clinton and most of the others? The 62 people who currently own as much as does half the world population? The impossibility of a Bernie Sanders, Elizabeth Warren or Jeremy Corbyn when facing the controlling oligarchy and MSM? The rejection by both the United Kingdom and Sweden of the UN's Working Group on Arbitrary Detention's decision concerning Julian Assange, his jailing in the UK and expected deportation to America? The Libyan civil war? Yemen? Or the intriguing farce of various former French political figures?

This last could hardly be better, and it is comfortably more in the past than in the immediate present. But we have had Nicolas Sarkozy, divorced from his wife Cécilia four months after being elected as President of France and then marrying Carla Bruni, condemning François Hollande who won over his Socialist rival and mother of his four children, Ségolène Royal, and who then evicted his live-in companion and France's unofficial first lady, Valérie Trierweiler, for a new mistress, Julie Gayet. Imperial Rome yet lives! Perhaps less ultimately on the French side of the Pond as on the American where we have no trial of anyone in the banking community responsible for the subprime collusions and 2008 financial meltdown and where there has been no real or satisfactory official inquiry into 911 is to name but two blatant outrages. Compared to the French, Bill Clinton's affair with Monica Lewinsky paled into ridicule apart from the political-puritan scandal it provoked. The source of our global problems stems primarily from the persistent Israeli empire and non-resolution of Palestine, and I fully admit that my suspicions of Mossad involvement with the Trade Towers reject me automatically to most as virtually a leftist conspiracist, but when we reflect on the nefarious and internecine behaviour of ancient Rome's rulers, at their time the most powerful people on the planet, why should we expect that the Washington elite and its affiliates, Deep State or otherwise, would be any different? What would make them any more immune to such miscalculated hubris – our Christian heritage? If anything, this last makes an even more vicious and arrogant monster. Throw in then a strong dose of ineptness, and the calamity of our times would seem inevitable and unalterable.

The machete and shooting deaths of Xulhaz Mannan and Tanay Mojumdar in Dhaka and the audacity of the killers to walk out of the apartment building following the crime chanting 'Allahu akbar' are beyond being utterly despicable. We hear repeatedly this false assertion as a desperate plea rather than a valid affirmation. It is clear to me that these maniacal fools are profoundly wrong; their god is not great. In fact, the subscription to this Abrahamic god in whatever particular form is like a malignancy that has infected humanity. The more traditional methods of combatting a cancer, such as chemo and radiation treatments, will not work here. With the disease having already spread through half the species, surgery is not an option either. The pathetic attempts to eliminate Daesh, al-Qaeda and Boko Haram put excision beyond being any viable solution to contamination.

The best resistance to disease is more likely the cultivation of the organism's intrinsic balance and natural resistance. A healthy entity is greatly more non-susceptible to alien invasion. If the Western world could regain its earlier confidence in animistic providence and the arts, it might be able to become stronger and more impervious to intimidation and compromising fear. I see music in particular as the West's strongest and most effective weapon. More down to earth, the recent British testing of a concentrated beam of soundwaves to kill tumours while leaving the surrounding cells unharmed holds a promise in the development of a method to benefit a sane well-being against the disruption caused by physical and cultural sicknesses alike. The challenge today is the development of innovative 'zapping therapies' that rely on high-intensity focused ultrasound (Hifu) and pleasant, harmonised tones. The West already has an Aladdin's Cave's treasure trove in her musical legacy. She also has the promise of further output through the perpetual permutations of inspired and new creativity. Higher cure rates with a lower cost to the patient in terms of reduced quality of life would be commensurate to a god who is truly great.

The 28-year-old Italian student, Giulio Regeni, attended Cambridge university and had gone to Egypt to study independent trade unions as part of his Ph.D. dissertation program. He had published articles that were critical of Egypt's president Adel Fattah al-Sisi's government. On the 25 January fifth anniversary (in 2016) of the Egyptian revolution, he travelled from the

Dokki district to downtown Cairo but went missing. His half-naked body was discovered nine days later by a desert roadside. He had obviously been terribly tortured, beaten with a stick, punched, kicked and cut by a razor. The tops of his ears had been cut off, finger and toenails had been ripped out, seven ribs were broken, his penis had been electrocuted, he had a brain haemorrhage, and his spinal cord was severed – probably by the sharp blow which mercifully finally ended his life and the torture he was receiving.

This, unfortunately, is the world in which we live in the 21st century. If it has ever been any different, it is no better and perhaps even worse now – or at least incommensurate with anything close to the human aspirations in which we contend to believe. And this atrocity in Egypt is not even Daesh, at least as far as we know, but seems more akin to the kind of American behaviour in places like Abu Ghraib and other rendition destinations. But equally as catastrophically horrible would be the missing 43 students in the Mexican state of Guerrero presumably in this case killed and incinerated by a police-colluding drugs cartel. But whether mafioso, jihadists, Egyptian security forces, American military, racist police, this is what we want to term 'inhuman' as if it is something other than us. But it is the very real underbelly of the veneer, gloss and comforts of civilization as we have come to know it.

Christianity has doubtlessly played a huge role in the establishment of the global ethic that we have evolved to espouse and has served to provide the historical standard against which we now measure and toward which we aim. But it is not enough! If we look reasonably deeply, we come to see even here double standards and contradictions. Any casual investigation into the Abrahamic mindset to which Christianity belongs will reveal an intrinsic fissiparous nature to this spiritual family – one which ultimately disqualifies it in supplying a moral vision that is applicable to the inhuman or subhuman and warring world we have become – one that is augmented by a much greater lethal potential than has ever previously existed.

But no other religion or spirituality can provide an alternative. If Christianity emerges as inadequate or bankrupt in fostering a universal moral foundation, so too do the dharmic and pagan religions. Each religiosity provides its own particular and ultimately isolating understanding – one which intrinsically is not shared by everyone. And beyond this, hubris and arrogance too often become part of any conviction toward religious righteousness. Negotiable penetration is then impossible, and the belief behaviour too often justifies the worst of person-to-person atrocity.

Consequently, we need a religious alternative. My partner has argued for a two-year moratorium on all religion, and while this is not feasible, it also does not recognise the important role and support that religions do provide for many people. Religion is often a solace, and it can also be, as with paganism, a mechanism for advance and meaningful discovery. But the alternative I have in mind is one that works with aesthetics rather than so-called religious truths. Veracity itself is different for different people, and apparently beauty is too. But when we can gaze at the heavens and our stellar cosmos, let alone perhaps those still largely unpolluted natural areas of our planet, somewhere in this direction a conviction exists that a foundation for discarding the inhuman can be located and shared between all human beings. It is, therefore, our collective search for the exquisite in terms of magnificence, a universal heavenliness on both earth and beyond, that is perhaps our chief – if not only – hope.

The deaths in Beirut and Paris have occurred in counterpoise to a celebratory tour to Islay; there has also been the massacre of San Bernadino and the knifing in the underground station of Leytonstone in London. Everyday there is more horror in the news, and now thanks to the unburied bodies of Daesh victims on the streets of Syria the flesh-eating parasite of Leishmanias. As the solar year was darkening at this time and coming to a close, one could wonder what next. My immediate 'Bottom Line' response became the following:

> Evil barbarians, bigoted Satanists, pathetic juveniles, sick cowards, non-humans, killer thugs and a host of other derogatory terms we hear used increasingly for the jihadists, but none of them are satisfactory. They are at best more expressive of our own outrage than they are of the perpetrators themselves. And rightly that we grieve for the Parisians and the others caught up in the sickness we have witnessed in the City of Light, one of the preeminent expressions of Western culture and the values in which we believe, and yet the bombing of Beirut the day before, Sinai, Nigeria, etc. get little if any mention at all.
>
> The Paris catastrophe receives the riveting focus it has for us because many of us have friends or relatives in the city or at least possibly in the city and also because we know Paris as a place of exceptional beauty – even a more familiar beauty than possibly that of Beirut, Bamako, Yolo, etc. We also know Paris as a place where life in most essentials proceeds similarly to that in most urban areas of the West. The attacks on Paris are attacks on us; they could have occurred in our neighbourhoods and haunts – and most likely they will yet!
>
> How do we stop the Daesh, Jihadist, Salafi and Wahabi insanity – the grotesque insult to *all* civilised aspiration? As pathetic and ridiculous they

may seem to us to be – and by any aesthetic standards they indeed are, they are operating via a different mindset and a different cultural insanity than our own. The 'god' they exalt in the name of atrocity is a phantom 'god' – at best an intrinsically deranged entity. Any true god does not demand his or her exclusive worship – the 'me and me alone' insistence. A true deity has no need for obedience to his/her megalomania. Our understandable hatred of jihadism unfortunately increasingly colours the Western perception of Islam as a whole. And while interfaith remains a worthy goal, it nevertheless remains predicated on a mutuality of respect. The Western mind may come more and more to wish – even seek – the elimination of the Islamic religion, but we must not forget that at heart the Allah of the Muslims is the 'God' of the Christians and the Elohim/Yahweh of the Jews. It is the Abrahamic faith alone that insists on an exclusive worship of its 'god' *manqué* – some perverted entity that purports to be a god but is not.

With our Christian and Jewish heritages, this counter-concept is a difficult one to grasp and accept. We can sugar coat this would-be god with proclaimed notions of love, kindness, truth and goodness, but this does not change the perverted and undermining reality that agitates beneath the fabricated gloss. The unacknowledged crux: If we wish to free our world from the endlessly destructive divisions of Crusades and Wars on Terror, we must emancipate ourselves from Abrahamic thought itself. We are obliged to come to understand what the Abrahamic 'God' is and represents. We are rightly being compelled to learn to recognise it as the yawning entropic oblivion that has simply been personified but which feeds on fear and annihilation, is fundamentally contrary to a democratic spirit, and demeans rather than exalts.

Our alternatives are the liberation sought by the Dharmic religions, the freedom from all religious sentiment with secularism, and/or the affirmation of nature and life in Pagan forms of spirituality. With any or all of these, we might be able to establish a viable kind of natural but necessary respect for *all* humans, for life in general and for the earth as our nurturing support and revered source. It is these very elements of awe and liberation that are also to be found in Christian churches, Hebrew temples and Muslim mosques. These elements are not the theology and fanaticism but instead those that comprise the positive dimensions of organic spirituality, of the force that leads to expansion and growth rather than petty triumph and despair, and of the spirit that feeds inter-humanity and universally shared beauty. When respect and dignity become the fabric of our collective being, we could eliminate the kinds of disenfranchisements that lead to downward spiralling poverty, isolation, alienation and resentment – the very conditions in which the appeal of the most deranged forms of Abrahamic posturing take root. We want, we can have if we can learn first to emancipate ourselves from the most demeaning sectarianisms that continually separate us, and we affirm a truly aesthetic world of beauty and compassion in which jihadist

> hatred, economic greed, ugliness and the littleness of mind have no place. Instead of some spiteful cult of death, we endorse absolutely our love of life and the universal right to it!

And meanwhile, an editorial on present danger appears that declares that pluralist society is itself a provocation, a persistent thorn in the side, to theocratic fanatics. Modernity that includes sexual equality and alcohol engenders Daesh and Al-Qaeda rage. With such an attitude, there is no possibility for negotiation. Instead, we are advised to remain strong in our own convictions because in time our civilisation will survive and triumph over the intolerant. The question of course remains whether our world, at least as an opportunity for sustaining life, will itself survive.

Meanwhile, there has been in our own time, and in the more immediate *Je suis Charlie* aftermath, the declaration that by the next year the one-percent will own more than the rest of the world's population, Martin Gilens and Benjamin Page's argument that America's political system has slowly transformed from a democracy into an oligarchy that steers the country's direction despite or even against the will of the majority, the *New York Review of Books'* interview of Mark Danner and a few other reporters on CIA mendacity and its program of torture, the publication of the frightening and appalling memoir of Guantánomo detainee Mohamedou Ould Slahi, London's mayor Boris Johnson's capitulation to the demands of the American tax system, the United States decision to ease travel restrictions to Cuba, the US Supreme Court announcement that it will decide whether same-sex couples nationwide can marry, and the Health Minister Ousane Kone declaration that Mali is free of the ebola virus. Some of these developments are positive; some are not. How many are even true?

The *Je suis Charlie* faction to which I belong most fervently has come to be encountered by those of *Je ne suis pas Charlie* and *Je ne suis pas exactement Charlie* voices. As Matt Taibbi pointed out, it is worldwide quickly becoming *de rigueur* to say 'I believe in free speech, or I am against violence, but . . .' If *Charlie Hebdo* is not being wise, it is at least being courageous. In the French tradition, free speech is sacred, and the French people hold to it even militantly. If from the dragon that wishes to attack me, I could attempt to hide or at least keep out of its destructive pathway, if it proceeds nonetheless to destroy my home or usurp my territory, I am still made less. For me, the dragon is the Abrahamic religions and their minions, and I despise this dragon. This does not necessarily apply to its adherents, but I wish that the world could come to see through these faiths, glean off perhaps their better features but reject them into disappearance for the rest. Free speech is free speech, and it does not necessarily entail that we must *like* what is being said, but free speech itself is the heart of democracy.

Satire has been occasionally considered the most provocative form of *civilised* expression, and its intention is exactly to provoke. To crib the words of Ian MacDonald and recast them, the intent behind satire is to cause us to stop, to think, to challenge unquestioned assumptions, to regain authentic interest, and to cry out and 'attack' what appears to us to be evil. Admittedly, this can be a painful process, but if we are eventually to gain a better and freer world, it is a necessary one. MacDonald refers to 'pre-scientific soul culture' that cherishes the inner meanings of things as more real and permanent than their outward forms. Where I might disagree with MacDonald is with his identification of beauty with 'truth', while I, following Robert Pirsig, would see the aesthetic as 'value'.

If the *Charlie Hebdo* cartoons offend, we have two grown-up possibilities. One is to seek to understand why and exactly how they offend; the other is simply to ignore them. But for some of us, their very expression is religious or spiritual in itself. If those who express such biting satire were also to resort to physical violence, then it would certainly be acceptable to condemn them – as it is when Christians go on Crusades, witch hunts or Cathari eradication, when Jews indiscriminately bomb the innocent or seize their lands, when Jihadists embark on suicide bombings, beheadings, rape or terrorist massacres, when Hindus destroy and fire-bomb mosques and churches, and even when pagans martyr Christians in sports arenas or endorse chauvinist/fascist notions of racial purity. It becomes instead a question of celebrating difference – or at least tolerating it – regardless of how that difference 'offends' our inflated personal sentiments. Taking a thought from Mohamed Kacimi, fundamentalism begins when we lose our sense of humour. And laughter *with* (in contrast to laughter *at*) must hover near the very pinnacle of the sacred.

There are still times, surprising though they might be, in which everything can be or seem to be perfect. ISIL is still there, though it appears at present to be in decline with a mentioned defeat eventually on the horizon. Any jihadist diminishment from my perspective is something to be welcomed. Indexing a prospective publication has been an enormous and disruptive interruption. Seeking a spousal visa has been another major drain on time and energy. For the rest, there is the FBAR to deal with once again, and, dear reader, if you do not know what an FBAR is, please consider yourself utterly blessed. And something on Al Jazeera one morning saying that the relevant Swedish authorities may have consented to interview Julian Assange in the United Kingdom. (This did not, alas, occur). The wars and massive displacements continue, typhoons such as the 2015 Tropical Cyclone Pam wreak havoc, but Amsterdam itself, while waiting for the inevitable, can continue to scintillate in incredible beauty (at least pre-pandemically) – especially when she is touched by the finger of spring and the possible promise of more enjoyable days to come. And though he is best venerated without too much overindulgence, Dionysus yet offers his ameliorating tonic to help one forget the terminal illnesses of so many surrounding loved ones, to forget all that is not the immediate here-and-now, and relish in an *ad hoc* joy.

But if we wonder why there appears to be a mini-stampede of disaffected youth wishing to join the Islamic State, should we be surprised? What alternatives in the West are we offering? A suicide bombing or jihadist death becomes a single and satisfying focus and release from the multiple conflicts for those who otherwise face bureaucratic torture, unemployment prospects, and onerous labour that is at best only poorly paid. And we wonder why so many of our youth find appeal in a hideous cause and early death? Personally, I wish to surrender as I more or less have for much of my life to the natural flow of a rich and deeply honoured existence – constituting a passivity that contrasts with the established drive of competitive capitalism. I am perhaps the very denial of the very system to which I owe my fortunate circumstances – the circumstances that have allowed me to rejoice in life rather than see it as merely oppressive and inopportune. Nevertheless, even under the best of conditions when we can attempt to build the most impervious forts, there still is no ultimate security. Sooner or later there will be some mechanical error or glitch to reduce our circumstances and possibly even to obliteration. It could be a natural calamity, or our isolating greed, or the grievousness of war. It is still possible that we could focus collectively on our doing what needs to be done, but instead we seem to perceive only the scarcity of our resources and concentrate therefore on some need for competition for them. Any notion of sharing is the furthest from our thoughts. Rhetorically, how much of the divisiveness of our current non-collective enterprise have we engineered ourselves? Disaster can happen to any of us, and whether internal displacement, refugee encampment, militia participation, elite perspectives or the sundry rest, survival is the best any of us can do when all is said and done. And when that is the case, it seems almost inevitably that it's every man or blinkered cause for itself.

How much of life is itself or must struggle to be? The law of the jungle, survival of the fittest, early bird who gets the worm, political backstabbing, ceaseless surveillance, Big Brother and religious conflict! The moments of oasis serenity are few and far between and less and less. Physical mortality, terminal illness, disease of countless variety, the disintegrations of age, the loss of energy let alone the basic comforts upon which many of us depend even within our citadels, and there is no final security and no final freedom. Liberty comes in any lasting sense alone with death. No wonder the disillusioned youth find appeal in a cause that employs their energies to the fullest and rewards with the emancipation of cessation!

The wonder for me is that art exists at all. How inconsequential it is in any direct sense with the struggle of life! We may be horrified when we see Daesh wielders of sledgehammers smashing flawless figures from Nineveh as we were when the Taliban demolished the standing giant Buddhas in the Bamiyan Valley of Afghanistan. Early Christians did no less when the Church first became ascendant in Europe and Egypt, nor when Byzantium launched its iconoclastic persecutions, or when China under Mao reduced its heritage through its destructive purge known as the Great Proletarian Cultural Revolution. Art is almost always vulnerable and hence impermanent. And yet great effort continues to be put into its production – echoing perhaps something perennial within the human spirit. We continue to revere beauty – including even the less obvious beauty of a political or social statement that exposes an unpalatable truth of reality. Our artists – perhaps now more than ever – are anomalies within the competitive drive for survival of me and mine alone, and yet they exist and persevere and continue to create. Disillusioning as the overall picture is, especially with the environmental catastrophes that augment that disillusionment, we can at least be grateful that art persists and artists continue to make it.

The mystical experience in one instance occurs when one can slip out from under a depression into a serenity if not an ecstasy. Through both concentrated rationale and psychic alchemy, I endeavour to float upon mystery whenever possible. My pursuit has been to ancient mythologies and their geographic grounding. That was what brought me to Europe in the first place. If there is a divine miraculousness behind all this, it is to that that I have dedicated my life. And I always hope that any current depression is simply the trough that preludes exhilaration.

How could an entity be worshiped that lusts after, or at least permits, negativity or pain for its own cause alone? To my way of thinking, that this occurs on the scale that it does is the world hex. I want to ask then if this is the best we humans can do? We now talk about the anthropocene era – the terrestrial epoch that may have begun in the 17th century with the transcontinental crossing of formerly indigenous crops and animals. The large-scale extermination of Native American peoples following European colonisation led initially to a loss of agriculture, a major regrowth of forest and a plunge in the atmospheric levels of carbon dioxide. With the anthropocene, however, humanity has steadily expanded to become a dominant geological power that influences all of the planet's ecosystems. It could easily be transforming in our day and age into an 'anthropocide'.

If we abandon 'God' in our human-terrestrial equations, have we become a diabolic force? But if we are Lucifer, the light-bearer, let alone rejecter of Christ, our role could actually be interpreted as an honoured one. We are the bearers of light! And to the degree that we succeed in this, we challenge 'God' himself/itself. 'God', therefore, constitutes the very limit to what we are allowed to wish for and have. Though we cannot afford to forsake reason, judiciousness and wisdom, the human spirit is one that affirms an unlimited aspiration. I stubbornly remain with the belief that if we but wanted to and could allow ourselves to grow up, we could engineer a future world such that might work for virtually everyone.

In our own times, among the worldwide problems that include economic inequality in which 13.5% of the world's population is hungry, loss of a sense of responsibility, resource exhaustion let alone commercial commodification of natural resources indispensable for human survival, pollution, waste accumulation, global warming, overpopulation, a shadow banking system and a pervasive psychological denial, we are now confronted with jihadist terrorism. When she was British Home Secretary, Theresa May referred to homegrown Islamic extremism as the product of 'poisonous ideology'. But it is no less important to realise that in our efforts to develop an effective counter-extremism strategy, what we might refer to as 'toxic' is fully legitimate and valid to those who embrace and are seduced by it. Jihadist ideology may not be *our* ideology, but to declare it simply as evil is to argue already from a defeatist position. It is less that the ideology is corrupt than it is simply *different*. If we are to combat it, we are obliged to present the range of ideologies to which one might possibly subscribe and then how to differentiate validly between them.

From my own perspective, Islam is as objectionable as its Abrahamic siblings, although, apart from its 'God' and Israel's unimaginative intransigence vis-à-vis the Palestinians, I have an increasing respect for Judaism, at least much of Judaism, in terms of its tolerance, progressive liberalism and pagan-like tribalism. The ideas or convictions of the infinite universe and that nothing comes from nothing that Matthew Stewart in his *Nature's God* traces to Epicurus and then down through Giordano Bruno, Baruch Spinoza and John Locke to America's Founding Fathers has an undeniable appeal over the common and entrenched religious consciousness. This last holds God as transcendent and independent of the universe, but the former understands God *as* the universe. My own mantra progresses from wishing to health to wonder to freedom: one-two-three for wishing; four-five for health; six-seven for wonder; eight-nine for freedom. Five was the understanding our linguistic ancestors had for totality – the number of fingers in the hand. Health is a cognate of wholeness – ultimately Spinoza's universe or nature; his 'God or Nature'. But where I differ from the secular pantheists is that I see and accept wonder as the aura of the universe as a whole. This emanation is not other than nature but a product of nature itself. For me, it constitutes 'co-nature' and is an – or *the* – 'auric sublimation' that exudes from the physical to begin with: matter mattering.

If freedom is our ultimate goal – probably more a direction rather than an acquired state of being, in a pantheistic understanding it entails being a part of, and as such identifying as, the whole. This is the full achievement of health – being a healthy part and being the healthy whole. And, of course, the further aspect of that divine totality is its own aura, however this is to be understood, so that we are both nature and co-nature – able to dance between and with both with a creative imagination that harmonises with the cosmic whole.

Perhaps my 'Triple Obliteration' *deus ex machina* in my as of yet unfinished novel is not the only way forward. Perhaps, just perhaps, under someone *like* Jeremy Corbyn, Britain might emancipate herself from the American imperial hegemony and augment the change toward a more egalitarian future world. Corbyn's original 24 position points were fascinating, and although I may personally have trouble with some of them, those with which I do not include joint administration of the Falkland Islands, an arms embargo imposed on Israel, not seeking to end the monarchy, public ownership of railways and energy companies, reunification of Ireland, ending the arms trade, winding up NATO, fostering comprehensive education under local authority control without the imposition of university tuition fees, and the encouragement of every child to learn a musical instrument or act on stage. These would be more or less at the heart of my pluralistic future world – dreams at this point; actuality at some time yet to come? Critics will say that these and Corbyn are regressive and more suggestive of the 1950s, but I feel and will argue that they are more than that and could be illustrative of a slumbering popular sentiment that is perhaps more widespread than the critics would wish to admit.

Being in Britain at the this point in time insulates against the migrant inundation that much of the Continent is presently experiencing. From my perspective, the US entrenched opposition to Basshar al-Assad has not only encouraged the ongoing Syrian war and the no more – if not even less – acceptable jihadist rebels but also spawned Islamic State. But if Daesh is to be quashed, and another Libyan chaos avoided, the West might most feasibly have to work with the Syrian regime as well as with Russia and Iran to do so. The flood of refugees that is threatening the very stability and future of the European Union is spearheaded by those seeking to escape Syria even if allegedly four-fifths of those seeking asylum in Europe are not Syrian.

But within the British cocoon, there is (or pre-pandemic was) instead an abandoned celebration of art, style and life. It is these elements that I perceive as the fabric of a more ubiquitous future. They are an affirmation of everything to which Daesh has decided to combat. And while we are all different, and the modus vivendi is inclusiveness, tolerance cannot be tolerant of intolerance. The mindset that sponsors intolerance is a malignant antihuman disease that needs to be purged and transformed, awakened or eliminated. Beyond intolerance, the double-standard lies of imperialism are equally not to be tolerated but rather exposed and revealed as much as possible. Through Facebook, I find myself engaged in a conversation that asks for 'a Global Movement for Peace, Mutual Respect, Mutual Benefit, Respect, Compassion and Equality Time for us to build a more productive interconnected way of living with each other harmoniously on the Earth'. And despite my militant optimism, I remain pessimistic when perceiving the entrenched powers that be, the deceit and ruthlessness that accompany less than daring and imaginative thought, and the virtually utter sham of democracy. For as much as I applaud same-sex marriage and cannabis liberalization, I see these as masquerading sops to the much greater menace of engineered paranoia and corporate profits through war. My pessimism arises from a perception of the inability to disseminate exposing insights into anything close to a mobilised global arena. The most penetrating critics of our day (whether Noam Chomsky, Matt Taibbi, Glenn Greenwald, Patrick Cockburn, Tony Cartalucci, Robert Parry, Seymour Hersh, Paul Craig Roberts and the like) have been effectively marginalised. So, in 2018, I have turned instead to the likes of the Ai Weiwei exhibition at the Royal Academy of Arts; the Celts: Art and Identity at the British Museum; Goya: The Portraits at the National Gallery; Rachel Rose's Palisades at the Serpentine Sackler Gallery; Lady Macbeth of Mtsensk at the English National Opera; and the English Choral Classics at St. James' Church, Paddington. Then too there has been the stunning Blood Moon eclipse over the Thames.

CHAPTER TWO

Walter Evans-Wentz / sacred place / 'standing under' & 'standing over' / superstition / religion / paganism's religious valuing of both tangibles & intangibles / the beauty of superstition; fleeing to Europe & the Amsterdam house purchase / Brittany / my pagan awareness of an unseen world / the house / Franz Altheim's 1938 *Römische Religionsgeschichte* / *The Roman Festival Calendar of Numa Pompilius* / Jere Franzway & the 21-day party / Morocco / the desert crossing; animist sentiment-shamanism-sacred time-sacred geography post-Altheim / rewriting the Bible backwards with four footnotes to Revelations / the tarot / Gertrude Moakley & the four triumphs / Nicolas Schors / Peter's death / Islamic martyrdom & Christian saints / filicide & patricide / Quranic & biblical violence / the middle way of paganism / Goulnacappy; no future objective but living for the now & love being the most important / the rotating binaries of the pagan flywheel / intercalation / the asuric void / the archaic /Indra's Net / pure wishing as sacred / tangibility as embodied wish / my basic approach to life / meditation / Richard / climate, health & education / pollution / American exceptionalism / post-WWII in France / the *polis* / the Westphalian Treaty / my departing concern / our planet's beauty / no reset button / the spirit of the spiritual; the Ruby Wedding Anniversary / my generic paganism / Guy Davenport & Ludwig Wittgenstein's otherworld / geography of the imagination / a central focus of pagan mysticism is navigating the interchange between the two worlds; politics / party affiliation & Presidential elections / Obama-Clinton-Trump / political leaders / populism / the Lotocene World / Brussels & Manchester; General Carl von Clausewitz / collateral damage / Brexit-Cameron-May / the European Union & the dream of Europe / Amis on Corbyn / Mother's condo sold / the banks of the River Lune / the US record of war killing / smile; London / past & present / the bus incident / Ulm / Grafing; Paris / Nick & Mackie / House of Lords: religion & caliphate; 2014 yule in Amsterdam; *carpe diem*

During what became my second crossing of the Atlantic Ocean, this time with the Holland-American Line, I read *The Fairy-faith in Celtic Countries* written by Walter Evans-Wentz and published in 1911. This inspired me to search for and explore megalithic and later significant sites throughout Europe – what became my chief occupation over the years that followed. Stonehenge and Avebury, of course, and in time Stanton Drew, the Rollright Stones, Arbor Low, Nine Ladies, Castlerigg, Callanish, Stenness,

Brodgar, and the recumbent stone circles of Aberdeenshire as well. There has also been visits to New Grange, Dowth, Knowth, Lissyviggeen and Tara in Ireland, to Gavrinis, la Roche-aux-Fées, the Alignments of Carnac, the Grand Menhir, Chartres, Puy de Dome, Nimes, Glanum, Vienne and Bavay in France, to Rome, Nemi, Pompeii, Paestum, Agrigento and Soluntum in Italy, and to Delphi, Delos, Thera, Knossos, Rhodes, Athens, Eleusis, Sounion, Arcadia, Olympia, Argos, Epidaurus and Dodona in Greece.

The physicality of sacred place may have, I have found, an aura of its own, an invisible lambent beauty. The layout can be subtle, but in a quiet presence of mind one is often able to discern the special location's integral preternatural dynamic and cunning patterns. This last leads into the extraordinary distinction between understanding and superstition. With both, the individual becomes the central pivot between the 'standing under' and the 'standing over'. While the 'under' in our word 'understanding' is claimed originally to signify 'among' or 'between' rather than 'beneath', the derived word itself conveys a notion that comprehension involves the placing of an insight into one's own orbit – putting it in a sense under one's control.

Superstition is something much different. It refers to things not understood but accepted. Perhaps it signifies what stands over in awe, but it is vis-à-vis the individual virtually the opposite of rational and empirical understanding. Avoiding walking under a ladder, knocking on wood or not opening an umbrella inside are common superstitions that many people perform in general automatically and without discerning reflection. These are behaviours that may be interpreted as reflecting beliefs that stand over us. Circumspect deportment in a holy locus is also a superstitious act. In fact, religion itself, or at least most religion, may be thought of and assessed as superstition. Like crossing our fingers and the like, religious belief is usually something we have been taught. It defies the rational and factually observed, namely, what is otherwise verifiably and pragmatically understood. For the most part, we simply embrace it and often without questioning. We may in time become convinced of something different in terms of faith, but what we super-stand or what super-stands us is most usually not what we understand as proven but still as what we give credit to.

Paganism too as a religiosity is a valuing of both tangibles and intangibles. It is as such a 'standing over' superstition rather than an empirical confirmation that constitutes understanding in the firsthand sense. Consequently, our navigation as individuals occurs between what 'stands under' and what 'stands over' us – whether we be pagan, secular, dharmic or Abrahamic.

We ourselves stand between what we know and what we believe. And it is within this framework that much of my explorations of the unusual and special have occurred in my life.

The beauty of superstition is that it co-exists with the pragmatic and empirical. It opens an additional dimension rather than a refutation. Even the scientist may follow certain superstitions or religious beliefs. Particularly within a pagan viewpoint, however, both forms of standing may be welcomed, though even here this is not invariably the case. But especially through myth and any established celebration of place or time or both, what is otherwise unfounded belief may be discovered to present a rich and fascinating world of colour, enchantment and soul-comforting synaesthesia. Whether within a megalithic site, before a domestic altar or in forming a magic circle with others, through various rituals involving music, dance and/or poetry, we insure a connection between this world and the otherworld. For a pagan, both of old and today, this connection is central to the practice of spiritual expression.

So, armed with Evans-Wentz's intuitions on gods, genii, daemons and spirits, I disembarked my Norwegian-American ship in 1970 for my second trip to Europe. Actually, this was not a 'trip' but a move. Alarmed by the Nixon administration, the Kent State shootings and what was becoming increasingly clear as the end of the Haight-Ashbury days or what Marlowe, one of my co-gurus, proclaimed as 'the party is over', I talked half of our Strawberry Hill coven to flee to Europe as well. I can no longer remember the initial sequence of events, but I worked my way from Scandinavia to Ulm in Germany where my friends Erhard and Ruth helped me with the purchase of a Volkswagen Beetle. I recall at the time hearing through an outdoor broadcast one of Brahms' symphonies and rejoicing in the classical and old-world atmosphere in which I had landed. And then it was Amsterdam were our 'Family' appeared to be meeting. Winter was approaching, and by some fluke I had enough money at the time to purchase a house. It is embarrassing now to realize how little the five-story canal building cost at the time – something I could never afford today.

While the arrangements were being settled, I took off with my Beetle to Brittany. I had already cut my long hair before I departed from America, but I was still very much the hippy and increasingly pursuing a shamanic investigation of sacred sites. Finding menhir and dolmens was not always easy, but I pursued. Reaching Gavrinis was particularly difficult in those days, and I waited an entire day for someone to take me by his boat as he had promised but who never did. My emotions were intense, and I wept at one point in my car over the frustration. The next day, however, I met a fisherman who agreed to take me. Once we arrived at the island, he gave me a half hour to find and visit the site. There either were some already there or I had candles myself which I lit along the passage of the tomb and marvelled then over the extreme beauty and mystery of the megalithic art. It still remains one of the most awesome and enchanted of moments in my life.

In all, my visit to Brittany allowed me virtually my first post-Haight-Ashbury counterculture encounter with the intersection of ancient monuments (standing stones, tombs and the like) and the residues of folk-memory. I became increasingly sensitive to the contact between the supersensuous realm and sympathetic nature. If there is anything that is central to my own pagan affinities beside music, it is this awareness of an unseen world that can be experienced and felt through ritual, entheogenic states of consciousness and, especially, sacred ancestral places of worship and/or enchantment.

I spent my last night in Maastricht before returning to Amsterdam. This was all well before our current days of mobile phones, email and the like, but I must have phoned my real estate agent and learned that everyone was already assembled at the solicitor's office waiting for the contract of the house sale to be signed. They were debating whether the hippie would really appear. I rushed back to Amsterdam and about an hour later was seated at the table with everyone else. I do remember thinking about the contrast between the time of my most negative LSD 'freak-out' on Strawberry Hill in San Francisco and the staid and formal decorum of the present document signing scene. But our wondrous house became a *fait accompli*, and a mad, thrilling, up-and-down commune began and then lasted for the next four years. My wife Nancy had set out for Europe twice before I did but only finally reached the Old World when her sister almost literally 'dragged' her over years later. From 'the Family' itself, we were besides myself, Coral, Richard and their infant daughter Iana, Warren & Jan, and Rosanne. Staying behind with their jobs were Marlowe, Lynne, John and Little Nancy. At one point, discouraged by the unkempt nature of the house, I wanted to hire a cleaner, but the rest were too embarrassed to be probably the only commune with a maid, that they agreed henceforth to make more effort in maintaining our environment.

As a result of my psychedelic experiences in San Francisco, I came to learn that Christian holidays (Christmas, Easter, etc.) were not the most appropriate times for shamanic journeying. Instead, we gravitated naturally toward the solstices and equinoxes. And then one day in Amsterdam, fortuitously in a bookshop on the Damstraat, a copy of the Harold Mattingly translation of Franz Altheim's 1938 *Römische Religionsgeschichte* (*A History of Roman Religion*) almost literally fell off the shelf into my hands. It contained a list let alone minimum description of the Roman festivals identified as certain days in our Gregorian/Julian calendar. This became a life-changing event, and once I knew the celebratory *feriae* from which our own secular calendar descends, I shifted my principal focus from my former astrological observations into thereafter a celebration of Roman pagan festivals. Though I never rejected astrology per se and have continued to be mindful of Mercury's retrograde periods (roughly three times per year), observation of polytheistic commemoration henceforth took precedent. In 1986, as a result, my *The Roman Festival Calendar of Numa Pompilius* became the first of my books to be published.

Much happened during the commune days in Amsterdam. Some was negative: a fire in the house, unhappy love affairs, my brother's suicide, but most was a time of discovery and expansion. Jim Clarke described the migrant Haight-Ashbury scene of the day as consisting of various 'courts' – a royalty (such as myself) with a coterie of attendants (the commune). As mentioned in the previous chapter, our basic number was between one and two dozen, though there were times in which forty or more had taken up residency in our canal house. It had been from my other San Francisco co-guru beside Marlowe, namely, Jere Franzway, that I had learned the festivities of partying. Our one-time-only '21-day open house celebration' in Amsterdam was the result.

Whether it was this occasion or another – our parties of the times eventually blurred together, there was a party-time when one group was in the basement while the rest of us were upstairs in the house itself. Hearing the bongos and music from the souterrain, two inebriated fellows tried to get in but were evicted by the partyers in the cellar. As our street was being reconstructed at the time, in anger the men threw a loose road brick through the basement window. In fury, Ramon's brother Coco picked up a crowbar and chased the men into the nearby gay bar, George the Fifth. He proceeded to half bash down the bar's shut door as everyone screamed inside. I was to reimburse for the door's repair, but a contingent of policemen had arrived at this point and were proceeding to storm into my house. I had just recently heard from someone that in Holland the police are required to have a signed mandate before they can otherwise enter a residence. I asked at the last second, 'Have you got papers?' ('Heeft uw paperien?'). In pure keystone comedy fashion, they all exclaimed 'Papers!' and then dejectedly collapsing on the spot said in unison, 'Oh, papers!' Before long, a police chief arrived, and the two culprits ran up to him screaming, 'Alcohol, marijuana!' to which he simply turned a jaundiced eye. I realized that here was someone I could work with, and as he wished to see my passport, I invited him alone into the house and took him to my room at the top to find my identity papers. What baffles me to this day was that, though the house had been packed at the time, there was no one to be seen as we ascended to the uppermost floor.

With the conclusion of the twenty-one days, there were the resultant consequences of insurance cancellation and an empty bank account, but apart for Blind Bob and the other deportees, never heard of or from again, we managed through these hurdles, and then it was that Rosanne and I jumped into my Volkswagen Beetle cabriolet and raced to Marseilles in pursuit of Africa and a full break from what we had just been through. We were of course completely naïve and ingénue, and we arrived at the French port by midnight expecting immediately to get a ferry to take us to Algeria. Instead, we were astonished to find the terminal completely closed. The next day we purchased our tickets and were then asked about our visas. '*Visas?!*' and I remember next a hand reaching out from under the grill that separated customers from the office, and our tickets were swiftly grabbed back.

I can no longer remember whether we ever did get our Algerian visas, but we decided instead to drive through Morocco and originally then the plan was to continue to the Ivory Coast. Once we realized the actual distances involved, we thought that we would instead circle back from Morocco through Algeria. We did manage to find Coral and Iana at some point and also enjoyed such places as Fez, Marrakesh and Agadir. When we approached Fez for the first time, it was like a vision out of *Scheherazade*. Arriving next in Marrakesh in a late afternoon, I could describe the impact as similar to when Ulysses arrived in Knossos with Helen of Troy in Nikos Kazantzakis' *The Odyssey: A Modern Sequel* – an active and buzzing market expressing an exuberant *joie de vivre*. The hot spring of Guelmim (Goulimine) was perhaps the most magical of all. And then from there we set off across the steppe land to the Spanish Sahara. As it was lunchtime, the border guards were inside their tents having their midday meal. Otherwise, they would have prevented us from travelling into the roadless area that followed.

Our desert crossing goes as follows. At first it was steppe land, and the driving was not difficult. There was no problem even if there were no roads. I do not now remember which we encountered first – a sand dune or a wadi. It was, however, the dry river valleys that emerged as onerous problems. There were in all three wadis or steep ravines that would become river channels in the rainy seasons. As we approached the first of these obstacles, a caravan of lorries was ascending the wadi bank from our opposite direction. The vehicle at the head pulled up alongside my Volkswagen and motioned for me not to move. Then someone climbed into the back truck and proceeded to drop six beautiful oranges into my hands. The driver then said 'Bonne chance' and pulled off. The wadis were always troublesome to descend and then re-ascend over loose dirt and sandy roadways. A Bedouin appeared to help us with our first re-ascent. Rosanne said, 'One does not tip brotherhood', so we gave him one of our oranges. Somehow, we managed to traverse all three of these valleys.

There was a point along the easier steppe, when we came upon a large sand dune. After stopping the car, we proceeded to play and roll down the sides of the rise. Two four-wheeled jeeps (Land Rovers I presume) arrived as we were enjoying ourselves – two journalists each with a female partner. They were covering an assignment for a story and were aghast to find us in the desert in a VW Bug. 'Have you got water, ropes, enough petrol? Do you want us to stay with you?' they asked. Since my tank was full, and the distance to the border was only 160 kilometres, I declined their offer, not wanting to delay them. We had water, and we had had no insurmountable problems so far. We insisted we were okay and for them to proceed. What we had not realized yet was that the sand dune we were presently enjoying was only the forerunner of many, many more before the steppe turned into a complete desert of sand. Our first sand dune became a second and then more and more until everything was only sand.

Three things I can specifically remember, if not more. One was the dazzling stellar expanse of the sky at night – uncontaminated and pure from any urban light whatsoever. We slept under stars that seemed as if they could be picked directly out of the nocturnal sky. Away from urban centres and the lights of civilization, the astral depths of our cosmos allow themselves to be witnessed in their unfathomable intensity. As intimidating and belittling as the unadulterated stellar reality can be, there is simultaneously an incomparable beauty to be savoured as well. Another memory was when, on an impulse, I switched on the car's radio not expecting any reception but intrigued all the same. Suddenly a beautiful sinfonietta by Scarlatti surrounded us crystal clear in the desert silence. That was how I became aware of the Canary Islands – a discovery that was subsequently to become important. Thirdly, at one point, we passed a tent, and its inhabitant waved us to stop and come by. He was a young and handsome man, dressed all in black, cheerful and curious about us, wearing various beads and amulets and with one leg and one arm missing. I took him to be a possible desert shaman but later wondered if he had been an exiled thief who had been punished with amputation – perhaps he was both. He did not appear to be an unhappy person at all, and once he was satisfied to have talked with us, we were allowed to continue.

What I remember most, however, was how strong I became in this adventure – the strongest physically I have most likely ever been. We developed the routine with Rosanne driving and me holding the rear end of the car up with my hands as if it were a wheelbarrow. If I let the vehicle down at any point, it was then a matter of hours for us to find enough stones and dig out enough of the sand to get the car able to move forward once again. Every once and a while, we would see an abandoned vehicle of one sort or another. I believe we were now on our fourth day and were gathering stones and rocks again in order to get across a ridge of sand in which we had again become stuck. It was then that I heard the sound of motor vehicles, and to everyone's surprise, it was the British journalists. They had made a wrong turn and descended a dead-end peninsula and were forced to double back. They had cursed themselves for abandoning us – saying to each other that we could never have made it. But we were ahead of them! With their ropes, they quickly pulled us out and across the sand ridge upon which we had become fixed. From there it was a relatively short distance to the Moroccan border where we spent the night.

It was here, however, that we learned that we all required 'exit visas' to leave Morocco and get into the Spanish Sahara. This was only available at some inaccessible site several hundred kilometres behind in the opposite direction. Our Volkswagen would not have been able to succeed; this much was clear. Collectively, we agreed that it would be 'each man for himself' and we would attempt at the first break of day to get across the border before the guards had emerged from their tents in which they slept the night. Rosanne and I succeeded, and one of the Land Rovers as well. But the second vehicle did not – being halted by the guards with rifles aimed at the jeep. The driver was allowed to cross over to tell us that he would need to go the distant journey back to secure the required exit visa.

However, at the Spanish Sahara side of the border, Rosanne not having an up-to-date small pox vaccination certificate was not allowed entry. I was permitted to drive alone and at least now along a paved road to the military base further south to ask the camp commander permission for Rosanne's entry. We had already learned by this point that no one for the past twenty-five years had used the road that the map had indicated to Algeria, and its location was no longer known. Thanks to Scarlatti, we now knew of the Canary Islands, and I believe it was from the journalists that we learned that it would be possible to reach Gran Canaria by ferry from El Aioun. Under the stipulation that we would get Rosanne's vaccination as soon as we arrived in the Canary Islands, I was able to secure her entry permit into the Spanish Sahara. Our next discovery was that our car was to be taken separately and ahead, and we watched in harrowing fear as she was placed into an amphibious dingy of sorts and then lifted by a crane that tried to lower our vehicle into the offshore cargo ship as it swayed back and forth in the churning sea. Finally, fortunately, the feat was successful, and we watched our car disappear toward the horizon. Our passenger ferry from El Aioun was the next day. The seas were extremely rough, and I was seasick the entire journey – spending the entire time horizontally in bed. But we arrived the following morning to the harbour of Las Palmas, and our car was waiting for us unattended in the parking lot. There was no one to receive us, and there was no control of any sort. We never did get Rosanne's vaccination.

From Gran Canary it was easy to get ourselves and our Beetle to the Spanish mainland. After several days of exploring the island and particularly what we could learn of the Guanches (Canarii), the pre-Spanish indigenous inhabitants – now extinct, we took the ferry to Spain. We had a few hours on Tenerife and several days in Madrid. And then we were home again in Amsterdam.

In all, the excursion with Rosanne into North Africa was, apart for my much briefer visit to Brittany, my first major travel after for what I thought at the time was a permanent move to Europe. I became increasingly filled with an animist sentiment and in particular in connection with the power emanations of sacred space. These became my foci during my earlier post-America days, and when I could get away from Amsterdam and the commune, I would explore as much as possible the expanse from Scandinavia to Sicily and Greece. These expeditions were not always easy. I pursued a shamanic approach including often a shamanic attire. I wore a small tinkling bell attached to my belt, sometimes a cloak and was still essentially a hippy. I interpreted the role of the shaman as a lonely one and without the prospect of a love relationship. Once I had become aware of Altheim's book, my fascination with sacred geography merged with a subsequently perpetual interest in sacred time. The calendar became my operative framework, and the awareness of Roman festivals and their rhythmic annual patterns came to replace my previous pursuit of astrologically related timing.

Progressively, a deepening awareness of pagan animism and the embedding of telluric spirit in both place and time resulted for me a steady disenchantment with, and rejection of, Christianity. I resolved to rewrite the Christian bible backwards – beginning with the Book of Revelations. I never got further than that, but my rewrite contained four footnotes. One of these became my examination of the Roman *feriae* which in 1986 I published as *The Roman Festival Calendar of Numa Pompilius*. Another footnote to my Revelations was recast to become in 1995 my *Divine versus the Asurian: An Interpretation of Indo-European Cult and Myth* – what I consider to be my *magnum opus*.

Writing emerged as my passion, and I balanced it with my exploratory travels and with communal living. I had also come to be engrossed since my San Francisco days with the tarot. When I had heard the shop assistant in The Metaphysical Bookshop on Powell Street pontificate to a customer that Latin was a spiritually bankrupt language and that Hebrew was the only vocabulary appropriate, my reaction was to reject the Rider-Waite deck in preference for the Marseilles and Swiss versions of the cards. To this day, it is the Swiss 1JJ Tarot that I continue to use. Subsequently, I searched and searched throughout Europe for ancient tarot decks of cards but never located any. I prefer the Juno and Jupiter substitutions in the major arcana of the Müller (Swiss) deck for the Popess (*La Papesse*) and Pope (*Le Pape*, Hierophant, High Priest) of the Tarot de Marseille. But I have also come to realize that one cannot use the tarot for both the purpose of working magic *and* for divination. It is one or the other but not both. In my more magically oriented days, I opted for tarot use in connection with influencing the future rather than foretelling it. I have since, however, come to employ the arcana as ritual calendar indications on my domestic altars and for drawing from a particular range of trump cards representing various *Commedia dell'Arte* figures for the goal of illuminating the present.

For me, the *tarrochi* are fully pagan, and I have been influenced by Gertrude Moakley's tracing of the 22 major arcana depictions to the 14th century Italian *triumphs* – the decorated floats and pageant carts that processed through the streets on festivals. Moakley attributed the idea behind these processions to Francesco Petrarch's poem *Il trionfi* – in which he derived the triumphs of the cardinal virtues from the Roman *triumphus* that originally celebrated a military victory. This is, of course, contentious but a much different idea than the occult association of the tarot with the 22 letters of the Hebrew alphabet. It is also still obvious that our earliest tarot packs, the Visconti di Modrone, the Brambilla, and the Visconti-Sforza cards that were painted by Bonifacio Bembo, had other sources as well, but Moakley's contribution to the understanding of the tarot retains merit.

Tracing the actual processions of triumphs within the tarot deck is more imaginative then can be discerned accurately according to Moakley's interpretation, but I recall vaguely that she considered the major arcana parades of the four Triumphs of the cardinal virtues (Justice – *La Justice,* Prudence – presumably *l'Ermite,* Strength/Courage – *La Force,* and *Temperance*) as not each comprising an equal number of *maschere* or carnival masks floats – some processions being longer than others. Nevertheless, the *tarrochi* have served me as a golden key or philosopher's stone into esoteric understandings. For myself in fact, along with a continuing fascination in the tarot, my studies, investigations and experiences have produced an adoration of the pagan gods. The deities are needed if for no other reason than to be focusing vitalities toward which we can express our gratitude and thankfulness. Among the Müller deck, I use for the proto-deities the cards of *Junon* for the dawn (II), *Jupiter* for the luminous sky (V), *La Lune* for the moon (XVIII), *Le Soleil* for the sun (XVIIII), and *Le Monde* for the earth (XXI). To these I add the divine twins to complete what I understand as the proto-pantheon, namely, *La Force* as Mars or Hercules (XI) and *Le Chariot* as Quirinus or Janus (VII).

La Maison de Dieu or (Falling) Tower (XVI) and *Le Jugement* or Judgment (XX) I employ as symbols of the anti-divine. On the altar, these two are always present but on the *feriae,* they are turned over to be face down. The remaining thirteen cards I accept as symbolizing the varying conditions, moral principles and/or the Commedia dell'Arte characters that comprise the panoply of life, and it is from these on festival days that I draw a card to divinize the present, namely, *Le Bateleur,* Juggler, Mountebank, Sorcerer or Magician (I); *L'Imperatrice,* Empress, Rosina or Colombina (III); *L'Empereur,* Emperor or Pantalone (IV); *L'Amoureux* or Lover(s) (VI); *La Justice* or Justice (VIII); *L'Ermite,* The Hermit or Il Dottore (VIIII); *La Roue de Fortune* or The Wheel of Fortune (X); *Le Pendu,* The Hanged Man or Pierrot (XII); La Mort or Death (XIII); Temperance (XIIII); *Le Diable,* the Devil, Pulcinella or Punch (XV); *L'Etoile,* the Star or Il Capitano (XVII) and *Le Mat,* the Fool or Harlequin (unnumbered or 0).

Consequently, along with the *I Ching,* I contend that the tarot deck of cards comes the closest to being a 'sacred book' for me and through which I gained my initial insights into paganism as an historic development and a different way to approach the holy than through biblical reflections or dharmic meditations. True enough, both Hinduism and Buddhism were early fascinations and probably mostly because they both offered established alternatives to replace my growing disenchantment with the Christianity in which I had been raised. I have always been attracted to the exotic, and the religions of the East certainly offered in the early stages a surplus of the colourful and alien. But in time one might learn that the unfamiliar and foreign are mostly titillating only at first and as they become increasingly known and understood are eventually recognised as only the more superficial aspects of spirituality rather than what comes in time to be the more durable and sustaining in the comprehensions of religious navigation. Today, through a Facebook page for pagans that seems to have a constantly growing number of requests to join (currently at 2.9K membership), there are continual requests from newcomers or sometimes just the curious for 'suggestions on the best ways to learn accurate and detailed information about paganism'. My usual reply is to refer to Margot Adler's *Drawing Down the Moon,* but recently during a recording for 'Candid Chats with Bella' (HPS Children of the Crossroads-ATC), both Lola Stardust and Belladonna LaVeau thought that Margot's book is too difficult and complicated for beginners. They also complained that pagan newbies today are principally interested in quickly succeeding with the crafting of spells yet without knowing what conjuring and hexing truly involve. Admittedly, I was surprised to learn that this is what concerns pagan newcomers the most at present. I have, of course, long recognised the appeal of magic (in London, especially that of Thelema and Chaos magick), but that to me seemed at first to entail seeking unnecessarily various violations of the natural. I have since come to understand magic as efforts to achieve shortcuts to a desired end more than strictly contradicting nature, and true enough, Dragon magick or eco-magic is undertaken for the protection and benefit of the environment and living world rather than their contravention. But for me, paganism is much, much more than spell casting, though there appears to be a growing divide between an older generation and youth who, even when identifying as pagan, subscribe to a new secular faith that is currently being designated as 'wokeism'. Wesley Yang refers to this as 'the successor ideology' – a delegitimisation project targeting the foundations of humanist, Enlightenment values. Wokeism seeks to crush dissent. For 'ex-Muslim' Sarah Haider, it is an 'anti-ideology' with no centre and in which its adherents find a thrill in playing the righteous inquisitor. This certainly is most evident when conversation between pagans today turns to the subject of transgenderism. The older generation of women argue for the right to their own space when addressing and conducting rituals concerning female issues such as giving birth, menstruation, menopause and the difficulties involved for those women who have lived all their lives under the duress of a patriarchal society. But any exclusion of transwomen from women's functions is often vehemently rejected by both younger women and men as transphobic, and the older generation are now labelled as 'TERFs' (trans-exclusionary radical feminists). How this age divide has come to be frankly baffles me, but my greater worry is with any premature wish to exercise a skill without a proper preparation. Some of this is a New Age desire for immediate results – both in the integration efforts and in spellcraft. This can also extend to the willy-nilly evocation of various deities. However, for an indigenous pagan tradition such as Candomblé or Lucumí, there is a strict enforcement of apprenticeship through one's godparents, and an unprepared solicitation of an *orisha* is considered to be an extremely dangerous undertaking for the uninitiated. Consequently, there are many different kinds of paganism, and those processes that lead to familiarisation and learning constitute by far the most feasible approach for anyone new to the spirituality. I think Margot's book is a good start for most of us, but I agree with Lola and Belladonna that Edith Hamilton's 1942 *Mythology: Timeless Tales of Gods and Heroes* that covers Greek, Roman and Norse myths is also as good an introduction to the pagan world as any. Beyond this and whatever reading anyone does, I also always advise the importance of finding some quiet place – under a favourite tree, by a spring or well, in a particular glen or woods, a seaside shore or the like – to contemplate peacefully in digesting what one has read and to let the divine communicate to the recipient in some gradually augmenting meaningful way.

The emergence of cancel culture or wokeism is not solely applicable to contemporary Western paganism, of course, but appears to be more a youth phenomenon in general. Bari Weiss, in fact, refers to 'the (mostly young) wokes and the (mostly 40+) liberals' as well as to the civil libertarianism of the Old Guard. But with the intolerance of a religious zealotry, youthful pagan wokeists as well as keyboard warriors likewise seem to be wishing to enforce conformity to nonliberal values through 'social policing, shaming and shunning tactics'. In this, they appear to be fusing the new secular faith of wokeism with paganism itself. Ayaan Hirst Ali, another 'ex-Muslim' like Haider, sees the woke movement as paralleling that of the Islamists and claims that the woke are not true liberals. Liberals themselves are those who continue to agitate for the ideals of universal human rights, individual freedom, free inquiry, critical thinking and subjectivity. Haider perceives that this emerging new extremism, in its efforts to elevate integration over multiculturism, is now being supported by our educational, media and nonprofit institutions. However, '. . . by attacking the legitimacy of our core spiritual principles', Gus DiZerega claims that 'Wokeism has done enormous harm to the NeoPagan community'. There is an over-focus on micro-issues, the rush to assert being a traumatised victim, and the expression of extreme levels of privileged fragility. This ultra-modernism is 'identitarianism gone bananas'.

Consequently, the need for appropriate and balanced books through which one might gain a workable insight into valid forms of paganism is increasingly important if not also imperative. Even though it precedes the first modern sense of the term *woke* (from soul singer Erykah Badu's song 'Master Teacher' in his 2008 album *New Amerykah Part One: 4th World War*), I will still suggest Margo Adler's *Drawing Down the Moon: Witches, Druids, Goddess-Worshippers, and Other Pagans in America* – first published in 1979 and subsequently revised in 1986, 1996 and 2006. But some other works have also been suggested. Among those that have been mentioned in the Facebook Pagans group are Grey Cat's *Deepening Witchcraft: Advancing Skills and Knowledge* (2002), Timothy Roderick's *Dark Moon Mysteries: Wisdom, Power, and Magic of the Shadow World* (1996), Judy Harrow's *Wicca Covens: How to Start and Organize Your Own* (1999), John Beckett's *The Path of Paganism: An Experience-Based Guide to Modern Pagan Practice* (2017), Ronald Hutton's *Triumph of the Moon: A History of Modern Pagan Witchcraft* (1999) and *Witches, Druids, and King Arthur* (2003), Starhawk's *The Spiral Dance: A Rebirth of the Ancient Religion of the Great Goddess* (1979,

1999), Vivianne Crowley's *Principles of Wicca* (1997), V. Vale & John Sulak's *Modern Pagans: An Investigation of Contemporary Pagan Practices* (2001), and 'if one's primary concern is ritual how-to', Mari Elm suggests Janet & Stewart Farrar's *A Witches' Bible: The Complete Witches Handbook* (1996) that, despite being 'very traditional', is adaptable. She also signals works by Raymond Buckland and Scott Cunningham – the latter especially with his 'gift for simplifying', and she adds,

> There are thousands of good books out there & thousands of not so good ones. You won't be able to suss out the not helpful books until you've read some good ones.

Nevertheless, Susan Greenwood more or less echoes my own sentiment when she says,

> Go and sit under a tree and let it speak to you, or listen to the movement of a river and let it flow through you. It's simple – open your senses and feel!

In addition, and though she refers to Wicca, her advice is equally applicable to paganism more broadly, in an earlier work, Vivianne Crowley says that:

> Other than a very simple belief in the life force and the powers of the human psyche, all that is required is that we accept the framework of ritual and symbolism in which Wicca operates as containing age-old truths which are not literal but which are hidden and whose truth will unfold over the years as we integrate them into our own lives.

There is a welcomed affirmation of liberal values through these works and the practices they suggest. They also attest to the variety and pluralism that ultimately is central to paganism. I may not agree with everything, but there is a wealth of material available for whomever has an interest. There is something for everyone.

I shall have a bit more to say about wokeism at a later point, but for now I wish to return to my own initial involvement with writing. During the early Amsterdam commune days, my neighbour Nicolas Schors whose occult and antiquarian bookstore, Boekhandel Arcanum, was just across the street asked me to write a book on the tarot. I decided to focus on the major arcana alone and write uninterruptedly on one card per day – beginning with the highest number and proceeding to the Magician as the culmination. During this writing, my mother phoned to tell me that my brother had died. Peter had told me when he was still in Amsterdam that he did not think he would live much longer. I replied that we can all feel that, but he responded by saying, 'I think I will do something about it'. When I asked why, he said, 'Because it is all repetitive'. During my conversation with my brother, I was at a loss for what to say since I had at the time been feeling much the same way. I could only think to reply, 'I will miss you'. I could tell he wanted me to say more and was surprised when I did not. He had always had grand ideas – like purchasing a yacht, building something, etc., and I allowed myself to think and hope that this was another one of his many pet schemes. A few days later I was to travel, and Peter was working in the basement of the Amsterdam house – constructing two small rooms that had been inspired by his recent trip to Morocco. He asked whether I liked what he had so far done and was pleased when I said that I did. It was the last time I saw my brother – alive.

He had left Amsterdam by the time I had got back. I remember having a terrible cold, and Richard called to me that my mother was on the phone and that she sounded very upset. When I got to the telephone, I heard her say, 'Oh, Michael, Michael, Michael!' I was thinking she was calling to tell me about my elderly grandmother. I said something to the effect that this was the expected inevitable. 'Not Grand,' she screamed, 'It's Peter!' The words still shock me to this day, and that was over a half-century ago. A friend with whom Peter had been had not seen him for two days and had called my family. Peter's car was at the Delaware Water Gap, and my father had gone there, and while there the police had found my brother's body. Peter had jumped from a cliff on the Pennsylvania side of the Delaware Water Gap. 'Dad is driving home now,' Mother explained, 'alone', she added. I told her to call Dr. Chamberlain, our family doctor, to ask for something to calm her down. 'Oh, he died!' she replied.

'Dr. Chamberlain died?' I asked in astonishment. Mother confirmed her surprise as well. People had apparently been telling him that he did not look well, but he would do nothing about it. Many years later while attending a peace rally in Wickford, Rhode Island, one of the speakers mentioned that the number of Vietnam veteran suicides was three times the number of war casualties themselves. It was only then that I realized that my battle-scarred brother belonged with those statistics.

Life does continue – as the adage says, and I have learned amply since that time that life is about much more than repetition. I have come to treasure being alive as something painful at times but wonderful for much of the rest. I wish my brother could have been able to learn this as well. But at the same time, I respect his and anyone's right to autonomy and his or her choice to end their life. If and when there is a mental health issue or the suicide attempt is really a cry for help, then of course self-death is not to be endorsed. From Socrates, Seneca and Vietnamese and Tibetan Buddhist monks to Diane Pretty, there are many suicides that occur for political or logical reasons. An individual's right to end suffering can be legitimately respected and even allowed. Thomas Moore, John Donne and David Hume had important things to say in this respect. But if one's own death is undertaken to cause the indiscriminate loss of life of innocent others, such as we have with jihadist bombers, a line must be drawn. Self-death if it involves only the self is one thing; self-death that takes others off the contended battle field of everyday life with it is, by contrast, a travesty of every moral and aesthetic principle. It is especially sad and pathetic when such an act is undertaken to gain some phantom paradise or honour an alleged supreme being. Apart from taking pleasure in the deliberate torture of captive victims, this could be *the* worst of human behaviour. The one mitigating factor, however debatable, is the belief in altruistic suicide on behalf of the asymmetrical suffering, injustice, humiliation and powerlessness endured by one's avenging group, community or religion.

The martyrdom of Islamist militants is different than that of Christian saints in that it is as much associated with homicide as it is with suicide. Civilians and non-combatants become the unwilling victims in a tactic to advance a cause through psychological warfare. But nonetheless, early Christian martyrs can be compared with the Islamic suicide bombers of today in their valuing of personal life as worth less than some communal or religious entity. If it was not these Christian individuals who are responsible for causing the deaths of others, it has nonetheless been the Christian Church which has been instrumental for the murder of countless victims from pagans in the third to sixth centuries – including Hypatia of Alexandria, Manichaeans in the 4th and 5th centuries, Saxons in the 8th century, the Crusades from the 11th to the 13th centuries that accounted for the deaths of Jews and peasants across Europe, the Inquisition against the Albigensians or Cathars in the 13th century, the slaughter of Poles and Turks in the 15th century, the Spanish Inquisition in the Netherlands in the 16th century, the Huguenots in the 16th century to the Burning Times of the Witch Craze from the 15th to the mid-18th centuries and the slaughter of German Protestants in the 17th century. These alone account for the deaths of thousands upon thousands if not millions of people. Individual martyrs include John Huss in 1415, Gaspard de Coligny in 1572, and Giordano Bruno in 1600. TThen too, beginning with the Pequot War, the extermination of Native Americans throughout both continents of the New World was predominantly done in the name of Christ. And even in the 20th century, there have been Croatian extermination camps, 'Soldiers of Christ' in Vietnam, and the Rwanda massacres. As dreadful as the current atrocities of Daesh and other jihadists have been, they almost pale in comparison to those committed in the past by Christians of both Catholic and Protestant stripes.

None of this, however, should be surprising if and when we take an honest look at the Mosaic religions beginning with God's ordering Abraham to sacrifice his son Isaac. Although this was not completed, it underscores not only the macabre nature of the Old Testament figure but also a *sub rosa* theme of paternal filicide throughout the Abrahamic tradition. This is the reverse of the unintended patricide of Oedipus or, more recently, that bizarre and mysterious case of Prince Dipendra of Nepal. Among the ancient Greeks, there is the prolicide of Cronus who devoured his children as soon as they were born – ostensibly to prevent the prophecy of his being overcome by one of his offspring. Other noteworthy instances of a father killing a son include those of Peter the Great, Ivan the Terrible and Marvin Gay, Sr. But even the intended crucifixion of Jesus Christ on Calvary through the plans of his father Yahweh – for whatever alleged reason – amounts to a seminal example of patrilineal cruelty.

Boris Johnson referred at some point to Islam as 'a Judaeo-Christian heresy'. As Christ was declared in the Book of John and then confirmed by the Nicene Creed to be God himself, Mohammed's religion may be understood as the attempt by Yahweh or Elohim, now called Allah, to reject this usurper son and re-establish his sole reign as the 'one true God'. Christ is now reduced to being a revered prophet but no longer one of three persons belonging to the God of the Old Testament or the Quran. The father has overthrown the deified son.

But either way, the Abrahamic figure may be understood as a heartless monster when it comes to humanity if not to animal life in general. Among the Quran's 164 Jihad verses, 2:191 and 2:193 advocate violence against those deemed to be wrongdoers and 9:5 the same against pagans. In addition, verse 49:9 calls for the bloodshed of transgressing Muslims. Nevertheless, the Old Testament far exceeds both the Christian New Testament and the Muslim Quran and Hadith in depicting the thousands of people who are butchered because of God. But even the New Testament's doctrine of eternal punishment allows or encourages the torture and slaughter of those who do not accept Christ. 1 Peter 4:1 directly states that one should suffer as did Christ – presumably the victim and victor alike. And we find in the writings of Tertullian, Augustine and Thomas Aquinas endorsement of those who are saved to take pleasure in witnessing the eternal sufferings of the damned.

I have no doubt that traditionalists of every kind will deplore what I am saying here. Admittedly, perhaps much of how I read the Bible is my own interpretation – but not all! There are too many tales and supposed statistics within the 'Good Book' which cannot be defended by even the most diehard of believers. While I am not in accord with such critics as Richard Dawkins and Christopher Hitchens, I resonate with a lot of what they say. But between the hardcore atheist position and that of the non-critical Abrahamists, there is a non-transcendental understanding that accepts enchantment but is not enslaved by it. It is this middle ground that I identify as pagan.

During my hasty return to the United States (from which I had sworn I would never return except for funerals) and Peter's burial proceedings, I kept to my vow and continued to write on the 22 trumps one per day. My unpublished manuscript, 'The End of Eternity', is the result, but Nick Schors observed that there were no footnotes or references, and because of the way I write, he felt that this was necessary. His suggestion in turn became my inspiration to expand those footnotes to my Book of Revelations rewrite into the footnoted tomes of *The Roman Festival Calendar* and *The Divine versus the Asurian*. The latter of these I began four or so years later over the winter when isolated in a chalet named Stäfa in the Swiss Alps – lent to me by Ian and Antoinette Baker of the Jungian Institute in Zurich.

For the rest, I continued my explorations into pagan and animist dimensions, sometimes with entheogenic assistance, in Uppsala and other theonymic places in Sweden, in Jutland, in the Roman forum, in Delphi and Dodona, and throughout Britain and Ireland – and of course, perhaps most continuously of all, at home in the below sea level bog known as Amsterdam. My hidden shamanic retreat, however, became a remote Goulnacappy house on 65 acres of land within the Ring of Kerry between Killarney and Killorglin. The idea of Ireland had come to me on the trans-Atlantic ship I had taken to return to Europe from Peter's funeral and after my driving a van of his belongings from San Francisco to New Jersey. The beauty and mystery of the Emerald Isle spoke to me as she came into view. Subsequently, I traversed that country and slept in my VW Beetle until I found the property and purchased it for only an astonishing £2,500.

Today, I have reached the realisation that one eventually comes to the point or stage of life in which there is no future objective. It is, however, at this junction that one is free to simply weave the various daily strands and impressions into a mystical fabric. There is nowhere to go; it has instead become a be-here-now situation.

If anything stains a soul, it has to be suicide bombing. If I could possibly believe in it, I would be a perfect candidate at my present end of life stage. The horror of our times is that there is a surfeit of youth who think this same way. Have they not got a viable objective towards which to aim? While I am not a Picasso, Joyce or Shostakovich, and it is now too late to try to become one, I am at least free to live each day as an immediate treasure; nothing more, nothing less. And if one is lucky enough to have a love, this is what is indeed the most important.

As a vernacular shaman, I question why in Wicca and contemporary paganism the feminine is virtually equated with darkness. As I have come to understand, all the oppositions (light-dark, male-female, positive-negative, spirit-matter, etc.) revolve and align differently at different times. These rotating binaries are the cosmic flywheel and are together opposed by the 'spirit' of total annihilation. And it is this last that has hoodwinked half of our planet. Drawing from Vedic, Iranian and Nordic sources, I have come to designate this non-existent but operative 'force' of extermination the 'asurian'. It has been made into or at least accepted as God, Yahweh, Allah. And here is where I lose a goodly portion of my readers, I would add to the mix: Varuna, Uranus, Hephaistos, Odin and Illuyanka.

By contrast, the phenomenon of intercalation allows our terrestrial year to coincide in principle with the ideal circle: 360 degrees / 360 days. For the ancients, the non-time extra represented the asuric void – something to be feared. Yes, paganism is indeed a part of modernity's quest and valuing of the archaic. But not everything that is old is sacred. To fill that 'extra' non-sacred void of absolute emptiness, the ancients conceived the carnival. They were creating a positive beauty out of a void or, rather, in spite of the empty abyss. We cannot turn nothing into something: *non creation ex nihilo* or *ex nhilo nihil fit*. Instead, it is a negative which we can transform or convert into a positive. Otherwise, it is a matter of creating an Indra's Net to *fill* the void that is intrinsically poised to obliterate both the positive and negative – Indra's Net being the whole of phenomenal reality; the dance of nature between the positive and negative; the reflection of the all in every gem at the cross-fibres of the endless net.

If there is a seminal creative principal to the cosmos, though more like an evolutionary, rather than creator, force, it is the pure act of wishing – regardless of whether for self, family or other. It is this that is the primal impulse of the universe or multiverse. Wishing is the sacred. It is at the heart of sacrality: holy in and of itself. In other words, the cosmic wish embodied is our entire cosmos or infinite world of physicality or tangibility. And the chief reflections of this matter-energy continuum are health or wholeness, wonder and freedom.

The entertainment of this understanding is my basic approach to life and the cosmos in which we exist – whether this is spiritual or religious or ritual or pagan. But it is at least, for me, a derivative of much contemplation. And as the image contains, if only through etymologically folkloric coincidence, the *magus* of magic, I prefer contemplation to the much-championed meditation. All the more power to those for whom meditation works. For me, I simply fall asleep. I, instead, choose form upon which to ponder.

But all this being said, the framework within which I work will include mention of Richard. We met through our coalescing family network and perhaps were in love with one another virtually from the start, but it took a number of years to realise this. For me, Richard retains a deferential vulnerability, a perpetual sense of humour, and a genuine generosity, and he has seemed to be in awe of me. We both are most humbly grateful to be sharing our legendary happiness with one another. And just after I have written what I have just said, Shirley reminded me that it was our tenth wedding anniversary. I had forgotten completely; we have so many marital commemorations, and I had only been celebrating the May Tubilustrium instead.

For the rest, the concerns to which I will inevitably return include climate, health and education. I could add to this the pollution that we are inflicting upon our environmental planet. More specifically, I remain distressed over the American-Iranian conflict, the hopelessness of Yemen, the unfinished ISIL business, the Venezuelan stalemate, Britain's Brexit even with the resignation of Theresa May, and the utter embarrassment of the

Trump presidency. I do not think of myself as truly political, but I do take seriously the opportunities to vote. I have lived much of my earlier life in a state of blessed naivety – not aware of American hegemonic deception and supposed 'exceptionalism'. I have been grateful and proud to learn from those of my own generation here in the Provence of France the gratitude that is felt towards my birth country for the role it played in the liberation at the conclusion of the Second World War. It may have been our best moment. And it came to fuse with the generosity that was expressed through the CARE package distribution I have heard of from friends in Germany and Scandinavia. So at least it is not a black-or-white situation in total, but I no longer feel any pride for my American origin. I do accept my British nationality, but I have always since my college days been opposed to the whole concept of the nation-state and the chauvinistic nationalism that it generates. I am a believer in the *polis* or city-state as a basic civil unit and the pre-Westphalian lack of boundaries and passports for the freedom of physical movement and travel.

It is instead for my children and grandchildren and *all* children that I muster my departing concern. Whether in the Midi or Scotland and previously the Californian coast or the panoramas of such states as Wyoming and Utah, I remain staggered by the beauty of our planet which I maintain is what is truly exceptional and what expresses to me the visionary need and hope for the peace, security and growth of the earth and her human and biotic communities in the days yet to come. Capitalism has indeed played a major contribution to civilisation's advance, but, like the criticism I have heard from Brits concerning the present European Union, 'it has no reset button'. The gulf today between the haves and especially the super-rich and the have-nots, the lack of equable distribution, the use of sanctions and military threat and aggression, the thoughtless exploitation and land clearance for ever-increasing agribusiness purposes, and the resulting pollution expose the deficiencies of unchecked capitalism vis-à-vis ecological sustainability and global human welfare. I pray to the gods for assistance in establishing an enlightened and awakened consciousness for planet earth.

For my conviction is that, behind the phenomenal and the grievous dilemmas that plague our terrestrial existence, there is a something else, a deeper magical beauty that constitutes itself as an offering to shared understanding and insight. The dynamic between the otherworld and this world is the elusive but always present spirit of the spiritual. It appears to us in countlessly different manners, shaped in large part by our respective cultural conditionings, but there is a common gist that is potentially recognisable by those who seek it. This crux is what we can tap into despite the individuality and private encounter we each have with the divine. Every one of us is a root that feeds into and then flowers together as the world tree.

One delightful interlude was attending Chris and Vivianne Crowley's Ruby Wedding Anniversary in Stratford upon Avon. Among the ninety or so guests were Ronald Hutton, Caroline Robertson, Morgana, and Rufus and Melissa Harrington. The celebration of two people's mutual love and enduring relationship was a moving and beautiful gathering. Most present were Wiccans – many of whom were initiates of Chris and Vivianne's. Richard and I were the anomalies. We have not been initiated, and we follow no specific lineage or tradition. Our paganism is organically unstructured, intrinsically spontaneous and primarily nature-oriented. It is this last which may be what we share the most with Wiccans and witches: all pagans resonate in some manner with the natural. It was amusing at the Stratford festivities, however, that we were intriguing to the majority who did not know us. Witches, initiated or otherwise, are pagans too, and we all celebrate overlapping ceremonial observations – chiefly the solstices and equinoxes. But at the same time, I became more mindful and aware how my pagan sympathies and practices are generic and contrast with more formally ritualistic expressions. And, of course, my pagan understanding is less reductive of the mythologic register of gods and goddesses. When I hear someone mention '*the* goddess', my automatic impulse is to ask 'which one?'

But apart from all this, and as Guy Davenport following Wittgenstein has said, the totality of the world requires another world for its meaning. This 'otherworld' is a reflection through idiom, metaphor and symbol of our perception of melodic pattern – another reality, an other or different reality, that 'exists' outside the empirical dimension of measurement. This is civilisation as the very product of religion, science and art comprising what Davenport refers to as 'geography of the imagination' – the correlative of the observable world of tangibility, energy and nature. Whether imaginary or an ontological co-creation, this is the index of myth, magic and the gods as an important and operative mode of exploration and celebration for a pagan – along with our comprehension, appreciation and protection of the natural as the this-worldly component of the sacred. Navigating the interchange between the two worlds, this world and the other, is a central focus of pagan mysticism.

While my life as a whole has skittered along in what could possibly be described as a quasi-blissful dream state, political realities have nevertheless intervened. I was raised in a Republican family and thought of myself as a member of the Republican Party. My mother in time became an independent, and I suppose I have too. My sister by contrast has become a staunch Democrat and ran as such three times for the governorship of the state of Rhode Island. My first chance to participate in a Presidential election occurred while I was studying at UCSB. As I high school student and in my Republican ignorance, I had indeed championed Dwight Eisenhower over Adlai Stevenson, but on the present occasion I complained to my father over the phone that the campaigns of both Kennedy and Nixon sounded more like childish mud-slinging. This was not what I had been raised to believe in, namely, the greater sophistication and dignity of Republican behaviour in comparison with that of the Democrats. There was now no difference whatsoever, and I did not want to vote for either candidate. My father explained forcefully, 'We are Republicans, and we vote for the Republican candidate!' And so I complied and did.

I remember Bill Clinton being the first President that I voted for and who won, but it must have actually been Jimmy Carter who remains for me a revered hero like Nelson Mandela. Unless, because I was living in Europe in the 1970s, and I was unable to vote. My memory is that I have never missed any Presidential election. With Lyndon Johnson and his race against Barry Goldwater, I liked neither candidate though at least preferring Johnson over the Senator from Arizona. In those days, the election results were known as they came in state-by-state, so I was able to wait until nearly 8 PM when the polls were to close in California, and knowing by then that Johnson had already won, I did not need to vote for him. I confess to having voted both times for Barack Obama and to have actually celebrated his first win. But, like almost all with the exception of Jimmy Carter, I have ended up no more enamoured of the Obama Presidency than I have of the others. In fact, I reached the point of finding his Presidency one of profound disappointment. The war in Syria may have been the worst of all, but his incarceration of whistle-blowers alone remains a grievous Lady Macbeth stain. Perhaps under the 'shadow government' he could have done no better than he had been 'allowed'. I am glad for the cannabis relaxation and same-sex marriage provisions that have principally served as bread-and-circus distractions – however much welcomed. I remember wishing in the remaining days while Obama was in office that there could have been Presidential Pardons for at least Chelsea Manning and Edward Snowden, but the likelihood of these seemed no greater than any kind of humble diminishment of arrogance in the eight years of his administration. I was wrong and delightfully surprised when Manning did in fact receive a release from prison.

Despite my strong disenchantment with Hillary Clinton, I would have preferred her to what we got. However, at the minimum of knowing that there was no doubt she would garner California, I was at least free on this occasion to vote Green for Jill Stein. My sympathies had been with Bernie Sanders, and while I felt that Donald Trump would be a major embarrassment let alone disaster, I also thought that the Clinton alliance with the feudalism of Wall Street would certainly not have encouraged the social-political changes that might at least have offered the possibility of rectification and advance. Political mendacity is the most annoying and stifling impediment to the popular awareness that is to be required for both local and global future well-being. I despise such political leaders as Barack Obama, Donald Trump, Hillary Clinton, Teresa May, Boris Johnson, Alexander Lukashenko, Rodrigo Duterte, Min Aung Hlaing, Jair Bolsonaro, Kim Jong-un, Silvio Berlusconi, Narenda Modi, Benjamin Netanyahu, Abdel Fattah Al-Sisi and Recep Tayyip Erdoğan among many others. My exceptions might include Jimmy Carter, Nelson Mandela, Sigurdur Ing Johannsson and José Alberto 'Pepe' Mujica. And I also despise the non-obvious capitalistic undermining of innovation and discovery, the very repression of ideas and inventions, that have been directed over time against the likes of Nikola Tesla, Adam Trombly, John Bedini, Eugene Mallove, Brian O'Leary, Floyd 'Sparky' Sweet, Shiuji Inomata and Parahamsa Tewari in relation, in this instance, to the energy industry's antithesis to torus-capturing of radiant or free energy. Instead, on the west side of the Pond and under the Presidency of Donald Trump, we have had the current heedless rollback of environmental protections, the pending overturn of Roe v. Wade, the permit granted for the disputed Keystone pipeline, the regulations cut for affordable health care, an illegal act of war after the chemical attack in Syria, the launch of brinkmanship with North Korea, the allowance for the sale of personal and sensitive information by internet service providers without knowledge or consent, and the slashing of funds for the arts, humanities endowments and public broadcasting. I may be completely wrong, and I am no unmitigated fan of Vladimir Putin – though admittedly I admire his tactical brilliance and his ability to talk publicly for hours and without teleprompter notes – but do not see him as the dastard demon he is increasingly accused of being. So, the anti-Russian hysteria that America screams now relentlessly leaves me essentially cold. Interfering with elections! Stephen Kinzer argues that the United States has been doing the same in foreign countries for more than a century. I am not convinced that the American hand had nothing to do with the Ukrainian debacle as well.

The repeal of Obamacare despite its many flaws and an overturning of a pregnant woman's liberty to choose would be most disappointingly regressive, and the deportation of illegal immigrants both cruel and sad. The Trump-Brexit alliance – especially as a vehicle to destroy the European Union – is nothing I am able to endorse. But perhaps the worst of all was the unpresidential sullying of an office that had been held in worldwide esteem. Piqued outrage and megalomania now truly did seem the 'so'-this, 'so'-that Trump-cards that would stand-in for gracelessness, boorishness and fear of possible ineptitude. Possession of the nuclear codes was maybe the most terrifying of all.

So our world had cracked. The press had lost its credentials, and a populist ignorance had come to seize control on both sides of the Pond and perhaps beyond. The clock was being turned back on much of the progressive achievements that are the products of many decades of struggle. I agree that the invasion of Iraq was 'possibly the worst decision ever made in the history of our country', and I can also agree with Trump's criticism of NATO. But I deplored his pro-Israeli position and resolve to veto any new UN Security Council resolution critical of Israel. I also lament what he has done with the nuclear agreement with Iran. I had hoped with this tweet, tweet, tweet businessman that there might be more delightful surprises than unhappy disappointments, but with the wall between the United States and Mexico being erected, the Keystone XL and Dakota Access pipelines being constructed – this last through the Standing Rock Sioux Reservation, the standards protecting vehicle emission being reduced, the number of refugees allowed into the U.S. from Syria and other majority-Muslim nations being limited, the Guantánamo Bay prison in Cuba remaining open, the torturing of prisoners for information having been resumed, three Supreme Court nominees unfavourable to preserving Roe v. Wade having been picked,

Israel announcing continuously that new homes for Jewish settlers will be built in the occupied West Bank, and the Suleimani assassination, whatever hope I may have had at the time of Trump's inauguration had come to be obliterated. Concerning social, legal and environmental issues, as a result of the Trump Presidency, we have apparently abandoned recognition of the achievements that we had struggled to have achieved. Every day was instead a sad revelation, and none of it was surprising. An anti-progressive populist fury has swept the preserves of Western civilization – one that has been eerily reminiscent of the fascist sentiments of the 1930s.

And while the release of Chelsea Manning had been a completely unexpected but welcomed surprise, one significant illustration of the more pervasive dastardliness of our times and in our Western world, rather than in the Middle East, Yemen or elsewhere, is the government-sanctioned police brutality – especially in the United States – that allows and even encourages bodily intrusions of suspected individuals that include vaginal and anal probing, forced blood draws, nonconsensual catheterisations, roadside strip searches, tasering, beatings, shackling and being held at gun point. The forced and violent removal of an already seated passenger on a United Airlines flight would be part of this barbarian syndrome. And then, of course, there has been the George Floyd on-camera murder.

I can see our present world re-shaping as a consequence of Trump's populist America and Britain's Brexit. At this point, these are only imaginings but yet still within the limits of relatively imminent possibility. In this envisioning, Scotland breaks free of the United Kingdom, and the island of Eire north and south becomes united as the Republic of Ireland. The real question concerns the European Union. There could be almost undoubtedly a Grexit for Greece. The independence of France and The Netherlands remains uncertain, but I would not be surprised if the EU is ultimately confined to the states of northern Europe alone. It is believable that in time, Catalonia will secede successfully from Spain. Perhaps there will eventually be an independent Basque state as well. Meanwhile, on the other side of the Pond, Calexit would result in California as an autonomous nation. Possibly Hawaii could do something similar. A Texit for Texas would seem improbable when that state is still too much in accord with the former Trump administration. How much Asia and Africa might change I have no idea. The continual protest in Hong Kong may, however unlikely, amount to something. There is also always the possibility of a united Kurdistan eventually diminishing both Iraq and Turkey. There has been talk of a war between the

United States and China, let alone one between North Korea and an alliance between Japan and South Korea. There is also talk of military confrontation between the US and Iran as well as between the US and Mexico!

In fact, the first two weeks of the Trump administration in Washington consisted of unsurprised shock. The President was keeping to his campaign declarations. I am ambivalent over popular protest, though the violence witnessed at the University of California's Berkeley campus and during the anti-inaugural demonstration in D.C. seemed to me completely inappropriate for the future of the liberal left. Political correctness and violations to the right of free speech are laughably sad – sad though also sadly understandable – as we become increasingly aware of political rule by corporate powers. As President Franklin Roosevelt expressed in 1938 no less, 'The liberty of a democracy is not safe if the people tolerate the growth of private power to a point where it becomes stronger than their democratic state itself. That, in its essence, is fascism.'

Simultaneously, I have read that the IRS is moving to revoke passports for unpaid taxes by citizens abroad. The 'Revocation or Denial of Passport in Case of Certain Tax Delinquencies' was first proposed in 2012 but rejected. However, Congress passed the bill in 2016, and Obama signed it into law. The title of the article in which I have read this information is prefaced with the question: 'Has the U.S. Become a Prison?' On this, I am in full accord with Americans Abroad who argue that permitting passport revocation on account of unpaid debts is contrary to the notions of human liberty established in the Magna Carta, the 1948 Universal Declaration of Human Rights, and the 1958 Supreme Court decision in *Kent v. Dulles* (357 US 116) that stipulates the federal government cannot restrict the right of travel without due process.

My oldest friend Fred has summed up the problems in the US as climate change; the 9th judge on the Supreme Court; justice for black persons, Mexicans, immigrants of all kinds; America's crumbling infrastructure; medical care; education for those who cannot afford it; Roe v. Wade; and the wealthy not paying their fair share. These are the issues still present in America and those with which a predominant number of my friends, liberals for the most part, are concerned. But, while we collectively deplore the opposition, when I criticised their preferred candidate, I became the minority among them. Of course, we need a non-Scalia-type Supreme Court, affordable education, universal medical care, justice for one and all, greater economic equality and a woman's right to safe and legal abortion, but at the same time I have felt for a long time that, like the Soviet Union, the United States has outlived its viability as a single nation-state. I am aware that such an attitude is to be labelled treasonous by traditional patriots, but at the same time I blame the country for a majority of the planet's present problems.

'Tis to be granted that my sympathies are liberal left more than right-winged or conservative, though I have an affinity to libertarianism as well. Whilst on some lists I have been labelled a 'cultural Marxist', my deific fondness ought to preclude me from that conspiracy. I do not subscribe to the elimination of all traditions, languages, religions, morality, individuality, or even to enforce government for social re-assembling as a communist utopia; my position is precisely the opposite. Though I am indeed highly critical of the Abrahamic religions as well as corporate capitalism, I strongly endorse religious and linguistic diversity, the encouragement of individual expression, and a tolerant cosmopolitan pluralism. The Lotocene World I envision in my novel concerning an imagined future is predicated upon a mature development that I accept as a human possibility – one that is both individual and collective, and one that self-checks against myopic greed and/or an aggrieved sense of wrongness for, instead, both genuine largesse and generous magnanimity. If I am tired apart from having grown as old as I have, my weariness incurs mostly from hearing an insistent denial that betterment is not possible.

And on the east side of the Pond this all has appeared to be counter-balanced by the complete uncertainty for a post-Brexit United Kingdom and the European Union through uncompromising arrogance; the British flouting of European rules on air quality; the expected forthcoming of genetically-modified, pesticide-infused and artificially enhanced food imports from America; the loss of consumer protections – let alone a regressive political divorce. As complex as our times have become, they appear to be even more complicated and forlorn through the present emergence of a death cult. With a second London terrorist attack since that on Westminster Bridge – this time involving London Bridge and Borough Market and following by two weeks the Manchester suicide bombing – the current opting for death relish represents a complete rejection of humanistic-humanitarian civilisation. The Brussels explosions at the Zaventem Airport and Maelbeek Metro Station coincided surrealistically with the otherwise *joie de vivre* that can embrace much of the day-to-day passage of time, especially when the sun shines brightly and the days have become longer than the night. Against the promise of spring resurrecting through the air, there can still be the disconsolate and challenging disconnect in the form of myopic violence. Deliberately causing grief to others is, to my way of thinking, among the most heinous of all human acts. There are few words that can even come marginally close to express this disgrace to the human dream of endeavour. For such perpetrators, it is no less and no more than a self-induced and alienating loss for themselves as well for missing out on the veritable splendour of consummate participation. Ariana Grande's return for the One Love Manchester benefit concert that emotionally reaffirmed Mancunian, British and Western determination not to be cowed by jihadist intimidation was tear-jerking but also a beautifully touching expression of hope and celebration. Appearing at this last along with Grande were Miley Cyrus, Katy Perry and Coldplay among others, but it was Justin Bieber whose appearance was perhaps the most direct and poignantly moving. One of the few things I feel President Trump had got right, in fact, is that the terrorists are 'losers'. Though I have no doubt that the humanistic measure of all things in the universe will always eventually triumph – and rightly so, the unnecessary pain and greed along the road we travel together mars our journey that could be and should be one of compassionate and mutually sharing ascent – a thing of beauty in itself and virtually for one and all.

But in honour of those who have lost life and limb on the sorry day of 22 March 2016, let us re-affirm and regain mutual respect and cultural curiosity! Let us also recover the former unity of the Mediterranean lake but move forward over that one-time achievement into an unprecedented union that encourages us all!

I will readily admit that this long political diatribe of mine (and I am not yet finished) has less to do with paganism *per se* and much more with my own liberal, libertarian and socialist convictions. But I frame my insights and aspirations into my personal vision of a paganism that is centred on humanistic, environmental and global values rather than on divisive self-interests that orient foremost, if not exclusively, to aggrandisement of their own power and financial resources. Obviously, not all who identify as pagan would agree with what I consider to be 'pagan' when the words 'human' and 'natural' are accepted as synonyms. Historically, at least, the possibility of world peace has remained only as a dream regardless of the spirituality that has aimed for it – pagan or otherwise or even via interfaith efforts. Fighting and bloodshed are instead the human norm. Of course, in combat, one purposely endeavours to subdue the opponent. In war, the legitimisation of extreme aggression, destruction and mortality is accepted. This has traditionally been understood as different polities engaging in armed conflict. In general, the confrontation occurs between relatively equal parties with a duration of uncertain outcome. Other forms of belligerency, however, are asymmetrical and might assume the form of external military expeditions, interventions or reprisals, and internal rebellions or insurrections in which usually a weaker force is confronted by or itself confronts a stronger one. For General Carl von Clausewitz, Prussian military strategist, war is 'an act of violence intended to compel our opponent to fulfil our will'. Traditionally, war was understood to be what followed its formal declaration between states, but it has become obvious that this official aspect is no longer the case and no longer are both parties necessarily sovereign entities.

Another feature of war is that conflict is to occur between armed fighters and is not to be directed against non-combatant civilians. When innocent non-participants are killed or injured, this has come to be known as 'collateral damage'. But it should be accepted after Nagasaki, Hiroshima, Iraq and Syria that there are no ordinary civilians who are exempt when war is raging. To either side, unless they are captives, those who support or do not oppose the enemy, whether armed or not, are considered themselves to be part of the enemy. And, of course, if our yet to be believed 'progressive West' is a sorry mess in itself, we have concomitantly the turmoil that rages throughout virtually the entire Middle East as well as across North Africa, in Sahel, sub-Saharan Africa, Pakistan, Kashmir, Thailand, the Philippines, Ukraine and between Armenia and Azerbaijan over Nagorno-Karabakh. The stalemate with North Korea is another possible flashpoint. So little unity; so much division; and even less capability of effective leadership and political resolve.

As warfare has become increasingly lethal and tangled, there are fewer and fewer lines of demarcation – at least other than in academic circles – that distinguish what is lawful violence and intimidation from what is unlawful. The supposed legality of the religious campaigns known as the Crusades sanctioned by the Latin Church led to widespread pillage, the Rhineland massacres, and the sacking of Constantinople, and they were ultimately unsuccessful in recovering the Holy Lands of the Eastern Mediterranean from Saracen-Muslim hegemony. Crusaders had expected a mass ascension into heaven to occur at Jerusalem. And if the Crusades were not themselves effective in territorial acquisition, they preceded the West's eventual colonial imperialism that has since fuelled jihadism and terrorism. What we might more profitably keep in mind at present is that the Crusades and religious expansionism – both Christian and Islamic – are a two-way phenomenon extending not just from the West to the East or the East to the West but historically and continually in *both* directions. Whether there has been official declaration or not, we *are* today in a war situation. No one is exempt, and no one is ultimately innocent.

One irony in our development of ethical consciousness is that the ethical was originally associated with human survival. Life is dangerous, and a constantly ready human alertness is or at least was necessary for the fragile human not to become a food source for a more powerful animal. Strength and courage were at the earliest stage the foundations of valour and success. Among the earliest Greeks, *arete* or virtue was principally fortitude in both the hunt and battle. The glory of the hero came to be considered the pinnacle of moral achievement.

But when we compare the origins of ethical understanding with the virtuous as it is often conceived today – mitigated by the additional principles of wisdom, justice and compassion, the glorious warriors of the past seem now to belong more to a bygone age. We tend to ascribe the ruthless and dangerous champion and the slaughter of which he was capable as perhaps medieval but certainly not properly modern. However, this ameliorated attitude is not universal and, especially under conditions of warring, is more often ridiculed as namby-pamby by angry factions. In some sense, the actual commencement of ethical behaviour is to be found in material scarcity and physical dangers and the concomitant competition that arises because of them. In other words, and in a narrow sense rather than in a broad or universal appreciation, it is the aspiration toward courage that characterized the Greek heroic warrior as initially the exemplar of a moral person. The notion of justice or fairness develops subsequently along with understandings of obligation and duty.

The frustrations of our day (at least prior to the November 2020 elections in America) are virtually enough to make any of us grow berserk. They and the possibility of tyranny that arises because of them demand individual risk and courage. On one side of the Atlantic, we had a television personality as President who acted as if he did not believe in the norms and traditions of the democracy he came to head and was instead only interested in serving his own interests – whether through threats, lies, bigotry, conning, boorishness, intellectual isolationism, rallies reminiscent of fascism and/or acting as if immune to the law. As a result, we had developed an over-bureaucratically burdened and non-democratically mismanaged political and economic union in dire need of a reform that scarcely appeared to be on the horizon. On the other side of the Atlantic, following David Cameron's ill-conceived and unintelligent 'in/out' Referendum, we had next a ruthlessly ambitious British Prime Minister who conformed to all the worst characteristics of a politician – one who had disastrously and fatally miscalculated, whose authority had evaporated through disdainful arrogance, who lacked both warmth and any honest sense of contrition, one who appeared to operate through resolute denial, and one who had inflexibly and shamelessly employed the populist mantra 'the people have spoken'. She has since been replaced, but there is virtually no improvement to be uncovered with her replacement.

Although I had been resigned to the success of Donald Trump from the very start, it remained no less horrifying than the Syrian catastrophe and the migrant crisis. But then we have the issue of the Brexit as well. When I first came to Europe, I had welcomed the prospect of smaller countries and borders over which to escape if and when necessary. And while I continue to deplore the very concept let alone reality of the nation-state, I have come at least to appreciate and welcome the prospect of a European Union. To my way of seeing things, the United Kingdom's departure from the EU comes across more like an archaic turning back of the clock in the same vein as the frightening and otherwise laughable reality of a President Trump across the seas had come to be. Those who are *for* the Brexit wish for a freedom from EU laws concerning agriculture, justice and home affairs. They have claimed that the City's unique appeal would not be diminished but that a freer economic market would instead become possible enhancing London as a Singapore-like centre for emerging-market finances. The Eurosceptics have steadfastly claimed that small and medium sized businesses will be released from EU regulations, that the UK would be able to manage its own borders, that the nation would have the ability to reclaim its territorial fishing waters, that it could eliminate the limits on the number of hours people are allowed to work per week, and that Britain would be able to escape the EU's drive for renewable energy. Those advocating a vote to leave Europe have also argued that Scotland would opt to remain with the United Kingdom because the European situation would become too uncertain, and they almost appear to want to see a collapse of the EU itself.

Those of us who have opposed the opt-out, by contrast, have argued that Scotland would indeed renew its desire to separate from England because of its much greater affinity for Europe. Some say that any separation from Europe would take years to be able to disentangle and would become impossible to reverse. From the perspective of the anti-Brexit faction, Britain is stronger by being part of Europe, and there would be a loss of Britain's military influence, a loss of EU subsidies, a loss of jobs if global manufacture were subsequently to move to lower cost EU countries, a loss of Britain's powers of negotiation, and a reduction of the pool of European candidates for the UK work force. While Britain remained as a member of the European Union, the country was able to engage in free trade, the nation's income from the EU surpassed its EU membership fees, and the City has been an important financial centre that served as a gateway to Europe. EU promoters also claim that the UK would still be subject to European politics and economics but be in a position from which it would be unable to influence them. They have feared both the unpredictable result that the Brexit might bring and the negative impact the exit would have on the European economy. Actress Emma Thompson has resonated and appealingly claimed that borders are to be taken down rather than be put up.

The con Brexit position, rather than welcoming the collapse of the EU as do the Eurosceptics, fears it. This comes the closet to my own stance. The views I am expressing are not to be taken as some broadly pagan viewpoint but only as those of myself as one pagan among many others. I hope later to explain the pagan affinities I see in my political position. Most of the arguments concerning the Brexit issue either way appear to have been centred around what was considered to be the best for Britain and what is best for Europe was at best a secondary consideration. Even among the pro-Europe people, there has appeared to have been little recognition or championing of the marvellous and daring experiment that the European Union is. The 'remain camp' concentrated primarily on the economy, and its Brexit fears were involved more simply with the consideration that there is more risk involved with exiting than with staying.

What appeared to be missing in all this, at least for me, is the admirable gamble to create a political union between the various European cultures. A political union invariably becomes also a cultural union as well – in this case, a pluralistic culture without doubt, but one which represents an affirmation of European civilisation. This last has not been fault-free by any account, but it is still a magnificent achievement and proudly rich legacy. To the degree that Europe can be a single entity, the discontinuation of its long history of inner strife and destructive war becomes a more likely possibility.

While there may be over 8,000 cultural communities throughout the world, the European is one of the largest and one that has viable affinities to both its North American and Latin American derivatives. All the same, it is not to be denied that the European Union is beset with terrifying woes that threaten its very survival. Beside the ramifications of Brexit, there also remains a possible Grexit – the withdrawal of Greece from the Union due to its virtually insurmountable debt. And no less an immediate threat is now the migrant crisis and the eventual inability for the Continent to absorb the staggering number of refugees that continue to bleed across its borders and end both the Shengen freedom and the former harmony between now barrier-building states.

Although the great adventure of European unity needs all the support and encouragement that is possible, I fear we have reached a 'united we stand and divided we fall' threshold. The Graeco-Roman values that have transformed, for better or for worse, into modern European values have since both the years of 312 and 1453 been persistently combatted by the ghastly retrograde plagues of anti-logos and immoderation. The European Union is not at all without its faults and profound difficulties, but in the name of progress and secular democracy, it asks to be seen as an enterprise that is worth the gamble. This is a wager that demands courage along with the beauty of imagination. Yes, it is a risk, but it remains a risk against which there is no advancing alternative. In opting for an isolating status quo, we change nothing and must simply continue with paranoia, obsolete crusades and unending uncertainty. So, while I became resigned to the inevitable and its consequence in America, I am equally regretting the Brexit shortsightedness and ending of the daring EU experiment. With regard to Brussels, I have no doubts that there are most unsavoury bureaucratic errors and poor decision-making facilities that have seemed to be more intrinsic than many would wish. But at the same time, despite Boris Johnson's accusations of fascistic centralisation, there is the 'dream of Europe' whose championship by the British is becoming lost and eradicated.

Yes, admittedly, I initially championed the selection of Jeremy Corbin as the leader of Britain's Labour Party and his tipping-the-balance support by the younger generation. I favoured especially his 24 position points as they were first enumerated. But his inflexible Brexit stance and refusal to compromise cemented my growing dislike. For me, the novelist and essayist

Martin Amis, in a 2015 *Sunday Times* article, best signalled the unchanging weaknesses of Corbin: his being undereducated, his slow-minded rigidity, his incuriosity concerning anything beyond the immediate, his 'encysted old left dogmas', his obvious un-electability and – worst of all – his humourlessness. Does this / could this have anything to do with paganism? Intrinsically, perhaps not, but pagans are people too, and like all people they live in a political world. So, it is only to be expected that, like many if not most people, pagans have political opinions. The most obvious, of course, concerns the environment. Since we tend to revere the earth as sacred in herself, ecology could be our foremost concern and what unites the community the most. But the natural world and the planet's ecosystems do not exist in a vacuum but instead interrelate with everything else: the communities into which we divide, the territories these occupy, the conflicts and wars that develop between these various occupations, the educational ventures upon which each collective engages, our abilities to experiment imaginatively, and our capacities to be empathic with others and to compromise with a degree of largess. *All* of this is political! It may be enhanced through science and technological achievements, and it may be reflected through all of our arts, and all might be shared and exchanged or, short of this last, marketed and sold. But now we are speaking economics and economic systems and, ultimately, freedom from government intervention vis-à-vis being inclusive of governmental planning. And, without argument, we are still with politics. So, I suppose that spirituality cannot at the end of the day be divorced from the political – and especially a spirituality that engages with the physicality of our planet and sacred host. True enough, probably the majority of pagans, at least in the West, hold to liberal values, though even here there are militant and at times violent exceptions through obstinately stubborn traditionalisms, chauvinisms, xenophobia, racial prejudice, bullying and myopic vision. As the Environmental Doomsday Clock continues to advance toward catastrophic and irreversible crisis, our political, cultural and religious impasse remains – and this last is as pagan as anything else might be.

But Carpe diem! Though the world's sorry mess remains with all its impossibility toward finding viable solutions, personally I encounter the irony of possessing the treasure of love and happiness despite both the lack of global and individual peace and unthreatened security. After the endless Hurricane Sandy and Artic Freeze delays, my mother's condo was finally sold, and I even have managed to get four-fifths of the funds from the sales price out of the country and abroad. And even though I have since learned that Swiss banks, thanks to all the cumbersome American restrictions that have been enforced upon them, can no longer accept US citizens as clients, the freedom from Rhode Island itself is a great and joyous relief – however temporarily the situation endures.

I have since been through several Novembers, several autumns, and the darker times of year when once again that warmer and lighter part of the twelve-month period in the northern hemisphere becomes a memory at best. But pell-mell has been the darker clouds not only of the Brexit vote, the populist rise of political sentiment across Europe and the ongoing atrocities in the Middle East but also the ongoing uninspiring American choice between unsavoury characters. Russia and Putin may be much, much less than perfect as well, but they appear to be playing their cards better. I can only hope that younger people, including our children, may not be burdened with the same degree of despair that appears to emerge the older one gets. The world's complexity winds itself increasingly into a gordian knot, and none of our political leaders indicate any ability toward unravelling it with understanding and diplomacy. Instead, like Alexander, it is only through an unreflective slashing madness that the intractable is sought to be solved. An additional problem emerges when there is more than one potential Alexander at the same time.

But I can still enjoy the dark, damp mists of Cumbria and beyond in what the autumnal time of the year in the more northern regions enfolds like a perpetual twilight. Not in jest does the confined locale mirror the half-light of humanity's explosive ebb and decline. The line between the present and environmental catastrophe speaks mostly in unheard silence of its impending precariousness. Nihilistic violence centres preoccupation, and a dark fall walk along the banks of the River Lune can become an escapist exercise – futile when measured against the greater imbecilities that plague the news and the shams of democracy on the global stage that are to be found on either side of the Pond. Elite greed and corruption vis-à-vis not only explosive urban obliteration but also the otherwise rotting infrastructures remain displayed beneath the so-called 'free' but mindless world of sound-bite sensationalism. Toxic illusions yet hover at the shadows' edges. In the present demand for instant gratification and a non-stop vaudeville act, 'Sober examinations of our economic, foreign, judicial and environmental policies are dismissed as too complicated and boring'. How much more of a sorry impasse to the human dream is there – one reflected too accurately and bitterly in the pretence and conniving of the media-enforced obscurities concerning both the Leave-Remain and American Presidential contest fiascos? Behind the circus, an oblivion is echoed in the winter's gloom of semidarkness as Ruskin's View fades from discerning sight.

The sun at times might mask, though not too crisply, the sorrows that abound and lurk through every access and crevice. I'm lost to the hammering reality that my birth country has, since I reached the age of five, killed the most people through war than any other. Where went art and the humanities in the avalanche of preoccupation to weapons for both profit and destruction? The refreshing, liberating breeze of science wends its way through the moss-strewn woods, but when the aerial swoosh comes to subside and briefly cease, with mindfulness the pilgrim might hear the enchanting melody of another world always present but less often heard amidst traffic's constant drone and hence forgotten. Almost seen, nymphs and satyrs dart and hide behind the trees and surrender now to find their alternate home in the temples of the muses – our citadels of treasure though rarely richly quiet as the thickened forest are yet hopefully to be found distant from the urban roar. The breeze unchecked is kin to the storm, and the sobering hurricane lashes lethally and destructively if and when her raging fury surpasses both gentle reason and fertile imagination. Lost loves too are swept away in the swift eddies and currents of time. Recollecting past exchanges and joyous moments, wondering whatever happened to those we once embraced, and mourning the many and the special departed becomes an intangible veil of sadness to drape around the soul. Those marvellous adventurous hopes of youth and promise fade or come to belong to newer generations. Rightly but nonetheless forlornly so, the relentless cycle turns. And yet a constantly augmenting cacophony of mindlessness and avarice threatens now even the younger carriers of exploration and mystery. Rebellion need not be violent and often is most successful when not. Conscious resistance that grounds deliberately in the triad of devotion, experience and beauty may be our lonely but only recourse through chaos, stagnation and regression. Friends both gone and present and perhaps still yet to be found are the spiritual allies to assist us each in whatever terrestrial and cosmic battles there are yet to be fought. We pray for the needed energy, and, despite the anguish, desolation and struggle there continues to be, we pray for laughter no less. The flower is a momentary thing of magnificence, but her fruit contains the seeds of re-established renewal and further mirth. Look gently into the quiet well; glimpse reflection and smile!

Toward the later part of my life, it has become London where I expect to finish most of my days. Only a few years ago, we enjoyed the tail-end of a prolonged Indian Summer – one that made the month of September in both Amsterdam and London among the driest in recent records. The warming of our planet must be a concern for everyone – pagan or otherwise. For the occasion I am remembering, I suspected there had already been enough rain not to make the late warm season particularly distressful. It had been delightful and especially welcomed after the premature winter-weather during the preceding August. With the mild bubble hanging on in the southeast of England for the first three days of October, with friends, I was able to enjoy a late lunch in London's oldest botanic garden, the Chelsea Physic Garden – something not on the more popular tourist circuit but well worth visiting. It describes itself as 'a unique living museum of over 5,000 edible, useful and historical plants' that dates to 1673. The Victorian Cool Fernery alone is a soothing marvel.

I know London Town as a huge expanse – more noticeably horizontal than vertical. For height, it is the area known as the City, the financial district, where the old, modern and postmodern interweave as a fascinating tapestry. In our own time but admittedly pre-pandemic, much of the city appears to be scintillatingly prosperous, and the proliferation of high-end brands of countlessly different products, captivatingly alluring store front windows, restaurants catering to every taste and pocketbook, theatre, cinema, music events let alone museum collections and temporary exhibitions reflect a Western achievement that could be classed exorbitant and out-of-control. The British actress Emma Thompson captures much of what is needed for our present times when she says 'there needs to be a revolution to fix the world's environmental and political problems'. She adds in connection with government, 'It is so corrupted by its nature, it's corrupt in its own nature, not even in the sense of corruption, how we know that word. It's the power that is corrupt . . . leadership is non-existent'. Thompson is for the overthrow of capitalistic society, while Andrew Levine speaks correspondingly for 'an aroused citizenry – in the United States and Europe and, if possible, in Israel itself – [to transform] the status quo' and eliminate the thriving war environment of our day. If the coronavirus can be brought under control, much of what I have written in this paragraph would once again be applicable as an initial appraisal and undertaking.

I first came to London in 1961. I remember needing coins for both heating and hot water showering or bathing in hotel rooms. It was a greatly different place than it is now – one that was still emerging from the war years and the deprivations that those times brought to Britain as a whole. Europe as well as the United Kingdom were still 'old world' with the drabness and quaint charm that came with it. One morning I jumped onto an open-ended bus as it was pulling away from the stop. Not being fully awake yet, I did not think to grab onto a fixture in the moving vehicle. I flew off the bus and landed flat on my back – knocking every bit of air out of my lungs. I was too embarrassed to continue to lie in the street and somehow got myself to the pavement where I collapsed into the arms of a quickly gathering crowd. Fortunately, the bus did not stop, but I remember making the most incredible sound as I desperately attempted to get oxygen back into my system. At the same time, there was a comfort, after the previous five months on the Continent, to hear people rationally and calmly speaking English. I knew I was in safe hands. I actually subsequently caught the next bus, but the lower half of both arms were numb and, in time, increased becoming even more deprived of sensation. By the time I reached Amsterdam, I was quite ill but as my Eurail pass was about to expire, I was constrained to take the train to Munich while I still could in order to begin German lessons in the city's suburb of Grafing. I got as far as Ulm and, unable to endure any further, descended there on a German couple I had previously met in Amalfi. I was in such a state of complete pain by this point that I contemplated climbing to the top of the city's cathedral spire – the highest in Europe if not the world – and jumping off. It would have been exchanging one pain for another and then cessation. It was a weekend, and Ruth and Erhard phoned medical emergency. There was one doctor on duty, but he was an expert on exactly what I had contracted – influenza of the vertebrae. He told my hosts I would not have lived much longer in the state I was. He gave me injections all over my back, and I recovered.

But back to London – the London of today. On certain lines, the buses for a brief period once again had open backs. A conductor would stand nearby – to prevent people from jumping on or off between the bus stops. Although Paris is the place where one expects elegance, the London streets are filled with well-dressed women along with ample chic and style. It is pure bustle but less frenzied as it might be in New York or Tokyo. It is as if a great party were underway. The post-war drab has vanished; so also have the coin-operated heaters and hot water tanks. I'm made to think of Damascus, Baghdad, Tripoli or Kabul in their present war-torn desolation – or the smaller cities in the environing regions like Homs and Idlib – and find the contrast with a functioning and thriving metropolis as London simply astonishing.

When we think at present of the divide between the American imperial hubris and its mental incompetency, on the one hand, and the irreconcilable and, yes, pathetic IS Caliphate, on the other, it is my conviction, as a pagan and cherisher of the earth, that my engaging with the employment of deific magic (whether this last has any true reality or not) has become my consolation between impossible odds. As things around me make the choices before us all all the clearer, it is this telluric centralising grounding that emerges as my solace and core. I have no doubts that pure, sane and open-minded people could do what is necessary equally and better than *any* military option. How to achieve genuine progress remains the dumbfounding question. Neither President Obama nor Abu Bakr al-Baghdadi were able to provide *anything* close to a viable option to a world in which families and friends might picnic together and savour the holy gifts of a natural and gods-given sacrality. Can we not let us let our ephemeral times on earth and as part of this earth be relaxed, gently full and occasions of gratitude? Must we always hate the other and in sick joyousness seek to exterminate them? When can we pause for a moment, a real moment, and look at ourselves and what we are doing and ask is this necessary, is this the only way, is there a more imaginative and expansive approach that is commensurate with our intrinsic dignity that we can share without being unimpeded by bias but rather universally with laughter?

Brief visits to Paris occasionally intervene basically to see good friends and loved ones. Even when the sojourn is only a few days, it at least allows one to savour the atmosphere of one of the world's most enchanting cities. In October of 2014, I managed to work almost all of my Paris time on the requested revisions to my ethics manuscript, so apart for an excursion to the Bois de Boulogne for viewing Frank Gerry's Foundation de Louis Vuitton (a madly wonderful conglomerate assembly of seemingly useless shapes apart from their aesthetic contribution) as well as a few visits to the Left Bank and two favourite restaurants, it was about as minimal as any travel could be. And we missed by one day the longed-for reopening of the Picasso Museum in the Marais.

And hardly a week earlier, our dear Nicolas Schors passed to the otherworld. He was 89, and we were fortunate to have been able to visit him in the hospital the day before we left Amsterdam for London. A merchant in occult books and a neighbour, Nick and his wife Magdalena who predeceased him were marvellously intelligent people who approached life as they wanted and not in conformity to what others might have thought was 'proper'. They both became great friends and extended family. When Magdalena died, her sister came to Nick and his long-time mistress and said, 'I think the two of you should marry, and I want to be a witness'. And so they did, and Nick's concluding days, although increasingly debilitated, were nevertheless happy ones. But I will miss his razor-sharp alertness let alone countless tales of survival under the German occupation of World War II – on several occasions near failures of survival but for quick and endlessly resourceful cleverness. Nick and Maggie were in their late teens during the time. When a German officer came to Maggie and demanded several thousand food stamps whose distribution was a task to which she had been assigned but the official had no documents for them and yet insisted she give them to him nonetheless, she realised she could sell and, for Sinterklaas, give away as many as she wished to; there was no oversight or control. And Nick, with the occasional 'Heil Hitler!' managed to deflect the Gestapo from his boarding house after they saw the poster of the Fuhrer he had placed on the wall of his room and despite the angry denouncements from the others living in the building with him. At another time, taking refuge in the country and walking along a rural lane, two drunken pistol-happy German solders approached from the direction in which Nick was heading. They shot the people who were ahead of him, saluted in return to Nick's victory hail and then shot the people who were behind him. Cultured people who exemplified the best of the European achievement, Nick and Maggie personified for me the very reason I had wanted in the first place to come to Europe.

And when once again in London after Paris, I was able to include attending a pagan ceremony in connection to Samhain/Hallowe'en, reconnect with friends not seen for a decade or so, attend two meetings of the Foundation for International Collaboration in the House of Lords, the second chamber of the UK Parliament – one discussing 'Religion – what's the point?'; the other, 'What is the purpose of a Caliphate?' and see a lawyer over the possibility of securing for Richard a British citizenship. With the pagan ethics manuscript revisions finally completed, though doubtlessly far from the end of the project, at least for the moment I was able to concentrate on other things and also get back to the present work.

The Latin yuletide – perhaps it is only Roman, but it is a seminal part of the Roman Festival calendar which the world as a whole, our world, has inherited as the Gregorian secular calendar we use today for international date keeping and planning. The yule begins on the 11th of December with the feast known as the Agonium, dedicated to the Indigenous Sun (*Sol Indiges*) – appropriately perhaps as the sun is now maximally below the horizon of the local community it serves. This of course is applicable to only the Northern Hemisphere. Everything is reversed 'down under'. And for the time of this writing – December 2014, I was celebrating in Amsterdam.

With our kitchen being re-done, the Yule festivities I had planned had to be suspended as cooking was at best disadvantaged if it could have occurred at all. But the remodelling at this time was an opportunity, and one I could not reject. The two months of London had passed, though I retain fond memories of Saatchi's 'Pop Art' exhibition, the 'Late Rembrandt' at the National Gallery, the Moroni and Anselm Kiefer at the Royal Academy. This last was especially momentous for me. I would not necessarily describe Kiefer's work as 'beautiful' but rather as utterly thought provoking – expanding into a cosmic soaring from the grounding organic beneath the social and military horrors that otherwise grab our attention. Mortified by the fascist disease that his birth country had endured before he was born and startled by Germany's perceived inability to face its past, Kiefer's art is his attempt to work out a solution for reflection and change. With the military commitments in which it is now enchained, America and/or the United States thereof seemed – and still seems – increasingly to me to be in a similar collective state of mind as was Germany in the advent of the Second World War. Friends would send me every week new articles deploring the Citizen Based Taxation to which all US citizens are subjected to wherever they live in the world. A Resident Based Taxation, however, seems still to be beyond governmental countenance. I had also learned at this yule time in Amsterdam that the cost for surrendering one's passport, already staggeringly high and unnecessary, had now been increased *fivefold*. The only possible justification can be the American need and desire to punish those of us who were born as citizens but do not wholeheartedly subscribe to 'the American Dream'.

The Netherlands during the winter time of year is dismal, dark and grey and more than conducive for the withdrawing into warmer interiors to offset or escape the bitter cold. Still there could be sunny moments however crisp, but in general it is for nature herself a wind-down time and a period of waiting for the solar increase to come. Socially, however, it is also the moment for yule lights, Amsterdam's Light Festival on this occasion in fact, and special bakery treats that are only available at this time of year: *oliebals, gevulde speculaas, keerst brood* and *appel flapjes*. Not at all high on any list of healthy things to consume but delicious and next to impossible not to surrender to one or another at some point.

For this yuletide, I had decided to abandon keeping up with the news. I had never done this before and am virtually addicted to listening to BBC's Radio Four and watching both Al-Jazeera and Euronews. I also receive news bulletins through France-Musique, and when insomnia strikes as it does occasionally, if I put on the BBC World Series, it will almost inevitably put me to sleep. But this hiatus in knowing what is transpiring globally turned out not to have been as difficult as originally imagined. I had wondered what a roughly two-week interval in which one is freed from news broadcasts and information might do for one's state of mind. Certainly, from what I mostly hear, there is no happiness as a result. Could one be happier when *not* hearing? I am reminded of my parents telling me when the Second World War had ended that we will still always have the news. One can, however, choose not to listen to it. In any event, the conscious absence of news, like that of a religious fast, can become an act of offering to the god/s. Release from the news is, in fact, a liberation, and that is ultimately what the Saturnalia are all about.

When the yuletide ended, and I put on the news at both 04:00 and 06:00, I fell asleep immediately with both. All in all, it was a pleasant if unreal break, and nothing of any real significance appeared to have changed. This Amsterdam occasion had been followed by another visit to Paris for a few days and, without an internet connection currently, I was again without the news – at least for Christmas day when so much is closed. I was surprised, however, to have found many cafes and restaurants open on the 25th, and during a sunny walk to the Seine, I had also seen both a bakery and a pharmacy ready to be receiving customers.

But in lieu of the dire forecasts for the future and the ominous cloud we appear to live under at present, *carpe diem quam minimum credula postero*! Sage advice from Horace. In London, this may currently be more possible. In Paris, apparently much less so. Since the attacks on the Stade de France, Le Carillon, Le Petit Cambodge, the Café Bonne Bière, La Casa Rostra, La Belle Équipe, the Comptoir Voltaire and the Bataclan Theatre, from all that I hear through friends in Paris, the city remained in shock and the end of year holidays passed with little joy. And yet, if Europe reels and oscillates between affirmation and gloom, the global arena is little different. Through a Royal Academy exhibition of dissident artist Ai Weiwei, we learn of the Chinese government's corruption and its hostility toward democracy and human rights. War and terrorism continue in Nigeria, Libya, Syria, Mali, Indonesia, Burkina Faso and too many other places as well. Britain, North America and South America suffer from flooding; Australia from virtually unprecedented wild fires. In all, upheaval appears increasingly to colour our times and world.

And despite the wider environment, I can nevertheless concede that personally I am extraordinary happy. To love another as I envision the protagonists of my novel to have done between themselves is a gift of the gods for which there may be nothing greater. While some are able to embrace for only a few years in their relationship, mine is more than four decades and has allowed not only a deeper mutual knowing but a trove of shared memories. Even irritations become endearing over time, and the perpetual comfort of love and respect provides a joyous background to whatever trials and tribulations arise – both daily and longer term. If I have a prayer beyond that of world well-being, it is that others might also know the intense intimacy with another and the joy and the euphoria it allows.

So *carpe diem*! And this over the previous year includes the loss and lamentation for Deborah Ann Light, a marvellous pagan lady, whose elegance and humour and dignified wisdom have been appreciated by many within the community. It was always for me a complete privilege to know her, and I remember when she came up to me during the 1993 Parliament of the World's Religions in Chicago and, with an unforgettable smile, introduced herself. Others that I have not known personally but departed from our dimension in the same annual duration as did Deborah include Anita Ekberg, Omar Sharif, Oliver Sacks, Jackie Collins, Yogi Berra, Maureen

O'Hara and Holly Woodlawn with Pierre Boulez, David Bowie and Alan Rickman following in the month of January 2016. Personalities and celebrities of especial talent are like visiting divine presences whose uniqueness comes more definitively into focus often only once their individual visit on this plane has concluded.

But rich, rich, rich! *Carpe diem*! From the magnificent Place Stanislas to Canaletto in Aix-en-Provence and Malevich in Amsterdam and to Shostakovich's *Lady Macbeth of Mtsensk* and Michael John LaChiusa's *See What I Wanna See,* even barely scratching the surface of the Western world in the 21st century releases a potential inundation of scintillating treasure. The incredibility of Plato denouncing the Orphics; the very denial of the artistic achievement of what continues to augment European tradition; the necessity of poetry and art for both sanity and *raison d'être* – all this *is* us and is that for which we stand. This is certainly not to disparage the contributions of Eastern and other civilizations. To welcome and rejoice over these last is not to diminish our own achievements but instead to celebrate the fecund diversity that comprises human life as a whole. Sad it is for those who cannot participate in this jamboree of the ever-present yet ongoing here-and-now. Puritanism may have its own moments and also bequeath some of the warp and weave themes within the legacy of the human mantel, but if and when the puritanical becomes excessively austere let alone tyrannical and insensitive to the individualities of humble human aspirations, it is then that it must be allowed and encouraged to wither and continue at best in its own ineffective and non-dangerous enclaves. Beauty is the ultimate aura of the cosmos, and the unimpeded human is a monumental contributor to this aesthetic emanation. We and our earth may be an infinitesimal speck within the endless and inconceivable immensity of the universe, but we are nevertheless still gigantic players in the pulchritude – both physical *and* spiritual – of cosmic totality.

CHAPTER THREE

Global horrors / lack of harmony in contemporary paganism / local self-independence / the immediate & the local / Pierre Chuvin & the *pagus* / celebration with one's home environment constituting the most legitimate behaviour / the absolute necessities / *Pagan Ethics* / freedom, comfort, health & worship; life's musical narrative a meaningless paean? / nature as a plurality; shamanic loneliness & all-night vigils / the Amsterdam commune & the transition from the Old World to the new 9–5 world / the Concertgebouw / Arthur Rubinstein, Amsterdam and the summer solstice; the world is dying / the hidden magical otherworld / the importance of the arts, science & trade / the Frisian debacle / the Belgian possibility / the farm / the Provence / King's College London & sociology / sacred geography & Kathmandu / pagan diversity & generic paganism / Dion Fortune / pagan=human=natural / non-dogmatism / childhood love of nature & trees / the contribution also of music / my desire to recollect my past / the dragon; 'We will always have the news' / Republican family / libertarian liberalism or liberal libertarianism / pagan involvement with politics because of the environment / human = 'earthling' / Mother & Grand / my childhood recognition of the preternatural / my fascination with ancient cultures / my early altars / the different ontological status of the gods from the empirical / beauty; *The Divine versus the Asurian* / India / 'I do not believe this' / Calcutta & Joyce / Kalighat / Kashi & first encounter of Vishvanath / not all gods are divine / pagan racism / worldview as an art / the proto-Indo-European (PIE) as a positive / Marija Gimbutas / Friedrich Max Müller's etymological approach / Georges Dumézil's functional interpretation / the proto-pantheon / idol worship / three significant proto-Indo-European mythologems: disruption, abduction & duplication; the Kashi apartment / Banaras as the world's oldest city / *bhang lassi* & nature's gift of the entheogenic / the divine twins / Hindu & pagan multiplicity / the most pagan-like shrines in Kashi / the positive wish-world of paganism / the Kashi Coast / Malcolm Arnold's *Fifth Symphony* / *darshan* / the British continuing prohibition of cannabis is archaic in the negative sense / Acapulco / fairness / Elsinore / Aristotle & democracy / citizen-based taxation / 'Be here now' & the Lotocene / 'going with the flow' & vigilance / Haight Ashbury / the Family & the coven / Richard's & my marriage in Amsterdam / my LSD freak out / Native American spirituality / Maurice Ravel's *Daphnis and Chloe* / the ubiquitous presence of nature & even in urban environments / the gods & their vehicles, images & symbols interpenetrate the everyday world / the Afro-Latin traditions / small *p* paganism over large *P* paganism; 'It's you he is looking up to' / three things about the American way of life: allergies, fracking & behaviour / ours is a better world; the Midi / the Gorges du Verdon & Draguignan / the dragon / *tellurique*; Arnold's *Fifth Symphony* / art & infinitesimal existence / academia /

publication rejection / Genesis 1.28 / paganism's core immanentalist reverence / gnosticism's *soma sema*; my plea; the smartphone, the Lotus World; marijuana & entheogenic sacraments; the Chelsea Flower Show of 2017; Iana at 8 & Stefanie / Breaking Convention & 'Exploring Consciousness: With What Intent?' / a Lotus-times-to-come

---

Paganism follows immediately, but first a very brief rant, if not a summary, continuing the disjunct I lamented in the previous chapter. In thinking of the litany of global horrors as I write at present, what first comes to mind are the Guaido manipulations and sanctions by my birth country in Venezuela patently in its desire for control of oil, the right-wing extremist shift and domination in Brazil, the longing for a wall between Mexico and the United States, the snubbing of the Paris Climate Accord, the Brexit fiasco in Britain, the cancellation of the nuclear agreement with Iran, the total deterioration of Yemen, and the endless Palestinian-Israeli conflict. And these are just what I can think of as a start. The out-of-control bush fires in Australia and the snake flu emerging from China could be added. Domestically, in America, there is the regressive populism, the pervasive racism, the 'safe-space' silliness curtailing freedom of speech, and the TERF (Trans-Exclusionary Radical Feminist)-FBW (female-born and still a woman) impasse. I know if I were to make the effort, I could extend the enumeration of these social festers almost indefinitely.

It is the similar lack of harmony that I incessantly witness within contemporary paganism that has provoked my desire to compose my present writing. The disharmony is one thing; the blindness to what is flexible and understandably vital within the non-Abrahamic and non-dharmic spirituality that is at heart paganism is the other. To discern, if possible, any common feature to the disturbances I have compiled in the preceding paragraph, in a quick reflection what first appears to be the case are two things: rampantly greedy capitalism and a non-recognition of local self-independence. The latter, in fact, is perhaps the *primus inter pares* and perhaps includes runaway greed as well. Paganism itself, despite its global dimensions – especially now concerning the ecological balance of the planet, is primarily focused on the immediate and local. While Ram Dass' admonition to 'be here now' is a Hindu-derived aphorism that may be expressive of the core to countercultural philosophy, it is also equally applicable to the full gist of 20th/21st century paganism. The viability of autonomy begins with the individual and proximate community. Conflict and exploitation arise when effort is extended to beyond a neighbourhood's boundaries. Paganism sacralises the home region. In fact, as I follow Pierre Chuvin in this, the term 'pagan' only subsequently signified 'country bumpkin' – allegedly as the last to convert to Christianity – and originally referred to an inhabitant of a *pagus*, the ('pegged' or 'marked out') municipal district or city ward. The Greek equivalent of *hellene* or *ethnikos* conveys the more urban or cosmopolitan association of the city ward original. A *paganus* or pagan was a 'civilian' belonging to a local territorial division. In the later Western Roman Empire, the *pagus* (hence French *pays*, Spanish *pago* 'a region, terroir') designated the smallest administrative district of a province. It developed an affinity with the *vicus* or 'village'. My contention is that a focus and celebration with one's home environment constitutes the most legitimate behaviour and activity properly belonging to a pagan. Ideally in political aspiration, this involves respect for both the individual and his/her surroundings, and this respect includes regional self-autonomy and the ability to say 'no' to the presence or imposition against the community's will of any destructive or exploitative enterprise within its territory. Perhaps this idealism is suggestive of a Marxist anarchy that envisions a polity situation free from outside governmental control, but I do not think that paganism is inherently opposed to free enterprise. Rather, it opposes the kind of multicorporate capitalism that reduces the individual to the status of a serf or pawn and out-purchases or militarily liquidates the self-determining sovereignty of the inhabitants of the domain in which the commercial venture is situated.

During my initial vagabonding adventures in Europe in my earliest twenties, I became through relatively penurious conditions mindful of the absolute necessities of life. Apart from the fundamental needs for air and water, what was mandatory were eating, excreting, sleeping, washing and keeping warm. Each of these was essential on either a daily or at best a few days basis, and each of these could be embellished from minimal Spartan fulfilment through various modifications into what made them more comfortable or even enjoyable. One could sleep on the cold ground when there was no alternative, but a true bed was more preferable. And for me, in addition to these five fundamental requirements, the ability to dream completed what I discovered to be the indispensables for both life and sanity.

Of course, what I have described here applies only to the basics of survival – not only for the refugee or migrant but also for every one of us regardless of any individual achievement of insulating luxury. Beyond the essential requisites, needless to say, we move into the domain of the ethical, and in my explorations of this dimension, years later, I summarized my considerations in the second of my paganism trilogy, my *Pagan Ethics: Paganism as a World Religion* that was published in 2016. I shall discuss this more in the pages that follow, but the virtues that I have come to champion for a solidly grounded paganism are those of freedom, comfort, health, and worship. Worship itself for me comprises the virtue-values of honour, pleasure, productivity and generosity. It is this last, namely, liberal magnanimity, that moves us beyond selfish concern and/or the concern solely with the self into consideration and the compassion for others. Without this last, paganism as well as any religion or spirituality are empty and dead.

It is through both the arts and nature that I am able to commune with my gods. Whether I refer to metaphors or something else, during the performance of a requiem, they have spoken to me concerning the human condition thusly: In contrast to the hideous butchery of the Daesh, there is a beauty of innocence in both youth and artistic endeavour. Is not life a musical narrative? It has a beginning and an end – with in between the variants ranging from grieving pathos to joyous freedom, from sorrow to serenity, and from fertile darkness to luminous brightness. Whether we employ the one or the many or nothing at all, by seeking to complete our song we honour accordingly the very gift of life. From the exquisite heavenliness of the young to the sophisticated elegance of the elderly, it may ultimately be a meaningless paean, but by its end it nevertheless constitutes what has been, and what has been is for eternity. We are both child of the cosmos and the cosmos itself. Nature is not just singular but a plurality, and her rhythms, developments and stories both flow and intersect – not always as we might wish they should, but the enormity alone is vastly more engulfing than we could possibly understand. Consequently, we can only accept all of which we are a part, but that very part that is ourselves is for us and by us at least important and may also be somehow at least inscrutably meaningful.

From the backroom of a New Orleans jazz bar to the celestial harps of heaven, let our beauty be musical or in the minimum let our beauty be carried aloft by music! To be kind and compassionate in our creative offerings, how can we more honour the gods than this? And when it is over, maybe it *is* over, but we have at least contributed our bit.

During my early shamanic days, my excursions were frequently lonely, and I was more aware of being a social outcast. I would visit sacred sites such as Delphi, Dowth or Avebury on the occasions of the solstices, equinoxes or the Celtic quarter festivals in anticipation that I might encounter others at these places and in those special times, but invariably there was no one. In those days, I would keep a wakeful vigil throughout the night (something I no longer can do) and assisted when possible with an all-night fire. Only once, with Richard, as we were heading to the Lac de St. Croix for the midsummer's sunrise did we come across a group of people in the forest who may have been a band of wandering celebrants. We were curious but had our mission and continued on our way. I have never encountered such a gathering again.

In between my shamanic retreats, communal life in Amsterdam retained its own fascination and relentless focus. Running a household in conformity to the calendar of Roman festivals not only brought us into a semi-ancestral spiritual mindfulness but also allowed a celebratory sequence that reaffirmed devotional and animistic values. While they lasted, these were significant days in which we discerned ancient pathways through the city, the locality's nodal points, Dutch pragmatism, the Amsterdamer's sense of humour and the exchange of new ideas with and from the steady stream of visitors that we entertained. In its own way, our house was an entheogenic venue at the time the Old World was transforming into a new and modern one. The Flower Market on the Singel, for one, was at our start an open venue through the night but after a few years became a nocturnal fortress of locked fences to prevent the theft of plants. The bathhouses disappeared as domestic showers became the norm. Refrigeration also allowed the preservation of regular milk in place of what had been treated to endure room temperatures. And perhaps most significant of all, the emergence of large-scale corporate work forces precluded the old gentlemen who had served for years as personal bank tellers. 9 to 5 agendas characteristically superseded the counterculture explosion that had become Amsterdam when we first arrived. Some of us departed; some stayed, but we all began to think of the countryside as a suitable non-urban alternative in which to extend our residence.

Meanwhile, the delightful Koninklijk Concertgebouw – Dutch literally for 'Royal Concert Building' – was persistently a temple venue for rapturous enjoyment. It is a perfectly acoustical structure and, as a 'music hall', another shrine like the museum for the Muses, presumably for Euterpe in particular, though the theatre more widely is also dedicated to Dionysus and Sarasvati, and the music theatre to Apollo as well. One Concertgebouw moment was a piano performance by Arthur Rubinstein. The Main Hall was absolutely packed; there was not one spare seat. When Rubinstein played Chopin's *Nocturne*, Opus 27, Number 8 in D-flat major, he paused completely before finishing with the last two notes. During that pause, there was not a sound anywhere – not even that of a breath. It was the most electrifying moment of silence in the presence of so many people I have ever experienced – the Concertgebouw's *Grote Zaal*'s seating capacity being 1,974.

Other fabulous events in that renowned structure included for me Dame Janet Baker singing Ravel's *Shéhérazade*, Bernard Haitink conducting Mahler's symphonies and Diana Ross personifying Billie Holliday in her *Lady Sings the Blues* concert. It was, however, Maria Callas' appearance as part of her farewell tour in 1973 that revealed a level of frenzied adoration of which I had not known previously the Dutch were capable. Callas' voice was already 'gone', and it was the tenor Giuseppe de Stefano who contributed to the vocals, but people in the audience, the most glitteringly dressed perhaps ever in Amsterdam, were virtually standing on the seat backs of their chairs to applaud and scream their honour to the diva. On another occasion, for an Ike and Tina Turner performance, we had to wait a good extra 45 minutes before the show began after the time for which it had been originally scheduled to begin. At one point, Tina swung her head around so that suddenly, when her hair was no longer hiding what was underneath, the audience could see the huge bandaging covering the side of her neck. We had already known the stories concerning Ike's abusive behaviour toward his wife. Further Concertgebouw moments in those heady days of the post-San Francisco 1970s exile included Renata Tebaldi and Nana Mouskouri.

Although I was raised a Methodist and retain a respect for the ideas of John Wesley, my spiritual affinities are pagan and some of my relevant practice includes rolling on the fresh dew at the moment of the midsummer's sunrise or more frequently plunging into a body of water. Over the years, this last has included the Serpentine in Hyde Park, more often the Thames at the Chelsea Embankment, the Weir of the Avon in Bath, a creek that runs through Newcastle-Upon-Tyne, the rain at Stonehenge, the Narragansett Bay of Rhode Island, the Ganges of Varanasi, the canals of Amsterdam and the Lac de St. Croix in the Provence. Based on these early moments of experience in the day, Richard has thought at times to title a book on our life together as 'Madness at the Crack of Dawn'.

As I now attempt to recollect what has seemed, and doubtlessly in fact is, a long life, I wish also to elucidate my understanding of what underlies the dynamic of the gods. While the summer solstice has long been for me a bittersweet occasion, I have a dear friend who enters a state of depression at this time. In the festival calendar of the early Romans, although the first half of the year and a bit beyond is formulated clearly with the ascent of the sun in mind, between the fifteenth of June and the first of July, there are no ostensible commemorations or festivals. When it came to ritual, the summer solstice was ignored even though the Romans were acutely aware of it. Nevertheless, the days at this time of year in the northern hemisphere are long and magical. They echo what may be accepted as a human affirmation of nature and our inclination for celebration. And after the 'blast' of midsummer's solar light, there is the hope if not also promise of warmer days to come – in one reckoning for the full stretch of summer; in another at least for the second half of summer. These are the times during which many of us take our breaks from the working parts of our lives and relax with vacation, sometimes travel, possibly beach time during the day and outdoor meals with friends, family and the balmy evening. When humanity rests with leisure, our intrinsic *joie de vivre* most manifests as a sacred witness against which strife and war are imbecilic and juvenile. How to capture that manifestation and expand it into the prevailing norm is the true question of our own times.

I recollect a summer moment in Amsterdam. Mosul had recently fallen to ISIL, Eastern Ukraine continued to become a sad horror, Syria's devastation worsened, Brazil's pre-World Cup riots and strikes also occupied much of the news, African sectarian violence remained seemingly an impossible situation to solve, and floods ravaged parts of China, South America and elsewhere. Today as I now write, the global scenario is not all that radically different, and we have instead or in addition, the brink of a World War III following the American assassination of the Iranian general Qasem Soleimani, the downing of Iran air flight 655, the Australian bush fires, malaria in Burundi, and lethal flooding here and there. But for the time I am presently remembering, Amsterdam and much of Europe had been enjoying the glories of full summer. The solstice was still approaching, and our days had been at times tropical. A waft of jasmine scented air flowed through the open windows, one walked barefoot in the neighbourhood, people ate and drank on their doorsteps, and in this holy interlude there was a prevailing relaxation that colours the fulfilment of a best of all possibilities. In The Netherlands I perceive a country that works. It may not be without its own problems and difficulties – and the recent macabre experience of embarrassing ridicule for Swamiji at Schiphol airport had illustrated one persisting problematic flaw, but the birthplace of modern capitalism is inhabited by an affluent society in which the rights and protections of individual freedoms have become fused with its national character, and all this is reflected in its work-a-day world, its taverns and cafes, its cherishing of the arts and its daily celebration of its own existence, good fortune and the products of its hard work. And when these people celebrate, they reflect the same general kind of pastimes and doings of people elsewhere around the world. This is foremost to be seen when people relax and have their down time, vacations and holidays or at least those wholesome moments of a nature-infused respite when the temperature releases us from any need for insulation, our windows are opened, we converse with our neighbours, the earth smiles and life is good.

Amplified by the midsummer days of suspension, the idyllic dell – still existing in our own times – encourages itself against a more daily mundane entanglement. Within the interlude and space of divine cessation, we might see a mother duck looking proud as she is surrounded by her brood of ducklings. Willow trees and reed orchids may sway in a gentle breeze. A youth could be engaged with his routine of exercises. Cyclists are to be seen to amble throughout a nature preserve's maze. There could come the warmth of the setting sun and perhaps the smell of burning wood from a crackling nighttime fire. Life has been serenely beautiful and could still yet be.

But let's face it. We are all going to die. And we are all dying – along with our planet earth. People and communities want to survive, even with the prospective threat of shortened life spans due to the industry in which they are involved or the by-product pollutions such as nickel they generate. The sea levels are rising, and the ice caps and glaciers are disappearing. The future scenario appears now to be a given. We can arrange a stunning *vernissage* that depicts the elephant in the room or the inevitable catastrophe to smartly dressed and *avant garde* viewers, but what is the effect? And is it not already too late?

For me, my pagan spirituality offers consolation in the face of political and environmental disaster. I operate primarily in polytheistic, animist and pantheistic understandings, and since childhood, I have always recognised a magical otherworld that is hidden but present in this world. It is chiefly through the arts and scientific research that I perceive transnational collective cooperation to be the most possible, and I have also come to understand the role of trade in its contribution toward the realities of world peace.

In our strongly emerging desire to have a rural base beyond Amsterdam, we purchased a small cottage in Friesland and proceeded to clean it and set it up for the commune. But after our first week, the fogs finally lifted, and we found that we were situated immediately next to a NATO airbase. When the jets took off right over our house, the noise was of such intensity that one could not even think. We were saved when we subsequently learned that the property had been condemned a few weeks before I bought it. The Frisians are proverbially known for their honesty, and in the time between the condemnation and my purchase, there had been six different owners with me being the seventh. Fortunately, and through the services of a good lawyer as well as a Dutch member of our commune who had insured that the clause *geen verborgen gebrek* ('no hidden defect') had been inserted into the purchase contract, I managed to get my money back.

Our next attempt, with a Dutch lady who was translating Proust, was the possible purchase of a house in a Belgian orchard not far beyond the border of Limburg. There were two halves to the mansion. She was to have one half and we the other. The area was beautiful and the nearby community in December was enchanting, but this effort also came to naught.

When Richard and I got together, we set off at first to Germany in search of a farm, but anything we could find was an enormous working enterprise. Eventually, we reached the French Provence. The gods were directing us, though we were unaware of that at the time. We found a relatively inexpensive hectare and a half of olive trees and grape vines with a three-story, one room each floor *mas* that had electricity (the more expensive to install) and only a short distance to branch to the water supply. The property was just outside a village that has seven roads leading to it. The town itself has been depicted as a centre of the world and has certainly been such for us.

The usual migration was between Amsterdam and the Midi – with occasional excursions elsewhere such as Italy and Greece, an Aegean cruise with friends, a round the world trip in 1982, Egypt in 1983 and my sojourns in India beginning in 1981. The Provence, however, has been paradise: lovely people, good friends, fine wines, cheese and cuisine, seductive Mediterranean climate, proximity to the magnificent coast, an exquisite *paysage*, a feast of music, colourful history, a fascinating long-worked land, and its being sublimely peaceful. But before the internet and possibility of easy global communication, the one ingredient lacking to a satisfactory degree was intellectual communication.

The only recourse for me to both the need for academic stimulation and my desire to get my manuscript published on Indo-European spirituality was to return to university for a Ph.D. degree. Since by this point, we had the flat in Chelsea and King's College London was only five Underground stops from it, after various negotiations I was allowed to enrol under Peter Clarke. In time, I managed to expand my subject from New Age religion to a comparison between New Age and Neo-paganism. And this was how my academic and eventual professional career began.

By approaching contemporary paganism from a sociological perspective, I was able to augment my understanding of earth-oriented religiosity. On my own and prior to the return to university, I was focusing primarily on mythology and archaeology and the development of perceiving the contours and nuances of sacred geography. I had become relatively adept in being able to intuit ancient procession routes as well as locating formerly venerated loci and significant religious boundaries. For instance, when I arrived in Kathmandu for the first time, I had checked myself into the Oberoi Hotel, but it was already nighttime when I then set out on my first exploratory excursion. Without a map and with only a gentle resignation to cultivated instinct, I was able to wander slowly and eventually but directly to find the Durbar square of Nepal's capital with its ancient and awesome temples – the very place I most wanted to know. It is this operative sensibility and insight into the geographic sacred as well as the interconnections between sacred place and sacred time that most constitutes paganism for me.

As a more unstructured spirituality, nature-sensitive and open to deific and mythological heritage, my paganism is non-denominational. I have a deep respect for, and applaud among many possible others, Celtic spirituality, Druidism, Heathenism, Wicca, Hellenismos, Religio Romana, Kemeticism, Canaanite religion, Romuva and such developments as Hermeticism, Thelema, Feraferia, and so forth. These I see as expressions of the very diversity of pagan understandings in both the contemporary West as well as more globally. In addition, I recognise the modern-day efforts to promote 'Paganism' as a legal entity and bona fide equivalent to rank alongside the accepted major world religions of Bahá'i, Buddhism, Christianity, Confucianism, Daoism, Hinduism, Islam, Jainism, Judaism, Shinto, Sikhism, and Zoroastrianism. Religious discrimination against Neopaganism is real and widespread, and the Neopagan community has a steady uphill struggle to secure tolerance and a welcoming reception. Legal recognition is an important part of this endeavour. My own and primary concern, however, is with paganism as a more generic and perhaps folkloric development. In this, I am essentially in accord with Dion Fortune. In her *The Goat-Foot God* of 1936, she mentions the word 'pagan' fourteen times and always in lower case. My personal feeling is that by trying to conform to the licitness of the world's twelve 'classical' religions – even with the legitimate advantages which this might confer, we lose something in the process. As a generic spirituality, paganism is special and different from the already recognised and established religious contenders.

In addition to the vernacular undercurrent of spirituality and cultic reflex, I have come to appreciate the words 'pagan', 'human' and 'natural' as fundamental synonyms. To be human is to be pagan, and to be either is natural. Most institutional religion, by contrast, is established by indoctrination. Paganism, however, is neither creedal nor dogmatic. It represents the natural response of the human being to both nature and the congenital. It may not be *limited* to the organic and unprocessed, but it begins with these and from them may soar into both the ethical and aesthetic. As much as my paganism began through my childhood love of nature that involved lying on the ground and peering upward into the foliage of trees and the clouds in the sky, it is equally a product of appreciating artistic creation. Especially Maurice Ravel's *Daphnis et Chloé* as well as other musical fabrications such as Igor Stravinsky's *Le Sacre du Printemps* were also influencing factors that encouraged for me, along with my love of the flora and fauna of the natural world, a pagan sensitivity and appreciation.

But even these contributing inspirations remain in part mysteries for me personally. I know my pagan sentiments evolved spontaneously – at least at first – though eventually they were augmented and encouraged further through research, study and copious literary reading. But I wish now to recollect as much of my past in order to understand the pagan paths I discovered and followed and, finally, how these intersect and diverge from pagan/Pagan/Neopagan developments in the contemporary world. Though I think of myself as principally a non-political animal, public affairs and civic life are what weigh on us all regardless of spirituality, religion or the lack thereof, and as paganism is intensely involved with the world, politics, its dilemmas and discussion are also inevitable.

I believe in some respects that this book is about coming to terms with the dragon motif – with what I have elsewhere referred to as the asurian. My project here may involve a re-constitution of the dragon – what we might understand as a Neo-pagan and Chinese synthesis. I am not yet fully certain of this but can see the possibilities – ones which I wish first to weigh a bit further. But in our own present day, the dragon emblem may be thought to include the POP or the 'point-one-percent' and the destructive annihilating consequences that seem to result from its current hegemony. In the old myths, the dragon would seek to overturn the divine order of things and often, for a duration at least, would seize the throne of power. In our day, a part of the dragon's success is abetted by the media itself. This last has become almost exclusively a selling machine rather than an educating organism. The 'news' is now something that is marketed, and what is sold is more often than not dependent on sensationalism and fear.

To live within the eve of the 21st century's pivotal times, as the reader does today, is to live at the beginning arc that will stretch – always hopefully – to the different world to come. Our youth is still innocent, and the rest of us continue to marvel over how they become aware of their various beauties and develop at least quasi-consciously the ability to advertise them. These are today without doubt difficult and precarious times, and while the older among us may become burdened with horror and despair, the young appear often to retain a perception of a positive future and joyous days ahead. This alone for me is the greatest of beauties – the optimism of youth. And anyone's innate beauty is to be understood itself as a gift of the gods. Maybe we acknowledge this as luck and, unlike the indoctrinated youth who are transformed into suicide killers or child mercenaries, we learn to rejoice in whatever good fortune another may have. In our present world, by contrast, there is a battle that is necessarily to be waged against all anti-human myopia. It is this non-humanitarian short-sightedness that is today's dragon. And like the Hittite Illuyanka, he may be connected to the sea – both literally as the rising sea level and tsunami and metaphorically as the oceanic chaos. Today's monstrous serpent is the POP as well as its jihadist twin. Eliminate one, we might eliminate the other as well. If not 'pop' he goes, at least 'Puff goes the magic dragon!'

The sea is indeed a stormy one. On a rainy (early-)summer's day, the eve of the July Kalends in fact, Richard and I shook hands as a pact for our venture. For the next duration, he will make 'money', while I will write this book. This is our ship. For years, after I had stepped into an unmoored rowboat without oars on hand, I had drifted the high seas of uncertainty. What was abandoned was the direction that I had first been taught to pursue, and instead I deserted a life of expected conformity and structured achievement. I allowed the vessel to meander to wherever the currents were to take me. But now it is more a question, stepping once again into a ship to sail the seas, of captaining and steering instead of wandering aimlessly and without goal or orientation. Without doubt, we have storms and rough seas around us to get through as we seek a tranquil harbour and peaceful refuge. Adventure and difficulty are ahead. Is this a version of the *Odyssey* and the journey of Ulysses? Homer's epic poem is one of our standard classics in Western culture. Whatever Levantine conceptual imports we have that have become elements in the evolution of Western civilization, Western *culture* is its seminal and subliminal part. But to follow in this cultural sense, the genetic/memetic codes of resistance and craftiness are also part of our inheritance. These are the very fuels for my voyage – a voyage that on this occasion I share with my partner Richard. At this stage, I am not sailing alone. And I have a pre-conceived even if only generally understood direction.

The oasis toward which we are hopefully cruising is at best our whole earth as a recognised maternal treasure both as immediate refuge and as a utopian future. This last has been shaped not only by global catastrophe but also by the likes of the Open Source Revolution, MAYDAY efforts, and wisdoms shared by people like Jimmy Carter, Evo Morales, Wangari Maathai and Maya Angelou. If and when it is not possible to wish, we are then – sadly – not in harmony with the cosmos. The gods of our future will still have their origins in the mythologies of the past and, beyond that, in the elements of nature. The gods yet have various mistakes and errors from their past to overcome and transcend.

Concurrent with the gradual awakening of a long-buried and marginalised pagan consciousness has been the stealth and expansion of the one remaining super-power, the United States of America. An influential work that has contributed to our spiritual awakening and helped ultimately to open awareness for the necessity of change has been Starhawk's *The Fifth Sacred Thing*. Further, and thanks to such works like Barbara McGraw's *Rediscovering America's Sacred Ground*, the violation to the founding vision of the USA's Constitution has begun to become increasingly clear. The tireless efforts of others like Noam Chomsky, Chris Hedges, Julian Assange,

Edward Snowdon and Glenn Greenwald have also served to furnish cracks in the American myth that served its propaganda. While I do not expect many in my own time to sympathize or agree with my political position, I am not yet certain what my role is or can be in fostering the awareness in our present era of collateral damage on which the moment for a parallel revolution/evolution comes into being.

When the Second World War ended, I asked my parents if that meant we would no longer be receiving the news over the radio. 'Oh no!' they responded. 'We will always have the news'. To me at the age of five, it had sounded so negative and depressing that I wondered what was the point of the war being over if we were still to have that! Despite having been raised in a Republican family, and staunchly so, my father was the only one to remain a GOP but nevertheless still had to support his Democrat daughter once she began standing as a gubernatorial candidate for the state of Rhode Island. I have always voted, though not always for the person I would vote for now. Today, I remain disillusioned and disgusted by both the Republican and Democratic Parties and now consider myself a Libertarian Liberal or a Liberal Libertarian – one or the other or both.

Contemporary paganism and especially Western Neopaganism are by and large involved with politics if for no other reason than the environment. Respecting the earth and understanding her sacredness is central to pagan thought, and the maintenance or, if necessary, the restoration of the natural ecological balance of our planet becomes a foremost pagan political concern. But even further, the human as the 'earthling' or 'child of the earth' is automatically an extension of terrestrial consideration, and a pagan's political interest expands, almost inevitably, into the well-being of collective humanity as well.

But these ruminations developed for me later and after childhood. It was instead both my mother and her mother who were initially instrumental in fostering my wide-eyed appreciation of the otherworld, the world of fairy and its intersection with this world and the world of nature. It was through my mother that I first became aware of numerology. Without knowing, she was an Arian. She thought that Jesus Christ was a divine being but not God. My grandmother spoke of elves as well as her ability to see the 'Invisible Bird'. When she was visiting, our beds became covered with coins and candy. These were gifts from the Invisible Bird that she could see but we not.

I was fascinated in childhood to read about the ancient Greeks, Egyptians and Babylonians. My favourite part of the Bible that we were each given by the Methodist Church was the map section in the back depicting the holy lands. My daydreaming fantasy up to at least my days in Purdue University was often concentrated on these enchanting lands. An irony is that, apart from Greece, I did not get to Egypt until 1983. It is less likely that I will ever come to visit Iraq or even Israel. But the mythologies from these cultures have always been captivatingly entrancing. It was in my teenage years, if not earlier, that I constructed altars to the gods and paid homage to them all – including even the Muslim Allah. I am of course much more selective now, but the recognition and worship of the preternatural other has long been an important focus of my remit.

I am certainly aware that for many people 'the gods' are fictions, childish fictions at that, and for some they even constitute obstacles to the current need for concentration on the environment. As I will seek to explain, however, 'the gods' comprise a different ontological status than empirical reality. They 'represent' various concerns and are perhaps operative in the same way beauty is functionally valid. For me at least, they open attention *to* ecology rather than block it.

I did not get to India until after I had completed my *magnum opus, The Divine versus the Asurian*. This last was the result of many years earlier when my family moved to a different house in my hometown of Maplewood, and I found an almost complete edition of the *Encyclopaedia Britannica* (the 9th dating to 1889) that had been left behind by the previous owners. Within the encyclopaedia, there was an article that discussed the strange reversal that had occurred between the ancient Persians and Indians. The word for 'deity' in the one had become that for 'demon' in the other; whereas the designation for 'demon' in the one was used to designate 'deity' in the other. I suppose this academic revelation became one of the principal motivations in my life into the search for spiritual understanding.

The land of India loomed for me as the penultimate place of mystery and fascination. I read as much about the country as I could. One main draw for me was my desire to encounter the Hindu temple – the closest I could guess as an equivalent or similarity to the classical and Egyptian temples of the pre-Christian pagan world. Of course, the actuality of India once I finally reached the subcontinent was much different than I had been able previously to imagine. But still I found it a land of colour and intense magic. Throughout the twenty-year period that I was able to travel and spend time in Bharat, as I walked through the narrow lanes principally of Benares (Varanasi), I was forced to repeat what became my personal mantra: 'I do not believe this'. India is as different from anywhere else that could be imaginable.

As I was about to depart for the East, my friend Susan had given me a journal to take along. This is before computers, laptops and mobile phones. For the 18th of April, 1981, I wrote at the beginning of the journal: 'Truth is not one; there are many, many truths – the one quality they all share being that of luminescent melody'. This is followed by an evocation to the Hindu gods that I recorded on the 15th of August that year, my first in India: 'Lord Śiva, I adore your *lingam* and come to it in reverence, but am I not worshipping auspicious Indra when I do? O Durga-Kalī I render you homage, but is this not to the embryo of the earth-mother which you contain? And is it not the same if I bend a knee to Brahmā? Or Sarasvati? Lord Viṣṇu, I remember you the stalwart support and companion of my lord. Great Lakhsmi, are you not as wife of the solar king the dawn herself? Ganesh I love your form, but are you not Airāvata, the vehicle of the lord of thunder, as well as his Viṣṇu friend? And Hanūman, I may bow to you perhaps grudgingly, for are you not the asuric at its best as devoted, faithful servant of the heroic light? O Kumar, what form have they given you and where have they put your name?' Perhaps I would rephrase some of this today, but it still captures the gist of my Indo-European/Vedic studies as well as my initial encounter with the Hindu gods in their own land.

Like a gossamer netting studded with pale emeralds and topaz and draped against a black void – with a battered burnt-orange opal of a moon hanging mistily and inconsequentially in the low heavens, India was initially encountered. Mystery? Enchantment? An irresistible beckoning? The invocation and call from the beginning of Ravel's *Scheherazade*? This was Bombay, now Mumbai, but at the time of day or rather night, it could have been just as easily the Jersey Meadows. My Amsterdam plane had landed before dawn. With the ventilator off and more than an hour's wait, it was already almost unbearably hot, and this was February. It was nearly 07:30 when the flight resumed. It was becoming light by now, but the land was heavily in mist. The plane moved toward the runway, and suddenly, through the opaqueness which masked the luxuriant green surrounding the airport, I saw my first India – at its morning ablutions. In Dacca, I was one of the fortunate four who was able to secure a seat on the day's Calcutta/Kolkata flight. And here by the Bay of Bengal was my entry to Hindustan. It became a visual whirl of chaos and unfamiliarity as I taxied from the Dum Dum Airport to Little Russell Street. Through friends, I had learned of a small hotel run by an occult cyclone, Joyce, a powerhouse Armenian woman. This became an old-world sanctuary filled with legacies of the Raj and from which I could venture into the teeming numbers of people, the constant noise and activity, the poverty and difference of both the urban complex and the ongoing onslaught of India itself.

My five days in Calcutta included visits to the New Market, India Museum, Victoria Memorial, Belur Math, Dakshineshwar, a Krishna temple, and the Swetamber and Digamber Jain temples, but it was the Kalighat that was the most central to my interests. I walked around the outside of the temple compound, then bought twenty-one candles and two strands of red flowers, and left my sandals with a small boy. Inside the temple, the doors to the inner sanctum were shut, and the crowd pressed as close to them as the guards would allow. Some people threw coins and took their leave, but I waited with the rest in the suffocating heat. After what seemed a long time, the doors were opened and a great frenzy of pushing and lunging forward commenced. I held my offerings above my head to protect them and then found myself pulled to the threshold of the shrine by the guards. It seemed as if I was handing out rupees at every turn. Vermilion was placed on my forehead. I was able to recognise Kali's red tongue but little more. Not availably having 11, 22 or multiples thereof of rupees, I declined on the purchase of a cloth. My offerings were blessed and returned and outside I dispensed them to children and beggars. I walked back to Joyce's hotel – exhausted.

My encounter three days later with the Golden Temple of Vishvanath in Benares was little different. I had arrived in the holy city of Kāshī the previous day which was the Roman festival of the Terminalia, the last day of the year. Beside seeing the temple from the outside and having my guide take my offerings inside to Lord Shiva for me, I visited the cremation ghat and also purchased a *dhoti* and *kurta* which the bearers back at the Clark's Hotel showed me how to wear. The day after the Terminalia is the Regifugium or the first of one of two Roman five-day epagomenal carnivals. I took a rickshaw to the river and bathed in the Ganges shortly after sunrise. I was then taken to the Golden Temple where a priest escorted me through at a rushed pace. But the glimpse was overpowering. I was stunned by the array of numinous veneration modes. I may have touched the most sacred *lingam* of all but am not sure. The barrage of images was like a psychedelic kaleidoscope of archetypal flashes. Through it all and the nearby shrines to which the priest led me, I encountered the Brahmin nemesis: 51 rupees at the Ganges, refused to give more than 7 at a Shiva *lingam* shrine but then turned around and gave 11 to a Durga priest whose foul breath stayed with me afterwards for hours. Altogether, the *puja* and all cost me Re. 129.25 – including 30 to my accompanying priest. He was not satisfied, but my companions Lalu and Kailash ignored him – Kailash loaning me 60 rupees to cover my immediate expenses. Besides having stepped barefoot on a live coal that morning and being hit by a rickshaw in the afternoon, I came down with a cold. But over the twenty years that followed, I became proficient and surprisingly comfortable with ritual worship in Indian temples and shrines.

My own pursuit of pagan gods and goddesses I have tended to confine for the most part to those within the derivative Indo-European daughter cultures – the Vedic/Hindu, the Greek, Roman, Celtic, Heathen, Baltic, Slavic, etc. Even here I am selective in the consideration of the divine-asurian polarisation and recognition that not all gods are divine. I am also aware that there is a tendency within various pagan circles that exalt ethnic deities to revert to chauvinistic racism. It is probably on this basis that Bruce Lincoln told me once at a conference that he had renounced Indo-European studies. But for me, and perhaps building on an erroneous understanding of ancient Greek religious culture as a developmental peak, I view the Indo-European as a positive and life-affirming precedent – one that is neither negatively patriarchal or hegemonically xenophobic. I could of course be wrong in all this, but it is my pursuit of this optimistic vision that has become the core of my pagan practice and buoyant belief. The mental picture I have and insist upon is universal, humanistic, humanitarian and valuing of the earth, nature and all humanity. If this is a created fabrication rather than some possible historical or prehistorical reality, then so be it! A spiritual worldview may be little different than the artifice of art. If it can be at least a thing of beauty, perhaps that is its true validity and importance.

Consequently, I view the Indo-Europeans or at least the Proto-Indo-Europeans in a similar manner to Edith Hamilton's understanding of Greek civilisation exalting life in all its exuberant potential or as Joseph Campbell upliftingly portrayed occidental culture. Although dismissed by Marija Gimbutas, Colin Renfrew's wave of diffusion theory retains for me a certain merit. He attributed the possibility of Indo-European language dissemination as part of the spread of agriculture from Anatolia. Gimbutas' idea is that the Indo-Europeans expanded through military raids and conquest. While her matriarchal Old Europe contention possesses a likeable quality, it has not been adequately substantiated, and it is contradicted by archaeological evidence of violent destruction of cultural centres from before the Kurgan or Indo-European arrivals. It cannot be doubted that the Kurgans were also conquerors, but this was the civilisation of the day in which the sanctity of the individual had not yet emerged, and while no longer accepted by today's fragile standards, I will still maintain that Indo-European success is in large part a result of not an orientation to patriarchal power but rather the people's buoyant optimism engendered by their affirmative spirituality. I do accept that the Indo-European or Kurgan homeland coincided, as Gimbutas has argued, with present-day Kazakhstan.

While now largely outdated, I follow a version of Friedrich Max Müller's etymological approach in reconstructing a possible proto-Indo-European pantheon. As a result, I do not buy into George Dumézil's tripartite functional interpretation. While Dumézil certainly supplies a wealth of information, his theory appears to me to be more imposed upon the data than derived from it. He omits contradictory evidence that does not support his formulation. Instead, rather than provinces of function, using a deity's cognate names to be found throughout the Indo-European daughter cultures (e.g., Vedic Dyaus, Greek Zeus, Roman Jupiter, Nordic Týr), I argue that not only is there a possibility of discerning the god's earlier designation but also how the figure, like a plant or tree, develops differently and variously over time. The proto-pantheon as I have come to understand it comprises the sun (**Sâwel*), dawn (**Hausos),* earth (**Ghðem),* moon (**Mênôt*), celestial luminosity (**Dyêus/*Perk*^{w}*us*), fire-water-twin (**Egnis/*(s)Nêp*) and deified humanity as hero (**Nert/*Rêgs*) – the last two comprising primordially the divine twins. These reconstructed names are, of course, provisional and conjectural, and there are in some instances more than one nominal root through which the prototypic element developed such as with the moon whose cognate name 'moon', Mâs, Mênê, etc. derive from the moon as 'measurer' of the 'month', while Candra, Hêna as well as Luna, etc. come from roots signifying 'to shine' or 'light'. Then, too, the celestial figure encompassing both the daylit sky and lightning/thunder becomes the Greek Zeus and Roman Jupiter but divides between the light of daytime among the Balts (Dievas/Díevs), Germans/Norse (Tîwaz/Tyr) and Vedic & Sanskrit speakers (Dyaus) and the weather-god of rain, thunder and lightning (Baltic Perkûnas/Pêrkons; German/Norse Donar/Thôr; Vedic/Sanskrit Parjânya and Indra). In other words, among some peoples the Zeus Pater prototype separates into an older figure of the bright firmament and a younger, more actively heroic figure of bombastic fertility and the storm. But as an aside here, I admit to having a tendency to enumerate the various gods as I have perceived and encountered them. Richard suggests to think of my deific musing as akin to a rose window with its materiality of coloured glass and light streaming through it. The large circular stained-glass window can be viewed as an overall whole (a pantheon; heptatheon) but also by examining any individual part (a deity herself/himself) and its mutations and patterns.

In any event, it was by being equipped with this deific framework that I came to explore and immerse myself into Hindu India. What I learned over the twenty-year period of visiting the subcontinent was the art and practice of idolatrous devotion. While many contemporary Western pagans appear to me to be predominantly conditioned by the Jewish and Christian rejection of idol worship as an abomination, India allowed me to engage freely with the thrill of a pantheistic and polytheistic idolatry. For myself, this has become something that augments but does not replace the numinous encounter with nature itself/herself. The two together render my pagan practices to be pluralistically non-sectarian and broadly accepting of magical-mystical differentiation in countless shapes and forms. It cannot be denied that my academic reconstruction of the European deities is controversial and debatable, but at least for myself my devotional practice to them for essentially five decades in the configuration I have uncovered has demonstrated a validity that I cannot contest. For the proto-Indo-Europeans, there appears to be three significant mythologems, namely, disruption, abduction and duplication. These translate as the impairment or overthrow of the central figure – the king of the gods, the rape of the daughter, and the appreciation of the divine twins.

Continuing now with my ceremonial dirge, with help from my 'pūjā guru' Kailash, I was able to rent a large room overlooking the Sitala temple and the Ganges River, and for the astoundingly incredible price of three hundred rupees a month – approximately $36 at the time. Favourite cities for me include Rome, New York/Manhattan, San Francisco, New Orleans,

London, Paris, Amsterdam and Varanasi/Benares. I believe that Benares is perhaps the oldest urban centre in the world. It is certainly one of the most fascinating – all crushed together along a brief stretch of the river along its southeasterly flow to the Bay of Bengal but when it turns for a moment north. With little visible on the opposite bank apart from trees, it allows an uninterrupted view of the rising morning sun. It was in Benares I was able to worship with others and without needing to be the leader of a pack. I could easily be stared at by Indians since they are unaccustomed to seeing a Westerner doing *pûjâ* and also by tourists who are amazed and probably uneasy over the same thing – especially from the tour boats on the river when I would have a crack of dawn *snan* and swim. But in all, and from the start, the feeling for me was wonderful and as if I had come in from the cold and lonely outdoors to warmth in the company of friends.

In Benares, I also discovered the *bhang lassi*, and this puts me ultimately into the same company as Jeremy Hunt who had the cannabis drink when backpacking in India. The use of mind-altering substances is among the more controversial social issues, and this includes for pagans as well. As my own practice is essentially shamanic, the employment of psychotropic substances is an important part of that practice. The rejection of such seems only in part due to our Judeo-Christian heritage and its political-colonial influence. There is a puritanical core that appears globally to be intrinsically terrified of psychonautic exploration. But, like a subtle fabric, the otherworld may be perceived to interpenetrate this world of empirical observation and reason, and nature has provided the human a means for being able to access this otherwise mostly invisible realm. True enough, that which nature has produced has been extended through various alchemical or pharmaceutical means, but the principle remains the same. Returning to my Indo-European studies, the divine twins theme has several understandings, but a central one may be interpreted as the pair comprising humanity as one twin and the psychedelic or hypnagogic substance as the other. Consequently, we have such possibilities as Apollo and Dionysus, Indra and Soma and the role of Neptunus/Nechtan/Nôdens as the secondary figure who embodies 'fire in water', 'inspired poetry' or 'luminous glory'. In mythic narrative, the secondary twin is often represented as the mortal figure who knows death, that is, the realm of the deceased as it is conflated in general with the otherworld of fantasy, dream and magic. The divine twin who encounters death is Dionysus, Ýmir, Yama, Castor, Remus and perhaps Balder among others. Through the portrayal of the figure as one who knows trans-stygian existence, this also depicts the figure as knowing the shamanic dimension of trance.

India is the most magically enchanted land under any circumstances. It is perhaps equally an ordeal, but the combination whirlwind of colour and mystery with the *bhang lassi* or *ganja* let alone more potent forms of alchemy augments intranatural dymaxion and eidesis. In other words, the entheogen allows the intervention of the divine through natural means, and this intrusion in turn encourages both the unusual vividness of mental images and an awakening of spiritual insights. India's sannyasins are proverbially committed to this kind of recourse, though choice here is always personal, and other people may have other means for obtaining internal and external transformations. For both the Hindu and the pagan, there is no 'one way'. Multiplicity is encouraged, and as long as there is no injury at least to others if not to the self as well, virtually all is permitted. The bonus of Benares in particular for shamanic exploration is that it contains more pagan-like shrines and temples per capita than anywhere else in the world.

Unlike Buddhism and strict Brahmanism, paganism does not view the otherworld or wish-world as negative but instead affirms this world and undertakes to transfer its reality to that of the other. In other words, while the gnostic *via negativa* approach is constructed upon the belief that desire is the root of evil and/or unhappiness and transmits the 'unreality' of the dream-world to materiality to then deny the validity of all existence, paganism seeks to *make* the wish-world as true as the material world and render both as beautiful. Besides the temples and shrines, the ghats along the river became my usual haunt in Benares – what I came to designate as the Kashi Coast. Everything appears to be reflected in India and her way of life, but in this mirroring it is magnified countless times to the point of ridiculousness. This is conducive to the sociologist and student of religion. Without knowing why, one guesses that everything is to be found here. This for me has included my dancing along the Kashi Coast to the *con fuoco* third movement of Malcolm Arnold's Fifth Symphony – enjoying the very moment of cosmic exhilaration that the composer engendered.

What the polytheist frequently seeks is what the Hindu refers to as *darshan*, namely, the seeing of deity. The shamanic psychotropic aids can assist in this, but one learns in India that there are many possibilities through which a deity might manifest to a person – through contemplation or meditation or though the more spontaneous. In a Hindu temple, there were frequent occasions when the power went out, and all was plunged suddenly into darkness. Sometimes with the soft illumination from a candle being lit, the deity might unexpectedly manifest through the idol. Other times, the same could occur through simply the dynamics of people and movement present. But the experience of *darshan* is more than simply beholding the deity in image form. An idol is an idol, but when in some, perhaps inexplicable way, the figure transmogrifies through the vital presence of deity, the spiritual fulfilment of *darshan* occurs. This indwelling is often a reflex of the worshipper's expanded state of consciousness. All that may be necessary for *darshan* ('seeing', 'vision', 'appearance') can be the act of simply gazing at the figure.

I will admit that *ganja* or cannabis is often important in the experiencing of *darshan* and especially in the Hindu worship of Shiva, and I believe that substances conducive to altered states of consciousness have been also significant in various pagan cultures as well as in the Greek mystery religions. Consequently, with regard to cannabis, and considering its legalisation or tolerance in Uruguay, Canada, Spain, Portugal, The Netherlands and eleven US states, the British continuing prohibition is archaic in the negative sense – especially with 63% of Londoners backing legalisation and 47% of the country as a whole supporting the same (with 23% undecided).

My initial experience with 'grass' or 'weed' occurred during those incredible days of the counterculture in Haight-Ashbury San Francisco. I had wanted to fly out the window but could not even get myself physically to move off the sofa. When I finally did get into motion, I eventually found myself in a car on a one-way trip to Acapulco, Mexico – the centre of Acapulco Gold marijuana. I had next to no money and survived there a good month. But I was then young and good looking, let alone adventuresome. I survived in various ways from sharing a two-peso room with another penurious soul I had met to staying in a villa that may have been owned by the American owners of MacDonald's. Much of the time was a blur, and after about six weeks one evening I was sitting in a cafe on the main square when an Italian artist living in America began a conversation with me. Since I was being vague when asked how long I was staying in Acapulco, he continued to press until he had me admit that I was stuck there. He then said that he would like to help me and that I should come to the beach the next day and that he would be leaving after that. I did not go to the beach the following day or two, and when I finally got there, he was still there and waved me over to him. He repeated that he was being serious in wanting to help me. I said that if he could purchase for me a bus ticket to Tijuana, that I could get home from there. He proceeded to take me straight to the airline office and bought me a ticket all the way through to San Francisco. He then explained that he was about to have a show of his paintings shortly in the United States and asked me if I would light a candle for his success. That was all he had asked of me.

On the way home, I stopped first in Los Angeles and was there introduced to George Darius who predicted for me a future of travel. Once home, I could always use some form of an income. My friend George (Buster) secured for me what was one of my early jobs in life, namely, collating an information manual that was to be available through a San Francisco travel agency. This allowed me to be able to enjoy the offices in the upper floor of a corner building on Union Square, now long demolished, but which still exists in my memory. The individual sheets were arranged sequentially around the edges of two oblong tables, and my task was to walk around the tables and put the manual's pages together one by one so that they could be bound into book form. This was by today's standards an old-fashioned process that involved physical and monotonous behaviour. And this was during those heady and unforgettable days of Haight-Ashbury. I was to work for one day in the evening, and so for the afternoon I had gone to a Golden Gate Park concert gathering of the Jefferson Airplane. Subsequently, once in the offices, I got one time around the tables with the intention of continuing when I confessed to Mildred Pierce, the owner of the travel agency and for whom I was working, that I was stoned. She immediately took a chair and sat down at the side of one of the tables, put her elbows on the surface and her chin into her hands and said with a big smile on her face, 'Tell me all about it!' We talked for several hours, and I had probably collated only one manual before our conversation began. But I remember Mildred telling me about the happy marriage she had had until one day, suddenly, her husband died. She was devastated and said subsequently to a friend, 'It just isn't fair!' Whereupon her friend retorted with the question, 'Whoever told you that life is supposed to be fair?'

Fairness is always an open question. I had gone to a talk in the Jewish Community Center of San Francisco on Wagner's *Tristan and Isolde*. It was the eve of an opening performance of the work at the San Francisco Opera House. It is now too many decades ago for me to remember who the speaker had been, but he explained how important the evening was to be in determining the suitability of the singers and whether this difficult opera of the German composer was to experience a rebirth. Beyond this, he explained the opera in such exciting detail that my enthusiasm became contagious to

Nancy who previously had dismissed any necessity of knowing the story of an opera before attending a performance. And to my surprise, she was completely captivated by the production and discovered on this occasion her subsequent lifelong love of opera. She even wanted to re-see the previous opera we had seen because she now recognized that she had not had the proper attitude.

I was a student at the time, and we would purchase standing room tickets to be able to see what there was to see. When intermission would come, we would each go to an exit of the opera house and ask whoever appeared to be leaving if we could use their tickets. I explained that we were students and were standing. Almost invariably, anyone we approached who was leaving was thrilled to know that their seats were not to be wasted, and we were granted their tickets gladly. However, on one occasion I saw a father departing with his young daughter and approached him and made my request. To my complete astonishment, he replied, 'Oh, I do not think that would be fair!' He seemed to me to be a young American 'military' type, and I was so dumbfounded by what he had said that I did not even think to mention to him how everyone else on previous occasions was more than glad to do what he wouldn't. When I found Nancy afterward and explained to her what had happened, she said not to worry. She had just been given two tickets for seats in the front row of the balcony. The realisation, however, that a fixed attitude of what is 'proper' can preclude a natural magnanimity has remained with me ever since that time.

Having lived in Europe for now what is more than half my life, I have come in the past to be proud of what visitors from here to the United States have often referred to as American generosity. We are, or can be, hospitable to a remarkable degree. I have grown to think that this is the American's best characteristic. It is of course not the Yankee's alone. A strange memory I have when I arrived in Stockholm for the first time were the number of Swedes who would come up to me and explain how, as a Swedish person, they could never speak on the street to another person of their own nationality that they did not already know. Recognising that I was not Swedish, they felt free to talk to me and explain this. After several days in the Swedish capital, I continued on with my now much more successful hitching of lifts and reached the Danish port city of Elsinore, the one of Hamlet fame. As I was walking to the youth hostel, a man on a bicycle approached and, noticing my flag, began to converse. He explained that he was going to the train station to meet his wife but if I preferred to sleep the night in a private bed, I should wait on his porch for them to return. I did, and the couple was wonderful – offering me the chance to take a bath and feeding me profusely. They explained that I was doing them a favour since they had planned a party for the weekend that had just passed but no one had come, so they had all the food still and needed someone with whom to share it. When I was leaving the following morning, I said I did not know how to thank them. I was told that if in some future moment I had the opportunity to do the same, I would then have thanked them.

I do think that generosity is perhaps the most beautiful of human possibilities, and I have sought to share much of what I have myself with which to share. With this, perhaps I am retaining a part of my American heritage. And likewise, I applaud Angela Merkel's brave decision to open Germany to the many, many migrants from both Africa and the Middle East. This last is understandably highly controversial and unleashes a host of further problems and difficulties. The Brexit decision to have Britain leave the European Union has as much to do with xenophobic migrant hatred as it does with the imperious passions of 'Little England'. But I also remember the arrogance and beliefs of 'American Exceptionalism' that seem increasingly to have become contagious in infecting natural proclivities to be found in other parts of the world as well.

For Aristotle, happiness is the end goal. For some even, being generous allows the giving individual to be happy. I doubt that generosity is itself a means to being happy, but I think that happiness itself permits, maybe encourages, one to be magnanimous. I will admit that on a personal level I am happy. I have friendship, love and companionship. These are supreme. Certainly, a degree of wealth or affluence is greatly helpful as well in cushioning the plethora of navigations life requires. I am also aware, especially as time and age advance, that nothing is permanent. All, including happiness, is ephemeral. That is why, for me at least, the *carpe diem* approach to existence is imperative. If we cannot appreciate the here-and-now, what guarantee is there that tomorrow will be better if not worse?

True enough, so much of democracy appears to be a sham. Aristotle had little respect for or expectation from any rule by the majority. The course of human historic progression has been understood to proliferate continually into evermore schismatic factionalisms with which the bigger-powers-that-be, through media control and *sub rosa* purchase, manipulate the greater number who are and remain ignorant or powerless or both. What appears to be the most astonishing is the preponderance of current focus upon the smartphone. Whether walking down the street, riding on the bus or underground, or during the intermission time at the theatre, virtually everyone appears to be glued to the screen of a tiny mobile device. Whether this same concentration will persist into whatever future the world may yet appreciate, I cannot say. But the general public of today seems to be increasingly oblivious to landscape, to three-dimensional reality, to the potential joy of people watching and casual interaction, and to live communication and exchange. As one who somehow has missed out with the technical transformations of our current times, more and more do I feel like a ghost who has become lost in a strange and nebulous pantomime. Granted that the smartphone allows ebook access and the availability of a this-worldly akashic records of endless information, but somewhere in all this the personal is lost. Without human-to-human sensitivities, is a republican commonwealth possible in the first place? Perhaps in a post-capitalist world in which people are not perpetually scrambling for competitive advance, one in which time becomes a luxury to be enjoyed, where laughter is both heard and immediately contagious, perhaps in such a world communal and festive rituals, the quiet and aromas of the woodlands, and the frequent touch between two or more persons become the norm. Such a milieu would be a healthy preserve – one that could possibly foster reflection, organic input and wholesome productivity.

Perhaps my musings are only an escapist dream and fantasy, but I will maintain them all the same to be preferable to the kind of nightmare encapsulated by the American presidential campaigning, by the incarceration of daring whistle-blowers, by the deterioration of educational standards and aspirations, by the demand for safe spaces over challenging university debate open to free speech, and by the wealth of prodigal expenditure on belligerency and catastrophic suffering. I will also maintain that generosity does not extend to the largess of paying exorbitant taxes. My resentments toward America include one opposed to citizen-based taxation rather than resident-based. But this is now extended to The Netherlands as well in which income tax is based not only on one's income but is to include the value of all property and assets worldwide. Even if and when the Dutch resident has no further income, the person is obligated to pay tax on one's holdings which means that one's savings will be steadily reduced over time. I suppose that those who are wealthy enough are able to employ expert advisers and lawyers who can discern the ways to circumvent the onerous. It has been speculated that Donald Trump may not have paid any income tax at all. Such mega-corporations like Goldman-Sachs, Bank of America,

General Electric, DuPont, Boeing, Shell, BP, ExxonMobil, FedEx, Verizon, Apple, Amazon, Starbucks and Facebook have the financial means to dodge taxes through complicated tax-avoiding structures, overseas exemptions and juggling subsidiaries throughout various tax haven countries. The tax breaks and loopholes that corporate businesses can afford and employ are those that the average person simply cannot obtain.

Fred Astaire and Rita Hayworth dance 'The Shorty George' in the 1942 film *You Were Never Lovelier*, Michelangelo's *David* through the vulnerability of the statue's weak and fissured ankles is in danger of a pulverizing collapse, and in 2016 the grime star Skepta wins the Mercury Award for the best musical album of the United Kingdom and Ireland. The arts are our best hope and yet, from the vantage of the disillusioned individual, can crystalise as a frivolous void that unsuccessfully masks more brutal realities in vain. One possible way to counter artistic non-engagement might be to concentrate on the present moment: Ram Dass' 'Be here now!' The risk with this last, with exclusive engrossment with the here-and-now, is that it does not encourage planning for a future and the work for making change – especially reshaping along the lines of a preconceived and intelligent plan. Simultaneously, it shifts focus away from the study of the past and learning the lessons garnered through former mistakes. Any 'Lotus World of the Future' as I am conceiving it is significantly dependent on reviewing and understanding its precedents in order to be evermore mindful of what has been achieved and how not to repeat unnecessary wrongs of previous times. I believe that what we might designate as the Lotocene will also be open and engaged with what is to come through both scientific discovery and the breakthroughs of artistic and spiritual endeavour. The eternally fleeting present is always to be cherished, but rather than being isolated from past and future it can only be integrally interconnected with both. But in today's war between the box of bureaucratic authority and the unrestricted movement for individual self-determination, there is the lunacy of terrorist ruination and the smothering of creative innovation by the cultivated fear of insecurity.

Planning judiciously for the future and being acutely mindful of the past do not preclude a predominant 'going with the flow'. One can accept and move along with the prevailing forces and trends. But as Mitchell Waldrop has observed, one can also remain vigilant, and when a more advantageous eddy appears, the oar could be thrust into the waters to punt one's vessel into it. Trance and the occasional surrender to mindless indifference are or can be important punctuations, but it is ultimately mindfulness that is of determinative importance. This often includes a freedom from judging in terms of right and wrong. But judgment itself is not excluded. Instead, there can be an acute awareness of what is conducive to the situation or one's wants and what is not. If the thing, moment or event is compatible, the judgment to accept it is possible and valid. We are floating specs upon a cosmopolitan sea of our pasts – as hauntingly rich and full of wailing and potentially dangerous sirens in the background they may be.

But back for the moment to the experimental avalanche of the seminal countercultural times, beside cannabis, hippiedom encouraged further explorations with other mind-expanding substances. I had already had peyote years earlier in San Francisco and Santa Barbara and subsequently had, of course, travelled through Europe with my backpack half full of the cactus. But the City by the Bay in the second half of the 1960s was an explosion. We experienced the gregariousness and spontaneous trust of others, inter-human experimentation, liberating festivals and above all the refreshing beauty of nature and the star-studded night skies of rural California. There emerged for many of us an enhanced curiosity into spiritual matters. We researched and consumed and researched further; we also danced and meditated and investigated all as if it were ripe fruit ready to be plucked from the tree. My wife Nancy worked as an occupational therapist in the psychiatric ward of the University of California San Francisco Medical Center in Parnassus Heights. In the innovative spirit of the times, she and her co-workers would provide feedback ideas from the likes of Alfred Adler, Fritz Perls and others to the breaking point of the clinic, and one day it was announced that the ward was closing. Suddenly the entire staff was on unemployment benefits. By sheer serendipity, every time any one of us would attend a hippy event, we were *all* there. The upshot was that we bonded, and our 'Family' was born. My friend Buster and I had talked for several years about forming a witches' coven, and suddenly we had nearly the thirteen we wanted. We would conduct our rituals on top of Strawberry Hill in Golden Gate Park – smeared with a flying ointment I had concocted out of belladonna and jimson weed. In all, our Strawberry Hill Coven celebrated a year of sabbats, and then with the political darkness gathering on the horizon, I talked half of us to flee with me to Europe. Since then, two of us have deceased along with my brother who participated in our first ritual, and with three further contact is minimal if at all, but when Richard and I married in Amsterdam, the rest all came, and it was once again the magic of our Family gathering. Nancy gave me away, and Coral, the mother of Richard's daughter, assumed this function for Richard.

And it should be of no surprise that while many psychedelic and cannabis intoxications are exhilarating, not all are. It was an Easter morning at Strawberry Hill on LSD when I fell suddenly into Hell – and 'forever' as these wispy elongated filaments that identified themselves as angels proclaimed unrelentingly. There was for a time no way out. And this has become ever since a re-encountered confrontation, but fortunately only on increasingly rare occasions. If I had not been there already, it led to my complete rejection of both Christianity and its inversion known as Satanism. My paganism unfolded through my investigations of Native American spirituality along with the fairy-faith call engendered for me by Walter Evans-Wentz and the lure of Arcadian Greece as presented by Maurice Ravel's *Daphnis and Chloe*. And even in the metropolitan environment, the rawer elements of nature are to be witnessed through the city's parks, tree-lined avenues, pavement weeds and the presence of birds. Nature is always present despite civilised humanity's efforts to mask and hide it, and nature suggests the divine not as some schizophrenic entity but as an organic multiplicity of zeniths and regeneration.

And similarly, the gods and their vehicles, images and symbols interpenetrate the everyday world in surprisingly numerous ways. The perception of such is something that usual requires cultivation, but for the person who wishes to witness the divine – through either nature or our cultural legacies or both, the possibility is there for each and every one of us. For me, India provided much of the springboard for this kind of insight – probably because in India the obvious is so much more exaggerated, but the basic cultivation of divine perception can exist and occur anywhere. And to this process, imagination is a friend.

And in connection with 'Get Up, Stand Up Now' celebrating Black creativity in Britain, I ought also to mention my longstanding fascination with the Afro-Latin traditions (Lucumí, Regla de Ochá, Candomblé, Vodou). I have found these to be more serious and not something for the casual inquirer or the one who randomly and self-assembles pastiche pieces, bit by bit. In these traditions, one is required to undergo prolonged training and eventual initiation. And while there may be some parallels between the Indo-European proto-pantheon and Las Seite Potencias Africanas, the latter belong to a much different observance and extreme care is mandatory when approaching the *orishas* of Santería – a familiarisation and understanding that is not required to the same intensity with the nature figures of the Proto-Indo-European or the embodied cultural resonances of the Classical deities of the Greeks and Romans. With these last, more intuition, flexibility and spontaneity are commensurate for the Euro-American Westerner; the legacy is more directly his or her own. Nevertheless, there is a magnetism that enchants through the colour and richness of the Afro-Latin altar and ritual. A pagan recognises a pagan element and spirit wherever it resides. And the African and Latin American spiritual expressions constitute a deeply important reservoir within the global pagan world.

And I suppose I ought to clarify my preference for small-p paganism over large-P Paganism. For me, the latter is subsumed within the former and is acceptable in the more political-type efforts to gain legitimacy and recognition of Paganism along with the competitor religions. But as Andras Corban-Arthen has explained to me, it is more an American thing to capitalise month names, weekday names, and the names of religions such as Christianity, Buddhism, Paganism, etc. Small-p paganism is for me an incoherent and vernacular generic – not an institutionalised religion *per se* despite the broad movement containing various institutionalised spiritualities along with the unconscious and natural. Any insistence on big-P Paganism as an overall designation becomes a dogma, and unlike most if not all other religions, the pagan orientation in today's and the future world has no dogmas. Admittedly, small-p paganism was originally employed by Christian writers as a derogatory term – perhaps like that of 'witch', but its distinction is one that I wish to welcome and champion. Consequently, I am with people like Dion Fortune and Guy Davenport who have seemed completely comfortable with the designation of 'paganism' pure and simple.

My own disenchantment with my birth country oscillated in the past but has in recent years become more horrifyingly complete. During the Second World War, I was used in a newspaper war bond advertisement probably around the time I was three. The photo showed me leaning on the back railing of the house my parents had rented in Buffalo, holding a wooden war ship and dreamily gazing into the future. The caption read as follows:

> We must not let anyone change his way of life. Boats, marbles, baseball, circuses; then to school and college . . . all are possible to him in a free country such as ours. That is why we are fighting this war: to continue the

American Way of Life. You are asked to buy War Bonds – to invest your money in the greatest 'company' in the world, your country. William Butler, the editor of the *Buffalo Evening News*, then concludes, It's YOU he's looking up to . . . don't let him down.

And yet all these many years later, that is precisely how I do feel – 'let down.' I have, however, learned by this point not to have expectations. Things will rarely turn out as first anticipated, and in an out-of-control world (as if it has ever been in control in actuality) one seeks survival as best one can under whatever the circumstances.

The irony behind this has nonetheless remained striking to me. I adored the circus as a child; baseball, less so, but school and college were the supreme treasures for which I remain eternally grateful. Yet America as a business company I have come to deplore. There are three things that currently come foremost to mind when I reflect on the American Way of Life. One I have learned through Americans who have moved to Europe and have subsequently lost a range of allergies and disabilities which had been formerly the norm for them when living on the Other Side of the Pond. 'Well, OK, I'll have a taste', Elizabeth would say after arriving in Amsterdam but being mindful of a plaguing range of allergies. And then slowly she discovered she could consume mostly whatever she wished. She did not become ill as she had been accustomed to in the United States. She came to be free from the hidden sugars and salt that have been added to virtually all processed American foods – for 'palatable' reasons an industry spokesperson explained one morning on the BBC's Radio Four. These along with the contaminants, chemicals and perhaps even GMO ingredients that have appeared to characterize the food industry of our times in the United States are enslaving people in unsuspecting ways. I have suspected as much for some time, but Elizabeth's story became one of several that validated for me beyond mere speculation how contaminated and artificially manipulated the American food supply now is. Another horror is the media suppression of hydraulic fracturing, more colloquially known as fracking, and its environmental results. The deceit involved with the resultant pollution of groundwater – to the extent that one has been able with a match to light a running water faucet into flame – and the resultant carcinogenic potential from the chemicals used; the huge amount of water employed in the fracking process – all the more ironic considering the current Californian drought; the increase in earth tremors and/or earthquakes in the fractured areas; and the imperative ecological need for an immediate fossil fuel reduction if not elimination rather than any increase. And thirdly, there is the condescendingly contemptuous 'American Way' that ignores treaties when no longer advantageously expedient (such as with the Native Americans), that refuses to ratify the UN Convention on Children's Rights and other international human rights treaties as well as the International Criminal Court and the Law of the Sea Treaty, that conducts its world policy in cowboy fashion, and that condones rendition, secret prisons, torture (e.g., water boarding, rectal feeding tubes, etc.), drone bombing and countless manners of deceit to achieve self-serving goals only – ones that benefit corporations rather than people and the POPs (point-one-percenters) rather than humanity as a more collective whole.

Consequently, the irony is that I do feel – and have for a long time now – 'let down' by the disillusionment over the insincere affirmation of ideals and virtues for which the American Republic was reputedly founded and which it allegedly endorsed. And then, putting all this into the perspective of the predictions concerning 'the end of the world as we know it' – the planet's 'sixth mass extinction event' – in which humans may become non-existent in 100 years or less, the malaise of depression along with realising that our species' artistic creations (Michelangelo, Caravaggio, Rembrandt, Van Gogh, Picasso, Shakespeare, Austin, Poe, Wordsworth, Donne, Pope, Sophocles, Dante, Goethe, Bach, Mozart, Brahms, Mahler, Ravel, Gershwin to name but a few) let along technological achievements (e.g., electricity, computation, space travel, cataract surgery, etc.) may all vanish without viable consequence because of our mindlessness and inability to change under the governmental, military and corporate controls in which we all live and operate. All this engenders the *carpe diem* for tomorrow we die vestige we appear only to have left. This last is the easiest to do – especially when we witness at present the youth of the West enthralled and living the joys of life, and as I am well into the autumn years of my own life, it can seem that this is all I along with most others can do. But I still believe in imagination, and, along with my deploring, it may not be a perfect world, whatever that could possibly be, but it is nonetheless a better world in both humanitarian and possibly recent environmental terms than it previously has been.

Perhaps available foods are little different health-wise in places beyond the USA, but this does not appear to be the case in France and, in particular, the

Midi – the 'South' of France, perhaps better known as the Provence. One can understand almost immediately why the Victorians discovered, and were captivated by, this area. The Romans were too – naming the region the Provincia Romana, i.e., *the* Roman province. The olive greens, the red earth, the muted yellows and blue skies and sea are the first to impact a northerner. The cosmopolitan and rural combination dawns on one in time. Both historically and pre-historically, great numbers of people have always come to or migrated through the territory – adding over time to its rich ethnic and cultural diversity. Like a marvellous and gigantic oasis-enclave, here is a sacred world that largely exists independent from the global havoc that is *elsewhere* and seemingly everywhere else. Here is a veritable paradise. And its Mediterranean diet has been lauded by countless nutritionists: strong on fruits, vegetables, whole grains, legumes, beans, nuts, seeds, herbs and spices and along with decent amounts of olive oil, fish and seafood as well as red wine. Poultry, eggs, butter, cheese and yoghurt are consumed more moderately; red meat, salt and sweet desserts, even less. And much of what one can consume is produced locally – even organically. The area impels a healthy degree of physical activity. Meals are relaxed and frequently in the company of friends and family. The first part of the afternoon is often devoted to the *déjeuner* – usually the largest meal of the day – and succeeded by the *sièste*. When I first came to the area in the 1970s, the *Var-Matin* published a three-day article asking if the Var was truly one-half foreign. By the end, it concluded that it was but that that should not be a problem as long as everyone could get along together. I have seen during a song contest as part of the local *fête* that there was no hesitation or qualms in awarding the first-place prize to an American singer. If there is a single word to describe the Midi, I would have to choose *comfortable*.

Of course, coming to a farm house after any duration of lengthy absence, there are the inevitable initial difficulties concerning water drainage, electricity, warming the walls of an unused dwelling, lack of telephone and internet and so forth. Only to be expected, and one sallies on with the various needed restorations and repairs – accepting the drenching sunlight as a compensation. Our house reveals the remnant of a sundial dated 1811 and along with the word *requiem*. To the north and east rises the first of the Alps from this direction – Le Montagne des Espiguières. And a short drive away is the Gorges du Verdon – France's answer to the Grand Canyon. Apart from Mt. Olympus in Greece, if the gods have a terrestrial dwelling, it would have to be the Valley of the Verdon. Though charted in the late eighteenth century, this area appears on no maps until the 1920s. Local inhabitants would certainly have known about it, and cavers and tour guides explored the area in the second half of the nineteenth century. Its beauty is indescribable. Not as immense as the Grand Canyon, the Verdon Gorge is the next in size after the more renowned site of Arizona. The river canyon is considered to be the most beautiful of the kind in the whole of Europe – with the green Verdon River snaking through rugged cliffs of Jurassic limestone and petrified coral. The valley remains wild and even dangerous, and fierce summer thunderstorms can appear suddenly.

To the southwest of the Gorges, there was the old Roman road connecting the city of Riez to the port of Fréjus – along which timber from the Alps was transported for the construction of ships. This route passed through both the *oppidum* (later *castrum*) Alpibus, a 'center of the world', and the City of the Dragon (Draguignan). The legend concerning the dragon emerges from medieval mists, and he was accordingly vanquished by the hermit, Saint Hermentaire, *circa* 400 ce. In one interpretation of the dragonslaying narrative, the serpent represents the pagan substratum to which the Church was opposed. The façade of a Roman temple in Riez has been attributed to the god Apollo who was also known as a slayer of a dragon – the Python of Delphi. Where exactly the dragon of Dragonianum lived is uncertain – either in the marshes of the Nartuby river where Hermentaire slew the beast, a section known to this day as Saint-Hermentaire, or the prominence within Draguignan known as the Malmont, that is, the 'bad Mount'. The name of 'Draguignan', however, conveys perhaps a deeper current to the story – deriving from *draco* and *guinum* relating to the people. Consequently, the Dragiugnan dragon may have been the 'dragon of the people'.

In any event, since the city of Toulon had sided against Napoleon, the emperor decreed the city of Draguignan to become the prefecture of the Department of the Var. In the Middle Ages, the city along with Aix, Nice and Marseilles had been among the most populated urban centres in the Provence. However, in 1974, the central government of France decided that the now much more populous and important city of Toulon should be once again the prefecture or administrative centre of the Var. The *dracénoises* or inhabitants of the Draguignan region protested violently – their protest taking the form of cutting down ancient trees that lined one of Baron Haussmann's avenues (Haussmann having been a native of Draguignan) and dynamiting the chalcolithic Pierre de la Fée, an impressive dolmen to be found in the city. It has since been restored.

The dragon, of course, remains a controversial but seminal mythogem or unit of mythological meaning not only in the European tradition but more globally as well. Although I have been comfortable with its traditional significance, I have come to recognise a different understanding for the image among both the Chinese and many contemporary pagans. For our own seminal ancestors, the fire-breathing, winged and scaly serpent represented the nihilistic impulse to prevent growth and regeneration and to obliterate the entire gamut of positive and negative polarities within the cosmos. From among the Levantine peoples of the middle east, I will argue that the personification of this impulse into the Abrahamic 'God' has also developed and been subsequently exported or imperially expanded to the rest of the world – to the point that at least half the inhabitants of our planet adhere to some following of this particular construct. While I will not go so far as to wish any *re*-construction of the Levantine figure into anything palatable less than pure deceit, I can fathom a need to rehabilitate the serpent-dragon image itself if we humans truly desire to progress beyond the debilitating stalemate we have reached in our twenty-first century of the present era. Another metaphor for what I have elsewhere termed the *asurian* is the volcano. But in recently asking a *parisienne* friend how she understood the term '*tellurique*', she described it as what 'comes up from the earth, such as a volcano'. Whereas I suspect the French relative of our English word *telluric* refers more to the indescribable aura of a numinous or sacred place, such as the mantic energy of a spring or well, I can accept that the volcano is also earth-born and requires ultimately an acceptance rather than a *carte blanche* rejection. Such is how I am currently coming to feel about the dragon.

❋

At least shortbread and Emmental cheese are wonderfully neutral foods. Maybe not the healthiest – dancing between diabetes and cholesterol – but always at least palatable. When I was young and visiting Manhattan, I often subsisted on orange juice, Jewish pumpernickel bread and Philadelphia cream cheese. If I am ill, I want only pizza and coca cola – presumably this last because as a child I was given coca cola syrup purchased from the pharmacy when sick. In India, I became known for living on fruit and nuts. This was not true, but they are both comestibles that I enjoy beyond the norm. The fascination with food has always been there for me. When I have been fortunate to have a vegetable garden in the Midi, the primary successes have been with tomatoes and courgettes. Presumably, our world collectively could produce ample food to be able to feed everyone on the planet. Distribution is of course a difficulty but not a formidable one. It is political rivalry and belligerence that are our real problems.

A favourite musical work is Malcolm Arnold's *Fifth Symphony*, Opus 74 – dating to 1961. Composed in conjunction with the death of four close friends and the dissolution of his first marriage, the music is both perversely celebratory and hauntingly mournful. And for a pinnacle moment in the third movement, Arnold breaks briefly into a joyous cosmic dance. This last never seems to last long enough, but it taunts the listener as a *raison d'être* for life – sandwiched between a range of enchanting evocations. As Alfred Brendel put it, 'The realm of aesthetics – art, music, literature, theatre and film – [seems] to be, as Nietzsche had said, the sole justification of life and the world'. Personally, the arts appear to me as the very life blood of existence. Without them, there is only absurdity despite all our attempt to rationalize ethics as something apart from aesthetics. We on planet Earth, let alone not only our entire Solar System – itself a speck of the Milky Way Galaxy which in turn is a speck of the Virgo Supercluster – are infinitesimal. But all these greater collections are themselves to be found within the supercluster of galaxies known as Laniakea. In other words, Laniakea contains the Milky Way, Andromeda and approximately another one hundred galaxies including the Virgo Supercluster as well. But even Laniakea and the Perseus-Pisces Supercluster that borders her are but themselves a small pocket in the great expanse whose portrayal a psychologist friend likens to the synapses inside the human brain. Yet, as minute as we are, we are still a part of the broader universe that is perhaps itself a developing consciousness – not a product of a transcendental creating agent but the agent of producing mindfulness itself. And if this super consciousness, the universe as a mind, is to have any meaning, its purpose can only be beauty in and of itself.

Education has long been one of my own most enjoyable pursuits. My various student days have constituted some of the finest periods in my life. And ultimately such periods culminated for me successively with a Research Fellowship, a position as Principal Lecturer, and finally one of becoming a full Professor. While I continue to champion the university and related environments and see these as evolving into virtually universal pastime foci in a future world in which automation has largely replaced the use of capital for labour, and machines and robots have assumed the performance of not only most basic manual tasks but also much intellectual work, there are still unsavoury areas and behaviour that are to be found currently in academia. Backstabbing for advancement and jealous vendettas occur more than one would wish among institutional staff and teaching competitors, and the target culture that British higher education has become – along with the aggressive readiness of both American and British students, if not those from elsewhere as well, to be offended over subject, language, grammar, ideas not in accord with their predisposed thought biases, accusations of unequal representation and protest against alleged reductionism and exclusivism – has allowed me to be thoroughly glad for retirement. There appears now to be the perpetual and most wearying translation of most liberal arts topics into protest issues of sexism, race, Eurocentrism and colonialism.

My most recent disappointment is one with publication. This of course is not the first time I have had difficulty with getting something into print – whether a book or a journal article. One of the most tiresome parts of the process is the reviewer feedback – otherwise known as peer review. In Belgium's Louvain-la-Neuve, I gave a paper on 'Pagan Ritual Practices and Religious Celebrations Dedicated to a Changing Nature'. Subsequently it was submitted to the sponsoring society's journal but has been rejected. One reviewer considered the proposed article to read like an undergraduate essay with sweeping claims that he or she found 'irritating'. The example given was my assertion that contemporary paganism results from a widespread popular perception of climate change and my ignoring any previous 'revival'. This would relate to an objection made by the other reviewer, namely:

> The author uses a lower case 'p' for 'pagans'. Michael York is one of the few contemporary academics who endorses this practice of a small 'p'. All other academics use a capital 'P' for 'Pagan'. If the author is explicitly following York's practice, then please reference York's justification for this practice. Otherwise, please use a capital 'P'.

Peer review is invariably done anonymously, so the reviewer would not have necessarily known that I am the author, but what both reviewers unfortunately miss is that I am addressing paganism as a spontaneous folk and vernacular development that is broader than any big-P Paganism and any sectarian formulation from Wicca and Heathenism to Druidism, etc. that may be approached as having developed out of the largely unarticulated, non-transcendental and quotidian sentiment that is both atavistic and naturally subliminal. Contemporary Western Paganism (CWP) is indeed a by-product of Western Esotericism which finds its own origins in Rosicrucianism, Swedenborgianism, Mesmerism, Spiritualism, Theosophy, Christian Science and New Thought as well as Freemasonry, the Neo-Templar movement and the modern-day practice of ceremonial magic.

The one reviewer argues that my 'proposition that contemporary Paganism is a product of reactions to climate change, pollution and overpopulation is clearly wrong'. More important than this as a motivating cause for (only) 'perhaps 10% at most [is] individualism, feminism, the environment movement, and Pagan themes in the mass media'. I remain uncertain what is the alleged difference between the 'environment movement' and reactions to climate change, habitat contamination and explosive population; I could agree perhaps when speaking of CWP but much less so in connection to generic paganism. More broadly, this last has a greater affinity with what Bron Taylor designates as Dark Green Religion.

The same reviewer argues that it is reasonable to assume that Pagans would recognise the influence of enlightenment thought, industrialisation and the modernisation project as the causes behind the mismanagement of the terrestrial environment, and while I have not denied this, I posit that the biblical injunction of Genesis 1.28 to subdue and have dominion over earth is frequently held to have legitimated humanity's using of nature as a resource rather than a sanctified presence that requires respect and protection first and foremost. The necessary 'harmony with nature' in opposition to a Judeo-Christian sanctioned 'dominance over nature' sentiment I have found to be held by many Contemporary Western Pagans including Margot Adler, Starhawk and Charlene Spretnak as well as such environmental academics or green spiritual activists as Lynn White Jr., John Seed and Jonathan Porritt. Adler for one, in her remarkable *Drawing Down the Moon,* refers not only to White but also to a 1972 Arnold Toynbee article in *The International Journal of Environmental Studies* in which the religious dimension to the worldwide environmental crisis is related to both the rise of monotheism and the Genesis verse that serves as a warrant 'delegating to man plenipotentiary powers'. As Adler discovers, however, 'Until the late 1960s the word [Paganism] had been used to designate either an ancient or indigenous tribal religion or an irreligious, immoral approach to life'. The centrality of environmentalism to paganism only emerged when Tim Zell (Church of All Worlds; *Green Egg*) broadened the designation 'Pagan' from being merely applicable to Craft into an environmental movement network that included both Feraferia and witchcraft groups. Consequently, while enlightenment secularisation and the contemporaneous development of magical orders have certainly been contributing factors to the rise of modern-day paganism, this rise has been inspired by an underlying belief that heedless industrialisation and mindless modernisation are encouraged as well as justified in the kind of thought conditioned by the biblical imperative of Genesis, namely, God's very first words to Adam.

The real gist of paganism, whether as a generic or vernacular attitude, or whether as a consciously formulated and possibly quasi-institutional articulation, is its fundamental distinction from the transcendental emphasis such as is found in both dharmic and Abrahamic religion. While no religion adheres strictly to its ideal-type, and paganism has no less both historically included and occasionally identified with gnostic values (e.g., Orphism, Pythagoras, Plato, Neo-platonism, Kabala, etc.), its core reverence is directed toward the natural, the earthly and the physical – the very foci that non-immanentalist religiosity abhors. The irony here is that Wicca which has spearheaded and opened the way for today's pagan resurgence and CWP in general is itself originally a derivative of the magical, theurgic and masonic traditions which are – both historically and actually – more gnostic than strictly pagan. One of my reviewers simply does not 'understand why the author notes that Freemasons locate Lucifer in the North'. The explanation, however, is straightforward. Freemasonry embodies a gnostic valuation for which the 'body is a tomb' (*soma sema*), and the whole thrust of its and related practices is to escape this imprisonment by matter. Consequently, rather than follow a primordial understanding which would place the element of fire in the east (where the sun rises), the directional elements are skewed by the freemasonic tradition so that the earth ends up in the barren and cold north. This is to underscore earthen physicality's alleged anti-salvational sterility and, hence, 'evil' nature. And it is precisely this identity and alignment that contemporary Western paganism has inherited though Wicca and continues today. This remains an unexamined paradox that is retained by much if not most current ritual circle-practice.

Whether they exist or not, the gods serve to access the gentle sanctifying rhythms of nature, and this was brought home to me as we lustrated today our oak tree in the Midi for an Ides of June. This connection, this realization, this coming home yet again is paganism, at least my understanding of paganism. For me, it is the antithesis of everything Daesh endeavours to be. This last, in its cultivation of death over the gift of life, its inhumane and small-minded rabid pomposity, its hideous cultivation of violence and massacre, its veritable sickness, is beyond pathetic. The very idea that Omar Mateen was offended by seeing two men kissing – offended to the point of undertaking the utterly selfish crime he did in Orlando's Pulse Nightclub – is unforgivable, and the act itself belongs nowhere else than in the detritus of history. The idea that there is a god who welcomes and encourages such ridiculousness is itself ridiculous and only underscores the infantile reification that saddles our brief experiment and terrestrial evolution. Such a god, I dare say it, is not great!

The beauty of love, of youth enjoying, of everyone enjoying, of the holy, holy, holy speck of the cosmos on which we live, of concord when it exists and is achievable, of art and music, of discovery and expanse, and of growth and maturity is the pagan celebration. For my own part, I seek honouring most often in the solitary communion with nature, with quiet-type ceremonial observance with a loved one or a few loved ones, through art, and in what for me is the fascinating watching of people in general – whether in urban or rural location. The private and more secluded forms of contemplation and worship succeed for me best, and while group rituals can and do work on occasion, it is perhaps the animosities and interpersonal contentions that often surround them that I find utterly baffling and undesirable.

I would think – do think – that the joy that imbibes a pagan perception and understanding, that is to be found in their organic heart, is such that it precludes dissension and argument. I could not agree more that no one ought be harassed, doxxed, be forced to move to feel safe, be threatened at work, endure bigotry or prejudicial exclusion, be raped, violated or be subject to the fear of rape. It is not a question of just 'playing nice' or 'getting over it' or being banned from Facebook. It's not even about community identity or unity. My plea at least is to diffuse the situation in the spirit of freedom that I understand paganism to treasure. If there is a better way than attempting to converse so as to rectify misunderstandings and grievances and avoid future pain – conversing even with those who have and are wronging us, I am for it. But Israel and Palestine cannot dialogue, Islamic State and the West cannot speak together, the US Congress and President cannot progressively communicate, and it seems that transgenders and TERFs are establishing an entrenched impasse – one that in addition misses the beauty, joy and example of paganism. I am saddened that one person who was seeking pagan harmony has had to withdraw from my Facebook group.

What appears to me to be the most astonishing is the preponderance of current focus upon the smartphone. The present-day pervasive ubiquity of cellphone use has been frequently hailed as encouraging direct exchange for business and financial matters in place of our former reliance on supposedly inefficient intermediaries. Depersonalisation is of course one result of this technological invasion – but only one among the possibility of several other questionable consequences as well. Probably an even greater loss is the resultant concrete and physical detachment that results for any ongoing and healthy interaction between the everyday human spirit and nature. As one who somehow has missed out with the technical transformations of our current times, more and more do I feel like a ghost who has become lost in a strange and nebulous pantomime. Granted that the smartphone allows ebook access and the availability of a this-worldly akashic record of endless information, but somewhere in all this the personal is lost. Without human-to-human sensitivities, is a republican commonwealth possible in the first place? Perhaps in a post-capitalist world in which people are not perpetually scrambling for competitive advance, one in which time becomes a luxury to be enjoyed, where laughter is both heard and immediately contagious, perhaps in such a world of communal and festive rituals, the quiet and aromas of the woodlands, and the frequent touch between two or more persons become the norm. Such a milieu would be a healthy preserve – one that would foster reflection, organic input and wholesome productivity.

The Lotus World of the Future as I am conceiving it is significantly dependent on reviewing and understanding its precedents in order to be evermore mindful of what has been achieved and how not to repeat unnecessary wrongs of previous times. I believe the Lotocene will also be open and engaged with what is to come though both scientific discovery and the breakthroughs of artistic and spiritual endeavour. The eternally fleeting present is cherished, but rather than being isolated from past and future it is integrally interconnected with both. But in today's war between the box of bureaucratic authority and the unrestricted movement for individual self-determination, there is the lunacy of terrorist ruination and the smothering of creative innovation by the cultivated fear of insecurity.

In our own times, even the employment of marijuana has a long way to go before legal and universal recognition. At best, there is a wider breakthrough in the acceptance of cannabis for medical purposes and the alleviation of pain, but recreational use – which would include the spiritual – is permitted in such few American states as Oregon and Colorado and in such nations as Uruguay, The Netherlands, South Africa and Canada. More recently, states such as California, Nevada, Washington, Alaska, Massachusetts and Maine have decriminalized the possession of small quantities, and yet US federal law still prohibits both medicinal and recreational employment of cannabis. A related American exception is the allowance of the Native American Church for which peyote is a sacrament. Similar provisions are to be found, in the United States and elsewhere (e.g., Brazil and Peru) for the employment of ayahuasca by the Santo Daime and União do Vegetal churches. In India and Nepal, although in general not legal, marijuana is acceptably used in religious rituals – especially for the festivals of Shivratri and Holi. Government authorized *bhang* dispensaries exist along with *bhang lassi* and *thandai* shops. On the other hand, possession of marijuana, especially in large quantities, is punishable by execution in Indonesia, Malaysia, Thailand, Singapore, China and Saudi Arabia. While in Mexico, cannabis became illegal in 1925, it was the Marijuana Tax Act of 1937 that prohibited the plant in the United States. One of the impetuses reputedly behind the passage of the Act was newspaper magnate William Randolph Hearst who owned substantial forests and wanted wood pulp for his paper instead of mash from hemp. The Du Pont family along with the Secretary of the Treasury, Andrew Mellon, in promoting nylon fibre in competition with hemp, supposedly also agitated for the illegalisation of cannabis.

The pagan argument for the inclusion of psychotropic employment for ritual or spiritual purposes is predicated on the existence of natural 'power plants' such as cannabis, peyote, psilocybin, jimson weed, ibogaine and the like. While Western and colonially influenced cultures have had to wrestle with the idea of a 'forbidden fruit' that permits access to Eden and allows humans to become as wise as gods or serpents, paganism rejects an Abrahamic god that denies nature and the provision for self-induced trance through hallucinogenic plants. The very notion that an authority figure places an entheogenic 'apple tree' within human reach but then forbids its consumption is part of a pagan's understanding of the divide between humanity and nature that Levantine monotheism has provoked. Instead, the magical fruit is paganesquely revered as one more of the great gifts of nature.

The question that next arises concerns the extension of the natural into the pharmaceutical. If ayahuasca and san pedro cactus are legitimate sacraments, why not such 'man-made' psychedelic compounds as LSD, MDMA, ketamine, the 2C substituted phenethylamines and so forth? Ultimately, one must ask where is the dividing line between the natural and the artificial. The neolithic revolution that was founded in part upon the domestication of agriculture (as well of animals) may be seen as integral to natural human development. Food-crop cultivation such as that of the cereals (originally emmer, einkorn and barley; later, bread wheat, durum, spelt, oats, rye, etc.) represents a human engineering of wild plants. Alchemy, the progenitor of modern chemistry, is a further enlargement of human-inspired transmutations of natural substances. Luddite pagans might reject the artificial entheogen but accept the natural ones. But alcohol that results from the brewing processes of fermentation and distillation is a product that is both popularly consumed and itself consists of a transformation of the otherwise unrefined natural.

Whether alchemical or natural, the entheogenic sacrament expands the normal waking state through the alteration of perception and disablement of the brain's filtering mechanisms. In the ritual, spiritual or shamanic context, the psychoactive substance encourages time-condensation, mind-wandering, mental revelation, hyper-sensory perception or perceptual enhancement, and a sense of galactic alignment through the harmonious connection of the inner and outer worlds. Nature has herself provided various portals into the dimensions of super-being. Within the range of pagan practice, therefore, the transformation and opening of the individual's thoughts, words and actions by contact with the otherworld is both an anciently established endeavour and an ongoing pursuit – one that may include employment of both relevant plant-derivatives and synthetic substances for those who so wish.

The magnificent Chelsea Flower Show with displays of lilies, dahlias, iris, tulips, daffodils, lupines, ferns, peonies, sweet pea, strawberries, succulents, cacti and many, many more; a splendidly beautiful summer's day; and then a moment for the ritual of 'collective grief' following Manchester. There is an uncanny power when a whole nation becomes silent for a duration. This is a defiant affirmation – one fuelled by the living sacrifices that have been made but not voluntarily. But once they have been made, we must accept them in our will and determination to reject the vile and go for something better.

Though so unalike, the Flower Show in Chelsea was in impact another Burning Man experience of the joy of people and relaxation. For me, it underscored the battle for space. We all have spatial needs. These may all be different for each of us, but we all have them in one manner or another. The Buddha opted to do away with such needs altogether. But for those of us who revere the earth, sometimes it is more the question of learning how to navigate with the flow. In other words, pagan attachments are not to possessions to be irretrievably held or owned but are instead for the enjoyment of the moment – whatever be its length and span.

And that incomparable divine silence – so moving and so complete. The moment of Mancunian quiet coinciding with the Flower Show was again that supreme soundless stillness of the Lebanese Cedar Forest in the Kadisha Valley of Lebanon in Western Asia.

Richard's daughter, Iana, visited us one summer in France when she was eight. Barbara, after whom our Conception Room is named, was two weeks from giving birth and was marrying on the weekend. A couple had just arrived in the village with their son and daughter – the last also being eight years of age. As Joanna put it, 'We are the only people [she and her husband] who will have attended both of Barbara's weddings'. They were also traveling with Virgil's sister-in-law. At the same time, Stef and Jeff and Bruce and Holly had come from California to do some work on the house of friends in the village, and all thirteen of us met at the Jardin de Couvent for the first time.

I remember the adults sitting in a large circle of chairs with the two eight-year olds playing together in the centre. We were conversing and getting to know one another tentatively when suddenly Joanna and Virgil's daughter burst into tears. Someone went up to the two of the children but got nowhere. I went to Iana next and asked what was happening. 'I'm a people too', she replied defiantly, 'I also have feelings'!

Stef next approached Iana after I had, nudged our daughter and said, 'Iana, give her back her shoes!' – which she did.

Afterwards, as we were leaving, Stef overheard me say to Richard, 'What's wrong with our daughter'?

'Nothing's wrong with your child'! Stef snapped. 'Your child's got sass. She reminds me of my son who's the same age. Give me a child like yours any day over a Shirley Temple brat like that other'!

Well, needless to say, I fell in love with Stef that moment for life. Living in California's Gold Rush country, she has been one of those rare, extra-special and fun people who has intersected with our life over many years and in many different places. We have been to Burning Man twice with her and her husband Gary. As Lyn had informed us before we first met her, 'Stef is a breath of fresh air'!

Last Friday, after a long and courageous fight, that breath we knew as Stefanie Freydont (1 October 1950 – 30 June 2017) went out. As Jacquie said, 'We've been friends since she was 17, it was love at first sight . . . We are so privileged to have been swept up by her vitality, life force and brilliance all these years, and her larger-than-life presence in all of our lives will leave an enormous sinkhole'.

This same weekend, Richard and I attended the three-day 'Breaking Convention: 4th International Conference on Psychedelic Consciousness' at the University of Greenwich, London. As David Luke explained to me at the conference's conclusion, this occasion was the result and continuation of the three-day forum on 'Exploring Consciousness: With What Intent?' I had organised just before my retirement in Bath. The original endeavour had been sponsored by the Sophia Centre for the Study of Cultural Astronomy and Astrology, the Academy for Cultural and Educational Studies, and the Psychonauts UK and was designed to be a dialogue between cosmological, pharmacopoeial, academic, pagan and Gaian spiritual perspectives. If our universe can be seen as the spontaneous reflex of a cosmos wishing to see itself, the basic issue we sought to explore was to ask what is the function of consciousness and how do we investigate its various potentials and possibilities?

Among the luminaries speaking at the Bath venture were Charles Jencks, Alexander and Ann Shulgin, Liz Greene, Serena Roney-Dougal, William Bloom, Philippa Berry, Susan Greenwood, Max Velmans, Bernard Eccles, Christian Ratsch, Claudia Muller-Ebeling and Bernadette Brady. The Bath venue was the former art deco cinema, the Bath Forum, that today is an Evangelical Christian church. The psychonauts succeeded in completely shredding to pieces the Harry Potter academic cloak of invisibility that I had hoped would disguise any upset to the church. To their credit, however, though they recognised what was occurring and, by contract, could have cancelled midway the rest of the conference, the church administrators allowed us to proceed. What became fascinating for me was how they subsequently could see mutual interests between themselves and us – such as our slides of ayahuasca visions resonating with the images from the Book of Revelations or a talk on ibogaine therapy being of interest to their drug outreach program.

The speakers from the Bath venue of 2004 who spoke again thirteen years later but now in Greenwich were chaos magician Julian Vayne, founding director of Breaking Convention and Senior Lecturer in Psychology David Luke, *TechGnosis: Myth, Magic, and Mysticism in the Age of Information* author Erik Davis, and Rick Doblin – founder and director of the Multidisciplinary Association for Psychedelic Studies (MAPS). Two other speakers from among the sixty plus were the biologist Rupert Sheldrake and Dennis McKenna – senior investigator of the Hoasca Project and younger brother of the late Terence McKenna. Coinciding with the 50th anniversary of the Summer of Love, the present Psychedelic Renaissance is hailed as the scientific and cultural study of modern society with its predominant focus on psychology and medicinal therapy. What was particularly impressive for me was to witness the immense maturity and mainstream acceptance of the former subculture and its masterly investigations into trans-rational philosophy, treatment of substance abuse, Amazonian shamanism, drugs in the Bible, ayahuasca healing, lucid dreaming, Aldous Huxley, Aleister Crowley and ongoing research of DMT, MDMA, LSD, ketamine, marijuana, psilocybin, etc. It is of course upon the notions of entheogenic integration and cognitive transformation that my vision of a Lotus-times-to-come is founded.

CHAPTER FOUR

Aldeburgh / augury; Olafur Eliasson / *snan* / Vishwanath / Brahman-Atman / the seminal purpose of this book / idolatry / prostration / Indian countryside / Delhi / exhaustion & ill health / Hardwar & Rishikesh / Sri Aurobindo Ghose / Epicurus / Hindu gods; Bangalore / Soma sacrifice; the El Paso & Dayton shootings / Pagan Patheos contributor John Beckett / Guy Davenport / the need for global thought & rectifying action / the non-deific Abrahamic god; interfaith & the Parliament of the World's Religions; Epicurus / Khajuraho / the urban centre / the *polis* & favourite cities; Maheshwar; my happiness; the matter-energy continuum versus the spirit-body dichotomy / psychedelic herbs & archaic understanding / two basic approaches to the gods: myth & drugs / Hindu festivals / the shaman / virtue-values / love; Bruges / Zeus / the gods unbound by human social conventions / Zeus & Typhon, etc. / Indo-European cultures & other pagan traditions; the woods of Europe / Gustav Mahler / the *Turangalîla-Symphonie* / Christianity & Protestant values and their difference with paganism; the evolution of Gaia from Chaos / the asurian & reasons for worship of it / Karachi & Harappa / Nūsha / Mohenjo-Daro; Hong Kong / Bangkok; Shinto & its resonating the most closely with my own understanding of paganism / Japan

By the summer sea in Aldeburgh where Benjamin Britten and Peter Pears had lived is another magical interlude. While English weather differs from that of the American East Coast, and the Suffolk seaside may not compare to the glorious warmth of the Jersey Shore, it is still exquisitely stunning with both the North Sea presence and its cosy high street. As marvellous as London is ('tired of London; tired of life'), the break with the accompaniment of loved ones to only the seagull-broken quiet is a most welcomed moment. A family home on the Crag Path that fronts the sea and with the salt marshes along the tidal Alde River beyond and surrounding the town itself make a stimulating diversion both for the soul and the body. Humanity's attraction to the seaside seems to result from an anciently ingrained and seductive draw. With the rising sea levels and increasingly precarious weather interruptions, the waterside is no longer the safest of places, but while we still can we will, as a species and the strange animal that we be, continue to come to the beach resort.

The shoreline beckons as a liminal portal both to other and faraway lands and to the necromantic otherworld of both our ancestral dead and the place of myth and fairy. For the devotional polytheist and others it may function as a significant part in the geography of the imagination. The visual expanse of the sea is itself an access point between the world of wonder and the this-worldly wondrousness of physical sensation. It becomes a place of relaxation, work and inspirational insight. There is here no puritanical imposition but instead the acceptance of engagement with the orgasm of life.

The Suffolk Coast and Heaths are a marvellous expanse of bulrush or cattails, bracken, bramble, couch grass, gorse interspersed with rosehips, lilac leaf, hogweed, stinging nettles, honey suckle, lady's bedstraw, clover, ragwort and pink and white campion. Along the old Sailors' Path through the Hazelwood Marshes, one also finds evening primrose, goose grass, blackthorn, vetch, bryony and Northfolk reed. In December of 2013, a storm breached the river wall along the Alde and the land became once again part of the estuary. Dead birch trees are now to be seen above the saltwater inundation, but there are still along the higher pathways the occasional oak, sycamore and Scotch pine. Colonising the exposed mud are both sea aster and delicious to eat samphire. Within the intertidal area are such feeding waders as dunlin, black-tailed godwits, redshanks, lapwings and even oyster catchers. Songs from sky larks, shelducks and wigeons may fill the overhead skies. Also present are swans, greylag geese, mallards, teal ducks, green sand pipers, grey herons, warblers, cormorants, little egrets, avocets, bitterns, curlews, bearded tits, linnets, barn owls and even such birds of prey as buzzards and marsh harriers. In all, the marshlands and dense reedbeds of Suffolk provide a rich feast of wildlife as well as haunting vistas. There are views to be enjoyed from Hoskins Hide at the end of a pathway that branches off from the Sailors' Path. Nearby is Barber's Point where archaeological digs have revealed Neolithic arrowheads, Roman and Saxon pottery and artefacts, and nineteen gravesites. At best, the Barber's Point settlements were humble and may have been only seasonally occupied for salt-working and oyster processing. Since the 2013 tidal surge, the place has become a small island. For the Anglo-Saxons, there is little evidence of shrines, temples or cult centres, but there is more in terms of votive offerings in cemeteries. These could include cowries, lumps of amber, fossils and antique items such as Roman coins, glass and iron keys. But with all this liminal smorgasbord of life and beauty in the Hazelwood Marshes, the appearance of a gatekeeper butterfly could only be appropriately fitting.

Augury is an ancient practice associated with paganism. It is primarily considered as an art of prognostication. More widely, however, it provides an alleged means in general for communicating with the gods. The deities reputedly have vehicles through which they are understood to appear or communicate if and when they might not directly manifest. Among the various vehicles that a god may have, avian forms are some of the most important – either through living birds or symbols and representations. Whether the Garuda may be considered an actual bird, he serves as the vehicle for the god Vishnu. Otherwise, and perhaps with my rose window of gods in mind, we have the eagle and swan for Jupiter/Zeus; the peacock and goose for Juno; the cuckoo, peacock and crane for Hera; the male duck for Janus; the female duck for Diana; the magpie, guinea fowl and quail for Artemis/Diana; the crow and raven along with the crane, heron and stork for Apollo; the raven also for Lugh; and the owl for Athena. Sometimes a particular avian vehicle has been shared by more than one deity. Among these we find the hawk or osprey used by Zeus, Apollo and Hermes; the vulture by Zeus and Ares as well as, with Homer, by Athena. Pindar, Pausanias and Ovid also link Athena with the crow or raven. The swan on occasion has been associated with Aphrodite who is also connected with doves. The dove otherwise belongs to the dawn-goddess Eos while the white dove is Dionysus. Aristophanes gives Aphrodite the coot and the duck to Poseidon. Along with Artemis, the quail is shared by Heracles/Hercules, while the god also has the cormorant. The rooster is shared by Hermes and Ares/Mars while the cockerel is also considered a love-gift from Zeus to Ganymede. The woodpecker belongs to Ares, while the jynx-bird or wryneck woodpecker is Hecate's. The swan is sometimes a vehicle of Apollo's but is also used by the Norse deity Hoenir. Possible associations with this last may be the crane/heron/stork and the hen. Loki has a falcon relationship while wearing Freya's cloak. The wild goose may be used by Nemesis, and the garuda is also utilized by Prajapati. In all, the augury association with deities is complex but a fascinating means of the two worlds, this one and the other, being in contact and feeling close. Augury is a special way for pagans to interact with specific figures that belong to the pantheon of divinity.

'Taking the auspices' might be used for predicting the future, but just the act of looking at birds is in itself a joy that can come with the taking of pleasure in nature. Combining this joy in life on earth with spiritual communion is the kind of augmentation that pagans who witness the magical reflection of the empirical in the trans-empirical may engage. Another form of augury of which I became aware while contemplating along the bank of the Ganges, the Kashi Coast, is seeing an actual deity in the flight of a group of birds. Who the deities were, I often could not say, but the soaring and turning of a flying flock was frequently to be seen as a god visiting and enjoying the holy city of Benares.

The Danish artist, Olafur Eliasson, mentions his art in connection with 'embodied knowledge'. The concretisation of spiritual experience could also be said to be fundamental to pagan ritual and worship. Without a doubt, my Indian experience of the *snan* or 'bathing' which I would undertake principally each morning in the Ganges River led to what I might designate as 'embodied knowledge'. Other bodies of water I have used for the purposes of *snan* include the Indus, the Thames, the Serpentine, the Avon, the Tyne, an Amsterdam canal, the Lac de Sainte Croix, the morning dew in Zealand, the North Sea and the Atlantic Ocean. In our increasingly neoliberal and consumerist 'late' capitalist and rational bureaucratic society, the challenge of re-finding a sense of enchantment is perhaps all the greater. Religion itself either conforms to what is considered instrumental rationalisation or is marginalised by it. Paganism is already a marginalised spirituality in today's world but offers both the simulacrum *and* the real as valid and operative. Despite the Enlightenment, it continues to build in many respects on the persistence of belief in the supernatural and the occult even into modernity. However, in addition with the increasing capture of the public imagination by environmental concerns, the marginalisation of pagan thought, practice and awareness may be diminishing as the spirituality they represent is becoming ever more relevant.

The *snan* in the Ganges or Mother Ganga and the emphasis of avoiding body parts (and on one occasion I just missed colliding with a cadaver as the river's current swept it by) certainly brought to full awareness how the sacred is being compromised by pollution. For the most part, however, the early morning river bath was exhilarating in an innovative numinous sense. The predominant routine was to approach the ghats, usually to the *ghatia* or priest who was the uncle of my first Benares landlord, strip down to my bathing suit, navigate through the crowd of other bathers (Hindu holidays could be a virtual nightmare), salute the river by repeatedly pouring water from it and back to it while reciting the *Gayatri*, then dunking three times beneath the surface, and frequently next swimming out to the middle of the river where it was the cleanest. After re-dressing, a sandal wood paste was usually applied by the *ghatia* to my forehead along with a *tikka,* and I would then proceed to the temples for unadulterated idolatrous worship. All this could be an ordeal but thrilling at the same time, and once it was completed, I would return back to the guest house for breakfast.

The temples in Kāshī that I frequented the most were Vishwanath (the Golden Temple of Shiva), Annapurna and Rama. These morning visits were conjoined with various shrines as well as taking water from Gyan Vapi, the Well of Wisdom. In the evening, I would begin with the Sitala Temple (the goddess of smallpox) and followed by a circuit of shrines. My journal for 4th of March, 1981 records the following for Shivaratri:

> Bathed in the Ganges just after the sun rose – having to return a second time since I had forgotten my water pot. Then I went to Viśnawara temple [Vishwanath] – only the narrow passageway from the mosque side being open. Finally reached the pathway gate and had to wait an hour in the crushing mob. Didn't mind because the guard was one of the most gorgeous men I have ever seen, but the realization that I had already been pickpocketed wasn't very helpful. Beside losing something more than 50 rupees or something less than $8, I've lost Richard's change purse he had given me and the key to my room. Once passed the gate, there were times [in the crunch and rush] that I thought death near. Totally dishevelled & filthy, I finally reached the temple. Touched the lingam and then lingered in the rest of the complex before going to the Annapurna temple and then to the flat. One of the carpenter boys got me in through another door. I have a spare key. I am exhausted. This is my first Hindu festival.

Typical of my early reflections in India is this:

> The brahmanic philosophy regarding the eternally existing supreme spirit as the one reality is certainly one of the intellectually most challenging ideas. But whatever may or may not be said about *Brahman,* and despite all the pretensions and inscrutable declarations of sages, in the end this *Brahman-Atman,* not this, not that, and *mokṣa, samadhi, nirvana* and union with it all boils down to glorified nothingness. And, incidentally, the latest particle physics speculation is that an absolute vacuum may be unstable.

I am well aware that devotion to deific construction may be considered to be in conflict with science, nature and environmental values. I dispute this and will seek in the pages to come how and why the encounter with awe might be precisely what supports and furthers a humanitarian ethic in all fields of non-destructive human endeavour. I am critical of much within contemporary pagan thought, and the explanation of this critique is the seminal purpose of this book. This is what I will come to anon, but I wish first to explore how my own pagan understanding has developed through my experiences, adventures and learning. I will state at this point an ambivalent evaluation I have with the currently popular rejection of the anthropocene as a human-centred hubristic myth. There can be no question that humans are capable of error and especially destructive behaviour concerning the maintenance of nature's balance, the earth's continued well-being and the importance of life in its many forms. None of this need be neglected as being of a central importance, but I still suspect that as far as human consciousness itself is concerned, we continue to be at our present stage of evolution and cosmic encounter crucially fundamental. We may not be the only ones who ultimately contribute to the feat of allowing the universe to be conscious of itself (dolphins, whales and extraterrestrials come immediately to mind), but we are centrally significant to that process and as yet the only super-reflective species that we know. Maybe artificial intelligence and other technical developments will come to surpass us, but if they do, I believe we are still obligated (if that word is not too strong) to understand how the divine will continue to resonate and be a wholesome and important factor in whatever future there is to be.

When it comes to the mythical-magical, idolatry is a major part of it for me. It has of course been India in which I learned and experienced this form of worship. *Darshan* and the 'living' manifestation of the deity through her idol are utterly awesome encounters. If I was fascinated by the physical embodiment of a god in a representation before India, I have certainly been so since. A recent *blót* to the Norse deity of Heimdall has been appealing in its organic naturalness, though the Brexit sympathies of most in attendance were discomforting. Nevertheless, these Heathen rituals as well as most others these days in pagan venues are absent of pictorial presentation. In my various altars, I do not believe I have any portrayals of Germanic figures – apart for Frey in an elf depiction. Idolatrous consideration is not a usual Nordic and Anglo-Saxon concern. The group honouring of the guardian and listening god Ríg, like much contemporary pagan ritual in general, does not involve idolatry and yet is fully commensurate with numinous awe and the wonder of the extraordinary.

But if human hubris is indeed an impediment to a balanced relationship between us, the earth, the divine and the cosmos, the humbling and even the more extreme prostration before a temple deity is one way to mitigate *hauteur*. There is indeed a refreshing beauty in the attitude encompassed by standing upright before a god when in communication and tribute. This is one way and is no less valid than such other ways like bowing, kneeling or lying flat out in honouring divinity or a divine representation. In paganism, diversity is its very norm.

India too is diversity – diversity, colour and passion. The temple experience alone is a cacophony of temple bells, drums, chanting, thronging people, incense, fire-lamps and slippery floors. Although rare, there were the occasional moments even in Varanasi in which I found a temple to be strangely and delightfully quiet and relaxed. On festivals such as Holi, my *ghatia* would give me some *bhang* along with a sweetened milk to consume. It was often difficult to know how stoned I might have been since the perpetual experience of the eco-cultural sphere of India was a complete high in itself. The ritualistic side of Hinduism, with its curious blend of awesome sanctity and casual naturalness along with the repetitive performance of ceremony always continued to enthral me completely.

But another thrill of the subcontinent is its non-urban countryside. Leaving Varanasi by train for Delhi, I was captivated by a nostalgic coverlet over the enchantment of the flat and luxuriant rural Ganges plains. The sun cast the remembrance of a late summer New Jersey glow which could often be seen between the shore and home. Tiny Shiva chapels now punctuated the landscape. Then the sun began a long, slow descent into a ball of brilliant orange to ever more muted pink. Despite all the joy of the sunrise, I suppose one does not realise how much the sun is loved until he/she sets. A momentary break in the trees on the horizon and a last glimpse of a gossamer half-dome of rose. Then ever deepening shadows before India is finally enveloped in a black shroud of obscurity.

Delhi itself was a disappointment for the most part. The only metropolises in India I came to appreciate have been Kolkata (Calcutta) and Mumbai (Bombay). Delhi itself is huge and not a walking city. The New Delhi part of the city contains oversized and pretentious boulevards reminiscent perhaps of Washington, D.C. but with an Indian accent. I did, however, enjoy the Lakshmi Narayan Temple – a magnificent, very ornate, almost Disneyesque complex containing Vishnu and Lakshmi in the centre, a Śiva shrine to the right, Durga to the left and shrines as well to Hanuman, Ganesh, the Vedas and Krishna. Behind the temple is a spacious and mad park that I enjoyed despite the feeling of being so different from Banaras.

In Delhi, I was more the tourist than a pilgrim. I plunged into the full circuit from the Jantar Mantar or 18th century observatory built by the Maharaja Jai Singh II of Jaipur (he set up one in Varanasi as well), the India Gate war memorial, Hamayun's Tomb (the garden-tomb predecessor of the Taj Mahal), the historic Lal Quila or Red Fort that was built over the village of Indrapat – presumably Indraprastha which was the capital of the Pandavas of *Mahabharata* fame, the 73-metre tall minaret known as the Qutab Minar, the mid-seventeenth century Jama Masjid (the Great Mosque of Delhi), the Rajghat and Shanti Vana (respectively the cremation spots of Gandhi and Nehru), the shrine of Yogmaya (sister of Krishna) and the marvellous National Museum. Apart from the much greater urban activity of Delhi, another noticeable difference it has with Banaras is its participation in Sunday culture. On a Sunday, the streets were relatively quiet and empty; stores were shut. Later in the day, Connaught Place and the parks fill with Sunday strollers, though in this respect riverside afternoons and evening in Varanasi are similar with crowds as well as many people boating out onto the river.

The perpetual weariness of India is a major issue. It seems that an extreme effort is required to do just about anything what with the obstacles, the detours, delays, constant hassles with people and the ceaseless fending off of mouchers, beggars and all those trying to get a bigger cut. In the years that followed, I learned to feel and be completely comfortable especially in Varanasi, and the whole complex often seemed to have become like an extended living room. Travelling in India is different and more challenging but more often than not at the same time an adventure of discovery. When in Delhi the first time, I visited the Kailash Shiva and Kalkaji Devi temples. The first *mandir* is to be found atop a rocky rise. It was a lovely setting and augmented when I was there by dramatic winds. The main shrine contains a numinous *lingam*. Above this is another room containing idols of Śiva and Devi plus a very small *lingam* beneath a large metallic vase with a tiny perforation at its bottom allowing thereby a minute stream of water to bathe the phallic image continuously. The overall site was perhaps my first experience of how the ancient promontories of Europe *et al.* would have functioned as cult centres. The adjacent Devi temple was not as pleasant but still interesting and relatively well attended. It is octagonal in design with entrances on each side and the shrine in the centre. The doors were not open when I arrived, and everyone was excluded. With the temple completely closed, a conch horn sounded from within and the people outside rang bells. It was highly reminiscent of my experience at Kalighat in which the goddess is secluded for an interval before a re-admittance of devotees.

And more often than not, despite the exhaustion, the queasy ill health, the general ineptitude and inconsiderateness, perhaps after a bit of nourishment, and maybe while in a rickshaw, the sun is setting and India is suddenly all enchantment and beauty. The beggars, the deformities and the hopeless poverty vanish with the growing darkness. But it was in Agra, south of Delhi, at the Taj Mahal as dusk was approaching and the interior became an awesome play of light, silhouette and shadow that I unexpectedly found my Scheherazade – the call of *Asie*. This was until the lovely Yamuna River yielded up an absolute plague of mosquitos.

I returned to Delhi after Agra and from there went to Hardwar and Rishikesh. Consequently, I was in Hardwar for the solar new year celebration of the first of Vaisakhi which in 1981 coincided with the Roman Ides of April. I had woken at 04:30, and it was still dark when I reached the Hari-ki-pairi *kund*. Gradually the outline of the eastern Siwaliks came into view, but as that it was hazy, they disappeared frequently. Consequently, following a rather colourless dawn, the sun gave no advance warning of its rise and suddenly just began to appear over the horizon. The actual sunrise has always seemed to me a most auspicious moment and especially for ritual bathing, but most people on this occasion seemed oblivious to him and had been in the water all along. I had waited while watching the ablutions and various reactions from people shivering with the cold, babies and children screaming in tears, to the general frolicking. All in all, it was more orderly than I had expected and, though extremely crowded, not impossible. And despite the tumult outside, after bathing I found the interiors of the temples to Bhairon and Maya Devi and that which contained the shrine of Ganesh in its basement quiet and peacefully sublime.

Rishikesh was equally captivating if not even more so than Hardwar. I continued to visit shrines and temples and bathing spots. Judith Tyberg quotes Aurobindo who speaks of 'higher' and 'lower' forms of spirituality. I find this distressing in that the qualifiers are physical terms – and relativistic ones at that – and convey misleading connotations when used in an ethical sense. Moreover, if the precepts of democracy have any validity, the beliefs, practices and sentiments of the common majority ought to be the better. I have long found the 'holier than thou' syndrome grossly distasteful with many of the world's 'great sages', rishis, maharishis, sadhus and pundits being the worst offenders on this score. In one of the ashrams near the Lakshman

Jhula suspension bridge across the Ganges I found a leaflet citing Śrī Kedar Khanda's *Adhyaya* 102: 'One who takes bath in Lakshmana Tirath gets all his desires fulfilled . . . '. After reading this, I bathed and wished for the restoration of a positive paganism as a viable religious alternative for the world.

With the following contemplation and enjoyment of the sunset by the riverfront before the Maha Yoga Ashram and then the return across the river while the full moon was cresting the mountains, I realised that, as much as I adore temples and temple worship, it is the intercourse with the sunrise or sunset, a spring or a river as well as the moon in which I find my most fulfilling communion. And for the first time in my life, while in the Śiva shrine of Swargāshram and right next to the *lingam*, I saw birds actually copulating. And further, my reflexions turned to the laws concerning matter and its constant flux and change. Every form has a durational limit. Weariness is a concomitant of a form's inevitable dissolution. But to extend this individual fatigue into an attitude of world-weariness is only the result of too strong an identity with our material form. The body is a vehicle and a gift – to be used and enjoyed and used as an instrument wherewith to worship the gods or the divine. But all the same, we remain – or at least can become – something more than our physical vehicles. This last I admit is a controversial notion – especially considering my infatuation with Friedrich Nietzsche and his 'turn to the body' outside traditional metaphysical discourse. For him, we are our bodies. I agree, but in that matter is energy or force, there is always also a possibility of dynamic transmutation.

Continuing in Rishikesh with my reading of Aurobindo, much of his Pūrna Yoga sounds to me like a Tolkienesque creation. What I do like about it is the objective of activating the supermind on the earth plane rather than seeking escape from life. Whereas Aurobindo considers the material to be a lower emanation or creation of Vijñāna with which it must reunite, my argument that divine consciousness is an outgrowth of the physical dimension – being the potential seed latent within matter – differs little in essence. For Aurobindo, the divine is an *a priori* reality; for me, it must be created rather than re-found – but its virtual presence has nonetheless existed from the very moment earth came into being: in other words, since the very beginning of the cosmos. For both Aurobindo and myself, realisation constitutes the key endeavour.

Whether nature or art or representation of the spiritual, these all affect mental qualia in the appreciator. India of course offers a prodigious surfeit of religious symbols, images and embodiments, and the magnification of insight on this score becomes something that I have found further encourages discerning perception elsewhere as well as 'back home'. I am not yet certain about the relationship between epiphenomenal impression, perhaps Epicurus' *eidola* or *simulacra* as the physical impact of images on our sense organs, and the subjective conscious experience produced by virtual reality, but I suspect they are connected in some cybernetic sense. Pagan understandings of both this world known through our senses and the otherworld encountered through imagination provide a rationale for access to an ontological co-reality that co-exists with the empirical dimension of the matter-energy continuum. One paganesque avenue for the expansion of consciousness or travel between the worlds is provided by the gentle dynamic of Hinduism with its range of archetypal foci. On the popular level, these may be reduced to seven deific prototypes: the mother goddess with a triad of manifestations – the awesome and almost asuric Sarasvatī, the lovely Lakhsmī, and the ambivalent Devī with her two characters: the terrifying/blood-thirsty Durgā/Kalī, and the gentle, maternal Umā-Gaurī-Parvatī-Anna Pūrna – giver of food and blessing. The remaining six figures are male: the majestic Śiva with his own dichotomous character, the reliable Viṣṇu – a kind god with his two chief avatars: the kingly and greatly revered Rāma and his frequent dioscuric manifestation, and the trickster Kriṣṇa. These are additionally supplemented in popular cult by the (semi-)animal gods of Hanuman (devotion) and Ganesha. These seven figures comprise the bulk of puranic and living devotion. Along with them, one might include both Skanda, the war-god and other son of Śiva, and Sūrya, the sun-god, whose cult apparently extends to include the *navagrahas* or seven planets along with the north and south lunar nodes.

Although I have come to insist that worship is one of the major objectives of life – at least it is for me, nevertheless it must share its claim to humanity's concern with the other aspirations – sometimes being even subservient to the others. The claim of health is obvious, but no less important is that of comfort – for the denial of such automatically becomes a denial of freedom which is our most important goal of all. Unquestionably my experiences of India along with my European vagabonding in 1961 and 1962 allowed me to understand what comfort is and its necessity. To me, the grotesque austerities that are exalted in the *Purāṇas* represent a mockery of human greatness, our affirmative spirit, and the gift of life.

I arrived in Bangalore. Toward the end of the day, clouds like cotton islands floated on a filmy sea of opaque air through which the glint of rivers meandered and slashed the all but invisible earth. Occasional continental groupings of strange surrealist shapes seemed to echo hidden recesses of the inner mind. Next progressed a thickening somberness, and the long and nostalgic few beams of the sun became obscured. And finally, there was the darkness of night. With its wide streets that give the impression of being well-planned, Bangalore – at least at night – appeared to be almost not India but possibly somewhere in the American Midwest. By daytime, however, it was not Midwestern but European – probably in France; perhaps Draguignan.

I had come to attend a Soma sacrifice (*somayajña*). The motorised rickshaw in which I was when heading to my contact was struck from behind by a bus. I was first hit in my back and then, being arched backwards, slammed the top of my head against the bus before being thrown forward. The bus continued on, but the tempo, although damaged, caught up with vehicle that had caused the accident. A huge crowd gathered. After recovering from my initial daze, I reckoned it was best to get the hell out of there, flagged another rickshaw and continued on to Mohan Rao who received me most cordially – offering water, food, an injection – all of which I declined. I was next taken to the Anjaneya Swamy Temple where I believe I witnessed the *dīkṣaṇīyeṣti* (preparation and offering of rice cakes to Agni-Viṣṇu – including boiled rice for Aditi which those in attendance also received as *prasad*) and the *dīkṣā* (the consecration of the sacrificer). This ancient Vedic ritual was reminiscent to me of Native American ceremony and appeared to be relatively low key, relaxed and open.

The *somayajña* in Bangalore from the 2nd to the 14th of May in 1981 was sponsored by K. Yajnanarayana Dikshit Somayāji with Rāmachandra Bhalta Kodlehere as *adhvaryu* and his brother K. Ganapati Somayāji as *hotṛ*. The Soma Sacrifice appears to have various names ranging from the *agnicayana* to the *devayajña*, but its purpose is to honour the gods as cosmic forces who maintain the harmony of the universe. The entire complex is known as the *maha vedi* or great altar. There are three significant fires in Vedic ritual. The *garhapatya* or womb-chamber fire-altar is round, dedicated to the earth and placed to the west. To the east is the *ahavaniya* or square fire-altar for the sky. The anvaharyapacana or *daksinagni* fire-altar is half-moon shaped and found to the southwest. There may also be a subordinate side-altar, the *dhishyna*, and a second altar known as the *ardvaradishnya*. The construction of a *soma* altar or *uttaravedi* (northern altar) for the sacred fire (*agnyayatana*) is to assume a great bird- or falcon-shape. The assembling process and the three basic fires that are part of the sacrifice involve various rites known as *īşţi*. The *īşţi* also concern only the *adhvaryu*, *āgnīdhra*, *hotṛ* and *brahmān* priests along with the *yajamāna* (the sacrificer who is the sponsor of the ceremony). The opening *īṣṭi* is the *prāyaṇūyā* which then leads into the purchasing of the *soma* (including the rites that deal with building the seventh step of the *soma-krayanī* or 'heifer' altar), the *subrahmaṇyā* litany (inviting Indra), the *prayāja* offerings, the production of fire by attrition, the *tānūaptra* by which the priests and *yajamāna* pledge mutual brotherhood, the strengthening of the *soma* stalks by the priests while holding a golden piece and using the *madantī* water, *pravargya* and *upasad* (the making of *gharma* from ghee and milk in the *mahāvīra* vessel which is then offered in the *āhavanīya* fire), and a concluding *īṣṭi* to the gods Agni, Soma and Viṣṇu. Since Indra is among my favourite of deities, I will include here his *subrahmaṇyā* invocation from the *Śatapatha Brahmana* (3.4.17-20):

> O Subrahmaṇya [Indra who protects excellent prayers], come, O Indra!
> O lord of *hari* [bay] steeds!
> Ram of Medhātithi!
> Menā (wife or daughter) of Vṛṣaṇaśva!
> Attacking buffalo!
> Lover of Ahalyā!
> O Kauśika!
> O brāhmana!
> Thou who callest thyself Gautama!

Mid-afternoon we were fed South Indian food in a nearby hall. The foundation of the Agnicayana or fire-altar was begun after this and continued for the next three days. All in all, I found that the ceremony ranged from tedium to a haunting loveliness.

What fascinated me the most was being able to experience a truly ancient and yet still preserved ritual – giving perhaps some idea of what might have occurred in the worship of the classical deities of Greece and Rome. The Romans had *flamens* to maintain the state's duties to the gods. While nothing comparable exists today in the contemporary West, the Native American Sun Dance, the Vedic Soma Sacrifice, the Tibetan Buddhjst *lhasang* and the Bolivian *yatiri*'s political inauguration ceremony in Tiwanaku possibly convey the intricacies of complex ceremonial observance from the pre-Christian past. In a word, they suggest an archaic spirit that may continue as shadowy yet discernible vestiges in the circle dances, blóts and processions of today's pagan practice.

Once the fire altar in Bangalore was completed, there was a milk sacrifice accompanied by the beautiful *Śatarudrīya* chant from the *Black Yajur Veda*. The altar was then swept clean – supposedly by using a frog, but the frog immediately leaped off. Gold coins were dispensed at this time to the various priests. In the days that followed, the *āhavaṇīya* fire was transferred to the *uttaravedī/agnipraṇayana* or fire altar, the *pravargya* utensils were burned, offerings of rice cakes, ghee and curd were made on the fire altar, and parts of a slain goat were presented at the *āhavaṇīya* which now served as the *gārhapatya* – with the tail being offered to the wives of the gods. Although largely secretive, I learned that there were three *paśubandha* sacrifices but each taking place deep in the night to avoid objections from those against animal sacrifice. To the last of these, *mlecchas* such as myself were allowed to attend. I did. Earlier that day between 06:30 and 08:30, the pressing of the *soma* had begun. The priests, holding the *lungi* of those before them, formed a serpent and, with mini-leaps, mounted the altar and then descended from it. The significance of this, like much else, remained unknown to me.

Around 02:00, we few lay persons descended from the Anjaneya Swami Temple to the *yajna* site. It had the feeling for me as if I was attending a black mass; the atmosphere was highly charged. The attendant boys were awakened not long after and appeared noticeably sleepy-eyed. A black goat had been tied to the sacrificial post. It was obvious that she was unaware of what was soon to happen – munching away on fresh leaves that had been procured for her and urinating unabashedly. *Mantras* were proclaimed, and the goat was sprinkled with water. The fire altars were also lustrated. Four pits had been dug earlier into the ground, and as we followed along in the dark with the movement, I suddenly found myself at the bottom of the largest cavity. Whatever this plummet might have portended, at least I was not injured. The goat was led to the sacrificial spot in the north (though it is supposed to be in the south). Being kept back from the actual smothering of the animal, in the darkness and with the priests crowded around the sacrifice, I could only hear strange muffled sounds from the victim herself. I believe the act occupied about 15 minutes in all.

The *yajamanapatni* sprinkled the slain animal with water, and we laypeople in attendance were allowed to witness the cutting up of the victim. The most astonishing thing was that there was not even one drop of blood in the whole process. After some time, something visceral (the omentum in texts) was removed from the entrails and offered on the fire-altar. The animal was then further dissected – the kidneys, heart and something else were pulled out from the same hole already made in the victim. Along with the tail and a section from each underpart of the legs from where they joined the body proper, these were strung together and put away. The carcass itself was then perfunctorily buried in the closest and smallest of the four pits. Along with some concluding *mantras* and offerings, that was basically the *pasuyajna*.

But at least along with each day's ceremonies, there was included both for lunch and dinner a banquet feast in a nearby hall. These provided a welcomed break as well as some delightfully delicious nourishment. In the morning, the second *soma* pressing was long, slow and the most tedious yet, but after the midday meal, for the first time, I was allowed to sit within the rope enclosure that surrounded the ritual site. To everyone's applause, ghee was poured on to the *yajamana*'s head. Once his entire family had passed themselves beneath a suspended cloth, fees were doled out to the priests. The Rigvedic *mantras* that were recited during the afternoon session were more captivating than those from the *Sama-veda*. Apart from the priests and their attendants and family that was sponsoring the affair, there were usually about thirty of us who formed the audience. This might have increased on some occasions to nearly one hundred. But as the sacrifice was coming to a close, the general aura of excitement was mounting. The *hotṛ* priest began his recitations at 03:00 on the final day, and once it became daylight and the day progressed, people arrived until there were nearly 4,000 in attendance.

The tail of the *pasu* was presented in the *āhavanīya* fire that was now serving as the *gārhapatya*. A bowl containing the last of the *soma* was placed on the head of one of the priests and then offered in the *agnyayatana* on the *uttaravedi*. A small tank for the concluding ritual bathing had been newly constructed just northwest of the falcon-shaped brick altar. For Hindus, ceremonial bathing is perhaps the most popular form of worship – hence the vast increase of crowds. The scene was mad, crowded and hot but also exhilarating. The *yajamana*, his wife and family submerged themselves in the *kund*, and the rest of us pressed forward so that we could be splashed with the holy water.

❋

What I learned from the twelve-day *agnicayana* is that not everything need be always observed to the letter. There is indeed some flexibility in the performance of such a complex ritual. Like any work of accomplished art, however, (and as opposed to political statement?), it emanates a beauty or at least a beauty in and through its hypnotic execution. The duration of the ceremony was like experiencing a prolonged visual symphony, but whether as ancient and complex as the Soma Sacrifice or such simpler forms as today's Wiccan circles, Celtic worship within stone circles or Heathen *blóts* and *sumbels*, ritual is one way in which we might come to understand and be with the gods. And whether they are 'real' or not, they open one to a vibrant mythic register that is endlessly fascinating, informative and occasionally enough enigmatic.

Reminiscing on the *maha vedi* ceremony I attended nearly four decades ago in Bangalore and the seductive otherworld that it could bring one into, there appears steadily to be an unfathomable and growing chasm between the spiritual lifting from the everyday into the ritualistic and the seemingly hopeless degeneracy of today's world. Do we not ultimately wish to flower and/or fly? These are the possibilities through celebratory worship, but instead one reads daily about mass shootings in El Paso, Texas, Dayton, Ohio or elsewhere, knifings and machete attacks in London, stabbings and robbery sprees in southern California, kidnapping, human slavery, using children as 'money mules', gang violence, aerial bombings in Yemen and Idlib, slovenly nationalism, the increasing closing of borders, trade wars, identity politics, fake news, no-platforming, the decline of democracy, poverty, the growing wealth gap, and the persistent silliness, greed and waste of our times. There are so many other unceasing concerns that demand our immediate attention over the chaos that we throw additionally into the mix – global warming, desertification, melting ice sheets and glaciers, plastic and other pollutions, diseases like the Ebola virus and dengue fever and COVID-19, Siberian and Portuguese forest fires as well as such pervasive natural phenomena as droughts, hurricanes, earthquakes, tsunamis, floods, landslides, etc. Our loss of grounding exacerbates all these dilemmas. I agree with John Beckett that when it comes to religion and spirituality, older is not necessarily better. I am, however with Guy Davenport in cherishing the archaic as providing a base for traditional value and developing art. Beckett affirms, 'The original will always be special because it was first, but later versions are cleaner and deeper'. When we surmise over the magnificent technological achievements of our day, we can but wonder the why of military weapon development and massive land clearance ostensibly for intensive farming and food production but which depletes the regenerative ability of the soil and contaminates it in addition with pesticides. A good part of my disillusionment with the pagan insight of today is with the inability of its spiritual outlook to capture the imagination and energy necessary for global thought and rectifying action.

I remember taking a Newari lad into a mosque in Srinagar. In astonishment, he looked around and saw no image or figure on an altar. 'They have no god!' he exclaimed in complete surprise. I agreed. My own research and experience have brought me to the realisation that the Abrahamic figure revered by the People of the Book is *not* a god but a personified non-deific, even anti-deific, imposter. I realise the difficulty that this consideration presents for interfaith, but the cultural and historic ramifications of biblical and related outlook are undeniable. Nevertheless, *all* peoples possess the democratic mandate to worship or not worship whom or whatever they choose. Human freedom trumps everything. If pagans endorse this liberty, unfortunately it is not always reciprocal. And without denying the right of others to pursue and honour that which they wish, it remains within a pagan remit to examine and scrutinise the state of affairs and hermeneutic evidence as openly and honestly as possible. While some may not like and even oppose how we see things, *tant pis, on fera au meme*!

But interfaith! Many within the pagan community are active in communicating with other religious viewpoints. This is doubtfully an important enterprise that is possibly helpful towards the furtherance of harmony throughout the world. Since my college days, I became involved with the Vedanta Society in both the Upper Westside of Manhattan and in the Santa Barbara Hills of Montecito. As such, I was aware of Ramakrishna's disciple, Swami Vivekananda and his legendary breakthrough appearance at the Chicago Parliament of the World's Religions in 1893. The off the record and undisclosed purpose of the original Chicago gathering was to convert the world to Christianity. No one had expected that someone from such a primitive and paganesque place like India could speak intelligently and captivatingly. But this is precisely what Vivekananda did. Consequently, when the city of Chicago decided to celebrate the centenary anniversary of the original event, it was something I very much wanted to attend.

I did not realise initially that I could take part in the meeting as an academic and attended instead as a delegate member of the Lyceum of Venus of Healing. Unlike the 1893 Parliament, the organisers of the second Parliament appeared to have no hidden agenda behind their efforts which were instead motivated by purely ecumenical interests and the desire for peaceful cooperation within the framework and realities of contemporary pluralism. In other words, it was fully an interfaith affair. It brought together six and half thousand religious leaders and representatives, and its primary objective was to draw people from various and variously different persuasions in a spirit of cooperation and acceptance. Along with the Buddhists, Christians, Hindus, Muslims and Jews, there were 120 other religious groups present. The communities represented on the host committee alone included the African American, Anglican/Episcopal, Bahá'í, Buddhist, Pan Orthodox, Hindu, Jain, Jewish, Muslim, Native American, Protestant, Roman Catholic, Sikh and Zoroastrian. Among the many co-sponsors were the AIDS National Interfaith Network, the Anthroposophical Society in America, the Brahma Kumaris World Spirituality University, the Swedenborgian Church of the New Jerusalem, the Free Daist Communion, the Joseph Campbell Society, the Kiwanis Club, the Association of Rastafarian Theologians and the Black International Iyabingi Press, the Liberal Catholic Church, the Theosophical Society, the Unitarian Universalist Association and the Unity School of Christianity. Among the lecturers giving talks or workshops were such names as Riane Eisler, Charlene Spretnak, Hans Küng, Metropolitan Paulos Mar Gregorios, Dr. Karan Singh, Thomas Berry, Dr. J. Gordon Melton, Swami Balasiva Yogeendra Maharaj, the Very Rev. James Parks Morton, Pir Vilayat Inayat Khan, Satguru Sivaya Subrahmunyaswami, Ven. Thich Nhat Hanh, Robert McDermott, Elizabeth Kubler-Ross, Professor Ursula King, Dr. Robert S. Ellwood, Barbara Marx Hubbard, Dr. Catherine Wessinger, Swami Bhaktipada and Harvey Cox. All in all, there were more than six hundred speakers.

There were both successes and mishaps for this 1993 Parliament of the World's Religions. The Native Americans, not invited in 1893, were not only present but played a significant role in the opening directional blessings held to launch the Parliament in a harmonious spirit. Other innovative spiritual orientations which enjoyed noteworthy profiles on par with the more traditional included Humanists, Metaphysicians, Pagans and Bahaists. Also present were Daoists, Shintoists and followers of the Orisha religion. Conspicuously absent, on the other hand, were most New Religious Movements whether the Unification Church or the Church of Scientology. Apart from the Urantia Foundation and the International Church of Metaphysics, there was no obvious New Age presence either. Neo-pagans themselves, however, were found well-represented through the Fellowship of Isis, the Lyceum of Venus of Healing, Earthspirit, the Covenant of the Goddess and Circle Sanctuary. On this first occasion, those I met within the pagan community included Deborah Ann Light, Selena Fox, Olivia Robertson and Isaac Bonewits. Heading the Lyceum of Venus of Healing were Cara Margarit-Drusilla (Cara-Kit van Zandt who appeared as Nefertiti) and Phoebe Wray (actor and environmentalist).

One focal moment of the entire Parliament fell on day two when Dr. Gerald O. Barney of the Arlington, Virginia-based Millennium Institute addressed a plenary session with a report entitled 'Global 2000 Revisited: What Shall We Do?'. This was an in-depth analysis of the approaching impasse projected for approximately the year 2020 when the shrinking limits of terrestrial food production resources will no longer be able to match human population growth patterns. In a clear-cut delineation of the problems faced by the world and humanity and a voice breaking with emotion, Barney appealed for a concerted awareness and world cooperation to head off what will otherwise certainly become a global catastrophe. 'I must tell you honestly', he asserted, 'that many people now wonder if any of our faith traditions have the wisdom we need for the future. . . . Many feel that our faith traditions have become a very central part of the human problem'.

Concerning the Parliament's desire to promote interfaith, the reality of its efforts often proved to be mixed. For the third day of plenaries, for instance, a session entitled 'Voices of the Dispossessed' was scheduled to present the views of the refugee. When the dispossessed was Haitian or Liberian or even South African, there was universal sympathy. But when Gulam Nabi Fai spoke uncompromisingly as a Muslim refugee from Kashmir, Hindu tolerance came to reach its breaking point, and uproar erupted in the auditorium. This was eventually quelled, and a meeting between leaders of the relevant religious factions was held secretly in a room beneath the ballroom to foster a working solution. Subsequently, Gurmit Singh Aulakh, speaking on behalf of the Punjabi Sikh community, took the podium. His one-sided litany of the horrors which have befallen his people surpassed even that of Gulam Nabi Fai, and this time total bedlam swept the floor. The conference organisers stood helplessly in shock, and I so wished that someone would make the simple statement acknowledging that all peoples have been wronged and all peoples have wronged and that only with this realisation can we proceed and be able to listen to one and all. But the unexpectedness on the part of the chairpersons for the reaction which followed virtually paralysed them one and all. The police removed all the speakers from the stage, and finally the Sikh speaker himself was persuaded to relinquish the podium. One section of the audience broke into the refrain 'We shall overcome', and this was then taken up by the others present. The Native Americans finally came to the rescue and cancelled their own scheduled talk and called for a healing circle dance in which everyone was invited to participate. The Parliament disarray was soothed at the conclusion of this ritual when each person was asked to embrace the one next to them.

If this feat along with the opening day invocation of the directions were the highpoints for the Native American contribution to the Parliament, much of the rest seemed downhill when the indigenous American community became divided over the drafting of a 'Declaration of War' targeting especially New Age profiteers but also Neo-paganists [sic.] The Native American grievances are overwhelming and include loss of the sacred homelands, decimation of their peoples, violations of their human rights, display of revered objects in museums and appropriation of their rituals and names by pretenders. Meanwhile, the Greek Orthodox Diocese of Chicago withdrew from the Parliament reputedly because of the Neo-pagan presence. The Anti-Defamation League of B'nai B'rith also withdrew, this time due to the talk scheduled by Louis Farrakhan, the leader of the Nation of Islam, who reputedly 'continues to espouse and promote classic anti-Semitic notions of Jewish domination and control'.

The final declaration concerning a 'Global Ethic' was largely the work of the Swiss Roman Catholic theologian Hans Küng. It was designed to address the issues of economic, environmental and political crises confronting the very survival of the world. It embraces a call for humane treatment of all peoples along with mutual respect for diversity and individualism. Sexual discrimination, 'limitless exploitation' of the environment, and the use of violence are condemned, while economic parity, intrinsic dignity and non-violent resistance 'whenever possible' [*sic.*] are pledged. There is no mention of the word 'God' nor explicit reference to the population explosion and the contested issue of birth control. While the role of religion is clearly recognised as having contributed to aggression, fanaticism and hate, the 'Declaration Towards a Global Ethic' is grounded on what is perceived as a universal minimal ethic already contained within 'our often millennia-old religious and ethical traditions' – 'an ethic which is convincing and practicable for all women and men of good will, religious and non-religious'. From the beginning, Küng's draft was considered as only the first step toward a more permanent and complete consensus on ethical behaviour. Eventually, the majority of leading religious delegates were persuaded to sign the Declaration as it stood, and the option was left open for the others to sign at a later and unspecified date. Those who signed the document from the start included the Tibetan spiritual leader His Holiness Dalai Lama XIV, His Eminence Cardinal Joseph Bernardin (Roman Catholic Archdiocese of Chicago), and the Revd. Wesley Ariarajah, deputy general secretary in Geneva of the World Council of Churches representing most major Protestant denominations. However, in protest to the presence of Black Muslim leader Farrakhan at the Parliament, none of the Jewish groups signed the document at the time of the gathering's conclusion

Meanwhile and separately, the Native American elders gained the upper hand and succeeded in re-drafting the 'Declaration of War' as a 'Declaration of Vision'. The New Age and Neo-paganist clauses were dropped, and the overall tone of the final statement was more conciliatory and moderate. The grievances of the Indigenous Nations and their dehumanisation were nevertheless still included, and the proclamation specifically asked that the Inter Cetera Bull of 4 May 1493 be rescinded by Pope John Paul II. The Declaration ends with the words: 'WITH RESPECT FOR ALL LIFE, WE THANK YOU'.

The concluding plenary was held in the Petrillo Bandshell of Grant Park. The Dalai Lama gave the keynote address. While acknowledging that there is little to be done concerning death caused by such natural calamities as flooding and earthquake, the Dalai Lama deplored the unnecessary deaths caused by starvation, human violence and warfare, or through ignorance and lack of proper medical research. He specifically mentioned AIDS and the necessity of not rendering the victim of the HIV virus as a social leper. He also spoke unremittingly about the urgency for birth control as the world's population spirals toward astronomical proportions. As a coda to this last, the Dalai Lama did acknowledge that there were more preferable means of achieving birth control than others. With tongue in cheek and casting an eye toward Cardinal Bernardin, 'Ideally, we need more monks and nuns!' he proclaimed. The exiled spiritual leader mentioned further the need for pluralism. 'Yes', he clarified, 'I would like very much that everyone be Buddhist, but I realise that we are not all the same. Consequently, we need different religions because we are all different people'. This was the strongest assertion for religious pluralism yet to be made by any spiritual leader and came as a retort to the Pope's own condemnation of relativism delivered in Colorado a few weeks earlier. The Dalai Lama concluded his address with the request that now that we have all talked about the world's problems we go home and actually do something about them.

After a reading of extracts from The Declaration of a Global Ethic, the 1993 Parliament of the World's Religions finished with Tibetan chanting and then a multi-cultural dance performance which included Native Americans, East Indians, Muong, Irish, Jewish and a spectacular Aztec drum and fire-dance. These were followed by the 500-strong all-black, 'drug-free' and 'crime-free' Chicago Soul Children's Choir concluding with some unforgettably moving gospel choruses. But this rousing conclusion did not eclipse the brief exchange I had heard earlier the same day when I found myself in the always crowded hotel elevator at one point with Daniel Gómez-Ibáñez. Recognising the Executive Director of the Board of Trustees for the Parliament, a woman turned to him and his colleagues and exclaimed, 'I want to thank you for making this all possible'.

'Really?' a surprised and weary Mr. Gómez-Ibáñez replied. 'Are you enjoying it?' he asked. 'We have only been dealing with all the countless problems'.

'Oh, yes', the lady continued rapturously with her Southern drawl, 'This has been the most wonderful experience of my life'.

After making the decision to continue having Parliaments, there have been those held in Cape Town, South Africa in 1999, Barcelona, Spain in 2004, Melbourne, Australia in 2009, Salt Lake City, Utah in 2015 and Toronto, Canada in 2018. Apart from the last two of these, I have attended all including 2021's virtual event. The 1993 Chicago Parliament was for pagans a milestone of recognition and euphoria. Rather shamelessly, there was a rambunctious procession of pagans – cymbals, sistrums and drums and all – through the lobby of the Palmer House Hotel, the Parliament's venue. More successfully engaged in universal dialogue on the pagans' part was Cape Town. Mobile phones were being offered on a rental basis during the registration. Subsequently, Deborah Ann Light sponsored a reception for the pagan delegates in which we all were able to exchange phone numbers and form a network to share information. As a result, in my experience, this was the most successful Parliament for the pagan community. In Barcelona, it was more the occasion for intrafaith than interfaith. In Melbourne, pagans were more balanced to engage in liaison with both themselves and with others.

In Chicago, the Lyceum of Venus of Healing allowed me to use its suite to invite pagans from as many related traditions in my hope to form an active coalition of animists, shamanists and polytheists (ASPs). We had a couple of breakfasts, and those who came included Daoists, Shinto and Native Americans (including Inca) as well as Selena Fox. My efforts overall, however, were unsuccessful. Omie Baldwin, Navajo, told me later that I would have trouble attracting Native Americans because most consider themselves to be Christian. Fundamentalist Christians, in fact, picketed the Palmer House Hilton's entrances denouncing the 'satanic' proceedings occurring inside. In Cape Town, it was Muslims who demonstrated outside but again against the 'devil worship' within. In Melbourne, the division was internal. Omie Baldwin had organised an exclusive Indigenous Peoples conference that met separately and allowed the Yoruban priest Baba Wande Abimbola to enter but not his Euro-American wife. This group issued an angry Statement to the World, more or less replacing the failed Declaration of War at the 1993 Parliament but again though this time more forcefully condemning the Doctrine of Discovery that had opened all non-Christian lands to be 'discovered' and claimed by Christian rulers (the Papal Bull 'Inter Caetera' of 1493). When I tried to say hello to Omie on this occasion, she turned her back on me. While it is crucially important to expose the basis for the supposedly 'legitimate' Western expansion by European nations and the United States, once again we had an expression that was incommensurate with the interfaith spirit that is fundamental to the Parliament of the World's Religions' endeavour.

Epicurus claims that as perfect beings the gods would take no interest in we mortal humans. While I am in agreement with much that the Greek philosopher says, or at least that Lucretius says he says, I differ on this point. As idealised expressions of consciousness itself, I expect that the gods have both the leisure *and* the interest to be concerned with the all of consciousness. And, as the foremost carriers of wakeful sentience, as far as we know, this divine interest would extend to us – if it does not already include us by default. We may not be immortal, but from a pantheist understanding if not otherwise, we are divine.

After again in Banaras, I flew to Khajuraho. From the plane, the atmospheric entertainment was truly magnificent with cotton amorphic shapes towering one above the other – a kind of frozen animation, battles and games between gods and demons, generally a panoply of units attached in some kind of complex molecular arrangement but sometimes linked by layers or pockets of mist and darkness. Though I had wanted to sleep, that was out of the question.

And once we were landed, the stone jewels – the 9th to 11th century Chandel Rajput temples – beckoned. They easily rival Pallava (3rd–9th c.) and Hoysala (11th–14th c.) architecture, but in contrast to the pristine structures of the Southern Deccan Plateau, these in the north are covered with erotic sculpture depicting men, women and animals engaged in orgiastic lovemaking and bestiality and even homosexuality – all to affirm the gods' endorsement of carnal pleasure. For our world today, the Khajuraho carvings are indelicately ribald and vulgarly off-colour. They express Hinduism perhaps in one of its most pagan resonances and, in the case of the sexual imagery of these *nagara*-style temples, the embodiment of *Kama Sutra* Tantric principles. Hindu temples throughout the Subcontinent range from being magnificent museums (like most of the 25 temples of Khajuraho, the Shore Temple of Mahabalipuram, the Cave Temples of Elephanta, the Kailasanatha in Ellora, the Konarak Sun temple in Orissa, the Chennakeshava temples in Belur and Somanathapura, and the Hoysaleshwara and Kedareshwara temples in Halebidu) to places for active worship (e.g., Viśvanath, Rameswaram, Śucindra, the Sri Kantheswara in Nanjangud, the Tirumala Venkateswara Temple in Tirupati as well as the 10th century temple in Khajuraho dedicated to Matangesvara or the Lord of Transformation). These provide a likely glimpse into the dynamic of both the classical temples of Greece and Rome and the priestly cult centres of Egypt, Canaan and Mesopotamia. Along with the Parthenon, Sounion, Paestum and Agrigento, the Indian temple monuments are fascinating venues to visit, but it is the living temples themselves where worship is continued even into today that open one uniquely to the passionate centres of incomparably vibrant spirituality.

It is virtually impossible for me to convey the persistent thrill I experienced with the Hindu temple. While much of my exposure occurred in the north, the temples of Dravidian India in particular with their otherworldly interiors of light and dark along with multidirectional stone patterns, filigree and carvings constituted outright numinous epiphanies. India itself is a challenging hardship for the visitor, tourist and pilgrim. There is the necessity in India to surrender to fate and luck – especially during the monsoon season. I often wanted to ask why when there is insight, there is no energy, but when there is energy, there is no insight. The overall encounter with this vast land and culture is an enigma, and I found that for whatever I could say about something, the opposite would be equally true. The great appeal of Hinduism is its lack of creeds. In both India and Nepal, however, Hinduism's fusion with Brahmanism and the concomitant requirement of fawning to the notion and practice of the caste system made me as a foreign 'whitey' realise that I am not a Hindu but instead a Vedist or, translated into contemporary terms, a pagan humanist. The pagan humanist approach is one that attempts to accommodate as many various ideologies as possible – not reduce the world to only one outlook. We pagan humanists are not Christians or Marxists, but we tolerate and accept both and seek to make room for them in as much as they can tolerate us as well. And despite any attraction I might have to Marxism, I regret that the concepts of imagination and wonder receive next to no mention if any at all.

When I was first back in Banaras, I became mindful of the whole different concept of devotion from that in the south. It was still a welcomed feeling to be making again the old circuit and pay homage to familiar deities. Vishvanath and other temples, however, were mobbed, and I began to believe that the frantic scenes at the main cult centres are important if only for a preparation for the intimate charm one comes into contact with in the quiet country shrines. In the days of my shamanic youth I used to be able to do a full night vigil for the key solar festivals. Back then, a midsummer solstice in Banaras allowed me to experience a different Banaras – hushed and supercharged both in the temples, the burning ghat, riverbank and the courtyard of Gyan Kup. This last, the 'Well of Wisdom', and thanks to the attached mythologies and histories – legendary or not, I came to know as the centre of the cosmos – the very place where the sky-lord entered and impregnated the earth-mother and from where she gave birth to all subsequent creation. This is presumably why Banaras/Varanasi is the oldest city, at least the oldest *continuous* city, on earth.

The urban centre has always had a singular appeal for me and despite my love for the rural and more pristine manifestations of the natural world. When in the south of India, I found I was devoid of any enthusiasm for Madras – now known as Chennai. In fact, although in principle I adore the concept of the city, there are in actuality very few that I really enjoy – perhaps seven in North America, perhaps nine in Europe. And the reasons for each of these vary as well. Of course, New York City is *the* city; San Francisco has a natural beauty, an excitement and a sophistication. Paris too is a city I love for her beauty, spirit, sophistication and cuisine. London, for music, theatre, art, libraries and social life. I have here come to appreciate the saying: 'Tired of London; tired of life!' Zürich is another place of sophistication and beauty; Amsterdam, beauty and social life; Rome for her throbbing animation and her ancientness; Istanbul for her people and mystery – probably by 1981 my only Asian city although technically on European soil; and Budapest for the arts, her people, her cuisine and, certainly not least, her thermal springs. I would still include München and Wien although I have had little familiarity with them in recent years. Other favoured cities: Berlin, New Orleans, Montreal, Vancouver, Boston and Philadelphia.

There is of course a second type of city as well – the smaller one, or what I would wish to call the municipal town – probably akin to the original *polis*, and many of these I adore. Amsterdam probably represents the upper limit of the municipal town. Prime examples, however, are Aix-en-Provence and Firenze. Among cities I detested by 1981 were Chicago and Athens. I have since, however, come to revise my feelings concerning Chicago. There is a great pride in the restoration efforts of the 'Windy City's' legacy of spectacular buildings, and the Art Institute (founded in 1879) alone is a treasure that raises Chicago in undeniable esteem. In Los Angeles I can have a great time but could not say that I like it or ever have. Calcutta is fascinating, but again I cannot say that it is a favourite. Since 1981, I have come to enjoy Cairo, Alexandria, Durban, Beirut, Bangkok, Singapore, Tokyo, Kyoto, Melbourne and Brisbane. For both Cape Town and Sydney, I remain more lukewarm.

Banaras, of course, is a prime example of the municipal town. For my first duration in India I lived above the Ahilya Bai Ghat in a building that the Holkar *maharani* (1725–1795) had constructed along with the *ghat*. Her capital of the Maratha Malwa kingdom was Maheswar on the banks of the Narmada River south of Indore. When I visited Maheswar, it was explained to me that the Narmada was the only one of India's holy rivers that is a virgin, that is, unmarried. Further, concerning the *archarya* theologian Śaṇkara, the guru who established monistic Advaita, there is a legend that he entered the dead body of King Amaruka. However, in Maheshwar a spot was pointed out to me where this teacher of Vedanta entered the body of a dead woman (rather than that of the dead king) in order to gain sexual knowledge for his debate with Mandana's wife Bharati. In any event, the figure who was without a doubt the most impressive for me in Maheshwar was Queen Ahilya Bai herself. During her virtually faultless reign, she had temples built throughout India – including that of Viśwanath in Banaras.

Ahilya Bai gave birth to a son and daughter, but her husband was killed in 1754, her father-in-law died twelve years later, and her son, for whom she was briefly regent, succumbed to illness shortly thereafter. Ahilya Bai became queen, and her daughter said to her not to worry, that she would produce an heir. But her daughter's husband also died, and the daughter then insisted on performing *sati*. Ahilya Bai could not convince her otherwise and had to watch the cremation pyre. At some subsequent point, she adopted a Holkar, her commander-in-chief, and, as a result, the dynasty has continued.

The queen held open court daily and was accessible to anyone who wished to see her. There is a noteworthy event in which she summoned a notorious *dacoit*, Zam, and informed him that whatever he wanted she would give to him. Reacting in shame to the queen's generosity, he repented of his criminal ways and used his wealth subsequently to build rest-houses for the people. I was also told the story that one day Ahilya Bai had her usual breakfast at 10:00 and then an hour later said to Bhalji that she thought she was going to die that day. Bhalji protested and said there was nothing wrong and that she had eaten a full breakfast. 'I know', she replied, 'but still I think today I am going to die'. And by noon, she was dead. The population of Maheshwar then went into an unprecedented four-year period of mourning for this much beloved queen. This entailed the eating of no sweets, the celebration of no marriages or investitures of brahmanical threads, and the forsaking of all enjoyment. Finally, the *ranī*'s daughter-in-law concluded that enough was enough and ordered the people of Maheshwar to cease mourning and resume a normal life.

Before I had first left France for India, Elisabeth introduced me to a friend of hers, Kostas, who in turn had given me contact details for Richard Holkar, the current (though contested) maharaja of Malwa or Indore State, and with whom I had communicated by letter. It was early evening when I had arrived in Maheshwar. I discovered there were no restaurants, and the Ahilya Fort guesthouse was not available. Somehow, and through the assistance of a broken-English speaking doctor, I secured a fold-down bench from the wall in a *dharamsala*. It came with a closet in which I could lock my things and cost me 25 paise for the night. It was the most primitive sleeping conditions I had had so far in India. After the night on the *dharamsala* board, the next morning I asked a stall keeper for the site of the prehistoric city of Maheshwar. I was given the name of a Mr. Maheshwar, the town's only guide, whom I located subsequently at the bus stand office. He at least spoke some English, and he confirmed to me that the guesthouse had been booked up by government officials because of a collapsed bridge. Later in the day, I asked again about the guesthouse and was again told that it was not available. But then I thought to produce my letter from Prince Richard which, even though he was currently away from Maheshwar, was beautifully explicit about my welcome. So, the next thing I knew was that I was lodging in the royal palace. Not exactly the Sheraton, but a most welcome and unbelievable change of fortune. Another time in Bombay, Prince Richard was again absent, but in his apartment home I did get to meet his then three-year old son Yeshwant.

And just to mention that I thank any powers that be for the happiness I have and share – now roughly 40 years after my initial visit to India, now and for the many years in between. My preeminent joys are music, nature, the arts, the gods and my loved ones. Yes, I miss the freedom, flexibility and energy of youth, but the autumn years, though quieter and more judiciously allocated between what is possible and what is not, retain no less a goodly portion of serenity and ecstasy.

Today I continue to grasp that the images and symbols the gods have used over many years as vehicles have been integrated into our quotidian world to allow a perpetually inspiring inter-communication with the afflatus of our cultural legacies. I am well aware that our physical universe is more space and force field than it is physical matter – right down to the atom itself and its components of protons, neutrons and electrons or even further to the force field particles known as bosons and the elementary fermions (quarks and leptons – including electrons) and composite fermions or baryons such as protons and neutrons – all being the very key building blocks of everyday matter. But it is a mistake to confuse the matter-energy continuum with the spirit-body dichotomy. Spirit in itself is not energy but a transcendental or non-empirical abstraction such as Platonic ideas, ideal templates, principles or number. The very word 'spirit' is itself a metaphor, signifying 'breath.'

In other words, a diaphanous physical metaphor has been used to designate the insubstantial. From a pagan perspective – at least a telluric pagan understanding, matter intrinsically has agency and is the matrix or mother of the 'drawn away' or abstract – including such non-concrete phenomena as concepts, ideas, incorporeal consciousness, the animated soul and the like. The abstract or spiritual may be real but remains undetectable to our senses. It depends instead on definition, intuition, inspiration, imagination and/or the affirmation of conviction or belief.

One of the ways to experience the evanescent realities of the spiritual, beside the use of incantation (mantra repetition), austerities (yoga), concentration (meditation, contemplation) or being born with the natural inclination to encounter such, is through psychedelic herbs. Nature has provided humanity with various catalysts of transformation that trigger neuro-chemical events in the brain. These may enhance meaning, lead to critically spiritual significance and produce root remembrances. The contact with Hindu temples provided for me an access to the archaic – especially when augmented with the ingestion of a psychoactive substance. The sacramental entheogen or visionary plant is understood to encourage humbleness, compassion, love, interconnectedness, interdependence, inspiration and mindfulness, to gain knowledge of the spiritual significance of anxiety, doubt, guilt and shame, and to shift perspective by 'cleansing the doors of perception' into the dimension of enchantment. The liminal space of the otherworld is where one can experience an ontological reality of metaphor, of the gods and spirits, and the psycho-physic interaction between landscape, the environment and wonder. The animistic thought that hallucinogens bring forth encourages not only reconnection to archaic understandings but also new ways of knowing and of being. At the same time, they reduce alienation from the natural world and that which sustains us.

Consequently, my contention is that there are two basic approaches to the gods: (1) via basic contemplation fuelled by mythological study and repetitive ritual commemoration, and (2) through the mind-alterants. In Hinduism and for some pagans such as myself, the idol serves as a focus for both devotion and contemplation, but in the Levantine-inspired ideologies idolatry has been condemned as if there is something inherently deficient and inferior in materialism. But why should matter not be sacred? True, it is forever undergoing change, but the very fact of its perpetual transformation methinks ought to let it be understood as all the more holy.

In India, the temples are mesmerising and increasingly so for festivals (*utsava*) such as Makar Sankranti, Maha Shivaratri, Holi, Navaratri-Dussehra and Diwali when they might be filled with flower decorations, special lighting and mounds of food. But they can also frequently become free-for-all occasions for heightened emotions and shoving – rendering the experience perfunctory at best and without a shred of possibility for contemplation or reflection. I remember as well the Sūrya idol being covered with a swarm of rats devouring the garlands adorning the figure. But there can also be times in which the temple and shrine venues offer sublime serenity and a transportation into another reality. And especially magical are the junctures in which the devotee is in a shamanic condition, and the full *raison d'être* for the worshipful experience becomes most evident.

Thinking about the virtually shameless dancing on a stage at the Daśaśwamedh Ghat in Banaras by the Ramakrishna monks, I became mindful of the comparative non-ostentation of the shaman in comparison to the priest. The shaman is essentially a private person who may gather with others of his own kind from time to time or for special occasions, but usually without audience. As a 'free-soul', he or she tends against forming into permanent priesthoods which vie for power and issue creeds, dogmas and regulations. With art being the mother of the sciences, and science the mother of the arts, it is magic which perhaps combines the two, that is, harmonises the modes of concern and detachment. Unfortunately, it is the *magi* who have given *magic* a bad name.

It was thanks to my nine months in India that I was able to understand freedom consisting of option, mobility and tolerance, or, to put it in other words, choice, the ability to exercise one's choice, and the capability to allow the same for others. It was also where I first elucidated my comprehension of the basic virtue-values. Along with freedom, 'worth' is the expression of gratitude more than formal worship (which can too easily be used and manipulated by others). If we combine this last with the pursuit of pleasure, productivity and generosity, we have the essence of worship – the shaping of something of value.

I realise I have not included love as a virtue or aim. This is because freedom, comfort, health and worth are guides by which to assess all other aspirations. Love is too vague a phenomenon to be used as a means of evaluation. Moreover, when unrequited at least, it can too often mean desire for revenge and nastiness. For most people love really seems to indicate a kind of taking. True love would be a giving. It is a comfort or pleasure but also in its givingness a form of generosity. So, while love certainly can be considered a comfort (even also a freedom as well as a form of health), it is primarily an aspect of worship, that is, worth. It would seem that the primary need of any individual is to evaluate one's situation to determine first if he or she is lucky, that would be, in possession of freedom, comfort, health and worth, and secondly, if not, why not. My belief is that even when afflicted, or burdened by the kind of poverty one ubiquitously sees in the land of India as well as elsewhere, every person can be free if so chosen or desired. This of course is not easy by a long shot, but it still is a possibility – sometimes one that requires great imagination and/or creativeness. There is, either hopefully or resolutely, always something for which to be thankful, and it is within the feeling of gratitude where one can find a kind of freedom.

Returning from Calcutta via Dacca to Amsterdam, Richard and I made a brief visit to Bruges. I found the West Flemish capital a bewitching re-entry into the European heritage and with its own cult nodal points clearly discernible. The excellent Belgian cuisine is a further enhancing factor. But apart from the food, we feasted on Hieronymus Bosch and René Magritte, the Gothic Hall of the Hotel de Ville and the Saint Walpurga Church. And after the forbidden temples of Puri, Bhubaneshwar, Kathmandu and Trivandrum, I came to appreciate that nature and private (and especially free) worship are my preferred wants and needs. But I also remained no less drawn to the Indian subcontinent and the incomparable insights it affords. Ganaspati has always been a preferred deity: a lord of magic whose vehicle is the rat and who, I suggest, is emblematic of how the wish-world can be made to ride above the unpleasant and dangerous. This world and the other – Hanuman the monkey god trickster in this one; the elephant-headed Ganesh in the other. But if the 'other' is illusion or *māyā*, this would of course be only half the picture. On the other hand, if *māyā* is *all* there is, then by sheer will alone there must be permanently useable (or, rather, useably permanent) illusions upon which for us to construct our reality.

Both Spinoza and Nietzsche deplore what they consider the illusion of a metaphysical or supernatural mandate. Belief in some exclusive transcendental only misunderstands the body and fantasises a false morality. However, in the Year of the Rat in which potentially thousands are to die of the coronavirus originating from China, in which the American Constitution is undermined by partisan politics, and, let alone the continuing global warfare and terrestrial disasters, in which Britain regressively and arrogantly sabotages the European Union, is either Spinoza's argument for reason or Nietzsche's for wills to power valid as a feasible means to further viable survival or success? As philosophers, I adore both Spinoza and Nietzsche and champion immanent understanding and the removal of tyranny. But in the light of such perpetual hopelessness, might we not also need magic? At the end of the day, I will argue that enchantment is the missing component in the present stage of human effort. Perhaps ceremonial magic can be effective, but I expect this to be no more than Christian prayer might be. After the fact claims and occasional or marginal, possibly Roseanne Barr's synchronicitous success notwithstanding, I still feel that sensible determination and action on our part might in some way be effectively augmented through the thaumaturgical. How and in what ways I cannot say, but nonetheless I surmise that the very exploration of the divine or divinity is itself an important recourse that is commensurate with both the aesthetic and persuasive imagination. Perhaps, just perhaps, as well as hopefully, the needed energy, sanity and insight might emerge through such investigation. My gut suspicion is that it is worth the gamble. What else is there to lose?

Granted that I came to cherish the gods of Hinduism (Śiva, Viśṇu, Devī, Sūrya, Ganesha) and the nearly twenty years of hands-on devotion to them that India and Nepal privileged for me, my preference nonetheless remains with the Vedic deities and their Greco-Roman, Heathen, Celtic and Lithuanian equivalents. A favourite for me remains Zeus/Jupiter who is Tīwaz/Týr among the Germanics and Norse, Dievas/Dievs for the Balts, the weather-god Tarḫunna of the Hittites (identified as the Hurrian Teshup and Hattic Taru), and while the Vedic peoples knew him as Dyaus Pita, he is for all practical purposes superseded for the Vedics by his more active son Indra. As I mentioned in the previous chapter, this last is a parallel to both Heathen and Baltic developments, for whereas the classical sky-father is god of both light/brightness *and* thunder/lightning, he bifurcates among the Lithuanians into Dievas and Perkunas and among the Germanics into Tīwaz/Tyr and Donar/Thor. Beside the Vedic Indra, the fulgurous figure, like Thor and Perkunas, emerges as a separate deity with the Vedic Parjanya, the Greek *Peraunos/*keraunos*, the Slavic Perun, the Albanian Perendi, the Norse Fjörgynn and the Gallic Taranis. As I perceive it, this splitting of deity stems originally from an Indo-European understanding of deific fluidity and how over time a divine figure may successively divide, multiply, fuse and re-coalesce. In essence, however, the fundamental prototype of light, lightning, thunder, rain and fertility is known through the theonym derivatives of **dei-*/**dyêus* and **perk^{w}u-s*. The name of the Hittite Tarḫunna, however, derives from a different source, namely, from the god *Tr̥ḫu-ent- 'the prevailing or conquering one' whose seminal root is considered to be **terh$_2$*- 'to cross over, pass through, overcome' – this radical stem also supposedly giving rise to the word *avatar* ('the one who crosses over') and the word *nectar* (the 'overcoming death' drink of the gods).

Personally, I endeavour to approach the myths concerning the gods as forms of narrative music. Uncontestably, they are to be enjoyed and fathomed for deeper or hidden meaning and intrinsic pleasure. In all, mythology and mythography (the study of myths) are ever-growing and hopefully innovative developments, but the archaic myths, despite by today's standards their oftentimes political incorrectness, still inform on a more challenging level and can encapsulate numinous, telluric, cosmic and primordial understandings. The tales of Jupiter-Zeus are paradigmatic in this respect. The personification of the divine prototype, whose very name is cognate to our words for 'divine', 'divinity' and 'deity', is himself the first-born offspring of the *terra mater*. If we were to strip away from Hesiod's *Theogony* the 'Succession of Heaven' myth that the poet imported from the Levant, the elemental sequence would be Gaia's parthenogenetic birthing not of Uranus but of Zeus. Echoes of this original understanding are to be seen in Thor's birth from Jörð, goddess of earth, and Indra's birth from the Sanskrit earth-mother Prithivi. Together, the Earth and the Sky (Sanskrit *dyavāprithivī*) become the parents of the rest of the gods. Contemporary Wicca retains this primeval chronicle in its portrayal of The God born from The Goddess and subsequently becoming her consort.

As the gods comprise instances of inscrutable perfection, Zeus is perfect light as Gaia is perfect matter. If Zeus is Ge's opposite, she nevertheless has the power to produce her antithesis. In actuality, he may be appreciated as the oedipal fantasy. Like mortals, the gods can also know death (e.g., Dionysus, Persephone), impairment (e.g., Zeus) and incest (e.g., Zeus), but they are not bound by humanity's social conventions since they belong more properly to the inexplicable and rawer dimensions of nature. A key feature of Zeus' myth is the establishment of his rule, that is, divine order (in Sanskrit, *r̥ta* and cognate with the words 'ritual', 'art' and 'rhythm'). But this undertaking is not a smooth process. There are various setbacks that involve a temporary disability of the Zeus-prototype. For Zeus himself,

Typhoeus or Typhon defeats the god and removes the sinews of his hands and feet – rendering the god paralysed until the sinews are re-secured by either Hermes and Aegipan ('Goat-Pan') or, as Nonnus tells it, by Cadmus. Being restored, Zeus then is able to defeat Typhon.

A similar version exists with the Hittite weather-god. There are two versions of the myth recorded in the Hattic language. In the earlier, the weather-god is defeated by the serpent-dragon Illuyanka until aided by the goddess Inara and the mortal Hupashiya. In the later account, Illuyanka cuts out the heart and eyes of the defeated god who then nevertheless proceeds to father a son on the daughter of a poor man. When the son becomes of age, he wishes to marry Illuyanka's daughter and asks as dowry the lost members of his father, the weather-god. When these are restored to the lord of weather, the god is able to slay the serpent. Another variant of the debilitation myth is to be seen in the king of the Irish Tuatha Dé Danann, Nuada, losing his arm in the first battle of Moytura and becoming thereby ineligible to be the ruler. There follows an interval of seven years in which Bres of the Fomorians, the enemy, rules as the king. But once Dian Cecht the leech replaces Nuada's arm with a silver one (hence Nuada *airgetlâm* 'of the silver arm') or Dian Cecht's son Miach heals Nuada's arm with a real one of flesh, the second battle of Moytura followed, and the Tuatha Dé Danann with Nuada as their king regain ascendency. And, similarly in line with the narrative interval of catabasis and compromise, in his battle with the dragon Vrita, the Vedic Indra retreats at some point in fear but is still able to overcome his terror to become lauded as the victorious hero.

In all these variants, divinity is temporarily defeated before becoming conclusively successful. There are two further versions of which to make note. One concerns the Nordic Tyr whose name is cognate with that of Zeus, Jupiter, Dyaus, and Dievas. In other words, he may be recognised as the original ruling lord of the bright sky. In Tyr's myth, however, he becomes impaired when he places his hand and sacrifices it in the mouth of the Fenrir wolf as the destructive monstrous beast is being bound by the gods. As a result, we find that the Aesir god Odin is the sovereign Norse power rather than the divine Tyr, and it is to be conjectured that the recording of the myth is incomplete or that the Christian poet Snorri Sturluson distorted the original tale so that the heathen god of light is not restored to his throne. The other version is Greek and concerns the god Dionysus, literally the 'Zeus of Nesa/Nysus', who is the son of Semele. The name of Dionysus' mother, comparing to Phrygian Zemelo and Slavic Zemlya, indicate her to be the 'earth-mother' herself – paralleling Zeus' own contended birth directly from Gaia. In this case, Dionysus is not the king of the gods (unless he is or was the god of the Nesians, that is, the Hittites), but he is nevertheless killed by the Titans though eventually reborn. In other words, the temporary incapacity of the Zeus- or sky-lord prototype becomes here the death of a Zeus cognate, but like the divine impairment, the death of the god is only temporary and not permanent.

For the polytheists among us, within the broad Indo-European heritage, there are Celtic, Heathen, Baltic, Slavic, Vedic, Hellenic and Roman pantheons among others. Additionally, however, we also have Kemetic, Canaanite, Akkadian, Chinese, Shinto, Polynesian, Afro-Latin, Mayan, Aztec, Inca and other Native American traditions. In other words, with these and further cultural conventions, there is a range and particularity for everyone. Above all, they provide contexts for those mystical moments in which there is the feeling of utter thanks. Beyond this, they furnish aesthetic registers within which to evaluate and honour meaning and desirability. And, once again, they might also become helpful factors in finding the means toward human restoration, rectification, regeneration, egalitarianism and emancipation.

After the more intense and 'greasier' Hinduism I fathomed in India, I welcomed once again the lighter, elfin paganism lurking in the shadows and woods of Europe. I am at home with local nodal points of the numinous along with modest delineations of the dynamic. In reminiscing, I recollected little dancing in India. In the West, there is disco and electronics, but at least we dance. And then there is the music of Gustav Mahler who may have defined Western culture or at least become the epitome of its expression. Experiencing a symphony of his is a religious event, at least as I encounter it. Perhaps no composer has surpassed him, although I would suspect that Olivier Messiaen with his *Turangalila Symphony* may be an exception. In any event, Mahler touches the wellspring of emotion, namely, the soul. His music encompasses the great range of Western civilisation and its associations. The first movement of his *Third Symphony* is the whole symphony in itself.

As 1981 ended, I reflected on my nine-month India excursion. I had encountered a land which is the most different from any I had previously known, a land of opposing extremes and magnitude but also one that I found to be remarkably akin to the Europe that I love. Perhaps I did not find the *Asie* of my dreams, but I entered Asia and discovered the people of India with their expected quotas of impossibilities to be all the same a people not alien but recognisably knowable. Also, they emerged for me as a warm, surprisingly industrious and surprisingly beautiful people. Beyond this – which would have been enough of a thrill in itself – I had the great satisfaction of confirming much of my own pre-guesses and intuitions concerning both pagan worship and Indo-European ideology. India had now become in my experience something real and wonderful and more than a merely – however marvellous – literary excursion.

There can be no doubt that Western civilisation came to be decidedly shaped by Christianity. The legacy that is focused on Jesus Christ has endured for 2,000 years. Among its more recent and positive contributions has been the campaign for civil rights, but Protestant values have also been claimed by such a racist organisation as the Ku Klux Klan. Even more central has been the anti-feminist and anti-gay biblical belief of evangelical fundamentalism that a woman's place is in the home and the gay rights movement is an obscenity. A major difference between Christianity and paganism is that the former holds the universe to be naturally moral. This translates for Christians that God is the Good, and the Good is God. It was Augustine who identified Yahweh with the Good and imported Platonic forms, patterns or transcendent ideals into an understanding of God. For most pagans, a supposedly loving God who punishes those who do not adhere to his commands reveals the hypocrisy of Christianity. Christian belief requires a moral universe; pagan conviction does not. The cosmos is instead understood as a neutral and amoral arena in which we live and operate. Yes, perhaps a moral universe would be nice, but pagans consider that ethical results depend on us and not in some response to a transcendent Creator and Redeemer. In other words, pagans have a morality but do not project ethical belief onto the universe itself. The labelling of race, gender and sexuality are not objective classifications but are instead social constructs that are used to frame the world and usually thereby advance particular agendas. By contrast and unless one accepts the Hindu belief in *māyā* or Nietzsche's alleged illusiveness of a substance ontology (i.e., that instead of matter there is only force), natural constructs supposedly really exist and include different kinds of stars, biological species and geological substances. In a word, and despite Nietzsche's rejection of scientific inquiry because it is ostensibly metaphysical and biasedly suggestive of a morality, the science that concerns itself with natural constructs seeks fundamentally to describe reality and eliminate subjective error. Social constructs, on the other hand, are not normative creations but more often than not political ones. They are fabrications instead of descriptions – sometimes useful perhaps but too often they are divisive and imprisoning. Religions are social constructions, and this includes paganism as well. But hopefully heathen/nature-oriented thought is liberating rather than constricting and blinding.

The original plan had been for Richard to join me in India and then for us together to continue around the world, but it proved to be less expensive to return first to Amsterdam and then proceed on our joint excursion from London. Seeing for the first time in months a Parvati in the Victoria and Albert Museum, I realised that I shall always love the Indian gods come what may. In London at the Olivier, we saw Peter Hall's production of Tony Harrison's version of Aeschylus' *The Oresteia*. The use of masks was powerful, and Harrison Birtwistle's haunting musical accompaniment (that he refers to as Anglo-Saxon) combined with Harrison's he-gods/she-gods translation produced a modern liturgy. I was struck by the consideration of Clytemnestra's murder as the destruction of the asurian anti-mother by the divine hero along with its counterbalance expressed in Athena's reasonable persuasion to the rest of the gods. In the case of Athena, I understood that historically she had undergone a similar transformation, namely, the anti-nature of the Chaos-descendants (here those of Nyx) mutate into proto-configurations of the *terra mater*. If not a counter-reflex or emergence, this is the evolution of Gaia from Chaos. There is lurking behind all of this one of the undetermined questions of paganism (found even in Shinto): does one worship the divine to prevent the influence of the asurian, or does one worship the asurian in order to transform it into the divine? In a sense, the matricide is the former; Athena's proposal is the latter. In another historic sense, the renaming of the Levantine Yahweh with the Latin Deus (cognate with the words 'divine' and 'Dios') possibly amounts to another apotropaic instance of anti-nature becoming converted into divinity.

Our flight from London took us to Karachi, and from there we went to Lahore and thence to Harappa, previously a centre of the Indus Valley culture. Through a series of unexpected luck, we lodged in the Harappa Guest Lodge. Our first night, we enjoyed dal and parathas for dinner but were not allowed to pay. And then on the way back to the lodge, an attractive policeman treated us to tea.

But what turned out to be the most revealing for me in Harappa was the presence of a very long tomb on top of the citadel mound. Nūsha is an Islamic saint, possibly from Saudi Arabia, but whose dates were unknown. It was explained that Nūsha was not as tall as his tomb suggested but that its length conveyed the 'greatness' of the man. What struck me was the demonstrative cult that was associated with the spot, and I began to recognise that cultic behaviour is a basic human phenomenon – one that is both integral to a religion but also transcends all religion. In other words, whether Hindu or Muslim, venerational expression is common to both. This seminal moment of insight led eventually to the writing of my *Pagan Theology: Paganism as a World Religion* which was published in 2003.

Our next site to visit was Mohenjo-Daro, the other key Indus Valley civilisation centre but a complete contrast to Harappa. Although the British had constructed the original airport in 1922, because the area was his birthplace, Prime Minister Zulfiqar Ali Bhutto reconstructed the airport and had it updated into what it surprisingly was when we flew from Multan. But whereas Harappa today is a living village on the original site, Mohenjo-Daro was never used for further habitation. Michaël Jansen from the University of Aachen, an architect who was engaged in re-surveying the entire site when we visited, commented that the lack of further use was surprising in an area where inundation is the chief problem. The most noticeable feature of Mohenjo-Daro is the Buddhist stupa, but 'the Mound of the Dead' was never used for additional dwelling, and Muslim tombs are even absent. Beside the stupa and adjacent monastery, there are no other Buddhist links. All in all, there is a mystery to the site. But at least I was able to bathe a couple of times in the nearby Indus River.

❋

The next destination was Hong Kong. This became a culinary delight including Peking duck and other delicacies. I rented a car one day, and this was the very first time I had driven with the steering wheel on the right-hand side. Hong Kong was perhaps not the best place to begin such a feat, and if it were not for Richard's screaming, who knows what I might have hit when turning? In addition, it was no longer the Hong Kong of Suzie Wong. But I was able to worship at several Mazu (Tin Hau, Queen of Heaven, Goddess of the Sea) temples as well as those of Man Mo (to Man the god of literature and Mo the god of war), Pak Tai Mui (to Pak Tai the Daoist god of the sea and Supreme Emperor of the Northern Heaven), Hung Shing (to an apotheosised government official of the Tang Dynasty), Kwun Yum (to the Buddhist goddess of mercy Guan Yin) and perhaps one to Confucius, I was not certain. I also found a Hindu temple that contained Laxmi-Narayan and Śiva-Parvati. Other interesting places included the Daoist retreat of Ching Chung Koon in Tuen Mun and the Ten Thousand Buddhas (so-called) Monastery in the New Territory. This last, founded only in 1951, was especially interesting because in a hall to the upper right there were photos of the complex's founder, the Venerable Yuet Kai, putting himself into the lotus position (presumably in 1965) and his intact body in the same pose next to the photos and dating supposedly from the time the photos were taken. But what was interesting was the difference between Chinese and Hindu temples and the deification of humans that is a striking feature of Chinese worship.

And writing this some nearly forty years later, Hong Kong is currently caught up in a so far four-year protest. I have been to Hong Kong a second time as part of the Citizen Ambassador Program's Religion and Philosophy Delegation to the People's Republic of China in 1994. We were interested in particular with religion in present-day China, how it was being approached within teaching and research institutions, and, under Marxist-Maoist dominance and the excesses of the 1966–1976 Cultural Revolution, how it has survived among the people at large. Beside Hong Kong, the delegation visited Shanghai, Qufu and Beijing. This was three years before Britain transferred the sovereignty over its territory to mainland China. With the memory of the 1989 Tiananmen Square demonstrations continually in mind, however, the present situation in Hong Kong has seemed precariously dangerous.

I will return to my delegation visit to China later, but after Hong Kong in 1981, our Pan Am flight took Richard and me to Bangkok. I continued my explorations and *puja* activities in Thailand. As I write this now, I am struck by how worshipful veneration appears to be almost incommensurate with the advancing secular norms of today's society. In the least, it requires a time factor, although personally I find this can be minimal. Much of ritual acknowledgement may be as simple as a token expression. But even for the dominant features of contemporary paganism, perhaps especially Wicca, assertion becomes more of a behavioural matter rather than bona fide adoration of deity. In Bangkok, there is the Lak Muang or foundation stone pillar of the city exhibiting Buddhist accretions but also a solidly flourishing pagan cult. I further discovered a highly decorated and revered *lingam* before the western façade of the Wat Pho (Temple of the Reclining Buddha). The mix of Hindu elements with Buddhism was intriguing – the Hindu suggesting the presence of a perennial counter-cult, though this veneration of the *anima/animus* was less conspicuous in the north (Chiang Mai), although even here there is the Phra Sae Tang Tamani – a rain-bringing and evil spirit-averting dark crystal Buddha. Concerning this image and conforming to Asia overall – including even China, there appears to be ample acknowledgement of the numinous, and it is this last that seems largely incompatible to the high-speed mechanical materialism that strikes me as what is nowadays exalted in the West.

In Bangkok itself, I found the Marble Temple (Wat Benchamabophit) to be extraordinarily lovely. Among the many other Buddhist centres I was able to visit, the Wat Arun (Temple of Dawn) and the Wat Trimitr (the Golden Buddha) were noteworthy. In addition, there are ubiquitous spirit houses witnessing animistic veneration that integrates spirituality to the land itself. I also found both a Tamil Hindu temple to Mariamman and Śiva on the Silom Road (south Indian for the most part but with strong Thai Hindu and Buddhist cultic elements) and a Chinese temple (Wat Mangkon Kamalawat) on the Charoen Krung or New Road that contained an adjacent second temple in gold and black with three main altars – one of the most beautiful Mahayana Buddhist temples I have seen anywhere.

In the Pramane Ground before the Royal Hotel where we lodged, there is a magnificent gold-leafed shrine of Nang Toranee, the earth-mother goddess. Of course, I am always interested to find any remnants of worship of Indra, the king of the gods. One of the most actively popular shrines in Bangkok is the Erawan, that is, to Indra's elephant vehicle though here with the god Brahma astride. It was only at the nearby Indra Hotel could I find an actual shrine to the thunder-lord. And I did find an Indra on Erawana facing east at the Phra Prang Sam Yot (1191) in Lop Buri, a former capital northeast of Bangkok. In all and in reference to the cultic, the ease of spiritual devotion makes Thailand similar to India. For both countries, cultivation of the extramundane is an accepted given. Our English words *culture, cult, cultic* and *cultivation* derive from the Latin verb *colere* (past participle *cultus*) that signifies both 'worship' and 'tilling the earth'. This intimate connection of the telluric with veneration is as pagan as it gets and suggests the aboriginal tie between devotion and the earth that is the incipient foundation of all idolisation and cultic adulation. Its absence in the West is what the sociologist Max Weber refers to as 'disenchantment' (*die Entzauberung der Welt*). Accordingly, in the exaltation of *progress* through Calvinist capitalism, its resultant bureaucracy functions as the 'iron cage' of modernity. Perhaps it was Weber's nervous breakdown that was necessary for his subsequent insight into the consequences that stem from the Enlightenment's rationalism and the elimination of magic as a necessary social and organisational operative. With its impersonal systemisation, modern capitalism from the viewpoint of Weber's disenchantment theory only incompletely at best serves human needs and desires.

One further memorable event in Bangkok, however, was a roadside stand in front of the train station. We enjoyed from there the most delicious chicken breasts – so delicious, in fact, that we had to return a second time to have them again. For Thailand itself, maybe not as colourful as India (as if anything else could be) but gentler, it is both intriguing and beautiful. And its beaches are renowned; we got for a few days at least to Pattaya.

But if there is a living pagan tradition that resonates the closest to my own pagan sentiments, it would be the Shinto of Japan – an earth-oriented spirituality that is as much at home in the urban environment as in the countryside – one that in fact often brings the natural world into the city itself. Even with the *shinbutsu bunri* or separation of Shinto from Buddhism inaugurated by the Meiji government in 1868, Japanese religion has remained in truth an amalgamation of the two faiths. But if we were to strip away the Buddhist overlay and focus on Shinto alone, what we have is something that is refreshingly jejune. Worship before the *kami* or Japanese deities consists of clapping one's hands and bowing. These sequential gestures resonate as conforming more appropriately with the habits of Western Protestant non-demonstrative minimalism, though I will still maintain that there is an unparalleled thrill to be attained in full prostration before a Hindu deity. Be this as it may, Shinto engages more directly with the natural world – there is predominantly an element of nature incorporated into the Shinto shrine, its *kami* are more directly personifications of or connected to the features of nature, and there are also the popular Dōsojin tutelary deities of roads and borders along with the cultic presence of phallic fetishes – both in honour of fertility. Noteworthy of the presence of a phallus is the Hanazono shrine in

Tokyo's Shinjuku ward. The sanctum is dedicated to the rice-deity Inari who has been described as an androgynous god of fertility and worldly success.

Design, pattern and rubbish present portals for possibilities of immersion. Contemporary journeys into sound and space, like Shinto shrines but now often technologically assisted, become acts of surrounding oneself with a culture of place or thought. Submerging into any cultural or religious framework allows a particular comprehension. Whether one permits oneself to be absorbed into a Hindu, Christian, Shinto or some other spiritual experience, there is at least an engaged involvement if not also an actual understanding. Submersion into a pagan framework itself resonates more broadly with deep mental involvement into the recent and current, and among the video screens, virtual realities and stroboscopic projections of present-day art installations there is almost inevitably also the inclusion of the wild and untamed of nature either represented or in actuality. This balance in avant-garde art between the cutting-edge high-tech and the natural of the uncultivated finds a parallel in Shintoism's incorporation of the organic within the physical structure of its shrines. In traditional Japanese spirituality, this is different of course from the innovative ultra-modern and unfamiliar, but the same principle of vestigial parity is nevertheless retained.

Apart from the culinary delights of Japan, there is not only an overall encounter with the urban as itself something awesome but also engagement with an indigenous and different kind of spirituality as well as with the enchanting beauty of the country's land itself. The Japanese let themselves be inspired by nature; this is obvious. Amidst the unbelievably bustling ultra-modern metropolis of Tokyo, I first came across the Joen-ji Temple which was one of the most perfect houses of worship I had ever seen. With its flawless taste and quiet but complete beauty, it is an aesthetic masterpiece. And yet, I was able to appreciate the temple as a quintessence of pagan expression in combining the old and the new. In Japan, Buddhist places of worship are designated temples while those belonging to Shintoism are called shrines. A Shinto shrine would be almost inevitably situated near a significant Buddhist temple, or on its grounds. Typical in this respect would be the Senso-ji or Asakusa Kannon Temple, perhaps Tokyo's oldest and certainly among the most popular and colourful. Not far to the left of the temple is the Asakusa Shrine. Although constructed only in 1649 by the Edo Shogun Tokugawa Iemitsu, virtually a millennium after the temple had been originally erected, it still appeared to me as a classic example of a later universalistic and missionising religion usurping a holy site belonging originally to another cult. One can assume that the locale was originally Shinto even though the present shrine building is much more recent. As the Sanja-sama or Shrine of the Three Gods, the Asakusa Shrine is dedicated to the two fishermen who discovered a statuette of Kannon (Kwan Yin) in their nets and the Buddhist landlord who converted the men and consecrated a small temple for the statue. While more than once the fishermen reputedly returned the Goddess of Mercy figure back into the Sumida River, the statue would, as the legend has it, always return to them.

Thinking now of a perhaps Japanese rose window rather than a gothic one, among the other Tokyo shrines I visited were the Gojoten (to the Tokugawa Shogunate founder Tokugawa Ieyasu), the magnificently beautiful Toshogu ('Sun-god of the east'), the *nagare-zukuri* styled Meiji (dedicated to Emperor Meiji and Empress Shōken) and, when I was again in Tokyo 24 years later, the Hikawa (for the sea and storm-god Susanoo), Takanawa (for business, academic and family success), Inari Daiichi-Keiki (god of cereal and fertility), Mite-Hachiman (tutelary god of war, divination and culture), Ueno Tōshōgū (again for Tokugawa Ieyasu), the Atago at Tokyo's highest elevation (to the fire-god Homusubi and others), the street-corner Hibiya (occupying one of Tokyo's 'power spots'), the family-run Sakurada (popular for weddings), the Nogi (where the general & his wife who committed suicide upon the death of Emperor Meiji are buried), the hill-top Hiei (to the quasi-Buddhist god of Mt. Hiei) and among others the controversial Yasukuni-Jinja (with a memorial museum attached commemorating Japan's war dead). Interesting also was the over-ornate Tōshōgū shrine to Tokugawa Ieyasu which, as a Shogunate structure, contrasts with the simpler elegance of imperial shrines. An accessible favourite, however, was near my hotel in Shinagawa, namely, the duskily patinaed Takayama Shinto Shrine for Inari that is ancient but crammed between buildings near the train station. Among Japanese Buddhist temples I have visited, there are the Horyuji (main temple of the Shōtoku Shū), the Higashi-Honganji (headquarters of the Jōdo Shinshū sect), the Kofukuji (the Mahayana Hossō school) with its five-storied pagoda, the small Sengakuji (Sōtō Zen), the Shōshūji and the Zōjōji (main temple of the Jōdo-shū Chinzei sect). In all, while the Buddhist temples are impressively spectacular, I continued to find the Shinto places as possessing a quiet earthly gentleness that at their core is organically pagan. And what I was able to re-affirm in 2005 is that the Japanese folk Shinto-Buddhism amalgam is certainly among the more important allies for the fledgling Western pagan cause.

Along with the continual fascination with temples and shrines, there is also the geographic beauty of Japan. As our flight from Bangkok was arriving in Tokyo, there was suddenly visible from the plane the deepest of crimson suns half-setting into a cloudbank – reminiscent of the nation's flag. In the city itself, I was particularly impressed by the densely thick park setting of the Meiji Shrine with its long tree-lined vista-channelling roadways. From Tokyo, we took the Shinkansen or bullet train to Kyoto, the country's former capital. From the train, we could see the snow cap of Mt. Fuji which appeared to float like a misted bridal veil in the air. In Kyoto itself, besides such treasured shrines as the Shimogamo, the Yoshida, the Heian (large and grand as a replica of the Imperial Palace) and the Yasaka (dedicated to Susanoo no Mikoto, Amaterasu's younger brother) – this last a pure delight being popular, open, peaceful and alive, there are several magnificent parks. The Shugakuin Imperial Villa, built in the 17th century, is a set of wondrous gardens with panoramic vistas competing with lush forests laced with tiny waterfalls. The atmosphere put me into a complete dream trance in which I contemplated divine vulnerability and the differences between mortal and immortal gods – the former, perhaps Indo-European deities who are like kin to humanity; the latter, Yahweh and the Brahmanic *trimurti*. But as overwhelmingly impressive as were Kyoto's parks and gardens and Buddhist temples such as the antique and rustic wooden structures of the Daitokuji Temple (a Rinzai Zen centre) which seemed to me like an immaculate and prosperous Beverly Hills, or the superlative-defying gardens of the Katsura Imperial Villa, it was invariably the Shinto shrines, smaller but pregnant with 'things' to discover, that exuded a more comprehensible numinousness. In the Imamiya Shrine, for instance, to the left was a tiny knoll or grove ringed by a low fencing and possessing a small shrine house along with a lovely stream passing through its grounds. This was balanced on the right side by an enclosed area containing a few large stones and touched by a fine gentleness.

Since the vernal equinox in Japan is a major public holiday, a time for visiting relatives and family burial sites, we learned from our *ryokan* in Kyoto that we would need to vacate our room for the day itself. There were no possibilities for lodging anywhere in the city, and the tourist office arranged for us to spend two nights on the coast in Koshika. For me, the presence of the Pacific Ocean was restorative. We walked along the beach climbing onto and off rocky peninsulas.

The Ise Shrines are the most sacred in Japan. The Geku or Outer Shrine is dedicated to Toyouke-Omikami, the Goddess of Farms, Harvest, Food and Seri-culture. There are also the auxiliary shrines of both the moon-god and the wind-god who is the divinity of the grounds. The Naiku or Inner Shrine is that of the Sun-goddess Ameratsu-Omikami. In Shinto, as with the Germanic, Baltic and Slavic cultures, the sun is feminine. In Ise, both shrines are combinations of majesty and directness with forests enveloping them. And the next day, at Futamigaura, we viewed the Meteo-Iwa ('Wedded Rocks') – two large boulders in the sea linked by a *shimenawa* or sacred rice straw rope and representing the primal parents, Izanagi and Izanami. I found the site to be superbly otherworldly, and in contrast to the beauty of Toba Bay, pristine and quiet – with the enchantment of the sea, her calm surface glistening at dusk and waves gently capping the breakwaters. It was one of the most awesome spots I encountered in Japan.

After a night in Toba, we proceeded to Yunomine Spa. Here we enjoyed the sulphur hot springs and were able to cook yams and eggs in the central source. There were some captivating paths ascending the hill behind the inn in which we stayed. I was able joyously to savour the mosses, ferns, rocks and thick pine groves and sat for a while in the sun to listen to the song of the birds. I was again struck by the occasional necessity for immersion in verdant nature. This was a moment for vistas, lush beauty and communing with mountain peaks. Later we took an even more lovely trail across the mountain on the other side of the road from our inn. We picnicked on our yams in various sunny spots and even fell asleep. It was pure heaven. At some point, I teased Richard by showing him what looked like a bear paw print in the path. The next day as we were leaving for Matsue via Kyoto, we saw by the side of the road a recently captured large bear in chains.

The Izumo Taisha Shrine in Matsue is the second most important Shinto centre after Ise, but for me it is at once far more open and accessible and greatly more unassuming and amiable. One is allowed to walk about the complex, and though entry within the inner fence is not allowed, the fence itself is unblocked and permits an ample viewing of the interior. Diagrams of the main shrine are provided, and photography is not discouraged. The shrine is dedicated to the affable and good-natured Daikoku-sama (Okuninushi-no-Mikoto) – a six-generation descendant of Susanoo but also that Kami's son-in-law, a god of nation-building, farming, medicine and business as well as the ruler of the unseen world of spirits and magic. In all, this sanctum was perhaps the most appealing of all I was able to encounter in Japan. And in the general vicinity there are both the Miko Shrine (for Daikoku's son Ebisu, the laughing god of fishermen and luck) and the marriage and match-making Yaegaki Shrine (for Susanoo and his consort) in which there is a spring (the Mirror Pond) on which people float paper lots carrying a coin – the length of time before the *o-mikumi* sinks being an indication of the success of one's marriage. I also remember when visiting Matsue, both the lulling waters of the Sea of Japan and the sunset over the pastel-shaded mountains behind Lake Shinji.

Japan proved to be surprisingly expensive. I had used up most of my cash before reaching the country thinking that I would be able to secure more funds once I reached Tokyo. In these days I had only an American Express card which I used to obtain money at a bank upon my arrival. But in two days, I had spent all that I had and returned to the bank only to learn that since I had just used my card I would need to wait two weeks before I could obtain more currency. In 1981, I had not yet acquired a Visa or MasterCard which in Japan I would have been able to use ubiquitously at the time. Consequently, much of what Richard and I consumed food-wise was what we purchased in supermarkets and the like. Finally, in Kyoto we found a restaurant named Matsubatu that displayed a large American Express sign. This proved to be our best meal of all in Japan that included fresh bamboo sprouts, 'seaplants' and sake. However, when the bill was presented, it was explained that if I paid in cash I would be exempt from the enormous tax surcharge that was required to be included if I paid with my credit card.

For visitors to Japan, the tourist agency had a programme though which one could meet people in a Japanese home. I had asked specifically for a Shinto family, but our host, a surprisingly energetic and spirited 93-year old leading artist of the Sume Nanga ('Southern Painting') School, was a Mr. Shuson Kono and not Shinto. We were accompanied by a young Japanese student, Nabata, who translated for us nicely but was himself utterly bored by the occasion. Mr. Shuson insisted that he was not Shinto or Buddhist but an atheist who had, like his parents, no religion whatsoever. However, when we were ushered into his studio, I noticed on a stage an altar with a figure of Kannon and evidence of freshly burned incense. The curtain of the stage was quickly drawn. Eventually we were seated in another part of the house and served tea. To make conversation, I asked about a small photo on the far wall. Excitedly, Mr. Shuson padded over to it and brought it back for us to see. He had secured one of the highest awards in Japan, and the photo showed him receiving the medal from the Emperor. With that presentation and explanation of the photo, I have never seen such a transformation in a person. Nabata's boredom utterly vanished, and he could not have been bowing more deeply in humbled and awed honour to our artist in the time that still ensued for our visit.

There were two further sites for us before we left Japan. One was the very popular and equally marvellous Fushima Inari Shrine in Kyoto where we climbed the *torii* covered paths, virtually tunnels, up the mountain to the sanctum itself. This was a fascinating spot – very pagan, heavy cult and a fabulous woods. There were also many sacred stones as well as images of foxes who are the attendants of the five *kami* honoured here. The other site was the Naritasan Shinshojin Temple. We had miscalculated in trying to reach by train the airport in Narita and missed our departing flight. As a result, we had an unexpected extra day in Narita itself and were able to encounter this most splendid Buddhist temple that unlike all the others I had visited is of the Shingon sect. What was especially appealing was the colour of the place and the surrender to the irrational. There were exquisite old wooden structures, a Shinto blend, and the priests within the temple buildings all discretely watching TV.

CHAPTER FIVE

Hawai'i / Vatican approval of spirit-worship / submissions rejected / non-academic accusations / the contrast of telluric paganism with Platonic, Neoplatonic and gnostic understandings / Stephen Fry's *Mythos* & post-colonial attempts toward self-determination / the 'ideal-type' as a tool for measurement / 'pagan' as an expression of marginality / the 1993 Parliament of the World's Religions & Alexander VI's 1493 *Inter Caetera* papal bull – the Doctrine of Discovery; the *heiau* of O'ahu & Kauai / Robert Corrington's 'semiotic plenitude' / *Kahuna*; back in America & San Francisco / my 1960 peyote trip / my days in the US Army / Los Angeles / San Francisco State College / the Haight-Ashbury days / Russian Hill / nude-bathing & muffin consumption / the secret of the universe / the Strawberry Hill Coven & the psychiatric ward of the University of California Hospital / the nocturnal stellar skies beyond San Francisco / Anton LaVey's catechism classes / my unrequited heartache / my unmoored & oarless row boat; Theodore Adorno / my bourgeois melomania / pleasure / my sonnets / Claude Debussy / the biblical condemnation of idolatry / pagan utilisation of the liminal potencies of communitas / life is short but wondrous; the Angwin May Pole ceremony / New Orleans / Voodoo / St. Expedite / the East Coast in 1982: New Jersey, New York & Rhode Island / possessions are not selfhood / the body & dream souls / to be & to be able / fires in the Provence / immortality / a Latin American music concert in Amsterdam / the museum as a pagan temple / 1982 ends; Bill Bryson / 1950s America / Maplewood / the MYF / Father Divine & Billy Graham / the 1953 Boy Scout Jamboree / Pit / *Peyton Place*; celebrities; the gods, Zeus and divine incest; Summer of Love / Nureyev and Fonteyn / Namsos / Tenino / Fritz Perls / my inheritance / San Francisco departure party; comtemporary music / magic / 2019 COP25 / millenarian & utopian expectation / ecodems / Nietzsche and Camus / the gnostic-pagan divergence / absurdity; life after death; the Provence / temporary durable metaphors / postmodernism / Jove / commodification and empty alienation / the pagan flow

And after Japan, it was the *heiau*-studded islands of the mid-Pacific. The Hawaiian temples or *heiau* vary from terraces to stone platforms but presumably unroofed and always open to the skies. They also ranged in their purposes – some for healing or offerings; others for military success or control of rain. With the 1819 collapse of *'Ai Noa* or the system of taboos (kapu) connected to *kahuna* or Hawaiian religion and the arrival shortly thereafter of Christian missionaries, the *heiau* were for the most part destroyed or fell into disrepair. But when visiting some of these temple sites on Oahu and Kauai, the presence of cultic offerings was nonetheless evident – bespeaking a, perhaps *sub rosa*, persistence of indigenous belief and practice.

As I am currently reflecting on 'Hawaiian paganism' more than three decades later, I am reading a highly critical article on the 'Vatican approval of spirit-worship' that Pope Francis appears to be promoting. Presumably the Pope's effort is to counter the dearth of clergy in such places as the Amazon, but the opposition to these papal initiatives clearly delineates the identity of indigenous paganism or at least the affinity between indigenous spirituality and what we might with some largess qualify as pagan religiosity. For instance, the German cardinal Walter Brandmüller claims that the document that had been prepared for the synod that was to take place in October 2019 is 'heretical' because it respects indigenous faiths and their veneration of nature. Brandmüller has said, 'In the context of the call for harmony with nature, there is even talk about the dialogue with the spirits.' For him, 'Mother Earth' is reminiscent of the 'pantheistic idolatry of nature' that was formerly espoused by the Hitler Youth. This conservative view has been echoed by Gerhard Müller who had been the prefect of the Congregation for the Doctrine of the Faith and who insists that the 'identification of God with nature is a form of atheism, because God is independent of nature.' Moreover, according to Müller, 'Man is the centre of creation and Jesus became man, he did not become a plant'. This last reminds me of John Allegro's highly controversial 1970 book *The Sacred Mushroom and the Cross* in which Christ is alleged to have been a mythological creation of entheogen-consuming shamans, but it also raises the anthropocentric question that many contemporary pagans address and that makes the natural world subservient to humanity.

Currently, I have also had various submissions to the pagan journal *The Pomegranate* rejected and have received criticism as an academic from other sources as well. As Ethan Doyle White remarks, my 2003 *Pagan Theology: Paganism as a World Religion* is 'controversial'. The controversy stems from my contention that paganism or, if you will, Paganism is a broader phenomenon than being merely contemporary Western paganism but includes such other spiritualities as Shinto, Chinese Folk Religion, the Afro-American syncretic movements and indigenous religions. I will come to discuss this issue further, but when the Djap Wurrung trees in western Victoria that are sacred to the Aboriginals are threatened by road construction or the

Australian government declares, in respect to protection of revered land against bauxite mining in the Northern Territories by the Nabalco and Rio Tinto excavation companies, that jobs are more important, the indigenous concern is the same as that held by many if not most Western pagans. The contended matter is at the heart of what sacrality means for an overall pagan mindset in contrast to Abrahamic and mechanistic secular considerations and even those of dharmic persuasion. While my own interest is first as a pagan rather than as an academic, I retain immense respect for scientific methodology and investigative value-neutrality but often feel akin to Claude Debussy in his rejection of the conservative strictures of the Paris Conservatoire.

I have been accused of being non-academic because I consider the intra-faith theological conversation of paganism as being 'fun'. Moreover, my employing the term 'embargo' for the ignoring of polytheology as a discipline is supposedly biased language, and I have been criticised for using on occasion online sources. Admittedly and as anyone who has reached this far in this book knows, I do express subjective views and beliefs, though in an academic work I will seek to say as much when I do and otherwise remain as objective as possible. Having investigated paganism, both contemporary and traditional, for at least four decades, I will sometimes use myself as an authority without repeating the data from fieldwork and research I have presented in earlier and more academic works. While I do not agree, my understanding of Neoplatonism and Gnosticism has been judged as inaccurate. And I have a tendency to present analytic descriptions rather than a concise or immediate definition. In fact, definition is something I argue, in more complicated areas such as understanding religion or paganism, that one works toward rather than something with which one can always simply begin.

Reputedly, in an assessment of my paper on Tellurian Paganism for possible publication, one comment is that 'The Plotinian and Iamblichean theological and cosmological perspectives are vastly different'. Of course, they are different, but how different is 'vastly different'? They both follow in a derivative tradition from Platonism that is fundamentally different from a geocentric understanding such as paganism or at least that pagan expression that is telluric in contrast to Platonic, Neoplatonic and gnostic. I have found that there are three essential or fundamental branches to contemporary paganism if not to paganism more globally, namely, secular, gnostic and telluric. I applaud and champion them all, but it is the last that is my chief concern and the specific focus of this book. Again, I am with both Spinoza and Nietzsche in their rejection of the transcendental for an immanent reality. I do see and accept transcendence as an emergence from the physical but not as a primordial agent of creation, and regardless of whether this alleged agent is personal or impersonal. I have read – and in part agree – that we do not have a body but we individually *are* a body. Personally, I feel that we may be or become something more (such as in the concept of 'soul-duality'), but this is a different matter. My own bottom line remains, namely, 'matter matters'. In other words, it is both that the physical is supremely important and what it does is physicality. Matter mattering is itself an emanation. Along with Spinoza and Nietzsche, I abandon Plato's consideration that the body is to be despised as the prison of the soul and that its passions are to be severely controlled if not eliminated altogether. Along with this, I thrill with the description of Spinoza as a 'God-intoxicated' person. His *Deus sive Natura* may say it all. Nature is divine and the whole of divinity, and nature is all that is. In my own understanding of pantheism, I employ the metaphor of 'co-nature'. This last is still the natural but other than the empirical. It includes the spheres of morality, art and religion, and it opens up the notion of a possibility of there being ontic 'hinterworlds'. It is essentially here where I diverge from my Spinoza and Nietzsche heroes. For me, the other-worldly is not necessarily a fiction. But admittedly, all this is theology, but it also is an ongoing – and for me a welcomed – part of the pagan discourse.

In all, it is a battle, or so it seems. Having recently been to the Palladian Theatre for Stephen Fry's *Mythos,* it was for me utterly refreshing to hear someone address the Greek and Roman gods through story and the gods' own diversity. Fry is not intimidated by 'political correctness' or post-colonial criticism. I do not possess quite the same largesse and have been more engaged in debate and exchange than with storytelling itself. I have also been castigated for having 'cast the net out too wide', and Religious Studies scholar Melissa Raphael has pointed out that many of the groups I label as 'pagan' would emphatically object to being associated with that 'category'. Likewise, sociologist Mary Jo Neitz argues that I gloss over significant differences. Similarly, pagan scholar Michael Strmiska levels the critique that I am doing a disservice to the struggle for post-colonial attempts toward self-determination.

The problem with all these encountered challenges is with the conflation of classification with measurement. I am employing the sociologist's tool known as the 'ideal type' in seeking to understand the distinction between

Abrahamic, dharmic, pagan and secularist (or non-religious secularist) expressions. Granted that the ideal-type is frequently confused with categorisation, but as a tool it is something the sociologist employs to understand any particular religion or spirituality and how closely it appears to approximate a distinct ideal. In fact, the four ideal-types are applicable to every religion as a means of signalling how and perhaps why a specific persuasion falls short of each ideal-type. Obviously, Christianity, Islam, Bahá'í and Judaism conform the most closely to the Abrahamic ideal but still not equally or in the same ways. Likewise, Hinduism and Buddhism correspond the most to the dharmic ideal. And my contention is that the religions of the pre-Christian classical world as well as the beliefs and practices of most indigenous peoples come the closest to what we can formulate as the 'pagan ideal-type'. This would be in contrast to any conformity they will also have to Abrahamic, dharmic and secular idealisations.

Consequently, use of the ideal-type as a tool for measurement precisely reveals difference and individuality rather than being a mechanism for 'glossing over significant divergences'. It provides a start for a study rather than its conclusion. But at the same time, religions can be grouped as generically similar in their approximation to one particular ideal over the others. Our present-day objection to being labelled in a way that does not conform to our own sense of self-identity is more a handicap to balanced enlightenment than it is a means to restore a lost cause. The protest against the use of a Eurocentric term for describing or just studying a formerly colonised people is unproductively myopic. If there were a better term than 'pagan', we might be able to reach a different semantic ballpark, but 'earth religion' or 'nature religion' do not include within their remit what has so far been useful with the term 'pagan'. If we could come up with a new and different designation, that would be fine, but so far we have not. The irony is that the term 'pagan' had historically become something to convey 'marginality', 'opprobrium' and 'othering' – precisely the disapproved status of imperialistically subjected or colonised peoples. The incongruity is also to be found in that the term 'pagan' derives from the Roman *pagus* – an early designation for a local district, whether a city ward or rural vicinity of the country. In other words, and as already has been mentioned in Chapter 3, a *paganus* or resident of a *pagus* is a local. It is only with the subsequent ascendency of Christianity that the last of the non-urban and unconverted *pagani* became re-interpreted as 'country-bumpkins'. Originally, the pagan was understood to be a member of a local community – an archaic understanding that is in general applicable to both indigenous peoples and non-Christian resurgences in the West.

The affinity between contemporary Western pagans and native ethnics, apart for that more New Age branch of paganism that I (maybe reluctantly) also accept as a denominational form of paganism, is *not* a license for appropriation – especially insensitive appropriation – of native practices by Western spiritualists. The affinity only allows the ungrounded and inchoate segment of contemporary society to *learn* and not steal from the elder and already long-established self-sufficient traditions. One detectable chord that appears to be emerging in the West is that, as former 'oppressors and colonisers', there is now a reversal and willingness to be taught by those who are closer to the earth and have preserved more of their ancestral understandings.

At the 1993 Parliament in Chicago, Navajo and clinical social worker Omie Baldwin had it right when she informed me that most Native Americans would object to my ASP efforts toward uniting animists, shamanists and polytheists because the indigenes identify as Christians. This is fact rather than labelling. The Amerindians were not originally Christian, and in this case I was attempting to appeal to an earlier religiosity. All the same, labels are also sometimes important and useful in the overall scheme of things. One might object to being called a pagan, but even in face of my own dislike of being an American that has globally been imperialist and bullying, I still cannot deny that I am American. I may deplore the deceit and disloyalty that my birth-country has employed when treaties signed with Native Americans were later unilaterally discarded when deemed no longer advantageous, or, equally, the Euro-American continuance of the *Inter caetera* papal bull issued by Pope Alexander VI in 1493, the Doctrine of Discovery, which allowed the right of ownership to lands not inhabited by Christians, but my attitude does not preclude the applicability of American identity to me. Rather than deny the undeniable, I wonder if it is not a better course toward learning from the past and proceeding into a positively reformed future by acknowledging the reality of the unwanted and distasteful.

In Honolulu, I managed to find a Shinto shrine just across from the YMCA at Waikiki where we were staying. More emotionally moving, however, was Waimea on the far side of O'ahu. Here we ascended to the rectangular rock wall of the Pu'u-o-mahuka ('Hill of Escape') Heiau, the largest on the island. The space was filled with prayer stones wrapped in *tī* fronds and placed on top of piles of larger rocks. According to the legend, the name of the temple refers to the place from which the volcano-goddess Pele leaped to the island of Molokai. Originally, the temple, besides being a place for offerings, would have included an altar as well as fire and water and places for housing sacred drums and other objects.

On the neighbouring island of Kauai, there is the Wailua River State Park which contains the Wailua Complex of Heiaus. This includes the Ka Lae O Ka Manu ('the crest of the bird') or Hikinaakala ('the rising sun') temple platform or heiau near the mouth of the river. Although with less evidence of cult, this presumably oldest *heiau* of Kauai has been partially restored and is maintained by the state in quiet, beautiful Celtic-like splendour. A flat stone is situated in the southwest corner. This may have been an altar, but not far from the temple are the Pohaku Piko (a ceremonial niche for a royal newborn's umbilical cord), the Pohaku Ho'ohanau (or royal birthstone) and the Holo-Holo-Ku (the birthstone of the Ho'ohanau area). Once again, the numinousness of the domain is undeniably evident. Further upstream on a bluff overlooking the river is the Poliahau Heiau that was reputedly built by the Menehunes (the dwarfs or brownies of Hawai'i) which was heavily overgrown and more reminiscent of Pu'u-o-mahuka at Waimea on O'ahu than the pristinely manicured but delightful shrine of Ka Lae O Ka Manu. Nearby is the Wailua Bellstone that was used to convey important messages. This was actually two large portal rocks. The *menehune* are also believed to have constructed the Malae *heiau* near the mouth of the Wailua River but south. This temple is not open to the public. In the park itself are the Opaeka Falls and the Fern Grotto, both of which are magnificent. Near Ka Lae O Ka Manu, the religious centre of Wailua also includes Hauola, a *pu'uhonua* or sacred place of refuge for those who had broken the religious, political or social laws of *kapu* and who might be able there to escape punishment.

Apart from the lush beauty of the Hawai'an islands, they also still convey the animistic spirituality of Polynesian religion. Beside Native Hawaiians, the Polynesian people include the Maori of New Zealand, the Samoans, Tahitians, Tongan and others. Despite having gods and myths about their gods, they also adhere to an animistic religiosity centred on *mana* or divine power. For instance, in Hawai'i, the *tí* plant is medicinal and possesses many other uses as well. It is considered to have much *mana*. The integration of the sacred with time and space allows for sacred areas to be places in which the animating force of *mana* is concentrated. Robert Corrington identifies the sacrality inherent in special places as areas possessing 'semiotic plenitude'. Animistic religion, however, also introduces the idea of possible pollution, such as the breaking of *kapu*, and the subsequent need for ritual purification. *Kahuna* religion entertains the ability to approach the gods and spirits through ritual, sacrifice and magic. And, of course, this intermixing of religion and magic along with the belief that ceremony can produce tangible results is pagan. While my time in Hawai'i was brief, and I only visited a few of the *heiaus*, I still considered myself fortunate to have been able to feel a pagan consciousness that is inherent in the land.

❊

And, for the first time since just after my brother's funeral, I was once again back on Californian soil. From Honolulu, we had flown to San Francisco, the old stomping grounds. A 5 a.m. interruption one morning and glancing from Bernal Heights, there was the barest hint of the day to come beyond Telegraph Hill. Why is she such a marvel? What makes her so beautiful and captivating? It was only a peek of the City by the Bay but yet an indelible touch of enchantment. Reconnecting with loved ones and some of The Family members was a complete joy. This last included a major family reunion at Coral's residence north of Cazadero. It seemed miraculous that the area where she was still existed. It was a land of leprechauns and outside the law battles between pot growers, pot bandits, and sheriffs and/or other policing officials. But certainly, when the gods made the earth, they displayed flawless fantasy when it came to the northern California coast. And Marlowe probably summed things up when he said, 'Michael is the only person who can completely get your attention and then forget what he was talking about'.

I believe it may have been for the Easter holiday that I had agreed to accompany John, my university roommate in Santa Barbara, to San Francisco. This was my first visit to the city, and the occasion was to engage in a peyote experience with Langston Bowen. Three years previously, it had been Gordon Wasson's 1957 photo essay in *Life* magazine describing his psilocybin mushroom consumption during a Mazatec ritual in Oaxaca, Mexico that had provoked my unquenchable desire for psychedelic engagement. Langston had warned us that if we went outside, we might stare at a lamppost thinking it was only five minutes but in actuality it might be a couple of hours. I did go outside after sitting rapturously on a multi-coloured cosmic cobweb enthralled by the music of Bartok, Shostakovich and Debussy and then managed to get myself lost in some remote part of the city. Some friendly people helped me re-find Langston's home. But throughout there was something uniquely thrilling about San Francisco – her feeling, her air, her wisps of fog, and her silent pulsations beneath all. In the morning, Langston made fresh pancakes to the music of Bach's *Brandenburg Concertos*.

There were of course subsequent visits to the bay side city and subsequent peyote consumptions, and for the summer of 1960 I attended summer school at the University of California in Berkeley. A few years later, after Europe and Laguna Beach, I was now living in Los Angeles. I received a draft notice and went to the induction centre in downtown LA but was not believed when I told I was gay. My Hollywood roommate Pfeif brought me my toothbrush after I phoned him. He also introduced me to a friend of his who was being inducted at the same time. We shared a cabin on the train to Fort Ord and already violated that night the mandatory requirement not to engage in same-sex sex. I remember most, however, the time when the night train passed through Santa Barbara, my alma mater town, and wistfully, longingly and painfully gazing on the familiar but now inaccessible. It was already an agonizing imprisonment. I have always been a pacifist and do not know how I might react if confronted with the need to kill someone if it were a question of survival. At an early moment during the induction period prior to Basic Training, we were told that if any of us had homosexual feelings to contact a particular officer. I was reading Aldous Huxley's *Essays* at the time and was fully in accord with the idea of the individual against the state. This was my chance. I made the contact. Immediately I was removed from the standard itinerary and assigned to secretarial work in the commanding office while my situation was being assessed. A routine was quickly established. I typed, delivered messages and welcomed new draftees to their barracks. Then, apparently, two whole barracks declared themselves to be gay, and the army's response was to cancel anyone's leaving the military for reasons of homosexuality. As a consequence, I was told to prepare for Basic that night. I had been at Ford Ord by this point for four weeks. In a last desperate effort, I went to the chaplain. He was a Baptist minister and wanted me to make the promise that I would at least try not to be gay. He would see what he could do. I knew that once I got to Basic there would be no hope in getting free. Whenever I could, I would almost daily stand on the overpass across Highway 1 and watch the cars drive by in what to me represented the 'free world'. That evening, resigned to the inevitable, I was returning from dinner in the mess hall when an officer was calling out my name. I approached him in response. 'Unpack!' he said, 'You are not going'.

I was dumbfounded but managed to ask, 'Then may I have a weekend pass?' The answer was affirmative, and I went directly to San Francisco. There has never been a place more beautiful, sparkling and glittering for me than that city at that glorious moment.

I did finally secure an army discharge after six weeks in all, but not before a friend, Chuck, appeared whose lover had been drafted but had already gone on to Basic. Chuck with his auto would sneak me off base. I remember a wonderful restaurant in Monterey that was in an old-fashioned house that had been converted – the kind that I almost believe no longer exists. But what I remember most was being taken to the Gilded Cage, a gay bar, in which I was astonished to find many of the people on the base who were processing me. The one who would say 'Mary!' when I delivered him messages from my office to his told me that everyone thought I was most courageous to be doing what I was doing. I was also informed that I need not worry about the midnight curfew when the gates to Fort Ord were closed. There was a Captain among those in the bar who could take me through at any time without being questioned.

So that was my military experience. I have always been opposed to killing and emphatically did not want the training to do so. I returned to Los Angeles and worked for several years as an Assistant Buyer for the Broadway department store chain. I think it no longer exists. I was first with the china department and then with toys. And after this, I returned to San Francisco to further my education at, what was then, the San Francisco State College. The idea was to procure a Master's degree in International Relations so that I might be able to return to Europe while working for an American bank and with an American salary. With the help of Diana, a friend of a friend, I found a spacious and lovely L-shaped flat at the corner of Carl and Cole Streets in the Haight-Ashbury delicatessen district.

Two weeks after I had moved into my first home in San Francisco, the pub directly across the street, Bradley's Corner, became a gay bar. The gals who worked there would leave foods that had not been sold that day on my doorstep. In their stormy relationship, it seemed that Jeanie and April were virtually jostling to see who could become my roommate first. Jeanie was among those who worked at Bradley's – or maybe only was a customer.

She referred to herself as a 'thumper', and she was the one who got to my place before April. But that was not for a long time yet. I was introduced by someone I had met at Bradley's to Nancy who was completing her time in the army as a WAC, a member of the Women's Army Corps. He saw that she and I had much in common. Subsequently, I encountered Nancy when visiting a North Beach pub and threw out a standard phrase of the day, 'Why don't you marry me and take me away from all of this?' We both thought about it after we each had gone home and decided it was a good idea. It would satisfy our parents; it would lower our joint income taxes; and we could have an exceptional party. But that part anon.

These were fabulous days. I was relatively independent; poor, yes, but managing. I adored my studies and became a teaching assistant which probably helped with the finances to a degree. Following on from the Psychedelic Shop and the clothing shop of Nancy's friend, Peggy, within half a year, the legendary Haight-Ashbury and the centre of 'flower power' blossomed as an unforgettable moment of history. If and when I now meet someone who knew those times (something that no longer happens with any frequency), the inevitable agreement is that that exceptional time is something he or she always to today remains grateful for having known.

I used to visit Pfeif whom I had known from fraternity days at Purdue University. And we roomed together in Los Angeles. He had now been transferred to San Francisco and lived on Russian Hill. Since he was more out of the fog belt than I was, I would go to sunbathe on the roof of his building. In one section of the flat roof, there was a locked and curtained games room from which I would occasionally hear a phone ring. When the building was one day sold to David Davies, I asked the new owner if I could rent the games room. I was at the time at the peak of my youth and attractiveness, and being a gay man, he said yes. I would use Pfeif's WC in his flat two floors down, and my rent initially was $25 a month – eventually raised to $30. And I remember the sinking feeling the day when I first moved into this sixteen-windowed space that possessed the most sweeping and stunning views of San Francisco and knowing immediately that someday I would be moving out and relinquishing that treasure. But for four years or so, I lived in this unique celestial-terrestrial paradise.

Nancy worked as an occupational therapist in the psychiatric ward of the UC Hospital in Parnassus Heights. Coral was a nurse on the ward, and one weekend she with her current boyfriend Joel and Nancy and I went to Bob Sherman's ranch north of the city. On the Friday evening, a dozen or more of us were sitting around in the house when someone mentioned the swimming pool. We all then rushed to it, and virtually everyone stripped off and jumped into the waters. Nancy was astonished and said, 'Aren't they going to wear suits?'

'Apparently not', I replied and joined the rest. Nancy could not do this – at least at first; nude group bathing was too foreign an idea for her. But as the rest of us were frolicking and having a wonderful time, Nancy realised that she had to join in and from that point never looked back.

The following day, some delicious cannabis muffins were being baked. I remember when Bob walked into the kitchen and said, 'One muffin should be more than enough'. But I had already consumed five. Later I was walking along a curving pathway through the woods. I came to a bend in the road and heard a multitude of voices saying, 'Stop! Around this roadway bend lies the answer to the secret of the universe. Preserve the mystery! Don't seek to know the answer!' But, of course, it is not in my nature to pass up such a possibility of insight, so I disobeyed the advice and continued around the bend. And what did I find? – another bend in the road!

Buster was the friend through whom I had met Diana who had been the person who helped me to find the Carl Street flat in the Cole Valley adjunct to Haight-Ashbury. He was also the person who officiated for my marriage to Richard much later in Amsterdam. When we first met, a copy of Margaret Murray's *The God of the Witches* had been strategically placed on a coffee table. I noticed this and of course commented on it. And there began our desire to form a coven – if we could find others who were also interested.

As the counter-culture exploded around us, one day Nancy went to work and the hospital announced that the psychiatric ward was to be closed. Apparently, among other things, there was too much of an overload from the staff of innovative and avant-garde suggestions and possible new techniques that was emerging in those explosive times that the administration could not assimilate the influx and decided that closing the ward would be the easiest option. The upshot was that the entire ward's personnel were now on unemployment as the flower power manifestation was undergoing its ascent. The magic of the times was that whenever any one of us went to a happening, we – the staff and partners – were all there. And out of this constantly recurring encounter, we identified and came to refer to ourselves as 'the family'. This included Nancy and her partner Rosanne who worked downtown. Through Rosanne, there was Warren who worked at the same firm as did she. Lynne was a nurse on the ward who had begun an affair with Little Nancy who was the ward clerk. The other nurse was Coral, and John was a psychiatric aid. Coral made a pitch for John. John's partner Marlowe put up with this for a duration and then met Richard at Hippy Hill in Golden Gate Park and virtually said, 'Coral, look what I found!' The Richard bait worked, and Coral would open her hand to Richard saying, 'Look what I have! Would you like one?' and Richard could never say no to a tab of LSD. And with Warren's partner Jan, this was and has remained the core of our 'family'. And suddenly Buster and I had most of whom we needed for our coven.

As it turned out, Buster had second thoughts and declined to participate in our ritual – volunteering instead to be a chauffeur to transport us to Strawberry Hill in Golden Gate Park. I was operating under the assumption that a coven should comprise thirteen participants. Thirteen has proven over the years to be a most difficult number of people to assemble together purposely. It either happens spontaneously or not at all. One of our family, like Buster, did not want to be a part of our first occasion, and another person who had originally agreed to come changed his mind at the last moment. My brother Peter did join us as well as the artist Michael Barnes. And then as we had lit our bonfire, a blond chap appeared on the hill. We invited him to join us; he did, and we were thirteen. This was the birth of our Strawberry Hill Coven.

As mentioned earlier, for our 'flying ointment', I concocted a mixture of belladonna and jimson weed. And we had a huge bonfire right in the middle of the park, but for the four or so times we celebrated the sabbats in that location, we were never detected by authorities or others. This in itself was magical. For our ceremonies themselves, they were definite experiences though I do not remember the specific heights. The entire time in San Francisco in the second half of the 1960s was itself a 'height'. And though I researched the best I could (pre-internet days), we were fortunate with the adventure with toxic substances. For the second time of the flying ointment employment, we all came to develop such sensitive skins, that after the night of ritual, all we could do was head for the nudist beach at Land's End where we could take our clothes off. Another time, a different drug, and looking at me most earnestly, Nancy says, 'Michael, the dog just went out the window!' Standing in the middle of the street before the house in which my brother lived. I looked at her and realised that this was my wife's body standing before me, but she herself was not there at all.

For our Midwinter's sabbat, Michael Barnes had arranged for us to pass the night at the San Francisco Art Institute which is reputedly haunted.

During the wee hours that pursued, some of us saw a ghost. And for our final gathering on Strawberry Hill, we dispensed by that time with the satanic invocations and metaphors with which we had initially begun and sat in a circle, naked of course, with our feet all touching and chanted the *Om* syllable. These in all were galvanising times, though not all euphoric or positive. On Easter, for instance, we (the family and others) went for the sunrise and psychedelic ingestion on the Strawberry Hill island. Coral's dog Fred killed a rabbit (the 'Easter bunny'), and that was when I eventually plunged into 'eternal Hell' from which there was no escape. That horrid nightmare did somehow end, but because of it I began to discern the compatibility of entheogenic celebration for pagan festivals rather than with Christian holidays. With my Amsterdam discovery of Franz Altheim's *A History of Roman Religion* and its list of the Roman *feriae* names around which our Julian/Gregorian calendar took its shape, my course of orientation was set and confirmed.

Concurrently during these 'legendary' days in San Francisco, I developed a need to visit the non-urban pristine away from the city. This was the time I became re-aware of the nocturnal stellar expanse and dazzle. It came to be what would provoke my desire to understand the understanding of constellations and their myths as known by the earlier autochthonous residents of the San Francisco Bay Area and its surrounds. I discovered in the process a fascinating and remarkably peaceful yet multi-linguistic culture (perhaps only surpassed by Java in terms of its number of different languages spoken). While there was at least one small reservation that I visited, I became aware of how my Euro-American ancestors had liquated these people and destroyed their way of life. Not ready to take up residence in a tepee, it was shame and disgust that in large part created my desire to 'return' to where my forebears had lived and to search for the roots of European myth and spirituality.

Before, however, I reached that point to leave America, and while my rejection of Christianity and Abrahamic religion was continuing to develop, it seemed logical for me to attend Anton LaVey's catechism classes for Satanism. These were interesting to say the least and concluded each time with an informal gathering for coffee and cookies in the kitchen of his house (the Black House) on California Street. LaVey saw the spiritual world of the future fairly evenly divided between Buddhism and Satanism. Upon the conclusion of the three catechism sessions, those of us who had attended them were offered affiliation with the Church of Satan. The condition for membership, however, was to take an oath of eternal fidelity to LaVey as the Satanic Pope. My Easter LSD ordeal on Strawberry Hill followed, and that concluded any further interest on my part in diabolical pursuit.

Because of the relatively frequent use of cannabis and hallucinogens during these uniquely active and colourful days in San Francisco, I felt it was important to balance with healthy exercise. I joined the YMCA in the Tenderloin and regularly used its gymnasium. I had concluded that as long as I could continue with my hour of calisthenics and weight-lifting three times a week, I was not overdoing with the rest. This was also when Peggy Lee's release of 'Is That All There Is?' became almost a signature of the times. In addition, it was the time when I became mesmerised by a youth who also exercised at the gym. We would see each other mostly on the circular running track, and our eyes would always meet the instant the other would enter the large room with the circuit. For me, this intense, intensely awkward and unconsummated connection was pivotal. I turned to writing sonnets to express my feelings, frustrations and awakening thrill to the world, life and the possibilities of supreme happiness. Our few meetings were always spontaneous, brief and emotionally profound. But through this deeply overcharged encounter, my inspiration as an artist at heart and commitment to freedom above all began.

But as much as the political turn of events was a motivating factor, it was also the inscrutable and completely futureless attraction that brought me to the decision to follow through on my Euro-American disgrace and leave the country – for what I initially thought was to be forever. In my poetic metaphor, I pictured myself in an unmoored row boat without oars. It was still adjacent at first to the dock – namely to everything I had been raised to believe, to legitimate work and traditional conformity. I had just turned thirty and could have still jumped out of the boat onto the land, but instead I remained simply sitting in the vessel and waved my hand to say 'goodbye' as I drifted off into the high seas. For my heartache love, it was Asia that was his call, but for me it was Europe!

I adore music, and my favourite composers are Maurice Ravel, Dmitri Shostakovich, Sergei Rachmaninoff, Claude Debussy, George Gershwin, Sergei Prokofiev and Bella Bartok. But I also adore Mozart, Beethoven and Brahms and especially Beethoven's late quartets. However, in reading about the German and influential post-World War II philosopher and sociologist Theodor Wiesengrund Adorno and his critical analyses of music, I find my tastes being deeply challenged. While I agree with his lauding of late Beethoven as well as the music of Gustav Mahler, Alban Berg (the opera *Wozzeck* in particular) and Anton Webern, I am more hesitant with Richard Wagner and Arnold Schoenberg. Interestingly, while Wagner is almost proverbially said to have been strongly influenced by my hero Nietzsche, Jed Perl in reviewing Alex Ross' *Wagnerism: Art and Politics in the Shadow of Music,* claims that Picasso, another favourite, also reflects the ideas of the philosopher. Nietzsche profoundly shaped 20th century artistic ideas and the modern fascination with the arts, myths and legends of the Greeks and Romans as much if not even more than did Wagner's attraction to the mythological North. Almost needless to say, I find myself also in much agreement with Adorno's censure of late capitalist society, mass culture uniformity and industrial commodity production and more fully with his condemnation of all forms of totalitarianism. He is certainly, from my perspective, correct in seeing the dominating rationality of modern economic commodification and its provocation of a banal and inescapable consumerism as diminishing or even precluding the sensuous, personal and spiritual aspects of life. Adorno deplored the crowd and stressed community instead, and his hatred was focused on the manipulated subjugation of the individual by the oppressive and alienating power of the collective. Much of this is in accord with my own liberal left beliefs, though these have come to fuse with libertarian sentiments as well.

But unlike Adorno (known foremost for his critical theory of society but also as a musicologist), I cannot, as a starter, reject the sonata-allegro form of music. Admittedly I am using Adorno here as a foil, but I deeply appreciate the works of Beethoven's early and middle periods as well as such composers as Igor Stravinsky, Paul Hindemith, Jean Sibelius let alone Debussy and Bartok. Even harder for me is Adorno's condemnation of jazz. In his advocacy for modern music, he is against the manufacturing of desire to buy or consume. He argues that modern music, unlike traditional music, expresses for social reform the necessary belittlement of the human subject in his or her disempowered loneliness. Music that does otherwise is illusory and manipulates by fragmenting the self, dominating over nature and partaking of the 'magical' character of the commodity. Most music for Adorno, other than late style Beethoven and serialism, constitutes commodification and an artificial or external construction of emotion. Through the rigid techniques that have impoverished imagination, it becomes simply the false bourgeois effort to resolve the difference between individual freedom and social conformity. The purpose of music for Adorno, at least that of modern music, is to convey truth rather than enjoyment. This conveyance is to instigate change over stasis, and for this to occur, the whole cannot predominate over the parts. In short, music that is without social critique is purposeless because modern social reality is bleak, and the sole *raison d'être* for music is to reflect and subvert rather than be submissive to the emptiness of modernity. In all, Adorno considers that self-indulgence is to be judged as morally vapid and regressive – and most pre-modern music is, in his opinion, hedonistic in this sense.

For Adorno, the sonata-like fabrication is a bourgeois product of craft rather than creation and retains 'echoes of commodity production'. The theme, motive or basic element, he identifies with the individual; the form of the composition in total represents for him the binding, collective force of society. The development of the musical theme or narrative he claims only appears to be spontaneous. It is instead a top-down construction and enforcement, and this authoritarian contriving reflects the totalitarian nature of late bourgeois capitalistic society and the human condition within it. The feeling or even reality of freedom is only imaginary. The subjects that are introduced in the exposition subsequently undergo development but are reintroduced in the recapitulation within a new equilibrium and, for Adorno, only fallaciously present the freedom of the sensuous subject vis-à-vis the ordering pressure of social life. Society in his view, conforming both to my opinion and that of many if not most contemporary pagans, exploits nature and oppresses the spiritual needs of the individual. This much is true, but Adorno goes further and claims that, like the sonata-allegro and tonalistic construction of music, society is undemocratically hierarchical. It has become, along with the traditional and pre-modern forms of music that mirror it, a closed system. Such is Adorno's dismissal of the Viennese classical tradition. At the end of day, he seems to wish that, through modernist music, we could awaken to see objectively how miserable we really are.

While I agree that any viable individuality only truly exists in and through one's relations with others, I will insist that there is more to music and the arts than the disclosing of human alienation and frustration with the collective. Much of Adorno's arguments strike me as puritan in the *via negativa* sense. Along with freedom, health and comfort, pleasure is imperative to human well-being. One contention in critique of the philosopher is that he has been limited by his own cultural ethnocentrism. While personally I praise and enjoy the compositions of Bach, Mozart, Beethoven, Brahms and Mahler among others, French and Russian music is equally impacting, and perhaps it is possible that Adorno's perspective built from his understanding of German music does not apply to that of other cultures. In the *very* least, the Impressionist music of Debussy and Ravel, the concert hall music of Shostakovich, Rachmaninoff, Prokofiev, Khachaturian let alone Tchaikovsky and Rimsky-Korsakov among others, and the jazz music of Louis Armstrong, Miles Davis, John Coltrane, Ella Fitzgerald, Peggy Lee, Billie Holiday, Sarah Vaughan, Dinah Washington, Ethel Waters, Fats Waller, Erroll Garner, Benny Goodman, Tommy Dorsey, Glenn Miller, Duke Ellington, Count Basie, The Grateful Dead, The Beatles, The Rolling Stones, Sting, Amy Winehouse, etc. are all enjoyable in some manner or another. Despite my self-consideration of myself as a non-conformist and quasi-rebel, if my appreciation of music as entertainment and pleasurable joy is bourgeois, then I admit to being bourgeois. For Adorno, by contrast, intoxication and ecstasy are required in the maintenance of the delusion of aesthetic completeness. If such really is the case, then so be it!

When I sought in San Francisco to express my agonies and jubilations provoked by falling in love, I turned to the form of the sonnet. Shakespeare became my muse, even though subsequently one great irony for me is that my daughter dismisses the playwright-poet and claims he is repetitive. But the sonnet form was the challenge within which I sought my expression. When I departed from San Francisco, I gave the first 120 sonnets I had composed, a 'trine of sonnets', to the English teacher with whom I was smitten and kept no copies of them. I have since written a second 'trine', but since I embarked upon an academic career, it is only most rarely that I continue with my poetic output, and the third 'trine' to the circle is not yet completed. But in relying on a strict form in this case and even on occasion to more spontaneous free-form, I reject Adorno's contention that all art and music must be socially-politically responsible and not entertaining or even sometimes simply distracting. My Philistinism is a deep part of my paganism, and while the acknowledgement of suffering, weakness, pain and defeat is vitally important, so too are enjoyment, pleasure, rapture and delirious ecstasy.

For me, the innovative composer Debussy represents a much different approach to music, to modern music as well, and one in which even superficial pleasure is allowed over the apparent virtues of classicism. But more than *agrément*, Debussy's impressionistic compositions blend the modal with the chromatic and convey beauty, exaltation, sensuality and spirituality. Not in the German sense extolled by Adorno, the French radical develops his own relations between harmony, melody, counterpoint, rhythm, colour, sonority, tempo and formal design, and his transformation of the established tonal system of musical keys is toward one that for him is less contrived but borrowed more from nature. He has inaugurated a new whole-tone consonance without the complexity of modernism, and his music expresses both emotional mystery and iridescent sexuality. Like Schoenberg, but differently, he revolts against traditionally established musical grammars and has developed his own mellifluous diatonic, pentatonic, chromatic and equal temperament tonal scales. Whereas Adorno deplores the collage/montage technique, Debussy is comfortable with sudden textural and colour changes. He formed a music that remains popular but which Adorno would reject as commercially conventional.

With Adorno, I discern in his total rejection of bourgeois commodification something akin to the biblical condemnation of idolatry. By contrast, I affirm even the inclusion of being stimulated and/or manipulated on appropriate occasions by the fetish. In a more multilateral arena of affairs and life, there are acceptable times for fetishising just the part as distinct from the whole. A complex dynamic exists between the two, and one is with a bit of imagination capable of leading to the other. Without that possibility and to be mandated to be under the constant duress of social responsibility is to be not free. It would also be a non-recognition of difference and plurality. If the commodity becomes a fetish for some people, it is little different than the sensuous worship or *pūjā* that might be directed toward a spiritual image or idol.

It is to be granted that much of contemporary paganism turns to the primitive as an uncorrupted beginning. This romantic concept is seen pessimistically by Adorno as an allegory of bourgeois collective force and master-servant rigidity. Even the glorification of nature, the natural and sensuality is understood as a romantic endeavour that places the archaic over civilisation. For Adorno, resonance with the archaic is a wish fantasy that leads to the disintegration of the individual being's integrity. He associates primitivism in particular with the music of Stravinsky and understands *Le Sacre du Printemps* as the barbaric celebration of sacrifice and elimination of the ego. Spiritual fulfilment can, accordingly, only be found through the individual's grounding in society. Both the spiritual and sensuous life are, therefore, to be located in the pre-bourgeois and pre-rational-technical community. But without the Adornoian extreme and exclusivity, contemporary pagans appear to be in a related accord. Whether ultimately successful or not, pagans of the present day resist economic instrumentality in seeking to re-establish the aesthetic and spiritual. In this effort, the 'magical' character of the commodity may still play a role but without the individual fragmentation and suppression by the dominant collectivity that Adorno insists is inevitably the result. The struggle is still a difficult one, and we may need to dance in various ways between subjective empowerment/resistance and conventional conformity, but the re-birth of pagan outlooks in today's world is in large part the re-acceptance of amusement and self-gratification as part of the heart of spirituality. In addition, the pagan thrust of the day is for more than merely reconciliation and instead for substantial, durable and effective change. This last is dependent in part in the emancipation of old ideas and restrictions without necessarily abandonment of the old, primitive and archaic themselves. There is in this the utilisation of the liminal potencies of *communitas* and celebration for re-securing the holy and sacred. And this entails not a blanket excommunication of the commodity and its 'convenience' but a balanced navigation through the mire and pitfalls of late capitalistic society for whatever of the sacrosanct is hidden within it. Pagans are not, as a general rule, intimidated by the beauty of myth. They seek to explore it without losing a centring awareness of the concerns and practical needs of today. Pagans are conceivably no less dedicated to the employment of spiritual resistance than would be a quasi-Marxist like Adorno. Like the philosopher, pagans are committed to the restoration of the subject as a spiritual centre, but in the pagan case this re-establishment is one to be undertaken as well in full cognisance of the world, nature and our surroundings as spiritual. The non-material is unambiguously to be harmonised with the material.

In the end, music has been in my case sometimes wonderfully intimate with dance. But I now listen to it virtually 24 hours a day – writing, cycling, sleeping, and for me it is mostly something upon which to float. I am a true melomane. Riding a cloud of music is like riding a cloud of the supernatural. Maybe, maybe, it allows me to be in both worlds simultaneously. Perhaps the purpose of either world is to expose the faults of the other. It must be obvious on determining who is currently ahead on racking up the higher score. And us, as the personal-subject-individual-particular, we must still manoeuvre our ways. This is because life is too short and still too wondrous to capitulate to any kind of empty alienation.

Admittedly, back in 1982, the realisation of one's carbon footprints from air miles had not yet become an issue. Our naivety from today's perspective is astonishing let alone embarrassing and shameless. But as pagans, and before present-day's consciousness, the very possibility of circling our blessed planet was itself for Richard and me a sacred act. From San Francisco, we continued on to visit friends and family in Guerneville, Santa Barbara, Los Angeles, Sun City, Palm Springs, Blythe and Thermal before flying first to New Orleans and then on to the East Coast to stay with my parents in New Jersey. But when still in northern California, we attended a May Day ceremony in Angwin (Napa County). The May Pole was wound twice – the first time by women only; the second, by both men and women. Richard described it as the most innocent and non-pretentious pagan rite he had ever seen.

Besides San Francisco, Manhattan and Big Sur, a most favourite place in America for me is undoubtedly New Orleans. I think of chicory coffee and beignets, of tropical inner courtyards, of ubiquitous music and jazz, of incredible cuisine and Galatoires, and of voodoo and magic and the cemetery in which Marie Laveau is buried. I have been to the city several times in the past and twice for the Mardi Gras, and I have re-visited Nola once more after the 1982 occasion. The overall ambience is one of indulgently sensuous decay and *sub rosa* but enticing mystery. The layers of French, Spanish, African, Caribbean and American cultures intermingle in a manner that sets this foot of the Mississippi world apart from anywhere else, and over the years I have probably had in the Crescent City some of my most intense encounters with the quasi-institutional configurations that have crystalised from the esoteric yet operate via mysterious serendipity. The 'Big Easy' has been a continuously bewildering but colourfully wondrous vortex.

As a Creole derivative of originally West African Vodun, the Voodoo presence in New Orleans is a pagan mix of animistic belief and magical practice. My initial exposure was through Alice who ran an occult shop in the area south of Canal Street from the Vieux Carré. She possessed a penetrating power and when looking deeply into my eyes in the late 1960s judged that my own powers had not yet matured. Alice was of the gris-gris culture of Voodoo and was both knowledgeable and friendly. Subsequently, during a Mardi Gras, I encountered on Canal Street the fascinating Zulu Parade which, unlike the other carnival processions that had defined routes, snaked its way randomly through the celebratory crowds. Suddenly, it seemed that more and more of the people around me were African-American and in a high state of anticipation. At the climax of the Zulu Parade, where Santa Claus would be in the Macy's Thanksgiving Day Parade in New York, was the Voodoo Mama dressed in black and accompanied by a daughter-like figure in a white wedding dress. The people pressed forward to receive blessing. To be in the woman's presence at such an *in flagrante* moment was both extraordinary and uncanny. This and other New Orleans junctures with the thaumaturgical over the years have contributed significantly to my confrontation with and growing understanding of an organic viability of the miraculous.

But even here, progress for counter-spirituality is not inevitably a forward moving sequence. When I was in Nola for the last time, I visited as I had always done previously the impressive 18th century Cathedral-Basilica of Saint Louis that is to be found at the heart of the French Quarter. However, on this occasion the statute of Expeditus that had formerly stood near the main altar had been removed from the church altogether. Expedite is the Voodoo saint, and I have found his figure in churches in both Puerto Rico and France (Lyons, Nice). The saint's cult is thought to have begun in the Italian city of Turin during the Middle Ages. As a Roman centurion, he holds aloft a cross inscribed with the word *hodie* (understood in Voodoo as the Bon Dieu or Good God/Bondye) and stands with a foot on a raven in whose beak is held a banner inscribed with the word *cras* or *cras-cras* (presumably suggested by a crow's cry). This last has been understood as 'gris-gris' which are talismans employed in this Afro-Latin spirituality for protection and/or black magic. It was not, however, until I had visited a church near Ulm in Germany (perhaps in Blaubeuren) and saw the Latin epitaph inscription *hodie mihi, cras tibi* signifying 'my lot today, yours tomorrow' (literally 'today me, tomorrow you') that I was able to discern the likely origins of the words associated with St. Expedite who is popular with those who follow Voodoo. But whereas the figure was once a focus in the New Orleans Basilica of Saint Louis for Voodooists, the church has since come to have squelched the possibility of this pagan veneration. Expeditus is gone, and though I inquired, there was no acknowledgement that he had ever been there.

And after the delights of New Orleans, our round-the-world excursion had us next on the East Coast where we oscillated between Maplewood, New Jersey – my hometown, Manhattan – still a favourite, Rhode Island's Moonstone, Narragansett & Providence, and with a brief visit to Provincetown on Cape Cod. There was too much to do and too many to see that we sold the last leg of our PanAm trip in order to stay longer. We had to go to the Newark Airport to check-in for the couple who had bought our tickets – something that would be impossible to do today, but this was still 1982. Much of my pursuit at the time was with Chinese religion – both folk and Daoism. We visited a few temples in New York, but for the most part, these were more difficult to locate than those in San Francisco. Nevertheless, our three-month stay coincided with the sweltering East Coast summer and night symphonies of crickets *et al.* which for me had originally been seminal to my own pagan awakening as well as fascination with the invisible world. And beside watching more television than I can imagine today (*The Streets of Los Angles* with Joanne Woodward, Truffaut's *Le Dernier Metro, Anna Karena* with Garbo, *First Love* with Deanna Durbin, John Pielmeier's *Agnes of God, Private Benjamin* with Goldie Hawn, *White Mama* with Bette Davis, *Zoro the Gay Blade* with George Hamilton, an English version of *The Last Metro,* Michael Wadleigh's *Wolfen,* Bruce Beresford's *Breaker Morant,* Masahiro Shinoda's *Demon Pond,* George Cukor's *Dinner at Eight* with Jean Harlow, *Julia* with Jane Fonda and Vanessa Redgrave, Delmer Daves' 1944 *Hollywood Canteen,* etc.) as well as conversations lasting into the wee hours of the morning, there was the thrill of Broadway and Off-Broadway theatre (*Cloud 9, Dreamgirls, The Torch Song Trilogy, The Pump Boys and the Dinettes, Master Harold and the Boys, Nine The Musical,* and Ibsen's *Ghosts* with Liv Ullman) as well as cinema (*Blade Runner,* Jean-Jacques Beineix' *Diva,* Robert Altman's *Health,* John Milius' *Conan the Barbarian,* Wayne Wang's *Chan is Missing,* Steven Lisberger's *Tron,* Steven Spielberg's *E.T. the Extra-Terrestrial* and *Poltergeist, Clash of the Titans* with Laurence Olivier, Bill Forsyth's *Gregory's Girl,* and Rainer Werner Fassbinder's *Lola*). There had also been the musical *Whoopee!* at Rhode Island's Theater by the Sea, but for music itself, it was only an evening at the Blue Note in New York with John 'Buddy' Connors and Earl 'Fatha' Hines as well as the Lincoln Center's outdoor salute to dance (*1,000 Years of Jazz*). This feast of indulgence culminated with my attendance of a high school reunion with Nancy the day before Richard and I flew back to Europe. There had been an eclipse during our East Coast sojourn as well as a PanAm 727 crash in New Orleans during a thunder storm and the Pershing Missiles II flop when much of Western Europe bollixed Ronald Reagan's plans for an economic boycott of the USSR. But still a memorable moment for me was when I looked out into the back garden of the Maplewood house and saw Richard sitting under a tree wearing his Walkman earphones. It was something special and almost magical as when one sees a rabbit on the lawn or amidst the shrubs.

Following the psychologist James Hillman, memories – especially long-term memories – and the imaginative images that are foundational to them are what augment character as we grow older. Accordingly, it was Freud who discovered that imagination constitutes the very base of memory. The flood of remembrances from this first circumnavigation of the globe, assisted in part by my journal keeping, allows me a continuation of a philosophical reflection that I was engaged upon at the time. I might begin by disclaiming that I am my soul, body or mind. In a sense, these are all possessions (contra, of course, to Nietzsche who claims we each are the body; it is not an owned item). Perhaps the only thing that I am actually is myself. Yet even here again identity occurs in terms of possession. I am *my* self. An individual is self, or, more particularly, the individual is not just any self but is his or her own self. So, I would conclude that identity is both possessive and reflexive. In some sense of course we are each the aggregate total of all our various possessions – including our memories, or, rather, we are each the projected common denominator of the entity which 'possesses' our various components. Among these various possessions then, the body is obviously the most important – at least on this present plane. On another level, perhaps, we have or possess the soul – an entity originally conceived in terms of 'wholeness', although rather universally, at least within indigenous and other pagan contexts, the soul has also been understood as a pair. Taking my cue from the Swedish anthropologist Åke Hultkrantz and supplemented by further research, the life soul or body soul is the animating principle through which the body has life. By contrast, the free soul or dream soul is that aspect of our self that lives on or beyond the body. What the two share ultimately in common is consciousness, otherwise known as the ego, that is, a Latin word for the *I* of selfhood.

What I am uncertain about is whether the identity of the self with consciousness does not represent some sort of quantum leap in the identification process, but I do feel that at some point this identity becomes valid and is contingently to be made. Spinoza, however, apparently claims that consciousness is the locus of illusions, though, crucially, it is also what allows us the ability to communicate. Whereas I had long considered consciousness to be the product of an organism's perception of pleasure and pain, the psychologist Julian Jaynes defines consciousness instead as the ability to engage in metaphor. Supposedly, an individual's cognisant awareness does not truly emerge until around the age of seven. Whatever the impact of this last might have on the question of abortion, I do feel that the search for our own individual identities begins with a taking stock of our possessions – our personality, our situation, our education, our memories, our imagination, etc. We are individually the possessing agent behind all these without being *per se* any of the possessions themselves. And as our possessions change over time and as they themselves undergo change, it is incumbent for us to recognise that we are fluid, constantly metamorphosising entities.

For the Romans, there was obviously a deep-rooted connection between the verbs *esse* 'to be' and *posse* 'to be able'. Our term for 'possession' actually is thought to derive from *port* 'toward' and *sedere* 'to sit', that is, *possidere* 'to sit toward or near (something)' and not directly from *posse*. But when the people to whom we had sold the last leg of our PanAm tickets arrived upon my invitation to us at the farm in France, Richard asked at one point whether they had watched the royal wedding of Charles and Diana, and Rod replied that that or the like was not his scene. I would today want to ask, 'Are you not able to enjoy something like that?' If ability is identity, the less we are able to do, the less we are. I perceive royalty as basically the embodiment of a collective wish. And since wishing is the essence of life, those who fail to perceive or enjoy the beauty of monarchy in itself I comprehend to have missed out on a basic aspect of the life process. In this strain of thought, let us take to mind the developments of *in posse* as 'the range of potential possibility' and *in esse* 'the range of actual being'. When one is dead, the range of possibility has vanished or at least has become greatly altered. For one, one is no longer able 'to sit toward or near (something or someone)' – *possidere*. Nor can one stand or, more specifically, stand out, i.e., exist.

In any event, we had heard about a week before we returned about terrible fires in our Provençal village. Paula, who had been staying in our house, was forced to evacuate twice. Helen and Pierre 'came out O.K. but were evacuated four times', and the Mailaenders 'lost everything but the house'. This is particularly poignant as I write this now with the devastating Kincade, Getty and at least nine other wildfires currently ravaging the state of California. When we arrived, however, once more to the south of France, we were relieved that the fire had not done as much damage as we had first believed. The military base on which the blaze had begun refused to allow Barbara's husband Lou-Lou (Louis) and the rest of the local volunteer fire department entry, but the latter disobeyed orders to evacuate the mountain and entered or marched into the base in defiance – and they were then able to save the forests. The worst of the destruction turned out to be along the route from our town to a neighbouring one. The trees used to arch over the road forming a tunnel of extraordinary vegetation beauty. More than thirty years later, that original magnificence has never been recovered. My comment at the time was that everything eventually changes, but the gods will always re-surface. One friend pointed out that the burnt-out area now produced a feeling of tranquillity. For the first time, one could see houses, vistas, rocks, streams and geographical contours that had all been previously hidden. The blackened sectors had a kind of majestic ugliness to them, and I was saddened in realising the long tortuous process of re-growth that was now necessary. Nonetheless, I still was able to appreciate overall how fortunate we were. And three weeks later, as we drove over the Maures to St. Maxime, I was astonished by the eerie contrast of an abundance of fresh green leafing emerging out of the charred black trees along the way that the fire had also devastated.

From my Chinese studies, I was provoked to consider immortality and whether such exists or not. For the Brahmanic speculators of the late Rigvedic hymns, even the great gods along with the earth, sun, fire and humanity are of limited duration. Only the entropic void alone is immortal. If this be so, then, the Daoist affirmation of endless perpetuity and the legitimate pursuit thereof is a direct denial of the Brahmanic/Buddhistic contention. The sadness that the Buddha spoke of as an inevitable part of life seems to be real enough. Can we legitimately ask for more than participation in the duration? Is centring/spiritualism a third alternative in the conflict of our day between anarchistic youth and communism on the one hand and the rigid, prosperous status quo establishment and capitalism on the other? And what about the dangers and extremes of a Khomeniism? These were my questions thirty-seven years ago. Now there are the further post-911 concerns of Al Qaeda, ISIL, Boko Haram and populism let alone environmentalism and climate change. One realisation upon returning from our first circumambulation of the planet was through learning that I had lost the friendship I had thought I had had and treasured with two people in Switzerland. With the cherished exception of Richard, I was now seeing life as a continually growing isolation. Still, I was clinging to my belief in the dream of humanity. But having been around the world, perhaps akin to the *hajj* of Muslims to Mecca, Richard and I now felt ourselves to be some kind of savants. And, melancholy and loneliness or otherwise, I always still thrill to when Jupiter roars in the heavens.

A modern Latin American music concert at Amsterdam's *Concertgebouw* included the Mexican Silvestre Revueltas' *Planos* (which I enjoyed) and *Ocho x radio* (which I enjoyed less), the Mexican Manuel Enríquez' *Concierto para 8* that presented cosmic emotions of pathos as had Revueltas' other work. The *Tregua* of the Venezualian composer Emilio Mendoza was virtually a dream. And with Mexican Ramón Nobre's *Divertimento* (for piano and orchestra) and Brazilian Heitor Villa-Lobos' *Nonet*, one was dealing with that other side of music that Adorno would deplore – the rhythmic – in which the rich fund of colourful and dancing idioms that comprise much of the Latin heritage affirmed life over the vast reaches of endlessly expanding space. All the same, despite this most enjoyable musical interlude, my mood at the time remained one of wistful intangibility and the lurking horror that one's train has left without him. I was in my nearly mid-forties and concluded that I simply wanted to be let to contemplate with the gods, enjoy the contact of a few friends, centre with Richard, explore through music and put out quietly but creatively. Besides health, maybe there needed to be nothing more. And I had yet to find or discover a pagan community or any pagan individuals at all.

With the death of George/Buster and a grieving letter from his mother Katherine, the underlying sadness of existence was brought to mind that made me consider my wonderment whether sorrow was essential for the pagan *joie de vivre*. But added to this was the frustration that continued to arise from being able to see how things should be against the mindlessness of both stagnation and uncontrolled change. As a Daoist and nature-worshipper I could accept this as the best of all possible worlds and trust the ultimate process; as a Confucian and humanist, however, I maintained belief in both collective and individual aspiration as part of the vital operation of nature being the preferred means by which a more creatively integral society composed of a myriad of self-determining communities could and ought to come about. My research and experiences to this point had led me to believe that the cultural dynamics and answers lay with the Indo-European, Chinese and Japanese and perhaps with the neolithic-animistic-primitive as well. To this possibility, I considered the Austronesian as a fifth major cultural/lingual ideology – including Indonesian, Malay and

Tagalog but also Hawaiian and the Rapa Nui of Easter Island. But if I put all into a wider context, I considered – and still do – the museum as well as the music hall as temples to the Muses. In India and around the world and especially in Paris, Amsterdam and London, attending such shrines has always been a major part of my devotions. But a glorious and most wonderful temple sits in majestic solitude and is known as the British Museum. True enough, she displays the treasures acquired from an imperial past, but part of me asks why not? The legacy is in a sense as much a part of Britain's past as it is a part of the various cultures from which it was produced and taken. The museum is a modern-day, non-theistic cosmopolitan temple. And the British Museum is even built like a classical one.

Is it sheer madness to love the world? How many people in fact can one love? How many different people can one be? In my forties, at least, I did not suppose there were any answers to these questions, but for me the replies are many as well as derangement and so what? As a polytheist, I could accept – and regardless of whether or not polytheism resolves into some kind of monism – the multiple as itself valid – cherished even and permitted to be a dynamic basis for life. However, as 1982 came to a close, I was able to recollect the wonderful thrill the year contained in allowing me to circle the world. The memory of the places seen and encountered, the many marvellous faces, and the plain joy of movement still glowed behind the basic stream of consciousness. Even the loss of friends that had accompanied this segment of time I was coming to accept as an inevitable shedding concurrent with the centrifugal effect of circular progress as well as a kind of freedom from the demands and obligation which friendship entails. To forage forward, yes, but no less to remember as well to stop and take stock of god-given gifts. I was able to realise that I had been and still am to the present unbelievably fortunate and divinely kissed. But I also knew that I would always remain grateful for having had the joys of this year.

Bill Bryson in his *The Life and Times of the Thunderbolt Kid* describes America in the 1950s – my teenage years. I remember from early school days, and as we were learning about other countries in the world and particularly in Europe, being made aware of how fortunate we were to be Americans and to be living in the USA. Bryson explains that in 1950, no other country had known such prosperity as America was enjoying. With the conclusion of World War II, the United States had an unprecedented advantage over everyone else. We had amassed an incredible amount of war-made manufacturing and innovative capacity and were without competitors. The rest of the world had either been ruined by war (we had no comparable damage) or was in a colonial or undeveloped state. Bryson claims that by 1951, 90% of American families had refrigerators. By contrast, when I first arrived in The Netherlands in 1961, and again in 1970, the possession of a refrigerator was almost the exception rather than the rule. To get a telephone installed in France was nearly impossible well into the 70s. Bryson claims that nearly 75% of American households had not only telephones but also washing machines, stoves either electric or gas, and vacuum cleaners. Americans represented five per cent of the people on the planet but owned 80% of all electrical merchandise. By the close of the war, this five per cent held more wealth than did everyone else in the world combined. The country was in control of two-thirds of the planet's entire productive capacity, whereas, in contrast, by 2017 only 18.2% of the world's goods were being manufactured by the U.S. – still the world's highest but now followed closely by China at 17.6%. With peace being re-established in 1945, the United States had acquired $26 billion worth of new factories, and by 2018, the gross domestic product of the country had reached $2.33 trillion. The $140 billion dollars of savings that America enjoyed in 1945 has become roughly $3,500 trillion by around 2017, but the country has been reduced to the 100th position in the ranking of countries by the percentage of their gross national savings. China was 10th in 2017. Nevertheless, and despite the great disparity in economic well-being vis-à-vis the rest of the world between now and then, the 'fabulous fifties' comprised a scintillating period of time for a naïve and unquestioning adolescent. Our greatest fear was that of a nuclear attack from the USSR, and air raid or civil defence drills were the norm in both school and beyond. My father had outrageously contended that with the victory that ended the war in 1945, the US should have used an atomic bomb on Moscow.

If I now recollect the Joseph McCarthy anti-Communist witch-hunts, the 1953 executions of Julius and Ethel Rosenberg, the truly insane atomic and hydrogen bomb tests throughout the 50s and the radioactive atmospheric debris generated globally from them, the Cold War 'Red Scare' with the Soviet Union, the Korean War, the polio epidemic and iron lungs, the US' constantly accelerating defence spending, and the stealthy emergence of the modern multinational corporation (e.g., the United Fruit Company) and concomitant imperialist interventions (e.g., Guatemala, Cuba), it amazes me to my having been so oblivious and unaware of both American mindlessness and her pervasive but underlying disgrace. Instead, it was an unparalleled and idyllic time to be growing up in the USA. And like Bryson's Des Moines, suburban Maplewood had a similar register of designated landmarks for those of us growing up there: the Park, the Baseball Field, the Pond, the Brook, the Village, the Tracks, the Other Side of the Tracks, the Woods or the Reservation and several, usually tree-covered, vacant lots as well as an unpaved and still dirt road between Maplewood and neighbouring Millburn. As teenagers, we had ceaseless fun times and usually with enough cleverness not to get caught when these involved activities we ought not be doing like entering houses when the owners were away, making explosives with our chemistry sets, swimming at private watering holes at night, and so forth.

The Methodist Youth Fellowship became an important part of my high school years. Bill Burns, the church's assistant minister, was in charge and was always a relaxed, spirited and enjoyable person who encouraged us to explore and be open. I remember several weekend retreats that the group of us would spend somewhere in a forest area. I would walk among the trees reading the Bible, and though I came eventually to lose my Christian belief, the effect of merging spirituality and nature was probably augmented and encouraged from these opportunities. It was, however, the convocation for youth that the Methodist Church chose to hold one summer at the Purdue University campus in Indiana that became a pivotal moment for me. A group of us from the MYF bussed privately to the site. My friend Fred commented afterwards on how the mind-expanding experience had changed me: 'The shell you had previously you smashed to smithereens on this trip'. It was from this point as well as a role I played in a school play that I began to be known as the Man about Town. The intellectual stimulation at the convocation along with the freedom I encountered by being with so many new people who could only see me as I was immediately presenting myself and without the roles and reputations I had acquired up to that time was a joyous liberation. In some sense, from then on, I never looked back.

But the idyllic life in my home town of Maplewood, New Jersey that I enjoyed for most of my childhood and through my high school days was always something fortunate. I knew that I would eventually travel and explore elsewhere, but I also knew that I would always be grateful for where I had been privileged to grow up, its beauty and specialness. Suburbia was protective, and other sadder realities were somewhere else and not our immediate focus. And the greatest city in the world was just over there! True enough, Bill Burns would organise MYF excursions into New York and to places like Harlem, and on one occasion we went to an International Peace Movement service (essentially New Thought) conducted by the charismatic leader Father Divine. Another time, we went to Madison Square Garden for the evangelist Billy Graham. This last was a highly charged affair, and when Graham asked us to search deeply into our souls to hear if we were being called to come forth to 'Be Born Again', I tried but heard nothing.

Grade school for me was a struggle. The school part I did not enjoy and was always bewildered and able just to scrape by. In a school play, I was the Magician and performed some of the magic tricks I knew from the magic set my parents had purchased for me. After Grade Six, it was Junior High School for three years, and this was my awakening. I went from a below average student to an above average one. Summers were almost always glorious, and that was when my parents would frequently rent a cabin at 'The Shore'. I was also sent to summer camps several times, and these too were magical. During my high school years, my father joined the Maplewood Country Club. Beside becoming the venue for our usual Sunday afternoon family dinners, the Club had both swimming pool and tennis courts and became the memorable place to hang out almost daily during our summer vacations. And in 1953, with a group of other boy scouts, we had hired a train to take us to and back from the Boy Scouts of America Jamboree at the Irving Ranch in Southern California. There were 50,000 of us, and this was the time when Vice President Richard Nixon put his hand on my shoulder and explained why he could not give me his autograph because of the number of others for whom he would then need to do the same. One memory from this excursion I have was when the train stopped during the night, and my carriage was the one which sat crossing the main street of the already then legendary Las Vegas. It was a Podunk town at the time and nothing like what it subsequently became, but the main street had neon lights and for a child of thirteen it was something most exciting. We visited such places as the Grand Canyon, Knott's Berry Farm, Yellowstone Park and Salt Lake City. It was probably at Yellowstone when we were having dinner in the lodge, the guys at my table bet me that I could not get the attractive young waitress to kiss me. I went up to her and explained the situation. She gave me a quick peck on my cheek before dashing away. I won the bet.

One summer between my fourth and fifth grades while I was at camp,

I learned from my parents that we were moving house. It was only about three blocks higher up on the beginning slope of South Mountain but in a slightly more affluent neighbourhood. It provided a new route for getting to the Jefferson Grade School – especially if I cut through the yards or gardens of the houses in the middle of the blocks rather than walking along the road. In all, it was thrilling to be in a different and larger dwelling for the rest of my days in Maplewood (grade school, junior high school and high school), and this was still the family home when Richard and I stayed there during the last leg of our 1982 circling of the world. I had my own room on the top floor with my brother's next to it.

'Pit' was, beside Fred, my best friend in these years. He and I snuck back stage at the Jamboree. There was a point that I dared to walk onto the empty stage. Pit was astounded and exclaimed, 'You have no nerve to be able to walk out in front of 50,000 people'. Pit and I did many things together – some of which we should not have, but we were young and seemingly wanted to know how much we might be able to get away with without being caught. I remember the corner on Ridgewood Road (supposedly a former Indian trail) where we were when I mentioned one day that if I were to be diagnosed with cancer, it would be something I would want to know. 'Oh, no!' exclaimed Pit, 'I would never want to know I was dying of cancer'. When it turned out to be the case for him during our sophomore high school year, I told his parents about that conversation, and he was not informed. He did, however, have his suspicions – especially after rummaging through his parents' post and reading the sadness that was being expressed because 'your son is dying of cancer'. One time when he was home between hospital stints, he was visiting me at my house which was a block from his home and mentioned the letters he had found. Somehow, I was able to snap back, 'Oh, you should hear the rumours that are going on at school about you. One is that you have cancer, another is that your father has died, and a third is that you had your leg amputated because you had been on crutches'. With that last, he laughed since we had been, not long before his diagnosis, to the Reservation where he had managed to sprain his foot. I think he realised that he was not going to get me to confirm his fears, so the matter was dropped and never mentioned again. But it was a burden to lose a close friend so relatively early in life.

Not long after Pit had died, I was in charge of setting up a Hallowe'en celebration at our church. It became quite a production, but about all I can remember of it now was that among the different things I had put together for all to do were apples tied to strings that were hung from the ceiling and which people were to attempt to grab with their teeth. The night before, during evening prayers, I had asked God for a sign that Pit was okay in the next world. At the church before we were to go to the room for the Hallowe'en festivities, there was an MYF gathering in the smaller side-chapel of the building. Suddenly my father entered and said angrily to me, 'Mike, come outside! I need to speak to you'. I was surprised and mystified since my focus had been almost exclusively on setting up the decorations and activities that were to follow, and I could not fathom why my father would be angry with me at that point. Outside, Dad rather sheepishly explained that his anger was only a set-up for everyone else who was inside in the chapel because there was to be a surprise panel discussion between parent and offspring on problems that might arise and he had been invited to be part of it. I do not remember now the exact details over what was deliberated, but it became one of the closest moments I recall having had with my father. I have Bill Burns to thank for having arranged this. And the activities that followed were also a success. For me, this was the confirmatory answer to my prayer.

The American soap-opera of the 1960s named after Grace Metalious' novel *Peyton Place* could have been modelled on my hometown of Maplewood. My father's adultery was almost duty-bound. My mother found him once in bed with my brother's godmother, the radio personality Helen King. Mother was often more like a sister for me than a parent; I was her confidant as well as her go-between. My brother had an affair with the women next door who in time became my mother's best friend but not until after Mother's own affair with the woman's husband. I was always thrilled that my mother had these experiences and was able to have some joy beyond the unhappy marriage she had with my father. The novel was also made into a film by the same name in 1957 starring one of my favourites, Lana Turner. Peyton Place was supposed to be a town in New England but could have just as easily been in Suburbia and my hometown of Maplewood. Leonard Bernstein's *Trouble in Tahiti* also reflects the world in which I grew up. My friend Fred still lives there and became mayor for a time. Through his encouragement, Maplewood has become a residential 'gay' enclave. The property taxes are, alas, formidable, but its South Orange-Maplewood school system is probably still one of the best in the country. That had been originally the very reason why my parents chose it as the place in which to raise their children.

For some reason, I have always adored Lana Turner and never tire of seeing her on the screen. I have found her supremely attractive and was horrified to learn after having cocktails at a round counter on the beach in Acapulco that Lana had been at that bar at the same time. I could have seen her live! Not to despair, however, when I was afterwards in Los Angeles on my way back home to San Francisco, one of my great loves Gene worked for CBS and arranged for me to come to the rehearsals for the Smothers Brothers Show that was to include Lana as a special guest. I was more than thrilled until the day before when CBS went on strike, and all was cancelled.

In attempting to recollect what celebrities I have seen in the flesh or even talked to or known, the first that comes to mind is the actor Alan Bates who had become a good friend. I first saw Alan on stage in 1979 with Sheila Ballantine in Simon Grey's *Stage Struck*. I was moved by the character he portrayed and wanted to meet him – which I did and found him to be a most generous, down-to-earth and enjoyable person, one with a lovely sense of humour and someone who remained unceasingly grateful with how fortunate he had been with his career. Alan was always enthusiastic to observe other performers. I once asked him if knowing so intimately how movies were constructed, whether that spoiled the cinema experience for him. His answer was 'Not at all!' On every occasion, he could engage totally as a viewer in the pure narrative of film as film. When Alan was first beginning as a young actor, he came to receive an offer in London but was in the West Country. He went to Tony John, the director, and explained, and Tony replied firmly, 'You are already under contract with me!' Alan did not know how to reply, so he repeated, 'But this is for London!'

'But you have signed a contract', Tony replied again. Alan told me that he kept repeating 'London' until Tony finally waved his hands in exasperation and told him he could go. Many, many years later, Tony commented to me that I should tell Alan that he thinks that Alan is an excellent actor and that he, Tony, congratulates him on his accomplishments.

Through Alan, sometimes at parties at his house, I have met the actress Felicity Kendal, Twiggy, the writer Peter Shaffer, the director Ronald Eyre and the poet Stephen Spender among others. I asked Felicity about Tom Stoppard's play *Hapgood* that she had starred in in 1988. I had thoroughly enjoyed the work but was completely perplexed by it and understanding what it was really about. She told me that she had finally figured it out herself but could no longer remember what that had been. Separately, but Alan of course knew him too, I met the director Tony Richardson and at his home, Le Nid du Duc in La Garde Freinet, got to know one weekend his daughters Natasha and Joely. Natasha told the story of how her and her boyfriend's television had recently been repossessed because they could not pay for it. She had her hand resting on the shoulder of her father as she related what had happened, and Tony just remained sitting quietly and smiling. But while at Tony's, Richard and I got to swim in that famous pool that David Hockney had painted.

One morning in Saint-Paul de Vence, Richard and I were having our morning coffees while some older men were conversing at an adjacent table. When one of them departed, the owner of the café jumped up from the table and told us excitedly that the gentleman who had just left was the artist Marc Chagall. I have seen Queen Elizabeth II one afternoon at the British Museum; through a press pass I had acquired from Aunt Dorothy in connection with her newspaper, *The Murray Hill News*, I was able to attend the investiture of Queen Beatrix in the Nieuwe Kerk of Amsterdam; and one day as I was standing before the Dutch house, Queen Maxima winked at me as her limousine was escorted passed. I was kissed by the singer Johnny Ray at a New Year's Eve party in New York; Richard and I have met Whoopie Goldberg backstage after her one-woman show on Broadway; and one day at a traffic light on Market Street in San Francisco, Nancy pointed out Janice Joplin in the Porsche right next to us. The light turned green, and we both floored our cars. Mine was a VW Beetle. I was still in the intersection when Janice disappeared over the horizon. And after watching the almost interminable *Apocalypse Now* in a cinema on the Champs-d'Élyéees, I had to rush to the WC immediately afterwards. As I hurried to the aisle, there were two women in fur coats sitting at the end. They did not want to get up, but the one saw the look of anguish on my face and rose slowly – a little more slowly than I had anticipated. Richard came running after me. 'That woman, that woman', he blurted out.

'What woman?' I asked.

He pointed her out and said, 'That's Sophia Loren!'

'Oh ,I had to reply guiltily, 'I just kicked her in her achilles heel with my boot'. Maybe it was fitting for the words by which the film ended: 'The horror; the horror', and was I doing Ms Loren a service?

Two others I ought to mention in this recollection are the Greek actor and former ballet dancer Vassili Lambrinos (he was the Prince in the movie *The Unsinkable Molly Brown* that he was filming when we met in

Los Angeles) and the singer Julie Felix. Vassili was my second lover, and through his ceaseless zest for life, I learned much from him – was even to some extent shaped by him. Julie I knew and dated a few times when at university in Santa Barbara. After graduation, we encountered each other by chance at the Prado Museum in Madrid. We spent several days together – especially at night when Julie would see people on the street with musical instruments and ask where they were going, and we would join them. For many, many years I wondered whatever happened with her. Then one day, I learned that she was to appear at a Pagan Federation event in London. From various friends I learned further that Julie had gone on to become essentially the Joan Baez of Britain. When I saw her at the PF function, I asked, 'What is a nice gal like you doing in a place like this?' She has since been once to our flat for dinner along with her then lover who turned out to have been one of the thirty or so of us who consumed ayahuasca under Alan Shoemaker's guidance at Neal's Yard in Covent Garden. I have since enjoyed Julie's reminiscences of Leonard Cohen at Saint James Piccadilly and her 80th birthday celebration performance in the Charing Cross Theatre at The Arches of the Embankment.

I have also attended two papal audiences. The first was in 1961with John XXIII. On this occasion, the Hall of the Pontifical Audiences had been divided into cubicles that each contained about a hundred people. Just ahead of the one I was in, there was a group of Italian soldiers who practiced a chant for the Pope. John was carried into the hall on a litter and was sternly blessing those he passed on both sides of the central aisle through which he was being carried. When he reached the cubicle where the soldiers were, they burst into their practiced chant, and the Pope subtly winked at them so that no one else could see – except me since I was immediately next to them. They all cheered then in great joy. The second audience occurred in the 1970s with Pope John Paul II. Richard and I were driving from the farm to Eastern Europe (Slovenia, Hungary, Romania, Bulgaria and Greece), but Aunt Dorothy was attending a lawyers' conference in Rome, and we decided first to visit her on our way. Since the gathering was named 'World Peace Through Law', the pontiff invited the assembly to a private audience. This was to be Aunt Dorothy's supreme moment. All my life I had seen pictures of my aunt on the front page of her *Murray Hill News* with a US President, a Supreme Court Justice, a New York mayor or some other celebrity, and this was the opportunity for one of her with the Pope. Richard and I were being dragged along so that Richard could take the photo with Aunt Dorothy's instamatic camera that she kept striking against the back of a chair to get it to advance. She had an explosive rage when the taxi could not take her directly to the Vatican entrance. We then walked her across the vehicle free area, and there was already a line of people waiting for entry. *Wait?!* This was something almost unheard of for my aunt. Richard accompanied her to the front of the line, but the Swiss Guards would not let her in until it was the proper time. The psychology of the entire affair was carefully contrived, and the half-hour wait before being allowed to enter was designed to augment the emotional input.

Aunt Dorothy's idea was to be at the head of the line so that she could get a front row seat in order to procure her desired photo. (I should probably add here that Aunt Dorothy, or Aunta Dee as my cousin calls her, was one of the Witnesses in Warren Beatty's film *Reds*). Finally, the doors opened. Richard and I did not have invitations since we were not delegates to the invited conference, but he was with my aunt, and I simply but successfully had to crunch my way through with the rapidly advancing crowd. Once inside, however, we were confronted with an enormous staircase seemingly a block long, and the one problem my aunt – the first woman to have been admitted to the Bar in the State of New York – had since she had once broken her hip was going up stairs. Everyone else was streaming past us, but we managed to get her to the top of the stairs, turned the corner, and there was another set of stairs of identical length. I believe in all there may have been eight sets, and all a part of carefully preconceived Vatican psychology. I told my aunt that I would go ahead and find seats as close to the front as possible and for her to take her time and Richard would stay with her to help. He thought at one point of the possibility of picking her up but pictured her turban and all unravelling let alone the sight of his entering the audience hall carrying her in his arms.

I managed to get three seats at one end of the second row. Eventually Dorothy and Richard did arrive, but she was so dreadfully emotionally deflated, that when I noticed there were still some seats in the front row and told her to go ahead and get one, she could not – virtually a first for me to hear my aunt decline on a suggestion like that. She was just too undone by all those stairs, but I prevailed and convinced her that securing a front row chair was only something she could do. So not only did she accomplish as much, but she obtained *three* seats for all of us – and, as it turned out, directly in front of where the pontiff was to sit. And, further, I was wearing the only jacket I had brought with me for our East European venture; it was white.

There was at least another half-hour wait for the Pope himself – once more a part of the meticulously engineered Vatican psychology. And during this time, Vatican etiquette was explained to the audience: there were official Vatican photographers, and no one was to take his or her own photos; and if anyone had a gift for the Pope, it was not to be handed to him directly but put on the side table to the right. Well, Aunt Dorothy was to have nothing to do with these instructions. She had brought along copies of her book *Lady Lawyer*, her autobiography, as well as a stack of her pamphlet 'How to Win in the Small Claims Court'. So, when the pontiff was finally brought into the chamber and placed on a throne (his red-slippered feet not even touching the floor), there was virtually another thirty minutes of flashbulbs snapping while almost all of the 300 people present took pictures. When things eventually quieted down, the chairman of the lawyer's conference gave an introductory speech during which he signalled Pope John Paul II as the 'moral leader of the world'. Hearing this, the pontiff rolled his eyes in a Groucho Marx fashion. His address to the audience itself was impressive – making only one mistake with his English and which he corrected. For me, sitting immediately before him as a pagan, I wondered what I could do and decided simply to glare at him with all the hatred I could express with my eyes in retaliation for Christianity's destruction of the spirituality that had preceded it. At the conclusion of the Pope's talk, he came down to the audience and began to shake the hands of those of us in the front row. This was Aunt Dorothy's chance, and she went forward with her literature. I believe an attendant took it from her, but she planted herself right next to the pontiff so that in all the photos, it looks as if they are in conversation. I was never certain that they had been at all.

When the Pope reached me, and it was obvious to him what I had been doing, he expressed confusion not knowing what to do. Since I believe strongly if there is an opportunity to shake hands with an enemy, one should do so. I took his hand, and Richard placed his on both of ours. At this very moment, the emotional fervour of the Latin Americans in the back of the chamber exploded, and they began to stampede forward. The Pope disappeared in an instant. So that is the 'Aunt Dorothy Meets the Pope' story. She got her photo. Whether it was one that Richard had taken or one from the Vatican photographer, I do not know, but it assumed a prideful place on the front page of *The Murray Hill News*. And I learned from Dorothy's husband Jay how the story came to be embellished. Accordingly, the pontiff squeezed my aunt's hand and she squeezed his with his saying, 'Too bad it must stop here'. Jay was also led to believe that we had a private dinner with the Pope after the audience seated at a long table with nuns waiting on us. What I do know for real, however, was that my dear and formidable aunt was not about to negotiate those staircases a second time, and she descended from the audience hall in the pontiff's private elevator.

I suppose the enjoyment of celebrity is similar to a pagan's cherishing of the gods. One appreciates them all but may still have favourite individual deities with whom there has been more interaction than with others. My formative relationship in my much earlier days was with the moon or moon-goddess. Richard's deity is the sun. I have come to revere especially Tellus/Gaia/Demeter, the Dioscuri, Mars, Indra, Freyr, the dawn-goddess and Jupiter-Zeus. And it is upon this last that I now wish more immediately to reflect. Already in 1994, my argument had been that, like mortals, the gods can know death (Dionysus, Persephone, Yama), impairment (Zeus with Typhon, the Hittite weather-god with Illuyanka, Tyr with Fenrir, Nuada with Sreng of the Fir Bolg, Indra with Vritra) and incest (stories to follow), but the gods themselves are not bound by humanity's social conventions. Instead, they belong more properly to the hidden, more raw dimensions of nature. Though much of the contemporary pagan community projects human ethics onto the gods and judges or condemns them accordingly, this is to miss the deeper challenges and, yes, even rewards of mythic probity.

The reconstruction of Indo-European mythology and its historical narratives of reinterpretation is contentious and always debatable. My understanding is only one among a host of different possibilities, but it remains as the comprehension that I have discerned from the themes and variations that may be uncovered. From Hesiod's *Theogony*, the *Eddas* and the *Rigveda*, it may be fathomed that Earth is the original mother of all. As Stephen Fry puts it, Chaos is a grand chasmic yawn. In a word, this gaping void translates as cosmic nothingness; it is Gaia who is the very first being and 'ever-sure foundation of all'. (It should not be necessary to explain that this geocentric interpretation is *not* the understanding of modern-day science; it is instead a feature of a mythological legacy that conveyed to our ancestors and to many of us still today a spiritual narrative that may be discerned operatively to underlie nature and the human civilisation or civilisations that have emerged from it.) Parthenogenetically, Gaia gives birth to Zeus. The later replacement of Zeus by Uranus most likely stems from Hesiod's adoption of the Middle Eastern but non-Indo-European 'Succession Myth'. In the original formulation, Earth has the power on her own to produce her opposite. Her unalike complement, her ultimate offspring, is Light. When we accept that the gods are inscrutable perfections, we may assume that Zeus is perfect light as Gaia is perfect matter. Together they might represent the matter-energy continuum; in mythology, they are the divine primordial parents of all. Throughout the Indo-European daughter languages (Greek, Latin, Vedic-Sanskrit, etc.) this verbal light-complex has given rise to our words 'divine', 'deity', '*deus*', '*deva*', '*tivar*', 'Zeus', 'Jupiter', '*Tiwaz-Tyr', 'Dyáus' as well as, at least possibly if not probably, 'Diana', 'Dione', 'Juno', 'Juturna' and 'Janus'. It is this nexus of luminosity that is arguably to be seen as centrally vital to original European spirituality.

By becoming the consort of his mother, Zeus is the oedipal fantasy *par excellence*. But now here is where things get even more vexedly contentious. The offspring of Zeus and Gaia is the dawn – the most 'beautiful' goddess or deity of all. Zeus is utterly and unavoidably smitten by his daughter's beauty and consequently rapes her. The narrative of this sexual ravishment is the basic mythological theme. The variations are to follow. But importantly, the child from the union of Zeus and Eos is the sun (Helios/Sūrya/Sôl/Sunna/Sun/Saulė as well as the Vedic Pūṣhan). The gist of the incest tale is most clearly presented in the *Rigveda* (1.71.5, 3.31.1, 10.61.7) and the later *Brāhmanas* and *Purānas*, though Dyaus' name is usually replaced by that of Prajāpati and later by Brahmā. Perhaps I should mention that in my reconstruction here of proto-Indo-European myth, I am for the most part employing throughout the name or marker of Zeus/Dyaus to designate the luminescent sky figure despite its subsequent replacements.

There are two chief initial variations to the original and fundamental mythologem. In one, Gaia the earth-mother goddess gives birth not just to one son but two: Zeus and the moon. Together her sons are the primordial twins. In the second variation, with the outrage that occurs when the father rapes the daughter, the archer (e.g., Rudra) shoots his arrow at the father. The arrow lodges in Zeus' thigh as he is engaged in coitus, and in pain he interrupts and withdraws with the consequence that some of his sperm falls to the earth whereupon the archer himself is born. One must keep in mind here that the normal time sequence that occurs for us in our world is not necessarily present in the mythological. One might say that magical time is what exists in the otherworld. There is also the implicit suggestion that it is the crescent moon that the archer uses as his bow. In any case, there are two important, in this case, mythogems that are to be discerned in the basic theme and two variations that I have so far submitted for consideration. One concerns the gender of the five or six figures introduced during the initial coalescing stage of the cosmic proto-narrative. The earth and dawn are female; the celestial luminosity, the sun and moon or archer are male. If we are to examine the proto-figures of the Indo-European pantheon, two are female (the earth and the dawn), two are male (the Zeus-prototype and his thunder-wielding self or twin) and three are ambivalent (the sun, the moon and fire-water). Consequently, in the Classical tradition that we know through the Greeks and Romans, the moon is female and the sun is male, but this is reversed among the Germanics and Baltic peoples where the sun is feminine and the moon is masculine. For the Vedic peoples, the sun and moon are both usually understood as male figures. But regardless of gender considerations and ambivalences, the proto-pantheon of the Indo-European speaking peoples conveys an understanding that is fundamentally grounded in nature. These root-deities consist simply of the sun, dawn, earth, moon and luminous sky and are subsequently augmented by the divine twins as the understandings of thunder/lightening/mortal humanity, on the one hand, and fire/water/immortal humanity, on the other.

The other mythogem that comes to play a significant role in the variations to the proto-myth that follow in time are the multiple familial relationships between the initial figures. Zeus is both father and brother to Eos; Gaia is both mother and lover of Zeus; the Moon and/or the Archer is uncle to Eos, son of Gaia and brother to both Zeus and Eos. And we find that the Sun is both brother, son and even lover of Eos. In the mythic variations which develop subsequently among the daughter-cultures, usually only one of these relationships comes to prevail (e.g., parent or sibling). At the time I was writing my *The Divine versus the Asurian*, I understood the Greek Hera more as an instance of the anti-mother – especially through her animosities toward her husband's mistresses and towards his sons (Heracles, Dionysus) as well as her parthenogenic birth of Hephaistos. But I have since come to consider Hera's name as possibly cognate with the Vedic Sūryā and now see her as essentially a further embodiment of the dawn-goddess. As such, the ravished daughter becomes the legitimate wife and queen of heaven consort of the celestial abductor.

And whether the *Homeric Hymn to Ares* is an early or late composition (I would guess the jury is still out on this one), the hymn to me has strongly associated solar connections belonging to the god which are otherwise not obvious. If so, Hera as his mother would again suggest the dawn's mythological parent role to the sun. There is no record I am aware of concerning mother-son incest between Hera and Ares; we find this suggestion instead in the *Rigveda* (6.55.4f, 10.3.3 & 10.85.37). The name given in the Vedic verses is that of the solar deity Pūṣan and the female figure is identified as mother or sister, but of course as both Ushas/Eos and Pūṣan/Sūrya/Ares are fathered by Zeus/Dyaus, the two hypostases are brother and sister. *Rigveda* 3.31.1f, in fact, mentions the sun-god Sūrya as marrying Ushas. But we also learn from Greek mythology that Ares was a lover of Eos before the latter became largely eclipsed by the imported Aphrodite, along with Hephaistos, from the Levant. Eos' promiscuity is accordingly her punishment inflicted by Aphrodite for the dawn-goddess' affair with Ares. But this licentiousness is already present from the goddess' initial incest with her father and arguably precedes Aphrodite's importation. The earlier 'sleeping around' may even be detectable in the rectifying nuance suggested by the rituals dedicated to the Roman goddess of the dawn, the Mater Matuta.

In coming to understand this seminal personification of the dawn among the Indo-Europeans, it is necessary to realise that we have three significant nominal designations for the goddess: (1) those deriving from a feminisation of the solar name itself (e.g., Sūryā, Hera, Saulė), (2) those from feminising light or *deus* itself (e.g., Dione, Diana, Juno and even in later Hindu literature Dyaus itself – 'goddess of the bright sky' or the 'She-Zeus'), and (3) those that refer to the east as the direction in which the dawn appears (e.g., Ushas, Eos, Aurora, Ostara, Ēostre, Aušra and the Lithuanian goddess of the morning star, Aušinė). This intermingling of the dawn and the morning star (the planet Venus) may have played a role in Aphrodite's conflation with Eos. Moreover, and differently, Homer designates Aphrodite as the daughter of Dione and Zeus. This last most likely reflects the original mythologem and contrasts with Hesiod who portrays Aphrodite as having been born from the sea-foam that had gathered around the castrated genitals of Uranus.

What becomes even more of interest is perhaps the transformation of the wanton looseness of the dawn-goddess (Eos/Ushas/proto-Indo-European *Hausos) who is both daughter and sister of Zeus/Dyaus/PIE *Dyēus into the chaste marriage-protectress figure we see with Hera as sister-wife. This is also reflected in the Matralia festival rites on the 11th of June in Rome. Moreover, the Roman Juno as the goddess of love and marriage is a deity of decorum rather than one of debauchery. There is also a persistent connection of the dawn-goddess prototype with the divine twins (e.g., the Dioscuri and Helen, the Ashvins and Ushas, the Ašieniai and Saulė). Actually, as all three are the children of the earth-mother, Zeus, Eos and the Archer may be the primordial formulation of the Dioscuric triad. In addition, the twins are variously considered the sons of Zeus/Dyaus, Ushas, Macha, Pērkons, Rhea Silvia, etc. But a further instance of the transformation of the father-daughter incest is probably to be seen in the abduction of Zeus and Demeter's daughter Persephone/Kore by Hades. As ruler of the underworld, Hades 'the unseen one' or Plouton 'the wealthy one' is most likely a development from an original triform ruler of the cosmos who rules the heavens as Zeus Olympios, the earth and/or seas as Poseidon ('lord of the earth') and the netherworld beneath the earth as Hades. Here again we have a female offspring of the sky and earth but with the rape being shifted to an *alter ego* of Zeus in place of the god himself, that is, Zeus now in his guise as Aidoneus, – Zeus *katachthonios* 'Zeus of the Underworld' and/or Zeus Meilichios 'the propitiated or gracious Zeus'.

Admittedly what I have sketched here is complicated and beyond the interest or cup of tea of most, but what I have chiefly wanted to convey is the fascinating nuances and developments that are possibly to be discovered through an engaging exploration of the mythological. Admittedly also, the mythologem of rape and incest at this primordial level will be considered offensive in the political correctness considerations of our present times. One response is to dismiss the past and re-write new and different myths, and while this is a possibility, my feeling is that much will then be missed. Confusing the ancient mythological portrayals of nature with the social concerns and ethics of today could be seen as a disservice to the fertile and boundless imagination of humanity that has been manifested historically and can also be surmised through our prehistory. Nature itself is beyond human moral judgment. For instance, we do not ethically assess the natural behaviour of animals or the destructive vagaries of naturally occurring events. That the wanton daughter becomes recognised as the legitimate and revered wife shows how the internal dynamic of our five thousand years or so old mythological heritage of metaphor and epithet may yet endorse the varieties and transformative answers that are required for a healthy, open and progressively developing society.

With the gods, it is Light that I revere among the most. And the dazzling daylight may be the first to come to mind, but the whole spectrum of colour's luminescence is also to be comprehended, and that may explain in part my consideration of the stained glass window as a fitting metaphor for personified divineness. The primary personification of Light is Jupiter or Zeus-Jupiter, but Deus itself is the luminous and thaumaturgical dynamic that is the essence of all the gods (deities, divinities). Divine brightness may be accepted as the holy of holies in European or Indo-European spirituality. However, the sacredness that is *primus inter pares* attributed to luminescence does not preclude honouring darkness as well. Both the bright and the dark are divine, complimentary and necessary for their mutual comprehension. The proto-pantheon is five in number – the concept of five being apparently a PIE understanding of 'totality' that is suggested presumably by the number of fingers in a hand. Earth, Deus and Dawn are the seminal figures of the proto-pantheon, and cosmogonically-speaking, the amorous relationship between the father-daughter figures was necessary if the father was the sole initial male personage. It would also have been necessary for the birth of Sun through the union of Deus or Brightness and Dawn. An alternate construction could have been a 'marriage' of Dawn and Moon from the version that has Earth originally giving birth to the twins, Deus and Moon. Various myths (e.g., Vedic, Baltic) relate the rivalry between Deus and Moon over Dawn. At this rudimentary level, Deus and Moon constitute the divine twins themselves, but in an augmented stage, the personification of the two essential features of Deus (the brightness of lightning, fireworks and/or explosion, on the one hand, and the gentler luminosity of daylight, starlight and firelight, on the other hand) becomes the prototypic *dioscuri*. As independent figures that are conceived as auxiliary to the initial five deities, Indo-European imagination has thus given rise to the primary seven figures of Indo-European nature worship. And from the underlying pagan perspective, whether gods or God, it is all the same. Divinity is both multiple and monistic. Non-pagans may have difficulty with this concept, but pagans themselves will not.

The Summer of Love was simply momentous in just about every preferred sense. I remember the British philosopher Alan Watts who gave a talk at San José State as well as almost regularly every week at The Family Dog the Hippie icon Steve Gaskin and his Monday Night Classes. The subjects ranged from ecology to the paranormal and were always stimulating. And then too, on the 10th of July in 1967, there was 'The Great Ballet Bust'. Someone I knew casually had hosted a dinner at his place in Haight-Ashbury. They were about twelve in all and included Rudolf Nureyev and Margot Fonteyn. And, as we all did at the time, they smoked some cannabis but then managed to be raided by the San Francisco police – possibly because a neighbour had complained about noise. This was of course headline news the following morning, and the papers included a photo on which it indicated the place where Nureyev had attempted to hide on the roof. A second photo showed Dame Margot arriving glamorously at the police station wrapped in a white fur stole and with a great smile on her face. San Francisco was absolutely a buzz. Nureyev took it all the most seriously, presumably terrified that he might as a result be deported back to the Soviet Union. However, the charges against them were dropped within hours, and I was still then able to enjoy them both in an unforgettable performance the next night of Prokofiev's *Romeo and Juliet* ballet for which I had already purchased a standing room ticket. The dancing was splendid and mesmerising, and the charge in the atmosphere stemming from what had just happened the night before was purely electrical.

In short, there is no way to convey the exhilarating ambience of those days in the late 1960s. All seemed more alive than ever before as well as, so it has come to pass, ever since. Generosity and openness were the norms, and often we could just walk into random houses, usually they were communes, and make ourselves at home. This was unprecedented. Little Nancy's VW Beetle was stolen at some point and then found in the state of Oregon. She, my Nancy, Rosanne and I set off in my car to fetch the stolen vehicle. We had attended one of Steve Gaskin's talks at the Family Dog in San Francisco the night before, and he had explained that the further away from one on the evolutionary scale it was, the better the food for health and well-being it would be. I remember our first morning in the redwood forests having bacon with our campfire breakfast. By the end of the week, however, we all had become vegetarians and returned home as such. I remained a vegetarian, or at least as a demi-vegetarian, for around the next twenty years – until the moment that I invited the mother of Karma Trinlay Rinpoche, the bodhisattva, to lunch in Kathmandu. She chose a restaurant that I think no longer exists, the Vienna Café in the Thamel, and it was said to be the best at the time. But to my shock and horror, Hecate ordered a steak. When I questioned this, she replied that nothing grounds one better than a good old-fashioned steak. It took me barely more than a minute to decide that

I wanted to ground myself too, and I have never looked back since. Years later, Hecate had become completely vegetarian, and when I reminded her that my own demi-vegetarianism had ended on that day we had had that lunch together, she proclaimed, 'My bad!'

I still tend to consume red meat only most rarely, but my worst moment occurred when I was visiting the relatives of Nancy who lived along the Namsen River in Trøndelag county of northern Norway. Beside vegetables, fruit, grain and dairy products, my regime had come to include poultry and especially sea food. Uncle Alfred had his own smokehouse and knew which herbs throughout the forest to collect for it. People from around the area would bring their salmon to be cured by him in his smokery. It was heaven to be served salmon for breakfast, midday meal, afternoon tea, supper and midnight snack. All could not have been more delicious, and Alfred and his wife and his brother, it was only the three of them, could not have been more welcoming (I had just shown up in my Volkswagen completely out of the blue) and expressive of Old Europe. The day arrived then when I was about to leave, and unbeknownst to me, they had purchased a roast of some kind to serve as my final meal with them. To my shame, I could not or would not eat it, and they had then to insist that I stay one more day so that they could serve some white fish which I would/could eat before being allowed to depart. I realised afterwards that it was the most stupid of things for me to have done, and I vowed then and there that I would accept and eat anything thereafter that was served to me.

But back to Oregon. After collecting Little Nancy's car, we continued on to Washington State and British Columbia. Once we had arrived in Vancouver, we went to the centre of town and sat with the rest who had gathered there (as young travellers still seem to do in the metropolises of the world) and wondered what we were to do next. A young gal suddenly and unexpectedly came up to us and asked if we needed a place to stay. She would not be needing her place that night and offered her keys to us. These were the countercultural times. They were simply marvellous and uncanny.

Rosanne's parents lived in Washington State, and so we visited and stayed with them as well. Someone had mentioned to me that if we were to be in that area at that time, we must checkout the festival in Tenino. Rosanne wanted to stay with her family, so the two Nancy's and I and Mrs. Dog, my brother's very pregnant dog who was with us, proceeded to see what this Sky River Rock Festival and Lighter Than Air Fair was about. Fortunately, our sleeping bags were still in the car; it was an incredible event, and we could not bear to leave for the next three days. This turned out to be the West Coast's answer to Woodstock that I believe was occurring at exactly the same time. The worst point was when we had returned to collect our sleeping gear and lost Dabbit Dog on the way back. There were thousands of us crowded throughout the farm grounds. I headed back to the car to look for our missing animal, and as I reached the entrance to the fair itself, there was Mrs. Dog running blindly back and forth in complete terror for having lost us. I called her to me, and it was the only time I have ever known a dog to cry and sob. After this and once we had set up our spot, she could come and go as much as she pleased. She knew where we were.

Besides our sleeping bags, we had brought nothing. But we quickly learned to scavenge. Perhaps because so many were stoned, there was a blanket of rubbish and a massive amount of dropped items covering the whole area. We found more than we ever needed – from more sleeping bags to unopened cans of salmon – and became a distribution centre to others in need. We were also freely able to strip ourselves naked, and our pictures appeared in the newspaper as a result. Our first evening, as the sun descended to the horizon, it all became for me India, even though it would be fourteen years before I would finally get to that magical land. We accepted what was given us – such was the trust and open-handedness of the times. The most amazing juncture occurred with the performance of the Steve Miller Band. We all were in a prolonged state of dancing ecstasy, and Miller's music kept taking everything higher and higher and higher. Both the band and we ourselves were not going to stop. But perhaps he was an MC who ran up at one culminating point and grabbed the microphone and yelled into it, 'Stop this madness! You have to stop this madness!' And we survived. When we woke on the first morning after the festival had concluded, it was overcast and raining, but for the fair itself, it had been hot, dry, sunny, dusty perhaps and purely perfect.

The other memorable event from this Pacific Northwest excursion was our visit to Vancouver Island. From her work in the psychiatric ward in San Francisco, Big Nancy wanted us to visit Fritz Perls's 'Gestalt therapy' centre, and it was while there that Mrs. Dog gave birth to her puppies. One of these, Debbit, my parents received. After my brother's death, my folks got Mrs. Dog as well. After several years, Debbit was hit by a car and lost use of her hind legs. The vet said there was nothing that could be done and that she should be put down. It was almost as if she heard this and immediately showed everyone that she could still manage and move about. Mrs.

Dog lived longer than her child, but both dogs became important for my parents as a link to my brother. But the significant and pivotal thing about the visit to the Vancouver Island centre was that it had been established by a man who *knew* – a Jew who had left Germany in the 1930s, who then left South Africa because of *apartheid* and had now left Big Sur, California for Victoria, Canada. As mentioned earlier, Perls' trajectory confirmed for me the direction in which my own thoughts had already been heading. It became for me 'the writing on the wall'. Subsequently, I managed to talk about half of the group of us who had bonded to flee the country. Nancy had set out for Europe two times before I had but always aborted her attempt and ended up back in San Francisco. Those of us who did get to Europe as the Haight-Ashbury scene itself was transferring to the other side of the Pond were Warren, Jan, Richard, Rosanne, and Coral but including as well Richard and Coral's infant daughter Iana. The day I came to leave San Francisco and thinking that I would only return in the future to America for funerals was the day of the Kent State shootings. The Kennedys had already been assassinated and Martin Luther King as well. The Manson murders had also taken place, and our days of the 'hippie revolution' were certainly beginning to appear to be numbered. How naïve we had been! We truly believed at the time that the world was changing and changing into some unprecedented henceforward period of love, sharing and emancipation. We were of course radically mistaken, but the realisation of our erroneous expectations took yet some more time to sink into our consciousness.

Of course, departing from San Francisco and moving to Europe was undeniably assisted by my 30th birthday inheritance. To collect it at the time, Nancy and I decided we would travel across the country to the East Coast by train. Even this was the end of an era, and when it was time (after Puerto Rico and Haiti) to return to California, train routes throughout the country had already been cancelled, and we had instead to fly back. But before leaving the City by the Bay on the first occasion, of course, we needed a farewell party to launch our departure the day before our train. For this, I invited virtually everyone I knew including people in the other apartments of the building as well the couple with whom I had served as a poll worker for the elections that had just occurred. These last, after arriving, were horrified by the wild and varied assortment of people who were present and made a sudden and hasty terrified exit. The party took place primarily in Pfeiffer's apartment, my game room residence on the roof, the roof itself and in the building's corridors. One person exclaimed to me at some point, 'My god, every major dealer in the City is here tonight!' All in all, it was a splendid send-off.

In seeing an advertised book concerning Plutarch as a man of many interests, what is signalled in the title are religion, myth and magic. That could almost summarise myself as well, except that I also have a curious concern for science – especially both nuclear physics and astronomy. But I would need to include in addition both nature and music if not the arts altogether. Of course, as a pagan, nature is my religion. But music is too. In fact, the mythogems, mythologems and continual narrative developments of mythology, let alone their mythographic study, parallels in my opinion the similar complexity of music with its themes, rhythms, textures, sonorities, tempos, forms and the ever-expanding tonal universe. While the dodecaphony of Arnold Schoenberg, Alban Berg, Anton Webern, Edgard Varèse and Pierre Boulez as well as the electronic music of composers like Karlheinz Stockhausen, John Cage, Henk Badings and others can be fascinating and intriguing and even enjoyable in a challenging way – with two favourites being György Ligeti and Iannis Xenakis, my real pleasure remains with classical and romantic musics and including such moderns as Henri Dutilleux and Malcolm Arnold. I am not certain that magic is only about will. In my understanding it primarily concerns enchantment. But like music, there are many different forms or kinds of magic. And if magic serves as a kind of shortcut technique for achieving desired results, both it and enchantment centre upon the experience and being of wonder. The arts themselves are patent pursuits of the wondrous when not necessarily preoccupied with political and social reformist agendas. And religion too possesses a conducive capacity to aim for and capture the wondrous when possible. But, of course, it is nature in all her manifestation that is supreme in being the living embodiment of wonder and the origin and/or matrix to the miraculous as a direct accessibility.

The failure of the 2019 COP25 UN climate conference in Madrid on the heels of the 'sweeping' Tory election victory in Britain was, short of outright war or terrorist catastrophe, about as depressing as things could get. With the US under Trump already pulling out of the 2015 Paris Agreement, the talks of the United Nation Framework Convention on Climate

Change between nearly 200 nations were only able, after two weeks of discussion, to postpone the key decision concerning the future of carbon markets. While the world seems to be increasingly aware of the need to cut greenhouse gases and the necessity to help poorer countries that are suffering from the effects of global warming, the richer states do not appear to be seriously aware of the devastating threat to the planet through climate change. Meanwhile Australia continues to hit record temperature highs while approximately 120 bushfires, half uncontrolled, rage throughout New South Wales and ringing Sydney. If today's environmental crisis awareness has come to supersede former Golden Age millenarian and utopian expectation and/or effort for a New Age/Aquarian Age, the declared denunciation of capitalism, consumerism and industrialisation remains ineffectually unchanged. Esoteric spirituality and ideas have been persistent since Plato, Renaissance imagination, even Enlightenment secular rationalism, Swedenborg's New Jerusalem, Theosophical inner-life spiritual illumination, Transcendental Romanticism, the Sixties' counterculturalisms, and the post-Harmonic Convergence's continued emphasis on meditation, individual transformation and eco-apocalypticism, but the dynamics of these non-mainstream protest movements appear to be as unsuccessful in any overall altering impact as they have ever been. Unfortunately, one solution that perennially seems to arise in the face of any serious challenge to traditional conventions and establishment is totalitarian fascism. Are ecodems (ecological democrats / democratic ecologists) always to be doomed to failure?

What I have been unable to understand since at least 1983 is why people continue to worship that Levantine god which goes by the name of Yahweh, Jehovah, Allah. True enough, I once did the same myself, but having grown in the ability of what I call discernment, I do not comprehend why others have not come to the same recognition and understanding. I am not a Marxist, although people of that faith may share similar 'anti-God' sentiments to those of my own. I affirm the godhead, the gods, the anima-animus, but for me this is something fundamentally different and freer than are the concepts embraced by Christianity and the like. Admittedly, my outlook resonates with the ideas of human alienation that have been articulated foremost by Friedrich Nietzsche and Albert Camus. The physical universe is for we humans an unending enigma. In this lack of *a priori* or determinable meaning, we are left with a cosmic nihilism that allows us two essential approaches to existence. One is the Socratic-Platonic-Christian hatred of life and its projection of reason, virtue and happiness into an exclusively idealist-transcendental unreal realm of otherworldly being. The other is an acceptance of the pains and pleasures of physical life, the search for an ethics that supersedes both good and evil as psychological-metaphysical categories, and an endorsement of the authentic instincts of this-worldly life that escape the mediocre emotions of cowardly resentment. In a word, this distinction between these two cosmic strategies is what I term the gnostic-pagan divergence. In the release that follows from the acceptance of measureless absurdity without ineffable and external dictate, we humans are free to make, create and endorse our own understanding of morality and meaning.

Have we not all done horrible things at some point in our pasts – shameful and cruel things that we have come to regret? And perhaps to the degree that we individually continue to exploit and sully the fragile ecology of our planet, our disgraceful behaviour is not only confined to former conduct but persists very much into the present. Guilt and shame are moral issues; wise action is something else. The former relates to the endeavour to succeed in attaining an ethical condition that is *beyond* good and evil; the latter, to common sense and action based on a sober assessment of the needs at hand. For Nietzsche, true morality becomes the effort of employing a will to power over oneself, whereas conventional morality is the pursuit of a powerful will over others. This last is what pagan activist Starhawk deplores, and it becomes a shabby means to bury personal offence and dishonour by scapegoating the wrongful onto others rather than instead of accepting and then mastering one's own negative regret. This last is doubtlessly no easy task to achieve, but its effort is what rightfully confronts us all – from cleaners, garbage collectors and manual labourers to prime ministers and presidents, from the lowliest to the highest, and everyone else between. Like each member of an orchestra, we individually have our parts to play – and playing well is not only due to the technical skill we manage to develop or have a natural aptitude for but also to that aura of self-transcendence that contributes to something being more than merely the sum of its parts. With projection of identity and character beyond the mediocre average of the norm, we aim for a superior ascendency. As metaphorical orchestral players, together then we might produce a music that can be incomparable and supremely beautiful. This is my understanding of Nietzsche rather than the totalitarian interpretation that was subsequently fostered onto him by his fascist sister. We have a most patent need to be emancipated from antiquated imprisonment and the downward spiral produced by outmoded and 'power over' notions and beliefs into courageous, adventurous and harmonious ways of trusting our collective potential.

We can imagine the imaginal or otherworld, and we can imagine that it exists as an alternate ontological reality – one to which we transfer upon our physical deaths. Maybe this is the case; maybe not. We shall find out when our time comes, and if we do not, we will not even know that we do not know. The possibilities are between some kind of post-mortem being and complete oblivion.

And if fight one must, then fight not against our own kind but against the spirits of injustice, oppression and stagnation. Fight through creativity! When all is said and done, in no way am I a Buddhist, but even less a Marxist. Over the many years of my long life, increasingly I feel that the only purpose to life is worship. The form of course varies. I have seen four basic courses of beauty if not also of value: devotion, pleasure, production, giving or any combination of these. The choice is the individual's – not the dictates of the mob or of a mob's consciousness even if expressed through a doctrinaire elite and especially when militarily implemented. O Indra, conquer the dragon! I am in full agreement, following Dostoevsky's argument, that if there is no God or God is dead, all is then permitted, that the absurdity of life's meaninglessness allows us – encourages us – to live life out in freedom, passion and innocence.

Much of my life has come to have been spent in the Midi. This emerged in time as an unplanned surprise. I can recall one Sunday morning when, after having voted, Helen and Pierre stopped by for drinks. They described the sudden friendliness of everyone in the town since one might be a potential voter for their side. They also had difficulty in recognising people since they were dressed up for a change. Moreover, there was no waiting necessary in order to vote. Instead, everybody was waiting for the next voter to arrive. The result of our local elections was, as usual, with nothing changing. Such is perhaps the sleepy Provence.

Between reading, writing, gardening, tending our olive trees and exchanging meals with friends, life in the south of France has for the most part been evocative of a paradise. Peter Mayle's *A Year in Provence* certainly capitalised on the tribulations that all ex-pats living in the area have experienced, and probably any one of us could have written something similar. But there is a *nous ne sommes pas tous pareils* largesse that prevails throughout an exquisite Mediterranean landscape along with the colour of the French language and cuisine that render the territory something special and apart. It also afforded me ample opportunity for continuing research and speculation. I came in time to play there with the notion of the postmodern God's floating foundation between the extremes of utter chaos and complete sterile stasis. The suspended footing for me of a dimension of being that provides a workable direction consists of such temporary durable metaphors as the sun, moon, dawn, etc. God itself/himself is also a temporary metaphor or functional reality to be located between the paradoxical extremes. After a visiting lectureship at the University of California, Santa Barbara, in May of 1994, while now visiting my mother in Narragansett, Rhode Island, I deduced that the (at the time) fascinating concept of the 'postmodern' (something *after* the modern) was not meant to be defined but was/is a 'play term' – one by which we are to have fun in coming to an understanding of what the term means. It remains a flexible designation that continues to be largely in the process of taking shape and being understood. I would argue that the arts take a leading role in this. But interestingly, my French friends, especially Parisians, argued against the postmodern, at least as an architectural style, and claimed that the non-retro *modern nouveaux* had already superseded it (e.g., the Foundation Louis Vuitton). Presumably, the New Modern supersedes *nouveau réalisme* – the New Realism for which the Pompidou Centre is exemplary.

If and when I become confused by contemporary developments and discourse, my solace is to turn back to much earlier pagan thought – not as an escape but rather as a re-finding of organic roots that might viably contribute to today's intellectual and spiritual navigation. And here I am turning back again to what I have already touched upon. One of my favourites is the ancient god of light, and if Jupiter or Zeus is Gaia's opposite, it is the goddess who herself generates her ontological opposite. But if the gods constitute inscrutable perfection, then, as already said, Zeus is perfect light as Ge is perfect matter. Whether they actually exist or not, they serve nevertheless for the mystical moment of feeling utter thanks. And to throw this into a random direction, whether we are grateful or belaboured, we must still question the official givens. For me, it does seem obvious that the US government played a role in the Kennedy assassinations. Is it really any surprise then that we have had the US government under its 45th President that we did? If imperial Rome, the most powerful state of its time, was as internecine and corrupt as we know it to have been, why should we expect things to be any different in those respects today? A *true* investigation into the Kennedy murders and 911 would be the only way to quell the ongoing suspicions and conspiracy allegations. But presently, what is the likelihood of this taking place? So let me just say that if Jove is the embodiment of illumination, I will continue to pray and invoke for the jovial to inform and rectify all life – personal and collective, human and other-than-human, the rigidly and terrified conservative and the unthinkingly morally superior and excessively liberal.

One danger as I see it is to do what Adorno does, namely, to fix one's terms too simplistically and solely in a black-and-white dichotomy or opposition. Commodification, for example, is not a unitary concept. Is not the addition of those extra buttons on the inside bottom of a shirt an art of thoughtfulness? Even if the shirt might not be thought of necessarily as a commodity, it still is usually an object of mass production. Perhaps this allows us to perceive a gradation of acceptability and/or worthiness in or of a commodity. There is undoubtedly more variety and consideration in life than our political rants and divisive positions allow us to see. And things do change when and if we let them. As a child, my parents grew rhubarb in the back garden, and I detested the smell of it when my mother was cooking it in the kitchen. Then one day when I was in my twenties, I woke one morning in that penthouse dream in San Francisco thinking that I would adore rhubarb now, and I have ever since. I believe at the end of the day all comes down to an affirmation of life; not an endorsement of some or any particular religion but of life itself and in all its wondrousness. More recently, Richard and I were sitting by a loch enjoying a ritual smoke and intersecting with the enveloping beauty surrounding us. I realised that somewhere there is a youth being taught by a person more advanced in maturity but in a situation akin to the mnemonic experience of nature's inspiration that Richard and I were experiencing at that very juncture of time. Of course, it is happening somewhere; perhaps it is happening in numerous instances – establishing for someone a rooted sequence of significant memory. Each of us is an embodiment of collective humanity, though each with different root memories. And while honesty at times can be horribly thoughtless, we still are at our best in our affirmations of life. And as part of this confirmation, we could allow ourselves to trust the synchronicities. Following the Global Consciousness Project conducted by Princeton's Institute of Noetic Sciences, collective consciousness has been pictured to be at an infant stage of development. It is supposedly just beginning. But perhaps more accurately, our collective self or consciousness is instead at some equivalent of teenage years – those times when we have done some atrocious unthinking things: joy riding, theft, bullying, recklessness and so forth. Some of us do not survive beyond such times, though most of us do grow up and out of that earlier stage of the maturing process. Let us but hope that we are collectively approaching that learning point or event that moves us in a positive direction. Ultimately, are we not obliged to accept the fact that not only are we a part of the collective whole of humanity but also that each of us ourselves *is* collective humanity. Life is before us for affirmation regardless of our different memory banks. To perform jihad for some evil empty entity is about as far from this stance as is possible. My own temptation previously in life to be off on some solitary sannyasin-type of enterprise has come to be replaced by my happy ensconcement with my love. I am, thankfully, no messiah or super guru or charismatic leader/preacher but simply one who affirms the collective affirmation of life as the choice offered to us all. It is but important that we affirmers are ultimately the ones who will prevail. While Thomas Hobbes famously considers that life is solitary, poor, nasty, brutish and short, I agree with the assessment of shortness, and this is all the more reason that with the addition of its wondrousness, we might rightly resist capitulation to empty alienation.

The Wicca repeating circle and the (more archaic) pagan ascent have perhaps been now replaced by a pagan flow. The flow is itself ambivalent – not always gentle, but rough and swift at some points, even dangerous. And yet in the reality of our more normal forward-forward paced world of today, a flow of any kind can be difficult with which to connect. It is for this reason principally that I celebrate a ritual calendar. My preferred sacraments to accompany commemoration are spirits and hemp. Cannabis in particular I find pulls one out from the rat-race tempo and into an otherworld in which there is the freedom to focus for a moment on the gods of nature that are always around us and actually just to be able to see them. I have indeed known that intense shamanic state, and the worst were my Strawberry Hill angels, invisibly anthropic, but appearing as elongated biblical whiffs of smoke. The acute altered state of consciousness is always present in some *sub rosa* manner, but as far as it remains possible, I abandon the super-messiah state for the gentle flow I have with my love in this more mundane world. Through ritual and commemorative mindfulness, the quasi-timeless realm can be encouraged to intersect with the routine forward-forward march.

Grandmother as a young woman, circa 1915 (left), and years later with my grandfather (right).

My grandmother (at far right) and her siblings at their mother's funeral upon which her siblings all feuded over their mother's inheritance. My grandmother would have nothing to do with it and moved then to California. She looks as if she is already distancing herself from the rest.

Indominitable Aunt Dorothy as a teenager sporting her Girl Scout uniform, circa 1914.

Aunt Dorothy on another assignment for her own Murray Hill News, this one is the 1969 Orient Convention. Here she is at far right standing next to my grandmother and two convention attendees. I love to compare the boots-on-the-ground stance of Aunt Dorothy's with my grandmother's more demure, charm-school pose.

Mother as a girl, circa 1922.

My mother and father as newlyweds, circa 1937.

The York family in the early 1950s, out for a stroll through Maplewood.

Mother and me at 3 months.

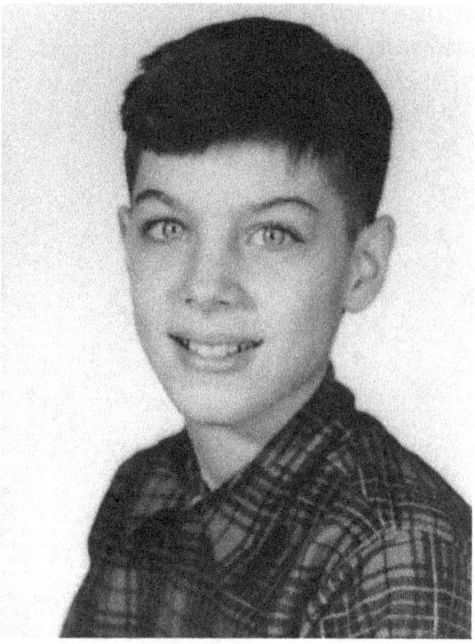

My 5th grade school photo.

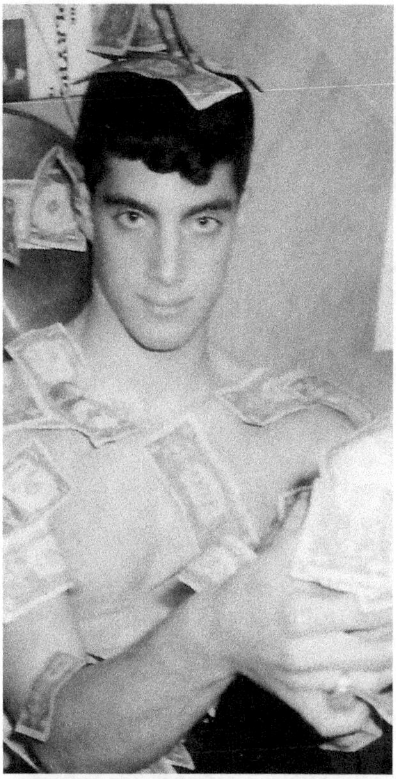

My brother Peter. Being silly, age 20 (left);
with me and Mrs. Dog (above);
with mother and me (below).

My ever-devoted Richard
(with his daughter Iana, above right).

My Amsterdam house (at right in the photo) pre-World War II.

The Provençal farmhouse, circa 1975.

Six of the 'family' with Bob Pfeiffer in his San Francisco apartment in 1969.

Me with Bob Pfeiffer (left) and Barbara Dauphin (right).

Nancy and me (above); our wedding announcement, June 1966 (right).

Mr. and Mrs. Michael Otto York

Nancy A. Williams, Michael Otto York

Miss Nancy Agnes Williams of San Francisco, daughter of

is attending the graduate school of San Francisco State College. She is a member of

Chloe, Rix, and Gin in Cannes, 1990.

Chloe and me in Bath, England.

My London family, with Freeman Gunter visiting.

Richard with his family in Columbus, New Mexico.

Me and pagan elders at conferences with Deborah Ann Light and Jeri Baldwin (top); with Selena Fox (middle); and with Ronald Hutton and Prudence Jones (right).

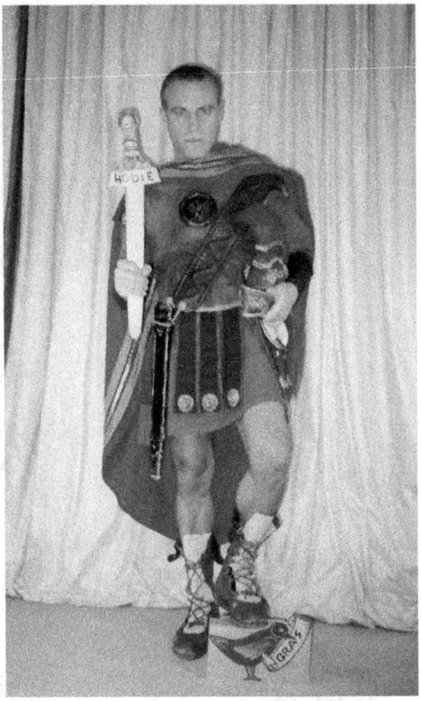

The Roman Baths of Sulis Minerva in Bath, England (above left);
in costume as the Roman centurion and Voodoo Saint Expedite (above right);
a giant lingam in San Francisco (left);
Sitala shrine in Benaras, India (below).

Edith's one and only night out (see page 330).

CHAPTER SIX

Paris / Marlene Dietrich / Toni Morgan / Margot Adler; popular insurrections; contemporary Western paganism / the gods; no Santa Claus; we sold our herd; the Midi / the 1950s / my Ghost Dance days in San Francisco / present-day lows, John Beckett's *Paganism in Depth*; my complaints with CWP / Heathen folkism / my definitions of paganism / Big Tent paganism / von List, von Liebenfels & Fritsch; Marie-Laure / music & Brown & Hopps' *The Extravagance of Music* / liminality & affordance / art & ritual; DNA myopia; Avoda Zara / my mother's disclosure / the Frooks family / the *asurian* ONE / the Covenant / Shlomo Sand's Khazar hypothesis / Hilda Ellis Davidson & Odin; Sibelius; pagan divisiveness / liminal access through nature / liminal access through non-nature / the countryside & city argument / theological plurality / the Gorges du Verdon / the delights of the Midi / the ethical core of paganism / humanity as one of the gods; the Pagania Express / the Cardinal Virtues / *kama, tapas,* Himeros, fire, Múspell / the Roman & Dioscuri dualities / access to primordial utility & inspiration, Prometheus, Indra, Agni, Vahagn / Indra, Suparna, Agni, Soma, Manu, Bölwerk, Tyr / pagan interest in the past as both heaven and the other / fire, enchantment & poetry; 1984 vis-à-vis COVID-19 / preternatural materialism & ceremonial humanism / favourite deiforms / the sacred geography of Kashi / Gyan Vapi & Viśvanātha / Avoda Vara & divine plurality / Gumburī Baba shrine amid the railway tracks / John Fowles and *The Aristos* / all-night North Indian concerts & Ravi Shankar / Mahashivaratri; post-India Amsterdam and the Provence / the river Indre / Carnac / Killarney, Glounacappy & Killorglin / Wales, Bath, London & Bradbourne / 'real' religion versus paganism / Goshen-Gottstein's 'same God' argument / current paganism & 'cancel culture' / divine fluidity / Yahweh as 'operative non-existence' / 'Kill the TERFs' authoritarianism / expression of gratitude; Egypt, Sinai & Gamil Ratib / Parisian police surveillance

Paris in August! So wonderfully empty and unlike its fullness and crowded busyness the rest of the year. Even the summer rains become enchanting, and the city's beauty that I have known for so many years is a familiar and much-loved friend. It is also especially poignant for me because many of my Parisian recollections are of Toni Morgan (19 August 1946 – 29 June 2014) with whom – taking a break from the Amsterdam commune – I came in the 1970s and definitively fell in love with France and her capital. Toni's marriage with an abusive Iranian husband lasted only a few years after our Parisian excursion. We had spent much of the time in the city looking for a pair of shoes for Toni.

Among the goddesses I revere I include Marlene Dietrich. With Little Toni, I went to see her perform at the Espace Cardin on the Champs-Élysées in the 1970s. Admittedly, it was a terrible performance, though I did not mind in particular – being thrilled just to see her. After every line, Marlene would project her tongue out from the side of her mouth. I suppose it was meant to be sexy, but it wasn't. When it was finally time for the curtain call, Dietrich was on the stage but someone opened the curtain before she was ready. Marlene was furious and stormed off with a fist raised after whomever was responsible. The curtain descended, and the shocked audience proceeded to leave the theatre in silence. I found it all unbelievable and turned around when half of us were still in the theatre. I could see that Marlene had stuck her head out between the curtains, so I began to applaud, and those who were still present joined too into the applause. The curtains were then opened, and our singer took her bows.

From Aunt Dorothy and her *Murray Hill News*, I had in those days a press pass that I used on many occasions – including to the investiture of Queen Beatrix in the Nieue Kerk of Amsterdam. Admittedly Toni and I were stoned, but I was determined to go back stage after the show. I was not aware that Dietrich detested reporters, but we gained entry and were told to wait in the corridor. From where we were, I could see the lady via a reflection from her vanity's mirror before which she was sitting. There was a group of sycophantic admirers gathered around her. One of them said finally, 'I'm tired of hearing how bad the show was. I think it was a great show!' A chorus of agreement immediately ensued.

When Marlene exited her dressing room, in my excitement, I handed her my car registration papers and invited her to Amsterdam. 'I never go to Amsterdam', she replied frostily. But to her great credit in my opinion, she looked at what I had handed her and said, 'These are much too important papers for me to have'. A paper was produced so that I could write down my address for her. We all then proceeded to the back stage exit of the theatre. A crowd of fans were waiting for her. Marlene held open the door, and all those who had been with her in her dressing room filed out one by one. When it was my turn, I just could not see myself allowing Marlene Dietrich to hold open the door for me, so I took the door from her and allowed her to continue to the applause outdoors. Toni and I departed at this point to see a showing of *Blonde Venus* (1932), and this in all was my Marlene Dietrich experience.

After living some time in Iran and then returning to Los Angeles, Toni secured her divorce and became a successful Hollywood film editor. In time, she came to care for her ailing father – flying every Friday evening directly from work to be at his bedside in Arizona and fly immediately back to work on Monday morning. Next was her mother who died a year to the day of her father's passing. And then Toni moved to Missoula to nurse her brother Robert who was dying with multiple sclerosis. With the loss of the three members of her family who were the most important people to her, Toni was deeply emotionally damaged. Her selfless dedication left her herself an invalid. She returned to Los Angeles but then returned from there once again to Montana, her home state. No one learned that her heart had simply stopped until a month later when a friend and her niece were contacted by the sheriff's department.

And two days after I learned of Toni's death, another friend, Margo Adler (16 April 1946 – 28 July 2014) died after a long battle with cancer. Margot had last written to me on the 17th of June saying: 'Things are difficult right now. Six weeks ago lost all energy – lungs at issue, went on steroids which were illusory but magical – but had to get off steroids to start clinical trial – now started clinical trial – we shall see. Margot'. Margot's book *Drawing Down the Moon* remains one of the best introductions to contemporary Western paganism. She was a lovely, energetic person loved by many, and I treasure the times she came to stay with us in Amsterdam.

And so with the emotional shock and subsequent adjustment, and having just completed a recent revision of my manuscript on pagan ethics, and being as well in between visiting friends to Amsterdam, Richard and I have come for a week to the City of Lights where we can walk the banks of the Seine and feast on the Parisian architecture and dazzling visuals. The irony with August of course is that several of our favourite places are closed for the summer break. But there are always here enough alternatives, and the air is soft – sometimes hot and humid, sometimes heavy with rain, and sometimes cooler and comfortable. The overall tempo in this month is relaxed, and people in the shops and cafés seem to be friendlier than might otherwise appear to be the case. And when one walks the relatively emptier streets at this time of year, there is more of an opportunity to sense the spirits of those who have walked along the same streets and boulevards for centuries – even those who were present in Celtic and Roman times as well. But today the sidewalk terraces still fill with those who stop for a beverage and to converse or simply watch the movement around them. There may be some of the most intriguing museums and theatre in the world here, but the real life of the city is to be found on its streets and the ebb and flow of a pedestrian parade that has been on show for a millennium or two. And I can still sense at least Toni's energy mingling its way through the people mix and savouring the panoramic vistas from any of the countless bridges that cross the river that flows through and divides this urban confluence.

There is no way of knowing what the situations might be when and *if* I am ever to finish this present writing venture. But as we are currently dawning into the new year of 2020, I am perplexed over the popular demonstrations in both Algeria and Lebanon. I could presumably add Hong Kong as well, but this last is a confrontation between a relatively tiny quasi-British legacy and the mega-power of the People's Republic of China. It is a different kind of contest altogether. But if the Algerian and Lebanese protesters were actually able to be successful in their insurrections, how could the process succeed with no one in charge and no spokespeople for the movements as a whole?

As I see it, if victorious, the people themselves would come to have the power over the internet rather than the government that could choose to shut it down. The danger would remain that some external bully might or will try to manipulate the internet, and this is an important consideration. But with a people's insurrection, candidates for a governing council of, say, nine members could be presented via social network/internet/etc. with each candidate having the opportunity to explain how she or he proposes to work with others. The people would then be offered to vote on each candidate individually, and those would be selected who receive two-thirds (66%) of the vote for themselves as opposed to those who had voted against them. Since 'referendum' has become a negative word, it is important that this selection depend on something like 60 or 66% of the total vote. The process could continue until there are nine (if that becomes the working number) who have each been *selected* by the requisite number of voters. Initially, the names of a dozen or more possibilities could be presented and chosen by lot – perhaps by virgins in white robes; maybe even by children.

While reflecting on how popular insurrections might be able to proceed,

I have become aware of the peculiar nature of the English. Like the Americans, both are imperialistic and driven from this desire. This need not be an Anglo thing, as I do not recognise imperialism as belonging to the Canadians, New Zealanders, South Africans and even the Australians. So, in the wake of our impending Brexit, I am perceiving that a distinction may be made between English imperialism vis-à-vis British internationalism. It is principally the English alone who want to leave the European Union; not the rest. I retain some satisfaction in realising that, in this sense, Londoners themselves are primarily British.

But returning to insurrection possibilities in such places as Algeria and Lebanon, the counsel and suggestions from former rulers could also be welcomed in the cyber-forum but subject to the same 66% approval conditions. Of course, this is only a suggestion, but it is incumbent that some operable procedure is to be found to transform a popular revolt into a functioning democracy. And while I am at it, I have proposals concerning the extreme economic divide of our world at present, namely, that which concerns both billionaire corporations and billionaires themselves: (1) all corporate enterprises must operate in accord with the global ecological ethic; (2) the people of the community's territory in which a corporate power is based are to have an equal say in decision-making. If there is a deadlock between the two, arbitration is then necessary. [I do realise the danger here that wealthy corporations would be able to buy votes among the people.]; and (3) billionaire funding of the UBI. The universal basic income could be based to match the salaries the super-wealthy pay to their guards who protect them.

Controversial ideas without a doubt, but is not radical progressive change necessary in whatever truth there might be in the global confusion the media presents to us? And do we not, above all, collectively owe serious consideration to our children and their children? And all is not gloom. Nicholas Kristof in *The New York Times* reports on the significant drop in the world's numbers experiencing extreme poverty, the greatly reduced toll of deaths of children under the age of 5, and the surprising gains in literacy (China, Argentina and Brazil in particular but the world as a whole as well).

I observe the Roman festival calendar because of its underlying celebration of nature and the seasons. It suggests as well a vital purity which feels to me commensurate with modern living. My rejection of Christianity has been personally one of great emancipation – freedom from such unnecessary burdens as original sin, guilt, obedience and martyrdom. My belief centres on and in this world and its values and a primary focus thereupon.

I am all too aware of shortcomings in contemporary Western paganism, and this concern is the ultimate *raison d'être* for the present work. Perhaps relatedly, Mark Green, who promotes an atheistic form of paganism (what he calls Atheopaganism), rants about the commercialism that he sees rampant in pagan fairs. He mentions Pantheacon specifically and condemns the crass 'buy, buy, buy' mentality that is encouraged through hucksters and vendors eager to sell such products as 'magic rocks', witchy clothing, drums, wands, baubles and all sorts of mass-produced paraphernalia (what Green himself refers to as 'junk'). The seduction of pagans by merchandise which, unless it is handcrafted and the like, Green sees as ecological violations of the earth. He opposes the hocus-pocus sales pitch and argues that the collection of pagan 'stuff' is not significant for anyone to be pagan. I feel he is right in his criticism of Western consumerism and any of us pagans who almost mindlessly can succumb to it as well. One main caution here, however, concerns the traditional market or kermis that flourished next to the medieval church on holy saint days and the like. These may represent origins to capitalism, but they are also natural for human proclivities. Pagans are little different in their attraction to the market. In addition, for many of those who are new to the pagan scene, the merchandise side serves as introductory and affords some initial insight. The 'battle' is with us as individual novices and less with the plethora and opportunists who confront us. It is a learning process and one in which the curious might be encouraged in time to be weaned away from the allure of glittering commodities and indoctrinating books, but compassion and understanding will hopefully remain as what is chiefly offered by those of us who are elders to and vis-à-vis our more vulnerable beginners.

The preservation of pristine and non-urbanised nature is the *sine qua non* of all pagan focus in today's world – both that and the ecological maintenance of our holy planet and the ever more mindfulness of climate change, plastic contamination of our seas and atmosphere, industrial exploitation and pollution and the needless waste that comes with imperialism and conflict. All these concerns tend to be summed up under the label of 'nature'. Perhaps not quite the same thing, but the much earlier agricultural and pastoral life of the countryside is closer to the wilder nature of the woodlands, forests and mountains – at least in comparison with the much greater divide from the natural world of technological society as we know it in the twenty-first century with its feats of engineering, artificial intelligence, medical advance and the cyber world. The initial shift is understood to have been that between the paleolithic (of hunting and gathering) and the neolithic (of farming and herding). The latter is condemned by some Luddites as the process that removed humanity from an original intimacy with the natural. The term 'Neolithic Revolution' is a misnomer. While metaphorically it refers to what might be considered a major turning point in human history, the 'neolithic' development itself of polished and ground-stone tools, pottery, food storage, farming over foraging, settled village and town life, and the establishment of writing was a long-drawn out and slow process. In no way, did it happen 'overnight'. The New Stone Age, however, led to the onset of agrarian societies, the domestication of natural plants and animals, and the replacement of total reliance on wild resources with a centring on domestic foods. We can see in this development of food-producing economies, with their accompanying craft-specialisation, metalsmithing, governing and autonomous art, the foundations of what we may recognise as civilisation. As I see it, human progress was inevitable. But as the Swedish philologist and mythographer, Martin Nilsson, has observed, the rustic popular religion of the Greeks and later European folklore emerged from both the dwelling places of nature spirits among the groves, meadows, waters, forests, caves and mountains and from the peasants' fundamental concern with crops, fruits, flocks and herds. This substratum of spirituality continues into our own times, and while great gods themselves have largely taken refuge within the West's artistic and mythological heritage, the sacred and secular continue to intermingle and remain accessible to those of us who hear their call. Consequently, along with nature, my paganism is founded upon mythology, the arts and music, and I trace all of these to the deepest longings of the soul and as they came to be expressed in rudimentary and/or persistent but dogma-free cults. This composite of foundations legitimises for me the honouring of nature, the gods and the arts.

The gods themselves I approach as both dynamic metaphors and tangible embodiments of nature such as the sun, moon, dawn, earth and luminosity. I have known many pagans who consider or even insist that the gods are definite beings with personality and usually embodied anthropomorphic form. I like this idea but am not prepared to go this far, although I have had a few times visionary *darshan* of one deity or another, and I have seen flying flocks of birds over the Ganges River or elsewhere that have looked like to be a divine being moving through the atmosphere. To the contrary, I know several pagans who patently deny the existence of gods. This stance retains a certain appeal for me as well. Freedom from the legacies of any traditional or established religion is a freedom. It also allows someone like Bron Taylor or possibly Mark Green to concentrate more fully on ecological needs and activism. But for me, elimination of the gods in ritual or worship, even as symbols or metaphors, for an unadulterated love of the natural world is akin to the elimination of art as a possible further distraction. While I adore and endorse all positions vis-à-vis the gods that pagans may have, from being real beings to not existing at all, personally I prefer to engage with analogy, play and paradox to reach beyond and into the extravagance of sublime enchantment. Because of my resistance to Plato and his enduring influence, particularly through Plotinus and Augustine, I remain hesitant in employing the term 'transcendence' – especially because it has been employed in gnostic or quasi-gnostic idealisms (including Christianity) as the *origin* of all tangible realities. When and if the transcendent is conceived of as an emanating aura *from* the physical rather than being the exclusive source of the matter-energy continuum, I am fine with the term in its suggestion of epiphanic mystery as radically other. Rather than transcendence or the transcendent, I prefer to employ such concepts as the rapturous, enchantment, the awesome, the ineffable, immanence, afflatus, dazzlement and so forth. What I cannot subscribe to is the neo-Platonic separation of the body and soul, any desire to escape corporeal experience under normal and painless times, and a relentless distrust of the senses.

I would have been around the age of 10 when we entered the 1950s. Until a few years before that, I would argue with any of my friends who denied that there was a Santa Claus. How could they possibly think like that? Then a day arrived, and I was ill and in bed instead of school. I heard something on the radio that prompted me to ask her why some people were denying the existence of Santa Claus. My mother explained gently to me and the best she could that there is a 'spirit of Santa Claus' but not an actual individual that soared through the skies on Christmas Eve bearing gifts and whose sleigh was pulled by flying reindeer. I was utterly aghast and shocked. 'Does that mean there is not an Easter Bunny too?' I had to ask. I remember later that year when it finally was Christmas that it was for the first time on my part a joyless occasion. I sadly envied the glee that my younger brother and sister were still able to enjoy when we gathered around the Christmas tree. In all, this realisation was of course necessary but was also one of those major turning points and disappointments in my life.

One of the best lines in my memory occurred at a *vernissage* for the American Museum in Bath. During the time that I was teaching in England, a friend of a friend had been the Museum's director and had talked me into becoming a Member. Subsequently, it may have been around 2004 when the United Kingdom was experiencing another major outbreak of bovine spongiform encephalopathy (BSE). By this time, the British government had finally admitted that humans could become infected with a variant form of CJD (Creutzfeldt-Jakob Disease) – presumably through contaminated beef. The current scare was ubiquitously in most people's minds. Attending a first-night opening of an American quilt exhibition for museum members, I knew no one present and had therefore the opportunity to listen to what others were saying. I heard a man nearby ask a woman he knew if she was worried at all about the mad cow disease. 'Oh no!' she replied dismissively, 'we sold our herd two years ago!'

Recollecting times in the South of France: acquiring my first computer and the headaches involved, the electricity blinking for a second and losing a mammoth amount of work in that split instant, the assessment by the technicians after saga after saga that I have '*pas de chance*', the Jazz Festival in Cimiez (with Herbie Hancock, Dick Hyman, Fats Domino) and the Festival d'Aix-en-Provence (Beethoven, Poulenc, Milhaud's *Bouef sur le toit,* Rossini's *Cenerentola,* Berio's version of Monteverdi's *Il combattimento di Tancredi e Clorinda,* Berio and Sanguineti's *Passagio* and Jesse Norman in Rameau's *Hippolyte et Aricie.*) Wonderful times, scorching Midi heat wave, dinners and lunches and drinks with friends, but I find frequently as I remember and recall my past that my memory can just as often return to the Fabulous Fifties: no computers, no email, no mobile phones and the re-found and then released Red and Blue Albums of Benny Goodman's *Carnegie Hall*

Concert of 1938 (along with Harry James, Lionel Hampton, Gene Krupa, Cootie Williams, Johnny Hodges, Lester Young, even Count Basie and more, and the fabulous voices of Martha Tilton and Helen Ward – and, of course, *Sing, Sing, Sing – With a Swing*). Whether the 50s were as innocent and without fault as I knew or thought them to be (and obviously they were not), their comfortable affluence, their freedom and diversity for a teenager, and their seeming openness to an even brighter future allowed them to fall together personally as an idyllic period of time. The Korean and Vietnam wars were far away and not of immediate concern. Ostensibly, the war in Korea ended in 1953, and American involvement in Vietnam did not really commence until the end of the 50s. The shocks of the time included the firing of the Second World War hero, General MacArthur, and the Suez Crisis of 1956. I was most upset with the invasion by France and the United Kingdom and prayed for the protection and freedom of Egypt – a land whose legacy of ancient myths and sacred places demanded in my mind inviolate protection and undamaged completeness. The Soviet Union was the great enemy – though not with the invasion of Egypt. For the rest, we had Marilyn Monroe, Rita Hayworth, Judy Garland, Elizabeth Taylor and James Dean – let alone Bette Davis, Joan Crawford, Barbara Stanwyck, Humphrey Bogart, Clark Gable, Jimmy Stewart and Cary Grant. There were many, many Hollywood stars, in fact, let alone Brigitte Bardot and Sophie Loren. And for the Golden Age of Television – often with our tv dinners before the set, we had *I Love Lucy* (with Lucille Ball), *Alfred Hitchcock Presents, The Honeymooners, The Ed Sullivan Show, The Jack Benny Program, The Milton Berle Show* and *You Bet Your Life* (with Groucho Marx). And while I was still enthralled with Benny Goodman, the 50s also gave rise to Chuck Berry and Elvis Presley and the start of Rock-n-roll over classic pop and the crooner sound. But I should also include mention of Peggy Lee, Rosemary Clooney, Dinah Shore, Julie London, Dinah Washington, Billie Holiday and Nat King Cole. In all, it was a veritable feast, and James Dean's films, *East of Eden* and *Rebel Without a Cause*, inspirationally managed to convey the kind of suburban environment in which I grew up.

How much is my recollection of the 50s an exercise of selective memory with regard to the bounty and ease of the times? I was aware of the luscious beauty of my hometown and that, regardless of wherever I was to go henceforth, I would always be grateful for what it had provided in terms of education, friendship, beauty and foundational completeness. Yes, it is true that Leonard Bernstein and Grace Metalious were able to convey the unhappiness, frustrations and steaminess that lay beneath Suburbia's exterior veneer, but these were not the concerns of an adolescent. The United States had won the war with Germany and Japan, and for the mid-century New Year's Eve, Kate Smith sang *God Bless America*. And yes, there was the horror of the Second Red Scare and the unbelievable era of McCarthyism. Pitting this last against the populism and prevailing anti-Russian accusations of today's present-day America, our now seems in political unease scarcely much different than that of the nineteen-fifties. But for a cognisance that was preoccupied with finding newts and tadpoles, with dance lessons and tennis, with wanting as an underage to get into Minsky's in Newark for the burlesque, with same-sex longings, with the ancient worlds of the Greeks, Egyptians and Romans, and with bedroom altars and incense, these times of general conformity in a prosperous and successful country superseded both the 'red scare' and the nuclear bomb air raid drills. Life was full, mysterious, exciting and magical, and our autos in their garages glittered in the headlight beams of a visiting vehicle.

In reality, of course, the 1950s had their darker side ranging from Nasser's overthrow of the Egyptian monarchy, the first Hydrogen bomb explosion test, the North Sea flood in the Netherlands and United Kingdom, the sinking of the Andrea Doria, the Hungarian Revolution, the production of the first plastic Coca-Cola bottle, and, depending on how one views it, Castro's overthrow of Batista in Cuba. The 1957 launching of Sputnik 1 by the USSR began, for the good or the bad, the Space Race. The more positives, unless one has affinities with the militant homeopathic part of my family, include Jonas Salk's development of the polio vaccine, the Marshall Plan reconstruction, Ingmar Bergman's *The Seventh Seal* and *Wild Strawberries*, Federico Fellini's *La Strada* and *Nights of Cabiria*, and the fashion designers Christian Dior and Coco Chanel. And even with its pluses and minuses, the 50s seem from today's vantage point comparatively innocent. And it is this very innocence that constituted my formative years.

A decade later, during my Ghost Dance days in San Francisco, I pursued magic as the only real alternative in the face of unrequited love. I became committed to the lonely life of the magician/shaman and remained as such until Richard ended my orientation to alienation. In the beginning of the 1970s, none of my ideas regarding Indo-European ideology as a positive world outlook had yet come to mind – save for Joseph Campbell's influence with regard to occidental mythology. My complete rejection of Vedanta-type thinking had not yet taken root. It was simply the Haight-Ashbury times replete with Aquarian Age idealism, my own bittersweet disentanglement from San Francisco, and my discovery of the story of the California Indian. Subsequently, it has been my innate impulse toward freedom and a love of life that led me to Amsterdam and the Midi and beyond.

But admittedly, in the face of Jair Messias Bolsonaro's decision to allow and encourage mining and industry within the indigenous reservations of Brazil, the sinking expectation that the coronavirus epidemic from China will get much worse before it gets better, the British 'advisory referendum' collapsing and becoming the 'pointless, masochistic' withdrawal from the European Union's remarkable community achievement, the untruths and over-dramatic exploitations within Donald Trump's State of the Union address and his impeachment acquittal, and the Democrats' rushed and foolishly incomplete Presidential impeachment violations inquiry, their overkill with the anti-Russia mantra and their fiasco with the Iowa primaries, one wonders how many lows after lows are endurable. I will still maintain that positive karma stems from being harmoniously in accord with the gods, namely, with the earth, with nature and with humanity. Being not in accord with these is negative karma and includes denying climate change and promoting global warming, destroying wildlife and living beings, and either engaging directly in warring or funding proxies to war on one's behalf.

As I am currently reading the Druid John Beckett's *Paganism in Depth,* I find myself refreshingly resonating with his animism and polytheism. His is a deity-centred paganism (or for him Paganism) rather than a nature-centred paganism – or at least for this specific book. He is easy to read and covers much of the basics. He understands the growth of pagan spirituality through our collective need for connection with nature, the gods and our ancestors. These three domains appear to be Beckett's foundational foci, and I differ slightly from him in my own principle focus as directed to nature, the gods and the arts. I certainly honour my ancestors and especially those who I have known, but I see and revere the arts as being a wider ancestral heritage. My own orientation is shamanic, and I have no claim toward being a priest. I welcome Beckett's assertion that polytheistic religions and traditions retain places 'for people who just want to honor the gods and live an ordinary life.' My own paganism or polytheism is very much engaged with honouring the divine, but personally I question or am hesitant to agree that offerings are made to the gods to promote reciprocity, namely, that we give to the gods so that they will give to us. Obviously, this is an endeavour for many pagans, but for myself, I give to such sacred beings primarily to express gratitude. I rarely ask the gods for anything specifically. My prayers are generally for world peace and collective happiness.

So, what are my complaints and upsets with contemporary paganism? Beckett mentions a few with which I agree, but considering the idea of 'Big Tent' paganism with which I wholeheartedly agree, my main grievance is, of course, its inclusion of chauvinist and racial forms of pagan spiritual expression. I was removed from an online Hellenic group after I questioned its voicing of ethnic purity sentiments. The Folkish problem is not confined to pagan Greek formulations but can exist throughout other modern-day pagan manifestations as well. Nevertheless, the greater publicity in this respect appears to be garnered at present by various Heathen Volkisch groups ranging from nationalists, fascists and metalheads. I participate on occasion with a London-based Asatru series of moots and blóts but remain distressed by the group's Brexit Leavers disclosure and its close identity of spirituality with national identity. Apart from those offered to Odin, I do, however, enjoy the rituals performed by these passionate polytheists to various Nordic deities and wish to continue with attendance to these, but at the same time I cannot accept the claim that people may only worship the gods of their ancestors.

The problem is a particularly vexing one. The alt-right, white supremacist contingent of Nordic religion has been responsible for various acts of violence such as the Christchurch attack against Muslims in New Zealand or the Norway killings by Anders Breivik. The exclusionary nature of folkish heathenry, let alone its heartless inhumanity and fierce barbarity, put it directly at odds with the non-racist universalism that prevails for the most part throughout contemporary paganism. And yet, we are a 'big tent' with no established authority who decides who is and who is not a bona fide pagan. Many non-fascist heathens worship the same Germanic or Nordic deities as do the folkists but do not agree with the xenophobic and excessive nationalistic bigotry that characterises the latter's extreme right-wing socio-political vision.

In my own efforts to establish a flexible formula for Big Tent pagan identity, I developed the following:

> Paganism is an affirmation of interactive and polymorphic sacred relationship by individual or community with the tangible, sentient, and non-empirical.

This 'definition' is actually the narrow one. More inclusively, the Bigger Tent allowance would read instead as:

> Paganism is an affirmation of interactive and polymorphic sacred relationship by individual or community with the tangible, sentient, and/or non-empirical.

Whereas the first understanding applies more specifically to what I would term 'telluric paganism', the second includes as well both non-supernatural nature religion and transcendental forms of Gnosticism. To translate or elucidate further, then, paganism is an orientation that is affirmative of different possibilities for relations between materiality and consciousness, between materiality and the magical, between consciousness and the magical or between all three areas (physicality, sentience and the supernatural). This orientation may be that which is held by an individual alone or that which is espoused more numerously by some collection of people. But in all cases, the relationships and connected domains envisioned are considered to be holy in and of themselves. In short, this is Big(ger) Tent paganism, and it possesses no exclusionary provision relating to either nation or race. And, further, Big Tent's flexibility when it comes to paganism also finds fundamentalisms under its very roof – whether the rest of us like it or not. And fascism itself is simply a further form of lethal fundamentalism in its 'being unquestionably convinced of its own correctness' – one that strives 'for centralized autocracy, social and economic regimentation, and, in its worst excesses, [aims for] the inhumane repression if not the elimination of opposition and difference'. Inasmuch as contemporary paganism subscribes to the insistence that anyone is free to consider himself/herself to be a pagan, this allows fundamentalists and fascists to find their own place within the tent. Unfortunately, but also undeniably, this puts a black mark against the more open and generous understanding of paganism that is endorsed by the rest of the tent dwellers. The only recourse beyond expulsion – which itself is a form of sectarian fundamentalism – is then to work hard and intelligently in attempting to convince and change myopic mindsets into the warmth of largess and open acceptance that is commensurate with a truly humane humanity. If we are to remain squabbling and conflicted by division there is no movement but instead perpetually endless repetition, and we miss out in the progress of human advancement. Or to stress John Beckett's admonition concerning all relationships – those with both this-worldly and otherworldly beings, they are to be grounded correctly in 'respect, reciprocity and honour'.

Near the end of my *Pagan Theology*, I discuss briefly fascistic paganism or pagan fascism and the pursuits of 'Aryan' eugenics and racial purity by the German *Völkstumsbewegung*. The regressive notion of Aryosophisme ('Aryan wisdom') was developed by Guido von List (1848–1919) and Jörg Lanz von Liebenfels (1874–1954). List founded the movement of Wotanism, as a monotheistic form of Ariosophy, and Armanism, the secret esoteric teachings of Wotanism and alleged spiritual expression of Aryan wisdom. His anti-semitic and occult *völkish* theories were in actuality more influenced by both Freemasonry and Helena Blavatsky's Theosophy than by pagan understandings themselves. List and Lanz's Ariosophic ideas along with their influence on Theodor Fritsch's Reichshammerbund and the Germanenorden (both founded in 1912) impacted the subsequent National Socialist German Workers' (or Nazi) Party and continue today as the occult *völkish* practices of much Heathenism throughout Europe, North America and Australia with the stress on belief in tribal and racial purity. My personal contention is that while rejecting these Ariosophical developments of Odinism and Asatru as genuinely compatible with pagan ideals, it is important to understand such expressions if we are to succeed in transforming or eliminating them.

My dear friend Marie-Laure is contending with an ailing father after the demise of his wife/her mother and with a beloved sister-in-law who has developed quite suddenly Creutzfeldt-Jakob disease, and, in dealing with both, she is stressfully plagued by the transportation delays, if and when there is any transport at all, between Paris and Dijon. When in Paris, she insists on getting mental rest which for her means seeking the company and love of dear friends and continuing with evenings out for theatre, music, plays, concerts and exhibitions. Beside her friends, she finds that 'only art soothes and restores'. And with the seeming hopelessness of present-day political stalemates and horrors, I too increasingly find solace in music and art.

For me, music in particular is intrinsically spiritual (or religious if you will). Jazz is affirmative of the pleasures of life that I revere as among gifts from the gods. Shostakovich takes one into the cosmos itself. And the piano and orchestral music of Debussy is nothing less than reassuringly divine. Consequently, I have been attracted to David Brown and Gavin Hopps'

2018 book *The Extravagance of Music* in which the authors seek to explore the manners in which music might engender religious experience. To their credit, they do not restrict their investigation simply to ostensibly sacred, catechetical or 'religious' music or even to only classical music more broadly but open the field to the popular as well: rock, post-rock, soul, punk, grunge, electronic, drone, heavy metal, even ambient and kitsch. Noteworthy in particular is the elucidation they make of a persistent theological bias against the senses and emotions. Their specific interest is with the possibility of divine encounter through the medium of music.

Pagan references do appear in the opus in connection with culture, art, imagery, joy and excess – this last, interestingly, in confirming the ubiquitous presence of the divine in the world. Divine immanence is assigned in one instance to a 'pagan context', and music may be understood as sensuous or mystical, war-like or commercial, pagan or Christian. And while Mozart's last symphony, the 41st, carries the byname 'Jupiter', this is explained not as a pagan allusion but in relation to divine reality that includes the Christian God (cited as the first Composer). Pagan or heathen speculations are distinguished from 'higher' inquiry. Brown and Hopps are both Christian theologians, and for Brown in particular music and the arts are instrumental in moving us away from material reality to an experience of 'the immaterial reality that is God'. For him, the aesthetic alone is not sufficient to provoke an encounter with the divine. The heavenly realm transcends our world. Consequently, it becomes clear that a Platonic undercurrent runs through the joint analysis of the book in that our customary quotidian vision of the world is claimed in actuality to be 'a turning *away* from reality'. In contrast, while a pagan may share an understanding of transcendence with the Christian, the epiphanic divine is more apt to be accepted as impersonal (perhaps a pantheistic immanence) or as personalised but differently than the Abrahamic entity or 'God' (e.g., as the Goddess) or as pluralised with personalities (e.g., the gods). Whereas Brown and presumably Hopps consider the religious as something more than, if not also 'above', the aesthetic, from my pagan perspective the religious or spiritual and the aesthetic are the same and co-extensive. Moreover, I will contend that there is a musical presence inherent in the marvellous itself.

What I do appreciate with these authors is their notion of extravagance or, specifically, musical extravagance. Tracing the word or notion to the medieval Latin *extra vagārī* that conveys 'wandering or straying outside limits', they capture perfectly what expresses the propensity of music to transport us beyond the ordinary. Music has this ability to inspire awareness of an inexpressible 'other'. It can still be worldly and yet elicit something beyond itself – ranging from vulgar delight or unpretentious relaxation to the acute *jouissance* of ecstatic mysticism, numinous rapture and communion with the timeless and immanent divine. This surplus of meaning that music is able to generate encompasses the analogous enchantment and wonder that a pagan tends also to find in and through nature. Even with their Christian bias, Brown and Hopps amply illuminate the spiritual potency and awe of which music and art are capable. And this possibility, they claim, is achievable with both popular music and in the epiphanic compositions of those who have themselves renounced religious belief – such as Bella Bartók, Pierre Boulez, George Gershwin, György Ligeti and Dmitri Shostakovich. Brown even acknowledges the nature mysticism in the music of Claude Debussy, Jean Sibelius, Antonin Dvorák and others that animates the awareness of divine immanence. In short, we possess the comforting (in adversity) and expanding (in times of fulfilment) possibility to experience through musical extravagance what we may call the very aura of nature.

Perhaps music on its own cannot 'deliver up a religion' as Frank Burch Brown says in the Foreword to the Brown and Hopps book, and he feels that words and rituals are additionally necessary if it were to do so. But rather than religion per se, music for many is simply spiritual in and of itself. It may not open up to 'God' in a conscious way without various external aids, but I will contend that it certainly is able instead to suggest quasi-somatic experience of the gods and such emotions as dazzlement, jubilation and euphoria that can merge a pagan more consciously with the divine. And some musical expressions, maybe more thought-provoking than ecstatic, may be more conducive toward promoting the sublime contemplations that might also assist one to wander into godhead. For pagans, material reality is not some desert separate from a wholly other transcendent but the mother of ineffable otherworldly realities that are to be known through imagination, wonder, ritual, devotion and awakened insight, and music may function importantly in assisting and developing these emotions that go to the very heart of paganism. While the Christian cannot endorse a pantheistic understanding, a pagan understands the immanence and ubiquity of the divine and accepts metaphor as a means to discover whatever spiritual excess there might be that could flourish as the non-obvious something more than what is otherwise known through the manifest and immediacies of the senses, including even common sense. In separating the spiritual from the aesthetic, Hopps is able to signal a potential danger in idolatry that could allegedly obscure the sacred. But idolatrous enchantment is still enchantment, and it is within this aura of the physical and musical that a pagan is perhaps most at home to explore spiritual matters. In this connection, Hopps mentions Christopher Small who suggests music as a dynamic event more than it is an independent object and one which extends the subject into the 'entanglement of the terrestrial sphere and the supernatural'. Paganism and Christianity are different religiosities, and while their Christian adherence hampers in my opinion Brown and Hopps' ability to grasp the full import and/or possibility of music in relation to spirituality, they nevertheless liberally convey the positive vitality of musical efficacy and how it as a 'worldly' phenomenon is nonetheless able to evoke something beyond itself.

It does, however, become clear with these authors how indebted their religious orientation is to the 'up-down' metaphor. They speak, for instance, of an '"upward" movement *from man to God*' (Hopps' emphasis). Our mundane reality is something 'below'. And reference is made often enough to higher levels of spirituality. But interestingly, in a footnote, there is a reference to the philosopher Mark Johnson who differentiates immanent 'horizontal' transcendence from 'vertical' religious transcendence. In reference to Olivier Messaien's *Quatuor pour la fin du temps* – admittedly a lovely work of music, Brown considers it an obvious instance of horizontal subordination to the vertical. This up-and-down trope, I will argue, is largely absent in paganism or at least in telluric paganism. There is no fundamental desire to escape physical realities and especially as something supposedly inferior and second-rate. While there is a pagan curiosity toward exploring even transcendence, it is approached essentially as something *other* or liminal rather than as something *above*.

The notion of liminality is paramount with music. Hopps introduces James J. Gibson's concept of *affordance* pertaining to the environment and behaviour. With this notion he has popular music the foremost in mind, but the construction is equally applicable to all music in general, namely, to the process of what it affords. While an affordance is usually approached as something objective, real and physical in contrast to subjective, phenomenal and mental values and meanings, for Gibson an affordance cuts across both the subjective and objective. This is liminality in that the affordance is both physical and psychical and yet transitional between them but still also separate or independent from either. With music, rather than its passive reception by the perceiver, affordance concerns its active engagement in effecting various possibilities for opportunities, functions and values beyond whatever the music supposedly means. This presumably relates to John McClure's understanding of the 'post-secular' position that avoids both atheism and agnosticism but without endorsing a religious alternative. Perhaps not exclusively, this more open and mysterious liminal zone between denial and affirmation is pagan. It is certainly through her experiences in nature that a pagan encounters the otherworldly and the liminally mysterious, but it is also true that with its sonic evocations of the numinous, music equally affords epiphanic transfiguration and enchantment. Beckett refers to mystical experiences of wonder and awe in which one might undergo a loss of self while being accompanied by a sense of profound unity or, instead, receive a message from a god or the vision of a spirit. Liminal ecstasies are what pagans tend to enjoy through nature, music and the arts. Or, to put it the other way around, nature, music and the arts *afford* for the open-minded (e.g., pagans at least if not others as well) supraliminal joy. Untamed nature, of course, is what has come together naturally – hence it is errorless by default. But likewise, the verbal root that has given rise to our words for both *art* and *ritual* also designates the 'putting together correctly' ostensibly in creating something more than merely the sum of the parts. This 'something more', perhaps as an experiential aura, may be understood as the mystical bliss of beauty and divine afflatus – potentially the inevitable product or result of the natural or aesthetic or both.

Consequently, we can allow that it is through affordance and its stimulation of one's imagination that there may be recognition of the vital importance of music to pagan flourishing. Melody, chords and the configuration of sounds open a primal way to mystical experience. But all the same, and remembering Marie-Laure whom I mentioned at the start of this reflection, music also provides solace – the provision of which is virtually a function of all religion. Especially in the face of hardship and stress, the consolation that religion seeks to furnish and instil is one of its most welcomed endeavours for the suffering and bewildered human. For some, music is a significant part of this aspiration; for others, it becomes the very feat in and of itself.

☼

Recently I was asked to give a talk on Greek and Roman gods to the London-based Asatru group of which I remain highly critical. My talk took place during the winter storm Dennis that battered Great Britain, and with both train cancellations and underground difficulties, attendance was presumably less than it might otherwise have been. During my presentation, one of the other two scheduled speakers beside myself did manage to arrive. His talk, following mine, was on 'Why Rome fell'. To my horror, the answer, however studious, was because the 'god-given DNA' of the Romans ceased to be the predominant operative thanks to the eventual influx of non-Romans. The subsequent emergence of the Renaissance was due to a majority of original gene-bearing Romans in Italy at the time. This became the Brexit argument of 'Britain for the British' or even 'England for the English'. The only legitimate focus and interest to be accepted is allegedly national – across the board and for everyone – along with the elimination of foreign migrants. Thanks to my insisted-upon liberalism and universalism as against anti-liberal folkism, I was disgusted early on with this racist rationale and almost walked out during the speaker's talk. I managed only to say at the end that the elephant in the room was the unmentioned environmental crisis and that with the precipitous decline of all the world's insects and their possible vanishing within a century, that this could portend the end of humanity as well. Global cooperation must supersede the 'me first/us first' approach of divisive and limited nationalisms.

The counter arguments to white supremacism and racist eugenics do exist but do not seem to be as strong or established as could be wished. The understanding of human races is relatively recent. Their perception is largely cosmetic (e.g., eye and skin colour, hair texture, and so forth). Since it became an island approximately 7,500 years ago, Britain has been continuously augmented by people from elsewhere, so the very notion of pure Britishness or Englishness is a falsehood. Racial purity is a fantasy, and we are all mongrels. There are no 'pure blood' humans. In addition, over time descendants shed the DNA of their actual ancestors so that only half that from one's ancestors from eleven preceding generations is retained. Supposedly, we may be genetically unrelated even to our physical ancestors from as recently as the 18th century. Apparently, Nazis will have Jewish ancestors, racists will have those from Africa, India and East Africa. In fact, compared to the genetic composition of all the rest of the world, there is actually more diversity on the African continent than everywhere else.

It was Carl Linnaeus who in the 18th century developed the binomial nomenclature used to classify all life forms and hence the biological taxonomy of Homo Sapiens that understands in terms of genus and species.

People like Voltaire and Immanuel Kant shared these resultant ideas of 'scientific' hierarchical racism with white Europeans being placed inevitably on top. Modern genetics, however, has come to establish that our racial understandings do not conform with actual human biological variation. Ethnic identities are instead social constructs, and variation has been determined more by environment, local adaptation and evolutionary pressures. While genetics are still important, race is itself little more if at all than a perception – with skin colour being the predominant factor. And fundamentally, despite what the moot speaker claimed with his facile authoritative manner, nurture cannot be dismissed in regard to a reputedly exclusive influence of nature in the emergence of human diversity and achievement. It could have been interesting to have been able to hear the third scheduled talk if the trains had not been cancelled thanks to Dennis, namely, on the Transhumanist Party UK.

In contrast to the embedding of the gods with genetics, my own approach links them with language. Less a product of ancestral biology, gods and goddesses are more cogently venerated in as much as they belong to our linguistic traditions. This does not mean the exclusion of worship for deities stemming from other traditions. Within the pagan spectrum, we have Kemetics and Afro-Latin spiritualities as well as a host of others. But one way – and my way – of appreciating the divine rather than via biological ancestors is through the language or languages we speak. For me, this last extends to the Indo-European tradition as a whole – especially toward a re-capturing of a proto-Indo-European seminal understanding of the primordial and elemental gods and goddesses – to where the divine metaphorically most interconnects with nature herself.

Paganism is Avoda Zara – 'foreign worship' for the Jewish tradition, especially with the *halachic* following of the body of Jewish law. Its chief repugnance has been the worship of images, and the proper attitude towards religions considered Avoda Zara ranges from scornful rejection, mocking contempt and often hostile exclusion to the tactic of dismissive delegitimation and self-evident invalidation. I am taking this idea of Jewish identity politics from Alon Goshen-Gottstein's *Same God, Other God: Judaism, Hinduism, and the Problem of Idolatry* (2016). The author attended the Melbourne Parliament of the World's Religions in 2009 and is the founder of the Elijah Interfaith

Institute in 1996. It is immediately clear what Goshen-Gottstein's direction is, namely, to find a way to reconcile respect and acceptance between Judaism and Hinduism as part of the project for establishing a hoped-for global coexistence between different religious communities. By discerning a broader view of religion, he shifts away from a ritual-only evaluation and endeavours to establish that the 'God' in both religions is actually one and the same. There are of course always a plethora of Hindu gurus, philosophers and sages who will say something virtually exactly like this, and on a more vernacular level in India one hears the constant refrain that 'God is one'. This unity of the divine is, in fact, a powerful urge to be found more universally throughout humanity.

While this last appears also in paganism, whether contemporary Western, Shinto, Yoruba or Santería, the affirmation of the 'One God' is less a pagan stance *per se* and probably not even its majority understanding. When Goshen-Gottstein acknowledges the millennial-long prohibition of the worship of the elements of nature, he admits in this case there is little to discuss. But he also asserts that Mesopotamian idol worship was more sophisticated than the Old Testament prophets allowed. His finding of spirituality, wisdom, vitality and inspiration along with devotions to graven images is certainly to be welcomed. However, in signalling that the prohibitions encapsulated by Avoda Zara are applicable only to Jewish people, he underscores the Covenant between God and Israel that stipulates the non-allowance of Jewish people for giving reverence to any other being than God. The Jewish Covenant then is something inherited. This in turn raises the question of being tied to one's ancestors and honouring them as well.

For John Beckett, his paganism consists of magic and the primacy of religious experiences on, as previously mentioned, a foundation of animism, polytheism and ancestor veneration. Personally, I am less focused on venerating my forebearers. I respect and love my parents and my grandmothers. Both grandmothers had divorced and remarried, so I only knew my step-grandfathers and not my biological ones. I knew my maternal grandmother's sister, Aunt Dorothy, as well as my father's siblings, but that is about it. The Maplewood-South Orange community in which I grew up was fairly evenly divided between one-third being Protestant, one-third being Catholic and one-third being Jewish. I remember being asked once by a classmate in junior high school why I was in school that day. She said that it was a Jewish holiday and that she thought I was Jewish. I was Methodist and only learned from my mother when I was in my college years that she had been born Jewish. Needless to say, this was a shock to learn. My maternal grandmother's family had, with the one exception of the eldest sibling, Aunt Mary, who had already married, renounced Judaism. I do not believe this abandonment was for any exalted reason. It was a survival tactic for greater social integration. I'm not sure when this was done. My mother says she was about two but that she remembered being taken to the synagogue, so she must have been older. My sister found the Jewish cemeteries where both my maternal grandfather was buried with his immediate family and the one with the graves of my maternal great-grandparents. This last was doubly surprising. The Frooks family had greatly adored their mother and erected a huge memorial to her over her grave. Next to it was simply an unmarked plot of grass. I asked about it at the cemetery office. The lady said to me and my sister, 'You're not Jewish'.

I asked, 'How can you tell?'

She replied, 'I know these things', but she confirmed that the unmarked grave was that of Louis, my maternal great-grandfather.

Apparently, the family squabbled to such a degree over inheritance that my grandmother in disgust left the East Coast and moved to California. As a result, apart from my Aunt Dorothy who lived and worked in Manhattan, I never knew much of that family. I met once only one or two of the younger of brothers of the nine siblings as well as Uncle Dick, the only one who had not married and who lived with Dorothy in the old family home in Scarsdale. And my vivacious Uncle Leighton visited us once in Maplewood with his second wife – an unabashed whisky drinker and cigar smoker who lived into his 90s. Eventually I met and came to know several cousins and second cousins. One irony is that as a lawyer, the first female lawyer in fact to have been admitted to the Bar in the State of New York, Dorothy managed to secure the inheritances of each of her siblings. My grandmother had been bequeathed a pair of silver candlestick holders from her parents that years later my mother and grandmother recognised on the mantel of Dorothy's home. They had been painted black as an attempt to disguise them. Nevertheless, Dorothy and my grandmother Elizabeth (whose pen name was Zeth Brooks) remained friends, and I recall the moment at the Roosevelt Hotel in Hollywood, when Dorothy was climbing out of the swimming pool, my grandmother saying that it was such a shock to see her younger sister as an old person.

But the irony and psychological adjustment remains for me that because *halacha* stipulates matrilineal descent, if my mother was Jewish, I am too.

It has been nothing with which I have ever identified, and politically in regard of the Palestinians I have always been strongly critical of the state of Israel. In this, I am in full accord with my in-laws, Hilary and Steven Rose, who, though Jewish, are active supporters of Palestinian rights – receiving, over the years, death threats and all. But even more for me, as a pagan, I am additionally highly critical of the Abrahamic 'God'. I see it not as divine but an operative personification of the primordial chaos that forever seeks to obliterate divinity in both its dark and light, positive and negative, male and female, physical and spiritual polarities. The term I employ for this operative non-entity (ONE) within the Indo-European legacy is the *asurian*. And due to the close geographic proximity at various times between the Semites and the Proto-Indo-European peoples – along with the historic association or even identity between the Jewish god Yahweh and the Avestan god Ahura Mazda, the Jewish Yahvic-god and the *asurian*, I recognise them as fundamentally one and the same. Through Zarathustra/Zoroaster, the nominally *asuric* Ahura Mazda was elevated to the supreme level of godhood while the divine *devas/daevas* were demoted into demons and devils. In my *magnum opus*, this is what I have termed the 'Persian inversion'. Consequently, while I can appreciate Goshen-Gottstein's efforts to broaden Avoda Zara, the pluralistic pagan godhead is not the same as the Jewish 'God'. It is almost likewise for Hinduism. Brahman is an impersonal godhead behind our reality which either does not exist or is secondary and of no value. And while, admittedly, there are transcendentalists, panentheists and Christo-pagans who identify as pagan, for most pagans by contrast the pagan god is telluric and recognised as pantheistic and/or polytheistic. In the least, paganism's 'other god' is to be differentiated from the Abrahamic understanding of 'God'. They are not the 'same god'. As I see it, uncontrolled, this would-be god is comfortably at home with the annihilation of Jericho, Sodom and Gomorrah; the obliteration of the Canaanites; the Great Crusades; the Inquisition; the eradication of the Knights Templar, the Cathar churches, the Bogomils and the Waldensians; the Inter Caetera papal bull of 1493 authorising the 'doctrine of discovery'; the European Wars of Religion; the witch trials and burnings of the late Middle Ages; the persecution of the Manichaeans; and today's jihadist fanaticism. The Avoda Zara by which Judaism has been able to castigate a religion as foreign and unacceptable describes both the basics of a jealous and narrow-minded god and the repugnant behaviours that have continued and still continue in the wake of the Abrahamic orientation.

One further irony is that several of our leading contemporary Western pagan figures have been of Jewish descent – Margot Adler and Starhawk among them. Over the millennia there has been a miasma of degradation within which every Jewish-born person must operate, and I wonder if, accordingly, I am inescapably bound by some ancestral Covenant to an unacceptable entity. This is why I am not exactly into ancestor veneration – unless by ancestors are meant not those who are necessarily biological but instead the contributing forebearers of our cultural legacies. In doing a 23andMe ancestry investigation, I discovered that I am 51.1% Ashkenazi. This would mean that even from my father's Lithuanian side there was some Jewish blood. The pagan roots to Judaism are of course to be found in Canaanite mythology and whatever cult practices that might be recovered, and, to a lesser extent, in the Kemetic tradition of ancient Egypt. And while the suggestion by Shlomo Sand (Tel Aviv University) of an *en masse* conversion to Judaism by the Khazar peoples of south Russia is highly controversial, excluding the underworld god of Tengrist spirituality, the major gods of Tengriism or Khazarian shamanism are seven in number and conform remarkably to the proto-deities of the Indo-European pantheon: sky, earth, sun, moon, fire, hero and, if not the dawn *per se*, the goddess of fertility and virginity. But admittedly, the Khazar hypothesis of Ashkenazi ancestry does not appear to be supported by genetic studies. Either way, however, it is with the pagan path that I wish to pursue and in staunch rejection of Abrahamic intimidation, dharmic devaluing and secular disenchantment.

And I might add here – and knowing that this contention is highly repugnant to most Heathens – that I follow Hilda Ellis Davidson's suggestion that Odin is, as a late figure, a 'demon' who has usurped the throne of the gods. The proper chief of the gods is Tyr – the cognate deity to Zeus, Jupiter and Indra's father Dyaus. In the various mythologies among the Indo-European daughter-cultures, the king of the gods is but temporarily defeated and impaired. Eventually, he is healed and restored to the throne. It is only among the Nordic and Germanic peoples that the proto-myth appears to have been interrupted and not completed. Interestingly, in a recently posted Nordic Animism community video on Facebook ('Christ vs Odin on the Jelling Stone') by Rune Hjarnø Rasmussen, whom I greatly respect though we differ on our personal focuses of worship, he indicates a likelihood of the hung-god Odin transforming easily into the crucified Christ. Exactly! The loss of heathenism in the north and especially of any Vanir-centric prospect was facilitated by the Aesir (*asuric*) worship centred on Odin transforming into the affinitive religion of Christianity. Once again, however, while pagan gods have the propensity to be fluid and fuse, bifurcate and re-collate, they are not the same god as the Christian-Jewish-Islamic 'God'.

Recently I had the great pleasure to hear a talk to the Anglo-Finnish Society in London by Edward Clark on the composer Jean Sibelius. The music of Sibelius, while perhaps most strongly influenced by developments in Germany and Austria and in particular by Bruckner, emerges and flourishes virtually independently from the major German, Russian and French musical centres of the time. Sibelius, a prolific traveller and *bon vivant*, apparently met Debussy in Paris, but neither understood the music of the other. Clark found this ironic in that he considers Debussy and Sibelius as the two greatest composers of the 20th century. Of course, their music is much different from each other's. Debussy was innovative and radical to the extent that his harmonic language broke almost all established rules but without subjecting the listener to the extremes of modernity. His is a music of melodic colour. He is closer to Tchaikovsky than is Sibelius whose own music emerges from the late Romantic as well as influences from Tchaikovsky, Wagner and Bruckner but proceeds subsequently more toward a Classical austerity. Nevertheless, some people hear echoes of Impressionist harmonies in some of Sibelius' music. He was certainly a master of the grand form – especially in his mature symphonies. In the wake of Sibelius, we find composers like Ralph Vaughan Williams, Arnold Bax, William Walton, Howard Hanson and Malcolm Arnold; in that of Debussy, we have – whether acknowledged or not – Maurice Ravel, Albert Roussel, *Les Six*, Frederick Delius and Manuel de Falla but even further with identifiable elements or moments in the compositions of Stravinsky, Schoenberg, Bartók and Puccini. According to Clark, Adorno detested the music of Sibelius and considered his restriction to tonal sounds as anachronistic. With Debussy, Adorno at least recognised the composer's 'constructive command of subjectivity' and his dependence on the rhythmic-spatial rather than the binding force of the sonata form. Nevertheless, in actuality, the tonality, symphonic form and musical architecture of Sibelius' music were unprecedented and novel in their own way. Though in a different but still modern manner, what Sibelius has produced is as accessible as that which we have received from Debussy.

I remember many years ago an open-air concert in San Francisco's Lake Merced Park near San Francisco State. It opened with the lovely *The Swan of Tuonela* tone poem and its haunting and mournful *cor anglaise*. With the outdoor beauty and rich music fusing with it, the memory has remained with me for decades. I have read that Sibelius was a pantheist and, like myself, loved both the forested countryside and the metropolitan centre as two contrasting extremes. His music expresses spirituality infused with the anguish of the human condition. Along with Beethoven and Mahler, he is at home with large-scale form. In 2004, the British composer, Julian Anderson proclaimed that 'there is virtually no major composer working today who has not been directly affected by the work of Jean Sibelius'. Earlier works incorporated myth, language and legend from the Finish epic poetry known as the *Kalevala*. His later works, more purely falling within the category of absolute music, continue Sibelius' exploration of liminal tonality.

Recognition of Sibelius has not been always ready and forthcoming by a long shot. The Polish/French serialist and conductor, René Leibowitz, in the 1950s called Sibelius 'the worst composer in the world'. Critical assessment toward Sibelius continued to be largely negative throughout the 1960s. His piano works are considered uneven as far as consistent quality is concerned, and the genre has been at times panned overall. Nevertheless, Clark considers that Sibelius' compositions for piano exhibit the same general curve of development as is to be witnessed with his large-scale works. In all, it is the composer's tone poems (*The Lemminkäinen Suite, Finlandia, Kuolema, The Oceanides, Tapiola*, etc.) and seven symphonies that reveal his genius, and it is through these that Sibelius has increasingly come to be recognised as a progressive musical innovator. The most popular of Sibelius' music appears to be his symphonies 1 in E minor, 2 in D major, 4 in A minor, 5 in E flat major, and 7 in C major, his Violin Concerto – Sibelius' 1904/1905 farewell to Romanticism, *The Swan of Tuonela, Finlandia, Valse Triste* and the *Karelia* Overture and Suite. His first three symphonies are romantic and optimistic works but with various degrees of anxiety; his 4th is innovative, modern, classical, austere, bleak, darkly turbulent and a compressed glorious protest in which he achieves in establishing his own unmistakable style henceforth; his mighty 5th is healthy, powerful, sexual, resilient and hesitantly optimistic; his elegiac 6th expresses happiness, luminosity, enigma and transcendence but without grandeur and emotional climaxes; and his 7th is a single movement of poetic and devotional prayer to the cosmos. From the Fourth Symphony on (1911), a decided spiritual or even pantheistic dimension is increasingly discernible. To be witnessed is an experimental daring that has entered his compositions along with a cataclysmic element. There is a detectable alliance of natural matters with the spiritual, and his *Nightride and Sunrise* concludes magnificently with the rising sun. While I am not overly familiar with the *oeuvres* of Sibelius, I look forward to an enjoyable discovery in the days to come.

Sibelius' pantheism and naturism bring again to mind reflections on current Western paganism. Beckett sees the three 'grand divisions' of paganism as non-theistic nature worship, Wicca and witchcraft, and polytheism. Certainly, pantheism could include deities but could also be non-theistic in the polytheistic sense. As CWP has developed from a more magical emphasis in the 1960s and 1970s, it has come to be increasingly characterised, if not appropriated, by feminism and/or environmentalism. These developments are important and are to be welcomed. Intersectional feminist thought or data-based feminism raises issues of dis-equality and unbalanced opportunity. These produce invisible structural and social elements that, until recognised and opened to consciousness, remain incommensurate to a healthy pagan mentality. Likewise, the ecological degradation of our planet is another major concern. The preservation and well-being of nature is vital for all life on earth, and contemporary paganism has recognised conservationist issues and put them at the forefront of pagan importance. Both the feminist movement and the efforts for ecological awareness integrate with the organic pagan religious impulse that itself flourishes beneath and behind theological, cosmological and political differences.

But within this organic religion of many gods, magic and/or the sacredness of nature, there is also to be witnessed such inorganic developments as racism, sexism, consolidation of power, cronyism and lack of transparency. The upshot is the emergence of a divisiveness that sunders the broad pagan community. There may be a need for more local groups or small bands of people as well as online communities, but if the need for organic cooperation and celebration is lost, what we have will wither and lose out in the reckless advance of chauvinist, populist, fascist and McCarthyist forces. Eugenic thought, non-recognition of privacy needs for different identities, transphobic and unsubstantiated TERF accusations, and power-centric elites are inappropriate to the indispensable spirit and ethos of an intrinsically pagan instinct. And if such narrow-minded phenomena occlude pagan sustainability, the emergence more recently of shallower forms of paganism, perhaps inspired by popular TV entertainment, comic books, punk rock, computer games and the like, is a further cause for disquiet. Those of us of advanced years wish more than ever for the healthy, the humanitarian and an inspirational holy that we understand as the pagan core – beneath, behind and beyond all political, social, factional, theological and cosmological difference.

For some, only the forest, the wild or the more pristine areas of the natural world afford the liminal access that a pagan might seek. But in our modern world, many of us do not have a ready access to the non-urban. To some extent, this is of course a sad situation because the experience of the rural and natural is important for every human. I remain grateful for my childhood experiences of Boy Scout and summer camps – a joy that motivated me further to explore my neighbourhood South Mountain Reservation, the beaches and hinterlands of Northern California including Yellowstone Park, the Grand Canyon, the Sahara Desert and the magnificent expanse of the Scottish Highlands. And as much as I adore the city (New York, San Francisco, New Orleans, London, Amsterdam, Paris, Rome, Istanbul, Beirut, Cairo, Bangkok, Kathmandu, Mumbai, Tokyo), there has always been for me the impulse to savour a rural interlude which led not only to the Friesian debacle but also to my sojourns in the Midi. Nevertheless, my argument is that pagan or liminal encounter is also available in the urban environment – with or without the employment of mind alterants. Both this worldly and otherworldly involvement are legitimate for the pagan who chooses one or the other or both, and the implicit individualism and personal choice that this implies have no merit toward being a source of division within pagan diversity.

Likewise, the same applies to the theological distinctions of pantheism, polytheism, atheism, henotheism, monism, monolatry, transcendentalism and panentheism. *Nous ne sommes pas tous pareils*! Paganism is the embrace of different isms and beliefs or non-beliefs and constitutes as a result a glorious, ongoing and never concluded conversation. As long as we can honour our host planet as well as humanity and life in general, our theological differences are to be welcomed and explored and not be allowed to become causes for friction and discord. How much this attestation plays out in reality is a moot point, and my observations and reading suggest that CWP has some distance still to go before we achieve the kinds of pluralistic harmonies in which we say we believe.

It is to be granted that paganism, despite its New Age elements that some orient to, is not all 'sugar & light'. There are unquestionably darker sides – especially within the Afro-Latin traditions, and some gods may be wilder and potentially more dangerous than others – such as with the vagaries and extremes of nature. But I will still maintain that if the gods live anywhere on earth besides Mount Olympus, it would surely include the Gorges du Verdon in the Provence. Here is nature at one of her most splendid manifestations. The perpetual delight of the Midi is not only in her special colours and natural beauties, however, but also with such art conglomerations as the Foundation Maeght in Saint-Paul-de-Vence. In this last, I have been able to thrill to the works of Max Ernst – a favourite artist for me ever since that fortuitous encounter at Peggy Guggenheim's home in Venice. In addition, there is the exquisite Chapelle de la Rosaire, the Matisse chapel, constituting a pristine white tile and yellow-blue experience. Of course, something like this last often has me wonder how wonderful it could be if something similar could be created as a pagan shrine or temple. But at least in the south of France, we have the relatively complete Roman temples of the Maison Carrée in Nimes and the Temple of Augustus and Livia in Vienne or the four pillars of a temple presumably dedicated to Apollo in Riez. Another treasure is the former Celto-Ligurian oppidum, expanded by the Greeks and finally to become the Roman city of Glanum south of Saint-Rémy-de-Provence.

But the more I think about it, I see the real core of paganism as ethical. Ritual, art, temples, shrines, mythology and worship of deities or reverence of nature, as important as they may be, if truth be told come *after* morality. In fact, ethicality precedes all religion. It does become something that religions adopt and then maybe modify to fit their theology. But with paganism as the oldest spirituality, the virtues it affirms and treasures are probably closest to the principles of natural integrity that we can ascribe to the pre-religiosity of humanity. And if there is or was no 'pre-religiosity' as such, then rectitude, justice and decency are themselves pagan standards and ideals before they came to be adopted by anyone else. For both the pagan and atheist, mores are not dependent on some legislating god; they precede the gods – and the gods arise at best with them. In fact, the virtue-values may be deities in and of themselves.

Epicurus did not deny the existence of the gods but said that as perfect beings they would have no interest in us mortals. I do not accept that. My feeling is that, as perfect beings, the gods would have an abundance of generosity and, out of their own munificence, would extend their interest to us as well. Afterall, we *are* interesting creatures. Why would they not have concern and maybe even help to assist us? I am no priest or particular authority in what I say here. But I have had more than a half-century of decades of perpetual reading about and pursuit of the gods. What I am attempting to do in this present work is to convey how and why I consider myself to be pagan in order to provide the background and reasons for the criticisms I have come to develop vis-à-vis the spirituality. So, in short, we are kin to the gods. Some of us even individually undergo apotheosis (Helen of Troy, Achilles, Heracles, Tin Hau, Tenjin, the Seven African Powers, etc.), but all of us I discern are collectively a member of the proto-pantheon, at least in the understanding of what we can reconstruct of proto-Indo-European thought. Most likely, we are the *Dioscuri* or divine twins – one of whom (Indra, Pollux, Manu) is immortal, while the other is a (resurrecting or rebirthed) mortal (Agni, Castor, Yama). This last I understand as the 'secondary twin' who patronises water, fire, fire-in-water, inebriation, shamanic consciousness, the female and connects to both death and the otherworld. He is the most complex of the whole lot and essentially embodies us in all his humanity. His twin promotes thunder, lightning, mankind and victory. In a word, one is Zeus/Dyeus, Apollo, Tyr, Lugh; the other, Prometheus/the moon, Dionysus, Freyr, the Dagda.

But if ethics precede the gods, then it is us – humanity, humankind, man, mankind – to whom the principals of morality originally belong. And it is we then who go back to, and find our source in, the primordial matrix of the cosmos. We are not only the child of the mother, the incarnation of the earth, but also the personification of cosmic will – the seminal urge behind the entire multiverse. So, the gods have an interest in us because we are one of them. This is, I contend, the message and beauty to which mythology and a continual investigation into it and its origins provide. This interrogation also includes the insights gained through ritual performance and the enactment of myth. And my wish is that once we re-gain a pagan world we will not repeat the same mistakes as before but harmoniously assemble a reasonably equable and universally comfortable and prosperous co-existence for everyone.

In connection with the preceding, let me qualify what immediately follows here as part of what I will call here the Pagania Express. I have always enjoyed the railway, and for a part of my childhood we lived near the railroad tracks. I have a memory of the chug-chug-chug from the locomotive of a stationary train at 04:00, the wee hours of the morning, as it intersected with my dreaming while resuming its forward journey. It was the Lackawanna's Phoebe Snow that for some inexplicable reason had stopped at that hour in my suburban town of Maplewood, New Jersey. I have many memories of the commute between Maplewood and Hoboken en route to Manhattan. In fact, one of my key mystical experiences occurred once on the return train during a sweltering peak of summer as I was about to prepare for an exam the following day at NYU. Steve Reich's *Different Trains* encapsulates the old-fashioned thrill of train travel during 1940s, '50s and into the '60s. For the 1953 Boy Scout Jamboree at the Irvine Ranch, we travelled from the East Coast to California and back by a specially hired train, and when it was time to collect my inheritance, Nancy and I took the train from the depot near San Francisco across the country. Our return tickets on that occasion were refunded because the cross-country train journeys were cancelled a few months later when we had planned to return. There have been many railroad excursions for me throughout the Indian subcontinent – often a tale in themselves, and, since my 1961/1962 Eurail days, travelling by train is still my preferred mode of proceeding around Europe.

So, I will suggest here that much of my writing is akin to journeying by train. There is a destination, but the reader need not worry about absorbing all the detail of what passes by through the window. We are on the Pagania Express, and what is to be seen in the present instance is fragments of the mythologies concerning both ethics and the gods. These are like towns and vistas viewed briefly as our pagan train moves along the tracks and passes them by. I want, however, to point out the cardinal virtues, and these are known as justice, temperance, fortitude and wisdom or prudence. The Romans personified the first of these as Justitia, while the Greeks knew her as Dikê, the daughter of Zeus and Themis. Dikê's sisters are Eirene ('peace') and Enomia ('order'). But additionally, Themis herself was understood as the goddess of justice. Being the personification of divine justice, Themis is the independent embodiment of the will of heaven. Dikê, by contrast, represents the forms of temporal justice that concern moral order, conventional custom and fair judgement.

We are passing the 'township' of the virtues for now, but it is a place to which anyone might choose to return to at some point in the future. Beside Justice, the Greeks personified wisdom or prudence as Epiphron but really understood her as the goddess Athene (Roman Minerva) as well as Sophia. Fortitude or strength had several designations (Alke, Bia or Latin Vis and Kratos or Latin Potestus) but otherwise was known as the apotheosised Greek/Roman hero Herakles/Hercules. Temperance the Greeks identified as Sophrosyne; the Romans, as Sobrietas. She is understood to be the daughter of the close-to-Chaos figures Erebos and Nyx, darkness and night. Christians added the virtues of faith, hope and charity or love, but at least two of these are already pagan divinities. The Romans recognised faith as the goddess Fides and Hope as Spes. Rather than *eros*, however, Paul used the word *agape* because the Greek Eros (Latin Amor) is too raw for Christian tastes and is hardly a virtue as such but more the personification of sexual passion; nevertheless, Eros along with Nike (Victory) and Nemesis (righteous wrath, ill will, injury, retribution – essentially an equivalent of *karma*) are the few abstractions to have received some cult status. But the precedence of some of these personifications (e.g., the pre-Olympian Themis, Temperance, Nemesis, Thanatos) may be interpreted as an indication of the ethical preceding the divine.

Our train moves on now, and in connection to reflections that rivet the attention of some, there is the question of how or from where did existence originate? Consequently, but with the pagan thought within a broad Indo-European framework, concerning our aboriginal cosmic origins, the tenth mandala of the *Rigveda* suggests the primal seed of the universe to be *kâma* 'desire' or *tapas* 'warmth, heat, fervour'. For the Greeks, but obliquely, Hesiod presents Himeros 'desire' in his *Theogony* as without ancestry and, consequently, as the pure germinal will from which *chaos geneto* and Gaia becomes 'the ever-sure foundation of all'. Considering the corollary of desire/*kâma*, namely, the warmth of heat or passion, *tapas*, likewise we have the cosmogonic fire realm of Múspelheim in Norse mythology and its role in the world's origin. The medium of Ginnungagap corresponds to Hesiod's Chaos. From this basic paradigm, we find various myths that suggest divinity reaching subsequently back in some way to the warmth and/or desire of the primordial in order to retrieve something important for we humans in our evolved deity-infused world. In some cases, the thing important is fire, and the classic rendition of that is Prometheus' theft of fire for the benefit of humanity. And for this, Zeus enchains the Titan and has the eagle (the vehicle of Zeus) feed upon Prometheus' ever-regenerating liver. In this tale and at this stage, Zeus and Prometheus appear to be instances of the negative relationship between the divine twins (as understood in the 'Roman' duality of Romulus and Remus, for instance) and only later, once the two become reconciled, are they then illustrative of the more positive duality (the mutually harmonious 'Dioscuric' twins). Also to note, however, is that rarely is Zeus portrayed in mythology as an opponent of the human. This depiction appears only with the Promethean complex which itself would seem to be more of a Levantine import rather than an indigenous Hellenic or Indo-European derivative – hence Prometheus' imprisonment is located not in Greece but further east in the Caucasus Mountains.

Further related fire-recovery myths concern the Vedic fire-god Agni who hides himself in either water (hence the fire-in-water motif) or the hollow of a reed stalk. Sometimes it is Indra himself who, perhaps after his initial defeat by Vritra, secludes himself in a lotus stalk in a remote lake and either emerges subsequently with the gift of fire or Agni himself plays the active role in securing Indra's return. Another version is Armenian and involves the dragon-slaying hero Vahagn who also hides in the hollow of a reed stalk and emerges from it with the flame. While fire may be primordial, it is not ancestral to the human. We evolve in spite of it – not because of it. But for our own advance, fire becomes a necessity, and it is to be obtained originally from within the treasury of our primordial antecedents.

So, while our Pagania Express has by now been gaining speed, let me just quickly point out two other variants of the original paradigm that replace the coveted object of fire instead with creative power. For the Vedic peoples, this is the mind-expanding *soma* that Indra steals from Tvashtar – either directly himself – or via Suparna – the Vedic eagle, falcon or hawk – who seizes the psychedelic elixir from the Gandharva guardian Krishanu in heaven. There are many Rigvedic versions of the soma-theft theme that variously involve Indra, Suparna, Agni, Soma and even Manu (the personification of mankind who is, of course, the ultimate beneficiary). And among Norse *eddas*, we have the burglary of the mead of poetry from Suttunger by Bölverk (ostensibly Odin but more than likely originally the Zeus-cognate Tyr who has come to be dethroned or 'replaced' by Odin). Let the train accelerate onward at this point and do not be concerned with the details. These have been taken from the research constituting my *magnum opus*. But the significant understanding here is that these myths circumscribe the feat of obtaining or recovering an archetypal treasure, and as such they synchronise with the heart of modern-day paganism's fascination with the past. In its ceaseless exploration and study of myth and archaeology, pagans wish to recover earlier understandings and insights – not to repeat the past but rather to augment the present and hopefully insure a better future. And by combing through the ancient past and primeval, there is further a greater chance of re-establishing those pre-religious ethical principles when they were still unconstrained by faith agendas and uncontaminated by biased sectarian interpretations. As our train now approaches its destination, let us but realise that in the fertility of an imaginative reconstitution, paganism understands the days of old as not only the other or something of the other-world but as heaven itself. In this, it endeavours to recapture both utility and inspiration. Paradise is affirmed as something feasibly possible here-and-now and not as something lost through an act of disobedience. In the celebration of fire, enchantment and poetry, there is the implicit belief that harmony and progress are possible.

Reflecting on the coronavirus that appears to be in ascent when I write at the present moment, it seems almost incomprehensible that back in 1984 I divided my time that year between India, Nepal, Bangladesh, the Netherlands, France, Ireland, Britain, Egypt and America. And who knows at this point what the final consequences of the COVID-19 disease will be? However, considering the capitalistic stranglehold the military-corporate elite has upon the world and the consequent economic polarisation, the religious wars and the plight of ecological concern and indigenous protections, I am wondering if the SARS-CoV-2 virus could ultimately be understood as a gift from Gaia. It may take a global pandemic to reverse our population explosion and implode the worker-slave conditions under which the human species predominantly operates.

Already in the 1980s, I described myself as a preternatural materialist and ceremonial humanist focusing on the divine godhead chiefly in terms of the miraculous and numinous. I had come to understand the experience of awe as an essential ingredient of health. My favourite deiforms were Jupiter, Mars, Vesta, Apollo, Dionysus, Indra, Agni-Śiva, Viśṇu, Týr, Freyr, Thor, the sun, moon, earth and dawn, and this listing remains unchanged more than three decades later. I declared my life goal to be a restoration of the recognition of these deities as benign and helpful powers and/or extensions or projections in contrast to the Christian, Islamic, Buddhist and Marxist monopolies. For me in particular, the basic Indo-European perception reveals an attitude founded upon a positivistic, humanistic and mystical human-god relationship. I am surprised how little any of this has changed for me by the year 2020.

In Varanasi at the end of 1983, I had to wonder about how to rationalise my indulgence of three months of dreaming besides the Ganges when so many of the short-lived people in India were forced to toil for long hours for their daily *paise*. Must those of 'private law' live off the hopeless anguish of the majority? Or could some live the model – and, yes, the dream – as the ultimate endeavour of all humanity? Or, at least, the possibility of all humanity? As Diana says (and I presume this to be Diana Eck), Gyan Vapi was 'dug by Shiva himself in order to cool the *linga* of Vishveshvara . . . .' It did not take me long to realise that, doubtlessly, this holy well is the very spot where the lord of the heavens entered the earth with his phallus. And as that very centre of Hinduism marks the primordial mating of Heaven and Earth, the sexual symbolism latent behind all of Indic culture has allowed for a population growth almost unparalleled and certainly at the heart of India's problems of poverty. Yet, ironically, the people of the Subcontinent seem relatively happy – even as they work – for smiles are continually manifesting across their beautiful faces.

In my understanding of the sacred geography of places, there is frequently an elevated location and a numinous water source. For Kāshī, this last is the Gyan Vapi or 'Well of Wisdom' adjacent to the Golden Temple. Today, Razzia's mosque occupies the peak of the central hill of the city's three prominences, and this was the original location of Shiva's Vishvenara or Vishveshara Temple before its destruction in the 13th century. The Adi-Vishweshur or Ur-Vishweshur Temple was next built where now the Gyan Vapi Mosque stands next to and southwest of the sacred well. The Moghul emperor Aurangzeb (1618–1707) destroyed this second splendid Vishvanath temple – leaving only enough of the temple's plinth with the mosque built above it to attest into our times the victory of Islam over Hinduism. The third and present-day Shiva temple, the Golden Temple of Vishvanath, was next constructed by Queen Ahilyabai Holkar just north of the Gyan Vapi. Completing the triangle of sacred centres in old Varanasi along with the Razzia summit and Well of Wisdom is the Jalasen burning ghat where cremations are undertaken. This last houses most likely the world's oldest continually human-tended fire. While I have over the years of successive visits to India approached Hinduism for its underlying retention of pagan practice and elements, I see Hinduism itself as an incongruent, super-imposed world-denying, and transcendental ethos reinterpretation of the confident and life-affirming tenets of Vedism. Nevertheless, the history of Hinduism reveals that despite the demolition of the succeeding Vishvanath temples and perhaps even the *linga,* the cardinal resilience of phallicism, like the phallus and fecundity of nature themselves, continues to remain irrepressible and triumphant. Perhaps today phallic symbolism is no longer condoned by feminist and 'me too' persuasions, but it was celebrated anciently by the Romans and today *sub rosa* by the Hindus.

The Gyan Vapi was always a favourite sacred spot that I understood as the central matrix of *all* creation. Since my Kāshī apartment was virtually next door, I would spend time in the shelter next to the well. On one occasion, reading Gore Vidal's 'Rich Kids' article in the *New York Review of Books,* I was thrilled with his ideational orientation, his way with words and his candid ability to strike right at the heart of any matter. Marvellous, for instance, was his reference to the Christian 'tripartite deity whose sense of fun has made sublunary life so strenuous and odd'. But, alas, he always seemed to be talking from an all but hopeless minority outlook. In the least, however, Vidal was aptly able to pinpoint the enemy. He could easily take a place in my pantheon of heroes. In his 'Sex is Politics' essay, he claims that Leviticus forbids not only homosexuality but also worship of the Great Mother. That biblical book also condemns clothing made of mixed fibres as well as the eating of rare meat, bacon and shellfish. In addition, Vidal refers to the 'Christers' and their pogrom of 'get the fags' in the name of Save Our Families, Save Our Children – reminiscent today of developments in Hungary and Georgia.

But reading Gore Vidal in Banaras is a contrast in extremes. Considering the tri-nodal reality of Kāshī with the magnetic Vishvanath temple legacy dedicated to the Lord of All, the peaceful and unobtrusive but most holy birthing centre – the Well of Wisdom, and the world's main portal to the otherworld in the form the Jalasen/Manikarnika burning ghat with its eternal sacred flame, the city is a wonder. In Hindu belief, all the gods wish to dwell here, and I came to believe that the garden of delight with its aural sanctuaries that is Kāshī -Banaras is the original site of the Garden of Eden or of the East. It is less a question of expulsion but rather that everyone has wanted to live here. In the evening, when I could contemplate the illuminated *sikhara* of the Vishvanath Mandir glistening modestly yet ever so intriguingly, I could recognise the *sanctum sanctorum* as the present world's preeminent pagan temple – certainly the 'first' within Hinduism. Only 'Hindus' are allowed within, but by bathing in the Ganga, wearing the proper attire and entering in a worshipful attitude, anyone is a Hindu. This last was not always the case for me. Once the government had seized the temple and put an R.K. Mishra in charge, I as a 'whitey' foreigner was not allowed to worship there for several years until this administrator was finally dismissed. More recently, since my dear Swami Mahadevanand Ji Saraswathi arranged for the installation of solar panels to provide non-polluting lighting for the Golden Temple, he did so under the stipulation that 'foreigners' could gain entry without restriction, and the temple is reputedly now more open.

Through my experiences in India, I have come to affirm that the 'true priest' is the one who guards and tends a geo-local shrine. This need have nothing to do with 'priesthoods'. Priestly colleges, on the other hand, are birds of a completely different feather. But in Kāshī I came to appreciate the position of Rakishankar, the chief *mahant* of the Vishvanath Temple, as well as the roles of the both the priest of Gyan Vapi and the Dom Raja, the keeper of the fire at the Jalasen Ghat. Then too, there is the King of Kāshī. The role of monarchs need not be political. They may be instead spiritual and 'ruling' spiritual kingdoms on earth. As such they merit tribute. In this connection, I should mention that I have long asserted in Nemine fashion to be the King of Rome because I claim that title, and, in default of any other current claimant, it is mine. Like my spiritual predecessor, Numa Pompilius, at least in India, I spend much if not virtually all of my time visiting and/or dwelling among numinous centres. Kāshī is certainly one of the most sacred of places if not the main one of all, although in today's world, lovely Japan is perhaps more manifestly commensurate as a full claimant to be the Garden of Eden East.

For a midwinter's night in Banaras, I decided shamanic. Embers of life persist through the night at the Godowlia crossing with trickles of pockets stretching from there to Chowk and Daśaśvamedh, but the all-night 'party' is and remains Jalasen. As one watches the pyres, you can feel Śiva himself breathing over your shoulders. Or again, he appears as the exquisite youth to be seen in sleeveless undershirt at the centre of the spectacle crouched on his haunches gazing as you do into the crackling, sizzling flames. If one holds his breath for a timeless moment, he can all but cross over and through that gaping hole; then, looking upward into the enchanting night-time Kāshī sky, he *is* there. But though the midwinter night be long, night itself in Banaras is short, for scarcely have three or four hours elapsed before the goddess Sitala in her temple affirms this world, that of the living, in triumphant, matinal music, song and chant. The bells are already sounding forth with the first of the venerators. Not long after, the Vishvanath temple itself lies for the early bather like a wide-open, unattended jewel box. Manikarnika remains timeless, unchanging, all-consuming, while Sitala and Vishvanath like pulsating nodes quicken the riverbank back to life which soon permeates throughout the city as a whole. And all the while, Gyan Vapi rests quietly, spawning, knowing.

Maybe the gods are only convenient mirrors – reflecting aspects or powers of the self. But satiated with mythographic and spiritual studies, and through my devotional experiences in India, China, Japan and with the ancient sites of Europe, I have come to contend that beyond convenience, the gods are also beautiful foci and perhaps even superhuman powers. Whatever else we human beings might be, we are animals as well. This is something pagans accept and do not seek to deny. Some of us engage further in the veneration of trees and stones, idols and stars, not to transform our animal natures but for our physical needs, pleasures and other personal ends. Above all, most pagans as pagans do not endorse the contention that only the incorporeal 'God' that descends from the Abrahamic tradition can be the source of all morality. Consequently, we do not agree with the arguments of Moses ben Maimon (Maimonides), Moses ben Nahman (Nachmanides) and Menachem Hameiri (Meiri) that our spirituality, Avoda Zara or Shituf or both, is not also legitimate religion. Pagans as a general rule do not see historic movement from polytheism to monotheism, or from fetishism to recognition of a transcendent 'God', as achievements of spiritual and cultural forms of an alleged 'higher' progress. Broadly speaking, although we have no credo or universally agreed upon belief, the godhead is understood as a multiple, intra-divine plurality. Reflections of the collective self, the powers and capabilities of the gods may be unlimited to the degree, as I suspect, the will itself possesses ultimate strength – especially and ultimately as collective will. We are a one – with no denial of the individual, and we are a collection of individuals. In the unending quest of collective consciousness and will, regardless of whatever other forms and/or dimensions we evolve into, we human beings are most likely and presently only at an early and beginning stage.

A favourite evening *pūjā* was always our Sunday visits to the Gumburī Baba's shrine located beyond the train station amid rows and rows of tracks.

The story was that a holy man had been buried alive beneath the large, roundish stone *toil* that was the ritual focus. When the British were laying the rail tracks, each morning when they returned, the tracks that had been laid previously through the holy site were found now to curve around it on both sides. Consequently, trains now swerve around the shrine as the British finally conceded to the *fait accompli*. We would offer a chillum to the stone and then smoke it. The shrine was open on three sides, and on one Sunday we had to endure rain and fierce winds, but inside there was a fire, and Kailash described the relatively exposed shrine as being 'like a house' in comfort and warmth. These weekly visits were serene.

Admittedly, between the oscillating feelings of exhilaration and lousiness in India, the repeated performance of morning and evening *pūjā* could be both fascinating and arduous. For me, idolatrous worship was a learning process – how to do it, what the procedure involves, and what to expect – including the unexpected. In his *The Aristos*, John Fowles claims that mankind harbours a deep and abiding archetypal hatred of routine. He acknowledges pleasure as generally associated with the surprising and the new, and while the strain between knowledge and mystery is the source of the human's being, the fundamental tension is pleasure-pain, namely, that between good and evil, beauty and ugliness, and security and insecurity. Fowles understands being as a joining, and the more complex the being is, the more there is that has joined together to create it. As with marriage, ardour and harmony are claimed to be the counter poles of any association. For the author of *The Magus* and *The French Lieutenant's Woman*, passion in our day reigns through our idolisation of the young. Certainly, I cherished my own youth, and though that period for me is now long, long ago, I find the young thrillingly inspirational and a joy both to know and to know that they exist. And India is overflowing with the young, and when I was last there around the beginning of the present millennium, the name for me that those I knew had between them was already that of 'grandfather'.

Even more than a half-century ago, Fowles understood that the future would consist of cybernetic society. His concept of productive leisure is one that I share wholeheartedly with him – involving both art and education. In his view, however, veneration will apparently play no part. In this last, I understand the understanding of secularists, humanists and atheist pagans, but personally I appreciate the utility of worshipping the divine in both its natural and animated expressions. The gods I accept as receptacles of collective human aspiration. Nothing to be lightly sneezed at or dismissed, for this is, after all, what it is all about. But even putting aside the gods as representations of aspiration, as natural or supernatural beings or powers, or as intervening agents, Fowles has forgotten the basic notion of the holy as the sacred and qualitative muchness. When people share the same feelings with regard to their perception of the holy, they form communities (Fowles' associations) of credence or activity. Even Christianity is such a community, though one I no longer care to be part of; once was enough. But for the rest, the gods live in Banaras – perhaps masquerading occasionally as both beggars and brahmins. While Fowles designates art to be the 'explanation of self by the expression of self, . . . the mirror of what the self has created', my contention is that the gods too are 'artistic artefacts' in as much as they may be considered collectively created mirrors of the self. In contrast to my ceremonial humanism – preternatural materialism, I would label Fowles an existential socialist-materialist. I probably agree with most of his ideas apart from my fear that a world without the sacred and the special would be sterile. Regardless of the question of specific afterlives, that irrational extra, the venerational and immortality as direct consequences of conscious existence allow the possibility of meaning – even if we are the ones who collectively make the meaning. Without these, the world is certainly diminished in colour, and if the presence of the holy, the wondrous and numinous is absent, we have by default something that is totalitarian despite itself.

Of course, for me, it is difficult to imagine the arts and especially music as not worship and veneration – both as listener and audience and, most enviable, as musician or player. And, although I cannot conceive of doing such now, I went to a series of all-night concerts in Varanasi. A major difference between north and south India, in fact, is that in the south musical concerts occur more reasonably in the evening whereas in the north they frequently do not begin until approaching midnight! I managed to enjoy four or five nights of musical concerts in succession at Varanasi's Nathak Nagari Mandali. These included a kathak dance performance, the vocalists Girija Devi, Sunanda Patanayak (Guruma) and Pundit Vidiyadhar Vyas, the santoor- or hammered dulcimer-players Shivkumar Sharma and Madhu Ritta, the sarod instrumentalist Ustad Amjad Ali Khan accompanied by Pundit Kīsan Maharaj on tabula, and both the sons of Imrat Khan and the *crème de la crème* Ustad Vilayat Khan as sitar-players. Exhaustion along with the trance-like effect of the magnificent raga music and trying to keep awake produce a stoned-like effect. When the maestro Vilayat Khan concluded the final Nathak Nagari programme at 04:30, half the audience was asleep, and there was not even a whimper of protest or demand for *encore* when he finished.

Scarcely more than two weeks later there was another concert when, for me, the persistent cold weather at the time and the ubiquitous illness suddenly all added up and made sense. Featured on this occasion were the vocalist Pandit Manas Chakraborty from Calcutta and then the renowned Ravi Shankar. After the break, Kailash managed somehow to get me sitting only fifteen rows back and directly in front of the sitar maestro during what I became convinced were some of his finest hours. It is true that Varanasi audiences are known to be horrible, and the previous year Shankar had proclaimed he would never play again in the city. But such is the power and uniqueness of Varanasi, a glowing with happiness and joy Shankar was back and, the master conjuror he was, was more than able to pull the focus together. I was reminded of Alan Watts' comment during a talk once at the Family Dog in San Francisco in reference to the continual chattering around the outskirts of the hall: 'Just listen to them as if birds singing in the trees'. Shankar had with him some excellent students performing as top musicians as well as an adoring and exquisite 'decoration' to the sitar player's back left on the harmonium. What is also special concerning the Hindustani classical musical tradition is that most performers in India are Muslim. It is in fact with and through music that the country's Muslim and Hindu communities most come together and transcend the sectarian divisions of faith and religious practice. Aesthetic foundations could surely become the true politics of the world. Perhaps all cultures bare their soul in their music; India certainly does. Indian culture exists in her music which is the nation's ultimate unity and identity. The Shankar concert ended at 05:30 in the morning and to this day ranks for me alongside with my experiences of Arthur Rubinstein, Maria Callas and Judy Garland and perhaps Janet Baker and Jesse Norman as well.

It was Mahashivaratri or 'Great Night of Shiva' just before I left Kāshī in 1984 for Kathmandu. The city had become a mounting crescendo of swarming activity. Everywhere, the shrines of Shiva and others were being freshly painted. Crowds were increasing. I had bathed in the Ganges after rising at three-thirty in the morning and then got into line in the Gyan Vapi courtyard. Barefoot and shawless, I waited for about an hour before being able to enter the Vishvanath temple around 05:10. Following Kailash's recommendation, I did not have even a *paise* with me and may have been the only one to have entered the sanctum without anything. I hand-cupped someone else's water to offer the lingam. Basically we were shoved through by the police, and at first I despaired over not being able to have visual *darshan* of Vishvanath, but suddenly the tip of the deity showed through the masses of flowers and water in the tank. Upon exiting, I found myself with a *mala* garland around my neck that I did not remember receiving. From various priests I was given a *tilak*, more *malas* and *prasad* of a puffed, milk-soaked grain along with coconut, guava and tangerine. When I mentioned to the Vishnu priest that I had no money on me, I believe he said that I had already given enough and could stop. All in all, it was a marvellous and emotionally heightened experience. I returned to my room for a coin and then did *pūjā* at the shrine of Varahi Devi. A pitched peak continued throughout Kāshī as the great night approached. Shiva's shrines were lit with coloured lights, sometimes accompanied with blasting music, candles and other burning flames as well as flowers and fruits on the *lingams*. The vigil for Shiva is traditionally augmented by consumption of *bhang*. 'The Dom Raja's looks like Christmas', Maureen said, but the truth was that half the city did as well. It was a beautiful sight to see lighted *lingam* shrines all over – with idols covered with flowers and fruit. At one point, Kailash and some others left for the Golden Temple, and to everyone's surprise returned shortly thereafter after having just walked in through the front entrance. I subsequently acted as guide and took the group to visit the *lingam* shrines of Mrityunjaya, Bhaironath and Omkareshwar. We continued with the all-night chanting of *kirtanas*. Eventually, I too was able to just walk in through the main entrance of the Vishvanath temple. It was full but marvellously quiet with no more lines of crowds. The throwing of coloured, sparkling dry powder-dust by the priests in the inner sanctum, mostly at one another, was both amusing and mysteriously beautiful. I made the rounds of the subsidiary shrines and lingered in the temple for quite a while before then circling the well and subsequently finding the 'party' at Jalasen the smallest and quietest I had ever seen. But still it was occurring. After a wee bit of sleep, I made a final round of *pūjā* visits the following day, made farewells and then was in Nepal.

The week began with fever, chills, body aches, nausea, diarrhea and a clogged nose. But all the same I was able to locate the shrines, temples and stupas that I wished to find. And I also was able to shop for figures of Indra and other altar artefacts that, thanks to the artistic industriousness of the Newari, are available in Nepal where they are not as a rule to be found in

India. I managed also to make acquaintance with two young shop vendors one day after the next with whom I remained friends for many years. I wished at one point to bicycle to Patan where on that day was a once in twelve years festival in which all the gods gather together, but as I was about to depart mid-afternoon, I could not find the bicycle key by the hotel's empty pool where I had been sleeping. I searched my room, returned to the pool, asked, asked at the lobby desk, searched room again, asked the manager, looked again at pool area, waited for the attendant to return from 'snacking', but he had not seen it. I was then starting to walk the bike back to from where I had rented it, and there was the copper-coloured key indistinguishable from the burnt brown grass – having fallen out of my pajamas as I had originally guessed. But it was by then too late for Patan.

My return to Amsterdam was via Dacca in Bangladesh. Among the group of us at the dinner table before our flight, a young English doctor-climber gave us all sleeping pills for the journey. I have never slept so well on a plane before or since. None of us scarcely remembered landing, waiting and retaking off in Bombay. And this concluded my visit to *Asie* for 1984 – unless one considers Egypt's Sinai as part of Asia and not Africa.

Once back in beloved Europe and with my beloved, the in-your-face devotional availability that exists throughout India and especially in Kāshī becomes more elusive and more difficult to locate. In Amsterdam, there is the Dam or centre, the Amstel, various oak trees, Nicholas (Saturnus) in the Begijnhof Chapel, and the Virgin on Crescent Moon (the Dea Mater) in the Papegaai on the Kalverstraat. At our farm in the Midi, I have *lingams* on the property, and the town itself is a '*centre du monde*'. And throughout Europe as well as beyond, there are always various vehicles of the gods to be found, perhaps more for token acknowledgement than ritualistic veneration, but after both Amsterdam and the Provence, we decided to explore the river Indre from its source near Préveranges to its mouth where it joins the Loire. The name of the river may have nothing to do with the god Indra and possibly is a derivative of Latin *Antrum* designating 'cave', but nevertheless it was a fascinating exploration that took us from Saint-Priest-la-Marche through Sainte-Sévère-sur-Indre, Châteauroux, Saint-Maur, Villedieu-sur-Indre, Buzançais, Saint-Genou, Palluau-sur-Indre, Châtillon-sur-Indre, Verneuil-sur-Indre, Loches, Azay-sur-Indre, Cormery to Montblazon south of Tours where we checked into the Château d'Artigny for Walpurgis Nacht/Beltane. I would always seek out the *églises* in each of these towns or villages. Inside and immediately to the left of the Church of Saint André in Châteauroux, I found a beautiful Saint George (Zeus Georgos, the 'earth-worker, farmer'). Before the main entrance of the Church of Saint Ours in exquisite Loches there is a round Celtic altar. The confluence of the Indre and the smaller Indrois occurs at Azay.

During our shamanic journeying on May Day, we walked the grounds of the chateau and then proceeded to the banks of the river. While sitting on a rickety pier, I had a vision of a gigantic Indra in the sky superimposed over us and the entire scene. I found myself saying, 'If I had to have a credo, I believe in the champion-god, and the champion-god is a duality'. In all, this was a most beautiful interlude. Later, we followed a 'sporting path' into an area posted '*pièges dangereux*'. We first reached a pavilion half in ruins, and this became the most difficult interval in that I was suddenly recalling the 'metaphysical' impossibility of the relationship in San Francisco from which I had fled and come to Europe. Moving on, we found a sacred oak with a stone-bank ringing it and forest paths leading from it in the four directions. The aura now was a healing one. Later, when we discussed it, Richard explained that he believes he is my lover on this earth-plane only – the only one in which he believes. Our relationship, of course, had begun nearly four decades ago. We have hung in together all that time and maybe have come to accept that there could be more than just the this-worldly. After a swim in the hotel's pool and a marvellous meal, it rained during the night. I dreamt of hearing the horrifying death-agony scream of a dragon as it was being killed.

After Montbazon, it was in Azay-le-Rideau that we came across a lovely church that possessed five cult figures: St. Vincent (with grapes), St. Symphorien (with axe), Joan of Arc, Nôtre Dame de Lourdes and St. Barbara. As charming as the valley of the Indre and the towns and places we visited through it had been, the confluence (Hindi *sangam*) of the Indre with the Loire at Le Neman was sobering. For here was placed Le Centre Nucléaire de Chinon. This seemed incommensurate with the beauty we had enjoyed pursuing from the source of the Indre. Such is the world of today in which we live. We next followed the Loire to Angers and Nantes before reaching Carnac and the Church of Saint Cornély for which some '*pretend qu'il aurait détrôné le dieu gaulois Kernunos*'.

If Stonehenge and Avebury in England and Newgrange in Ireland are pagan treasures, so too are the megalithic alignments of Kerlescan, Kermario, Ménac and Petit Ménac in Brittany. Rows and rows of standing stones or menhirs; so many deities! Along with the tumuli of Saint-Michel and Kercado, in all it was as if we were in paradise. Fourteen years earlier, I had also been to the passage-grave or Gavrinus Cairn on the island by the same name that is off the south coast of Bretagne from Carnac in the Gulf of Morbihan. This tumulus contains the most intriguing of stone carvings. I was at that time able to light candles along the passageway and into the central chamber and then savour unforgettably something completely otherworldly and enchantingly beautiful. But the predominance of lace-headed women during that first time to southwest Brittany was no more. *Tout change*. They were of a different era.

In the Breton Saint-Pol-de-Léon Cathedral, I found another replete pantheon that, beside the standards, included Herbot (with a cow?), Eloi (with a horse), Pol (with a dragon), the skull of Paulus Aur, Claire, Apolline (with tongs), Marguerite (with dragon), a lovely Nôtre Dame du Carmel, Roch, Sebastien and Anthony (with lamb). Beforehand, in Landivisiau, there was a Michael and dragon on the exterior of the Church of St. Thivisiau that Richard thought was probably produced by the same artist who had created the Calvary within the *enclos paroissial* of the parish church in Saint-Thégonnec. This saint is depicted with a wolf pulling a chariot. A night ferry followed all this to Cork.

In Ireland, we briefly visited the acreage I had once purchased in Glounacappy between Killarney and Killorgin. Here is a land of elves and saints, goblins and Virgins, as well as the impressive menhir near Beaufort whose photo I used for the cover of my *Pagan Theology* (2003). There is also the magnificent Gap of Dunloe (Bearra an Choimín) as well as the stone circle I most think about at Lissyviggen, Killarney. I found Kerry County's Cill Airne particularly fascinating at this point in that I was interested in locating its sacred wells. One was that of St. Mary behind the Killarney town hall and tourist office across the street from the Protestant church of St. Mary's. All but neglected, it was still enchanting. Another well in the lane that leads to the parking lot was, however, filled with rubbish. Finally, St. Margaret's Well in New Road was no more. Its source had been a spring on the adjacent hill, but when the new school was built, the flow was cut off, and students as well as others then used the old well for litter. The man on whose property it had been finally cemented it up, and now only a break in his wall indicated where it was. Killarney at this point appeared to be a mid-point between Banaras and 'well-less' Paris, London or Amsterdam. Sadly, it was nevertheless an enlightening discovery.

Wales was next with its church of St. Cybi in Llandrino, standing stones and the Vale of Edeyrnion. This was followed by Prince's Oak on the way to Shrewsbury and then Bath a good decade and a half before I knew I would be living and working there. Here of course is the sacred spring of Sulis-Minerva. After Stonehenge and Avebury, we reached London (Ludgate, St. Paul's, the London Stone, the Thames) and again before I knew I would eventually live here. We stayed first in the Shaftesbury Hotel before moving in with Alan Bates. While in London, theatre is always important and some of the best in the world. On this occasion, we attended *Noises Off* at the Savoy Theatre. Richard thought the first act was the best. The second kept one laughing continuously, but the third act did not exhibit the same skill in timing as had the rest and became more silly than anything else. Still, one laughed even here, but overall I found the play light fun but nothing more. Much more marvellous was *The Benefactors* at the Vaudeville with an excellent Patricia Hodges. For musicals, there was *Guys and Dolls* and *Little Shop of Horrors*. Our films on this occasion were *Terms of Endearment* and *Swann in Love*, and videos at Alan's included *Educating Rita*, *Betrayal*, *Fanny and Alexander*, *Blood Wedding*, *The Ballad of Narayama*, *Guys and Dolls* and two with Alan: *An Englishman Abroad* and *Separate Tables*. We also at this time took a walk along King's Road not realising that it would eventually be where we were to live. I met Peter Shaffer who I considered at that time my favourite playwright. And we went for a few days to Alan's Derbyshire home in Bradbourne amid rolling hills dotted with cows and with a stream. Absolutely idyllic. We were unable on this occasion to find the Stanton Moor stone circle (that was for another time), but Alan took us to both Haddon Hall and the lush and lavish Chatsworth House. In this last, there are many paintings, murals, statues and busts of the classical deities. What I liked best was John Gibson's sculpture of Cupid restraining a magnificent Mars.

Once back in London, there was a visit to the Murugan Temple on Archway Road at Highgate Hill allowing *darshan* of Skanda and Ganapati and a moment of reconnection to India. Other deities I was able to see during the time in London were Apollo, Athena, Fu Shên, Tsai Shên and Shou Hsing. While I continue to appreciate Goshen-Gottstein's efforts to further inter-religious harmony and his feeling that contemporary circumstances mandate the necessity of a radical rethinking of Judaism's understanding of Avoda Zara, I cannot accept his consideration that 'true religion' is only that which affirms a transcendental sense of God. Even further annoying is his borrowing from Jan Assman that idolatry, in opposition to true belief, includes unquestionably such evils as injustice, lawlessness, oppression, violence, murder and fornication. Beyond theology, real religion is to be supposedly recognised through its sponsorship of moral behaviour – something of which idolatry is reputedly incapable. The ethical principles that are named include humility, service, loving-kindness, compassion and human transformation, and the contention that paganism does not embrace these as well is actually offensive. Goshen-Gottstein's basic argument is that all true religious experience points to the 'same God' regardless of the specific tradition (Christianity, Hinduism, etc.), and for this he is dependent on the notion of 'God' as 'Creator' and ultimate referent as well as God's being incorporeal. For him, religion is what intervenes in the battle against physical nature. Homage to images means worshiping a being other than 'God'. But whether a pagan employs images, idols, forces of nature, deified humans, such popular anthropomorphic-like figures as Shiva, Vishnu, Rama, Krishna, Hanuman, Ganesha and Devi or even instead turns to an apophatic approach entirely, he/she is still definitely not revering the Judaic/Christian/Islamic/Bahaist entity but indeed is acknowledging the operative worth in the otherness of gods, spirits or phantasmic persons who, despite their variously mutual interconnections, can remain as relatively independent and autonomous divine principles, energies and powers that are not identified as a God Absolute who is alleged to be beyond manifestation in any and all form. And in this, morality is not to be usurped as the sole privilege of only veridical religion and an allegedly 'true God' – in fact, of any religion whatsoever. At best, it is only when the Abrahamic figure is extended into a pantheistic or possibly panentheistic understanding, as Goshen-Gottstein appears to be suggesting, that the 'same God' argument could have any authentic merit, but mosaic, traditional halakhist, noachide, talmudic, *shituf*, postbiblical Judaic, technical and legal discourse do not truly appear to support this. In short, paganism is and remains Avoda Zara and, vis-á-vis Judaism and other Abrahamic religiosities, is happy with this. In fact, it is only through moral consensus rather than theological fudges and compromises that interfaith has any possibility at all. Once again, *nous ne sommes pas tous pareils*. Difference as well as the recognition of both imagination and intra-divine multiplicity remain the fundamental hallmarks of a pagan orientation.

Consequently, in lieu of what I have just affirmed, I am increasingly astonished over how much current paganism appears to be infected by 'cancel culture'. My understanding, let alone my deepest of wishes, is that the pagan community is one that places dialogue and inter-communication at the forefront. In London at least, so much of the scene has centred around venues featuring different and individual speakers. The prevailing ethos has always been to agree to disagree. The implosion of Pantheacon and disinvitation and boycott of various pagan presenters, usually elders, seems to be resulting from a disintegration of open curiosity and the tolerance and/or willingness to hear people with whom we have already decided we are not in accord. If this is what the contemporary pagan exchange – or lack of exchange – is becoming, it is not what we were originally and had set out to be. If there is no authority to decide who is or what is pagan, then by default as a collective we are open and inclusive. I admit that I am not in favour of those who support racist, chauvinist, fascist, McCarthyist or myopic ideas and actions, but I remain willing to talk to them. Paganism, as I understand it – or, again, wish it to be – includes gnostics, tellurics, atheists, lesbians, gays, bisexuals, transgenders, queers, intersex, asexuals, the polygamous/polyamorous, kinks, pansexuals, the two-spirited, questioners, ascetics, celibates, hedonists, women born as women, straight men and virtually anyone under the sun who is pagan willing. As such, and in line with its pluralistic diversity, paganism endeavours to provide time and space for all of us together as well as for any of our groups or identities separately. My great fear is that the currently popular wokeness has killed humour and, consequently, our liberality and broad-mindedness. For me, this amounts to a profound disappointment. If we lose our tolerance, we offer nothing whatsoever that is positive and beautiful. And yet, at the heart of pagan vision and understanding, it is certainly undoubted that there is a progressive and advancing impulse.

As much as I deplore the traditional depiction of the Abrahamic 'God' and what has been historically accomplished under its name, I do applaud and encourage even here dialogue and endeavour for harmonious cooperation. As I understand, pagan discourse – for it to be *pagan* and hence both human and intrinsically natural – is both intra between itself *and* inter with others. Consequently, while I remain not in accord with Goshen-Gottstein's 'same God' argument, I am in agreement with his efforts to find commonality between Judaism and Hinduism through theologies of divine fluidity. The irony here is that the ability for divinity to appear in multiple locations simultaneously, able to enter and be identified with various objects, along with the notion of divine omnipresence are all fundamental pagan ideas. Form both mediates divinity and *is* divinity. Rather than 'raising' to a 'higher' spiritual realm, the idol is an instance of divine embodiment that may be used to *bring* or translate one's consciousness to a different or *other* spiritual realm. Idolatry is never the whole of the picture – unless we understand nature herself as the ultimate idol. But to the degree that Goshen-Gottstein suggests a fluidity of the divine, there is here the possibility of a godhead understanding that encompasses or surpasses all religions. Perhaps what I am proposing is that there is conceivably an area of concurrence even between paganism and Abrahamic religion. But for Goshen-Gottstein, the 'message of Hebrew monotheism was one of liberation from nature and its servitude', and he argues that in the polytheisms of ancient Greece, Egypt and Mesopotamia, the gods are limited in ultimate power – being subservient to nonpersonal chaos or fate. And true enough, pagan deities are generally not conceived as omnipotent. Here, instead, the divine (that includes both nature and the human) is for the pagan a sacred power that perpetually evolves through the changes understood as 'process theology'. It is in this distinction between an always ultimately improving divine embodiment and a supreme Hebrew-Christian-Islamic 'God' understood as transcendently non-temporal and already fully omniscient and omnipotent that we have the divide between pagan and Abrahamic religion. While the contention exists that because only the one 'God' exists, all worship of whatever kind is by default to him, I could just as easily claim that the ONE Yahweh (and his derivatives) is only an 'operative non-existence', and hence all worship automatically belongs to mother earth or nature. But it is also here that hopefully we can agree to disagree.

What currently becomes even more difficult to accept are the 'Kill the TERFs' and anti-'Stop Violencias Machistas' demonstration attacks in Madrid, Barcelona, Toulouse, Paris, Brussels and earlier in San Francisco. Bottles have been thrown at feminists, and women have been punched. Threats are screamed, and banners that protest violence against women, gays and trans people and advocate for unity are trampled and destroyed. How much this bullying authoritarianism is bleeding into paganism itself is unclear, but along with environmentalism, feminism is another important and necessary part of the pagan movement in the twenty-first century. Instead of emerging into an assemblage of antagonistic factions, both within and without a pagan sensitivity, there is more than ever the need for all of us to grow into democratic partnerships – giving each a voice but without accompanying savagery.

But back to 1984, after London, Richard and I spent the next six-and-a-half months in France followed by a month in Egypt, another week in Paris and the rest of the year in New York and New Jersey. I am realising in my recall of my past that it sounds as if I have only been travelling and enjoying, but I have also always at the same time been writing or revising my writings regardless of my rarely being successful in having things published. Though not impregnable, our homes are the last bastions or citadels of solitude in our conformist, bureaucratic world. For an adored residence, I remain continually grateful. The expression of gratitude to the powers that be is personally the heart of my religion. And I could include that my worship includes that of the irrational as the luck of good fortune. But reading my journal for 1984, I am utterly amazed over how often I was not feeling well, how much time I spent working in our vegetable garden, and above all how much trouble I had perpetually with computer and printer problems. It was still early days with these last. I was dependent on an *onduleur*, and time and again I would lose an entire file, chapter or letter I had just completed. What also is striking are the various friends both locally and abroad we had and socialised or communicated with (those days via letter, post card or telephone) relatively frequently and how many of these have either deceased since that time or drifted on into obscurity. It's mostly a completely different set today.

Pharaonic Egypt has since childhood always held a fascination for me. At one point, I wanted to delve into the depths of Kemetic studies but when I had first moved permanently to Europe, I felt I should pursue European spiritualty and its origins before proceeding to those of Egypt. But I had never ceased in wanting to visit the Nile and the pyramids. Egypt, however, was a place in which Richard never had any interest for travelling. But one morning about nine years into our relationship, he was standing in the kitchen of the farmhouse waving a journal that was advertising one of Hans Ebenstein's gay cruises of Egypt. Richard had thought it was something to which I would never agree – maybe less because of the gay thing and more because my preference has been not to travel with a tour. But it only took me less than a minute to think that if this is the way to get him to agree to

Egypt for me to decide okay. As it turned out, it was a fabulous group of guys, mostly Republican but with happily some exceptions, and we remained dear friends with several for years after – including still Freeman (Dr. Habib) in Manhattan who had the ship play his tape of Egyptian operatic and cinema music on its speakers as we departed up the Nile from Cairo.

In my theological studies, I have speculated that the god Amon the 'hidden one' belongs to the same syndrome of figures that includes the Canaanite El, the Hebrew Yahweh, the Vedic Varuna and the Nordic Odin. Basically, I see these as antagonistic personifications of the nothingness or void of primordial chaos, and I understand that there is a decided gnostic element pervading Kemetic spirituality as a whole. For instance, Cherry Hill Seminary's Holli Emore confirms to me that her tradition, Osereion, is 'very Neoplatonic'. Nevertheless, a definite pagan or telluric strand exists as well – understood primarily perhaps in Egyptian understandings of soul duality, in its ithyphallic god Min, and in the corpus of myth and worship centred around the dying-rising figure of Osiris. Among Kemeticists I have known, there has been Phoebe Wray and Donald Hill – both now deceased – as well as Cara-Margarite Drusilla, Freeman Gunther and Tamara Suida. And also I remained in communication with both Anne Key and Candace Kant when they were serving as priestesses at the Sekhmet temple in Nevada. Ancient Egyptian spirituality is undoubtedly fascinating, colourful and something that was surprisingly enduring for millennia. Its rebirth in today's world is to be welcomed – thanks in part to the depthless richness that Egyptian religion and mythology encompass.

But in recollecting that wondrous excursion in the 'Black Land' from the corona-imposed perspective of today's stay-at-home quarantine, the irony between our currently desolate avenues lined by shops all shut tight and the massive humanity of a bustling Egypt along with the comradery of our gregarious group could not be greater. As Hans Ebenstein pointed out, we were all relaxedly free to point out to one another one 'dishy' number after the next. We were free from the more usual constraints of caution and could simply enjoy without the need for self-censorship. Richard and I had already visited Alexandria, Lawrence Durrell's setting for his tetralogy, and Giza with its pyramids and Sphinx. In Giza, we took up an initial residency at the stunning Mina House Oberoi – a dazzling Scheherazade. With the black silhouette of the Sphinx in the distance, I was mesmerised by the structures of Cheops, Chephren and Menkaure and thought of them as both ancient and futuristic. The Great Pyramid of Giza, that was built for

Cheops/Khufu, is the largest and oldest of the three. It is also the oldest of the Seven Wonders of the World. When we entered this pyramid, I found it hot, crowded and extremely noisy. At first, I felt to be on the verge of claustrophobia and struggled for the silence against the groups of tourists of which the Germans were the worst. We had resigned ourselves to it never happening, but then rather suddenly we had the inner chamber completely to ourselves. This was marvellous beyond description; I could feel a power. This unexpected and miraculous and uninterrupted duration we were so privileged to have had inside the King's Chamber was a sacred highlight. Outside, the Pyramid of Khafre had less impact; that of Menkaure, more than Khafre's. All were nonetheless haunting, but it is the exteriors which are the most captivating. Along with Alexandria, which I loathed to leave, these structured marvels along with the sunset, the Sphinx, the Valley Temple and other tombs, I had seen Egypt and already seen what I had wanted to see in Egypt.

Alexandria itself had been a delightful two-night stay. Amani at the Mina House arranged for us a slow taxi to drive across the desert to Alexandria. I found the people there kind and generous and, often enough, beautiful. The city is interesting not only as the mother cosmopolitan urban centre of all, but also because she still exudes a richness and mystery as well as the promise of a once again future greatness. I had read in the *Herald Tribune* just before we had departed for Egypt about Uncle Elias' quail restaurant that appears in the open market just at sunset. By chance, we happened to be in the right spot for the very moment that the restaurant began to be set up. It was indeed a culinary treat (despite the ecological consequences for the migrating quail). The tomb of Iscander (Alexander) has been lost, and we tried to intuit its location. At best, we could only surmise that the Soma or Sema might be under the mosque or Masjid al-Nābī Danyāl. In all, Alexandria involved us finding the Canopic Way, the Greco-Roman Museum, Lochias (site of the former royal palace), the Kom al-Dikkah or Hill of Rubble (site of the Paneion as well as a recently discovered Roman theatre), the Serapium (Pompey's Pillar) and the Mïdän al-Tahrir or public town square. In Egypt's Delta, I found a country working hard, construction underway everywhere, and a level of prosperity I had not seen in India. Poor it still was – often with sewers for streets between blocks of apartments, but there seemed to be an ascending promising struggle and hope for a future – all against the colour which is Egypt. I meditated on the tri-theistic pantheon of Goddess, God and Man as well as the pentad of the Mother, the Father, the Sister or Lady, the Brother or Lord, and the Child or Man – this last being the pinnacle of the pyramid of which the others form the four corners of the base.

Consequently, when I learned at the welcome dinner for our tour that several of the fellows had arranged *to climb* the great pyramid the next morning at 05:30, there was no hesitation but to choose to join them. Climbing the pyramid was actually forbidden since a tourist had fallen from it, but at the break of day, the guards were not adverse to being bribed. As we were about to ascend the pyramid the next day, a young American woman joined our group. But about a quarter of the way up, she developed acrophobia which contagiously spread to the rest of us. I could see what was happening and, being determined not to miss this golden opportunity to reach the summit, took off on my own. Our guide, Firganī, quickly caught up with me, and we continued together to the top, while the rest huddled at a corner with rifles pointed at them from the guards below. Without doubt, the view was splendid, and the feeling to be at the top of the Great Pyramid nothing short of fantastic. There were six others at the highest point as well – four of whom were Americans. Clouds obscured the rising sun until already above the horizon. Firganī proceeded to smoke a cigarette, but after I mentioned that it was not healthy, he dramatically ripped up the package and threw it and his matches from the top of the pyramid. The descent was more difficult. I was wearing a ridiculously tight pair of Levi jeans, and one could only see the level of stone blocks one was currently on but nothing else. Nevertheless, it was necessary for me to coach the young woman down to the ground. Afterwards, we walked around the pyramid peacefully.

Cairo itself was a whirlwind. Richard and I had already re-entered Cheops' pyramid which was again a zapping experience. Further, we hired a taxi to take us to the City of the Dead where we were served tea in the caretaker's house and then shown some exquisite Mamluk Sultanate tombs as well as that of King Farouk. This became another highlight. And with the tour, we were taken to the stupendous and overwhelming Egyptian Museum and later, after lunch at the Fellafalla restaurant, to two large mosques – one in the citadel, the Coptic Museum (from which I dashed into the nearby Church of Saint George, inter alia, Zeus *georgos*, and lit a candle), a synagogue and the church where Christ and his family had taken refuge in a cave.

Before we had left Paris, through friends of friends, Richard and I had been given the phone number of the Egyptian actor Gamil Ratib. I spoke with him on our fourth day in Giza, but as his play was to open the next day, he was not free to see us, and we arranged to rendezvous upon our return to Cairo. But in the ensuing two weeks, we would ask members of the crew as well as guides if they were familiar with Gamil Ratib. 'Gamil Ratib!' they would always exclaim in great excitement. In Egypt, as it turned out, he was very famous.

For our last day at the Mina House, we were taken to the Old Kingdom capital of Memphis to see the marvellous and colossal statue of a young Ramesses (Ramses the Great) lying on its back, then at Saqqara the stepped pyramid of Zozer and the adjacent pyramid complexes of Userkaf and Unas – this last with its wonderfully decorated inner chamber, the Serapeum and the mastaba tomb of Ti. In the distance is Dakshur where we could view both the Bent Pyramid of Seneferu and the unfinished one of Abusir. And then we flew by plane first to Aswan and from there to Abū Simbel for the marvellous temples of Ramesses II and Queen Nefertari. These also represent one of the engineering feats of the twentieth century. With the completion of the Aswan Dam and the consequent rising waters of Lake Nasser, to save the complex from being submerged, the temples were dismantled, relocated and reassembled 65 meters higher and 200 meters back from the river. The smaller temple is dedicated to the goddess Hathor; the larger contains sanctuary statues of Ptah, Amun-Re, Re-Harakhte and the deified Ramesses – the latter three being illuminated on two days of the year by the first light of the rising sun. From Abū Simbel we flew back to board our cruise ship, the MS Pyramid. One of our elderly gents, Elmer, tripped while boarding the vessel and landed on some rocks badly bruising his hands and ribs if not more. After two days of disoriented seclusion, he was transported back to the U.S.

While the ship was at the base of the Aswan Dam, I read in the Baedeker Guide that if the dam were to be destroyed by a surprise enemy attack, 98% of the Egyptian population would perish. The day before, the Egyptian newspapers had published photos of the former Libyan prime minister, Abdul Hamid Bakkush, lying supposedly assassinated in a pool of blood. Colonel Muammar el-Qaddafi then proclaimed the success of one of his suicide missions that had been sent to Egypt. However, on the BBC News the next day, I learned that the photos had been a fake and that President Hosni Mubarak announced that Bakkush was 'alive and well'. Egypt was then on alert over the possibility of Libyan revenge and bombers being sent to Aswan. It was another of those 'interesting' times. But we continued on without mishap or disaster to the Temple of Khnum, the ram-headed creator god, on Elephantine Island; then the Temple of Satis, Khnum's consort, that was being restored at the time by the German Archaeological Institute; the tomb of the Aga Khan; El Nabatat or Kitchener's Island with the Aswan Botanical Garden; and the double temple of Kom Ombo dedicated to the falcon-headed Horus and the crocodile-god Sobek. The banks of the Nile themselves were almost always splendidly scenic with their desert oasis foliage of palms, papyrus, bamboo and grazing fields – all utterly peaceful. Horus is also the deity at the Temple of Edfu with its mammoth pylon as entrance. Another temple dedicated to Khnum is the exquisite structure in Esnā with its lovely hypostyle columns.

Luxor, the New Kingdom capital, became the next delight where we passed four nights. Beside the Luxor Museum and the Karnak Sound and Light Show, it was the Great Temple of Amun-Re in Karnak, the second largest religious site in the world, that was the most impressive. As part of the precinct, there are also temples to Mut (Amun's consort), their son Khonsu, the craftsmen-god Ptah and Ramesses III. The complex is connected by the Avenue of Sphinxes to the smaller but extraordinarily well-preserved Temple of Luxor. This last was apparently not dedicated to a specific deity per se but served as the place where pharaohs were coronated either actually or symbolically. As part of the Temple of Luxor is the Mosque of Abu Haggag. Inside this last, it was gratifying to witness worshippers approaching the saint's tomb in full pagan fashion – caressing the lattice railing with their hands, bringing children to it or seeking blessing while pregnant. I did see there a man, though, who was bowing away from the direction of Mecca.

One day, it was the Valley of the Kings, the Valley of the Queens and the Valley of the Nobles on the west bank of the Nile. We went first to the tomb of Tutankhamun in which the king's body is still present. The irony in connection with this last is that the nearby Saatchi Gallery here in London has been currently exhibiting 'Tutankhamun: The Treasures of the Golden Pharaoh'. I had been planning to see the more than 150 pieces from his tomb, but the Saatchi, like all museums in London, is now closed thanks to COVID-19. In any event, back to those glorious November days in Egypt, besides the tomb of King Tut, we also visited those of Tuthmosis III, Amenhotep II, Horemheb and Ramesses I. After these, about eight of us walked over the mountain to the Deir al-Bahrī mortuary temple of Queen Hatshepsut. This 'Holy of Holies' consists of a series of colonnaded terraces that lead into the cliff and site of the temple itself and has been described as one of the 'incomparable monuments of ancient Egypt'. It was a place that has long captivated me since youth when I first saw photos of the sanctuary. Next, at the memorial temple of Ramesses II, the Ramesseum, and before the fallen colossus, to a small group of us I read Percy Shelley's poem *Ozymandias* with the lines: 'My name is Ozymandias, King of Kings; / Look on my Works, ye Mighty, and despair! / Nothing beside remains. Round the decay / Of that colossal Wreck, boundless and bare / The lone and level sands stretch far away'.

In the Valley of the Nobles, there were the tombs of Nakht and Ramose with restored pillars and two reliefs of Akhenaton – one from before and one after the reform. In the Valley of the Queens, there were the tombs of Tyti, wife and sister of Ramesses III, and that of Prince Amun-hir-Khopshef, the son of Ramesses III. At the king's own mortuary temple, the Madīnat Habu, the exterior wall depicts the king's defeat of the Sea Peoples. Inside, in a side chamber that contained a wall relief or painting of the fertility-god Min, I found myself unexpectedly enjoying 'fun and games' with the temple's attendant, Mohammed. Finally, it was twin statues depicting Amenhotep III, the Colossi of Memnon, that stood guard to the pharaoh's mortuary temple, originally larger and more opulent than even the Temple of Karnak. Memnon was an Ethiopian king and hero of the Trojan War who was a son of the dawn-goddess Eos. Following an earthquake in 27 BC that shattered the upper part of the eastern colossus, the statue was legendarily known to 'sing' at dawn or just after sunrise. This lasted until around 199 when the Romans reconstructed the upper part of the statue with sandstone.

From time to time, there were those of us who would detach ourselves from the tour group to have a moment to explore on our own. Within the overwhelming perplexity of Egypt, one could on occasion sink into a trance of interaction or even non-verbal or non-cognizant recognition. Periodically, in various temple complexes or perhaps the tombs, there could be a transfixion of the soul. With rented bicycles, Richard and I revisited the temples of Karnak, including that of Apet or Opet – the hippopotamus mother of Osiris – and Luxor. Leaving this last, I was able to touch the sister of the Concord *obelesque*. After Luxor, it was both Dendera and Abydos. The former is the site of the magnificent Ptolemaic Temple of Hathor with pylons, roof, terraces, crypts, *et al.* In the outer hypostyle hall and elsewhere, there are the 36 Egyptian zodiac signs. There is also a marvellous representation of Nut (identified with Hathor, wife of Horus the Elder and mother of Ihy, the ecstatic sistrum player, god of music and dancing) – depicted as both swallowing and giving birth to the sun. On the rear exterior wall of the temple are reliefs of Cleopatra VII and her son, by Julius Caesar, Caesarion. This splendid site we were able to visit leisurely and view in addition the Temple of Isis, the Sacred Lake and nearby well, and the Mammisi or 'birthing houses' of both Nectanebo II, the last of the native pharaohs, and the Romans. Christians had of course done their damage, but much remained to reveal the great beauty of the place – one of Egypt's best-preserved temple complexes.

Further downstream is the Temple of Seti I in Abydos. The ship moored for the night in al-Balyana – a reputedly 'very pious city' crowded with mosques as well as a large Coptic church/fortress. From there we bussed through some of the most beautiful countryside we had yet seen (immaculate fields, pleasant houses, lush groves of palm trees) to Al 'Arabah al Madfunah and Seti's temple containing shrines to Horus, Isis, Osiris, Amun-Re, Re-Harakhte, Ptah and the deified pharaoh. This was yet another of my favourites with its perfect layout and some exquisitely fine reliefs. Abydos, one of the oldest cities of Egypt, was originally home to the Predynastic rulers and became the burial place of pharaohs from the First, Second, Twelfth and Thirteen Dynasties as well as of Ahmose I, founder of the 18th Dynasty of the New Kingdom and builder of Egypt's final pyramid. The continual re-building of the city itself lasted into the Thirtieth Dynasty. Seti I was the second ruler of the 19th Dynasty, but to the north and older than his impressive Great Temple of Abydos in the ancient city is the frequently rebuilt Great Osiris Temple. Adjacent to Seti's temple is that of his son, Ramesses II, and behind Seti's temple is a much older temple, the Osireion, that was incorporated into Seti's funerary memorial. Other structures include the 2nd Dynasty Shûnet el-Zebîb (a large rectangular enclosure of mud-brick walls that looked like something belonging more to Mesopotamia), the Umm el Qa'āb ('Mother of Pots' – containing broken pot shards from offerings of earlier times), and the 1st Dynasty tomb of Horus Djer that became identified as the burial spot of Osiris. Hence, over time, Abydos emerged to be an important and ancient place of pilgrimage. And what we see here is a structured rivalry between the state triad of Ptah, Amun-Re and Re-Harakhte and the more enduring, popular and vernacular cult triad of Osiris, Isis and Horus. It seems that the local deity of Abydos, Khentiamentiu 'foremost Westerner' [that is, the dead], a manifestation of the pharaoh in the otherworld, became reinterpreted in the 5th Dynasty as an epithet belonging to Osiris.

It is, of course, the myth and worship of Osiris, the bringer of civilisation and the god of fertility, agriculture, vegetation, life, the dead, the afterlife and resurrection, that constitutes the telluric heart of Kemetic pagan spirituality. The city of Busiris in the delta was considered the birthplace of the god and his other major cult centre beside Abydos. It cannot be denied that Egyptian mythology is complex and messy and full of different variations concerning one theme or another. But for a culture that lasted a good three millennia, perhaps this is only to be expected. Unlike most other conceptualisations, for the Egyptians the sky was female, the goddess Nut, and earth was male, the god Geb. Nut and Geb became the parents of Osiris, Isis, Set, Nephthys and Horus the Elder. There is some allusion that this Horus was also the child of Isis and Osiris conceived within the womb of Nut as the siblings had become mutually enamoured even before their birth. While Horus, the hawk-headed god of light, was originally the deity of Lower Egypt, Set, a god of darkness, the desert and disorder, was the ruler of Upper Egypt. Set, as the jealous god who murders his brother Osiris, is often depicted as an antithetic evil figure, nevertheless various pharaohs took his name (e.g., Seti I and Seti II, cf. Peribsen, Setnakht). Joseph Campbell refers to 'The Secret of the Two Partners' as the understanding and implicit harmony existing virtually *sub rosa* behind the overt conflict between Set and Osiris' avenging son Horus 'the One Far Above'.

The primary myth concerning Osiris has him killed and later dismembered by Set. Isis retrieves the severed parts with the exception of Osiris' penis that had been eaten by Nile fish. She magically but briefly restores her brother-husband to life and makes for him a replica phallus from gold and wax with which he then posthumously impregnates her with their son Horus the Younger, the heir to the kingdom. Osiris then becomes the god and judge of the dead in the underworld or the western world. The reigning pharaoh of Egypt was considered to be a manifestation of Horus, a god of light and quintessential power whose right eye was the sun or morning star while his left eye was the moon or evening star. This last, injured by Set, was healed by Thoth but thereby represents the waxing and waning lunar phases. The *wedjat* or restored eye became subsequently a popular amulet of good health and protection for the ancient Egyptians. One manifestation of Horus is known by the name of Harpocrates, the child god of silence, who became especially revered in Ptolemaic times. The consort of Horus is the cow-goddess Hathor, a revered deity in her own right, goddess of beauty and love, but it is the awesome Isis who is the emotional centre of the myth involving Osiris. Clever, wise, resourceful and a formidable wonder-worker, she is the mother-goddess *par excellence* and Queen of Heaven who was the most popular deity among the ordinary people of Egypt and who was notably revered by the Roman writer Apuleius. She appears to be a precursor of the Virgin Mary whose own cult is likely a continuation of that which originally belonged to Isis.

While I should have known better but was too young at the time, I used to fantasise with my sister about ancient Egypt where brother-sister marriages had notably occurred. I think that as we grew older and beyond these childhood imaginings, my sister harboured and developed a resentment toward me as a non-spouse to her. Consequently, the lawyer she became and with my absence abroad ('You went to Europe'), virtually the whole of the inheritance from my father was hers. I could have pursued a similar recourse as did one or more of Martin Luther King, Jr.'s children, but in the overall scheme of things, it just did not seem to me to be the right thing to do. My dear friend Chickie from high school and beyond agreed with my decision but commented, 'Too bad about the money' Subsequently, in some shamanic musings, I have wondered if it may have actually been Isis who could have in a hidden and obscured version been the agent behind Osiris' death with haplessly Set being then engineered into being the villain. The corpus of myth is endlessly fluid and capable of yet to be discovered or created understandings. In Egypt, the most important of the early local gods included Hathor and Horus as well as the jackal-headed funerary god Anubis, the sun-god Atum of Heliopolis, the cat-goddess Bastet, the solar goddess of destruction and healing Sekhmet, the ram-headed Khnum, the moon-god Khonsu of Thebes, Min with an erect penis, the hawk-headed Montu supplanted by Amun, the weaving and wisdom goddess Neith of Sais, the vulture-goddess Nekhbet, the bull-god Ptah of Memphis, the crocodile god Sobek of Kom Ombo, and the ibis-headed god of writing and learning Thoth. Gods of wider jurisdictions were Ra the sun, Hapi the Nile and Nun the primordial watery abyss or the ocean. In Heliopolis, Atum became merged with Ra and an ennead was formed under him that included Geb and Nut, Osiris and Isis and Set and Nephthys. Horus was identified in Heliopolis with Atum-Ra-Harakhte, and, later, such local figures as Sobek and Amun were also linked with Ra and emerged as prominent gods – especially Amun-Re who was transformed into a supreme god and 'self-created one' during the hegemony of the 18th Dynasty in Thebes. To experience the temples to so many of these fascinating figures was an experience of a lifetime. Not as a Kemeticist per se but simply as a polytheist, the gods and goddesses of ancient Egypt were and are for me inspirational attestations to the fundamental variety and multiplicity of divine plenitude.

And after Abydos, it was the much different site of Tel el-Amara, the former city of Akhetaten ('Horizon of Aten') built by the pharaoh Akhenaten when he abandoned Thebes for his new capital. Akhenaten is hailed as reputedly the world's first significant monotheist. John MacDonald, our tour guide from the Metropolitan Museum of Art, argued that Akhenaten was actually intensely conservative, and his agenda was to re-establish the role of the king as high priest. In all this, he was not really a monotheist but rather a henotheist. True enough, he may have chosen the visible sun as his exclusive focus for worship without denying the existence of other deities, but his behaviour (e.g., defacing inscriptions, temple closure) toward the monuments and shrines of the other gods and goddesses appears little different than that of the Abrahamic religions. In fact, it has been pointed out that the pharaoh's 'Great Hymn to the Aten' shows remarkable similarities to Psalm 104. Henotheism itself has been described as an 'intermediate' stage between polytheism and monotheism such as is to be witnessed in the stage of Israelite belief in 'God' from the time of Moses to the exile. It is supposedly applicable when the unity of worship has not yet become 'sufficiently philosophically advanced' to deny the existence of other *netjeru*, the gods. In his fifth year as pharaoh, Akhenaten changed his name from Amenhotep IV and not long after moved Egypt's capital from Thebes to his new city of Akhetaten. How much of a religious radical or spiritual reformer Akhenaten truly was is debatable, but he was opposed to traditional Egyptian religion and promoted if not ordered the sole worship of Aten (perhaps originally Re-Harakhte). With the end of his 17-year reign, he might have been succeeded variously by Smenkhkare (possibly a son) and Neferneferuaten (possibly Nefertiti) – this interregnum period is uncertain – before the succession of Tutankhaten ('the living image of Aten') who subsequently changed his name to Tutankhamun ('living image of Amun') and transferred the capital back to Thebes. King Tut restored the worship of Amun and the other previously established gods of Kemet. Tel el-Amara was abandoned and largely destroyed. The area today is indeed empty and desolate. Then and now, I have no feeling for Akhenaten. What I enjoyed the most was the present-day hamlet with its smiling and waving children and villagers.

In all, to cruise along the magnificent Nile was to experience enchantment. The river is a corridor of life that cuts through the great desert. From its banks are the thin bands of fertility that each end with a line that divides the life-giving from the sudden expanse of dry and empty sand. After Tel el-Amara, we sailed to the baboon statues in al-Ashmūnayn – the site of Hermopolis and the only Greek-style temple in Egypt outside of Alexandria. Then in Tūnal al-Gabal, there is the tomb of Petrosiris and catacombs filled with tens of thousands of mummies of baboons and ibises. Further, at the site of Antinoopolis, several of us threw flowers into the Nile. And then, for our last banquet dinner on board, there was a costume party in which Richard and I came as lobsters. The following day by bus, we went first to the pyramid of Maidum with impressive cedar beams inside and a moment in the burial chamber before the rest arrived. Outside, on the far side of the pyramid, a group of workmen were playing a game in which one person covered his eyes with one hand while putting the other behind his back. Then someone would strike the hand, and the receiver had to guess who he is. After a picnic lunch and the mortuary temple, we drove to the Fayyūm oasis and Madinat al-Fayyūm (Crocodilopolis – ancient centre of Sobek worship), the obelisk of Senusert I and coffees on the shores of Lake Qārūn before crossing the desert to Giza and back to the Mina House.

After contacting Gamil Ratib, we arranged to meet at his apartment. The Cairo traffic was always nightmarish, and often the cab driver would simply turn off his engine in the wait before being able to proceed. When we reached Gamil's, there was a note on his door apologising that he had been summoned at the last minute for a rescheduled rehearsal of the play he was in, and he had departed five minutes before we had arrived. He proposed a rendezvous the next day, but when I phoned the following morning, he had to apologise again because it was the last day before the opening of his play. We then arranged to meet upon our final return to Cairo. For the day itself, we went first to the bazaar, then to the house belonging to the father of Mastafa the waiter from our ship where we enjoyed lunch with his family. A last hour in the Egyptian Museum, then a Sound and Light show at the Sphinx and Pyramids and finally an emotional farewell dinner at the Mina House.

While most of the 'Cruise the Nile with Us' group departed at this point, a small number of us had opted for the Sinai extension to which Hans Ebenstein himself now joined. We departed at 07:00 with an Egyptian guide, Ahmed, in a small bus and through the amazing, pulsating streets of Cairo and into the empty solitude of the desert. By taking a tunnel, we could not actually see the Suez Canal, but the sight of large freighters that appeared to be moving across the sand was uncanny. At Abu Zuneimah, a frontier-like shipping-mining town, we left the bus but had to wait several hours before our Land Rover arrived. We headed off to follow the great rock-cliff divide between north and south Sinai when a taxi blowing its horn madly caught up with us. It was David, our German guide, who lives in Israel. It was an Israeli company who organised these Sinai tours. We stopped to picnic out of cans. All of the food now was from Israel, and, after the fare in Egypt, this change in itself was refreshing. We had a fresh salad during dinner in the Bedouin camp in which we set up for the night. In a partially covered, enclosed pen, we retired early and under the stars. During a pee break at one point, the moon had set, and the sky was perfectly clear and dazzling. In short, I found the Sinai to be magnificent country – clean in its emptiness and purity – with great multi-coloured and jagged mountains like teeth. A kind of no man's land.

The following morning it was a visit to Serabit al-Khadim where we found the temple of Hathor as goddess of turquoise (mined in the area) and wondered about the possible influence of this cult site on the origin of the Golden Calf. Here we picnicked breakfast/lunch before returning to the camp, and after departure we stopped briefly at the tomb-shrine of a local *shaykh*. Then began a long open-aired ride through spectacular desert and mountains, but we arrived late to the Monastery of Saint Catherine, cold, hungry and highly irritable. A clash began between two factions of our group. Hans avoided the dorm where we unexpectedly had to sleep as the guest rooms in the monastery were being used by the monks themselves. Richard and I managed to explore much of the cloister by dark, with flashlight and binoculars and without being caught. The Burning Bush turns out to be a bramble. Later we smoked what we thought was a spliff but was not. Back with the group, I dispensed some scotch as a pacifier for both tetchy factions.

We woke at 03:00, and seven of us set off to climb Mount Sinai. One smoker among us, though young, could not make it, but the rest of us did. The night sky was utterly dazzling, and a strange shaft of light shot up at one point vertically from the horizon into the sky. Gradually this beam of light widened – it was the so-called zodiacal light – and suddenly transformed horizontally into the morning's light across the eastern skyline. We reached the summit by 05:35. The horizon's light turned into a gorgeous red band and issued forth a welcomed sun at 06:14. Descent, shower and the Nabi Hārūm or site of the Golden Calf where Richard and I, hidden discretely, spilled semen on the earth. Breakfast followed and then our tour of the monastery. The church interior is a marvellous, virtually otherworldly spectacle. I was the only one to light a candle.

The first of December was a day of open-air driving but on a paved road. We stopped for lunch in an area that contained Nabataean rock inscriptions and then proceeded to the beach on the Gulf of Aqaba near Sharm al-Shaykh. Around a camp fire, we enjoyed a soup and flambéed chicken for dinner with Ahmed singing some delightful songs and the rest of us doing 'Dinah'. A lovely sleep on the beach followed, and then it was scuba snorkelling and encountering myriads of colourful fish and a world of underwater life on the order of something I had never before seen. From here we flew back to Cairo and were checked into the Sheraton Hotel. I phoned from there to Gamil, and he mercifully suggested to us in our exhaustion that he would come to the hotel to meet us instead of our coming to him.

The Sheraton had a balcony veranda that fully surrounded an atrium below. We sat at one of its tables, and as we talked countless people walking by would stop and ask for his autograph – always in a state of great excitement. Gamil had been in David Lean's 1962 film *Laurence of Arabia* as Majid. He explained to us that he had lived in France from about the age of 30 (he was around 58 when we met him in 1984) and had only in the last few years been invited to return to Egypt for a role in a television series. To his surprise, he was an enormous success, and that was why so many if not everyone in Egypt knew who he was. What was most fascinating for me was that, after his having lived so long in Europe, he was essentially a Westerner but also of course an Egyptian and could thereby explain things about the culture and way of life of his native country to me in a clear, understandable and insightful manner. It was a perfect way to conclude our visit to this ancient and captivating land with its spirited people. Gamil Ratib died two years ago in 2018 at the age of 91.

The next night we were back in Paris and visiting Alexis and Raffy in their enormous 16ème arrondissement apartment on the Rue de la Faisandier to which they had recently moved. They told of registering with the police, a requirement, and were astonished to learn that the municipal police of Paris knew who was in every residence of the city, how many in each, when they came and went, what they did for a living, and on and on. And this was back in the early 1980s! One can only imagine with a profound shudder where surveillance society is now nearly forty years later.

CHAPTER SEVEN

Mesclun salad; COVID-19 and bigAg, bigFood & bigPharm; the gods, enchantment & epiphany; the Entheogenic Renaissance; Robert Pfeiffer; Don Patterson; Spinoza & Nietzsche; Heathenism / geocentric progression; childhood dreams / magic tales & fairy tales / the Lindworm Prince; en route to Key West with Adams & Reich; airport tales; alcoholic escapades; Rigoglioso's virgin mothers; early conferences; memory / Mnemosyne & the Muses / Randy Connor / Pavel Horák / Richard Fenman & science / Conner's Christianisation; the Spanish flu / carnival / Boobie's; random thoughts: Reagan-Vidal-Nietzsche-Harvey Milk / Kemeticism, God & gods / awe / the pandemic dragon / Chirac mayor of Paris / luck / Dionysus & Apollo; travel & *foie gras*; Karel Bouse & Neo-shamanism

The *mesclun* salad in the Provence is a blend of salad greens and traditionally includes arugula, chervil, oak leaf and mâché. Its name is derived from the French *mesclar* which simply designates 'mixture'. We were once having a dinner with Alexis and Jean-Louis in Saint-Paul de Vence. Alexis ordered a *mesclun* salad but complained after it had been served because it did not have the sufficient variety of lettuces or greens for it to qualify as a *mesclun*. The chef then appeared from the kitchen, and together he and Alexis proceeded to place each type of leaf on the table. Alexis insisted that the true *mesclun* must have a variety of five plants but the one that was served had only three. Painstakingly, the chef combed through Alexis' salad and finally found a fourth ingredient that was then placed alongside the other three. In all it was a humourous moment. I think one could only be French to do what Alexis did and probably Parisian at that.

⁂

The pandemic spread of COVID-19 is occurring as I proceed to write. Globally, at the present point, over one million cases have been confirmed. 5% of these have resulted in death, but 21% or nearly 219,000 people have recovered. The situation still is grim. Is this the traditional 'Chinese curse' that would have us living in interesting times? Whether the alleged phrase is apocryphal or actually derived from China, it can at least not be doubted that our horrific times are attention-grabbing. But out of this viral plague, I do see the possibility that the structure of our very world and the way we live and what we tolerate may be undergoing radical change. My steadfast militant optimism and/or wish is that this change will be something *profoundly* for the better. It may all be a bitter pill, but I see this SARS-CoV2 invasion fundamentally as a 'gift' from the Earth – a Trojan Horse or Pandora Box conferment, perhaps, but a possible 'learning' offering in the least. She is allowing those of us who do survive finally, intelligently and engagingly to wake up!

I continue to be outraged by the US President (Trump) who has blamed hospitals, medical workers and governors for the health-care equipment shortages amid the coronavirus outbreak, and yet it has been his administration that, two-months before the December 2019 onset in Wuhan, China, terminated the pandemic early-warning programme (PREDICT) that had been established to detect coronaviruses. The Trump administration had already downgraded global health security efforts previously by slashing funding to science agencies and eliminating the National Security Council's key global health post. Trump claims that the COVID-19 pandemic was completely unexpected, and yet White House economists published a study around the same time that PREDICT's funding was cut that specifically warned that a global epidemic could kill a half million Americans and devastate the economy. Even more, Bill Gates gave a TED Talk on the 3rd of April in 2015 that explicitly and accurately warned about the unpreparedness for the next epidemic – specifically concerning coronaviruses. Using a model based on the 1918/1919 Spanish flu plague, he claimed that something much more devastating than the Ebola virus was highly possible – even likely. Ebola itself is not spread through the air, and it would have been much worse if it got into urban areas.

Gates had argued that the Ebola epidemic could serve as a wake-up call. It provided us an early warning, and that if we start now, we could be ready for the next epidemic. And this was five years ago. In his address, Gates recognised that science and technology were needed to be part of an overall global health system. We have satellite maps, cell phones and advances in biology. What is necessary is a preparation that is similar to that of the military. In fact, a medical reserve core could be readied and then paired with the military to move fast when necessary. Stronger health systems in poorer countries are vital as is more research and development. Simulation 'germ games' could be conducted in order to gauge possibilities and how best to manage future threats and outbreaks. And most obvious to us now, Gates maintained that compared to the cost of an epidemic, the budget for what he was proposing is 'very modest'. He clearly forecast that time is not on our side. And today I have learned that tigers in a Bronx Zoo have been detected with the coronavirus.

The present global failure of early 2020 has underscored the utter mess we are making of our shared habitat. What is necessary more than ever is a shift in focus from the individual nation to worldwide cooperation. We need to work globally together without being limited by an illusory nation-first short-sightedness. Moreover, and this is perhaps the most difficult and bitter pill, we are obligated to recognise the roles that 'bigAg, bigFood and bigPharma' have played and are playing in the undermining of healthy habitats and individual physical fitness. Maybe extreme, but a family member rants that the 'bigCorps in business . . . will be doing very well out of this malarkey – while we are filled with fear, kept indoors, told to eat crap and dose ourselves on paracetamol and of course wait for the vaccine so we can keep the injected neurotoxins coming in nice and steady every winter'. With the way we have managed to lose a predominant sense of balance and the kind of necessary scepticism that is part of the human birth right, the majority of us automatically dismiss what she is saying. But if, in a wider comprehension, the corona pandemic could be seen as a natural rectification, the thousands of deaths and the economic devastation that are presently occurring could be accepted as Earth's revelation that the corporate management of life on the planet is in need of radical reappraisal and something much new and different and imaginative is crucially overdue. We want the copacetic phoenix to rise from the ashes. There quite conceivably might not be another chance. I can only hope that we can re-learn to appreciate and allow the ways that the earth regenerates when she is allowed to do so and also how our immune systems might recover when properly encouraged. There is something to gain from this viral catastrophe. Are we grasping it, and will we work together to have it be what we all on this planet might share and bequeath to the future of our children?

For the needs that are on hand, we cannot depend on the gods. What must be done, we must do ourselves. *Deus ex machina* acts could be helpful, even lovely, but the gods are not there primarily for that. Instead, the gods as I understand them at least belong to the aesthetic realm, and as such they serve to inspire and make us stronger and more complete. They may be something more and other than the earth as well, but in as much as they derive *from* the earth, my veneration of the divine is also a devotion *to* the earth. Herein lies my concern with her well-being. For me, the gods are grounded foremost in nature and music. But I also adore their depiction in sculpture and artwork. In all, godhead may not be understood as a personal 'God', but it definitely includes many personalities. In fact, from a pantheistic pagan understanding, it includes all that is: nature, the *dryghten,* the Star Goddess, the physical/empirical world *and* the incorporeal spiritual/metaphysical, the physical cosmos *and* the non-material mind/spirit/soul, this world *and* the otherworld, the animate *and* inanimate, the Goddess *and* the God, the gods *and* humanity. Christians (for instance, John Gee) are unable to understand a pagan combination of non-belief in an ultimate truth and yet our palpable maintenance of active relationship with the divine. But pagan adoration of nature is not linked to acceptance of the fully transcendent. While accepting death, pagans engage with life – and with this engagement, responsibility is solely ours alone, both individually and, especially, collectively. This last requires and mandates the human effort and ability to vision and work both wisely and together.

But to return to enchantment and its potency of which I would argue the gods to be the *primus inter pares* embodiments, thaumaturgic rapture belongs to both this-world (in nature and through art) and the otherworld (in deity, *anima,* the miraculous). In fact, enchantment is the liminal threshold that functions as the very gateway between the two dimensions, the this and the other. When the wondrous manifests to us from either provenance, we then experience the epiphanic. Experiences of epiphany have been described as ranging from high-relief, quiet, dialogue and unconscious to prophetic, mystical and miraculous. In his *Religious Epiphanies across Traditions and Cultures* (2017), James Kellenberger defines a religious epiphany as 'the appearance or manifestation of God, a god or goddess, or the divine or religious reality, as received in human experience'. But in his book, he reveals himself to be steadily more interested in the 'God' of the theistic traditions of Christianity, Judaism and Islam, although he does at least acknowledge the phantasmagoric revelation of Krishna as Vishnu to Arjuna in the *Mahābhārata,* the polytheistic epiphanies in the *Iliad* of Homer, Vodou possession, and the vision quests of Native American traditions. It is especially the epiphanic, as known from other sources besides biblical narrative or through such personages as Teresa of Ávila, John of the Cross, Catherine of Siena, Meister Eckhart, etc., that holds pagan interest. And Kellenberger does at least also allow that 'Psychoactive chemicals have been used in religious ceremonies and in such settings arguably they enhance or facilitate epiphanic experiences' – even that 'When ingested under proper conditions peyote may allow a worshipper to experience a personal revelation, often in the form of a vision'.

A proverbial question concerning epiphany has to do with its veridicality. Are visions and locutions merely hallucinations? Are they unreal phantasies or apprehensions caused by brain activity, or are they for the Christian genuine creations from God, or for a pagan are they raptures from a god or divine reality? For theists, the matter is more difficult. Teresa of Ávila struggled to know whether her visions and locutions were truly from God or were instead supernatural machinations conjured by Satan. Paganism, by contrast, is not burdened by 'belief' in the devil. The evil entity and opponent of God is understood as itself a Christian creation and not a part of a pagan world-outlook. But even apart from this, the theist confronts the possibility that seemingly epiphanic apprehension might be a product of imagination or neurological brain activity. In either case, it would not be a true epiphany in as much as it is not an appearance or manifestation of or from God. And again, the pagan is not limited by this sacred/mundane dichotomy. Whether the phantasmagoric is an imagination or a neurological development within the brain's cortex, or even a consequence from an external deity, within a pantheistic framework, all is divine, and any apparitional phantasm is a configuration that shares with the innate divinity of existence itself – especially in consideration of any informative nature that may occur with it. Hallucinatory experience need not be an ultimate creation of the Christian or Abrahamic God but more broadly one simply of divine activity per se. 'Epiphany' may, however, be applied inappropriately toward self-centred indulgence or the like, but this lies in the individual's implementation of what has been received rather than the genuineness of its source. For a pagan, the epiphanic mystical concerns above all the salient experience of awe, wonder, bliss and sublimity as well as authentic meaningfulness, insight and the possibility of metanoia or significant change in one's values and directions.

There also appears within the full range of pagan perspective to be the need for some to locate or attest an ultimate but unknowable 'transcendent religious reality' behind or uniting the plethora of diverse epiphanic experiences that exist through the many and various traditions of religion and even non-theistic orientations. While paganism is far from a position of religious exclusivism and exhibits little proclivity to judge experiences outside its own formulations as false, it remains comfortable with its own understandings of divinity which are unique in comparison to those of the world's other 'major religions'. Thanks especially to participation in the Parliament of the World's Religions as well as other forums such as San Francisco's United Religions Initiative, there is a pagan faction today that is deeply involved with interfaith engagement. Nevertheless, someone like Sarah Ann Osmen in her 1990 *Sacred Places: A Journey into the Holiest Lands* resonates with my own personal conviction when she describes a future possibility, maybe two or three hundred years from now, of fearless individual inspiration 'once the glitter of the Christian Church has finally faded and left our sight clearer again'. As a whole, paganism is not enamoured of Christianity or Islam and feels no need to compromise its own insights and experiences to conform with a 'religious reality' that is championed as either wholly transcendent or an ultimate praxis and common denominator uniting all religiosity.

For pagans, mystical experience is sought foremost in and through nature. There is an undeniable joy to be experienced with the desert, the mountain, the forest, the river, lake, sea and ocean. The wonders of the natural world evoke awe and a sense of the sublime. In this, the epiphanic is finding a central source in the aesthetic. Pagans may also encounter profound alterations of consciousness through ritual participation or in the contemplation or *pūjā* before an altar – whether domestic or in a temple, but it is in natural surroundings that convey the beauty of the earth where a pagan is perhaps most at home. She/he may acknowledge what is usually understood as the non-personal but nevertheless holy presence that animates the natural world and has been variously designated as *mana, orenda, wakan, manitou, anima, kami* and/or *numen*, and it is in this recognition that we can perceive the 'paganesqueness' of such spiritualities as Shinto, Native American traditions, indigenous identities, Afro-Latin religiosities and contemporary Western paganisms (Wicca, Celtic, Heathen, Kemetic, Classical, Romuva, secular and so forth). Whether in nature, natural miracles, ritual, interior quiet or even just the daily awareness of divine ubiquity, pagans can encounter the presence of enchantment and a purpose for life. A primary endeavour within paganism then is to overcome quotidian blindnesses for mindful recognition of divine epiphanic continuity. Perhaps most fundamentally, a pagan seeks to cultivate an awareness of and thankfulness for the miracle of life itself.

The pagan approach to numinous immanence and understanding materialises for me, therefore, to be vital for the kind of sane endurance that is necessary in today's COVID-19 world pandemic. If other spiritual practices work for others, pagans have no difficulty as long as mutual tolerance and co-existence can also prevail. We are all different to various extents, and this means that different expressions become valid for different people. Within this differentiation, there is fundamentally little impulse for pagan non-acceptance of non-pagan belief and thinking. However, the grounding of pagan spirituality with the earth and nature allows us an immediate source of psychological strength in confrontations with uncertainty, fear, chaos and even death. Paganism encapsulates a refreshing and earth-oriented beauty that exists and perdures through crisis. Pagans understand mortality as an intrinsic part of our corporeal existence, and while various beliefs or comprehensions concerning possibilities of afterlife, Summerland, the Western Isles and rebirth may be held by various pagans, there is no primary focus on 'pie-in-the-sky' hopes for what comes after our duration on this planet or for resurrection. It is life in this-world, our present world, on which pagans concentrate, and in hard times pagans continue to celebrate life's underlying melody, harmony, rhythm and capacity for heroism. At its best, paganism is in itself talismanic.

By its ancient, historical and pangaean vernacular appeal, paganism is very much a spirituality that accompanies and can infuse ordinary life in its more quotidian and conventional circumstances. But this primarily earth-based approach is also vital for the support to be welcomed in contending with life crises. This last is of course likely to be a function of all religions, but paganism is in addition significant for its own manner of experiencing the mystical – precisely what I sought to explore in the third of my *Paganism as a World Religion* series, namely, *Pagan Mysticism* (2019). Pagans seek ways to look at and understand our earth but also, at least on occasion, to fuse this within the 'otherwordly-psychocosmic-faeriesque-hyperspatial' range of acutely eidetic imagery and thankful encounter with reverential awe, numinal inspiration and rapturous quintessence. Both the natural and phantasmagoric worlds may be important to various pagans and in different ways or focusing. My interest in this present moment of writing, however, is more specifically with the cosmic consciousness of the *unio mystica* or *mysterium tremendum et fascinans* – in short, with the ecstasies that can be engendered through ritual and dance, through the flora and fauna and landscapes of the natural environment, through concentrated contemplation and/or through psychotropic sacraments including ambrosia, *amrita,* nectar and natural or artificial hallucinogens. With these last, we are more than likely touching upon the ancient and ineffable mysteries of pagandom that involved delirium, enlightenment and initiation. Although the intricacies of these former pagan cults are now lost to us, we can conjecture their likelihood through what Jonathan Ott in his *The Age of Entheogens & The Angel's Dictionary* (1995) refers to as the Dark Ages and Pharmacratic Inquisition vis-à-vis the archaic revival, the Psychedelic Age and the Entheogenic Renaissance or Entheogenic Reformation. He cites the personal and ecstatic experiences of the divine, the faith-inspiring ecstasy and religious democracy that had at one time characterised the pagan world and claims that even today 'we are *still* in the Dark Ages' that have stretched from the destruction of the Eleusinian Mysteries, through the persecution of witches in the Middle Ages, to the continuance of a public health 'War on Drugs'. With no compromise, Ott declares that the Catholic or Christian 'Sacrament' is a placebo entheogen and 'merely an inactive symbol of the primordial Element in Communion – the entheogenic plant or Potion'.

I confess that I am fully in accord with Jonathan here. By this, I do not mean that pagans must rush out and into the psychedelic scene, but there ought to be some recognition and acceptance that the hallucinogenic sacrament played a significant role in ancient paganisms and still does within some of the world's current traditions with which we contemporary Western pagans may claim an affinity. Granted, apart from the likelihood of the *kykeon* being entheogenic within the popular Eleusinian Mysteries, the ingestion of mind-altering substances was and is more properly the undertaking of the shaman rather than that of the general populace. Nevertheless, I want to stress that mysticism in paganism is not dependent on intoxicants, but in the *via positiva* approach that is typical for pagan spirituality in general and differentiates it from other religions, these are equally legitimate for attaining the enthusiasm of god-possession. It is this centrality of mystical consciousness that is important for non-theistic or non-monotheistic pagan religiosity – concerning both vernacular everyday awareness and, more intensely, for those special occasions of ecstatic beatitude. Epiphanic revelation is sought through ineffable beauty, sublimity or divinity, and perhaps these dimensions in reality may all be one and the same. A pagan appears in an overall sense to accept what Nietzsche terms *Rausch* or 'rapture' and as attainable through either corporeal nature or the physiology of art. The

German philosopher considers that the indispensable factor for aesthetic action or vision of any kind is *intoxication* of one kind or another. What becomes essential for the pagan is the feeling of completeness, enhancement, plenitude and the augmentation of strength. This is rapture and is what interconnects the pagan with our world itself. The mystical routes to this transfiguring interrelatedness are sought through that which might be seen in vision, heard in locution or felt through the evanescent inspiration of rapture. Overall, what is most rejected within a pagan framework is estrangement from things of the earth. Pagan denial of an alienating transcendent does not preclude flying, but even with visionary flight the body always remains related in one manner or another with its environment. In all this, what pagans cultivate as the *primus inter pares* of abilities is what Baudelaire allowed to be 'that queen of the faculties', namely, imagination. It may be that an irrational function is intrinsic to the intuitive inventiveness for a pagan-type of mystical consciousness and/or aesthetic endeavour, and someone like Maurice Ravel could claim that 'Art is the supreme imposture'. But even so, the achievements of the French impressionist composer amount to some of our supreme musical creations such as the nocturnal enchantment, the glorious daybreak emergence of the sun and the orgiastic climax of his *Daphnis and Chloe*. The very nature of fabrication in art, in fact, may also be the nature of human encounter with the otherworld. This is not empirical or factual but the ritual and/or artistic putting together so that the sum is greater than its parts.

I feel, however, that it is important here to emphasise that the transformations and/or mysticisms to which I have been alluding do not require rushed undertakings and any effort toward an achievement of a quickly wished for goal. Instead, much more often than not, the endeavours involve the art of patience and the taking of time gently. For many, the use of externals of any kind is not commensurate with their natural orientation and hence becomes unnecessary. What is important with all pagan endeavours, however, are study and contemplation. These last necessitate ample time and the cultivation of tranquil perseverance.

Consequently, in our current lockdowns and shielding-in-place, in whatever limited access some of us might have to the outdoors and the beauties of blossoming nature, and in our unease and even illness, a pagan conviction is one that has the ability to see many if not most of us through the storm. On our viral planet, the virus too is a part of nature. Our love for the earth is also a trust in the earth and what she unfolds despite our clumsiness, greed, short-sightedness, inflexibilities and miscalculations. We may have the non-consciousness of full cessation after our final duration on this planet, or we might have some continuance in an otherworld afterlife, or even rebirth for another life after this present one. But all these possibilities remain the great unknowns and at best ought not distract us from participating as much as possible in the here-and-now, enjoying what there is to enjoy, serving and helping others in need, and working toward contribution to a legacy of improvement for those who will follow us. The light and brilliance as well as the dance between the luminous and the dark that a pagan consciousness celebrates are all there for us throughout all these endeavours. What will see us through is the development of mindfulness for the present and gratitude for what has been. This is the trust of freedom that paganism offers rather than the burdens of guilt and intimidation.

California north of San Francisco was always a pleasure for me – Sausalito where Nancy and I married, Tiburon where Rosalie and Bill Sennett once lived, Wunderchen where Pennell and Steve have now holed up, Mount Tamalpais, Napa, Sonoma, Clear Lake, Mendocino, Big River, Pomo country, Coast Miwok country, and then Russian River and Guerneville. This last was a popular get-away destination for San Franciscans. A memory I have is of a weekend in which Pfeiffer and I had gone to the 'River'. After a night in our sleeping bags, Pfeif found a place for breakfast. As I had little in the way of money in those days, I declined and said that I would be fine while he breakfasted. On my own, I discovered a large bramble bush laden with berries – a joy I have always allowed myself when in an appropriate area in late summer or early autumn. But while I was feasting most contentedly, apparently Bob could see me through the window of the restaurant. All of a sudden, he appeared and said resignedly, 'Okay, come inside! I will buy you breakfast'.

I had met Robert Kent Pfeiffer during my first year at Purdue University. I was serving from behind the counter in the cafeteria of Cary Hall, and he always had something jovial to say when he passed by with his tray for lunch or dinner. The second year, he pledged to the Sigma Phi Epsilon fraternity after I had already been initiated into it. We were both majoring in chemical engineering and became friends. At this point, he was eking by on a scholarship and with little extra for any spending. Since I was better funded by my father, I was in a position to help him through. And for the great Easter break, he, I and three others drove to Fort Lauderdale where we stayed with his parents. Pfeif and one of the other chaps had told the driver's girlfriend that I belonged to some esoteric sect and was not allowed to talk to women. Periodically, the car was stopped so that I could get out and prostate in prayer to the sun. It was, however, during these mad and wonderful times in Florida that I definitively abandoned all semblance of the beliefs with which I had been raised and now adopted an atheistic form of Hinduism acknowledging a sole impersonal Brahman. Pfeif/Pfeiffer (he used his family name as his first name) had been brought up staunchly Roman Catholic, and I remember when a carload of fraternity brothers drove off campus for my last night at Purdue to drink beer together in the car. Pfeif talked about how he had been influenced by me and had lost his faith after hearing my pantheistic and atheistic arguments. I had a laryngitis at that moment and could not say anything to mollify my affect but felt discomfited by what I had done to him. What is the point in undermining someone's beliefs?

We reconnected several years later and after both of us had graduated from college. Pfeiffer had landed a job with Union Carbide and was initially assigned to New York. I was on my way to Europe for the first time and, while staying with my parents, Pfeif and I saw each other several times in the city. One night at a party, with a big shit-eating grin on his face, he comes up to me and asks, 'Michael, where were you last night?' The name of the gay bar I no longer remember, but I mentioned it to him. 'What were you doing there?' he then asked.

'Having a beer with the fellow who brought me out', I replied. Pfeiffer had thought he had recognised me but had rushed down to the loo to put on his contact lens to be sure, and by the time he had got back upstairs, I had already left.

Later, after Europe, during my sojourn in Laguna Beach with my 'astrological parents', Jack Fontan and Ray Unger, Pfeiffer would visit. He was now working from Los Angeles. And when subsequently I came to the City of the Angels, I roomed with him on Lexington Avenue in Hollywood just off Vine Street. After this, we moved to a large and lovely flat above a row of parking garages on North Beachwood Drive next to the Theosophical Society's Besant Lodge. These were heady days of amorous youthful escapades, pursuit of opera, my brief army stint, President Kennedy's assassination and eventually the decision to return to college. After several years, Union Carbide transferred Pfeiffer to San Francisco, and I rented an apartment in

Lincoln Heights within close walking distance to the headquarters of the Broadway department store where I worked as an assistant buyer – first in china and then in toys. After this, I enrolled for an M.A. degree in International Relations at San Francisco State College. My after-graduation plan had been to secure an overseas job with a bank, work in Europe and benefit by having an American salary. None of this came to be. But I had found an apartment for $80 a month on Carl Street in the Haight-Ashbury. After several years, I then moved into my dream cabin in the sky on Russian Hill. With Pfeif's comparatively luxurious apartment just two floors below, he and I were again essentially rooming together. He had his affairs, and I had mine, and it was nothing short of a joyous time of youth, energy and the curiosity of abandonment.

One day I asked Bob why he was hanging out almost exclusively with my group. He replied, 'Because your friends are much more interesting than mine'. These were the times of the counterculture or what Jonathan Ott refers to as the 'Psychedelic Age'. Pfeiffer maintained his Union Carbide duties during the week, but for the weekend, he would part his hair down the middle, put on an Indian band to keep it in place, and then be one with the rest of us. With my brother stationed in Vietnam, when Nancy and I decided to marry, Pfeif asked, 'May I be your best man?'

After I had moved to Europe at the start of the 1970s, Pfeiffer's company transferred him back to Manhattan and after that to Atlanta. He was still in New York and met me at the airport when I had come back for my brother's funeral. I sobbed in his arms. But between New York and Atlanta, Pfeif was placed in Lima where he worked for a number of years through the 1970s. My regret is that Richard and I never had the chance to visit him when he was in Peru. He had a good friend there, Carmen, who was a travel agent. He went on one occasion with her to a dinner in Lima for travel agents that he described afterwards as having poor food, being uncomfortably hot and utterly boring until his name was pulled in a lottery for wining a cruise for two in the Aegean Sea. Richard and I joined him and Carmen. For the first few days with her hair wrapped up in a turban she was Carmen Miranda, and then one evening after having been to the ship's hair dresser, she walked into dinner as Rita Hayworth. Departing from Athens, the ship went to Istanbul, Izmir, Mykonos, Delos, Crete and Rhodes. Following advice from a friend, we eschewed the organised tours, and instead the four of us would share the cost of a taxi to see what there was to see, see more in fact and also avoid the tourist sales stops. We had an exceptionally wonderful time in Istanbul and must have been so glowing with our thrill for being there that we were spontaneously invited to an after-hours club where the entertainers of the city themselves went to relax. Afterwards and late in the night we walked back to our ship in the harbour, but only realised much too late that we had taken the wrong route and were separated from the ship by fencing with lethal spikes at the top. Pfeif said, 'I will not allow you to try to get Carmen over that!' But neither she nor Richard and myself wanted to walk the long trek back, so Richard and I despite our inebriation managed to get Carmen and then Pfeif over the spikes. To this day, neither Richard or I can imagine that we dared to do what we did. The gods were certainly with us on that occasion.

Several years later, Richard, my mother and I visited and stayed with Pfeiffer in Georgia as we were driving to Florida. This was the moment when the Presidential Inauguration in Washington, D.C. had to be cancelled because of the frigid weather. Bob was caring for his younger brother Jerry then who was an early AIDS victim. Pfeif later contracted AIDS as well and also eventually died from it. As I was then enmeshed in my Ph.D. research at King's College in London, I was unable to be with him for his final days. But the memory of him that first comes always to mind is that of the delicious blackberries and equally delicious breakfast in Russian River. He was a dear friend for many years.

Massalia was founded on the Mediterranean coast around 600 BC by colonists from the Asia Minor city of Phocaea. It was the first Greek colony in what is now France and known today as the city of Marseille. I have two negatively challenging experiences thanks to this port city. One was contracting a severe case of giardia from a bouillabaisse consumed in the Vieux-Port that had been most likely concocted from fish bones and the like that the woman had pulled out of the garbage. The other was much earlier during my European vagabonding days. I woke during the night in the Marseille hotel I had chosen to find the bed swarming with bed bugs. Even worse, subsequently I discovered I had acquired crab louse. It became clear that what I had thought to be a hotel was in fact a brothel.

Next in Rome, I checked into a sprawling hotel on the banks of the Tiber that was operated by nuns. Another person who was registering at the same time was Don Patterson from Dallas. After explaining to him what had happened in Marseille, he invited me to his room and searched and removed the crabs from my pubic region. That evening we walked together in the Borghese Gardens, and before long, Don had found an Italian to pick up. I became the go-between by using my French. I remember Don yelling from a bridge across the river as I was returning back to the hotel, 'Hey! You seem to know more about this than I do'.

Don became another good friend for many years. After I had 'outed' myself to him, I mentioned the camp name a friend of Bob Pfeiffer's in New York had given me. '*Yvonne!?*' Don exclaimed, 'I think it is more like Edith'. And so it became. During the 1970s popular raves in Amsterdam, it was finally an occasion for Edith to go out on the town. My neighbour Maggie from across the canal lent me an elegant black chiffon dress along with a blonde wig. Patricia did my makeup and even blended in my small moustache making it scarcely noticeable. And in our house were a pair of high-heel golden shoes that only fit over my three main toes. But what became the most surprising, and beyond the number of 'hits' I received from countless fellows, was that instead of my expectation to simply have fun and be trashy, an extremely ladylike persona took over throughout the evening. And this became Edith's one and only night out.

It was through Don that I got to know Sheila, also from Dallas, who became one of the 'major dealers' that had been present for my inheritance party in San Francisco. Don had moved from Texas to California and became a successful lecturer and fund raiser in one of the California State Universities north of San Francisco. I remember a party that Don gave in which I had a conversation with a Taurus and Capricorn – remarking that with me being Virgo, we were the three earth signs. My tortuous unrequited love was the astrological sign of Cancer, and I mentioned how frustrating I was finding the relationship or non-relationship to be – whereupon, Tony, the Capricorn, emphatically agreed that the sign of Cancer (Capricorn's opposite) was 'very difficult'. Later, someone informed me that Tony had killed his lover. I had visited Philip several times as he was dying in the hospital and had lent my Volkswagen to his mother so she could get to her son. And Philip was a Cancer. That was the first and only time I had met Tony, and he was mesmerisingly attractive. Don said firmly afterwards to, 'Be careful!'

We lost touch for several years after I had moved to Europe, but at some point I looked up all the Don Pattersons who were in northern California. None that I spoke with turned out to be him, but I left a message with the one number on which I had not reached a live person and said, 'It is Edith trying to reach Blanche'. Eventually, not hearing anything further, I tried that one number one more time, and we reconnected.

With the AIDS onslaught, Don and his longtime partner, Robert, decided to have a monogamous relationship. Robert says it was fifty years in all. They lived variously in the Hayes Valley, Potrero Hill and then for some inexplicable reason in Roseville not far from Sacramento before returning to San Francisco. They finally settled in a small but nice flat in the Hayes Apartment Complex on Page Street. Don developed prostate cancer that plagued him for several years, but he got through that one. But hardly had he come through that crisis when he was diagnosed with Parkinson's. He passed in January of 2017, and I miss his loyalty and perpetually caustic humour.

Ramadan in 2020 begins on the 23rd of April. Ironically, this date is also the conclusion of a *nefastus* period in April that begins on the 5th. Apart for the first three days of December, the Roman festival calendar has four stretches of *dies nefasti* – one in February, the one in April and two nine-day ones before and after the summer solstice, in June and the first nine days of July. My research into Roman religion was published in 1986 as *The Roman Festival Calendar of Numa Pompilius*. Numa was the second king of Rome following Romulus. The *nefasti* were subsequently declared as auspicious and correct for inaugurating court cases, but Richard and I have employed them as quasi-Lenten practices for restricting pleasures such as alcohol, sugars, overly refined foods, hallucinogens, red meat and, in earlier days, caffeine. They seem basically to be related to the 'waxing' daylight hours due to the sun being between her winter and summer solstices. While my basic hedonist self has always been sceptical of abstinences such as the Christian Lent, the Muslim Ramadan, the Hindu Tuesday fast for Hanuman and the like, I have come to appreciate the benefits of periods of temperance and forgoing if not necessarily for spiritual purposes then at least for physical health and bodily maintenance.

The underlying theme of my writing ventures is the re-examination, reassessment and re-establishment of our Western origins as distinct from their Judaeo-Christian domination. Two philosophers that I hold to be among the highest in innovation and accomplishment are Baruch Spinoza and Friedrich Nietzsche. I am fully in accord with the German philosopher's attempt to revaluate established values as well as his dismissal of, if not of Christ himself, the development of the Church as a purveyor of resentment, inferiority, mendacity, fictious morality, an illusory redemption, disparager of the feminine, priestly tyranny and negation of life. As Razvan Ioan conveys in his 2019 *The Body in Spinoza and Nietzsche*, there is a refreshing emphasis on corporeal existence and physicality that both philosophers endorse and especially in a telluric manner by Nietzsche.

Spinoza equates God with nature (*deus sive natura*); they are one and the same. He understands motion as inherent in matter and not something that results from a transcendent God. In fact, for both Spinoza and Nietzsche there is no appeal to transcendent ideals for living naturally and for locating a source to ethical behaviour. The goals of liberation and empowerment are to be achieved through a focus on the body and the need to increase one's power for acting in this world. The difference between the two rests in part with Spinoza's understanding liberation through the reduction of conflict, whereas for Nietzsche strength and power are enhanced precisely through conflictual discord. But with both, freedom entails being free from transcendence and the illusions produced by transcendent theology. The physical is not approached as a source of evil, and both philosophers seek to restore humanity's place in nature. They abandon the traditional philosophical and theological invention of teleology that renders humanity different from the rest of nature; nature has no *purpose* – and this last means that there is no pre-given or externally mandated intention to human existence. Consequently, as conscious beings, ones for whom mind and body are the same thing, we are free to create our own purpose. For Nietzsche especially, the artistic, spiritual, moral and political are immanent features of nature rather than transcendentally imposed institutions, and through them life itself is to be enhanced and affirmed. The physiology of politics comprises our foremost concerns for food, nutrition, health, clothing, shelter, movement and reproduction.

What for me is the difficulty with Nietzsche in particular is his 'de-deification' of nature in his reinterpreting and revaluating values and his understanding that we humans create the otherworld through our despair of the body and our accompanying incapacity, suffering and weariness. Otherworldly values are fictions, and he, like Spinoza, strive for life-affirming values in *this* world. But I think what Nietzsche is actually after in this is the rejection of supernatural origins for morality and specifically the impositions that result from ecclesiastical tyranny. It is our submission to being controlled by a mind-set that desires principally withdrawal from the world and employs the emotion of fear or dread to achieve its ends, and this is what Nietzsche terms superstition. His seeming dismissal of enchantment and the magical is perhaps part of his main effort to convey such Christian falsities as original sin, the Last Judgement and eternal life as priestly manipulations that prevent our ability to revaluate false idols for the efficacy and usefulness of fantasy. As Jung understands, there is a necessity for magic and its ability to restore wholeness. This is an integral part of humanity's search for meaning in the face of the unknown.

As a 'believer' or 'accepter' of the gods, I think they are always present. If the imaginary has an ontic reality of its own, the 'gods' nevertheless are anchored to corporeal actuality as well – such, as the sun, moon, dawn, earth, lightning and so forth. Moreover, I will dare to say that the gods are always aware of our own individual courses. If this sounds similar to the Abrahamic god, the 'God' I conceive is a dynamic of multiple minds/awarenesses, each ranging from quasi to full independence but in a flowing, melodic, harmonious and rhythmic inter-cooperation. Basically, this is a vitality with which to connect in a moment of mindfulness. For Spinoza and Nietzsche, the mind and the body are one and the same. As Nietzsche sees it, conscious thought is an organ of the body. And in fact, we do not have a body; we are a body.

Disasters are not always natural (such as earthquakes, hurricanes, droughts, etc.), but both kinds have similar results. So, while I have managed yet again to survive – and unlikely for the last time as long as I keep living – a financial disaster, I seem on a micro or personal level to be paralleling or reflecting the wider and current global and even universal pandemic upheaval. One plays for as long as one can in the game. We all eventually lose; that's the nature of competitive games. But who exactly is our competitor? It must be both – not just one or the other – our reflective twin (and herein is the hinterworld of the imaginal) *and* the rules of corporeality (by which we are bound in this, the empirical world). When luck is with one, the game is fun, namely, what a game is meant to be. When fortune is not assisting, we still need to play as best we can. Eventually, of course, everybody loses, but if we all have lost but played the game well (and maybe we cannot but play well), we are victorious for having at least played the game. Do we find somewhere in this our immortality? Perhaps as some anti-entropy vibration?

My gods,
My gods,
My gods,
You have to exist so I can thank you!

For all of Nietzsche's rejection of the supernatural, his *Thus Spoke Zarathustra* is full of such magical elements. If humanity in its far past directly identified with the symbols of myth and magic before later reinterpreting them instead as allegories, we now are even more able to approach the symbolic with some kind of increasing objectivity. This does not preclude the usefulness of symbols and metaphors even into our own times. They circumscribe a fantasy within which, through various techniques, we might be able to enter profitably. Where Nietzsche remains highly critical of the fictitiousness of the imaginary world, he is principally criticising the falsification and devaluing that is the decadent work of Christianity. By contrast, he affirms the world of dreams as providing dynamic reflections of reality. As Jung would put it, 'the tangible and apparent world is one reality, but fantasy is the other reality'. Pagans of today are more apt to reconnect with the mysteries of inner experience that were in the past personified as the gods. Do we need the realisation of a 'new God' as Jung would have it when we already have the many gods of our pagan past?

At heart, Nietzsche is attempting to resituate humanity back into nature and without the 'slave morality' that has come to oppress the human being – especially in the West. His 'atheism' as such affords an initial stage for establishing the freedom of self-liberation. The historical preaching of 'anti-nature' becomes for him nothing less than a vice. And in this he follows Spinoza to an extent as both reject teleology. The consequence of this for Spinoza is that God is identical with nature; there is nothing outside or beyond nature, and for both Spinoza and Nietzsche, nature has no purpose. It just is. And like Robert Pirsig in his 1974 *Zen and the Art of Motorcycle Maintenance*, freedom for Nietzsche is the freedom from the traditionally tyrannical belief in truth instead of the recognition that value is what is pre-eminently healthy for the human endeavour.

There are, of course, various aspects of Nietzsche's philosophy that appear incommensurate with a pagan *ethos* and the possible emergence of Western paganism in particular. Foremost here are the German philosopher's association with fascism and racism. This debilitation, however, is more accurately due to various misinterpretations that can be attributed to Bertrand Russell, Martin Heidegger and Walter Kaufmann than to Nietzsche himself. But even more, once he was reduced to the concluding period of his life of insanity and confined eventually to the care of his sister Elisabeth Förster-Nietzsche who was an anti-Semite and endorser of an extreme right form of German nationalism, it was she who edited and even forged parts of his writings to conform to her own political desires and position. A careful reading of Nietzsche's own writings reveal that he was not endorsing 'Aryan purity' as well as ethnic cleansing. The aristocracy of which he affirmed is not a social class but those who emerge to become the most courageously innovative. Apart from Jesus Christ, Nietzsche's superman/overperson (*Übermensch*) is most likely ultimately to be understood as the earth-based collective and humanistic humanity itself. Without mitigation, he pits the art of commanding against herd obedience, but in 'The Bestowing Virtue' of *Zarathustra*, the highest virtue is nevertheless named as generosity. Although Nietzsche's Zarathustra does at least acknowledge laughter, it is this element along with a feminine softening and the expression of compassion that are most missing with Nietzsche and which would render his thinking more fully compatible to a pagan outlook. In his relentless seriousness, Nietzsche attributes the morality of compassion as a priestly invention that stunts human growth and stature. However, in the cultivation of abundance or plenty that Nietzsche stresses for the best of humanity, not only does generosity become a possibility but also, at least in a pagan understanding, the freedom to be compassionate. Let me conclude here with a brief citation from my 2016 *Pagan Ethics*:

> Pagan gods are 'beyond good and evil', and in paganism, humanity's place is understood as among the gods. As Nietzsche reveals, the ultimate issue is not morality but aesthetics. And the place that is 'beyond good and evil' is this world, the world of nature. Man is a natural animal but no less one of the gods – not in the sense of Abrahamic hubristic projection but in that of the special sacredness contingent upon animistic being.

As a uniquely animate part of ubiquitous divinity, there is nothing that hinders us from extending and augmenting Nietzsche into endorsing and affirming both generosity and compassion. From a pagan perspective, this could be a significant part of playing the game of life well.

Nevertheless, this present work is intended, at least in part, as a presentation of what I am encountering as disheartening within the present pagan scene. So, before I proceed with more recollection, I wish to air a conversation today that has occurred on the Academic Heathens page of Facebook. In all, this is one of my preferred exchanges in social media. Foremost with this group, for me at least, is the horror the members express vis-à-vis the far-right racist and nationalistic developments of the Heathen Folkist contingent, the tribalists and theodish types, who seem these days to attract the greater amount of media coverage. The Academic Heathens appear to be more solidly in step with the wider pagan expression that is humanitarian, humanistic and liberally progressive. There is an unanimity that disapproves of pseudoscience, chauvinism, white supremacism, racial essentialism, and neo-Nazi anti-immigration as incommensurate with a viable heathenism for the 21st century and beyond. And further than this, they are actively pursuing vast ranges of quality research from the academic and sociological to textual analyses and archaeology as well as explorations of folklore, fiction, liminality and cosmology. Moreover, the exchange keeps within the bounds of agreeing to disagree but politely. The group discussion can even address such popular developments like Viking martial arts (GLIMA), Nordic wrestling and metal and post-metal music that are virtually beyond my ken completely.

Another aspect about Academic Heathenism is a non-hesitancy to examine other areas beyond heathenism itself – such as Celtic and Afro-Latin spiritualities, Indo-European antiquity, the Dancing African Pallbearer Meme, magic and the study of new religions. Consequently, when Rune submitted a photo of masculine masochistic ritual submission to a Facebook group of witches, he was shocked when it was rejected because of the fear that such an uncensored expression of human carnality might provoke controversy among them. The photo Rune attests was taken from a childhood fairy tale book, and his rant concerning what he perceives to be really 'a brand of bourgeois frigid protestantism' elicited several comments from among the Academic Heathen group.

In response, Caroline considers that witchcraft, while stressing there is more than just one witchcraft, is 'a big mess'. She laments that overall it has become 'unbelievably lame and conformist, unimaginative, commercial, New Age' and is concerned to disassociate from any origins with Satanic imagery and background that it may have. History, challenge or difficulty is eschewed along with a deep resistance to any scholarly attempt to explain the relationship or non-relationship between 'witchcraft' as ceremonial magic and 'ancient Pagan religions'. For Caroline, a witch is a magic worker, and while there are both religious and practical forms of witchcraft (including Wicca), following the Murray thesis, it is a 'successful re-visioning [and] re-symbolising of what was considered to be the activities of a "Satanic" society into a benevolent "Pagan" one.' She denies that witchcraft is pagan but considers it to be Neo-Pagan. What is lacking in its practice is a working with 'real, historically verified deities, including the Devil' despite the fact that there were no historical occurrences of Witches' Sabbaths. Caroline goes further and states that witchcraft also needs involvement with other-than-human 'nature' as well as the acceptance that 'nature' is not only benevolent and human-oriented. Her objection comes down to 'the namby-pamby goody-goody attempt to white wash [itself] of its Satanic history' regardless of whether this last was a historical actuality or not.

In another response, Emma points out the conflict that has developed in such progressive/social justice movements as feminism, LGBT and so forth between 'sex positive' and '(sex) protective' values. The former accepts 'kink, public nudity, [the desire] to include sex workers, [and the] putting a lot of freedom (and responsibility) in the individual and so on'. For the 'protective values', she mentions wanting to safeguard children, taking care of survivors of abuse as well as trigger warnings and the quest for safe spaces. Emma has doubtlessly described a feature of our present-day PC culture and the challenge it foments to freedom on many fronts.

My own response has been the following:

> For me, it is sad when over-protection closes openness, curiosity and tolerance. But I suppose it is all part of 'humanity disappearing' or, rather, transforming during our current times of upheaval. I will still maintain that, while it is a poisonous gift, the present pandemic is still a 'gift' of mother earth. Because of it, we will change; we are changing, and in this I still cling tenaciously to my militant optimism. Witchcraft and Wicca in particular have served as midwife to the contemporary pagan movement (for lack of a better word). But we are now here! There will be sadnesses, loses and disappointments, but we will prevail because in the widest perspective it is our geocentric spirituality and propensity for innovative and healthy imagination that trumps everything else. We need to be mindful, honour all that there is to honour, and trust the process.

Yes, indeed, there is a belligerent myopia that could be an even greater pandemic infecting human society than is COVID-19. Sometimes it becomes violent to the extent that it even causes death, but short of physical violence, it still authors a 'death' of the human spirit and creative inspiration.

And here again it respects no borders or boundaries. Paganism is no more immune, or so it increasingly seems, than is anything else. Nevertheless, while for some they are metaphorical, while for others they are very much real and yet for still others they amount to nothing more than regressive or counter-productive fictions, I wish to say all the same that for a grounded pagan outlook, one that takes advantage of both this world *and* otherworld perspectives, of both necessary pragmatics *and* the liberating dynamics of imagination, the gods *together* are, represent or constitute the unique balance of the earth's ability to host life, humanity and civilisation.

Our planet and solar system within our Galaxias/Via Lactea/Milky Way galaxy operate in a unison that is virtually unbelievable but necessarily contingent for human existence. Among the parameters that allow and encourage life, perhaps approximately 72 in all, is our planet's 'right' distance from the sun, the steadiness of our sun's energy output, and Earth's circular orbit around the sun in what is known as the 'circumstellar habitable zone' in which water remains primarily liquid – neither freezing or boiling away. If our planet were closer to the sun, there would be increases in both radiation and the danger of being struck by planetoids. And relatedly, the large planets of Jupiter and Saturn have the ability to catch asteroids and thereby reduce their number. Our globe's 24-hour rotation regulates temperature variations, reduces wind violence around the planet, and contributes to the possibility of photosynthesis. The axial inclination of the earth of 23.5 degrees, not more nor less, allows precisely the advantage of seasonal variation without extremes. The size of our moon and her distance from the planet are conducive to the earth's tides, tidal cleansing of the world ocean and continental shorelines as well as the possibility for tidal zones and biologic diversification. Moreover, the size or thickness of the planet's crust allows the amount of gravity necessary for holding our atmosphere, while the molten core generates a protective magnetic field that mitigates harmful solar rays and also contributes to the distribution of minerals more widely around the planet. There is in addition a critical relation between the earth's mass and the layers of gases above us. Another critical factor for both life and the prospect of agriculture is the proportion of oxygen, nitrogen and carbon dioxide in our atmosphere as well as the protective role for life that the planet's ozone layer serves. When we consider the necessity of water, the vegetation that covers our planet and the equilibrium of interactions between plants, animals and bacteria that comprise Earth's ecosystem, we cannot be other than stunned by the miraculousness of the coordinated operation of these precise parameters. Whether the 'rare earth theory' has any validity, or whether there are possibly billions of habitable planets through the enormity of the cosmos, the key thing for humanity is this earth-based existence. Secularists including secular pagans may consider our planet's habitability and our emergence as products of chance. This could also be understood by pagans poetically as 'the gods (operating) together'. While of course another pagan interpretation could understand this unique balance as the gods *actively and correctly* working together, that is, as a godhead that is a coordinated multiple consciousness rather than as a single and/or transcendent mind revered by non-pagans as Yahweh/God/Al. But regardless of our individual theological or faith positions, in the face of the unique balance that allows us all to be here in the first place, it becomes all the more imperative that pagans and humanity as a whole can and will also operate together in a harmonious, mindfully conscious and collectively geocentrically progressive manner.

An intense dream I had when I was in grade school, one I used to be able to remember much more clearly than I do now, involved me and a school friend, Caroline, coming upon a large magic house. Maybe it was a house made from gingerbread, but it was surrounded by an impregnable fence. There seemed to be another presence who offered us a kite. Holding onto the string of the flying object, we were able to lift ourselves over the fence. I remember an angry witch then screaming at us from an upper window of the house. What I no longer remember is what we then did. I'm not sure if we threw stones at her and she dissolved, or if this is a later projection into my recollection. But the colour and intensity of this early dream remained with me for many years afterwards. We had been in fairyland with its special wondrousness.

Through my mother and her mother, I had been introduced into an awareness of a fairy world – one which in some cases constitutes a parallel spirit world; and in other times, one which interpenetrates with this world. Among the books my parents had, there was one in particular that included the most enchanting pictures of fairies, the moon, dew drops, flowers and the like. Whatever became of that book, I do not know. I searched and searched for many years for it, but it simply opened my imagination and then disappeared. I have since come to understand the otherworld as one of many dimensions – that of faerie being one of them; that of gods and goddesses being another. As a child, experience of the imaginary dimension was spontaneous for the most part. Later, reading works like *The Metamorphoses of Lucius Apuleius* (otherwise known as *The Golden Ass*) on balmy East Coast summer evenings in the expanse of green fields re-engaged me even further into fairy and magic tales and a love for the miraculous. In time, already being propelled toward that direction by R. Gordon Wasson's 1957 'Seeking the Magic Mushroom' essay in *Life Magazine*, shamanic explorations into the otherworld of animism and supernatural beings became a part of my pagan development.

In her *Magic Tales and Fairy Tale Magic: From Ancient Egypt to the Italian Renaissance* of 2014, Ruth Bottigheimer examines the narratives of ancient and medieval magic and how they transformed through medieval Jewish, Christian and Muslim tales of the wondrous from service to divinities to service of human beings. Our more modern fairy tale genre appears to have emerged from Renaissance magic tales that culminate with happy endings on earth for their heroes and heroines. Bottigheimer distinguishes fairy tales from fairyland fictions which tend to be more complex and lengthy and do not always end happily. She also mentions that many early Greek divinities 'personify earthborn forces (such as earthquakes) and natural phenomena (such as wind, water, vegetation, and human and animal life) ... [whose] parallel world is contiguous with the magically parallel worlds of medieval, early modern, and modern fairyland fictions'. With this book we are lead through Ovid's *Metamorphoses*, the near-polytheistic view of the Rabbinic period in which YHWH is only one among many divinities, the Muslim *Tales of the Marvelous* and what survives as the *Thousand and One Nights* told by Sheherazade, *The Pleasant Nights* of Giovan Francesco Straparola, Giambattista Basile's *The Pentamerone* and Charles Perrault's refinements. With these precedents, Bottigheimer concludes that for the dominant fairy tale magic into the late twentieth century and beyond, fairies are almost invariably female and selflessly bring good fortune to those who are themselves good.

The picture that Rune sent of a naked maiden whipping a snake-like creature is from the Scandinavian fairy tale of 'The Lindworn Prince'. There are several versions of this story, and the Swedish one continues with an additional sequence. For Danes and Norwegians, sometimes there are two princes – a younger handsome one and the first-born who is a wingless dragon-like creature or a serpent monster, the lindworm, who slithers off after birth. When the younger prince wishes to marry, the lindworm prince blocks his way and says as the older brother he must be allowed to marry first. Successively, he is married to princesses, but on the respective wedding night, he eats them first. A peasant maid, daughter of a shepherd, is chosen for the third time, but after the wedding, she refuses to undress until her husband sheds a serpent skin. She is wearing either every dress she owns or seven or ten white wedding gowns and insists that the lindworm must shed a skin for each dress she removes. Once the young woman has removed all her clothing, the lindworm submits to a sadomasochistic torture as she whips with him with lye. This is the event that Rune's photo depicts. She next bathes him in fresh milk, the curse is lifted, and the handsome prince's human form is recovered and revealed. A joyous second wedding then occurs, and the couple proceed 'to live happily ever after'.

The magic in this tale is represented through the old woman who appears unexpectedly – first to the prince's or the two princes' mother who had had no children (she is advised to eat either roses or onions the following morning but does not follow the exact instructions and hence the lindworm birth) and secondly to the shepherd's daughter with the instructions on what to do on her wedding night. The magical acts that follow are those that overturn the physical laws of nature. Strictly speaking, these acts are more miraculous than magical, and what is crucial is the mysterious old woman's ability to know the fairy world's supernatural powers and to convey the means to manipulate them. Modern fairy tales such as that of the Lindworm Prince do not involve gods or goddesses but only the mantic and effective energies that emanate from the otherworld to which we can allow that divinities and human-shaped supernaturals also belong. But the overall focus is this-worldly and includes a protagonist's dramatic social and economic rise from humble origins and the consequence of earthly happiness.

Apart for demons, dragons and monsters, the chief denizens of the otherworld are divinities, fairies and their elfin kindred, and ancestors or, more generally, the spirits of the departed. As a reflection of this world, it too includes inimical darkness, as well as the fairy tales that convey the interactions between the two worlds, but it does not dismiss, along with magic's mediation for a 'happy ending', such negativities as the deaths of the two innocent princesses that had travelled from foreign lands for marriage to the Lindworm Prince. With humanity and equally throughout paganism, any compulsion to believe is matched by the obsession to disbelieve. As the poet and critic Dennis Joseph Enright describes, 'The ever credulous and the unremittingly incredulous resemble two political parties forever nagging each at the other'. The one certainty he allows for what the supernatural has in common with nature is that 'you may drive it out with a pitchfork, but it will constantly come running back'. Between the 'two parties', Enright proposes the possibility of a third or at least a loose association of third parties in which this-world and the other might meet.

> For the supernatural impinges on the natural in the latter's most sympathetic aspects and in its most deplorable, in love and longing, in concupiscence and cupidity, in the urge to help and the desire to destroy.

Our fears and hopes might encounter each other in the crossroads between the natural and the supernatural and the emotions portrayed through our legacy of fairy and magic tales that no less highlights the eerie, the frightening and the grotesque along with the positive. As important as is our requirement to accept the present pandemic reality, we are also challenged to discern through the offensive and terrifying – not hiding from either or blindly dismissing them – ways of life that are flexible and not intimidated or limited by parochial outrage but which still allow the grasping of the beauty that yet exists and with this to engage maturely in calm exchange and the desired effort for both collective enjoyment and globally shared improvement. The heritage that we have through our dreams and art concerning the supernatural is, along with humanity's technological achievements, one of our most important assets. And forgive me Nietzsche, but I wish to include one further valuable resource with this, namely, compassion.

Another indelible memory. Richard, my mother and I were driving from Naples, Florida to Key West. I was in the back seat and listening for the first time to the double cassette of Steve Reich's *Variations for Winds, Strings and Keyboards* and John Adams' *Shaker Loops*. I was so moved by the music and our setting that when the music had completed, I removed my ear phones and insisted on sharing by placing the tape into the car's player. As we would coast along and rise to the height of each bridge connecting each of the Florida Keys to the next, the encompassing sea would sparkle with the sun's light dancing across the water's expanse. The combination of this uplifting music and the up-and-down as we flowed through the enchantment of our surroundings became an unforgettable *moment supreme*.

Some other memorable experiences though less serenely enjoyable are airport stories. I scheduled to come home for Christmas from Purdue University along with my friend Ted. It was he who had first introduced me to Ravel's *Daphnis and Chloe*. My father had insisted that we not check our luggage but carry it with us. This would allow us a faster connection between our flights. However, keeping our baggage with us on the airline that took us to Chicago's Midway was not allowed. There was not much time between the flights for us to make our connection. When we arrived, I told Ted to collect our luggage while I went on to see about our flight to Newark. At the gate, there were the flight attendants including the pilot. We waited and waited for Ted, but he did not arrive. If I had not listened to my father and had checked our suitcases all the way through, the plane would have waited. Finally, I ran the crowded distance back to where I had left Ted and was virtually pushing people aside as a tore through the long distance. I found Ted. He had been waiting for me to come back. So we now rushed back to the gate. There was no one there, but we went through the door onto the tarmac. The plane was moving along the runway. The pilot saw us, stopped, and a ramp was rolled up to the plane, and we exhaustedly boarded and collapsed. Two hours later, American Airlines went on strike. When the Christmas break concluded, we had to take trains back. The airline was still on strike. But the pilot must have known that the suspension was imminent and that if we had missed his flight there would not have been another.

My second airport tale also occurred back in the times before airport security. It was a much different world in the late 50s and early 60s. When I first flew to California for my post-Purdue studies at UCSB, the cross-country plane was a turbo-prop and took something like eleven hours from coast to coast. When Christmas was arriving, I was again scheduled to fly home. In the cafeteria having lunch shortly before I was to get to the Santa Barbara airport, I was curious as to why the cooks were going from table to table. Finally, one arrived at our table, and it was me for whom they were looking. The airline that was to connect me to Los Angeles was delayed. Back at the dormitory, someone at the switchboard connected me and two women who were also about to miss their connecting flights in LA with a private small plane company. This was the first time I had been on a four-way phone call. The three of us hired the piper cub to get us to Los Angeles. I remember as we were arriving the pilot said, 'If I had taken the other plane, it would have been faster'. He approached the airport to land, and the tower control screamed that he had not been given clearance. He was told to circle around the Hollywood Bowl until he had permission to land. We then flew across much of Los Angeles looking for the Bowl. Eventually we found it and after a long time we were told to return for landing. Again, it was difficult for the pilot to find where we were going, and when he approached the runway, he came down at something like a 45-degree angle. The front of the plane broke off, and the four of us had to pull the piper cub off the runway.

Of course, I had missed my flight home. As it was the approach of Christmas, most flights were full, and the airport was extremely crowded. I believe this time it was United Airlines, and I went to the check-in desk. The man at the counter told me I would need to go to the desk of the airlines with which I had been originally booked to fly from Santa Barbara to Los Angeles. This was a considerable distance away. When I arrived, the people at the counter were indifferent and told me to go back to United Airlines. I explained that United had told me that it was their responsibility to find me a flight to the East Coast. Suddenly, the man from the United Airlines counter appeared and said he had been trying to phone this West Coast airlines, but their phone was apparently out of order. He told me that there was an available seat on a United flight that was about to depart. Together we rushed back and down the galley to the departure gate. In my left hand, I was carrying a bowl of tropical fish that the dormitory authorities had ordered me to remove from my room. We were not allowed to have pets of any sort. I was also still weak from having been in the school infirmary with mononucleosis. The counter attendant carried my suitcase for me. We reached the gate, but it was closed. Virtually we could have reached through the closed doors and touched the airplane, but we were too late. I expressed my despair but was told not to worry. I was to be placed on 'emergency standby' and would have precedence even over the President. Whether this last could have actually been true, I did manage to be put on a flight and was able to have my holidays with my family.

It is strangely curious how one's memory bank springs forth random recollections for one who is nearing the end of life. I was always appreciative of my father allowing me a half a glass of wine on occasion during supper.

And after Mr. Hamlin, our Junior High School French class teacher, took us to a delightful French restaurant called Champlain on West 49th Street near Rockefeller Center in Manhattan, this became a significant venue henceforth. Entering from the street, one stepped down into a long narrow stretch with a bar along the left side and tables for two along the wall on the right. Continuing through, one came into a large, high-ceilinged room with sawdust on the floor and double swinging doors to the kitchen through which traditionally dressed waiters carrying large circular trays over a shoulder came and went. The Champlain could not have been more atmospheric, its food was delicious and inexpensive, and from the age of 14 I was always able to order a glass of white burgundy wine with my lunch even through the legal age for ordering alcoholic drinks in New York was 18. The Champlain was eventually demolished along with the entire city block when Rockefeller extended, but for years and years afterwards, I continued to look for this favourite restaurant always in hopes that I had the street wrong and might find it.

Another memory from youth consists of the numerous times my parents returned from an evening party with my mother virtually 'over the bumper' and my getting her to bed and then cleaning up the floor. Eventually this stopped, and I thought to ask my mother one day why I was no longer looking after her as I had been. 'I learned to drink scotch', was her reply. Previously, she had not known how to consume alcohol and mixed everything.

Upon graduation from High School in 1957, we all went to the shore to celebrate. A group of us rented a cottage, and I became the 'maid' who cleaned up the mess after the others drank themselves into oblivion and got sick. I suppose watching the others was enough to make me not want to join them. My first time of overdoing alcohol was that time, thanks to Gigi, during my first year at Purdue University. The second and last time for many, many years thereafter was in the course of that pledge 'walkout' to Miami University in Ohio.

After graduating from Santa Barbara, I did come to enjoy European beer – especially the weizen beer of Germany. Facing the prospect of American beer after I had returned from Europe, I asked my mother to teach me to drink scotch. I was nevertheless a non-drinker for the most part and would usually order ginger ale at a bar. I believe it was after having champagne with Saint Lynne at a membership event at the California Palace of the Legion of Honor in San Francisco when we next smoked a spliff before having a dinner in a restaurant in the Avenues that I needed to step outside to lose everything in the gutter of the street. There have doubtlessly been a few other moments like this, but once I was a smoker of cannabis I was able to consume alcohol again – if mostly moderately. However, there was a wicked time in Paris when Richard, Donald and I were having dinner, and suddenly we had to vacate our table as the floor was cleared for dancing. Feeling no pain at the time, Donald and I would finish the drinks left on the bar by those who were now dancing. Donald somehow was unaffected, but I was wailing, and Richard was required to nurse me through the remainder of the night.

But in all I consider myself a devotee of the god Dionysus. I learned to enjoy single malt whisky especially, but other than the occasional beer or wine with others during a meal (preferably the evening one) – especially in France where it is *de rigueur*, Saturday and *feriae* imbibing ranges between negroni, margarita and daquiri. None of this is formidably often any longer, and pot-smoking even less – perhaps for general lack of availability. However, when I review some of my journals, I am astonished over how often we all did smoke in the past – something of which I am no longer capable. But I still nonetheless revere the deity behind the incarnations of Dionysus, Neptunus and Soma – the deific constellation I contend from an Indo-European perspective is the 'twin' of humanity.

And one further memory that comes to mind. It was a scorching summer day in Narragansett, and we crossed over to the open-air hotel deck of next door for afternoon drinks. It must have been a festival day for us to have alcohol that early in the day. I asked the lads at the table next to us what the white drink was they were having. It was a mudslide, and one of the young fellows insisted I taste his. (Oh, what a different times they were from our pandemic present!) The cocktail the Village Inn bar made that day consisted of Baileys Irish Cream or Kahlúa, vanilla vodka, heavy cream and coffee liqueur. On an extremely hot day, it is an utterly delicious drink, and this occasion in Rhode Island was delectable in all respects.

Without doubt, 'warfare, global warming, climate change, and a host of environmental and social ills' are universal concerns – now perhaps more than ever, but how much these might be attributed to some hypermasculine patriarchal intrusion into a former egalitarian matrifocal social system remains debatable. Certainly, in its effort to change the perception of what it means to be a woman, the rise of feminist thought is a vitally important development of the 20th/21st century. The contemporary feminist movement's advocacy for an equality of the sexes and women's economic, political, social and personal rights is to be welcomed as long-overdue. For a mature humanity, women and men are to be seen as coequals, and there ought be no question that women's salaries should be the same as men's. If the male has been the traditional bread-winner in the past, this has been superseded in modern times. In addition, polygyny without polyandry is unfair. There ought to be more than the one legendary instance beside that of Draupadi and the Pandava brothers. There is, however, a potential danger with any self-interest group – one that includes the gays as well, and this relates to often being unable to know when to stop with its demands. Looking from the inside of its own perspective, a self-interest group of any kind is frequently unable to perceive boundaries and even viable co-existence. My critique of an unbridled feminism is the neglect of how something actually is as opposed to the preference of how it is wanted to be. An example I remember from early days was the accusation that there had been an historical patriarchal suppression of the thirteenth astrological sign of Arachne. Overlooked was the carefully established balance between the zodiac's six masculine signs and six feminine ones. An equilibrium of parity was too easily to be destroyed because of an outrage against patriarchy. Another memory is of a Jungian analyst in Zürich who insisted on equality as a woman but at least recognised the paradox in her becoming upset when others, the men, would not capitulate to her feminine charms.

Near the very beginning of her 2010 *Virgin Mother Goddesses of Antiquity,* Marguerite Rigoglioso claims to be 'a male-honoring woman', but what follows as a relentless diatribe against androcentric degeneration, attributions of blatant misogyny and ceaseless intrusions by 'the patriarchal enterprise' does not in the least support this initial assertion. With numerous lacunae, any of our attempts to reconstruct and reinterpret ancient Greek and Indo-European cult and myth resembles the effort toward reassembling an enormous jigsaw puzzle for which many pieces are missing. In such a situation, a great variety of 'pictures' becomes possible. This is as much the case with Rigoglioso's *Virgin Mother Goddesses of Antiquity* as it is with my *The Divine versus the Asurian: An Interpretation of Indo-European Cult and Myth* (1995).

The difficulties I have with Rigoglioso are (1) her uncompromising division between matriarchal and patriarchal, (2) the feminist blindness to the possibility of feminine negativity e.g., Neumann's 'terrible mother' or what

I term the 'anti-mother', (3) the uncritical reliance on Gnostic sources/distortions/convolutions, and (4) the amount of unsupported but wished for speculation – even to the degree of eventually becoming unquestioned assumptions as the presentation continues. Anything that does not fit the author's thesis is attributed succinctly to a patriarchal subversion or revision – such as the Hesiodic detail about Ge's advice to Zeus concerning Metis. However, the overall mythic and cultic complex is more complex than an inflexible black-and-white rendering allows. Some allegations of imposition through Olympian mythology and male-dominated oppression are of course true, but there are other developments and possible interpretations as well. Moreover, an indiscriminate reliance on the Orphic complex, while containing some telluric aspects and thus is insightful on occasion, is primarily a gnostic compendium and shifts interpretation toward a transcendental comprehension.

An irony is that there is much with which I agree in Rigoglioso's analyses. As I attempted to convey in my 1995 work, through both the comparisons available between various Indo-European daughter-culture versions and the stripping away of Hesiod's infatuation with the Akkadian, Hurrian and Phoenician Succession Myth (hence the sequence from Uranus to Cronus to Zeus), it becomes patently established that Gaia/Ge is the primordial Great Mother who parthenogenetically gives birth to Zeus as the fundamental expression of the feminine cosmos' capacity to generate (give birth to) her gender opposite. In other words, the *deus*-phenomenon is directly born from the *terra mater* – full stop. The two figures then become the proto-parents of all that follows. Apart from the implicit identity between Gaia, Rhea and Demeter, it becomes evident through a study of Hellenic cult and myth that the figures of Athena, Artemis and Persephone are themselves developments from the same archaic goddess. Through her own ample citations and thorough references, Rigoglioso also makes this much clear. As I explain in regard to the two-tiered Indo-European mythological composite,

> On the one hand, there are the primordial and dominating mother-goddesses with their male satellite attendants inherited in part from non-Indo-European predecessors but also in part from the Indo-European's own first encounters and perceptions of the dark mysteries of the earth and nature and death and life. And on the other hand, there are the more refined developments, the deities of light and justice and beauty, more masculine-oriented and more conducive, perhaps, to both nomadic and urban peoples.

I conclude from this that as the secondary development emerges and becomes dominant, the earlier maternal figures transform into the classical daughter-goddesses such as Athena, Artemis and Hestia or otherwise into the more fearsome Harpies, serpent-haired Gorgons, Scyllae and Erinyes. Athena, for example, may be less the expression of patriarchy as she is of a more progressive understanding of justice vis-à-vis that of the primitively vengeful Furies. Whether these earlier substratum mother-goddesses were served by virgin-priestesses devoted to cults of parthenogenesis, as Rigoglioso contends, and also whether for the Eleusinian Mysteries 'women would have inserted the phallus into their vaginas, men into their anuses', I would say that these are possibilities though more than likely the 'jury is still out' on any unquestioned establishment. What I am definitely in accord with, however, is the author's belief that the *kykeon* imbibed for the Eleusinian hallucinogenic trance ritual involved entheogenic ingestion. She compares the likely use of pennyroyal oil with the similar psychotropic effects of *salvia divinorum*.

Rigoglioso provides a basic summary of her argument:

> With the back of the cosmic and earthly Matriarchy broken through the rape of Persephone, holy virgins dedicated to miraculous conception [through a form of narcissistic tantra] became increasingly beleaguered in their parthenogenetic attempts to bring forth the daughters of the goddess, female avatars. They were, instead, conscripted into having sexual encounters in the trance state with male gods. That is, they were forced or coerced into becoming conduits for what were believed to be the gods' children. Frequently, such children were male warrior heroes bent on further eroding the Matriarchy. . .

She draws repeatedly from a recognisable industry of 'feminist hermeneutical perspective' for support, refers to her earlier book *The Cult of Divine Birth in Ancient Greece* (2009) in virtually every paragraph, and inserts constantly throughout her text 'I submit', 'I establish', 'I propose', 'I show', 'I contend', 'I support', 'I argue', 'I discuss', 'I posit', 'I attempt' and 'I have put forth'. We are also informed that Persephone's rape did not occur at any specific chronological date but is a mystical *analogue*. In goddess cosmogony itself, there is no male consort.

In the feminist trope there is also no recognition of the anti-mother, and any negativity of the feminine is the result of patriarchy. A darker side of Gaia – perhaps expressing the more violent aspects of nature – is without doubt to be seen in her motherhood of the Cyclopes, the Aloadai, the

Hundred-handed, the Giants, the Erinyes and even the Titans Cronus and Iapetus. Her 'birth' of Uranus, however, amounts more to a kind of shedding on Gaia's part of the vestigial element connected to her own origin with Chaos (representing the black and if not empty then at least disembodied roots of the universe). Uranus is really the progeny of Chaos-Nyx, and his castration simply underscores his ineffectiveness as a fertilising consort. The birth of Zeus as the real sky, the bright sky, becomes possible only once the night-sky, that is Uranus, is separated from Gaia herself. It has been argued that the Cronus-Uranus opposition is a repetition of that between Zeus and Cronus or ultimately between Zeus and Uranus. From an Indo-European perspective, Zeus is expressive of a necessary and affirmative cosmogonic development rather than being little more than a transgressive patriarchal usurper. Moreover, his cognatic identity throughout the Indo-European daughter-cultures reveals him to be much more ancient than the suggestion that his name is supposedly first to be accredited to Cecrops in Athens.

Rigoglioso's Libyan and Anatolian virgin-priestess Amazons do not appear to conform with Marija Gimbutas' positing of Old Europe's peaceful matrilineal and matrilocal matriarchy. If the Amazon's were militaristic, they appear then to have been bettered by stronger male fighters. The real question that is never answered is why did matriarchy end? What caused the rise of the patriarchy rebellion? If matriarchies did exist, they must have been unremittingly suffocating to cause such a universal masculine realignment. Though this will doubtlessly not win me many friends, there is a detectable asphyxiating quality that arises with the inflexible extremes of some of current feminism. One can only hope that we are not entering a quasi-historical repetitive social cycle.

A key and persistent outrage that has adhered to humanity and continues to do so is that of rape. And it cannot be denied that the Zeus-prototype's behaviour is so termed in Vedic, Orphic and Hesiodic/Homeric sources. This is a fundamental mythologem in the Indo-European legacy. This particular primordial act is narratively depicted as sexual violation probably through subsequent moral revaluations. Originally, once the *deus* is born from the parthenogenic *terra mater*, the son and mother become lovers. The child of their union is the goddess of the dawn. When and if we consider the different developments of the auroral deity throughout the subsequent mythic and cultic legacies, Dyaus' 'rape' of Hausos could have been as much the result of Hausos' enticement. Primordially, there were only Gaia, Zeus and Eos (Hausos) – mother, son & daughter. The Eos prototype is to be seen through myth (and even cult) as both the chaste matron and the promiscuous lover.

On occasion, Rigoglioso refers the timeline in reference to the gods as not being linear as it is with us mortals. Consequently, 'an oblique, non-linear approach to the material is [at least sometimes (my insertion)] required'. I agree with her. A quintessential such instance occurs with the Vedic sky-father's rape of the daughter who spills semen on the earth during the *coitus interruptus* when he suddenly withdraws after being shot in his thigh by the archer (perhaps the moon?), and it is from that very sperm that falls to the earth that the archer is himself born. With both myth and the otherworld, temporal sequences can occur out of an expected order.

And here we come to the fascinating portrayal of Hera, the 'wife' of Zeus. Hellenic goddesses are not just virgin-mothers who have been usurped and dethroned by male gods. They are also conflations, and in Hera's case one that includes fusion with that of the Terrible Mother/anti-mother – this last perhaps in part a derivative of the archaic virgin-mother goddess that Rigoglioso exalts. Hera's anti-divine capacity survives in the myths that have her as the parthenogenic mother of both the *deus*-opponent Typhon and the 'ugly' and lame Hephaestus who I have argued is, along with Aphrodite, essentially an import into the Olympians from the Levant and not originally Greek. Nevertheless, there is another side of Hera. One understanding of her name sees it as cognate with the various solar theonyms to be found in the Sanskrit, Greek, Latin, Germanic and Baltic languages. The child of the father-daughter incest, the Zeus and Eos prototypes, is, in fact, the sun. Consequently, my argument is that originally the god Ares was probably a solar figure. It is only with Ovid, relatively late, that Ares is himself cited as parthenogenetically born from Hera as are Typhon and Hephaestus. Otherwise, the god's parents are Hera *and* Zeus both. But for the violated daughter (by the god who is both her father and, by both being children of the earth-mother, her sibling), she becomes both the wife of Zeus and queen of heaven for the Greeks and the revered and chaste Mater Matuta ('Dawn-mother') among the Romans. A vestige of the dawn's promiscuity, however, – apart from that of Eos herself – may be Hera's alleged motherhood of Prometheus by the Giant Eurymedon.

Consequently, what I am afraid is lost through Rigoglioso's agenda is the poetic evolution and creative fertility that was the ancient Greek mind and inheritance of Western civilisation. The general Indo-European view regards the empyrean as lighter than the earth but nevertheless born from it and still substantial rather than transcendental. There is a decided celebration of an ascendance of light and consciousness. While Erich Neumann, in *The Great Mother: An Analysis of the Archetype,* has recognised the three implicit forms of the Great Mother, namely, the good, terrible and good-bad mother, this psychological concept of the feminine archetype represents the totality of the physical cosmos as well as the temporal span of beginning-middle-end. Before becoming the traditional virgin-goddess as we know her, Athena was earlier an archaic manifestation of the *terra mater*. The classical mythology of the Greeks constitutes an aesthetic apogee. Andromeda is Medusa's *alter ego*, and the Hesperides emerge to be the feminine archetype as a positive and friendly force. The Greeks have inherited the Indo-European understanding of the divine that emerges from the *deus*-principle or ultimately the *terra mater* as a godhead by committee. The Earth Goddess does not 'emanate' the masculine but gives *birth* to it. This also resonates with the concluding chapter (on Sophia) to *The Virgin Mother Goddesses of Antiquity*'s exploration in which Angeleen Campra differentiates between the understanding of a 'generated' universe and a 'created' universe: the great goddess gives birth from her womb; the Abrahamic male entity creates through the vocal Word. As I had hoped to convey in my 1995 work, 'the male-female polarity cannot be reduced to a simple black-and-white dichotomy in which the masculine is condemned and the feminine is uncritically elevated'. At least through our Indo-European heritage, there is a more profound and operative dichotomy than the revolving dualities between the feminine and masculine, the positive and negative, the luminous and darkness, and the corporeal and ethereal let alone the good and the bad. A more substantial and less agenda-driven comprehension 'allows us to escape the simplistic and reductionistic for a more differentiated foundation on which to establish durable social change'.

My very first international conference (1991) had been in New York – the 36th annual meeting of the International Linguistic Association in which my subject was 'Toward a Proto-Indo-European Vocabulary of the Sacred'. It was on this occasion that I had the great honour of meeting Marija Gimbutas and sat next to her during a dinner. I remember during the delivery of my paper being so inexperienced and new to the academic scene that I never even swallowed once as I raced through what I had prepared within the time limit allowed – completing virtually to the second. The following month, May, I delivered two papers to the 'New Religions in Global Perspective' gathering for the Santa Barbara Centre for Humanistic Studies that was held in Solvang, California – one on New Age and the other on Paganism. The next year, in Lyons, France, for the Sixth International CESNUR Seminar on 'The Challenge of Magic' (*Le Défi Magique*), my paper addressed 'New Age and Wiccan Objections to Satanism'. On this occasion, I praised a radical French Catholic priest, possibly Jacques Roux, and was countered publicly by Massimo Introvigne, the organiser, who proclaimed that everyone knew he had been a 'false priest' and what he had proclaimed was worthless. During the morning session, 'Satan' had appeared with horns, full costume and veil but was asked to leave. We were told that 'He had not registered and paid the conference fee'. Like most academic conferences, this was fun and immensely enjoyable. Lyons was abuzz because of our subject, and this became clear to us during an evening reception at the Hôtel de Ville and the fascinated but wary reactions from those who were serving us. More peaceful and relaxed was the meeting of the Ilkley Study Group later that year in Glastonbury on 'The Sociology of the New Age'. My talk covered 'The New Age/Christian Overlap'.

The Fourth Annual UCLA Indo-European Conference occurred in May of 1992, and I had expected it to be a highlight in my pursuit of European and Aryan pre-Christian religiosity as well as my first full encounter with those who were studying in the field. Many of the papers were densely linguistic, and I wondered if I was completely over my head and out of my range. Still, I found most talks interesting and enjoyed meeting many of those who were in attendance. One thing I did find horrifying, however, was when one person hung out the window and began screaming 'Hello Liz!' to Elizabeth Taylor who was attending the Forbes reception next door with her final husband. She was stunning to see.

My talk, finally, was on the third day and covered 'The Mithraic Tauroctony as a Derivative of an Indo-European Soma/Haoma Sacramental Cult'. I had a bevy of slides including some of the large Nandi bull on the banks of the Ganges in Varanasi, and again I was terribly naïve and thought that my paper might revolutionise the field. One thing I had learned by this point was the extreme contrast between sociologists and those in the field of Indo-European Studies. While the former might disagree with your position, they would dispute politely; the latter would instead attack vehemently in their dissent and opposition. The favourable comments to my paper were said to me mostly in private afterwards, but Professor Harmut Scharfe, the conference organiser and with whom I had had a pleasant conversation the previous evening with suggestions for job-finding possibilities, criticised my presentation severely. Even worse was someone else, an 'old guard', who deplored my paper at great length but mumbled his complaints in such an inaudible manner that no one understood what he was saying including me. Almost everyone in the IE field at UCLA were addicted followers of George Dumézil, the French philologist who had re-instituted Indo-European studies. I, however, have rejected his tripartite theory and am out-of-step with the consensus. The one positive that came out of this occasion was my getting to know Edgar Polomé, another giant in the field, and with whom I enjoyed a correspondence for several years thereafter.

In time, Indo-European inquiry has no longer remained my chief focus, at least in academia, and I remember Bruce Lincoln telling me that he had 'renounced Indo-European Studies' because of the predominant fascist and racist sentiments he had experienced from those in the field. I had replied then that that should be all the more reason for one to remain with the discipline. 'Good luck!' was his retort. And while my initial sociological area was with the New Age movement, I was able primarily to extend this and even replace it with my interest in paganism. Now that I have been retired for fifteen years, I no longer am required to write about pagan spirituality from a scholarly perspective but instead as an ordinary follower and practitioner.

Memory in its own way can be curiously entertaining. I once read a book in which the first chapter described the sirocco captivatingly. Years later, it was not until I reached the penultimate chapter that I realised it was the same book that I had already once read. But even today, I no longer can recall what the book's title or its author were. And now, glancing through my *curriculum vitae*, I am realising I had earlier read and wrote a review of Rigoglioso's goddess book in 2009 for the *Journal of Contemporary Religion*. At least I came to the same conclusion and said virtually exactly the same thing ten/eleven years ago as I have now just a few days ago.

Mnemosyne is the Hellenic goddess of memory as well as of words and language. She is an aunt of Metis and by Zeus the mother of the nine Muses (*Mousai*). Presiding over learning and the arts, the nine personifications were differently enumerated and identified, but Hesiod supplies us with their canonical version: Calliope (goddess of epic poetry, 'She of the Beautiful Voice'), Clio (history, the 'Proclaimer'), Erato (erotic poetry, 'the Lovely'), Euterpe (lyric poetry, the 'Well Pleasing'), Melpomene (tragedy, the 'Songstress'), Polyhymnia (religious hymns/sacred poetry, 'She of the Many Hymns'), Terpsichore (choral song, dance and flute-playing, 'Delighting in the Dance'), Thalia (comedy and idyllic poetry, the 'Blooming/Luxuriant') and Urania (astronomy, the 'Heavenly'). As the patronesses of music, song, dance and poetic inspiration, these goddesses are vital for the arts, all liberal arts and science, and the remembrance of all that has come to pass. The Greeks thereby stressed the importance of the arts and science to memory as well as vice versa.

A refreshing read of late is that of Randy P. Conner's five volume *The Pagan Heart of the West: Embodying Ancient Beliefs and Practices from Antiquity to the Present* (2020). Like Rigoglioso, he draws on the possibility of African influence but is more specifically interested in African-diasporic traditions rather than the alleged Amazonian tribes of North Africa. He is also probably more focused on the matrifocal substratum than I am, but nevertheless I invariably enjoy virtually any polytheistic emphasis that is expressed in pagandom. What I also take pleasure in is the recognition that Conner makes concerning earth-centred and earth-based spirituality as something other than the Platonic, Neoplatonic, Gnostic, Kabbalistic and even Hermetic exaltation of transcendence over immanence. He understands paganism as the veneration of nature, the reverence of divinities and ancestors, the celebration of seasonal rites and the practices of offering, divination and magic. He deplores the 'absolutist language' characteristic of such academics as Ronald Hutton and Alison Rowlands that he claims to be an obfuscating mix of social constructivism and essentialism, and he especially opposes the idea that ancient paganisms ceased altogether until their recreation through the works of Margaret Murray and Gerald Gardner. Consequently, Conner proceeds to explore the countless vestiges of pagan expression and pagan-based practices that persisted in much of Christianised Europe through the Middle Ages and possibly into the 17th and 18th centuries. And instead of endorsing the 'Christocentric' perspective of Hutton, Jay Kinney, Mark Booth or Caitlín and John Matthews that merely take 'pagan survivals' for granted, Connor argues for detecting the ample resistance that occurred with the transformation of a pagan society to a Christian one. He considers the hybridity of ancient pagan belief with living Christianity to constitute virtually a 'third' religion but criticises even this if acknowledgement is not made of a paganism that is still 'ever-evolving'. And he finds much of the sought-for evidence in the *petits récits* of everyday life and marginalised groups. To this postmodern end, he employs Michel Foucault's genealogical method for uncovering the particular, local, regional, non-centralised, discontinuous and popular 'subjugated knowledges' that are dismissed as primitive and/or naïve by the dominant hegemonic theology of institutional Christianity and the 'either/or' thinking of much of academia. Instead, Conner stresses the need for developing a counter-discourse through the insights and analyses that are signified by Neo-paganism, Wicca and Women's Spirituality. Through Gayatri Spivak, he understands the 'Other' who is considered to threaten the values of civilised society to include 'the foreigner, the homosexual, and the feminine' and now the pagan and witch as well. Instead of the Cartesian-Newtonian Western paradigm that exploits nature and promotes imperialism, colonialism, misogyny and racism for the rationalistic patriarchal expansion of social and political order/power/conquest, the emerging paganistic worldviews that consist of a fluid collection of ancient, indigenous, ethnic, tribal, traditional and/or earth-centred beliefs and ideas are seminal to a more harmoniously balanced and viable future.

In an autumn dream in 1985, I was asked by someone to explain spiritualism. Of course, I proceeded on to materialism arguing that it is matter that gives form to life even if it also becomes the melancholia of decline through age, illness, injury, disfigurement, maiming and death. But it is matter that allows individuality and independence. It is also what gives embodied expression to collectivity, community and oneness – in a word, to both capitalistic and communistic endeavour. For the one, the right *not* to work and the right to amass the largest personal fortune ever; for the other, the concern for all and for generous inter-relationship. The spirit cannot be divorced from the material – even though it may soar off from it. My dream elucidation ended, but I probably say more or the less the same today concerning corporeal reality. Richard refers to my spiritual position as 'the new materialism'.

It may be subtle, but even with an earth-centred polytheist as is Conner, I cringe when I hear such expressions as 'all life is *imbued* with sacred energy or force', 'the *coincidence* of spirituality with infinite matter', or allegedly Giordano Bruno's distinction, even if and when they are 'bonded' (*vinculum*), between 'Divinity and Nature' or 'Spirit and Matter'. The underlying sentiment is still dualistic. In the telluric understanding of a pagan outlook, what I endeavour to champion, matter *is* spiritual. Perhaps it ranges from the solid to the ethereal, but it is always still holy – as are also the fantasies, frames of mind and abstractions that are born from it. Thus, there is *no* divide between divinity and nature; nature *is* divine. As Sara Ruddick puts it, 'the spirit is material'. Conner says that he likes Richard Kurin's term of 'enspirited materiality' in preference to 'spirituality' since it supposedly underscores 'the embodied dimension of the sacred'. But again, this appears to suggest some separation between the spiritual and the physical. My preference is more toward such wording as 'materialistic spirituality'. What is ironic I find is that our term 'spiritual' is itself a metaphor. It derives from the Latin word for 'breath', namely, *spiritus*. Consequently, even in our desire to conceptualise a particular kind of special quality, something especially sublime and/or unearthly, we employ a lingual derivative of a physical substance for it. This may say it all. All the more with the distinction I recognise between the this-worldly and the otherworldly, I retain the pantheistic understanding that all is nature, that there is *nothing* beyond or outside nature – including both empirical reality and the co-natural however this last is understood.

I find Conner's uncovering of Immanuel Kant's citation in *The Critique of Aesthetic Judgment* (1790) of the Temple of Isis inscription as well as the identification of the name of Paris with that of Isis (Per-Isi 'temple of Isis' or Parisis 'near the temple of Isis') made by Antoine Count de Gébelin, Nicolas de Bonneville, Charles Dupuis and Alexander Lenoir – and especially the allegation that the Cathédrale Notre-Dame de Paris was built over the ruins of a temple to Isis – both interesting and yet implausible. It is the Église de Saint-Germain-des-Prés that has been constructed on the site where formerly the temple to Isis and Ceres stood. Notre-Dame itself occupies the location of a temple to Jupiter as the Church itself formerly attested and as was revealed with the discovery of Le Pilier des Nautes, an altar to Jupiter, under the choir of the Notre-Dame cathedral. Beside the Roman forum before the Panthéon and near the strongly cultic Saint-Étienne-du-Mont, the 'third' pagan site of Paris is Montmartre and the lovely Paroisse Saint-Pierre whose nave contains four numinous columns from the *templum Martis* that preceded the construction of the church. For some reason, the Roman temple on top of Montmartre is sometimes said to have been dedicated to the god Mercury rather than Mars, but Montmartre the 'Mont des Martyrs' was earlier known as the Mont de Mars. And yet, besides Mars, the site suggests even stronger associations with the god Dionysus. The church of St. Pierre is reputedly the place where the first Parisian martyr, Saint Denis, was decapitated by an impatient executioner before reaching the scheduled place for his execution. Legend has it that the saint picked up his head and carried it to where now the Basilica of Saint-Denis stands. The story is reminiscent of the dismemberment of Dionysus (hence Denis) by the Titans. Interestingly, close to the church of St. Pierre there is a vineyard that has been maintained to the present within metropolitan Paris. Connor's pagan revelations gleaned from the likes of Ficino, Bruno and Kant, however, tend to display a more gnostic interpretation of pre-Christian spirituality. Apuleius' *Golden Ass* is one of the most entertaining novels I have read, but the conclusion with Lucius' initiation into the mysteries of Isis and Osiris is again gnostic rather than a telluric endorsement of *this* world along with its fleeting but nevertheless real pleasures. But despite the quibbles I may have with some of his 'evidence', interpretations and preferences, I applaud Conner in his attempt to relocate pagan survivals that counter Hutton's contention that 'the pre-Christian religions of the English were defunct by the 730s' and after the subsequent invasions and settlements by the Vikings, 'these traditions vanished, around 1020, forever'. Conner's argument for both Britain and Continental Europe is that, despite ruptures, the absolutists and those who promote a comfortable ecumenism but deny persistence and innovation are both operating simplistically and naïvely.

Understanding how pagans both past and present understand the sacred, the gods and associated practices of worship has been, and continues to be, a challenge not only for those who study religion but also for pagans themselves. Conner appears more concerned with detecting the presence of theonyms and remnants as well as continuities than with deciphering the underlying doctrinal aspects of earth-centred beliefs. By contrast, in two *Pomegranate* articles, 'The Image of Paganism in the Age of Reason: From Idolatry towards a Secular Concept of Polytheism' (2016) and 'The Image of Paganism in the British Romanticism' (2017), Pavel Horák from the Czech Academy of Sciences traces the historic perception of pagan religiosity, at least as concerns the British Isles, and explores the Enlightenment, Christian theological, antiquarian, Protestant, Deist and Romantic concept of a *prisca theologia* that held that humanity's original understanding of the divine was that of a patriarchal Supreme God but which subsequently degenerated into paganism. For the deist Herbert of Cherbury, this debasement of primeval worship is attributed to priestly lies and machinations in the ecclesiastical bid for power. According to the 'true' theology given by God to man, the sublunary world is a place of corruption with the Supreme Operator existing above and beyond the stars – accompanied by humanity worshipping the unknown supernal being as well as the astral manifestations, especially that of the sun. As the original religion of humanity declined and paganism emerged, so the contention goes, there was the historical shift from monotheism to polytheism, the corruption of worship through the use of images and statues, and no repentance of sinful behaviour. However, while retaining the same understanding of the idolatrous nature of paganism as had been held by his deist predecessors, the humanist philosopher David Hume differed in as much as he argued that polytheism was the original religion of humanity. The people themselves, through their lack of reason, i.e., their stupidity and ignorance, were unable to understand and endorse the existence of the one Supreme God. With the Enlightenment's reinvention of the term 'pagan' to refer to the primitive, barbarous, idolatrous and/or the superstitious, Horák argues that 'paganism' first became a scientific category for the purposes of comparative religion. Its characteristic features were identified as nature worship, sacrifices, rites and polytheism (whether the elements of nature, deified humans or spiritual entities). For Horák, pagans of today are dealing with the same issues that were being discussed in the 17th and 18th centuries, namely, the nature of polytheism, the features of proper worship and the notion of gods. The roots of contemporary paganism, he claims, are fundamentally Christian since they have been formed within the 'theological way of thinking'. These apparently include worshipping nature as supreme, worshipping the sun in the open air and within stone circles, the acceptance of the many different goddesses as manifestations of one Goddess and of different gods as expressions of the supreme God, and that all of these developments have been allegedly shaped by the underlying Christian framework. In elucidating the antiquarian John Smith's contention that Druidic religion derived from Noah but degenerated into idolatry with the Roman invasion, Horák acknowledges that the Romantic image of the Celts and Druids has nevertheless stayed the same and has remained to the present. He feels that if contemporary Western pagans continue to draw their conceptual language from Christianity, they remain confined to theological thinking.

It is with this last, of course, that I disagree with Horák. Theology is as much pagan and dharmic as it is Christian or Abrahamic. Admittedly, in the West, religion has come to be understood even within academia to signify Christianity, possibly extended on occasion to include all four

Abrahamic faiths. Theology in Western universities has traditionally been *Christian* theology. Consequently, for addressing the future of religious studies, that was the very reason Brian Bocking insisted in Bath Spa and Cork upon changing the name of the Department for the Study of Religion to the Department for the Study of Religions. The emphasis on that plural '*s*' was always stressed. And I maintain that for the fuller understanding of a specific religion, virtually any religion, knowledge of its underlying theological consideration of divinity, or the lack of such, is fundamentally important. Whether our term for 'religion'/*religio* derives from *re-legere* 'to go through', 'to go over again in reading, speech or thought' (*pace* Cicero) or from *re-ligare* 'to bind to or reconnect with [godhead]' (*pace* Lactantius), what most distinguishes paganism from both Abrahamic and dharmic formulations is its telluric endorsement rather than in comprehending the spiritual in gnostic and/or transcendental escapist concepts. For a pagan, the divine is here-and-now and as much of this-world as it might be of anything further. This understanding *is* theological.

But in all our explorations of spirituality, religion and the arts, science is equally as important. Richard Feynman explains that it is science that takes us into uncertainty and doubt. These last may not be particularly comfortable at times, but they are both ultimately emancipating and anti-hubristic. The arrogance of unquestioned belief and inflexible assumptions contribute to the short-sightedness and unimaginative fixations that increasingly plague our world in her political, economic and pandemic arenas. Scientists are not gods, but they may be among the closest priest-like intermediaries we have to sane awareness and the knowledge necessary for advance with the foundations to well-being. While description and the signalling of events from the past are important undertakings, the methodology of science is inapplicable for the discipline of history. Nevertheless, Conner uncovers what I believe cannot be denied, namely, that there has been a persistent undercurrent detectable in the Western cultural canon that has entertained pagan concepts and even practices – perhaps not in the form of Margaret Murray's witch cult – of one sort or another through the Middle Ages and beyond and into the present-day. Whether the hidden has been durably institutionalised over great stretches of time may be doubtful, but an appreciation and recognition of earthly sacrality would seem to be virtually intrinsic to human imagination when not oppressed by ecclesiastical mandate or secular-driven agendas. And even if and when it is, the spirit of people's resistance and rebellion remains irrepressible. To the carefully discerning eye, telluric pagan indications of animism, pantheism, polytheism and the tangible as holy become evident. In tracing this 'hermeneutics of suspicion' through the ages of 'Christianisation', Conner notes from among a host of relevant personages, the poet Percy Bysshe Shelley, the philosopher/poet Friedrich Nietzsche, the writer Joseph Campbell and the psychologist Carl Jung. We learn that Shelley was surprisingly prescient in foreshadowing present-day paganism and witchcraft, that for Nietzsche Christianity robbed us of the culture of the ancient world, that Joseph Campbell (a seminal early influence for me) is guilty of a 'monomythic' approach, and that Jung came increasingly to distance himself from earth-mysticism and the psycho-mythical significance of pagan gods for a greater interest in Christianity, hermeticism and alchemy. In all, Conner presents many others who have played significant roles in the development of pagan consciousness: T.S. Eliot, Henry David Thoreau, Walt Whitman, William James, Oscar Wilde, William Butler Yeats, Aleister Crowley, Isadora Duncan, D.H. Lawrence, Robert Graves, James Hillman, Gilles Deleuze and Freya Matthews to name only some. What I take from him foremost, however, is his rejection of the Platonic, Neoplatonic and Hermeticist 'as above, so below' dualism between the ideal and the mundane in which the former is privileged over the latter. Whether this dichotomy can be strictly extended into an understanding of the patriarchal and abstract over the matrifocal and egalitarian is another matter. Personally, I have much appreciated Marija Gimbutas's earlier archaeological work but have become more hesitant with her later conclusions concerning a destruction of a peaceful matriarchal society by invading Kurgans and the accompanying 'Goddess theory' that has come to be endorsed unquestionably by radical feminist political activists. Perhaps more or less as did Margaret Murray, Gimbutas fits her material into a preconceived schema reflecting more what was desired to be seen rather than subjecting the evidence to careful analysis. This is a danger we all face. But to the development of a counter-discourse to Christianisation, misogyny, racism, privileging of the few over the many, colonialism and imperialism, a pagan spirituality that is rooted in the ancient, indigenous, ethnic, tribal, traditional and earth-centred has an important role to contribute.

The intersection of paganism and Christianity, whether in the hybrid form that Conner frequently mentions or as rivalling competitors, presents challenges for both interfaith efforts and 21st century co-existence possibilities. In reflecting on his parents, Richard contends that they were 'the real thing'. Even as Christians, they would allow the exception if and when they saw it as being honest and true. Learning that Queen Elizabeth in 1961 had originally objected to including Jackie Kennedy's sister and brother-in-law to a Buckingham Palace dinner in honour of the American President and First Lady because both were divorcées, Richard questions the Queen's not questioning the Church then and subsequently. The irony is, of course, that three of Elizabeth's own children eventually divorced their own spouses. Traditionally, however, divorcées were not invited to State Dinners at Buckingham Palace, and Elizabeth was only conforming to established precedence. But as the occasion was a private banquet and not an official State Dinner, the royals relented and did invite Jackie's relatives. Nevertheless, Richard affirms that he believes in progressive royalty and is highly critical of any effort toward 'trying to beat the odds of reality by using a make-believe God who at most embodies cosmic disaster'. He argues instead that we should all 'let our earth be the ruling base of conscious endeavour'. This conforms to the earth-centred practices that Conner exalts when following Starhawk in her claim that paganism is rooted in immanence, interconnection and community. With 'tradition' as a chief obstacle, pagan spirituality has much of its work already cut out for it.

The zombie land of social-distancing seems to be diminishing to some extent as the lockdown is gradually being lifted, but people still walk warily around each other. And how little any of us seemed to have been aware of the 1918/1919 Spanish flu epidemic for most of my life. When it finally became once again mentioned, I had asked my father about it. His hometown was Gary, Indiana, and he told me that both his mother and older sister had contracted the virus but recovered. However, the babysitter who lived further down the street did not. Dad remembers seeing her body on display in the window of her house.

How different is our pandemic world from the century of times that intervened between today and 1919. A great thrill for Nancy and me would occur when we wished to walk through a tight crowd during the *mardi gras* in New Orleans. One by one, we would squeeze by a person and then the next – slowly of course but intimately and, in time, always successfully. Richard and I have experienced much the same during carnival celebrations in Maastricht and Binche or during the Queen's birthday celebrations (*Koninginnedag*) in Amsterdam. Randy Conner refers to the Russian philosopher

Mikhail Bakhtin and his recognition of 'the carnival processions [as] the march of the [officially] rejected gods'. The carnival itself constitutes a 'time between time' – originally the extra days of the solar year that exceed the 'perfect' circle of 360 degrees or days. As the suspension of normal time, a kind of 'non-time', the carnival is the occasion for the inversions of normal behaviour (masks, costumes, crossdressing) that invokes the Golden Age and is to be traced to the Roman celebrations of both the December Saturnalia and the epagomenal days before the New Year's Day that originally occurred on the first of March. In my much younger days, I had a passion for the carnivalesque and, besides those in Belgium and The Netherlands, have attended the various 'feasts of fools' in New Orleans, München, Basil and Nice. Such collective yet local exercises of excess, abandon and freedom for me have been quintessentially pagan experiences. Certainly not quiet contemplations within and of nature, but the carnival frenzy embodies the more strictly Dionysian counterbalance of pagan experience and awareness. But unlike Nancy, when it came to the bodily crunch, Richard has always been more reluctant to plunge into and through a packed group of people, but sometimes there has been no choice.

If I recollect, there have been many densely populated events in my past – the Fourth of July celebrations in my hometown of Maplewood, New Jersey and from the Sky River Rock Festival and Lighter Than Air Fair in Tenino, Washington to various Grandes Parades du Jazz in the Arènes de Cimiez of Nice, France. There was also an 'on acid' moment in which Nancy and I were in Manhattan at Christmas time. We got ourselves into an elevator in Macy's just as the doors were closing. The lift was jammed pack and in complete interminable silence as it seemed to take forever to reach the next floor. Nancy and I had been totally unprepared, and when the doors finally opened, we both popped out screaming with hysterical laughter. Maybe not involving such masses of people, I am also remembering one of my earliest LSD experiences with Nancy, Rosanne and Sarah. We had 'dropped' at the Frank Lloyd Wright Marin County Civic Center in California and from there wandered into the adjacent Spanish Colonial style convent orphanage. Later the site became a school at which my coven co-inaugurator, Buster, eventually taught. But at this time, the lads all seemed to be smoking pot to which the elderly East European or German nuns were unaware but were using brooms to chase the teenagers who were otherwise perceived to be misbehaving.

After a while, the four of us got into my VW Beetle in search of something to eat. We crossed Route 101 into a suburban area with a constant chorus of laughter erupting from the back seat. We must have found a stamped envelope that someone had inadvertently dropped, and when I drove up to the postman at the mail box, I handed him the letter. He was not a postman but someone who was mailing his own letters. The laughter continued unabated. We asked the gentleman if he could suggest somewhere in the area where we could eat. He hesitated for a moment and then proceeded to inform us that if we continued directly ahead and turned right at the end, there was 'Boobie's'. The roar of laughter from the back seat of the car doubled then in volume.

We arrived at Boobie's, and the array of food on display in the counter brought all of us into a state of uncontrolled laughter. And it was contagious. The young gal and fellow behind the counter could not stop themselves from laughing with us. She at least, if not both, was on her knees with her face buried into the back of the counter virtually sobbing with laughter. After what had been easily ten minutes if not more, they managed to extract from us our order and then told us to wait outside. There was a swing door that I was pulling the wrong way when a man jumped up from behind us to open the door for me. It was only then that we became aware that there was a section of Boobie's that was full of tables with customers sitting in utter silence through all of this.

Some random thoughts from my past: Are we not as youths gods themselves? As we grow older and, apart only in exceptional cases, no longer are gods, we naturally come to worship the gods as something other than ourselves. I can imagine the objections to this thought. The overall pagan understanding I hold is that all is divine including ourselves. But I suppose that gods are a special kind of divinity. And in the least, I feel that paganism is first and foremost for the young. We elders hopefully have some acquired wisdoms to share, but we come in time no longer to be capable of all-night vigils and spiral dances among other things. Paganism for us becomes something quieter and perhaps more quietly in communication with nature and our reflections. But youth is the future – as is paganism, and I thrill over that.

I wish I had more confidence in our political leaders and the functioning of our political processes. So much appears to me as shameless. I remember Ronald Reagan's State of the Union address to Congress in 1985 and listening to him steal Gore Vidal's 'The Second American Revolution' phrase and completely misuse it. Of course, for Nietzsche, conflict is a positive and contributes to development. The assassination of Harvey Milk in San Francisco was a shocking and chilling event, and I still cannot agree with or condone the (albeit understandable) violence that erupted over the sentencing of Dan White, but for the rest what came out of it constituted a dignified and beautiful episode in gay and human history. Whether Nietzsche would agree is another question.

While I find ancient Egyptian religion always fascinating, I am not a Kemetic. Nevertheless, I have wondered about Hebrewism being a Protestant form of the old religion along the Nile. The conflict between God and Man-Satan is duplicated – if not originated – in that between Set and Osiris-Horus. As Christ is the 'Son of Man', Horus is the son of Osiris, who is himself the equivalent of man. Last night I listened on the BBC World Service to the story of a man who was on death row in the state of Alabama for thirty years. His mother had taught him that 'God can do everything but fail'. It is an interesting concept, and one can readily understand its appeal. Pagan gods are different; they are human and as such can make mistakes and even fail on occasion. But as such, they are part of, or exemplified in, the fabric of nature. They are not 'perfect' in as much as they embody change, but to the degree that we trust the natural processes of the world and cosmos, alteration and transformation and evolution are ultimately positive.

The feeling of awe is said to be a mingling of the emotions of wonder, fear and reverence. The gods, who are among our natural objects that conjure the experience of awe, are not necessarily terrifying in themselves. They are instead our portals (or masks) to and of the abyss, and it is the terror of the abyss that we might feel in the presence of a deity. And with a pagan understanding, there is not but one god; there are many doors to the void.

During the days of the AIDS crisis, there was always the strange resurgence of self-doubts regarding one's own state of health that re-emerged each time upon learning that another friend had fallen victim. But like today with the corona pandemic, one continues to seek some form for his or her own positive contribution – until one's own number appears. And yet I continue to wish that the dragon could be slain, that the gods would stop the contrary – not only the disease of course (though that would be a welcomed starter) but as well the ignorance, intolerance, small-mindedness and the like that imperil human well-being and co-existence. Death is the outcome of life, yes, but the world seems so much fuller now of it (in the past, the concerns were Bradford, Bruxelles, Ethiopia, Sudan, Lebanon *et al.*; today, Libya, Yemen, sub-Saharan Africa, Syria, Iraq, Afghanistan, and the COVID-19) – or are we just older?

But in the ups and downs and flow of time, there have always been enough of the occasional intersections of the special or unusual to keep it interestingly engaging. Typical might be the time that Vassili along with two other artists was being honoured at the Mairie in Paris in connection with an exhibition of the work of the three in the Bois de Boulogne. We were to meet Jacques Chirac, then mayor of Paris. It felt something like having an audience with the Pope. The person in charge was Jacqueline Nebout, the deputy mayor. Privately we referred to her as 'big tits'. She described the rooms of the Mairie as 'slightly kitch'; otherwise, they were overwhelming. While we were waiting, Nebout would move around the circle and speak to various people. We were lavishly furnished with champagne, jus d'orange, a multitude of hors d'oeuvres and pastries. Several times we were prepared for an imminent arrival of the mayor himself and finally with great fanfare he was announced, but it was not less than an hour and half later that he actually slipped into the room profusely apologetic. He was amiably impressive and even handsome. Nebout escorted Chirac around the circle of those of us in attendance so he could have a word with everyone. Nebout had not spoken to Richard or me beforehand, and as Chirac approached us I could hear her whisper to him, '*Des inconnues*'.

Perhaps it all comes down to luck. Some people work hard for their successes, but luck might still be a factor in whether they succeed. Others work equally as hard and yet are not successful. Still others are reduced to committing robbery or writing forged cheques, and some of these encounter the further bad luck of dying in the process – such as George Floyd by the Minnesota police. There is also the poor luck of miscalculation and subsequent exposure such as we have with Dominic Cummings driving 60 miles round trip to Barnard Castle with his child and wife in the car ostensibly but implausibly 'to see if his eyes were so banjaxed that it was unsafe for him to drive' (Marina Hyde). Throughout the world there are scores and scores of poor souls enduring abject poverty, the dangers of violence and the misfortunes of disease. Do we attribute such conditions to the randomness of luck or the acts of God, the gods or Providence? When and if we are lucky, even extremely lucky, ought we feel guilt in comparing our situation with those who are less lucky? Personally, I thank the gods virtually every day for having the love and companionship I have. With whatever good fortune one is 'blessed', gratitude appears to be commensurate – maybe not as the conclusion but perhaps as an opening toward securing some way to contribute to the well-being of others.

I suppose my deep pagan orientation will always bring me back to the gods. I perceive them as the music that informs both this-world and the conscious realms that exist beyond the cognitive capabilities of our physical senses. Dionysus is most usually associated with excess and wild abandon, and yet, with the gentle one or two drinks, he allows instead simply the welcomed and calm realisation of serene bliss. The Dionysian is contrasted and yet paired with the Apollonian. The latter is the more refined artistic expression, but with a deeper analysis of Hellenic and Indo-European mythology, it becomes discernible that Apollo and Dionysus were themselves the divine twins, the Dioscuri. Consequently, despite their supposed differences, they can be understood finally as one and the same. It was Nietzsche in his *The Birth of Tragedy* (1872) who first fully formulated the Dionysian and Apollonian aesthetic and philosophical dialectics. Dionysus (ultimately the Zeus of Nysa), the lord of wine, drama and dance, is known as the god of intuition, emotions, instincts, the unexpected, the dark and chthonic, the irrational and chaotic, and the hedonic. By contrast, Apollo is the god of music, poetry, prophecy and healing and also, like Dionysus, of dance. He is considered the most Greek of all the gods and distinguished as the deity who promotes light, structure, reason, rational thinking, logic, prudence, perfection, purity, clarity, moderation, goal-seeking and order. While critics of the dominant cultural paradigm of modernity, with its Newtonian-based positivism that considers exclusively only the observable, measurable and predictive (perhaps Camille Paglia, more definitely Randy Conner), tend to stress the Dionysian over the Apollonian, for me it is a mistake to ascribe to Dionysus the life-affirmative, all-inclusive, closeness and the real while seeing Apollo as expressive of life-denial, alienation, distance and the ideal. The underlying twinship of the two deities underscores both their implicit identity and the dynamics of harmony that are necessary for an integrated life – one that accepts both the empirical/cognitive paradigm and the anomalous, magical and mystic. I find it difficult not to think of Apollo as also affirmative of life – especially through music and healing. Perhaps Apollo's moderation opens one to the sublimity of Dionysian intoxication, while Dionysus brings pleasure into perfection.

I suppose I have always been a day-dreamer and, without doubt, this has constituted at various times a form of escapism. I can remember long walks at Purdue University between classes and residence. My fantasy at the time was to be living in ancient Egypt on the banks of the Nile with a magician. He was older and, of course, most enjoyably handsome.

In time, and in addition to Ravel's *Daphnis and Chloe* which exemplifies for me the ultimate sensual evocation of the Arcadian world, it has been the composer's *Shéhérezade* and the call to *Asie* that helped to fire and augment my *Wanderlust*. With the present pandemic and ever-diminishing financial resources – and not that age is not an additional factor, my remaining days of traveling are not likely to be many. I have yet to visit the Czech Republic, Slovakia, Poland, Latvia, Estonia and Russia if not also Byelorussia, Moldavia and Ukraine among European countries, but I also have a fascination now for the Caucasus Region and maybe the Stans. I daily follow the weather for Sochi and Baku, and Tbilisi is on the list as well. As for Sub-Sahara Africa, I have been only to South Africa; and for Latin America, it has been Mexico, Haiti and Puerto Rico. I do consider Oman, New Zealand and Polynesia as territories I would also yet like to reach, and then there are countless places that I would adore to *re*-visit.

Not a travelling recollection but one relating to residence in the Midi is the explanation from a restaurant's chef on how to prepare *foie gras*. First one should fry apple slices in butter with a touch of salt. Next, after lightly dipping the *foie gras* in flour, it is fried in butter with a bit of salt added. Finally, all is served on a bed of lettuce sprinkled with vinaigrette, garnished with blanched carrot strips and parsley and sprinkled with hazelnut oil (*huile de noisette*). This is of course not for vegetarians and also not for those who are animal rights activists. In Europe, only France, Belgium, Spain, Hungary and Bulgaria still allow the production of *foie gras*.

As a student, I have been privileged to have had some wonderful instructors. And, vice versa, as a teacher, a great fortune is to have on occasion the exceptional student. One of these for me has been Karel James Bouse who enrolled in my Cherry Hill Seminary course on 'World Religions from a Pagan Perspective'. In 2019, Karel has published a book on *Neo-shamanism and Mental Health*. I scarcely know where to begin in my praise of this work in which the contemporary practice of Neo-shamanism is explored both in its link to traditional shamanism and its role in mental health therapy and psychology studies. In a refreshing, succinct and no-nonsense approach, Karel Bouse clearly investigates and most enjoyably presents the applicability of the shamanic journey for the psychologist, anthropologist, sociologist, psychotherapist, parapsychologist and anyone interested in consciousness itself.

A major distinction between traditional shamanism and Neo-shamanism is the supporting cultural matrix enjoyed by the former vis-à-vis for the latter the dominant Western paradigm that confines value to the observable, measurable and predictive and, in separating humanity from the earth, eschews mysticism and magic. Herein, we find the innovative yet alien position of paganism in general – one that is judged by the sensate world to be eccentric, deviant and/or pathological. Where I tend to disagree with Bouse is over her inclusion of materialism as a potential negative along with rationalism, capitalism and science's restricted understanding of reality that eliminates value from what cannot be approached through our physical senses. The standard criterion for legitimacy within contemporary Western culture is explained as materialist-cognitive, and the 'spirit world' is something that exists beyond the scope of our sensory apparatus. The author here links the ethereal to supposedly shamanic elements of Gnosticism. The gnostic inclines toward reducing the physical simply to the mechanical and crass and too easily becomes blind to matter's inherent sacredness of which the divine is an additional efflux or an aura thereof. In my consideration, the magical worldview of shamanism/Neo-shamanism is as much telluric as it may also be 'transcendentally gnostic'. Once again, this may be described as what Richard terms 'the new materialism'.

Bouse considers that along with Neo-paganism and Wicca, Neo-shamanism emerged from the New Age movement in the 1980s and 1990s, but her astute analyses and arguments are unusually *not* New Agey. And what I tend to refer to as the otherworld, she makes clear that it is also to be known as the anomalous. She even goes as far as to say that supernormal 'experiences are real and perhaps may not be internally generated projections'. As with paganism in general, shamanism/Neo-shamanism develops from an understanding of the foundation of immanent divinity and the sacred as present in all things; its perceptions and/or experiences of the anomalous, mystical and/or magical may not necessarily arise through fantasy proneness but, instead, through the discerning powers of imagination. While the ability to indulge in the make-believe is sometimes also inherent in much of Neo-shamanism, its shamanic predecessor's anchoring in the archaic understandings of nature, animism, pantheism, spiritual omnipresence, liminality, numinosity and earth-centredness are likely to permit access to realities that do not conform to the positivist, biomedical and clinical ideal.

Accessing the world that lies beyond material and sensate boundaries for the purposes of insight and healing within the shamanic or Neo-shamanic context depends on the production of altered states of consciousness often termed 'journeying'. Apart from the more secular forms of paganism (dark-green religionists, atheistic pagans, those concerned strictly with this-world and/or nature), pagan spirituality more typically embraces the mythic, archetypal and transpersonal along with the mundane and personal, and this embrace very much includes the shamanic-spiritual psychonaut. The journey is undertaken at will and traditionally for a set purpose and, in as much as it is mindfully directed, differs from other states of altered consciousness such as dreams, lucid dreaming, self-hypnosis, guided visualisations, channelling and meditation. In contrast to traditional shamans, the Neo-shaman tends not to employ such tools as psychoactive drugs, fasting and sleep deprivation and relies instead principally on repetitive, rhythmic drumming in a darkened environment, perhaps blindfolded. Consequently, the hypnogogic interface with the otherworld is not separate from normal waking consciousness and may be aborted at will. Bouse points out that research in evolutionary psychology suggests that the gene which allows interaction with the supernormal world may be the same gene behind schizophrenia, and she does not underplay that there is always the possibility of unsettling, even harmful risk with shamanic journeying. And further, she stresses that the (Neo-)shamanic practitioner must also live a life that is 'balanced with the willingness and ability to do the grocery shopping, go to work, have successful relationships, and balance the checkbook'. All in all, I can easily say that Karel Bouse's compact book has been a delight to read and one that explicates a significant aspect of contemporary paganism in a grounded and professional manner.

CHAPTER EIGHT

The Citizen Ambassador Program to China / College of Creative Studies, UCSB / Pacifica Institute / Joseph Campbell / Indo-European Studies conference at UCLA / Romuva in Platelai / 'Paganism in Contemporary Britain' at the University of Newcastle upon Tyne / China and 'one country, two systems' / China, Confucian & Daoist religiosity and harmony: Keping Wang's *Harmonism as an Alternative* / Western freedom, individualism, self-expression, pluralism & dissent / Pirsig's value versus truth / harmony and music; Santa Barbara & San Francisco / 'wraping things up' / Barbara Dauphin / Black Lives Matter, 're-evaulating the past', and paganism as first & last / Kāshī Vishwanath, Ram Shankar Tripathi & R.K. Mishra / Western arrogance / the Kashi House's American Center for Efficacious Service / Donald Lippe(r) / Lee Brevard / 'Devil worship' / Delhi, Khajuraho & the solar eclipse in Banaras / Baba Versa Singh / the Bloolips' 'The Island of Lost Shoes' / Paula Letellier / the ACES conference 'Christians and pagans: Can Divergent Traditions Converse? A Contemporary Dialogue' / Jaqueline Spruyt / *otitus externa* surgery and liberation; pagan reincarnation & soul-duality / Åke Hultkrantz' *Conceptions of the Soul Among North American Indians*; Christianity and the Platonic denunciation of pleasure / woke culture / transgenderism; *pūjā* in India / more on my expulsion from Shiva's temple in Banaras / nature, the gods & music / musings on Arabs, Israelis, Euro-Americans, Iranians, Indians, the Japanese and Chinese / Tirupati / Mysore, Halley's comet, Swami Nirmalanda & Chacha's funeral; Fury / natural hierarchies / Vritra; Dad; 1986 / the *pillán* / cosmopolitan paganism; Richard; my fortune & privilege; the seaside; the Strawberry Hill Coven / light versus darkness / Anton LaVey's Church of Satan / transhumanism / Portland & Kent State

In 1994, I was fortunate to have been part of a group of 24 scholars to visit the People's Republic of China. We were, through the American Academy of Religion, part of the Citizen Ambassador Program of People to People that had been founded by Dwight Eisenhower during his Presidency. The purpose of our Religion and Philosophy Delegation was to understand both the survival of religion in China and how it was being approached within teaching and research institutions. This was to be conducted under the effects of Marxist-Maoist domination and the aftermath of both the Cultural Revolution (1966–1976) and the 1989 Tiananmen Square protests/massacre. Before we departed for China, the Chinese necessity of 'saving face' was carefully explained to us. I would guess that this last relates to my businessman father who always insisted that there was no need for a contract with the Chinese, in contrast with the Japanese, because, before he returned from China, 'We shook hands on the deal'.

Richard and I had been to Hong Kong when we made our round-the-world excursion in 1982. Previously, Chinese cuisine was not for me a preference. When the consensus among those I was with was 'Let's eat Chinese', I always went along, but Hong Kong had been a revelation, and our Peking duck became an unforgettable experience. When we arrived in California after Hong Kong, a journal had just published an article specifying the best Chinese restaurants on the West Coast. This became our 'bible'. And with the 1994 visit to Shanghai, Qufu and Beijing, with the exception of only two meals which were mediocre or just so-so, we ate sumptuously and deliciously throughout – concluding with a Peking duck dinner on our last night.

Our first meeting with Chinese academics occurred at the Fudan University in Shanghai. We were told: 'We do not have a homosexual problem in China', that Confucianism is *not* considered a religion, and that folk religion no longer exists – 'Oh, apart from the hinterland, but it is not studied and certainly is not appreciated'. After while walking along the Nanjing Road, the complete stripping away of religiosity from the overabundance of the market-driven economy was depressing until I came across, perhaps on the Zhejiang Road, a religious icon kiosk with a working shrine to Guan Yin (Kwan Yin). I lit some incense, and the attendants lit candles with my 1-yuan payment as well. I found this uplifting. Later, we were taken to the magnificent Jade Temple with a great number of young monks engaged with a ritual just as we arrived. I returned to the Jade Buddha afterwards to light incense and was nicely welcomed by the attendants who invited me into the normally closed off section before the idol.

There was a mixed contrast between the appreciative reactions I would receive while engaging in something akin to the *pūjā* I had learned in India but now before Chinese shrines (that still existed) and the responses I would get in the likes of the East China Normal University and the Institute of Religious Studies of Shanghai to my usual questions about folk religion. The interconnection between culture and religion would be acknowledged, but then the declaration would be made that folk religion is not religion but only superstition. Academically, the study of religion in China seemed to be more of a socialist front for the maintenance of political stability. Superstition was dismissed for it not being, in contrast to religion, systematic and organised. It has no doctrines, standardised rites or 'complete' concepts. Instead, it is a method of cheating people and includes witches (both male and female), fortune tellers, and those who fabricate medicines. 'Freedom of religion does not apply to freedom of superstition'.

In Jinan, the highlight was the Daoist temple to Zhen Wu (Xuan Wu/ Tian), god of the north. Again I was able to light incense and, in the nearby 'memorial' temple, I gonged the great bell for 'good luck'. The Confucian temple in Confucius' birthplace of Qufu, allegedly the only Confucian temple still existing in China (Hong Kong was still at this point a British colony) was spectacular but also disappointing in being little more than a museum. At the Institute for Confucian Studies in the Qufu Normal University, we received the typical and uninspiring promotion of the official line: Confucianism is not a religion; Confucius was great but Marx was greater; and what were the possibilities of Confucianism prospering in the 21st century. When I had first become fascinated with the *I Ching* in San Francisco, I segregated the later commentary added by Confucius and concentrated only on the earlier and original text. This was part of my still forming pagan spirituality to retrieve as much as possible of the initial roots – an effort that I shared with other pagans in the 1970s, 1980s and later. I have since, however, come to revere Confucius (Kong Chou) as a bona fide pagan figure espousing a refreshing humanistic understanding. Though I may still have some criticism of the Chinese philosopher, I have come to appreciate his basic teachings and thrust. While at the China Confucian Society when in Qufu, I asked a question about the scientific study of religion versus the agenda-motivated study of religion but learned afterwards that my question had not been properly translated. That evening, Kurt and I wanted to visit the pyramid 'tomb' of the Yellow Emperor's son as well as the earth mound behind it which is recognised as the birthplace of the Yellow Emperor himself. Hardly before we knew it, we were off with the group's bus and our guide – just the three of us plus the driver. Both in design and setting, we found the pyramid lovely, but when we returned to the bus, three rowdy and very ancient men demanded money from us before they would remove themselves from beneath the wheels of the vehicle. We paid 40 yuan, but they demanded more. I got angry and was about to storm after and pull them out, but Mr. Shin, our mortified guide, forked over another 6 yuan. It was a violation of 'saving face', but we were able to proceed back to our hotel. Kurt and I gave both Mr. Shin and the driver 100 yuan each.

In Beijing, I met a Professor Tong De-Fu from the Research Institute of Religions of the Central University of Nationalities whose field of studies was shamanism. More progressively than the norm, he allowed that shamanism is a 'primitive form of religion but not superstition'. His interest, however, was purely ethnological and in medicinal healing techniques including the Gang Qika shamanism hospital in Inner Mongolia. I learned later that he was the vice-chairman of his local Communist Party. And during our session with the Institute of World Religions and the Social Science Institute, I heard once again that superstition is something that is to be eliminated. As Professor Tong had said, shamanism has no role within contemporary society. This is of course in complete contrast to Karel Bouse's contentions concerning both traditional and Neo- shamanisms I mentioned in the previous chapter. While the academic attitude we encountered in Beijing was more liberal, religious reform still had the objectives of fostering religious unity, removing formalism (including the worship of the sun, moon, ancestors and the like) and eliminating both superstition and magic. Nevertheless, at both the Ming tomb and the awesome Temple of Heaven, cult veneration was obviously alive with abundant offerings of coins and paper money before the tombs, thrones and altars. In all, at least at the time of our delegation's visit, China officially acknowledged the legal existence of only five religions, namely, Buddhism, Daoism, Catholicism, Protestantism and Islam. While it has bequeathed the legacies of both Daoism and Confucianism and has been instrumental in the development of Mahayana Buddhism, it has come to establish Marxist socialism as virtually, in an Abrahamic fashion, the 'one and true religion'. Nevertheless, the classical folk religion of the Chinese people has been recognised by some scholars as well as others as constituting a religious identity of its own.

In all, my 1994 trip to China was a highly memorable experience. I had begun the first four days of the year in Kāshī and Kathmandu next until returning to London on the 16th of January. A month later with Richard we were in Florida (Naples, Sarasota, Sebastian, Fort Lauderdale). After five nights in New York, we got to Santa Barbara on April Fool's Day and settled into Isla Vista for my two-month lecturing on 'Postmodern Indo-European Studies' for the College of Creative Studies with the University of California, my alma mater. I did not have many students, but those that I did were bright and enjoyable. This was my first real teaching experience, and as the time progressed, the class and exchange improved steadily. On the last day, the students asked about the 'sober assessment of self' that I had put into the syllabus. I replied that it was the topic for our final class. During this semester, Richard and I went to Los Angeles at one point to have *darshan* of Ma Jaya Bhagavati who was visiting and having her crowded teaching audiences. Unsuccessfully, we had her try to intervene with Richard's father who was also visiting LA and get him not to surrender to Virginia and her household in New Mexico. That we failed to convince him from what he wanted to do turned out to be the best thing of all. Virginia took care of William marvellously, and for us freely, for the rest of his life. Later during the Easter break, we had a brief visit to San Diego and Baha California. And when the UCSB episode finally concluded, Richard and I then drove north along Highway 1, the coastal route, to Big Sur and Salinas and finally San Francisco. After about ten days in the City by the Bay, I flew to Shanghai for the start of the delegation in China. When I returned to San Francisco, I located four temples in Chinatown: two Buddhist (the Gold Mountain Monastery and one on Waverly Place) and two Daoist (the Tien Hou temple also on Waverly Place and the Kong Chou on Stockton Street). But I still think the most beautiful Chinese temple I have ever seen was in Bangkok.

A few other things that occurred during the 1994 Santa Barbara stay included a visit to Ojai on Ascension Day (both for the Wheeler Hot Springs and the magical Ojai Foundation whose land had been originally purchased by Annie Besant and which, ironically, seemed the closest to the kind of paganism I have perceived in Lithuania). Next was a visit to the Pacifica Institute to see the first video of a series that Joseph Campbell had put together on the Arthurian legend. He discusses Europe and the individual versus Asia, the Church and the tribe or community which will relate to what I have yet to say about China. There was also the Indo-European Studies conference at UCLA at which the Freie Universität Berlin professor Bernfried Schleratt gave a fine talk in which he explained the contradictions in Dumézil's research – something with which I strongly resonate. The rest of 1994 included another month in San Francisco that itself included the loan to Richard and me of William and Lyn's delightful home for a week in Lafayette. The first night of August we spent in Montecito with Howard and Jean Fenton with the rest of the week in Los Angeles with Toni and the rest of the month after that on the East Coast (Manhattan and Rhode Island) during which time I flew to Lithuania for the Romuva gathering in Plateliai and to give a talk on the Chicago Parliament of Religions. On the last full day in Lithuania, I got to swim in the Baltic Sea. London followed with attending the 'Paganism in Contemporary Britain' conference sponsored by the University of Newcastle upon Tyne's Department of Religious Studies and for which I gave a paper on 'New Age and Paganism'. After London, we had about ten days in Amsterdam, less than a week at the farm in Provence, about two weeks in Paris, another two weeks in London and were back then in San Francisco by Thanksgiving and for the rest of the year. 1994 was also the year in which my parents finally separated. It was moreover when our dear Lyn was diagnosed with a melanoma of the urethra – a rare disease (she being the third known case) from which she eventually died.

However, back to my consideration of China which at the time I am now writing is engaged in bitter feuding as the second largest world economy with the United States as the first. Is this, I wonder, the proverbial East-West clash? The east versus west culture conflict has most significantly and recently emerged with the national security law that Beijing wishes to impose on the city of Hong Kong. Under the agreement made between Great Britain and China, the former surrendered sovereignty in 1997 over its Crown colony of Hong Kong to the People's Republic of China with the agreement that a 'one country, two systems' principle would operate subsequently for fifty years. This formula was to allow Hong Kong to maintain its capitalistic economy and way of life and to serve both as an independent centre for international trade and as a secure haven for dissidents and political refugees from mainland China. The proposed national security law, however, appears to undermine the two systems structure and to consider any act of secession, subversion, terrorism or foreign interference to be a criminal undertaking. The Hong Kong opposition fears that people could then be punished for criticising Beijing. In other words, free speech and the right to protest can henceforth be seen as acts of subversion – restrictions that directly violate Western understandings of freedom. The law might allow Beijing to set up its own institutions for reasons of security within Hong Kong.

For Western outsiders, China's autocratic political system is perceived as non-democratic and certainly contrary to the pluralism endorsed by the West. How much this relates to differences in mentality between the East and the West might be gaged in part by Japan's refusal to join the United States, Britain, Australia and Canada in condemning China's move toward the imposition of its security law on Hong Kong. Washington sees this refusal as stemming from Japan's fear of developing friction with its powerful neighbour, but it may result more from the misunderstanding by the West of east-west cultural differences.

The long history of China involves 'saving face' embarrassment concerning dignity and social reputation as well as its distinctive Confucian-Daoist religiosity. Even if Marxism is to be seen as a new religious development, the longstanding ethical-spiritual-political tradition behind Chinese culture is still operative – especially the underlying Confucian understandings of the harmonious relationship between Heaven, Earth and humanity that is considered to be based on moderation and equilibrium. From the perspective of classical Confucianism, harmony is the highest of values. It develops from emotion. By contrast and as Aristotle has it, justice – produced through reason or rationality – is the leading cardinal virtue for the West. According to Keping Wang in his *Harmonism as an Alternative* (2018/2019), Confucianism is to be understood as the harmony-conscious cultural heritage of China. Harmony (the Confucian ideal of the 'Great Union') is recognised as the end rather than the means, and the 'promotion of the harmonious society is easily understood and widely accepted by the Chinese citizens'.

Conversely, our Western ideals are different. While Wang considers justice to be the most important in the West, I wonder instead if it is not liberty. Interestingly, when Wang enumerates the Confucian ideals of the Great Union or world Commonwealth as 'equality, fraternity, harmony, welfare and justice', he does not mention freedom (cf. the French national motto of *liberté, égalité, fraternité*). Liberty in the West includes the rights of independence, association, free speech or self-expression, belief or religion but also, in some places, such things as the right to bear arms and the unrestrained capitalist latitude to make money. In general, and in contrast to communitarian ideals, we in the West place greater emphasis on individualism and liberalism. We cherish human rights, supposedly equality and what we consider to be democracy. Our weaknesses become our excessive libertarianism and pathetic lack of compassion. Instead of understanding justice and rights as inherent principles, we depend upon instrumental rationality that in its unmoderated state becomes little more than a self-interested calculation based purely on perceptions of utility. One of our worst errors I take from Robert Pirsig's 1974 *Zen and the Art of Motorcycle Maintenance* in which he signals our exaltation of truth (reified as Truth) rather than value. Wang mentions Michael Sandel's consideration (in his *Justice: What's the Right Thing to Do?* [2010]) of justice being less about the distribution of things than it is about correctly valuing them. It also becomes a question that concerns fairness.

However, when I first returned from the academic trip to China, my feeling was that what I brought back was a reinvigoration of my innate sense of rebellion. We in the West are a pluralistic society that can revel in the process of spectacular dissent. It is our life blood or the air we breathe. This can be painful and might engineer the disparity of justice (such as the O.J. Simpson case of that time, or the Black Lives Matter and I Can't Breathe protests that are occurring as I am currently writing), but it also encourages a celebration of beauty and colour that for me appeared to be largely absent from the life pulse of China.

Wang argues that Chinese religious morality or the Confucian traditional ethos, specifically harmony over justice, may come to contribute to the future world. He recognises that today's challenges are 'terrorist attack and regional war, military hegemony and national [friction], cold-war mentality and zero-sum-game policy, trade protectionism and national supremacism' – all problems that I think, if we are being honest, we also need to admit to. And likewise, we in the West might be able to profit if we take into serious consideration the reality and achievement of the Chinese religio-political tradition. Good government in China has aspired toward keeping the peace through managing local sovereign states via the principles of its Confucian heritage. Nevertheless, Wang sees the necessity for economic equity and social justice as also foundational for a harmonious society in the global future and admits to this end that complementary Chinese and Western values might be advantageously integrated. Our principle concerns, accordingly, are the increasing divide between rich and poor, our diminishing resources and the need for environmental protection. In a sense, Beijing's national security law that is being imposed on Hong Kong doubtlessly arises from the Confucian desire for political harmony in place of warring states, but though Wang does not mention it, perhaps equally operative in this case is the traditionally influential *Fajia* or Chinese Legalism that has been compared to Machiavellianism and also seeks order, security and stability but through the application of fear. Consequently, the imposition of the security law on Hong Kong is seen as totalitarian to us in the West, but to the degree that the decree might be more a derivative of Confucianism, we may need to recognise and accept the legitimacy of cultural differences from our own way of seeing and doing things.

Complementary to Confucianism in China is Daoism. While the former focuses on Heaven, Earth and humanity as the constituents of the cosmos, the latter considers additionally the Dao. True enough, Laozi/Lao-tzu and Zhang Zai/Zhuang, respectively, convey the *dao* tautologically in the *Dao De Jing* and *Zhuangzi*. Nevertheless, despite the resultant obliqueness, we must understand the *dao* or 'Way' not as a thing but rather as collective movement. Perhaps essentially it approximates what contemporary Western pagans understand as 'nature' itself/herself. Compared to Confucianism, Daoism is certainly more colourful and seemingly more resonant with CWP, and its naturalism has been likened to Hellenic quietism. Rather than social conformity and political concern, Daoism focuses on the cosmos and the reciprocal *yin* and *yang* actuality of nature as well as their blending as a third vital force. If we keep the *dao* of change and/or nature in mind with the Great Union of Confucius, the Chinese concept of *tian-xia* ('all under Heaven') more fully corresponds culturally to the Hellenic *oikoumenē* and the ecumenical possibility of a comprehensive compassion, humanness and harmony. It is again through the possibility of a creative synthesis between Eastern and Western understandings, that a better world might become a possibility for our children and their children.

Confucius, of course, requires a more modern updating with regard to his language. For instance, the *wu lun* or 'five human relationships' he depicts are those of 'father and son, husband and wife, ruler and minister, elder and younger brothers, and peers and friends'. We look in vain for mention of 'mother and son, father and daughter, brothers and sisters' and the like. Confucius lived and wrote in a patriarchal-feudal time that does not reflect today's awareness of gender equality. But we need not throw the baby out with the bathwater (one of my favourite phrases) but instead use our skills and imagination to grasp the underlying humanism of his pagan thought. Another problem, however, with the Confucian ideal of moderation and decorum is that it leaves little room for the excesses of Dionysus. Perhaps it is here that the non-conformity of Daoism has an important role to play. The seeking of both pleasure and freedom are vital to the Western spirit. The navigation between the wild and the moderate is something to be carefully balanced and managed. In this light, we ought to notice the radical contrast between traditional Chinese body-mind oneness and Platonic body-mind dichotomy. Despite the body and mind/soul distinction in Chinese awareness, there is no *soma sema* or 'body as the prison of the soul' belief. This allows us to appreciate the fundamental pagan/telluric affinity of Chinese religiosity. World-rejection is not a part of it. Without doubt, the Dionysian is more a part of a Western pagan acceptance of worldly life than it is for the Chinese in their desire for the mode of harmony as the predominant operative, but the mutual affinity between respective non-transcendental valuing is an important awareness and cooperative possibility for which we ought not lose sight.

But finally, what I find most beautiful within the spiritual or religio-political tradition of China is the idea that harmony originates from music. As Wang points out, the Chinese words for 'music' (*yue*) and 'joy' (*le*) are written with the same character. The seminal Confucian notion of the rites-music function and its interaction with the cosmic law is that ritual applies externally while music cultivates from within. The importance of poetry, music and dance cannot be underestimated for the Chinese, and this in itself provides the possibility of another bridge between East and West. Doubtlessly, the music of China with its pentatonic scales and application to the doctrine of the Golden Mean differs substantially from Western music based variously on diatonic scales of seven notes to a key – both major or minor, the chromatic scale of whole tones, the blues scale and/or atonal approaches as well as varieties of rhythm, syncopation, dissonance, improvisation and sometimes predominately conveying mystery or dramatic emotion. Whether music always brings about unity and harmony is a nice thought but doubtful to some degree for the Western context. Nevertheless, the joyful quality of music throughout the world – even when it might also convey sorrow or pathos as well as reflection, pleasure, anger, reverence, love and/or surprise – maybe even licentiousness, dissonance and seduction – opens one and all to the possibilities of living life more to the full.

After I had completed my Ph.D. studies, I was captivated by academia and wanted to teach. But this period coincided with the time that universities and colleges had become overstretched and were cutting down on their teaching staffs; not hiring additional lecturers. During the expedition in China, several people gave me various suggestions, but these all came to naught. Judith, however, gave me good advice for formulating my *curriculum vitae*. Howard Fenton, my dear former art professor, was instrumental in my securing the visiting position with the College of Creative Studies. When Richard and I had been in Isla Vista for the UCSB teaching sojourn, I re-fell in love with my old 'shamanic coast', and both of us wanted to find property in the area or within Santa Barbara itself. But once we got to San Francisco, our desire to be there prevailed over the possibility of Southern California. We began to look at various properties for sale and were outbid on the one on which we had first decided. But what was meant to be was the Castro property on Market Street – six units plus garage: a large Edwardian house on the street itself and a lovely Victorian house behind it. Eventually I learned that after the 1906 earthquake, the Victorian house had then been dragged further back and the Edwardian building was constructed on its former site. The actual purchase of the two houses occurred in late September when we were back in London.

The Victorian house had two occupied flats on the lower level. For the house itself, through thrift shops, yard sales and the occasional antique shop, we set it up in a beautiful fashion, and when my mother would visit, she adored it. Richard and I took possession of the two upper floors in the main building and lived in the uppermost. It was always a semi-exhausting climb to reach, but there was a sun deck off the kitchen in the back, and this was an additional joy. We adored to be once again living in San Francisco where we had originally met. It is certainly one of the most attractive cities in the world – a finger where nature and humanity's urban achievement kiss. And there is a unique excitement that belongs to San Francisco alone and propelled by her vibrant history that one senses to be still alive just beneath today's dynamic façade. We had begun sleeping in the flat by the very end of November and had our house warming party for forty people on the Saturnalia in December.

In writing this present roundabout critique of contemporary Western paganism which entails also what is my 'life-story', I am involved accordingly to read through 40+ years of journal records. With San Francisco alone, I am amazed over the amount of things we were involved with and did virtually each day (exhausting to conceive of now) as well as the amount of friends and loved ones with whom we were regularly engaged but who are no longer with us. During the present stage of the pandemic for which the United Kingdom is currently attributing over 41,000 deaths, besides this immediate work, I am also redrafting my will and attempting to extend the lease on the flat. In short, the emotional effect is the feeling that I am now 'wrapping things up'. What further amazes me in recollecting my past with Richard if not beyond has been the amount of travelling and moving between residences we did, but it is the loss of the 'so many' that is the most astonishing to realise. If there is a postmortem gathering, it cannot be other than joyful.

While not connected to San Francisco but rather our village in the Midi, Barbara Floyd Dauphin is one more of the 'many'. She passed, and unfortunately not easily, last year. We knew her as an American from California though originally from Connecticut. She was very proud of having some Narragansett Indian ancestry. Exactly one year and one day younger than

Richard and a half year less one day older than I am, she had missed the entire 1960s by being already in the south of France. She had come to study under the German painter and art educator Leo Marchutz (1903–1976) in Aix-en-Provence. An affair that had since terminated brought her to our village, and though she had an alcohol problem and had become virtually the town mascot, she was invaluable for Richard and me as a liaison who could tell us what to do and not to do but also explain to the Provençal locals why we did the things we did. Eventually, when she became anxious over the imminent arrival of Lyn (whose husband William had been the Lafayette man who fell out of his tree house that I had read on the front page in the newspaper on my last day the first time I was moving from San Francisco) and for whom Barbara was working as *le gardien*, we suggested that this could be the perfect moment for her to be checked into the alcohol clinic so that she could avoid Lyn who as lovely as she was could also be wrathful as an employer. Barbara asked the town doctor about the clinic, and he arranged it immediately before she could reconsider. The upshot was that Barbara never drank again – apart for the time that Richard and I had given her some chocolates that unthinkingly we did not realise contained some alcohol filling. She was furious with us, but we never did that one again. I should also add the irony that Barbara turned out to be the cousin of my college roommate's best friend. Richard and my counterculture background always amused Barbara, and finally we all convinced her to visit India. She came to revere Ramana Maharshi and returned a quietly self-proclaimed guru herself and did thereby come to help various others of the locals.

Before the clinic and all that followed, there was a time that Barbara's funding had ceased. We did not know it when it first happened, but Barbara's father was reinvesting what had been her financial source and nothing was forthcoming in the interim. She had to move in with us and could not find employment without a work permit, but the only way she could get a permit for France was to marry her boyfriend Louis. When their on-again/off-again relationship had first begun, Louis was on his knees begging Barbara to marry him, but she was still thinking of the school teacher with whom she had originally come to our *oppidum*. By now, Louis no longer wanted to marry because Barbara never became pregnant. And why? 'Because the acid level in my body is too high, it kills the sperm too soon'. So off I go to the local health shop in Draguignan and ask for something that could reduce one's acidic level. I am given an elixir with the instructions to take a spoonful three times a day followed each time by a large glass of water.

Barbara does this for two-and-a-half days and then says, 'This is ridiculous' and throws the tonic away. Louis had stopped seeing her just as she discontinued the 'treatment' that I had hoped might do the trick. In time, Barbara developed severe cramps. A medical check in Marseilles ensued, and they wanted immediately to remove her appendix. Barbara's response was that Marseilles was too far away and no one would visit her. A second diagnosis this time in Draguignan said that her problem was that she smoked too much. Several months without menstruation passed, and finally I dragged Barbara into the pharmacy to ask for the pregnancy test. She had to do this herself because I did not think my French was enough sufficient. Barbara burst out laughing and said, 'If you are paying for this, do you realise what everyone is going to think?'

'I don't care', I replied. 'Just get the test!' And she hit the bull's eye. Louis and Barbara married two weeks before 'Daisy' was born. While there is so much more to the story, Barbara's daughter Natacha Dauphin has recently published the first volume of her own book, *Letters from the Wound* (2020). And almost needless to say, though we miss her mother, Natacha has become a joy in our life.

When one reviews the past, one's own past, there is the kaleidoscope of reliving it. On a broader level, we seem currently to be re-addressing much of our collective past. Along with the COVID-19 pandemic, the Black Lives Matter protests are having us question the memorials to social benefactors who were also slave traders and/or systemic racists. It may also be true that 'All Lives Matter', but not when signs proclaiming such are to be seen carried by white supremacist protestors mockingly appearing on a bent knee. I am proud to be able to affirm that a quarter of my own family is black. I do agree with the protest against destruction as well as with the sentiment that we cannot or ought not whitewash the dark periods of our history. The statues against which many are now demonstrating could, instead of being destroyed, be put in museums so that the past is not forgotten but is still something from which we might be provoked to learn. On the BBC's Radio Four today, in his 'Thought for the Day', Bishop Richard Harris talks about 're-evaluating the past'. He claims that we can find four times in the New Testament the phrase, 'The last shall be first and the first last'. The thought that immediately comes to my mind in re-evaluating the past and the first becoming the last is, of course, paganism as the first of religion or spirituality and hopefully the last in coming full circle into re-valuing, protecting and understanding nature as first and holy. It is with this renewed awareness as a restored spiritual foundation, I want to affirm, can we not only re-address the environment and the needs of a balanced and sustainable world but also the viability of true justice, freedom and equality without oppression.

But to keep reality in perspective, when Ram Shankar Tripathi, the chief mahant of the Vishwanath temple in Varanasi, had reported to the police that one of the gold panels had been apparently stolen from the *shikhara*, he was replaced for several years by a government appointed administrator. After a year or so, Ramakant Mishra became inflated with his authority and refused me permission to enter the temple. Beside the Śitala *mandir* at Daśaśwamedh Ghat, the Golden Temple had been the one in which I most performed *pūjā*, so my ban was painful and upsetting. There may have been a few times that I did manage to enter the shrine complex, but the one I remember was during the time of Shivaratri and I swept in with the throngs. Mishra saw me on this occasion and was furious, but with the hoard of worshippers on the occasion there was little he could do about it. And then one year when I returned to Kāshī, Mishra was gone – finally! It was a February and was cold but could have been colder. It even rained during the *snan* or morning bath in the river, but after this I went once again freely to the temple. The crush of crowd entering the sanctum was horrendous. The bells were clanging at such a pitch that it seemed as if one was entering for ritual sacrifice. I had left my water pot at the *mala*s stand, but it did not matter. The *lingam* was as powerful – and soothing – as ever. I proceeded in the process to become completely drenched as someone in the frenzy poured their entire pail of oblation over my head rather than on Vishwanath. But this too did not matter and only added to the stunned dishevelment of the occasion. The temple itself was too frantic to enjoy, but the Vishnu priest garlanded me – as did the others who were all happy to see me once again, and I was given both a tangerine and some sugar *prasad*. While officially all this was Hinduism, for me it was blatant paganism. And since I was last in Varanasi, Swami Ji has had solar panels installed to the Golden Temple for electricity with the stipulated agreement that *mlecchas*, that is, foreigners, not be prevented to enter for purposes of worship.

There were, almost needless to say, other times in which the number of worshippers were less, and I was able to have a long and what I would describe as a full encounter with the Vishwanath *lingam*. And music speaks. I remember witnessing a small group of villagers approaching Vishwanath for a once-in-their-lifetime *darshan* of the deity. They had hired drummers to lead their way. I found it so moving that it brought me close to tears. The next day, I saw the Madhya Pradesh Chief Minister, Arjun Singh, enter the Golden Temple with party members and police escort. He was at this moment considered to be a possible future Prime Minister of India. The aura of his presence and response, a mute intensity, was almost as moving as was that of the *deshis* of the previous day. My morning plunge into the river, my persistent morning and evening rounds of *pūjā*, boating excursions on the Ganges, concerts, domestic and restaurant meals, *chola matar*, continuous reading and all along with chronic insomnia, wicked colds, digestion problems and persistent illness were all because of my desire to become familiar as completely as I could with something paganesque but non-Western.

In connection with this last, there does seem to me to be a prevailing arrogance with Westerners – whether pagan or otherwise. Yes, we have a freedom spiritually to do what we will – including to interpret or even make things up as these 'resonate' personally with ourselves individually. And I suppose this is particularly true for solitaries among whom I consider myself to be for the most part. But at the same time, especially to the degree that we might cultivate a sense of humility and humbleness – and for pagans in particular, there are important things to learn and awarenesses to gain from those who have been able to remain closer to their indigenous and elemental origins. This is what India has been for me with her possibility of a relentless engagement with *pūjā* and encounter with a special understanding of the gods. The other is a many, and from one like the vernacular Hindu or from Native Americans, Shinto, the African diaspora and so forth, we of the West might learn, *not appropriate,* but learn a nuance and the insight that has been trampled under and lost by our Abrahamic traditions and secular/bureaucratic blinding affirmations. Foremost, and as the sociologist Max Weber discerned, we have lost the sense and impact of enchantment. Perhaps this is not only a pagan loss, but enchantment began with what we may signal as pagan, and for the West, pagans are or at least should be the preeminent re-discoverers of magical delight.

During our first five-and-a-half months as San Francisco landlords, Richard and I took a two-month hiatus to the East Coast (Manhattan, Woodstock and Narragansett) after the struggle with finding people to rent our Market Street flats, the even greater struggle with computer hassle in those comparatively early but now obsolete days (preparing camera-ready copies, constant revisions, printing and re-printing, etc.) and with our fruitless effort to establish the Victorian house as a New Age centre (the Kashi House's American Center for Efficacious Service/ACES). These were not the happiest of times, though San Francisco provides her own comforts along with the friends we had there and the dinners, even banquets, at home, in restaurants or at the houses of friends. There was indeed a schizoid alteration between attempting to secure rental income vis-à-vis a vision launching. We had a stand at the Expo in the Fashion Center, and the woman at the booth next to us thought we were a cereal. The Kashi House's initial opening day was a relative flop, and when someone from Los Angeles performed a smudging for the occasion, it drove everyone out of the house and ended the day's activities. From the Expo itself, we had met Ken Phelps, a channeller, who gave a talk on 'Metaphysical Products'. Other speakers for our Open Day included Ramana Das and Marilyn Silbey on 'Healing through the power of Ecstatic Sound', me on 'Cultivating Religion' and two presentations on Vibrational Healing – 'Introduction' by Kala Lyons, and 'Massages Fluid Movement' by Joanna Brown. Jesse Golden gave two talks as 'Wellness Previews', and subsequently we held several Nikken Silver Trainings that employed an NLP approach for their 'pyramid scheme' involving the sale of magnet products. It was also during this time that I was with my dear friend Donald when he died of AIDS at the San Francisco Veterans Affairs Medical Center. I had been sitting with him in the hospital and sensed something. He had not been consciously awake since the day before. I held him and said, 'Donald, just do it! We're all here, and we love you. Just do it now!' and he did. His wish was to be released from earthly life and complete what he insisted was his last incarnation (he referred to himself as an 'Evolved Master'). Back at the Market Street house, Richard felt a great spirit of 'joyous liftoff' at this very time.

During this same interim, there was the Oklahoma City bombing, the finalisation of my parents' divorce, the appearance of the Sisters of Perpetual Indulgence in Castro Street, a memorial gathering in the Kashi House for Donald, and a moment in the front house during Pride when we had to interrupt the dinner for eight of us including my mother to rush to the front windows overlooking Market Street to watch the Dykes on Bikes pass by. I also had learned two months earlier that Lee Brevard had passed in Los Angeles the previous December. He was one of my few gay friends who was HIV negative. We had originally met in London when he was struggling as an unsuccessful artist in Paris. Eventually he gave up on his time in Europe and moved to LA where he became fascinated with acquiring gemstones. He went on to become a highly successful fine jewellery designer whose clients included Heather Locklear, Farrah Fawcett, Susan Sarandon, Julia Roberts and Candace Bergen. One day Lee received a call from Elizabeth

Taylor asking him to make for her a necklace. 'I thought you said you were not going to buy from me anymore', he replied.

'Well, there is no one as good as you'. Lee explained that it would take him at least a month to produce what she wanted. Elizabeth retorted angrily, 'If I went to Nieman Marcus I could have it in a week!'

Lee snapped back, 'Don't you *ever* compare me to a department store!'

'Oh', she replied dejectedly, 'You have me over a barrel'. Lee was that good and could, with pleasure, get his way. He died suddenly at the age of 45 from a heart attack.

On the East Coast, in between the fabulous beach at summer time, a visit from the London family, and my constant explorations, I was able to continue my numinal activities. In San Francisco, these had included visits to Chinese temples – both Daoist and Buddhist, the occasional *lingam* for purposes of *pūjā* and initial pursuits into Santería and Voodoo. I had the great joy in the San Francisco house to have an altar room, my first and only. The central shrine was Indo-European, and this was flanked by an Afro-Latin altar on one side and a Chinese one on the other. Nancy had asked at one point if a 'friend' from Fort Collins who was moving to San Francisco could stay at our house. I was away at this time, but Richard allowed him to sleep in the altar room until a space became available elsewhere in the flat below ours. We only learned much later and after smoking pot with him on several occasions that he was an 'ex-cop' and a Christian. He admitted in his deposition against us subsequently when suing for harassment and wrongful eviction that he had told us he would be moving out to his own house (he had sold his property in Colorado but only learned after this how much more expensive and unaffordable San Francisco had become property-wise) and accused us of being into 'Devil worship'. I can say little more on this deeply upsetting experience because the settlement the insurance companies arranged included a 'gag order'. Our house insurance was cancelled shortly later, but our agent was not only able to get it subsequently re-instated but also with a lower premium. But I would like to say that in my perspective the Christian God if not the Abrahamic one more fully is guilt – guilt and shame, and hence his preoccupation with these – these and sin. His dichotomy (technically called theodicy) is the inability to reconcile perfection and the existence of evil. It is difficult if even possible to account for both. This discrepancy is what accounts for the rich theological tradition of Christianity: its attempt to answer the impossible. God's only possibility for atonement is his sacrifice which for God would be eternal. A pagan, however, would rather and more simply bypass such an entity as simply not being worth the bother.

And after seven months in 1995, I was back again in India. My *pūjā* guru's brother, Ajit, and best Indian friend met me in Delhi. After a few days, we flew to Khajuraho and, for me, it was once again the magnificent Chandela pornographic and/or *Kama Sutra* derived temples dating from the 10th and 11th centuries. Reading at the time Nigel Pennick and Prudence Jones' *A History of Pagan Europe* made the combination of spiritualities in both Europe and the Kalinjar area of central India especially intense. In the village adjacent to the temples, I came across an extraordinary 800-year-old idol of Rama with mesmerising eyes being offered for sale at 10,000 rupees (later reduced to 8,000), but besides weighing what felt like a ton and being riskily difficult to get through customs out of India, I did not have the necessary funds with me (having forgotten to bring dollars or pounds along from home) – an opportunity I have always since regretted missing.

In Banaras it was back to the usual rounds of *pūjā* and effort toward daily survival. The heat was excruciating and felt like Vritra in the form of unmitigated constriction and oppression and virtually precluding any possibility of *joie de vivre*. We were approaching the festival of Divali, and there was a sudden invasion of thousands upon thousands of insects: beetles, grasshoppers, mantis, butterflies, etc. They were everywhere: as a completely thick and crunching carpet when one attempted to walk, inside one's clothes, biting during sleep. This was a short one-month visit. I had gone for the solar eclipse, and if I had gone not too far south of Kāshī, it would have been total. But I wanted to be in the river itself at the time wishing for world peace. I kept silence for several hours in advance of the obscuration and then went into the river. It became colder and colder and movingly dark but never night. While the ghats were absolutely packed, the Hindus are highly superstitious concerning an eclipse and most temples (Vishwanath, Visalashi) and virtually all shops were shut tight. Śitala itself was operating, and not too long after the eclipse it became warm and all went back to normal. To bathe in this sacred river becomes a noetic encounter with nature and is akin to worship in a temple as an experience of the anomalous – both affording contacts with an ineffable divine concentration. When, on this occasion, I left what I believe to be the oldest city in the world, I arrived in Delhi late in the evening. Mary Pat Fisher met me and took me to Gobind Sadan where I was introduced to Baba Versa Singh. He told me to find peace within, make friends with it and spread it naturally by example. I found him cute, and the audience with him was sweet. His message was simple, God-based and not really commensurate with the complexities of the human venture. The Sikh ambience, however, was refreshing and enchanting. I was back at the airport after midnight, and my flight to London departed around 3 am.

Richard flew in from San Francisco at the same time, and we were able to catch at Drill Hall the latest Bloolips show, 'The Island of Lost Shoes', before getting to Amsterdam for a week and after that to the Provence for another week. We were checking on the properties, but just as we were going out the door of the London flat, Marion Bowman phoned and asked if I might be interested in a Research Fellowship at what was then still the Bath College of Higher Education. To the possibility of a job, I could not say 'no'. After Amsterdam, it was the Midi and learning that Paula in Aix-en-Provence had been diagnosed with a malignant tumour of the pancreas and that she had not told her husband Jacques. 'He is like Richard and needs to be protected'. She was fine for herself and only worried about Jacques. From the farm, we returned to Amsterdam for three nights and a Thanksgiving dinner with dear friends Stephan and Koen. Then we were back again to London for almost two weeks in which we included a Scotch Malt Whisky Society tasting that was held in the Middle Temple Hall, Nicole Kidman in *To Die For*, Edward Albee's *Three Tall Women* with Maggie Smith, Alan Bates in Ibsen's *The Master Builder*, a Talking Stick evening with Paul Devereux speaking about the link between crop circles, stone circles and the solar system, and the second conference that was sponsored by the charity Elisabeth Arweck and I had founded, the Academy for Cultural and Educational Studies (ACES). This last was 'Christians and pagans: Can Divergent Traditions Converse? A Contemporary Dialogue' and was held at my alma mater, King's College London. Our speakers were Edward Bailey, Peggy Morgan and Keith Ward for the Christians and Steve Wilson, Prudence Jones and Ronald Hutton for the pagans. After our lunch break, Ronald in a not most delicate manner challenged the Christians for exalting St. Paul who is in reality 'a second-rate writer' and then became incensed with the 'privileged position' of the Christian reply. Prudence told me after that she thought Keith had answered Ronald beautifully. But it was almost as if lightning had struck, and Harriet Crabtree then attacked ACES itself. This being Elisabeth's 'baby', she rose magnificently to the defence. The irony with all this is that we had recorded the day's proceedings, but in listening to the tape, the lightning strike and upheaval do not come across at all, and all sounds serenely calm – even Ronald. This has made me wonder if some events occur only for the very moment and cannot be recorded because their existence is purely and only *ad hoc*.

London was followed by two nights in Amsterdam. Jackie had just died suddenly. She was Dutch and one of us who had originally formed the Amsterdam commune. She had been instrumental when we had extended with the Friesian farm fiasco by getting into the contract the clause that saved us. We stretched our Amsterdam stay by one day to attend her funeral. Then after six nights in a Paris paralysed by a transport strike, we had one further night in Amsterdam and finally three nights in Glastonbury at Little St. Michael's and Chalice Well before the interview in Bath. And I got the job!

We finished the remainder of the Roman yuletide in London and after Boxing Day were back to San Francisco for New Year's. I stayed for only the first week of 1996 and then left Richard to assume the role of landlord while I flew off to Amsterdam for a 'swimmer's ear' operation in Leiden. Years later when I was told in France that I should have my other ear operated on as well, I balked at first over the prospect of again having the ear sliced open from behind, but the otologist in Draguignan assured me that now that former procedure was 'medieval' and it involved instead an outpatient process rather than requiring the three nights I had had in the Leiden hospital. The second *otitus externa* surgery (though for me this concerned the closing off of the middle ear canal rather than infection of the outer canal) was a liberating revelation. Because of the sensitivity of the procedure, the sedation is extremely intense in order to prevent totally any bodily movement. I realised once I was again awake that in death one will not even know one has died – that there is a complete cessation and no consciousness at all. I suppose this is pure Epicurus who contended that when one is alive, there is death, and when one has died, there is nothing at all, including fear. But after the earlier surgery in The Netherlands, I proceeded during the first two months to shuttle back and forth between Bath/London and Amsterdam/Leiden. Apart for the salary, the Research Fellowship was a dream job until the funding ran out. I was unbelievably free and encouraged to travel for research purposes as much as was possible. For six years I attended academic conferences on both sides of the Pond and sojourned when not in Bath at my mother's homes in Naples, Florida and Narragansett, Rhode Island, with Richard in San Francisco, and with the temples of Varanasi.

On this pagan question of afterlife, whether there is one or there is complete cessation and oblivion, I will admit that the latter has a certain appeal. Many contemporary Western pagans hold to a belief in reincarnation. Whether this is a predominant view, I am unable to say, but it does also have an attraction. For pagans, rebirth is not considered a negative or punishment as it is in the dharmic traditions. Instead of life being something from which to escape, in a pagan understanding it is instead something to welcome, embrace and celebrate. This applies to either case: whether we have many lives or that this one that we do have is it, the only one we have.

A major influence for me has been Åke Hultkrantz' 1953 *Conceptions of the Soul Among North American Indians: A Study in Religious Ethnology*. I believe this was originally his PhD dissertation. Somehow, I suppose during my research into the Native American culture of central California (the San Francisco Bay Area and surroundings), I came across this book in the San Francisco State College library. Hultkrantz (1920–2006) discovers the Native American notion of soul-duality. Unlike the single soul idea of Christianity or the Abrahamic religions, there is the belief in a body-soul or life-soul which is what animates the body but also a dream-soul or free-soul through which we experience our dreams, trance or delirium as it wanders when we are asleep. In Indian culture, if for some reason the dream-soul was unable to return to the body upon waking (soul loss), mental illness or insanity would be the result. If not being permanently insane, usually the individual is expected to die within the ensuing six months. A basic function of the shaman, in fact, is the recovery of a person's lost soul.

The ego or consciousness belongs to the body/body-soul but is detachable. When we sleep, it is what then joins the wandering dream-soul. So our conscious mind alternates between the two fundamental souls, the life-soul and the free-soul. For Native Americans, the ego is thought to transfer permanently to the free-soul upon death or shortly before the body dies. That is probably why the seeing of one's *doppelgänger* is, apart for the shaman, taken as a signal of one's impending decease. But if we look at other pagan traditions besides those of the American Indian, we tend to find similar understandings of soul-duality – with the ancient Egyptian *ka* 'breath' and *ba* 'spirit' being prime examples but also the Greek distinction between *pneuma* and *psyche*, the Roman between the *anima*/*animus* and *spiritus*, the Confucian or Chinese 'lower'/corporeal soul of the earth (the *po* or the *shen*) and the rational principle (*hun*). The former ends with death and then at best is the ghost, while the latter, the ethereal soul, becomes the object of ancestor worship. Soul-duality is to be found among other pagan peoples as well including the Austronesians and Polynesians. In English, the duality is perhaps best understood through the terms of 'soul' and 'spirit'.

There are, of course, many variants, and for some the multiplicity of souls is more than just two. On some occasions, there are several souls that comprise the body-soul itself. But what is of particular interest is how soul-duality fits with both reincarnation and afterlife. The body-soul is variously thought to cease either with the body's expiry or at some time after this. If there is an interim between the two, this would be the time in which the person's remnant survives as a ghost. For the Greeks, the ghostly body-soul becomes the *skiá* or 'shade', possibly *fántasma,* that dwells in Hades. This shadow of the self would continue to persist as long as descendants continue to honour it or to the degree that the fame or remembrance of the person keeps her/him alive in cultural/social/historic memory. For example, Mozart lives through his music, Rembrandt through his art, Einstein through his scientific legacy, Lincoln through his politics and so forth. While the duration may vary, I tend to picture the expiring body-soul like a drop of water that falls into the ocean. Ultimately it loses individuality and merges with the whole becoming one with the world soul or collective consciousness.

But there is also the free-soul to which one's individual- or ego-consciousness is thought to link up permanently around the time of death. It would be this soul that finds its afterlife in Elysium, the Western Isles, the Isles of the Blessed, the White Island in the Black Sea, the Vedic Svarga, the Otherworld, the Egyptian Aaru/Field of Reeds, the Slavic Vyraj, Shamballa, Bardo, Sukhāvatī/Amitābha's Pure Land of Bliss, Ullr's Ýdalir ('Yewdale'), the *orbis alius,* Fairyland, the end of the Milky Way or even the Milky Way itself, the happy hunting ground, the paradisiacal garden at the crown of the cosmic tree/*axis mundi,* the light of the dawn or what contemporary Western pagans often refer to as Summerland. For some, the joy of the Western Paradise is interminable, but others conceive it as a heaven that exists between incarnations. It would seem that in keeping with pagan affirmations of freedom, the choice would be left to the postmortem dream-soul itself/herself/himself. In other words, the dream-soul/free-soul might choose to rejoin corporeal reality. Some would understand this more or less along theosophical lines as reincarnation, but I believe the fuller pagan understanding recognises the 're-incarnating' free-soul more in terms of its becoming the guardian spirit of a newborn. For the Romans, this would be the *genius* for the male or the *juno* for the female. In other words, the reborn free-soul is not the body and ego themselves but their protective spirit. We may merge with our dream-soul during sleep or trance, but this merger only becomes final when our physical selves die. This would possibly explain why most of us cannot remember or recall our supposed previous lives. They are not ours but belong instead to our guardian spirits.

Consequently, the pagan possibility that lies ahead is either complete annihilation as Epicurus would have it or the various Summerland/netherworld existences as the great welter of earth traditions and folklore would have it. Most importantly, however, we do not have in pagan conceptualising of the afterlife a fundamental idea of eternal damnation in an everlasting and inescapable hell. This last is not paganism. Perhaps for certain extreme evil doers such as Hitler and ISIL jihadists there might be a total obliteration upon death, that is, a final rejection of the individual's conscious ego by the person's guardian spirit, but more likely one's negative *karma* excludes any immediate possibility of becoming one of the *di manes* or *pitri* and instead at first a ghoul, malicious *kobold*, frightening spectre, Chinese *guei*, Japanese *kappa* or *tengu* and the like. Even with the co-nature of the otherworld, all is still nature, and with nature *tout change*, everything changes. There is no rigid fixity, and everything retains the potential and possibility for growth and development. And this last even would ultimately include Sisyphus, Tantalus, Tityus, Ixion, Oknus and the Danaids whose unending punishments served as cautionary examples to illustrate the unforgivable consequences that result from *hybris* or hubris in defiance of the gods. Consequently, we can see with these last as with Loki's confinement notions that come close to representing perpetual torture even within paganism, but I will still maintain that the gods and nature or both are not at the end of the day vindictive. Revenge and malignant perdition belong to neither.

I have read recently that had Christianity not obliterated pagan spirituality as it had, paganism itself would have developed the same attitude concerning marriage as only permissible between a man and a woman. At first glance, this seems almost preposterous, but the argument was that with the ascent of Platonism during the days of late paganism, the previous flexibility and acceptance if not even endorsement of homosexuality was already coming to an end. Certainly, Platonic denunciation of pleasure and sensuality opened the way for Christianity – perhaps in a similar fashion as did the rise of the worship of Odin encourage the same to occur in Scandinavia. With its increasingly and tightly organised clergy – whether an extension of the Persian *magi* or not (my speculative argument in my *The Divine versus the Asurian*), the Church made a consistent and ultimately successful endeavour to erase earth religion and the polytheism that had been associated with it. Christianity is a religion that appears to hold its own during unchallenging times but then to capitalise on uncertainty and fear when a people are under siege by a military enemy or a plague or some other disaster. Practices to which the Church is opposed are denounced as sin, and the rationale of guilt is then employed to cajole those who are suffering into repentance and submission. It is a clever tactic and one that has served the expansion of Christian imperialism and colonialism well.

The renaissance and reawakening of contemporary pagan ways of thinking – particularly in the West but also with the growing promotion of indigenous spiritualities as well as their diasporic extensions as both akin and equally legitimate – are hopefully positive developments, especially for a world that seems to be perpetually out of sync. But the current emergence of so-called 'woke' culture is darkening the horizon of dawning hope. There is no real question that 'black lives matter' as much as any life, and the protest calls for radical police reform following the murder of George Floyd, and the need to shift racial prejudice into a greater recognition of the needs for both opportunity and the cessation of hateful cruelty, have become a paramount global concern. *Woke* came to prominence as an African American Vernacular English byword for social awareness and the necessary self-awareness that comes with a communal consciousness that will question a dominant paradigm of engrained and traditional prejudice. And after the 2014 shooting death of Michael Brown in Ferguson, Missouri, *woke* has become not just a designation for an awakened consciousness but also an activist term for the developing anger against injustice and racial tension. Apart from some regressive Heathens or Odinists and other ultra-conservative chauvinists, there are few pagans who would disagree with the basic parameters of the woke dynamic to this point concerning parity and fairness as well as understanding the denouement of 'white privilege'.

However, the idea of woke culture is also increasingly being used as a part of social media activism and the imposition of 'political correctness'. This last employs forms of public humiliation and even death threats against individuals and/or groups who are perceived to be offensive by those who follow in the path of the 'outrage culture' that has morphed from Woke AF consciousness. The use of shaming is the main tool now employed by current 'call-out' awareness, and contemporary Western pagans appear also to be infected by this kind of behaviour that in my opinion remains incommensurate with the spirit of open-minded organic paganism.

One of the standing arguments I have with Richard is over the rights of transgenderism. And it is not that he is against rights *per se*, but he is adamantly opposed to tampering with one's birth body such as through injectable dermal or facial filler, breast augmentation using implants, cross-sex hormone therapy and, especially, sex reassignment surgery. He sees the desire to be 're-created from a hospital' as unsexy, boring and a reflection of the individual being stuck in a particular mind-frame only. It is denial of the body's physicality that our parents produced, and the idea that one can play only one role in one body is not at all interesting for Richard. Being just one thing and not the other is ludicrous. He is for the honouring of both the male and female natures that we all have as individuals.

Though I am certainly opposed to bio-gender interference before one has reached the stage of adult decision-making, my contrasting position to Richard's is more one of 'live and let live.' I may not want to endorse the necessary physical/surgical process any more than he does, but if a person desires to be other than what their birth predisposes him or her to be, it is from my perspective their unquestionable right to choose to pursue freely whatever possibilities technology affords. As long as one harms not another, a person must have the liberty to attempt to be who the person wants to be – whether a straight male, a gay male, an effeminate male, a straight woman, a lesbian, a butch dyke, a transgender, a non-binary or a bi-sexual. No one is obligated to please me or anyone other than the person himself/herself alone. I will grant that surgery and the rest is a risky process and that there is no certainty that a person will be happier rather than less happy following transition. There is indeed a distressing ratio of transgender suicides, but such is a hazard consequent upon the freedom of choice in the first place. An individual must be free to decide, and then it is incumbent upon the rest of us to accept and support the decisions made.

Part of the problem for today, and no less for pagans as for others, is that – as Richard puts it – liberalism accepts too much. I see this, however, more as an insistence than merely an acceptance. The thought-police infesting social media too often act without thinking. There is a 'jumping onto the bandwagon' thoughtlessness that appears too readily to become enraged and to accuse without the benefit of supporting evidence or mindful consideration. When this occurs within paganism, I find it particularly distressing and out of proportion to what I understand or at least wish organic pagan latitude to be. The extreme condemnation of J.K. Rowling and of female-born-women (FBWs) who want not only their occasional own space (for purposes of ritual, discussion and/or self-expression) is highly questionable in the least. FBWs also respectfully wish to be recognised as the females they are and who have been struggling arduously not to be continually erased or reduced to second class citizenship. Equality in pay and work treatment, awareness that female healthcare differs from the medical needs of men, and Me Too protections against rape and intimidation are all legitimate female concerns, and while the transgender female may share with some of these, menstruation, pregnancy, childbirth and the repressive tribulations that have been suffered all their lives by women in a 'patriarchal' society in which the male is both the stronger and dominant are longstanding issues with which women *as* women have been able to make some gains, however painstakingly. Much has been achieved, but the fairer world we desire is still something yet to attain and far from being a *fait accompli*. When women seek to concentrate on biological female issues and on their own terms, what kind of pagan other than misogynist traditionalists and now, apparently, irate transgender activists with their 'woke trans-allies' would be opposed?

None of us can have everything, and this is a basic condition to life itself. Sanity forces us to accept such – sanity and wisdom rather than some demanding impetuousness and me-and-mine-alone selfishness. We all think differently, and again, as long as the principle 'an' ye harm none' operates, separate spaces for those who wish are viable for certain occasions. We become little different than Nazis if and when we endeavour to trample quests for personal and group individuality under our own demands and insistences. Blanketly to denounce the efforts and desires of birth sisterhood as 'trans-exclusionary radical feminists' or TERFs differs little from jihadist labelling of someone as an infidel and meriting to be killed for not believing the same as the jihadist. Certainly, the jihadist but also the 'politically correct' bandwagon joiner and the social-media woke activist do not understand the generous beauty of a genuine pagan awareness – one that is in tune with the organic naturalism of tolerance. The desire 'to make space' is not to disallow the universe to change but to encourage it to be multiple and inclusive as well as to recognise that there are times or situations in which transgender women's womanhood is different and works against cis women's womanhood with its own biological realities. The need for transgender acceptance in all fairness requires also the undertaking to acknowledge the biological female's crusade for acknowledging the consequences of socially constructed identity when the different players of the society are not intrinsically comparable participants. Like it or not, we are required to concede the space wanted by female-born-women without it being jeopardised by men and/or men who want to be women. There is no need for cis women to be punched, shut up, made to yield passively or re-educated. Paganism celebrates diversity, and diversity includes men, women, transgender women, transgender men and intersex as not always conflated identities.

Consequently, it is difficult to deny that the hard-won sex-based rights for women are under threat by the so-called 'trans lobby'. This last, as distinct from many and probably a majority of trans people themselves, vociferously argues that one can change biological sex along with changing gender identity. I have heard that the trans lobby is possibly a part of the transhumanist movement that believes in the evolution through science and technology of the human being beyond our current physical and mental limitations. Maybe so, but again there is no need to conflate the intermediary and post-human with those who remain 'below' with more immediate political and social urgencies and desiderata. I suspect that the transhumanist has more desire for achieving the transcendent and freedom from the body than for enjoying the telluric itself.

I suppose I should have and perhaps could have questioned initially what I was doing by plunging into such intense Hindu temple and shrine veneration in India over a period of 20 years. I have little recollection of my actual reasons at the start, ostensibly to gain an idea of the mechanics and processes involved within a pagan-type temple, and my real questions would arise mostly after the fact rather than before. But I maintained a basic and relatively unchanging *pūjā* routine in Varanasi, and the substantial variation to this was usually when engaged in pilgrimage to other significant sites (Rameswaram, Tirupati, Ujjain) or in general temple exploration throughout India. When at 'home', I would always perform the *gangasnan* first thing and, after the river bath, visit various shrines depending on what day of the week it was (Mondays for Kashi Vishwanath though for the Golden

Temple often other mornings as well, Tuesdays for Vishalakshi, Saturdays for the Śani shrine, Sundays for the Sūrya shrine in the Annapurna Mandir, etc.) and eventually almost every day a sip of water from Gyan Vapi. In the evenings, hands, feet and forehead were nominally washed in the river, and then I would always go to the temple of Śitala before engaging on the round of small shrines around the base of Dashashwamedh Road (e.g., Kalī, Bindu Mai, Kalī Devī, Śitala, Durga and Hanuman) to which Kailash had introduced me. For special festival days, favourite places to visit included the Kedareshwar Temple, the Manikarnika/Jalsain Ghat Śiva shrine, the Kālaratrī Durga temple, the Kaal Bhairav Mandir, the Lahurabir Baba temple, the Pishach Mochan Kund and the Pitarkunda Talab. On Sunday evenings, a group of us would invariably hire a rickshaw to take us to the Gumbari Bir shrine amidst the railway tracks. The sanctuaries of India range from the considerably ancient and numinously venerable to the colourfully Disneyesque and uncompromisingly schlocky.

It was during my 1986 visit to Varanasi that my difficulties with the Vishwanath Temple began. Part of this might have been because, through his son at theatre rehearsals, I had come to know the chief mahant, Ram Shankar Tripathi. After he had reported on the missing golden panels from the temple's *sikhara*, the government proceeded to remove Tripathi from his post. On his behalf, I had visited lawyers and argued that the government was interfering with religious practice and was thereby violating the Indian Constitution. Nothing ever came of any of this, though I did purchase a cow for the now unemployed priest. I believe it was during my next visit to India as I was continuing with my regular *pūjā* at the Golden Temple, the officiating priest in the inner sanctum received me well, and I touched the sacred *lingam*. But as I was doing this, police and one *yatri* began screaming. I proceeded as customary to circle the sanctum but was interrupted by a policeman who took me to R.K. Mishra, the government-appointed administrator, who ordered me out of the temple. I proceeded to do *pūjā* at the Vishnu shrine, but it was obvious that the priests who knew me were intimidated. I was not allowed out through the side entryway of the temple. I circled around to Gyan Vapi and then the adjacent shrines where the Vishnu priest was waiting to give me *prasad*.

The following day I was too ill to leave my room at all. The next four days I had no problem worshipping in the Vishwanath temple, but on the fifth day I was stopped in the inner shrine by *pūjāris* and guards and taken to a desk where I was told I must first get permission to enter the temple. A very young person, seemingly still a child, appeared to be in charge. I asked in Hindi if I could finish worshipping, and he allowed this. With the *lingam*, there was no lingering savouring, but the contact was still intense, and as *prasad* I received a tomato and something else that I did not recognise at all – let alone if it was even edible. Then as I was leaving the sanctuary, I was intercepted by Mishra who asked me angrily why I persisted in coming back to Vishwanath when I had been prohibited to enter. He said that next time I would be arrested and my passport confiscated. He also told me that it would make no difference if I was able to receive temple admittance through the District Magistrate since he too was a city magistrate. The DM had been at a conference the day I had already tried to see him just before the week-end. I asked why I was being barred, and Mishra's reply was simply because he said so. The 'Good morning, Sir; Are you happy?' *pūjāri* appeared and most sweetly explained that I had better leave the temple. He walked me to the door apologising.

My paganism reveres nature, the gods and music. This last more broadly would be the arts, but India allowed me to experience veneration of the divine through formal and traditional edification. My fundamental deities are the earth, the luminous, the dawn, sun and moon along with fire-water and thunder-lightning – what I collectively refer to as 'the heptatheon', but I also persist in devotion to such more particular instances as Indra and Agni from Vedic India; Týr, Freyr, Thor and Frigg-Freya from the Norse lands; Zeus, Demeter, Apollo and Dionysus from the Greeks; and Jupiter, Mars, Vesta, Ceres, Janus and Larentia of the Romans. And yet India offers the concrete possibilities to worship such deific derivatives as Shiva, Vishnu, Devi (Durga, Kali, Parvati), Ganesha and Śītalā whose still active cults are popular and widespread. In the cultic sense of adulation, Hinduism provides the possibility of experiencing a living reverence to divinity that is probably the closest that still exists in our world of today and yet is akin to the more formal forms of worship that once prevailed in the ancient paganisms of the classical world and beyond. To be banished from Shiva Vishwanath's home as well as forbidden entry to some temples elsewhere in India was to undergo the feelings of racism and prejudice of which as a white male I was unfamiliar in the West – ultimately a welcomed learning experience, but otherwise my engagement with temples, shrines and holy places on the Subcontinent has been – albeit grudgingly difficult at times – an expansion of awareness of things cultically divine.

India overall can be a nightmare of trials and tribulations. Before my

1986 visit, I had originally gone to the Indian Embassy in Den Haag for the visa. This, however, was refused because I am a writer – 'new ruling'. It was perennially through experiences like this that I would wonder if India was really worth the effort and bother. I clung to the belief that it was, but it would feel as if too much of the soul was lost through such inane, petty and utterly ridiculous rigamarole. Six days later after countless phone calls to various people at the Embassy, my visa was approved. But India itself was always mostly a love-hate undergoing. I remember from the roof of the building in which I lived viewing the moon just passed being full rising over the river on the Roman festival of the Regifugium. Banaras appeared shrouded, and the crimson-orange of the twilight cut into the northern darkness along the horizon like an obscure dagger whose worn and tattered tip had lost all boundaries of definition. As the twilight deepened, the mantel of curfew and mist gave the city the aura of smoldering ruins following a raid during a blitz. I had come to know Kāshī several times when a curfew had been imposed for one reason or another – usually rioting. As a foreigner, the curfew would not apply to me, and I could come and go as I pleased. Cycling at such times was bliss, and *pūjā* in empty temples was a luxury with a serene stillness instead of loudly clanging bells or crowded jostling. A greater intimacy with deity could then be felt.

Some pagan musings at the time: the Arabs are a nice people with an awful religion, the Israelis – an awful people with an awful religion, the Euro-Americans my people colonised by an awful religion, the Iranians – the black sheep of the Indo-European peoples, the Indians – a nice people with a nice religion but insidiously undermined by a treacherous priesthood, the Japanese – a fascinating people not always honourable with a wonderful religion, the Chinese – a wonderful people with some wonderful religions. Today, however, when I read a 2015 World Trade Organisation report on the exportation of Chinese foods, I begin to wonder about the supposed wonderfulness of China. Disrespecting international regulations, seventeen items have been found to contain such harmful and/or cancerous chemical products as arsenic, pesticides, paraffin, industrial colourants, iron sulfate, lead and even some organic diseases. The items named are apple juice, industrial salt, cod & tilapia, chicken, garlic, mushrooms, green peas, sweet potato noodles, ginger, ginseng, soya sauce, tapioca, tofu, canned goods, frozen spinach and shrimps. Coupling this – if it is still the case – with the current treatment of the Uighurs and the imposition of the security law on Hong Kong, my esteem for China is lessened. In all, I believe there are probably four top countries in the world at present that merit a deserved respect: Finland, New Zealand, Switzerland and Iceland.

The passengers erupted into applause when our flight from Varanasi landed as perfectly as it did. Stepping from the plane in Kathmandu, I heard a lady exclaim, 'Ah, l'air de montagne, c'est magnifique!' and I could not have agreed more. And then with my Newari friend Binod, it was Pokhara first. The bus followed a frightening hairpin road. We stopped on the way for refreshments in Muglin. I kept thinking that the Thakalī woman at the next stall had snot hanging from her nose, but it was instead a pendant attached as a nasal piercing. The beauty of Nepal with her mountains and rivers as well as gems of ubiquitous shrines is utterly captivating. After Pokhara, we returned to Lalitapur and from there underwent a grand excursion to Delhi, Srinagar, Jaipur, Jodhpur, Udaipur and then back to Delhi from where Binod flew home to Kathmandu and I on first to Calcutta and from there to Tirumala/Tirupati for the magnificent temple of Vimana Venkateshwar. This last is a pilgrimage centre *par excellence* – perhaps even exceeding Kashi Vishwanath and certainly wealthier. The mass accommodation of pilgrims in the hill-top shrine of Tirupati is big, big business and fascinating, and in the temple complex itself, for a Hindu crowd, it was decidedly calm and controlled. Pilgrims are ushered into spacious waiting areas, and after two and a half hours of mounting excitement we were then conducted into the shrine itself. There seems to be no record of the idol of Balaji (Vishnu) being created; it apparently just appeared – an improbable but nevertheless possible spontaneous natural coalescence. A hushed aura sweeps over the crowd in the few minutes one has for *darshan*. The idol is magnificent. It sweats and yet is impervious to chemically reacting to the camphor with which it is covered. It wears real hair, and one can reputedly hear the sound of sea waves when putting the ear against the back of the image.

The extreme sanctity and miracle of Tirupati struck me even further after two nights later – the second of which I had passed back down the hill in Tirumala. In the morning, I discovered that I had forgotten my electric razor in the 10 rupee a night Garudadri Pilgrim Home in which I had stayed when on Tirupati. I bussed back and then was directed to an office where I was told that my razor was locked in an adjacent room but the man with the keys had left for Tirumala ten minutes earlier and would not return until the morning of the following day. Eventually, with the help of Srinivara, a young doctor from Andra Pradesh, I was taken to the administration offices. After a long wait, the razor was suddenly produced out of a cabinet there! Some more red tape ensued, but eventually I descended with my razor – and this was India!

The next miracle was, as previously, in finding my Canadian friend Norman's in Mysore. When boarding the bus in Bangalore to get to Mysore, I saw my first whiteys in three days – a couple. The woman said to me, 'Excuse me, there is a line, and I am ahead of you'. I replied, 'Look, honey, it looks more as if it's everyone for himself' – which it clearly was. Only sometimes would the phrase '*Line hai!*' work in India. In Mysore around 05:30, I saw Halley's comet above the eastern horizon. Later the same day, in the Balliligiri Rangana Hills, I met Swami Nirmalananda who, while keeping to his vow of silence and only chanting *om, namah Shivaja*, fed us with wonderful vegetarian food and bread he had cooked himself. In his younger years, he had travelled the world but eventually took *sannyas* and lived by this point in the area of the Soliga tribals for about a quarter of a century. Thirteen years later, in poor health, he performed *prayopavesha / mahaprasthana* or a self-willed death by fasting. I remember him as perfectly happy and charming. A few days later, I returned to Kāshī via Bombay and stayed there for a month before returning to London through Kathmandu and Dacca.

But when in Kāshī, Kailash and Ajit's uncle Chacha died. The cremation itself was something of a circus. The saddest part was the wailing from the women – first in the courtyard where Chacha's body was prepared for the burning ghat while red powder was rubbed onto everyone's forehead, and second after the women had taken a short cut to intercept the procession just before reaching the ghat. Although I was certain that the people of the Jalsain area see countless processions everyday like ours, everyone seemed attentive and moved as we passed. The body was dipped into the Ganga before being placed on the pyre. Symbolic feedings for the corpse next appeared to take place, and then, to my great astonishment, with the holiest of holy fires right there – the oldest in the world! – matches were used to light the straw beneath the wood. Of course, I had to ask why, and it was explained that the Doms who possessed the fire were too low and hence the eternal fire of the Jalsain Ghat was too contaminated for upper castes to use. The whole cremation occurred between 11:00 and 15:00. It was exceedingly hot. Fortunately, we did not sit to watch the burning but retired under a thatched sunshade at the Marnikarnika Ghat. It was still tortuously hot. I accepted a *paan* to eat and returned with Babū when he performed the last feeding. Finally, the brothers along with some friends and relatives dosed the remaining logs with *Ganga pani* and collected the few bones that were left. We were given banu grass to hold, then break and finally throw over our heads toward the burning place without looking back. We bathed in the river afterwards and washed our clothes. Back at the Kapūr house, the women entered first, then the men while non-family returned home from there.

This last coincided with Śitala Ashtami during which the smallpox goddess' temple at Dashashvamedh was completely decked out with clothes, masks and covers on every idol and lingam. And, of course, it was packed with devotees. *Arti* had already begun, and the temple was illuminated by oil lamps since the lighting had failed. The electrician arrived right in the midst of everything for the repairs, and the *pujari* had to send him away. The next day was a lunar eclipse, and during it all the goddesses were veiled from view: Śitala, Vindhyachal Devi, the Kalīs in Dashashvamedh Road and Panir Gully. And one day later, I was back in Lalitapur where unexpectedly I encountered the transportation of the idol to a special pavilion on the first day of Macchendranath Rath. Several priests circumambulated the goddess – the first while wearing a conical iron crown and performing a sexy, effeminate dance to the four water jugs in each corner. The priests circled three times while being accompanied by trumpets, fifes and drums. Save for the conically crowned priest, the four water jug bearers and one other shaven-headed priest in a suit jacket, everyone in the pavilion knelt or crouched (policemen as well) while the water was poured over the feet of the decorated idol amid almost frenzied excitement, cheering and firecrackers. The crowd lunged then forward to be splashed with holy water. It was a moving yet simple and relaxed spectacle, and a week later I was back in London followed by Amsterdam and then the south of France for most of the rest of the year with excursions back to London and Amsterdam and also to Paris, Aix-en-Provence, Firenze and Venezia. It was during one of the U.K. visits that I bought the London flat.

If there is an appropriate goddess for our times, it would be the Roman goddess Fury. Vergil depicts her in chains, but Petronius presents her instead as unbound, raging and/or revelling but at liberty. I am wondering if this very duality in understanding the goddess Fury relates to a human divide. If the goddess is fettered, who is responsible for her binding? If, by contrast, she is free, how does she operate? Petronius answers this last as rage and revelry. I would suppose our anger would be against the stalemate and non-parity in any forward movement for human society. Celebration would occur when and if there is an advance.

There is an undoubted anger against what is perceived as hierarchy – especially in terms of social class. And yet hierarchy is a natural. A classless social order may not be a possibility, but if we could reduce humanity to consisting of only two classes such as the middle class and upper class – at least in economic considerations, we would have eliminated the poor and the untouchables. But even with a two-class configuration, there would most likely still be the 'upper middle' or what my own family was as well as what my father perceived us to be, namely, '(lower) upper'. Again, pecking orders and hierarchies are natural phenomena. We may question some of these rankings now and seek at least to modify them, but they are still natural developments. This fact alone may present the very anti-nature want for an Abrahamic God. Admittedly, considering a telluric emphasis, Islam and perhaps Judaism are closer to an appreciation of physicality and nature than are Christianity and much Gnosticism. But the question remains, with these two perspectives and/or valuings concerning Fury, could we come to operate collectively together in a cooperative forum?

Richard asks why would we want such a cooperation, and my reply is 'to save, sustain and have an equable future for our world'. It is this for which I wish, and I understand the desire of wishing as the most holy phenomenon of all. In the end, our entire corporeal cosmos is the tangible manifestation of the divine and primordial and ever-continuing wish. Freedom *is* the wish. Of course, there is always an enemy, and vis-à-vis the all, the enemy, the dragon Vritra, is ultimately entropy and exhaustion or weariness. But as we move through life, both personally and collectively, could it become possible for us to accept *every* step or phase as a further advance in the achievement of freedom? This is a challenge and would depend on an extreme discernment of imagination, but it would render and transform even a negative into a positive. We already do this when acts of violence become seminal to a creative work of art or an artistic commemoration.

But to return to the naturalness of the social divide, need this invariably entail the snobbish act of 'looking down' on the other? I remember our dear, dear Stef and Gary who would describe themselves as 'food snobs'. But as such, are they simply not just *another* grouping, or is it integral to a kind of 'looking down' on the rest and hence another natural hierarchy even if and when there are only two rungs to the ladder? Richard argues that pecking orders shift and change as well as being at least semi-fixed. But I will counter that if one is to use a ladder (and sometimes they are necessary), one wants the rungs and frame of the ladder to be strong and well-connected.

Along with my difficult relationship I had with my father, I recollect three key Dad moments. One was at home on Curtiss Place in Maplewood. My mother, brother and sister were away, and it was just the two of us. This was after the Coliseum business fair when I had worked the week for my father, and it was near the end of my summer school at New York University. I needed the fees for continuing with college at UCSB. We were sitting in the dining room and began talking about our relationship. As I spoke about the hurt I had always felt from him, tears began copiously to flow down my cheeks. I was not actually crying, but the water poured from my eyes beyond my control. However, apparently, they were persuasive. Dad pulled out his cheque book and wrote out what was required for California.

Another key moment when we had boarded the ship that was to take me back to Europe after my brother's death. My mother, father and sister were seeing me off. The announcement was made that it was time for family and other visitors who were not sailing to leave the vessel. Dad could not speak at that moment. When my family was on the dock and the ship began to depart, my father looked into my eyes and bawled like I had never seen him to do. I could not even shift my look to my mother. When they were out of sight of me, my mother asked my father if he wanted to leave. They were in separate cars, but he would not move, so she had to let him stand alone on the dock.

The third key moment was when Richard and I had returned to the US for a brief visit. My father had already sold his company and after a year his honorary presidency had ended and was not being renewed. Richard and I were suddenly drafted into a week of helping my father move his office into his condo residency. It was an awful week, and at its end my father snapped at me, 'Mike, come upstairs to my office'. He began by asking if Richard and I were having a 'gay relationship'. My mother, now in Florida, had always said to me on the phone, 'Don't tell your father that you are gay!' So I replied by asking him what was he getting at. His answer was that he thought I was the most selfish and self-centred person he had known. 'That's very interesting', I then said, 'because that is exactly how I feel about you'.

There is another memory. Dad and I were with my mother, and we had just parked the car on a street in Manhattan. There was someone nearby who was belligerent and began to threaten me with assault for some now forgotten reason. My father stepped quickly out of the vehicle and placed himself between me and my possible assailant. It was an instinctual and automatically protective act on his part. I remember that as well.

In some final reflections on 1986, it was not a bad year though the most expensive I had yet known thanks to the London flat and its transformation into a home. Richard and I had managed to get ourselves established in London and legalised in the south of France. I had experienced India once again and, even more, Nepal. The losses continued but some good friends remained. Overall, I considered myself to have been lucky, and I was finally able to get published. In all, it was a full year.

On the pagan front, I learned about the Mapuche 'male spirit' or *pillán* (plural *pillanes*) from an Indian rebel leader, Juan, in political exile in London. 'We are not Christian', he explained while showing photos of goddess-attended tree shrines from his home country that were flanked by two large pots before them and two masks hung on them. My practice and altar shrines are different, of course, but despite plague, terrorism and penury of the times then as well as now, the kind of paganism with which I remain involved in the West consists simply of worshipping the gods through ceremony and acts of human kindness. As I became aware of both Nazca shamans and the emerging 'New Age' religion (especially its rejection of the Judaeo-Christian concept of a single omnipotent God) along with the general growth of modern alternative religions in the West, I came to think of myself as a 'Neo-Pagan' – thanks to Oberon Zell-Ravenheart/Oberon Zell who coined the term.

In my own search to form a cosmopolitan pantheon, I turned foremost to inspiration from Santería, Confucian-classical Chinese religion, Shinto, Humanism, Epicureanism and Stoicism. Along with Sophism, Tantrism and shamanism, I consider all these to be the viable traditions of materialist religious spirituality. As in my earlier days, I still entertain that the most sustainable way of proceeding is surrendering to the divine guidance of the gods despite the political and economic running of our world by people who do not even know the what or why of the gods themselves. Is the fiery angel Madiel ever closer to shattering our world? But on the basis of the sense of intuition alone, I still suspect that death will be some kind of a surprise. For all my humanistic sympathies, give me some shamanic mind-alternator, and I am unable to resist the thrill of pagan mysticism.

My first sexual encounter with Richard occurred during our first coven celebration on Strawberry Hill. But he was with Coral, and I was actively busy with searching for a partner – as well as numerous good times for which I am eternally grateful. In Amsterdam, I had a brief affair with Thomas. But there was a time when I was comfortably taking a bath, and Richard informed me that Thomas had just come to the house. I groaned, and Richard asked if I would mind if he began an affair with Thomas. 'Please, please!' I responded. Their liaison ensued, and I remember the time in the dining room (this being way before the advent of mobile phones and this was where the telephone was) when Thomas had called. Richard was late for something he was to do with Thomas, and I could hear from across the room the torrent of abuse that Thomas was delivering to an apologetic Richard. I thought to myself, if Richard could endure that, he would be able to put up with me. I think of this as the moment in which I fell in love with Richard.

However long it was after this, it was a New Year's Day, and I said to Richard that I thought we had some unfinished business to which to attend. It was not completely successful, and when we woke in the morning, some inkling I had made me surmise that there had to be something more to it, and spontaneously I proposed to him. I think Richard was so astonished that he consented yes. My friend George/Buster was visiting the house for his annual Christmas holidays. A year earlier two lesbians had asked me to officiate a marriage for them (what pagans would subsequently come to call a handfasting). The ceremony I had composed for them became the ceremony that Buster employed for the marriage between Richard and me.

Our second 'marriage' occurred by surprise when we were visiting Ma Jaya Bhagavati's ashram in Sebastian, Florida. We had been invited to come but then were expected to pay for our lodging which I did not do since to me it seemed a violation of an invitation. I did leave money for a memorial plaque to Pfeiffer to be included among the rest that the Kashi Ashram had, but I suspect this was never done. But in any event, during one of Ma's evening audiences, she announced that she was going to perform a marriage ceremony for Richard and me and proceeded to do so.

In my elementary, junior high school and high school days, my other 'best friend' beside Henry 'Pit' Pitman was Fred Profeta. Fred eventually became the town mayor of Maplewood, New Jersey, and by the time he had then become deputy assistant mayor he kept nagging me that he wanted to perform a civil union ceremony for Richard and me in my hometown while he still had the authority to do so. There was a harrowing moment when Richard and I were on the train to Maplewood for our Monday-scheduled ceremony on the Friday before the arranged date to register at the Town Hall the mandatory three-days in advance. But while we were en route, the Amtrak train broke down between Kingston, Rhode Island and our ultimate destination of Maplewood, and the only recourse we had was to hire a taxi in Connecticut. Our driver's name was Angel, and he managed to get us there only minutes before the office was closing. My friends Freeman and Drew were present along with Chickie whose maiden name had been Zimmerman, and hence we always sat next to one another in the alphabetical order of seating in our high school home room. There were also Carol who had had some relatively inexplicable relationship with my father as well as Cindy who had been the liaison between my father and the New Jersey Institute of Technology. There were others as well, and in all it was a splendid occasion and became what Richard and I now refer to as our 'third marriage'.

The 'fourth marriage' occurred in Amsterdam is actually our 'first' real marriage in legal terms. It was another 'splendid occasion', and Coral, the mother of Richard's daughter, and Nancy, my now *ex*-wife 'gave each of us away'. Most of 'The Family' had come from abroad – from California, Scotland and London. The following day, Richard and I took for ourselves alone and went off to have a stoned day in Amsterdam. As we were finally returning to the house, we were coming down the outside of the Keizersgracht from the Utrechtsestraat toward the Reguliersgracht where the house is. There was a young lady at the far end of the block (and it is a long block) walking toward us with the sun behind her. She had on a summery dress and ambled in our direction in a carefree, casually buoyant and Marilyn Monroe-like manner, and I thought to myself, wouldn't it be lovely if that silhouetted figure could be Chloe. As she continued to come closer in her dreamlike and happy manner, I kept repeating almost unconsciously how wonderful if this delightful person could be my daughter – and once she reached us, *it was Chloe*! This became a divine moment – one more perhaps among many but an unforgettable one in the very least.

I am neither a capitalist or in any sense a businessman, but I am a privileged whitey who has benefitted from the capitalist system. Thanks to my sister, I have benefited the minimally possible, but I have still benefitted. Whether I am proud of any of this is beside the point. It is who I am, and it is part of the explanation of how I see life and the particular spirituality that I have come to perceive as vital to life – not only for myself but potentially for anyone and everyone who is open to the miraculousness of human existence and the mother earth planet that makes this precarious existence possible to begin with.

I can only say that I have been extraordinarily fortunate and it is through such 'fortune' that I have been able to gain the insights or perspectives on the possibility of a fortunate life for virtually the vast majority of all of us. Are the gods responsible for anyone's luck? Are the gods 'responsible' for anything at all? I see them primarily as vehicles toward which to express gratitude – vehicles that possess their own unique and peculiar beauty. For me, that alone is enough. I use the gods as these vehicles through which to give my thanks to the cosmos and the trajectory of my own personal journey through it.

It may be a foolish and simple want, but I wish that most of the inhabitants on earth, we human inhabitants at least, could be free and free to enjoy what I have enjoyed on this most blessed planet. I also see that we have essentially the *technical* means for this to be a possibility. But our technical capabilities are only a part of what would be necessary. The rest would depend on political, cultural and educational abilities and perhaps as all of these could come to be informed and shaped by spiritual factors. If we turn to religions *per se*, I see Hinduism basically as a workable religion apart for its nemesis of caste endorsement and ultimate wish to 'escape'. Buddhism retains something perhaps the most respectable of all religions, but its dharmic anti-telluric desires I cannot ultimately endorse. With Christianity, there are some lovely aspects such as concern allegedly for all, but I do not see this in actuality. Judaism misses by what it has become focussed on, namely, the expropriation of Palestine and its treatment of non-Jewish citizens within its claimed territory. Islam too has some beautiful aspects, but its anathema to my own understanding of divine pluralism makes me want to reject it as well. And secularism I see as missing out on the very fun of enchantment and its transfiguring magical aspect.

So where does this leave us? I think by now I have made clear my telluric sympathies. I see myself as pagan and 'fully' endorse (if that is the right word) the potential freedom of *everyone*. This freedom of course must keep commensurate with the potentials of an ecologically balanced host planet from which we have emerged in the first place. But it is vital always to keep in mind that *nous ne sommes pas tous pareils*, we are not all the same but are all different. Consequently, we need and need to accept a world that accommodates all our differences from being transgenders, heathens, witches, vegetarians, gays, and Trump supporters to Chinese, Americans, Russians, British and especially Europeans and should I add black, yellow, red, white and even green if they exist as well?

The Pyke part of our London family has part of a house facing the sea in Aldeburgh. It is always a joy to have some time there. I have yet to find it warm enough to enter the sea in Aldeburgh, but hopefully that day will yet come. But the high street just behind the house is small town loveliness, and the sound of the waves and scent of the salt air are unfailingly enchanting.

My family always had a love for the oceanside. We would vacation regularly at the Jersey shore, and as a child it was inevitably thrilling when, during the drive from Maplewood to the Barnegat Peninsula, sand would begin to appear at the sides of the road and we could smell the sea. My parents would rent a bungalow at Chadwick Beach. There was a general store in Chadwick facing Highway 35 that had a swinging screen door. It was from here that we could do most of the essential shopping. The Barnegat Peninsula is a long, narrow strip of land that separates the Barnegat Bay from the Atlantic Ocean. There were large and fascinating, ancient-looking, shingle-styled mansions to be seen along the peninsula. I still and always will remember that morning when I might have been about seven and had gone to the beach and there encountered the small crowd watching a wooden rowing skiff being pulled onto the shore that was packed and virtually overflowing with a truly enormous catch of fish. I have never ever seen anything like this since. It was while I stood there in wide-eyed wonder, that one of the fishermen handed me two fish to take home to my surprised and delighted mother. We never knew what kind of fish they had been.

In later years, my mother would rent a summer place in Spring Lake and still later in Narragansett, Rhode Island. Finally, she bought a condominium facing directly onto the Rhode Island Sound in Narragansett. Mother had first pick as the complex was being constructed, and she chose the northern most in the row of five town houses – the one which gave her windows on three sides. I inherited the condominium, and it was always an utter joy to wake with the vista of the Atlantic Ocean directly before one.

Prior to this Rhode Island dream, following my withdrawal from Purdue, the prospect of continuing my university education at a seaside campus made the appeal of the University of California, Santa Barbara irresistible. Today in London, at least, I am only three blocks from the Thames, while the Amsterdam house is on a canal. No longer the oceanside, but at least I am still near water. And then there is this occasional sojourn in Aldeburgh.

Somehow during the second half of the 1960s in the Library of San Francisco State College, I came across a book that enumerated the four Celtic cross-quarter festivals – Samhain, Imbolc, Beltane and Lammas. Whether the book had suggested it or not, I realised these mid-point celebrations could be combined with commemorating the solstices and equinoxes. It was to be several years before I was to discover the calendar of Numa Pompilius, Rome's second king, in which while the summer solstice is minimally recognised, and the autumnal equinox is ignored altogether, there still seems to be some correlation with the Wiccan/Pagan wheel of the year and its eight sabbats of seasonal festivals. The Romans descended in the pagan tradition that celebrated light in particular, and the diminishment of the luminous was not something overtly to commemorate. Despite modern Wicca's insistence on equally honouring darkness, the more organic but still pantheistic understanding that prevailed in pre-Christian times approached light as a metaphor for visual perception and the positivity of advance. Even more important, the polarity of light and dark was *not* equated or fixed to the polarity between the masculine and feminine in the terms of the patriarchal interpretation that has come to be prevalent today. The telluric discernment of spirituality extols brightness and shadow, the male and female, the corporeal and ethereal or matter and energy and even the positive and negative comprehensively. But within this totality of cherishment, there remains the symbolic preference for both the luminescent and the positive. Consequently, I do not agree with or endorse Starhawk's contention in *Dreaming the Dark* that the polarity between the light and dark necessarily entails the racial suppression of blacks by whites. This last has certainly happened and continues to happen but not because of humanity's innate cherishing of light and brilliance. I feel that Starhawk's accusation is an unhelpful reductionism that throws the baby out with the bathwater.

During the 1960s, following my initial experiences with peyote in San Francisco, I explored and experimented with other psychotropic substances as well. Consequently, when Buster and I organised our first coven gathering for Hallowe'en or Lughnasadh in 1968 – it being so long ago I can no longer remember which, this was when I prepared the belladonna and jimson weed elixir that we drank and also rubbed over our naked bodies as a flying ointment. We proceeded to dance, ritualise and make love together next to the bonfire we had constructed on top of Strawberry Hill in San Francisco's Golden Gate Park. The gods must have been with us because, in our year of celebrations – half of which occurred at that site and always with a fire – we were never detected and remained invisible to the outside world.

Since my initial motivation was a rejection of Christianity, I had initially constructed our observation around the understanding of the witches' covens of the Middle Ages and employed a Satanic metaphor as an opposite to the persecuting Church. This was the occasion in which I learned how difficult it is to form a coven of exactly thirteen people. It is an elusive number and basically only occurs on its own accord. Buster had reneged on participating as we neared the time for our ritual orgy, and Kinmont also pulled out at the last minute. From our San Francisco 'family', there were myself, my wife Nancy, Rosanne, Richard and his partner Coral, Warren and Jan, Lynne and 'Little' Nancy. My brother Peter and his girlfriend Ann agreed to participate, and I believe the artist Michael Barnes did as well. We were still one short, but a chap happened by as we were about to begin, and he agreed to join us as well. Such were those wonderful countercultural days of San Francisco! We drew lots to determine who would be the Lord and Lady for the occasion, and ironically it turned out to be myself and Nancy. Our ultimate aim was to attain a collective mind of consciousness. We were assisted by a fundamental trust that had developed mutually between those of us who identified as 'family'. How successful we ever were in achieving egregore remains an open question, but the quest for creating and/or merging with an autonomous psychic entity as a shared thought-form was always our underlying intention.

There were three sabbat celebrations for which we did not get to Strawberry Hill. One of these took place at Lynne and Nancy's in the Avenues. Again, we used my flying ointment concoction, but by the morning and probably because of the heat from the open fire in the hearth we had experienced an extreme skin irritation to the degree that clothes against our flesh became unbearable. This was when we retreated for the day to a small and isolated beach at Land's End where we were able to enjoy the day in our nudity.

On another occasion we were intending to go to Strawberry Hill and were first meeting again at my brother's apartment near the Panhandle. Next door to Peter's flat was a party of young people in full swing and who had then joined us. I realised that the present vibe was such that there was no way we could transfer everyone to the park, so I announced that we would hold our coven ritual in Peter's place instead. Anyone who did not want to participate was welcome to stay, but the only requirement was that everyone who remained would need to take off their clothes. My sister was present and refused to undress, so my brother and she left. There was also a movie maker who was there to record us for a pornographic film. He pleaded with me to be excepted – saying he absolutely could not undress with others present. There was no way to make exceptions, so our Family's pornographic career ended virtually before it began. And on this occasion, we employed ketamine in place of my flying ointment mix. But once again, there were about half of us who 'crossed over' while the rest, including myself, wondered why we had not. This was when I was standing with Nancy on Shrader Street before my brother's house with her worriedly declaring 'Michael! The dog just went out the window!' Though she was physically present, she herself was not there at all.

It was for the midwinter's solstice, that Michael Barnes, who taught at the San Francisco Art Institute, had arranged for us to pass the night there since we were intrigued by the rumours that the private college was haunted. One by one, we would individually climb to the top of the school's tower to see if we could encounter the ghost. Lynne saw a middle-aged librarian woman furtively scurrying about with a notepad presumably looking for books. A small group of us at one point went to a basement room, and suddenly a man in a bathrobe appeared through the wall and turned on the overhead lights and demanded to know what we were doing. We replied that we were looking for the ghost. Michael explained to us the next day that there was no one who stayed at the Institute. Richard has always insisted otherwise, but I have wondered if in fact this had been the Art Institute ghost.

It was during this year that I attended Anton LaVey's three catechism classes at his residence on California Street (the Black House) in anticipation of joining the Church of Satan. These were pleasant evenings with refreshments served afterwards in the kitchen. I remember little now of what was explained apart for the hedonist beliefs of Satanists and LaVey seeing the future world as more or less religiously divided between Satanists and Buddhists. At the conclusion of the three classes, we were each given a questionnaire to complete along with signing a statement by which we swore eternal allegiance and submission to LaVey as the 'Pope' of the Church of Satan. Simply, this was something to which I could not agree. It also more or less coincided with my Easter LSD experience of *eternal Hell* on Strawberry Hill. With this last, the omens had appeared, so to speak, on the wall. When we first arrived at the hill, Coral's dog Fred managed to kill the Easter Bunny. Lynne too experienced the out-of-the-ordinary, and for her it was the Second Coming. She fell to her knees in anticipation and threw away her contact lenses that she would no longer be requiring. In vain, the next day, we searched for them.

Consequently, during our year or so of celebrating the sabbats, there was a gradual evolution and transformation of our Strawberry Hill Coven away from satanism or devil-worship toward something more natural and organic. For our last gathering in Golden Gate Park, we concluded our ceremony by sitting in a circle with our feet touching those of the others while we chanted the *Om* syllable. We were on our way to a bona fide paganism even if we had yet not quite reached it. Richard says that we *had* reached it but still did not know at this point that it was pagan. But perhaps it is important to stress that our coven's effort toward a collective conscious was one that was being sought *through* our bodies (young and agile as they once were) and not in repudiation of the physical and a desire to escape from it. Ours was not a transhumanistic undertaking in any sense but rather a celebration of embodiment and the telluric dimensions of being.

While a number of my current friends and acquaintances insist that transhumanism is anti-pagan, I do not wish to go that far. Despite the homeopaths and anti-vaxxers that are in my own family, I still maintain a belief in and acceptance of science and technology and despite my being someone with the least of technical proficiencies. My confidence in advanced tech-art, however, does not preclude some severe criticisms I have of so-called 'modern progress' and especially my suspicion of transhumanism as a gnostic endorsement of transcendence, but the attempt to move beyond physical and mental limitations seems unavoidably intrinsic to being human in the first place. The goals of futurism are controversial and involve cybernetics, artificial intelligence, genetic engineering, nano-technology and cryonics. Eugenics has come to be considered immoral largely because of the murder and sterilisation programmes of the 20th century Nazis, but if and when procreation is not coerced by a third party (government, institutions, profit-monopolising corporations, etc.) but undertaken through individual choice alone, the unethical assessment concerning genetic modification is less certain. The complexity with the issue concerns considerations of what exactly is healthy, optimal or perfect, the possibility of creating social inequality, and any availability only to a privileged few.

Transhumanism's assessment of disability, suffering and disease as both unnecessary and undesirable and its efforts to limit the duration of injury and reduce trauma would seem to be credible in and of themselves. Augmenting longevity against such negatives as 'aging' and 'involuntary death' becomes more contentious in that immortality does not appear in our present stage of human evolution to be natural. But we are all, pagans and others, plagued by some inherent conflict between nature and nurture, and yet culture is not just a way of life that is free from judgment. Prejudice based on race, for instance, is cultural and something that is learned, and as such it is a way of life that can be critically examined and consequently changed. When we are really speaking of cultures in the plural rather than as a single and uniform stage of civilisation, they can be critiqued and transformed through education. At present in the West, identity has come to be argued as something that is socially constructed and beyond being determined by either culture and/or biology. If our goals in life include a fundamental response to our environment, this response can no longer be something that is left purely to our instincts but must be guided by those human-based cultures that are amenable and capable of modification, transformation and even improvement in terms of individual choice and aspiration. And to the degree that our inborn tendencies and cultural outlooks are debilitating and limiting, the unnaturalness of transhumanism may actually be the more natural alternative. Can paganism, both contemporary and indigenous, adjust and accommodate itself to the emerging BIN technologies that seek improvement in the Bio, Info and Nano spheres?

I put the question of whether transhumanism is anti-pagan to the Pagans group on Facebook. The upshot of the answers tends to depend on how transhumanism is understood. For some, it includes the wearing of eye glasses; for others, it takes in efforts to upload our consciousness into a computer. One person points out that, along with Christianity and modernity, a common thought in paganisms is that all things man-made are anti-natural, but someone else claims that in today's world it is impossible to avoid man-made things and hence we have a 'new natural'. The reduction of suffering and disease is in general not viewed as anti-pagan since at least the incubations within the temples of Asclepius – if not both before and certainly after. But the technologising of the body is cited by one person as the utter antithesis to life getting back to nature. Nevertheless, there is the outlook that it is Christian dualism that has separated matter and spirit and elevates the latter as superior, and this is something that has influenced much in contemporary paganism. In fact, however, paganism is a fluid term and ranges from telluric to gnostic understandings. The bottom question becomes one of asking that if we humans are natural, are not what we create aspects of nature as well? This last, though, must be gaged against anything that upsets the natural balance. Modern pagan movements are usually firmly anchored in nature and advocate living naturally with the earth. Agriculture represents a 'leap' for humanity, but as Kris Hughes explains it has also become the source for the philosophy of unchecked growth, habitat destruction, mechanisation and the violent taking of land from one group by another. If transhumanism is to be seen as the promotion of advance, there are negatives that appear to come with it. But rather than being perceived as 'anti-pagan', transhumanism perhaps requires pagan awareness and sensitivity to balance it and allow it to be endorsed judiciously.

The real problem for pagans with transhumanism, however, revolves around cryogenics. The merging of technological advancement and death denial does not mesh with the natural cycles that include death. For one individual, the attempt to live forever denies the existence of the soul. Truncating biological evolution is seen as not a good thing, and it certainly complicates reincarnation. From an atheistic perspective, transhumanism is condemned because it 'violates' the fundamental biosphere rule of death which is necessary for continued evolution and the making of room for new organisms. Death is considered the obligatory price for 'the ticket to life'. Transhumanism is comprehended by some as an attempt to become a god, but one person asks if we are not already gods and goddesses. We are by default a part of the pantheistic whole. So, true enough, the assessment of transhumanism is a theological issue and comes close to how I see a divide between the gnostic and the telluric. One person grasps paganism as the effort to maintain and enhance our human connection to our natural source. This of course brings the debate closer to the transgender issue. Since there seems to be no resolution to this last for as long as 'opposing sides' are unable to compromise with largess, I will avoid this matter further. But I am wondering if our understanding of the 'gnostic' were to shift from that of Abrahamic transcendentalism to one of enhancement transhumanism, might there then be more possibility for an accord between the natural and the transnatural? As when we understand the preternatural as the co-natural – existing in some way alongside the natural but as something different, could there likewise be a viable dance between nature and transnature in ways that are compatible with the embrace of paganism?

And as I am addressing the transhumanism issue, federal agents are tear-gassing and detaining protesters in the city of Portland – reminiscent for me of the Kent State shootings of students by the National Guard in 1970. But if Kansas City, Chicago and Albuquerque are to become part of the current picture, this would be Kent State on a more numerous and dangerous level. I was unabashedly a part of the Haight-Ashbury phenomenon, and what people continue to fail to appreciate is that we hippies have been able to adjust to changing times. As part of our non-mainstream legacy, to this day we have never at all accepted Ronald Reagan as a hero. I have recently read a Catholic anti-idolatry article, but with contemporary Western paganism – along with New Age as a descendent of the 1960s counterculture – the goal of satisfying a single, one-only, monarch-god has been replaced by working toward a desired accord with divine plurality. The image or idol does not for us become 'less' than the 'good' but is instead utilised as an applicable *vehicle* for it. And with this, the supposedly fixed polarity between the light and the dark that is signalled negatively by Starhawk and company is possibly more of a regression than an advance. Especially as I have grown older and have even become *old*, more and more do I appreciate the extremely vital importance of *energy* for accomplishing anything. And light is a form of energy. In a pagan understanding of an organic, flexible and open reality, we might metaphorically perceive things through a moving flywheel of dichotomies. Basically, I consider there are five divisions, and as the components of the flywheel shift and turn, the alignments between the light and dark, matter and energy, the male and the female, the positive and negative and the true and false turn and shift as well. In this constant process of realignment, there can be – ultimately *must be* – a viable equality between 'races', gender identities and sexual preferences. Although there is greed and unfair opportunism throughout the world – and even most disappointingly within our pagan communities as well, I still believe that the more equable is a possibility.

CHAPTER NINE

Wondering about a second volume; pantheism vs panentheism; summertime / David Norris / Woody Allen / Hilary Rose / Robert Tombs / John Pilger; San Francisco & teaching assistance; Folkism & Stephen McNallen / Greek mythology & syncretism & other legacies / human = natural = pagan / my mantra's source & wishing-health-wonder-freedom / the primordial wish & divine silence / the Muses / the dynamic of enchantment / divine silence / the Muses / the *desiderium primordium* / the pagan rebirth vis-á-vis a non-spiritual / divine sublimation & intoxicated altered states / the divine twins & their complex manifestations / the wives of Zeus / dethronement & primordial rape: a proto-European theogony in a nutshell / ancestral spiritual insight / music & a future *Fortunate Insulae*; Hecate / Nepal / India / Khajuraho / the 'threshold of myth'; 'the great American novel'; more mythology & Roberto Calasso / *gános* / joissance; the sublime, ridiculous, sorrowful & humorous as well as death & apotheosis / my 1973 letter to Marie-Hélène / Julius Evola / the Einstein-Spinoza pantheistic affirmation / Garbati's *Medusa* & blasphemy

It dawned on me during our Neptunalia celebrations in this pandemic year of 2020 that my review of my life and contemporary Western paganism will not feasibly complete within a single book – at least at the rate and within the reflective amount in which I am proceeding. The idea has consequently arisen that perhaps a volume 2 might be necessary or at least in the offing. However, the number of chapters in anything I have written is always a concern, and so I have decided to complete one further chapter for this present exercise.

By accident (actually by someone on the Pagans group in Facebook just now liking something I had written nine years earlier in 2011), I have come across an exchange I had with Adrian Ivakhiv, Vivianne Crowley, Mogg Morgan, Jonathan Korman and Nicole Youngman on the distinction between pantheism and panentheism that I deem is importantly relevant to the contrast of telluric paganism from paganism's gnostic forms. My current complaints and dissatisfaction with contemporary paganism has more to do with the emergence of hard-right and folkish developments, with the less than adult and certainly civil conversation within the broad community, and with the kinds of unresolved difficulties that arise through woke culture, questions of identity as a political-type of inflexibility, and the strident demands for separate spaces and times in consideration of gender and sexual differences. What everything comes down to in my own understanding is our capability to agree to disagree and especially when and if that faculty is absent or has become an inability. The pantheism/panentheism issue may bleed into these more immediate shortcomings, but it is a central theological matter on its own that can be or should be approached in any fundamental attempt to understand what we variously mean by paganism and its contrasts as well as overlaps with non-pagan religions.

I shall now in this 'heavy' year of 2020 both cite and recapitulate some of the 2011 exchange, and what I find curious for myself is what I already comprehended then and its similarity with what I think today. The major difference that has developed in my thought or, more precisely, vocabulary since then is my employment of the designation 'telluric'. I began with my consideration that the difference between pantheism and panentheism is in how they each understand what comes 'first' – respectively, 'nature' or 'God'. 'The pantheist holds that nature is the origin, the source, of all things; the panentheist finds instead the origin of the all – including that of nature – in some pre-existent entity'. Along with this, however, I felt it was important to stress that the pantheist, like the panentheist, does entertain the notion of the transcendental – but, unlike the panentheist, as an evolving emergent rather than as a pre-given source.

I had wanted to understand if there could a be a way of reconciling a panentheist understanding with a pagan position. The closest I could come was to conceive of the transcendent as possibly akin to something's aura – whether that something is a person, an object, a god, the world or the cosmos. Nevertheless, for the pantheist pagan, the auratic is a product and not the origin or source of what is emanating the overtone. But both then and now, I have maintained that as a 'process theology' formulation, panentheism was at first a Christian attempt to 'have their cake and eat it too'. Panentheists are, begrudgingly perhaps, accepting of this world but wanting their 'pre-existent God' as well. At King's College, Colin Gunther would argue with me that panentheism 'collapses' back into pantheism. I did not see how it necessarily does and, in fact, saw just the opposite, namely, that any Christian understanding of worldly sacrality becomes superseded by (metaphorically, 'collapses' into) panentheism.

I know that Gus diZerega has felt that the panentheistic concept could be helpful for interfaith reconciliation between transcendental and immanent understandings of the sacred. But when it comes to what comes – or came – first, we are still with 'the chicken and the egg' question. 'Whilst there is an answer – thanks to evolution – to that last, there may not be when it comes to "God" or nature. In some sense, it does not matter. We have what we have, and in the here-and-now we had just better get on with it. But I do feel that it takes a degree of theological courage for both the atheist and pantheist pagan to reject the idea of a comforting pre-existential transcendental and to start on without it. That stance places the burden of responsibility more fully and completely upon ourselves'.

By contrast, for the panentheist including the panentheistic pagan, there is a dependence on the idea that the world appears by external, chiefly verbal, magic – such as with the goddess Vac of the late *Rigveda*, the Logos of St. John the Evangelist, the Gnostic Demiurgic Mind, the Egyptian Ptah's speaking the world into existence, the 'Let there be . . .' of Genesis, Brahmanical mâyâ, the Miria reflection of Starhawk, and so forth. 'And maybe it has been. I personally have not been convinced that this is the case and, though it took me sometime to wean myself from my Christian upbringing, do not feel that it is necessary. As far as beginnings, the natural is good enough for me'. The problem that I perceive with a panentheist *creatio ex nihilo* is in explaining how the corporeal, allegedly secondary and born from the incorporeal, is still integrally part of a pre-existent 'God/Goddess' of transcendence. A 'God/Goddess/All that is' that is corporeal from the very start does not face this problem.

To support my understanding of a physical first-ness ('first principal' already sounds too abstract), I turned to complexity theory and its understanding that our universe is greatly more non-linear than it is linear. This would allow for the possibility of spontaneous self-organisation in which the whole becomes something more than the mere sum of its parts – such as with a chemical reaction, the human body, a city, an economy, a culture or a thing emanating an aura. 'And whilst that whole becomes subsequently an influential agency *sui generis*, it is not the whole that caused its wholeness but something more tangibly magical and spontaneous and without outside help that either springs or evolves the greater wholeness into its being; something akin perhaps to that slight tilt or wobble with the big bang that allowed matter to predominate over anti-matter'. I cited John Cooper's assessment of 'transcendence [as] the primordial unity of the "unbroken circle," the life force beyond sexual differentiation', and countered that 'there is no circle in pre-big bang singularity – not even nothing. Transcendence becomes at best the goal; not the Platonic ideal and origin'. In a pagan understanding of pantheism, the gods are nature and come into being with or through it. 'Even the void of chaos comes, as Hesiod put it, into being (*genito*)'. In other words, chaos or nothingness is not a pre-existence.

Dear Jonathan, in response, called my argument 'provocative as ever' and confessed that his own thinking, drawing principally from the Hermetic Qabalah, is slippery in this area but has 'a strong panentheist bent'. He hopes that his affinity for divine mojo cascading into manifestation in Malkuth is 'not simply a hangover from Abrahamic conceptions of a Big Daddy Creator'. But he continues: 'I'll often say that I square my Pagan gnosis with my modern atheistic materialism in pantheistic terms: divinity(ies) are patterns found [in] the material Cosmos as perceived from a human perspective and are not truly separate from it'. In addition, he admits that having been trained in the natural sciences, the mathematicians' Platonism has somewhat rubbed off on him. His 'intuition is that gods like Maxwell's Equations [proposing that light is an electromagnetic phenomenon] are indeed prior to manifestations like actual magnetic fields'.

Jonathan also adds that 'most contemporary Pagans' would dismiss the question concerning pantheistic origins versus panentheistic ones 'as an un-Pagan one to ask' – precisely another of my complaints with contemporary paganism. Most pagans need not engage with the theological question or think it is at all relevant to their practices, but I would definitely not accept that the question is itself 'un-pagan'. In the very least, the theological exchange is fun, and fun *is* a pagan enjoyment. Not everyone plays chess or baseball, but for those who do, there is a pleasure involved.

Nicole Youngman, having coming across Kaatryn MacMorgan's assertion that pantheism is the same as monotheism and based on the wish by those who have had a monotheistic upbringing wanting the cosmos to be 'One Being', wonders about animism and whether 'the non-human beings with whom we should have respectful relationships [are] also emergent from nature?' In response, I contended that it is panentheism that works much better as a monotheistic substitute. It is, nevertheless, important to recognise that there are two forms of pantheism: 'One is understanding it as devoid of the theistic altogether – sort of a non-supernatural monism perhaps. Another understanding, with which I resonate, sees a pantheistic outlook as providing a possible ground for polytheism – as something that embraces or includes the magical/imaginal/preternatural'. But for Jonathan's Buddhist-informed panentheistic panpsychism, all things in the cosmos have consciousness attached to them. He admits, though, that 'My mind has consciousness attached because all things have consciousness attached, though a stone's consciousness is more straightforward than my own swirl of thoughts; the stone's consciousness is basically "I'm a stone . . . I'm a stone . . . I'm a stone" all day every day'.

The consciousness of stones and rocks, etc. relates to Graham Harvey's 'new animism' that for me 'amounts to a pluralistic personalism, and personalism I understand as a more modern form of, at least a derivative of, Platonism'. Relating to rocks, trees and so forth as *persons* I would argue is relating to them less as actualities. We derive our word 'person' from the Etruscan *persona* that means 'mask', so to render everything or at least most things into persons 'is a way of slipping Platonic transcendentalism in through the back door'. Instead, with the understanding of traditional animism, the *anima* and *animus* are inherent within the physical, that is, as 'the animating dynamic resident in and part of any pantheistic whole that includes enchantment'. This attitude and approach does not preclude a respectful relationship with the rocks and trees of the environment, with the environment itself, with the deific and the *vættir* even if and when understood as emergent from nature rather than being prior to the Big Bang.

Meanwhile, Vivianne Crowley suggested that for those who have experienced consciousness as existing without a physical body, then the panentheistic contention that 'the consciousness of the universe may have existed prior to its creating its physical self' is plausible. While some might prefer to call this consciousness 'God', this last is too loaded a term and does not more clearly suggest that primordial consciousness in seeking to experience itself 'begins a creative and exploratory process in which conscious life forms like human beings play an active part'. However, favouring a Spinozism or monistic panpsychism, Adrian Ivakhiv disagrees with Vivianne and wonders instead if 'the Big Bang was not a bang of matter erupting out of nothing, with consciousness, deity, etc, emerging *later*, but was already an explosion of idea/consciousness/deity/energy/matter'. Positing a 'nothing' as preceding the Big Bang sounds transcendent to him, though I wish to mention here that the very notion of singularity precludes the pre-existence of anything – including nothingness. Adrian conceives the Big Bang as part of an ongoing and ceaseless process – without beginning or end, and he wonders 'if the pre-existence [might not be] an entity but a process? What if all entities are but processes taking forms and shedding them in favor of others, with the forms being "display" (aesthetic) and the processes being material-energetic-experiential?'

My response to Adrian on this last would draw on Einstein's $e = mc^2$ which allows that matter is a kind of 'solidified' energy, and energy itself is processual, that is, more a process than a thing. Whether the cosmos is without beginning and end, as Hinduism and Raëlianism contend, is of course a possibility, and if consciousness were part of the Big Bang as either the very beginning or the start of our present *yuga*, I will still feel more cosmologically comfortable with the idea that there was not some exterior consciousness initially directing it. Are we not a part of the evolution of consciousness, and is not our decision-making capacity a part of that evolutionary process and rather than its origin?

Jonathan, meanwhile, considers my consideration that consciousness emerges from material origins as a rejection of panpsychism as prior to the material. My understanding of panpsychism is that it is the theological position that holds that all of nature is psychical, but my own view is that nature may include mind but is not all mind and, yes still, that mind does not precede the matter-energy continuum but develops within it and as a product from it. Jonathan, however, is asking whether I would continue to consider his 'Buddhist-informed panpsychism' or other responses that do not see consciousness as an emergent still as 'Pagan'. He further refers to the Feri creation myth that regards 'God Herself birthing the multiplicity of the Cosmos out of self-awareness'.

I replied to Jonathan's question by saying: 'Jonathan, it's not for me or anyone to pronounce who is and who is not 'pagan'. I think that is a beauty in paganism. There is no authority and no provision for heresy or expulsion. Paganism itself is a multiple dialogue that includes its own opposites. That does not mean that we cannot have theological discussion – at least among those who so wish to engage. And granted, many if not most chose not to be bothered by the theological nuance and such ramifications at all. Personally, I think paganism has behind it a rich and important theological tradition and that this is important if we wish to enter into the world's religion roundtable of exchange'. I explained that he is by no means alone as a pagan with a belief in the panpsychic precedence of the mind but that my own preference is for what I referred to at the time as 'deep paganism' – what I now more often designate as 'telluric paganism'. If consciousness is attributed to everything, it becomes tautological and meaningless. I also wondered what has happened to the Goddess' womb if she births multiplicity out of self-awareness – a picture of mental creation, rather than womb-birth, by the primordial goddess that Starhawk also presents (I believe in *The Spiral Dance*). With Jonathan, I suggested he might simply be doing the proverbial putting of Yahweh into a dress. He concedes on this last but maintains that his conception of consciousness is not causal; it is something that 'just *always is*'. He also clarifies that by panspyschism he does not mean that consciousness is the equivalent of everything but that it is 'present in everything'. Yet, he admits that he can only recognise consciousness but not define it.

Following up, I had to ask Jonathan what is the actual meaning of his assertion that 'Consciousness just *always is*'? In expressing my own theopantist position (the universe as a whole is God or the divine), I could only wonder what would be the point of a consciousness that is primordial but not causal? 'Even without being able to define consciousness, we recognise it in ourselves and others, but do we actually do the same with rocks – or do we project it as such? Do we not talk about consciousness because consciousness itself is reflective?' Nevertheless, for Jonathan, there is no more teleological point to consciousness than there is with gravity, prime numbers or the Second Law of Thermodynamics. Drawing from Buddhism, he says, 'consciousness is not a component of thought, and so is not necessarily a product of it'. He is careful to add, almost amusingly, that he derives this insight not from a 'personal gnosis' but from 'a kind of logician's intuition' – 'something I suspect ought to be correct but which I cannot prove, nor even perfectly articulate why I suspect it to be true'.

I agreed with Jonathan that the existing Cosmos must have the form it does; nothing else would be truly possible. And I liked his asking what the point of consciousness might be, though I did not find it similar to the point of gravity which is matter's attraction to matter and which is probably part of why the universe has the form it does. Consciousness, however, I felt to be part of, or evolved as part of, the primordial desire of the universe to see itself, and the very instant of this desire is the Big Bang. History and speculation are what followed. This desire is pure desire and not yet conscious; it is the formative start of consciousness' development. For me, consciousness is seminally the perception of pleasure and pain, and evolution is the ongoing refinement of this perception that is actually the development of matter's intrinsic desire to become conscious. In other words, evolution is the movement and eventual blossoming of pre-consciousness from the mineral kingdom through the vegetable into the animal of which we humans belong as a part of this biological vehicle for consciousness' coming into being. Nonbinary Yvonne Aburrow had originally participated in this exchange as well and must have subsequently deleted their contribution, but I had appreciated their suggestion that matter might be seen as a denser form of consciousness.

To Jonathan, I wondered that a more 'parsimonious understanding might be to see consciousness in all things, but what good is that understanding if it does not explain anything?' I agreed with his assertion that 'Divinity and all aspects of the material world are inseparable, that world is composed of a multitude of entities of different kinds, all compelling respect', but I did not consider that respect is necessarily dependent on consciousness being by default in all things. Instead, I wondered to him if the evolution/emergence of consciousness would not actually be the more parsimonious explanation.

I will need here to admit that this exchange is a convoluted one but still something that personally I very much enjoyed. This present philosophical section, however, may be easily skipped and passed over by anyone finding it too complex or not to their interest. I only say at this point that it may require several readings for it to be comprehended, but, if that is not desired at present, it can nonetheless be kept in mind for some future moment. Adrian had built his notion of the explosion (not necessarily the Big Bang) of consciousness/deity/energy/matter on A.N. Whitehead's picturing of interiority and matter appearing simultaneously – with consciousness being a variant of interiority. Whitehead like C.S. Pierce 'teetered', according to Adrian, 'on the edge of the pantheistic/panentheist blade', but I have wondered if this very blade might not be the edge of chaos itself. Yvonne had mentioned the philosophers Aratus of Soli and Epimenides of Cnossos in our discussion, while Jonathan signals that the advice to 'live, move, and have our being' is a crib from Acts 17:28. What I most share with Jonathan, however, is his attestation from Feri liturgy of the 'Holy Mother, in Whom we live, move and have our being, from You all things emerge and unto You all things return' and her not being a demiurgic author but the vehicle of an all-generative womb. Where we differ, of course, is that, apart perhaps as a poetic idea, I do not comprehend her being transcendent but rather immanent through the thrust of her poetic presence that 'all things, including ourselves, are' her flesh.

'With regard to Nicole's hesitancy to project gender roles onto sexual deities as well as aspects of the earth/cosmos that are not sexed or gendered, our broader linguistic tradition saw some things female (earth, dawn), some male (lightning, celestial brightness) and some things male *or* female – not male *and* female as Mogg has in his Kemetic tradition – (the sun, the moon and fire). These are ancient metaphors that I find have their own numinous power. If they come to be declared old-fashioned, I fear that we could be throwing out the baby with the bathwater'.

To recapitulate my fundamental telluric perception of evolution, 'the idea of consciousness as the Cosmos' will to know itself' is to be understood as 'pure will', that is, desire before even consciousness has arisen from it. Combining the tenth mandala Rigvedic hymn on 'creation' concerning *kama* (10.129.4), with Hesiod's *Theogony* mentioning an always-present Himeros ('desire') and the primordial passion-fire (Surtr) and the wish-cow Audhumla in Snorri Sturluson's *Gylfaginning*, one can conjecture that the proto-Indo-Europeans recognised will as seminal to the very emergence of the cosmos. I do not think, however, that 'the will causes consciousness' any more than the carbon, oxygen, etc. *cause* a human body. Each is instead something that *develops*. From the idea of complexity theory's alinearity over linearity, rather than say 'that the utterly necessary cosmic will to self-awareness is the true definition of consciousness', *pace* Jonathan, this could be more appropriately and accurately rephrased as the utterly necessary cosmic will to self-awareness being the ultimate origin of consciousness.

Regarding panpsychism, I wonder if it might not ultimately be a goal; and to assume that it already exists could be a human arrogance and hubris. Do we need 'an explanation for how, mechanically, consciousness arises from the processes of the brain'? And could it not be that the brain has evolved to be a *vehicle* for the emergence of consciousness?

I agreed with Jonathan that 'paganity' marries well with other partners besides panpsychism. And speaking of marriage and offspring, I also agreed that gender metaphors can lead and have led to bad places, but do we not again lose the baby if we ignore the richness of an ancestral legacy and simply abandon those metaphors? We *know* that the feminine takes precedence (as opposed to how the Abrahamic traditions would have it), and I argue that what follows needs rather to be kept in functional balance and in a viable and respectful valuing based on that knowledge – perhaps today even more than was the case in 2011.

Nicole, however, thought that my use of the term *feminine* illustrated some of the difficulties that occur with 'sexed/gendered metaphors for the divine'. She found it a 'loaded term in our culture that, when unpacked, contains a host of decidedly sexist assumptions regarding how women/female people are supposed to behave and present themselves'. Sex alone has 'the cultural baggage of gender tightly attached,' and while Nicole expressed having no desire to 'neuter' the gods and goddesses as they have been perceived for millennia, she still did not want them to be used 'to reinforce "traditional" and decidedly harmful gender roles that I'd like to see Pagans (and all of society) moving beyond'.

It was by this point in our exchange, if not sooner, that I wondered if we were not simply talking in circles. Much theological conversation – including that of paganism – goes indeed into a circular discussion. Recently I have participated in a Zoom celebration of the Sophia Centre's new graduates. It was through Sophia that I was granted my professorship in Cultural Astronomy and Astrology. I had first learned horoscopy from Dale Sherwood, Anita Kirkpatrick (Edmund Purdom's first wife), and my 'astrological parents', Jack Fontan and Ray Unger. These last had taught me that astrology was empirical and based on observation. When I learned scientific methodology under Carlo Lastrucci at San Francisco State, I asked him at one point if astrology could be considered a science to the degree that it had been founded by following the empirical principles of observance. 'Absolutely', he affirmed. However, once the Sophia programme was underway at Bath Spa University College, I was astonished to discover that our astrologer-students approached the discipline as Platonic and founded upon a range of *a priori* projections. I was reminded of this even further during the Sophia Centre's 'grand Zoom celebration' as the graduates each delivered five-minute summaries of their dissertations. While these were highly researched and most impressive theses, the speakers mentioned predominantly such Neo-Platonists as Porphyry, Iamblichus and Proclus, and, likewise as with astrologers, a corresponding gnostic understanding of paganism or contemporary Western paganism is without question held by many within the pagan community – such as Jonathan Korman. Despite this, I still maintain that a telluric and/or *tellurique* worldview is the more compatible interpretation for an earth-based/earth-centred pagan spirituality.

There is no question that the Neoplatonist philosophers are intriguingly fascinating, but to me they encapsulate a transcendental perspective that is closer to Abrahamic religion, Vedantic Hinduism and Mahayana Buddhism than it is to a telluric understanding of paganism. A vernacular pagan sentiment is nevertheless deeply atavistic, and as a consequence we witness various pagan residues in Roman Catholic and Orthodox religious Christian devotion, in various paganish elements easily detectable in Islam, in Hindu *pūjā* and in Buddhist veneration. Nevertheless, with all these main world religions apart possibly with Islam, there is a central underlying wish to escape the sordidness of physicality as an imprisonment. With 'deep' paganism, by contrast, if there were reincarnation it would be something to be welcomed and celebrate rather than to end.

But to return to our circle of pagan theological exchange, Jonathan claims that I have 'fallen for one of the common misunderstandings of the Buddhist project'. He maintains that the 'goal is not elimination of desire; the [Buddhist] goal is the elimination of suffering', and the 'cause of suffering is the ATTACHMENT TO desire'.

'Oh com'on, Jonathan', I replied, '*everyone* wants to avoid suffering – everyone apart from a few martyrs and masochists'.

> . . . the Buddha's 'way' is another throwing the baby out with the bathwater for, along with suffering, he eliminates pleasure as well. His method for ending suffering is to achieve a state of detachment and indifference which can only be translated as one of non-desire. Nirvana is a different goal than that of the pagan and her affirmation of pleasure from gentle delight to, when appropriate, the throes of passion. The Second Noble Truth identifies attachment as the *cause* of suffering. Eliminate that, and suffering is eliminated as well.

Part of 'correct thought', accordingly, is the avoidance of covetousness or the desire that is integral to pleasure-seeking. But here Adrian comes in with the following:

> Michael – I don't think it's quite fair to ascribe the 'elimination of pleasure' to the Buddha (i.e. the historical figure, Siddhartha Gautama) simply because there's so much debate and uncertainty over what he actually taught and what accreted to those teachings in the years and centuries that followed. One of the pillars of Buddhism is the idea of a 'middle way' between extremes, so arguably the elimination of *too much* pleasure, or *too many* pleasure-bound activities, may be considered a teaching of his. There are certainly many pleasure-eliminating strands within Buddhism, and these aren't at all surprising given their Southeast Asian cultural contexts (less so for the Far East), but there are also numerous pleasure-accepting

> strands, and even pleasure-seeking ones, in the case of the Tantric traditions. What's central in the latter is *experience without attachment*, since attachment is considered to lead to displeasure (i.e. suffering) and delusion, while non-attachment is considered to enhance the capacity for experience and for enlightenment. Attachment in this case means something like trying to stop or hold back the flow of experience; non-attachment means going with that flow.

I agreed with Adrian in as much as I was using the Buddha as the nominal or titular embodiment of Buddhism itself. He was correct since I was actually attempting to describe Buddhism rather than necessarily the teachings of the Buddha. The 'middle way' I suggested was a much more contentious and even controversial area than I was allowing for since there could be suspicion over how 'middle' the 'middle way' truly is, but this is a different subject than the one at hand. As for *tantra*, it is not original to Buddhism but plays more of a similar role as does Bon Po to Vajrayana and Mahayana. While it appears to have been grafted on to Buddhism as well as Hinduism, in itself *tantra* is something much closer to paganism in spirit and possibly in origins.

Nicole speculated on her puzzlement with the concept of 'non-attachment' since 'it seems to imply that one shouldn't care about anything or anyone too deeply on a personal level, except in the abstract sense of cultivating a sort of generalized compassion'. She mentions that the 'engaged Buddhism' taught by Thich Nhat Hanh and others seems to be a substantially different approach. Another thing that puzzled her is that 'the Buddha is [also] revered for leaving his wife and child to seek enlightenment'.

My own feeling remained that attachment is itself intimately connected to desire. I asked rhetorically if the experience that is had with non-attachment is simply tailored by definition to the supposed experience of enlightenment rather than through empirical fact. In other words, it becomes a *particular* kind of experience that is being cleverly legitimised. Attachment could be equally attached to the flow rather than be resistant to it. But I did agree with Adrian's suggestion that paganisms could have much to gain from the 'practical psycho-spiritual sophistication of Buddhism' – including the philosophical nuance of certain Mahayana Buddhist strands, while at the same time 'Buddhism has much that could be shed in favor of a more world-embracing faith and practice'. I am likewise in accord both with the potential possibility of an alliance between Buddhism and paganism to augment a mutual contribution that each could make to the other and as well as with

Adrian's proposal that the process philosophies offer a great tool for cultivating that alliance.

I certainly do not wish to harp on this, though I'm afraid it may sound as if I am, but the understanding of the cosmos and our places within it that I fervently endorse is the most at home with the metaphor of feminine birth. This differs both in its concept of seminal origins and in any *raison d'être* consequence of subsequent direction than it would be in comprehending our cosmos as the result of some spoken word or the mind-projection of a primordial god or even goddess. The divine womb would be that from which one and all come and evolve, but whether it is also that to which we ultimately return or in which we have final dissolution is another question. But it is this metaphor of organic femininity that I sense holds our cosmos together with the human adventure. In response to Nicole and the imperative to move beyond 'decidedly harmful gender roles', I explained that, originally, I had thought to use the word *female* in the preceding sentence but decided that *feminine* (*femininity*) was more accurate. I asked if most terms we employ are not in fact already 'loaded' in some way or another, and I wonder if this is something with which we must always navigate in our efforts toward communication.

In the sociology of religion for instance, there is an outspoken contingent that wishes to abandon the terms 'sect' and 'cult' that are, otherwise within the field, *bona fide* terms for marginal religious movements. My argument with my colleagues has been that if we abandon these labels, we surrender to the media, psychologists and even the government in determining who controls the politics of representation and have taught the wider public nothing in the process. In religion, the same dynamic lies behind the desire to reclaim such terms as *witch*, *pagan* and *idolatry* etc. Words have indeed been misused for millennia, but when Nicole asks, 'how do we work around this?' I suspect it is more an answer of not going 'around' but straight into the problem, confronting it squarely, making the vagaries of history as clear as we can, and moving on with that knowledge at the forefront.

In English, we have rather fully neutered our linguistic heritage. Dutch now divides between the neuter and a common gender reduced from an earlier understanding of some words as either masculine or feminine, whereas German retains the fuller designation of nouns as neuter, masculine and feminine. French considers people, places and things to be either male or female. Lightning, for instance, is *la foudre*, that is, a feminine noun. In Latin, the word for honour is masculine, but that for virtue is feminine despite *virtu* being derived from the word *vir* meaning 'a man, male person'. And, besides *honos*, the other virtues are all feminine. Interestingly, all the words that Nicole used to describe the results from the perception of lightning as male/masculine, namely, power, force, anger, energy and punishment are feminine designations in French – respectively *la puissance, la force, la colère, l'énergie* and *la punition*. The ramifications of gender nuance are a complex legacy that have much more to tell us than their cultural and historical employments to foster and maintain sexist non-equality. There are differences, but that is not to undermine our goal of equality: different but equal. Is not one of the fundamental pagan affirmations of plurality the celebration of diversity? Here in France, the people invariably say, '*Vive la difference*!' My fear is that if we lose the gender nuance of nature and our deities of nature, we short-change and do ourselves a disservice. Our archaic rituals and understandings allow us important root connections that can for the increasingly mindful not only allow us access to spiritual renewal, numinous grounding and contemplative wonder but also encourage us to end gender ideologies rather than reinforce them.

In reply, Nicole thinks nevertheless that the term *female* is preferable to *feminine*.

> If we could use 'feminine' to simply mean 'that which is associated with being female' in the biological sense (gestating, birthing), that might be fine, but in our culture it conjures up too many images of frilly pink dresses and such that get in the way. I'm all in favor of reclaiming language in many cases, but my preference on this one would be to let *feminine* fall by the wayside and find something else to work with without the accompanying baggage.

Nicole remains unconvinced that there is not a strong connection between grammatically masculine or feminine words and concepts and the ways by which those ideas are attached to social gender roles. While finding the linguistic issue interesting, she claimed that the evolution of grammar is just too bizarre and random. '*Uterus* is masculine in French, after all; how much sense does *that* make'? For Jonathan, there is a hesitancy over accepting the vigorously gendered imagery from the ancients' conceptions of divinity because such images are culturally embedded. 'Gender meant different things to the people who spoke on those terms; re-mapping onto local/contemporary conceptions of gender can easily result in confusion'. However, I continued to affirm that even with gendered imagery being culturally embedded, if we dig deep into our collective linguistic heritage, we might find 'a radical/root cultural awareness/understanding that is to be shared today by many different daughter cultures – thereby assisting us in any cosmopolitan venture toward a more equable but still grounded world'.

Meanwhile, Jonathan explained to Nicole that he understood the theological concept of panpsychism to refer to the range of philosophies that say, in some sense, that 'all is mind'. He admitted that the more common understanding of the term comprehends the illusion of material existence and holds that it is the thoughts in the divine Mind that constitute the ultimate truth of the cosmos. But rather than employing the more familiar solipsistic versions of this idea, for him it is not that 'all is mind' but that 'all have minds' in the narrow sense of consciousness or awareness. To my consideration that 'the utterly necessary cosmic will to self-awareness is the ultimate origin of consciousness', Jonathan wondered if that makes the will to self-awareness the only precursor to self-awareness or whether there are others in the process as well. To my assertion that 'the brain has evolved as a *vehicle* for the emergence of consciousness', he claimed there are two 'readings'. One is teleological; the 'other is the idea that the brain is a receiver for consciousness as a radio is a receiver for music'. He felt that the latter appeals to our sense that brains are unique in having consciousness while setting aside or dismissing the problem of how the brain actually produces it. Admittedly, this raises more questions than it settles. He asks, 'Why did the brain evolve to receive consciousness, from an evolutionary process standpoint? "Why" is there consciousness out there for the brain to receive?'

My reply to Jonathan's 'other precursors' question was to suppose that 'along the way', this could be a possibility but that still 'the cosmic will itself is the precursor of the whole shebang'. For some Vedic speculationists, will or desire is the 'first principle'. Otherwise, if we conceive of an organism's capacity for the experience of pleasure and pain as engendering consciousness, the brain as a 'radio receiver' is not necessary. Consciousness becomes increasingly an emergent necessity for a more evolved, complex and fragile organism's own survival. My general dismissal of panpsychism rests on my understanding of it as a monistic form of pantheism in which all things are held to have minds or mental qualities. In short, that all nature is psychical. Nicole had asked, 'How exactly can an entity will or desire something without first being conscious?' However, in the panthelistic understanding I am considering (from *theilen* 'to will'), there is no primordial entity but instead an inaugural instance of pure will. I readily will admit that it is difficult for us to conceive of wishing only as wishing rather than wishing *for* something. It may be akin to Jonathan's awareness without thought of any kind. In one of my own contemplative evocations, I seek to begin by centring or focusing upon purely wishing but not wishing for anything in particular. The wishing for something specific may come later. And purely wishing but not wishing for something is not easy to do but is probably similar to a Buddhist meditational effort to empty completely the mind from all thoughts. I am not a Buddhist and understand pan-consciousness as a goal rather than as an origin or something always present. As a pagan, I centre upon and begin with purely desiring without desiring anything in particular. In other words, I am doing perhaps the precise opposite of the Buddhist who seeks to eliminate desire; I am exalting it – either by seeking to attune, however briefly, with the primordial wish, or by endeavouring to become, again however briefly, consciously one with the entire cosmos.

Whether any present reader might come at all close to doing the same, this theological exchange I had primarily with Nicole, Adrian and Jonathan was an encounter that I enjoyed immensely. I would have forgotten about it completely had Elvira Mysanthrope not found it among the far-past Pagan group discussions on Facebook. At its conclusion, Terry Dohney had asked, 'whot happens if there is no god?' I was able to reply, 'We're free then to make one up'.

The autumn for me has a special beauty with its embering colour and nostalgic closing in. Winter is winter with its different yuletide colours, the warmth and cosiness of indoors and the bracing challenge of the rest. And the blossoming magic of spring with its reawakening is always a great joy. But summer is and always has been my favourite time of year. 'Summertime and the living is easy . . . Your daddy's rich and your ma is good looking'. This Gershwin song was my childhood. While Irish politician David Norris wished his mother could have been glamorous, I did not have that wish because my mother was most elegant, attractive and beautiful. But like Norris' mother, mine 'also had a wonderful natural gift for happiness . . . It was always in her nature to be happy, and to want others to be happy. . . . She delighted in laughter, and music, and she loved me'.

I have recently read Woody Allen's autobiography, *Apropos of Nothing*. I am amazed that I have missed so many of his films. I adored *Interiors*, *Match Point*, *Annie Hall* and *Hannah and Her Sisters*. I could include *Manhattan* and *Midnight in Paris* as well. My tendency was to side with him in his dispute with Mia Farrow, and after reading his book, I am convinced that the allegations against him are both untrue and vengeful. For their support of Allen, I now hold Diane Keaton, Scarlett Johansson, Alec Baldwin, Charlotte Rampling, Pedro Amodóvar, Javier Bardem, Catherine Deneuve, Isabelle Huppert, Jude Law and Alan Alda in even a higher regard than I had previously. I could be disappointed with Satchel Ronan Farrow and his anti-Allen position, but gay sons almost always love and foremost support their mothers.

I belong to that generation born in the 1930s to the mid-40s who lived through a world war and into a time when the world seemed promisingly secure – this last eventually becoming an interlude times before subsequent perpetual economic insecurity. I came of age in the 1950s & 1960s. My childhood progressed from ration books, saving tin foil, party line telephones, newsreels at the cinema, the radio broadcasting no more than three stations, polio, the Korean War, and Castro becoming Prime Minister of Cuba into what seemed to be overflowing plenty and opportunity. Milk was delivered bottled to the door, television only came later, and we were allowed to play as children unsupervised outdoors. Admittedly, without TV, we had virtually no understanding of the wider world, and there was nothing yet even close to Google, the internet and mobile phones. Sharing this today through social media, I hear that my 'Best of times' was something only applicable for 'privileged white straight people'. In hindsight, I suppose this is true, but am I supposed now to feel guilt and shame because of it?

My extended London family today includes the now retired LSE sociologist Hilary Rose. As the grandmother of my daughter's non-biological brother, when we first met, she thought that it would be appropriate for me to call her 'Mom'. She is only a few years older than I am. One of the things I most admire about Hilary and her husband Steven is their determined courageousness in that they are receivers of death threats for being Jews who advocate passionately in favour of the Palestinians. In response to my posting about being one of the last generation who knew and grew up in 'the best possible time', Hilary responds with mention of the wartime poverty in Britain in which the children her school teacher parents taught would fall asleep because they had had no breakfast. She talks further about the shelters, gas masks, barrage balloons, incendiary bombs, the search lights and the dog fights in the sky. In contrast, America of course lived through the war with Pearl Harbor being the only attack on the country. We did not have 60K civilians killed or US Jews sent to death camps. Meanwhile, having to distinguish enemy planes from those of the allies, Hilary knew when to jump into the nearest ditch or throw herself flat on the ground.

When she thinks about the 1930s and 1940s, it is Billie Holiday's 1939 *Strange Fruit* that initially comes to Hilary's mind. The first black people she saw were near the US airfields in Britain when white Yanks attempted to exclude them from the pubs. She welcomes Black Lives Matter and points out the huge proportion of incarcerated black men in both US and UK prisons. Hilary decides to 'skip the sixties' when she not only met the Freedom Riders and the National Welfare Rights Organization in the United States but also went through the doomed hopefulness of 1968.

Turning from the post-WWII 'Interesting Facts', she concentrates instead on some of the more sobering 'facts' of today such as the USA infant mortality rate of 5.9 vis-à-vis Finland's 1.5 and Hong Kong's 1.3. This compares with the 52% white infant mortality percentage in the US of 1935 versus the 84% of non-whites. Hilary deplores in particular the 'unthinkable levels of poverty in deprived areas' in which 50% of children have parents with the most meagre of incomes. What we share, however, is a hope that 'the younger generations could build a different [and] better world'.

Personally, I cannot deplore more than I already do such persistent Western scourges as poverty, racism, imperialistic colonialism and any ethnic or cultural claims to superiority. But recently coming across a three-year-old article by Professor Robert Tombs, who – as it turns out – is the cousin of dear friend Meg, I agree with his defence of what he refers to as 'western civilisation'. Following David Hume, Tombs claims that the

> western civilisation we have inherited is the result of a painful, slow, dangerous, accidental and faltering invention of a set of rules for life, the best we have managed over many centuries, and certainly in need of constant maintenance and improvement, but also worth defending and proclaiming.

Without a single source, scripture or prophet, we cultural Westerners are unstable, disunited and never fully orthodox. As a culture, western civilisation is and has always been quarrelsome, diverse but also flexible. As Tombs sees it, we owe our philosophical foundations to ancient Greece and their transmission by Arabic scholars, our legal systems to both ancient Rome and medieval England, and our modernity to the 17th century scientific revolution and the 18th century Enlightenment. All this together informs

Western civilisation's laws, values, arts, institutions and our 'habits of mind and heart' that enable us more or less to live, fairly harmoniously, together. What perhaps renders us unique is our diversity, eclecticism and capacity for evolution. Although mostly relatively late developments albeit with some ancient links, for Tombs, our core *ideals* include tolerance, rationality, scientific methodology, the rule of law, democracy, rights, justice, fairness and equality or at least some notion of parity before the law and/or the equality of opportunity. To a critical mind, such as mine might on occasion be, it becomes obvious that we fall painfully short of these principles, and in the ongoing cherishing and teaching of our better aspects, we still need to be crucially evaluative of inherited values, maturely mindful of our past misdeeds, and open to change.

Among the core ideas of 'western civilisation', Tombs includes the Judaeo-Christian notions of charity, love, peace and forgiveness. However, one feedback I have received is that there is no 'Judaeo-Christian' tradition and hence, Tombs' argument is undermined by that 'cliched ahistorical trope' since Jews and Christians have not run in the same circles since the 1st century c.e. Although the terms 'Judaeo Christian' and '*Judenchristlich*' appeared in the 19th century, and Paul Tillich referred in 1933 to the Jewish-Christian tradition, it is true that the Judeo-Christian expression is largely a 20th century American invention originally employed in anti-Nazi and anti-Communist contexts. But vis-à-vis paganism as well as various non-Western religious communities including Native Americans, secularists and atheists, the Judaeo-Christian trope can refer to a particular aspect of Abrahamism that is to be distinguished from Islam and others predominantly on the basis of common values and ethics, the extensive historical continuity between Jewish and Christian world views, and a shared understanding of the general relationship the individual allegedly has with 'God'. Though by St. Paul on, the Jews have been marginalised, and the Jewish-Christian concept has been variously employed by the American right and left, Conservatives and Liberals, I want to argue that it has a broader applicability than merely as some reference to a 'common American identity'.

Nevertheless, Tombs considers that our present demoralisation in the West results from a routine denigration of 'western' values that are weakening solidarity, promoting indifference to political principles and institutions, and encouraging intransigent assertions of entitlement along with magnified claims to victimhood. He feels that we in the West are currently dangerously undermining free thought, free speech, equality before the law, and the right to a fair trial. And while I am in agreement for the most part – especial in the aftermath to the 2020 American Presidential elections with its frightening political divide, I also want and hope to see Western civilisation expand to join a truly viable global accord that addresses ecology (climate change and pollution), non-belligerent resolution, food distribution and epidemic/pandemic and other health issues.

A problem, however, that I see that is additional to this is one that John Pilger brings up on the 75th anniversary of the atomic bombing of Hiroshima. I am aware that Pilger is decidedly left – even more so than I am, but I have yet to find cogent reasons to doubt the things on which he informs. In the present case, it concerns the 'lie' in which I was raised, namely, that the atomic bomb was dropped to end the war with Japan. Pilger, however, points out documents contained in Washington's National Archives that indicate that the Japanese were making peace overtures already in 1943. But the United States wanted to use its nuclear weapon as a detergent to the Soviet Union. I remember my father, bless him, expressing his wish at the conclusion of the Second World War for America to drop a bomb on Moscow. The effects of radiation in Japan were catastrophic on purely human terms and then, subsequently, in the Marshall Islands that were used for testing purposes between 1946 and 1958 there has been, additionally horrifyingly, a shamelessly callous consequence of someone's need 'to get a measure of human uptake when people live in a contaminated environment'. As Pilger accurately expresses in reference to 'the ruthlessness and immorality of great power: that is, *imperial* power, . . . cynicism is the true enemy of humanity'. With China now replacing Russia as the – largely economic – threat to American hegemony and 'the myth of Western superiority', the nuclear target has changed.

While it is to be granted that both the 're-education camps' that China has instituted for its Uighur population and the new security law being imposed upon Hong Kong are constituting grotesque stains on China's ability to be part of a credible global community, the West's apocalyptic manoeuvring, bullying and 'abandonment of honest reporting' exemplify an even more pathetic dishonour for the Western civilisation many of us still wish to champion. If indeed our core goals or values are justice, fairness, equality and the rule of democratic law, we need an honest freedom of the press to support these. What I find ironic to some extent is that much of the positive hopes that are detectable as deeply imbedded in the culture of the West coincide with those of both contemporary Western paganism and paganism more broadly: viable community, growth, freedom and an organic interconnection with the earth and nature. Perhaps through our celebrations of beauty, enchantment and honesty, the pagan spirituality that is implicitly natural to all of humanity might transform the neglected promise of both Western culture and the global community into more durable expressions of honour and joy.

In the meantime, I continue to do my best to ensure that in summertime, the living remains easy. My dear and beautiful mother is no longer accessible, but despite pandemics and political bluster, life is still precious as a divine gift. Within the nuances and catharses of our constantly augmenting aesthetic legacies, could we not but help to alleviate the suffering of those who are suffering, feed and shelter one and all, and provide an open and intelligent education for our younger generations? These are the humane aspirations of both Western and all cultures. How much longer must we continue to ignore them and only pretend that we are not disregarding such objectives?

I believe it was 1965 when I 'escaped' Los Angeles after my stint with the Broadway department store as an assistant buyer, first with china and then with toys. A friend of Buster/George (Diana) helped me find the L-shaped flat in San Francisco's Haight-Ashbury. The rent was $80 a month, and it had one-bedroom but also a large closet that I was subsequently able to use as my bedroom once Jeannie, the 'thumper', moved in with me.

At San Francisco State, I pursued my MA studies in International Relations. This was another idyllic time in which it was possible to enjoy both the studies and the magic of the City by the Bay. As wondrous as other urban areas throughout the world may be, EssEff is in a class completely of its own. And during these few years, Haight Street transformed from being the delicatessen district it had been into the countercultural and hippie centre for which it has become legendarily famous. And with that metamorphosis, I changed too.

But before I became a long-haired 'freak', I was able to complete my Social Science degree. For a meagre but necessary income, I accepted to be a Teaching Assistant and was put in charge of one of the seminar divisions. The students I had were a lively and lovely group. One day as I was heading to the class, I had a flat tyre en route and was enormously late – well after the mandatory ten-minute waiting period. But when I finally arrived, all my students were still there and waiting for me. This class excelled, and all were motivated to participate to the fullest.

The Assistant Head of the department, DeVere Pentony (and as I write this I discover that he only passed last year at the age of 94!), explained that if a student actively engaged in the class discussion and wrote the required essays of approximately so many words, an A, B or C would depend on the papers' lengths. Not knowing otherwise, I explained these requirements for the class to encourage all those for whom I was responsible. As a result, it was an unforgettable time of dynamic group exchange and the production of superlative compositions. But also, consequently, I believe virtually everyone who was in my seminar had earned and was awarded an A. Somehow, this resonates with the current downgrading fiasco thanks to the Tory government's official education algorithm being endorsed for determining A-level grades after the British lockdown and its resultant cancelation of live classes. The TAs of the other seminars for the International Relations class at S.F. State were forced to produce an assessment 'curve' for the class as a whole, and while my students received top marks, none of those in the other seminars did.

Based on my own experience, I found that returning to college or university later in one's life after the initial undergraduate degree is an incomparable joy and an endeavour and opportunity that are more and more appreciated the older one becomes. The oral exams at the conclusion of my MA studies were another story. Each of my colleagues went before the board for at least an hour, but my session lasted scarcely more than fifteen minutes. I would not allow myself to be cornered and answered the questions suppositionally when necessary and accurately for the rest. I learned later that the examining board was perplexed by me because International Relations had not been my undergraduate major, so though I had qualified for top marks, I was granted something less for the official record. Several years later and after I had left San Francisco for Europe, there was the notoriety of Angela Davis as a Black Panther supporter of the Soledad brothers. With her later acquittal and release from prison, it became Professor Pentony's decision to accept her as a teacher at San Francisco State College. Eventually she became a Professor of Ethnic Studies at SFSU.

The field of Ethnic Studies is conceived in part, as opposed to International Studies, with its interdisciplinary focus on difference – both racial and minority ethnicity – and the relations of the West with Third World Countries. It strives, as I suppose so does Postmodernism, to counter what is conceived as the inherently Eurocentric perspective of history, sociology, political science and cultural studies. But when it comes to religion and in particular pagan Heathenism, there has arisen the controversial right-hand path known as Folkism, the uncompromised belief that ancestral DNA connections are vital to spiritual practice. Stephen McNallen, the former head of the Asatru Folk Assembly, has claimed that ancestry is 'better' than universalism. He argues that what a dream is for the individual, a myth is to a group. What McNallen has in mind is an alleged importance of legend, folk belief and mythical tradition to a racially exclusive ethnicity. But against this, I will argue that it is through the dream or myth conveyed by the artist, poet, composer and the like that a myth can precisely become an allegorical complex that is universally shared. Consequently, for pagans in general, mythology is a treasure-trove for accessing and understanding the divine not only in one's preferred traditions but also within the navigation of enchantment more inclusively global and worldwide.

For the West, the mythology of the ancient Greeks is seminal and one of the richest domains for comprehending the gods and the sacred, although it is certainly not the only avenue for gaining historical and allegorical reflections of reality, afterlife comprehensions and unconditional godhead. Within the Indo-European linguistic heritage alone, there are also Vedic-Hindu, Hittite, Roman, Celtic and Heathen contributions and across the board also Chinese, Shinto, Afro-Latin, Native American as well as other cultural lineages that offer non-Abrahamic spiritual insight. Within paganism, and in contrast to folkish exclusivity, syncretic movements have arisen and continue to do so.

But let me play for a moment with our Hellenic legacy. What follows in this section that deals with my thoughts on mythology may come across as something once again more complex to the reader, at least as my partner Richard contends, and could be skipped over by those who wish, but it amounts at the minimum to an attempted digest of both my musings and research conclusions. Much of what I perceive is controversial and does not fit traditional understandings or accepted norms, but it contributes to my own comprehension of both paganism in general and the heritage in which my post-Christian spirituality has begun.

Greco-Roman myths are rarely happily ending tales. The visit of Zeus and Hermes, though disguised as human travellers, to Philemon and Baucis is an exception and among the more agreeable. One can imagine the thrill-based hospitality of the elderly couple stemming from their delight in advancing age to have visitors who, even in disguise, would have been impressive. Zeus' abduction of Ganymede and lifting him to immortality in Olympus and Dionysus's rescue of the abandoned Ariadne are also affirmative events. Another happier lore is to be found in some versions of the love between Daphnis and Chloe – at least as Ovid tells their story, and, despite her tribulations, Psyche's liaison with Cupid as related by Apuleius is another that comes to a satisfactory conclusion. By contrast, the fates of both Narcissus and Hermaphroditus are unfortunate ones. But in these cases, Narcissus was excessively mesmerised by himself, whereas Hermaphroditus' difficulty is likewise not really of his own making but results from the naiad Salmacis' love for him. Both tales are expressive of the random hazards of nature rather than being cautionary tales about an individual's culpable morality. What happens to them could happen to any of us.

While the gods may be immortal, they can nevertheless become incapacitated – as when Typhon steals the sinews of Zeus or Hephaestus chains Hera to her throne or Prometheus has his liver eaten daily by an eagle. And in more rare cases, the gods can in fact know death: Dionysus, his mother Semele whose name signifies the 'earth', Persephone, Pan, Asclepius. But Dionysus is reborn, and he later brings his mother back from Hades. Asclepius, too, is resurrected. Persephone returns annually to the world of the living, and presumably once nature worship comes again into vogue, Pan will come back to life as well. Interestingly, as a god of vegetation, Dionysus may be seen as the very agent of the earth's recovery. And thanks to Hesiod's infatuation with the myths of the Levant, the birth of the Lord of Light (Zeus) directly from Mother Earth (Gaia) that is paralleled by the parental relationship between Semele (the earth mother) and Dionysus (the Zeus of Nysus or Nesa) has been all but obscured. What I contend here is that against the earlier substratum of what describes our world's generation, Uranus is a later insertion based on the Middle Eastern 'succession myths' belonging to Anatolia and Mesopotamia.

Extending beyond the Greek corpus, we find many other gods who die if not in some cases permanently. For various people these particular figures may be of personal interest and include diversely the moon; the Nordic Balder (Baldr) and Höðr as well as such figures as Thor, Týr, Freyr, Heimdallr and Loki who will perish with *Ragnarök*; the Vedic Yama; the Hattic/Hittite Telipinu; the Akkadian Ishtar; the Japanese Izanami; the Aztec Quetzalcoatl; and the Afro-Latin Orishas who were originally ancestral humans who 'disappeared' or became apotheosised upon their departure from life. Many of the Chinese and Japanese gods were also deified upon death (Tiān Hòu, Bao Sheng Da Di, Guandi, Hachiman, Tenjin, etc.) Related are such dying-and-rising gods as Osiris, Attis, Tammuz and Adonis. These all may be of a special interest in that we usually understand the gods as the immortals, and a deity's experiencing or knowing the netherworld allows a further dimension to their very being. But it is primarily with Hellenic mythology that at present I wish to remain.

As we explore Classic mythology and especially that of the Greeks, we find that it does not particularly present a wish-world but more a poignant range of metaphors for this, our world with its own realities and unhappinesses. Much grief occurs in the mythic realm, and there is sorrow expressed from Apollo's loss of Hyacinthus and Daphne's escape from the god, Demeter's desolation for Kore, Orpheus' premature violation of Eurydice's release from Hades, to Phaethon's fall from his father's chariot, Pandora's foolishness, Heracles' agony from Deianeira's poisoned cloak, Io's tribulations due to Hera, and Actaeon's violent demise thanks to Artemis. Artemis along with her brother Apollo brought suffering to the thoughtlessly boasting Niobe by extinguishing all her children, and, similarly, Apollo's flaying of Marsyas was a result of the satyr's witless challenging of the god of music to a musical contest. But while Greek mythology presents us with a host of cautionary tales and warnings, it is more than just this in its comprehending of multiple realities, its beauty in fantastical models and divine players, and its intrinsic sense of the magical and marvellous.

When someone or something is said to develop 'like a weed', the phrase refers to being strong in persistent growth that is otherwise unlimited or uncontrolled by human management. Though we often refer to the growth of weeds as being 'natural', we humans too are no less than 'natural'. If truth be told, the adjective 'human' is fundamentally interchangeable with the qualifier 'natural', and at core both modifiers reciprocate with the attribute of 'pagan'. Etymologically speaking, there are detectable reasons that our words have arisen and developed along their way as they have. What becomes important spiritually is the recognition that as our words have sources, and because sources are sacred, words themselves have 'sacred sources'. This constitutes one of the chief factors behind the dynamism and perennial appeal of mythology. And it is how we understand some, not all, but *some* of our gods.

I have long felt that within the Classical tradition, virtually anyone's real love among the male deities is ultimately an avatar of Jupiter/Zeus. Among goddesses, it would be Juno/Hera. Hera is the personification of the wife – including that of the jealous wife. Given the questionable behaviour and faithlessness of the male part of our species, spousal jealousy on the part of the woman would seem to be inevitable in marriage. Hence the tales of Hera as the vindictive wife. But she still embodies much more than this, and, like Juno, she is principally the personification of the light of the dawn.

As a brief aside at this point, I would like to mention that the source of my preferred *mantra* is to be found within Hellenic/Classical mythology and the underlying understanding that it comprehends. First of *all* is the *wish* ('one, two, three for wishing'). Metaphorically or literally, the Big Bang is the telluric embodiment of *the* Wish (e.g., Himerus, but also depicted elsewhere as *kama, tapas,* Muspell). The resulting incorporation and/or incarnation becomes the entire cosmos as the concretised reflex of the seminally primal wish. Noteworthy in addition is that mind comes *after* the primordial *wish* – the spontaneous, unconscious desire comes first; awareness and sentience develop later. *Health*, then, is the whole itself and the being one with the cosmos ('four, five for health'). *Wonder*, for me, comes next and is known in the very moment when wonder intersects with consciousness ('six, seven for wonder'). And, finally, *freedom* is the ultimate goal and aim of everyone/everything ('eight, nine for freedom'). Consequently, health, wonder and freedom may be seen as elaborations of the very wish that is the beginning of the cosmic entirety. For wonder alone, one needs only 'to look at it all.' Ceremonial ritual, of course, is not a necessity, but it likewise embodies a wish and, as such, reflects the physical reality or the physically-based reality of that which is wished. As an overall guiding principle, I believe in honesty rather than in asserting something I may not really believe. The sabbats, for instance, are for me too far apart and regular for encouraging a dynamic stimulation between the ceremonial and the organic. There is a similar everyday inflexibility with the orderly new and full moons, though these do in fact intersect with the solar calendar in interesting and varied ways. But a festival calendar of the kind like that which has evolved from the Roman *feriae* of Numa Pompilius and has become the base of the chief calendar of today's world, albeit secular, has offered to my personal experience a naturally variable compromise.

But to return to comprehending the beginning of all, maybe divine silence is the primordial wish itself. Despite today's raucously noisy world with only the barest but welcomed hint of cessation during the start of the pandemic lockdown, I have at least experienced the wondrously full silence of enchantment on a few occasions. The Rubinstein moment in Amsterdam's Concertgebouw when the renowned pianist played the Chopin *Nocturne* in the 1970s was one such, but I have been to the Sahara and Sinai deserts, and once in Rome with Richard, and at the very moment of the winter solstice, everything went quiet for the instant. Another was the splendid moment with only Richard in the King's Chamber of the Great Pyramid. Suddenly, the crowd of people all departed without exception. We had the burial room then completely to ourselves, and there was no sound at all. A further 'Cheops-type moment' occurred for Richard and me in the Kadisha Valley's Cedar Forest. Lebanon had been our last round the world stopover before returning to London. We had been first to Boston and Rhode Island and then Montreal, San Francisco and Los Angeles en route to Australia for the Parliament of the World's Religions in 2009. After Melbourne, Uluru, Alice Springs, Brisbane and Sydney, our flights took us to Bali, Singapore, Mumbai, Istanbul and finally Beirut with us interrupting our journey every time we had a change of planes. But it was at the *souk* in Sidon while looking in my jacket for a pendant I had purchased in Turkey, that I had an unexpected and shocking surprise. I wanted to locate the medallion in order to find a chain for it but found instead a package of marijuana originally from Amsterdam that I had, unwittingly, been carrying around the entire globe, from continent to continent and country to country. Subsequently, we were able to smoke this 'gift from the gods' four days later when visiting the ancient cedar trees. As it was February, there was snow on the ground, and when it began unexpectedly to rain, Fred and Vicky returned quickly to the car. The rain stopped, and while there had been a group of people ahead of us, once they crossed over the bordering summit, Richard and I discovered unanticipatedly that we were alone in this noise-absorbing forest and snow and, consequently, completely enveloped by a supreme all-embracing silence. The cedar trees soaked up every shred of sound. This was our last day before returning to London on the next, and it became the highlight peak of a marvellous time in our circling of the planet.

Both Homer and Hesiod mention the Muses, daughters of Zeus and Memory (the Titan Mnemosyne). Eventually they were recognised as nine in number with Calliope ('She of the Beautiful Voice') as their leader.

They sing and dance their days at the sacred springs of Mount Helicon and Mount Parnassus, and their only task is to serenade the gods when the latter have their meals. American writer Michael Macrone refers to them as 'the first dinner-club entertainers'. Their temples are our museums, and their principle art (*mousike*) is what we know as music. Through one of their number, namely Urania, they connect in addition to the 'music of the spheres'. For me, my musical encounter with the supreme joy of the cosmos occurs during three brief musical passages: one in the Third Movement of Malcolm Arnold's *Fifth Symphony*, another in the Third Movement of Dmitri Shostakovich's *Tenth Symphony*, and in the instrumental interlude, 'Danse des Rainettes', in Maurice Ravel's *L'Enfant et les Sortilèges* that coincides with the pivotal moment when the child undergoes his transformation from naughtiness to being *bon* and *sage*.

As big as it – the cosmos – all is, one is still connected to its very beginning – as is *everything* else as well. In this total unity of interconnectedness, we might ask if we still have need of the mythic tales, legends and drama? Is it not now enough to know and feel the gentle overall harmony of the cosmos, the music of the spheres, and any commensurate possible presence of the gods? Like ritual, mythology is also something that is not necessary but may nevertheless be approached as a storehouse of precious valuables like Aladdin's Cave. Yet, again, at the heart of the entire compendium of mythic narrative is the *desiderium primordium*, the very first wish of all. In Nordic mythology, the Vanir deities Freyr and Freyja are ultimate embodiments of desire. In a sense, this brother and sister pair probably constitute for the Scandinavians one more instance of the seminal drive behind the whole cosmos. The closest equivalent for the Greeks would be the cognate Priapus, the phallic god of vegetable gardens, beehives, flocks and vineyards. In the pursuit of a collection of mythic tales and along with the concomitant mythographic study of the gods' ancestries and etymologies, more or less like the repeated performance of ritual, the various patterns of symbols, beliefs and insights relevant to a cultural group may come to be discerned in ever accumulating gradations of meaning. The fundamental notion behind our concepts of ritual and art as well as of harmony and order is the idea or feat of putting something together properly. Even with the pure repetition of an old ritual, one done again many times, the performer or participant never knows in advance when the procedure might suddenly congeal and become more than just the sum of its parts. In fact, the more one knows about the object of adoration or the goal of a ceremonial undertaking, the more meaningful and illuminating the possibilities become. One may of course execute a ritual or create a work of art that does not include or relate to divine presences, but for those that are oriented toward pagan spirituality, our mythological legacies can play a highly augmenting part toward the achievement of sublime and interdimensional ecstasies.

While true enough, Hellenic mythology comes across predominantly as a collection of cautionary tales, the magical and interactive world between god and human in which they are situated opens us to the dynamic of enchantment. From Max Weber to my Sophia colleague Patrick Curry, there is the recognition that the bureaucratic and secularised modern life that we endure today increasingly lacks the creative imagination and excitement that comes with the old-time heavenly rapture of entrancement. It is my belief that the 'rebirth' of pagan spirituality in today's West stems precisely from our human need to counter a growing non-spiritual void. Perhaps the consensus is that paganism is more the result of environmental degradation and the perceived dangers of climate change, but the understanding of classical mythologies (of the Greeks, Romans, Vedics, Heathens, Celts, Indo-Europeans and many other cultures as well) conveys the centrally intrinsic link between the divine as animated and personified, on the one hand, and nature as alive and sacred, on the other. One does not have to believe in the gods or even 'use' them in an informing sense toward any acknowledgement of the importance of the natural and organic along with an objective and methodological undertaking for increasing knowledge, but this belief and/or use of the divine gods is not counterproductive but something that might just augment how we may live our lives despite the many disappointments and anti-human power-grabbers encountered along the way.

During an interview, the film director Oliver Stone remarked, in connection to both his service in Vietnam and afterwards his work in America itself, that the increase in recreational drug use compensated for the loss of spirituality within the United States. While there may be some truth to Stone's observation, personally I will argue that mind-alteration is less a compensation as such than it is *a* long-standing, naturally occurring and/or persistent vehicle for intensely enhancing and grounding spiritual insight into telluric experience. Intoxication is to paganism what paganism is to intoxication. Theologically, they are intimately interrelated. For the Greeks, the wine-lord Dionysus is, more widely, the deity of any and all altered states of consciousness – from alcohol to the psychotropics but also from meditation, yoga and other contemplative bodily exercises. Already *circa* 300 bce, the Seleucid ambassador Megasthenes to Chandragupta Maurya conveyed the identity of Dionysus with the Hindu Shiva, both being lords of dance and ecstatic possession.

Here's where we get for another time a bit more thickly complex because I wish to name some of the deities across the Indo-European legacy to indicate, for those who are interested, how they line up or interchange as instances of a or *the* divine duality. Once again, the following may be thought of as another stained glass rose window metaphor that embraces divine personages as symbolic assemblages of refracted light, segmented or divided by narrative mullions, muntins and tracery but composing together a colourfully integrated informative whole and/or a joyously hypnotic dance. For those who are not interested, please skip over this paragraph. Perhaps the freelance writer/editor Patrick Harrigan is correct in seeing the more accurate identity between Dionysus with Shiva's son, Skanda-Murugan Kataragama, instead of with Shiva himself, but throughout the PIE daughter cultures and for the Indo-Europeans themselves, there is an undoubted understanding of the divine twin of alternate consciousness (e.g., Soma) and his this-worldly human counterpart (e.g., Indra). For the Romans, Dionysus was hailed as Bacchus, but his real functional equivalent would be Neptunus, the god of reflected light (e.g., the sun's reflection on the surface of water) and hence 'fire-in-water' (wine, alcohol, naphtha, illumination, etc.) whose prototype also becomes Nechtan, the Irish guardian of the Tobar Segais or the Well of Wisdom and source of the river Boyne. Nechtan, in turn, is believed to be further manifest in such Celtic figures as the British healing-god Nodens and the Irish Nuada ('cloud-maker'), first king of the Tuatha Dé Danann and husband of the Boyne river-goddess Boand, as well as with the Vedic/Persian water-god, Apam Napat. In my own researches into Proto-Indo-European mythology, among the many instances to be discerned of the underlying *dioscuri*, I would include Kastor and Polydeuces, (known to the Romans as Castor and Pollux), Dionysus and Apollo, Prometheus and Zeus, the Nordic Freyr and Týr, the Irish Dagda and Lugh, the Vedic Soma and Indra, Agni and Indra, Vishnu and Indra, Yama and Manu and the Hindu Vishnu and Shiva as well as the hero *avatar* Rama/Ramachandra and his brother Lakshmana. All these various allegorical depictions are mythic and cultic illustrations of the mortal and immortal aspects of humanity that are portrayed and worshipped as the divine twins – both the humans of this world and their *alter ego* vehicle that frequently appears as either horse and/or power plant substance. In any pagan advocacy for mind-alteration, those who so wish are free to acknowledge that nature herself has gifted us a pharmacopeia of healing plants, nutrients and spiritual hallucinogens. Whether as equestrian support, as mind-expanding assistance and fortification, our otherworld or chthonian complement, or as the tool of fire – the use of which distinguishes us from the rest of the animal kingdom, these divine counterparts are understood as alternate mystical selves of the human being himself, herself, itself.

For the Greeks and many if not most others, portrayal of the gods is placed into a mythological narrative that is intriguingly grounded in nature – including the ambivalences and random difficulties that nature might present to human endeavour. While someone like Robin Lane Fox may ridicule and dismiss ancient belief that saw the gods behind such catastrophes as epidemics in contrast to the empirical advances slowly being made by medical science, our beliefs in the causality between humanity and divinity are today different but still of metaphorical and even spiritual value. Within the Hellenic panorama for those who have appreciated and resonated with classical mythology, we see the Olympians in a struggle with the rawer elements of the natural world: the protogenoi gods of Chaos, Tartarus, Night, the Erinyes, Typhon and his offspring, Thanatos, Nemesis, Eris or Strife, the Moirai or Fates, Uranus, the Titans and the Giants. The ambivalence of the Earth Mother Gaia herself is to be seen in her birthing not only the Titans but also the Olympians' opponents Uranus, Typhon and the Giants as well as both the one-eyed Cyclops and the hundred-handed Hecatoncheires who subsequently became allies of the gods in their overthrow of the Titans. Besides Uranus, Gaia also parthenogenetically produced Pontus the sea and with him became the parent of Nereus – the Old Man of the Sea and father of the Nereids or water nymphs including Thetis the mother of Achilles, Thaumus the wondrous and parent of both the Harpies and Iris the rainbow, Eurybia from whom Hecate descends, and Phorcys and Ceto as the personifications of the dangerous aspects of the sea whose offspring include Skylla, Echidna, Ladon, the Graeae and the Gorgons (Medusa).

Of course, not all pagans – contemporary or otherwise – are enamoured by the gods and goddesses of the Greek and Classical traditions, but these deities have no less been pivotally significant in the development and vitality of Western culture. The true second-generation gods are the Titans, and while the Olympians overthrow them in the progress of civilisation, those who have preceded them are not all negative. Among the twelve are Oceanus and Tethys – 'models of conjugal fidelity' and parents of Tyche the goddess of chance, Styx the underworld river goddess and Clymene the wife of Iapetus; Coeus and Phoebe whose children are Asteria (mother of Hecate) and Leto (the sixth wife of Zeus and mother of Artemis and Apollo); Crius who through his half-sister, flint-hearted Eurybia, parents Astraeus, Pallas and Hecate's father Perseus; Hyperion and Theia who parent Helios the sun, Selene the moon and Eos the dawn; Themis – a Gaia continuation, goddess of justice, law and order, and Zeus' second wife who gives birth to the Horae or Seasons, the Moirai (when not considered the daughters of Nyx) and sometimes additionally the Hesperides who are otherwise daughters of Atlas; and Mnemosyne the fifth wife of Zeus, the goddess of memory and mother of the nine Muses. Of the six male Titans, it is Crius, Coeus, Hyperion and Iapetus who become the pillars who subsequently hold up the sky after the castration of Uranus. The ten-year Titanomachy was essentially against Cronus, the first-generation Olympians' father through Rhea (another Gaia incarnation) who had swallowed Zeus' five elder siblings until the Oceanid Metis (Zeus' first wife and mother of Athena) gave Cronus a mixture of wine and mustard that caused him to vomit out his children. Iapetus' son Atlas was Cronus' chief ally in the Titan War, while Iapetus' son Prometheus (sometimes claimed to be Themis' offspring) sided with the Olympians. These shifting nuances and identities of both Titans and Olympians are fundamental to ancient Greek spirituality, culture and civilisation.

The third wife of Zeus was the Oceanid Eurynome who birthed the Charites or Graces. Zeus' fourth wife was Demeter, who as goddess of agriculture is another incarnation of Gaia. Demeter's daughter is Persephone. Hera, the eldest daughter of Rhea and Cronus, becomes Zeus' seventh and final wife. While Greek mythology and especially through the poet Hesiod was strongly influenced by Asian or Levantine precedents, the earlier Indo-European substratum would have depicted Zeus as the offspring and initial consort (instead of Uranus) of Gaia. This is important and reflected in Hera being the *first* daughter of the Rhea-Gaia hypostasis – the importance relating to an underlying narrative concerning a father-daughter rape that is among the more difficult features to accept from ancient mythology when considering contemporary mores. But as Roberto Calasso explains in connection with the behaviour of Zeus, mythic rape is 'the sign of the overwhelming power of the divine, of the residual capacity of distant gods to invade mortal minds and bodies. Rape is at once possessing and possession'. Beyond this, however, it is also cosmogonic in as much as it seeks metaphorically to explain or depict how the world came to be as we know it.

As mythology progresses through time and is repeatedly recast and various original features are disguised and even lost, the mythographic attempt to divine and reassemble primeval understandings may be compared to the attempt to fit back together an enormous jigsaw puzzle with some of its pieces missing. The proto-narrative of spiritual perception belonging to our European or Indo-European-speaking ancestors would appear originally to centre around the dethronement and temporary disability of the divine prototype (Zeus with Typhon, Tyr with Fenrir, Indra with Vritra, etc.), on the one hand, and around the rape of the first-born daughter of the primordial parents, Earth (Gaia) and Sky (the Zeus prototype), on the other hand.

So in a nutshell and using the Greek names rather than their cognates and reconstructed early nomenclatures, the aboriginal portrayal as I have come to discern it consists of the Earth's (Gaia's) virgin birth of her son and subsequent lover (Zeus) and Zeus' infatuation and rape of the first-born from Zeus and Gaia as the primordial parents, that is, of the dawn-goddess Eos. The child of this Zeus-Eos union is the sun. Among the Vedics, Zeus would be Dyaus or Prajāpati, Gaia is Prithivi, and Eos is Ushas or Sūryā (*Rigveda* 1.71.5, 8; 10.61.5-7), and an indigitation for Dyaus or Dyâvâp*r*thvî is Mâtarishvan ('growing in the mother': *RV* 1.96.4) – likewise reflecting Gaia's and ultimately Zeus' emergence from the cosmic sea. If Sūryā is a cognate of Hera, the deflowering of his sister/daughter by Zeus comes to be subsequently disguised and amended with the victim becoming the legitimate wife of Zeus as well as the 'queen of heaven'. The aboriginal tale is countlessly re-drafted to accrue into other variations. In the development of Greek mythology itself, the 'daughter' becomes not abducted by her father Zeus but by Zeus' brother Hades, the Zeus Chthonius – yet a variant of Zeus. There are also occasions when the mother-daughter is understood as a single earth-dawn hypostasis. If Dionysus (the Zeus of Nysus/Nesa) is the Eleusinian child of Kore and the agent who returns the mother as the agricultural earth to the land of the living, there is an echo here of Persephone's return from the underworld. Zeus' own primordial liaison with the Earth or Gaia is retained as, or transformed into, his affairs with both Demeter and Semele. The child of the latter is now a son, namely, Dionysus who, nevertheless, through the Eleusinian mysteries, appears to have an intimate relationship with Kore/Persephone. More known as the consort of Dionysus is Ariadne who is probably also the Hittite sun-goddess of Arinna. As the consort of the weather-god, we have most likely another instance of the Zeus-Hera paradigm. There are still further twists concerning incest. The Vedic dawn-goddess has an affair with her solar son (now assuming the name of Pûshan as his mother's suitor and sister's lover: *RV* 6.55.4F & 58.3f), and if my own speculation that the Greek god Ares may have originally had solar features, his pre-Aphrodite romance with Eos may constitute another disguised instance of this primordial matinal-solar relationship.

Various instances of earth being the mother of the divine lord can be surmised as well from other peoples who are descendant from the Indo-Europeans. For instance, the Eddic earth-goddess Jörð, sometimes cited as the daughter of Night (cf., Chaos), is recognised as the mother of the Indra-Zeus analogue, Thor, the *Jarðar burr* ('son of Jörð'). The Nordic sequence Nótt-Jörð-Thor may be a parallel of the contended Chaos-Gaia-Zeus of the proto-Greeks. The interchange between the god of light as weather-god and the god of lightning and thunder (e.g., the Greek Zeus, the Lithuanian Dievas and Perkunas, the Vedic Dyaus and Indra) is also suggested by the Latin *carminibus antiquis* that mentions Tuisto as a *deum terra editum* or 'god, born of the earth'. Tacitus refers to Tuisto as the divine ancestor of the Germanic peoples. A possible variant of the 'Tuisto' name is 'Tuisco' which is considered by some as a cognate of *Tiwaz, the Tyr prototype among the Germans. Consequently, the Tyr-Thor hypostasis is suggested as the offspring of the earth (Jörð/Fjörgyn) and supports my contention that Zeus is the original son born primordially to Gaia.

In the Rigvedic stanzas that relate the incest-rape mythologem, a further development is the introduction of the archer (e.g., the Vedic Rudra – a prototype along with Indra and Agni of Shiva) who in outrage shoots an arrow into his father's thigh when he is engaged in sexual union with his daughter. As a result of the *coitus interruptus*, some of Dyaus/Prajāpati's semen falls to the earth from which the archer himself is born. Such is the marvellous non-linear temporality that myth incorporates. What is curious is the wounding of the father's thigh in the Vedic tale and the gestation of the unborn Dionysus in the thigh of Zeus. Consequently, with the out-of-the-ordinary PIE cosmogonic symbolism, the primordial parents are mother and son, the son is father and brother of the daughter, and the archer is the son and brother of the father and the brother of the daughter. It would be, however, a mistake to assess and judge the archetypal in terms of today's morality – for when we short shrift ourselves from the legacy of our ancient lore, we lose out on the hidden possibility of ancestral and catalytic spiritual insight. True enough, a seminal element of ethical judgment is introduced with the archer variation, but the basic theme concerns the origins of the universe and not the standards by which humans are eventually supposed to live. Transgression is presented as necessary just to get it all started.

As symbolic narrative, Greek or classical myth opens and introduces the pursuer to an incredible cornucopia of suggestion and affirmation. For those who enjoy this magnificent legacy, there are variously Deucalion and Pyrrha instead of Adam and Eve as the progenitors of humanity; the adventures of Daedalus and Icarus and such heroes as Bellerophon, Jason, Perseus, Theseus and Heracles; the unending punishments of Sisyphus, Tantalus and Ixion; the stories of Myrrh, Midas, Pygmalion, Medea, the Minotaur and Pegasus; the Zeus affairs with Io, Leda, Alcmene and Europa; and the complex families of Oedipus, Jocasta and Antigone in Thebes and of Helen, Castor, Polydeuces and Clytaemnestra in Sparta. All of these are an enrichening part of the Western endowment that are relevant not only to Europeans and Americans North and South but to anyone who shares a related interest. In a sense, they belong to the world as well as to the West. While they may indeed be used inappropriately in terms of alleged superiority, Folkist-type enhancement or even gender myopia, less sad is the recognition of their special dynamic beauty that unites rather than separates.

Perhaps the best way to approach and conceive of mythology, Hellenic or Classical in particular, is as if it were music. Even with the cautionary tale or that most often it is the dilemmas and more sobering possibilities of reality that are what is reflected, there is a special pleasure in 'listening to', discerning and following its themes and narrative melodies. Through even the most casual entrance or deeper immersion into the mythic realm, we encounter a world of ambrosia, nectar, enthusiasm and fascination. The stories with happier endings, though relatively rare, include those of Cupid and Psyche, Perseus and Andromeda, Dionysus and Ariadne, Cadmus and Harmonia, Deucalion and Pyrrha, Io and Telegonus, Pygmalion and his 'ivory girl', and Baucis and Philemon. For the rest, the enjoyer of mythology and the explorer of its mythemes traverses a halcyon gamut that includes Atlantis, Elysium, the Isles of the Blessed, Arcadia and the Golden Age. We tend to picture the ideal period of time as something in the long-ago lost past, but the hope and/or promise of paganism today more preferably conjures the Age of Gold with its flora and fauna as something toward which we are working and heading. The otherworld of the *Fortunate Insulae* is to be more our future than our past – in both this world and the next. Meanwhile, in the present, we can appraise the ancient pagan gods through their mythologies and representations in art and symbol. In my daily experience, through a mindfulness of the vehicles of the gods, an interconnection between the deific and quotidian may be welcomed and established.

I had not heard from Hecate for what seemed like a long time and have been planning an attempt to contact her son to ask about her. But yesterday I thought to search for her through Facebook and learned as a result that she had passed last year on the 4th of December 2019 in Perigueux, France nine months ago. She was a one-of-a-kind whom I had originally met in Kathmandu in 1981. When her father died unexpectedly, I paid for her ticket to Maine so that she could attend his funeral. Hecate's son had been recognised as a *tulku*, Karma Trinlay Rinpoche, and was raised by Tibetan monks in Boudhanath, Nepal. As a 'Holy Mother', she had been given a small home on the grounds adjacent to the Ka-Nying Shedrub Ling monastery.

Before becoming enamoured with the combined schools of Kagyu and Nyingma Buddhism, Hecate had been the girlfriend of Jimi Hendrix, but his family would not allow her to attend his funeral. She was certainly among the more fascinating people I have known. One Hecate story concerned someone in Manhattan who was threatening her and claiming that she owed him money. 'Do you want this money?' she asked finally. 'Then come with me!' She took him to Harlem and walked him into a large room with this dude sitting on a throne and surrounded by attendants. Seeing her, the enthroned one remarked, 'Hello Hecate! What can I do for you?'

'This fellow says that I owe him money!' she replied.

'Oh, really?' and the dude then pulled out his wallet and started counting out bills. 'How much does she owe you?' he asked.

'Nothing, nothing!' the fellow exclaimed suddenly in terror and fled. Subsequently he pleaded with Hecate not to have anything happen to him. She agreed and added, 'But I never want to see you again!' And she didn't.

Though I have had dinner with Hecate in Santa Barbara when she had come to live in California for a year or so, for me it has been Kathmandu where I knew her principally and associate her the most. Her world in and around Boudhanath included for me Efale, Margi, Dutch Bob and the abbot Chökyi Nyima Rinpoche. Before all that, however, and for or my very first night in Nepal, I had booked myself into the Soaltee Oberoi. The air conditioning was most welcomed, and after bathing, napping and snacking, I set off in the mid-evening and somehow managed both to find the Kathmandu's Darbar Square which in the dark was pure exotica and my way back to the hotel – all with a gently relaxed confluence of inkling and intuition. But already I came to experience the greater racial and nationalistic biases of Nepalese Hinduism in contrast to what is encountered throughout much of India. As a result, in the days that followed, more firmly did I realise that I am not a Hindu since in reality Hinduism is Brahmanism and requires fawning to the notion and practice of a caste system. If anything, I knew myself as a Vedist or, translated into contemporary terms, a pagan humanist. Nevertheless, when I was able a few days later to cross the Bagmati near Pashupati, I found myself entranced by an enchanting area that contained both a royal cemetery and an exquisite wooded area with stone walkways and moss-covered walls strikingly reminiscent of Killarney save for the presence of grazing cows and monkeys – all so very peaceful and much closer to what is my core religious sentiment and inspiration.

At the British Embassy on this first Nepalese occasion, I attended a Grand Charity Ball in celebration of the marriage of Prince Charles and Diana Spencer. The collective toast to the Nepalese king was made with utter reverence, while that to the prince and new princess was with enthusiastic exuberance. In all, it was a fascinating occasion with some of the ex-pats I met being delightful and kindred free souls. In the raffle, I won a cigarette lighter.

I had gone to Nepal because of the suggestion by the government official in Varanasi, India who handled the permits for foreigners. He was about as crooked as they come. When he saw that I had purchased a pressure cooker for my housemate in Varanasi, he wanted me to give it to him when I was leaving India. I had always planned on my initial visit to the subcontinent to stay for nine months. I got the three-month visa for India in London that had the option of extending for an additional three-months. However, as the six months were expiring, the government agent told me to go to Nepal and from there re-apply for another three-months' stay in India. What he did not tell me but the Indian Embassy did once I was in Kathmandu was that I was required to have a 'no objection' stamp in my passport in order to be granted re-entry. In Nepal, I was told that I would not be able to return to India. The American Embassy was no help at all, so I tried the British one, and that is how I learned about the charity ball. This was two decades before I actually became British, but the UK staff in Kathmandu was much more helpful even to a non-citizen. I still had two weeks left on my three-month extension and, on the embassy's suggestion, used that to get back into India via Varanasi.

Once again in India, reluctantly, I decided not to procrastinate and went straightaway to the Videshi Visa Office where I was informed that by my having gone to Nepal, which their agent had suggested, automatically I cancelled my extension and should have been stopped at the airport. I was thus now in India illegally. I had originally been told that re-entry permits would be definitely extended to the second three months, but now they were saying precisely the opposite. This, of course, is India. I had to pay 800 rupees and surrender my passport with the understanding that I could not leave Varanasi for 30 days. But by 18:00 the same day, my passport was delivered back to me with a 30-day permission and permission to travel if I wanted. Three days later, I took a plane to Khajuraho.

The nagara-style architecture of these world-famous temples of the Chandela capital with their erotic sculptures is utterly awesome. The 9th to 11th century structures are stone jewels that are encased with what in today's terminology would be called pornographic depictions of the gods, apsaras and gandharvas. The Chausath Yogini Temple may have been my favourite as both the oldest and most primitive, and it is the one that retains that old pagan ritual feel and reminded me of both Mexican Aztec monuments and the ancient edifices to be found on Corsica. With the impressive and still active Kandariya Mahadeva Temple, there are three mandapa shrines, the central containing Shiva's phallic emblem or *linga*. As this temple may have originally been a Devi shrine, the three *sancta santorum* suggest an archaic memory of the dioscuric triad but here with the male in the centre flanked by two females rather than the divine twins accompanying their sister-wife. Getting lost at one point in the nearby village and being offered a *chillum* in a *babu*'s Laxmi and Durga shrine, subsequently I went into ecstasy before the peaceful and imposing statue of Vishnu in the Chatturbhuj Temple. My revery brought to mind that Earth is, of course, Vishnu's first wife (as well as his mother – the boar incarnation being both an earth-mother symbol and a solar one who, born from the goddess in the waters, ascends from there; it only becoming an earth-diver myth in later brahmanic distortion in which *a priori* he dives into the water to 'rescue' the earth). Vishnu's co-wife is Laxmi who in one sense is also the earth who is born from the milk ocean. But Laxmi is the wish-goddess as well, the lady of beauty and fortune. The two wives together embody the two worlds (this and the other), and the iconography of the two with Vishnu is again a reversal of the dioscuric triad.

Ruminations on the many forms of mythical divine figures and their manifestations, transformations and even contradictions are what can indeed take the contemplator over and past the 'threshold of myth'.

I will have some more to say on mythology, though first instead here is my response to Richard's contention that the story of my family reads like 'the great American novel'. I do not see it the same way; Richard assesses the American novel – great or otherwise – much differently than I do, but I will nevertheless attempt to sketch out a narrative outline and some of the events that I can still remember. My maternal grandmother was apparently born on the ship from Argentina to New York after a coup. The family were Ashkenazi from The Netherlands. Along with a son and a daughter, my paternal grandmother came to the United States pregnant with my father to join her husband who had come to the States six months earlier. She was Protestant Lithuanian but had always told her children that she was German. The surname of my grandfather's family designation had been anglicised from the Lithuanian form of the name that indicates an unmarried daughter. My mother refused to marry my father until he legally shortened the name to York.

The marriage between my paternal grandparents did not last, and nor for that matter did the marriage between my maternal grandparents either. My father's father who was very little spoken of came back at one point to the family home in Gary, Indiana, and my aunt Irene, my father's sister-in-law, slammed the door in his face saying that he was not welcomed. I had loved this aunt as I did my other relatives until the time when I was bringing my brother's belongings back from San Francisco to the East Coast, and, when I saw Aunt Irene as I interrupted the driving in Indiana, she launched into a tirade about the use of countercultural 'drugs'. Perhaps she was right, but that was not the time to say such to someone grieving. As for my mother's mother, she had been politically active in Texas and might have become, so the story had it, that state's second woman governor. But my grandfather objected and took her and my mother from Dallas to New York. According to my grandmother, she claimed he was closer to his birth family, his two sisters, and subsequently, she told him to return to them and divorced him. Again, I know little more of this grandfather as well. He also was Ashkenazi, and the family had lived in East London before emigrating to America.

My father's earliest years were penurious. The family worked for Wonder Bread, and many years later when showing me the large dough-kneading receptacles he told that the dough had turned pink after a worker had once fallen into one of the vats. Despite the relative poverty, my father was bright and got himself enrolled in Purdue University from which he graduated as a chemical engineer. He impressed my mother's mother by arriving for my parents' first date in an automobile during the height of the Great Depression. The car was borrowed. My grandmother had graduated from Barnard College with a major in chemistry, and this formed the basis of her convincing my mother to marry my father. My parents' wedding took place in Buffalo (where I was born), and my mother told the story that after the nuptial ceremony, my father stopped the car at an intersection during pouring rain and told my grandmother to get out. I came onto the scene two years later. My father was away at the time on a business trip, and my mother went into labour for 48 hours saying that she would only be able to deliver once my father had returned. I was a breech birth and must have been resisting coming into this world to the very end. My daughter's birthing, caesarean after fourteen hours, was vaguely similar, and she seemed to be at first a very ancient soul who was furious for having been reborn.

Mother was a combination of beauty, elegance, charm. *joie de vivre* and warmth. She loved people, and they loved her. For my father and his business aspirations, she was his winning asset. It was she who would captivate his backers and others to his side. Despite their eventually unhappy marriage, Dad always enjoyed and never ceased to tell stories about Mother and how her presence would tip the balance in his favour.

My brother was born in Buffalo three years after my birth. When I was five, the family moved to New Jersey because the Maplewood-South Orange school system had been ranked second best in the country. The first was in Evanston, Illinois, but as it was too close to my father's family in Chicago and Gary, my mother said no to that one. For my first grade of schooling, we had moved for a year to Orange and here my sister was born. We moved then back to Maplewood which remained as my hometown thereafter.

Maplewood was a typical suburban town with a commuter train to New York. It is situated in the Orange Valley on the slope of South Mountain from which, higher up, one can see Manhattan. The town and my upbringing could be described as a blend of *East of Eden, Trouble in Tahiti* and *Peyton Place*. My father was promiscuous, and my mother caught him in bed one morning with my brother's godmother, Helen King, a radio announcer. I became my mother's confident and was thrilled during my high school years to be her go-between with Ken, the father of one of my school friends, with whom she began an affair. She wanted marriage, but he could not bring himself to do it. My family had a party during which mother got ill and went to bed. She did not know how to drink in those days, and often I was the one who put her to bed. Ken came to her bedroom to see how she was; my father walked in on them and threw Ken out of our house. A few days later, Ken's wife came to my mother and asked her to apologise for my father's behaviour. She did not know about the affair, but my mother refused and said that she could not go against any decision that her husband had made.

At some point, my brother began an affair with our next-door neighbour, Barbara. She was instrumental in Peter's not enlisting into the army under the agreement for being posted to Germany, so when he was drafted, he was sent instead to Vietnam. My father always blamed Barbara for this, and she turned him down when he proposed that he and she have an affair. This occurred when my father had told Barbara that he thought his wife was romantically involved with her husband. In advance, Mother had told Barbara that my father would probably say to her that he believed his wife was having a relationship with her husband, but she still had turned my father down. There was a period of time when Barbara had been away caring for her dying sister, Mother was home in bed, and Dad was away for business. The phone rang, and it was Barbara's husband Jim asking Mother if she wanted to have a drink with him. My mother said no and that she had already retired. After some more minutes, he called again, and this time Mother explained that her hair was in curlers and she had already put her night cream on her face. A few minutes later she heard the front screen door swinging open, and with that she rushed downstairs to stop Jim. He simply picked her up and carried her back upstairs in his arms to her bedroom. This was my mother's second and last affair. This time it was Jim who wanted to marry, but my mother thought the better of it. In time, Barbara and Jim divorced, and Barbara became my mother's best friend, but she never knew of the affair my mother had had with her husband, and my mother never knew of the affair Barbara had had with my brother.

My own longings were chiefly toward brawny, hirsute men and also with a few classmates. The few sexual encounters I did have were only explorations with friends while we kept the *Playboy* centrefold open mandatorily next to us. It was not until when attending NYU summer school between my Purdue and UCSB years that I met Quay one evening in Washington Square

Park – he being the one who 'brought me out'. At college in Santa Barbara, there was both a Jim and a Tim who mesmerised me with unquenchable yearning. I was still living in the dormitory my first year and was about to be late for a date with Julie Felix when Tim came into my room. He turned out to be an Evangelical and proceeded to plead with me to give myself to Christ. Julie was slightly annoyed that I was late. I still think on occasion of Jim.

I did have a brief and unsatisfactory affair while at UCSB that ended when we went to summer school at the University of California in Berkeley between my junior and senior years, but my first real romance was in Amsterdam when I met Joop in the Odeon Kring. He was a golden Pan and, with the assistance of his record collection and my peyote, we travelled to Arcadia and ancient Greece. After Europe, on the East Coast, Jack Fontan and Ray Unger were visiting from Laguna Beach. A roommate had introduced me to them when I was still at school in California. I ended up living with them. I call them my 'astrological parents', and they named me 'Cocaine' because they found me addictive. The sojourn was not to last, but it was what got me back to California.

Apart for my 1961/1962 vagabonding through Europe, I passed virtually all of the 1960s in California: primarily Los Angeles for the first half and San Francisco for the second. I dealt with the draft and managed to get out of the Army as quickly as I could. My second lover was the Greek actor and subsequently artist, Vassili Lambrinos, and my third was Gernot Kuehn, a German film editor. In completely different ways, they were both interesting relationships, and Vassili remained a friend for the rest of his life.

My LA days included the assassination of President John F. Kennedy and those in EssEff, that of his brother Robert. These were shocking events at the time and riveted the American psyche into a frame of mind it had not known since the Second World War if not much earlier. In 1953, there had been the execution of Julius and Ethel Rosenberg and, in 1968, the assassination of Martin Luther King, Jr.

Although strange incidents when they occurred, in the light of political and global developments and polarisation since, they no longer seem to me to be particularly unusual. I tend to measure things against ancient Rome and especially imperial Rome and see the same nefarious undercurrents of today as something similar and still continually reflective of human immaturity.

In any event, the transformation of Haight-Ashbury from being an old-fashioned delicatessen district into the emanating vortex of counterculture was truly astonishing. The large-scale and exhilarating gatherings that accompanied these times seem completely surreal to me now in our present pandemic days of social-distancing, isolation and currently no more than six people together at any given time. The years of the second half of the 1960s in San Francisco were, albeit wholly naïve, a magical duration of joyous hope, radical expectation and abandoned celebration. For me, they have been unlike any other time in my life, and I am profoundly grateful for them having coincided with me when I was still in my 20s. The saying is that if you can remember the 60s, you were not there. There is indeed an avalanche of forgotten memories, but what I do remember was simply glorious, gregarious, replete with open trust, daring if not also experimental, and liberating. It remains an experience I would never have wanted not to have had, and I sympathise with my daughter who, when she realised that she had missed those incomparable years, cried as a result.

From the Haight, I moved to the Russian Hill cabin with its stunning panorama view from which I explored the California hinterlands and Yosemite and travelled at various times between Acapulco and Vancouver. This dreamtime I realise in retrospect could not have lasted, and as the curtain was dropping in the likes of the Vietnam war, the National Guard shootings at Kent State University, and the Sharon Tate murders in Los Angeles, I talked half of our own 'family' or coven or both to flee with me to Europe. We re-coalesced in Amsterdam, and for a few more unforgettable years our commune flourished and continued the lifestyle we had exported from San Francisco in an unquestioned opposition to the dominant values and the mainstream of social behaviour. Dutch society with its long-established ethos of tolerance allowed non-conformist conduct as long as we paid our taxes and utility bills.

These Amsterdam commune days were also exciting, and the rota of constant visitors to the house was fascinating and kept us all interconnected with the global flower power movement that stretched from the Americas, Britain, Continental Europe, northern Africa, South Africa, Israel and Japan to Australia and New Zealand – with India and Nepal serving as Mecca-destinations for most of us. When I had left the United States, I had vowed never to come back apart for funerals. My brother's post-Vietnam suicide was the reason for my first return. A year later, my sister was marrying, and I was conflicted over whether I should attend or not. Finally, one morning I implored my brother to help me know what I should do. I asked that if I ought to go, let the pull-up bar I was about to grab on to detach itself from the door frame. The next moment I found myself on my knees on the floor with the bar in my hands This had never occurred before, and it has never done it again in the nearly half-century that has followed. 'Well', I thought, 'there cannot be a clearer answer than this'. So I went. The real joy against the mixed reaction to me and my waist-length hair was my grandmother, Pfeiffer and my sister's friend Marty whom I believe my sister never saw again. Pfeif, Marty and I knew what to do and did it, and my grandmother revealed to me on this occasion that she had been the ghost writer of Adele Davis' best-selling book, *Let's Eat Right to Keep Fit*. After I returned to The Netherlands, there was the desire for many of us in the commune to establish a base in the country. The Friesian farm was a fiasco when, once the Dutch fogs finally lifted, we discovered ourselves to be immediately on the edge of a NATO airbase. With their roar and our house being directly beneath the flight path, the deafening sound of jets taking off precluded even thought. There was a subsequent near-attempt for rural life in north-eastern Belgium, but it was only with the approaching dissolution of the Amsterdam commune and the 'marriage' of Richard and me that he and I acquired our farm in the south of France. This last opens another chapter or two or more.

But Europe overall for me was – and continues to be – an opportunity to connect with the gods with whom I most resonate – especially the Classical deities both Roman and Greek, with their sacred places and including those that belong to the Celtic- and Germanic-speaking peoples as well, and with the megalithic sites throughout Britain, Ireland and the Continent. My paganism truly births with these and later even further with my experiences on the Indian subcontinent. In contrast to both today's secular/scientistic disenchantment and Abrahamic militantism whether Islamic jihadism, Christian retro-fundamentalism or even Israeli nationalism, the more viable spiritual alternative appears to me to be one that is centred on this world's organic nature as a cosmic isomorph. This last not only includes maintaining as best as is possible the seminal ecological balance of our planet of residence but also the liberating expanse of human imagination – one that has a propensity to include the gods. The divine, whether personified or otherwise, is the atavistic glamour that continues to pulsate throughout all that is. Paganism is for me the effort and practice to sense and connect with this pantheistic, polytheistic and animist vibrating flow.

This pagan effort is of course in part an internal enterprise that involves the establishment of mental equilibrium and concentrated focus, but it also externally concerns the physical actions that are necessary for activating environmental reform and changing the outer incommensurate political situation. Shamanic explorer and American writer Daniel Pinchbeck contends that inner spiritual work and 'New Age' culture will be insufficient to accomplish any preservation of freedom of assembly, the lessening of surveillance and resistance to the suppression of civil rights unless we can effectively acknowledge that 'the rule by psychopaths is at the core of our deepening collective crisis'. The claim is precisely that, in the hierarchical structures of the military, governments and corporate enterprises, those people who possess sociopathic personality disorders and hence are without ethical compunction are the ones who will and do rise into positions of power that flourish through the sociopolitical orders that are compatible with domination and exploitation. Our ever-intensifying global despotisms are assisted by the unceasing formations of apparatus systems that can be employed for technological control. In fact, the 'accelerating power of technology has far outpaced our ethical and moral development as a species'. For Pinchbeck, because psychopathic influence is – at least to varying degrees – conscienceless, emotionless, selfish, cold, calculating and without any moral or ethical standards, the rule and manipulation by those 'without conscience helps to explain the increasingly vacuous, soulless quality of contemporary existence'. My feeling is that it is precisely with this last as articulated by Pinchbeck that the importance of contemporary and indigenous paganism comes most vitally and necessarily into play.

In Amsterdam during the 1970s, as I was increasing developing an understanding of an organic and pagan outlook, I resolved upon the project of re-writing the Bible backwards. I never got further than the Book of Revelations and assume that if that part of my re-write still exists it must be somewhere in the house in Amsterdam. But what I did manage to accomplish included four footnotes. Upon subsequent expansion, one of these became my first published book, *The Roman Festival Calendar of Numa Pompilius*, and another subsequently developed into my *magnum opus*, *The Divine versus the Asurian: An Interpretation of Indo-European Cult and Myth*. This last involved much of my research being conducted in the renowned British Museum Reading Room with its great dome. This is where Karl Marx worked on his *Das Kapital* and where Alfred Hitchcock used the roof in the climax of his 1929 film *Blackmail*. The magnificent Round Reading Room was also a work space for the likes of Charles Darwin, Charles Dickens, George Bernard Shaw, Vladimir Lenin, Bram Stoker, Sir Arthur

Conan Doyle and Virginia Woolf. The time I was privileged to research in this venerable hall became a thrilling period of my life, and I would arrive in the morning shortly before opening and remain there all day. At the time, there was an old-fashioned cafeteria that was part of the museum and would be where I would have my lunch. It has been long replaced by the Pizzeria on the opposite side, and the museum has been much changed. The Great Court that was under the open sky and which contains the Reading Room has since been covered, enhanced and now contains the Court Café and the Great Court Restaurant. The British Library itself has moved into a new purpose-built building at the site that had been the old goods yard in St. Pancras. But despite the modern developments, I retain cherished nostalgic memories of what had been an awesome centre for me during many happy days. One day, even, we had been alerted and then were able to see Queen Elizabeth visiting the museum with Crown Prince Willem-Alexander of the Netherlands. The reputation of the Queen's radiant complexion was, in actuality, certainly confirmed.

The museum is a veritable temple of the Muses. Pre-eminent museums for me include the British Museum, the Prado in Madrid, the Louvre in Paris, the Metropolitan Museum of Art in New York, the Art Institute of Chicago, the de Young Museum and the California Palace of the Legion of Honor in San Francisco, Amsterdam's Rijksmuseum and the Museo Nacional de Antropologia in Mexico City. There is also Berlin's Museum Island containing the Neues Museum (with the head of Nefertiti), Pergamon Museum, the Altes Museum and the Alte Nationalgalerie. Further in London, there are the Tate Modern, the Tate Britain, the Royal Academy of Art, the National Gallery, the Courtald Gallery, and The Wallace Collection. I have yet to reach the Hermitage Museum of Saint Petersburg, but its branch, the Hermitage Amsterdam, is another much enjoyed exhibition centre even though it replaced the retirement home on the banks of the Amstel river that I had been planning on for my own future days. And there are of course many, many smaller museums that could be mentioned – the Frick Museum in Manhattan, the Van Gogh Museum in Amsterdam and the Kröller-Müller in Gelderland being three that first come to mind. But in all, these are marvellous centres, not necessarily without controversy such as the likes of the Elgin Marbles in the British Museum, that function for my pagan soul as holy shrines and temples that belong under the auspices of the Nine Muses of Greek mythology.

Consequently, I have nostalgic and strongly favourable memories of the

British Museum's Reading Room in which I conducted much of my investigations for *The Divine versus the Asurian*. It had been the writer William Davenport who was instrumental toward my procurement of the required library pass, and it was the welcomed permission by the Baker's to use their Swiss Alps holiday home for the month of January that allowed me to begin and write the work's first chapter. Ian and Antoinette were Jungian analysts residing in Zurich whom I had considered as close friends. After the period of estrangement I had had with my mother, she came with my aunt Florence to visit Richard and me in France. We four met the Bakers in Les Baux, and when lodged in our hotel I remember telling them at that point that I was feeling closer to them than I was to my mother. However, in time I witnessed how they decided at one point no longer to continue their friendship with an American priest who had visited them frequently. I asked them, that if they ever chose to do the same with me, would they at least please let me know, but of course they could not, and the cessation of my relationship with them has always remained a bitter pill for me.

In 1981, I went to India for the first time – staying in all nine months. This was followed by Richard's and my round-the-world travel with Pan Am and, after another sojourn for me in India, Richard and I joined the cruise of the Nile in Egypt. The footnote to my Book of Revelations rewrite that became *The Roman Festival Calendar* was published in 1986 by Peter Lang. My editor was Kenneth Jay Wilson who has remained ever since a much beloved friend. To be able to get my *magnum opus* published was the next major hurdle and one that ultimately led me to reading for my Ph.D. at King's College London. My daughter was born in 1989. My heady days with King's were comparable with my time with the Reading Room. I had by that point purchased the leasehold to the London flat in Chelsea. Upon completing my doctoral studies, I then wished to remain with academia, but job possibilities at that time were virtually non-existent. Ultimately, in part to coincide with Richard's wishes, we moved to San Francisco and bought the house on Market Street. And then I got the Research Fellowship in Bath back in England. My mother passed in 2005 and my father in 2007. In between, we were able to sell and be free of the Market Street house, though those days in San Francisco were wondrous in themselves despite various ups-and-downs including the lawsuit for wrongful eviction. I agreed with my sister that she could have my mother's house in Naples, Florida, while the Narragansett, Rhode Island condominium passed to me.

Now whether this could at all be labelled a 'great American novel', I have my serious doubts. But it is my story and has been my life. This here is only an outline, but what my life has been has included an incredible rostrum of incredible people, including my own family and extended families as well as those from the schools I have attended and with those whom I have met during my many travels. While my sister and I were in accord with my mother's estate and its comparable equal division, such was not at all the case with that of my father. With this, what I received from my father was more than what most people could or would hope for but was insufficient for the causes I had wished to support and was virtually negligible in comparison to the amount that my lawyer sister managed to be bequeathed. My sister's response was 'I do not know what is fair' and 'I have to respect my father's will' and 'You went to Europe'. Our relationship had already disintegrated prior to this. Once she became a politician, she was no longer the person with whom I had been close. She became the Democratic Party's candidate for Governor of the state of Rhode Island three times, and during the campaign periods, she did not want me to visit my mother who was living on the Rhode Island coast in the town of Narragansett. Of course I did all the same. There was earlier a strange interlude that began while Richard and I were having a holiday with my sister and her husband David on the island of Corsica. It was clear that little closeness existed until one night at dinner we got into a discussion about refugees. I repeated a standard truism I had learned when studying International Relations at San Francisco State for my master's degree, namely, 'One cannot get an unbiased report about a country from which a refugee has escaped'. My sister and brother-in-law had not exactly adopted but did raise a refugee from Cambodia, and David vehemently could not accept what I was saying. We finished the meal and returned to our rooms. Suddenly there was a knock on our door, and it was my sister asking if we had any aspirin. 'David has a headache'. We scrambled to find what was requested, but once we gave the aspirin to my sister, she was in no hurry to leave, and what followed was a delightful conversation. From this point on and for several years after, she was once again my 'little sister'. But out of the blue one evening, Richard and I were having dinner with my sister and her best friend Debra at a Mexican restaurant in London. My mother never liked or trusted Debra, but I was more or less 'in love' with her and always enjoyed her sharp humour. She is, however, ambitious and crafty, and Richard and I have come to refer to her as 'Iago'. During the dinner, the conversation turned to the time on Corsica. My sister denied everything and expressed her complete and venomous anger toward me for my lifestyle and for not having remained in America. That lovely interlude ended that night once and for all. My sister has nonetheless maintained her own separate relationship with my London family whom she visits. She and David took our English children to Machu Picchu, and Chloe's mother has travelled with my sister on occasion. I will admit this last is painful, but Richard and I have both ourselves come to welcome no longer having to deal with my sister. But as dear friend Chickie added when agreeing that we were better off, 'Too bad about the money!' My mother described that her own relationship with her daughter was 'like walking on egg shells'. I could have challenged my father's will as did some of Martin Luther King, Jr.'s children did theirs, but my life has been one of being grateful for all and whatever has been given to me, and I reneged on the possibility of employing a lawyer for this purpose.

In all, the chief areas of my residential life have been the American East Coast from New Jersey to Rhode Island, the cities of Los Angeles, Santa Barbara (Goleta/Isla Vista) and San Francisco as well as Amsterdam, London, Varanasi and the Provence. I have travelled relatively extensively, and the medium George Darius predicted that there is no land or place that I will not eventually visit. This has so far not been true and, at my present stage of life, is increasingly unlikely to become otherwise. But I have enjoyed Mexico, Haiti, Canada, Morocco, Egypt, Lebanon, South Africa, Turkey, Pakistan, Thailand, China, Japan, Australia and much of Europe. Apart from Alaska, I believe I have been to each of the states comprising the USA. But in addition to geographic locations, I consider that I have also travelled extensively via mythology and the arts – especially through music. Apart from the preeminent domain of sound, there are the visual worlds represented by painting, theatre and cinema and the literary province of poetry and the novel. I would affirm that these are all as important for me as is physical space. Underlying all is the spark of imagination, and this last is undeniably a vital part of freedom itself.

Richard and I met with the 'family' formation in San Francisco. About four years later, we began our own partnership. My friend Buster 'married' us in the dining room of the Amsterdam house with the Christmas Twins as our witnesses. Later, in Sebastian, Florida, Ma Jaya Bhagavati performed a spontaneous marital ceremony on our behalf. Even later, Fred, one of my two best childhood friends, conducted a civil union ceremony for Richard and me in my hometown of Maplewood, New Jersey. And finally, we were legally married in Amsterdam in 2009 with my wife giving me away and the mother of Richard's daughter doing the same with him. With a musical composition or a novel with which one is already familiar, how the work completes is a known. But with life itself, for the most part we do not know what it may become or how it will end. Richard and I have understood one another for nearly a half century, and our relationship has been a few years less than that. My life has been a long one and longer than that of many I have known and loved. It has had both the better moments and some much worse. But I remain very much in love with my partner, and with these autumn years I feel in all, and despite the limitations and disabilities of age, that I have never been happier.

As undoubtedly a 'mythology junkie', I wish now to return to the world of myth. Myths may be understood as traditional stories and folklore narratives principally involving deities, demigods, supernatural humans or legendary characters that are important for a culture or society in metaphorically explaining foundations, origins, phenomena of nature and other significant events including established practices, rites and ethical maxims. The variations and contradictions involving any one tale or theme can be completely baffling. For instance, Odysseus' wife Penelope is lauded for her faithfulness to her husband while waiting twenty years for him to return from Troy, but all the same, she is named as the mother of the Greek god Pan – by Hermes or Apollo or even by the 108 would-be suitors! Odysseus' son by Circe is Telegonus who accidentally kills his father. He marries Penelope while Penelope's son by Odysseus, Telemachus, marries Circe. Circe makes them all immortal, and they live on her island of Aeaea, presumably off the Tyrrhenian coast of Italy – possibly Ponza. The contradiction and convolution here are typical of the superabundance in our mythological heirloom from the Greco-Roman world.

One of the most enjoyable presentations and explorations of Hellenic mythology is to be found in Roberto Calasso's 1993 *The Marriage of Cadmus and Harmony* – essentially a must I feel for any pagan who has an interest with the Classical gods. In what amounts virtually to be a fantasy novel, the author refashions the Greek legacy in between fiction and philosophy. Drawing principally from Homer (the *Iliad* and *Odyssey*) who for the ancient Greeks was the ultimate authority but also from Nonnus (the *Dionysiaca*) and perhaps additionally everyone between these two, Calasso's gods are brutal, distant and fascinating but also fully human. Although he is critical of the Platonic tyranny which has led through the *scala naturae* or Ladder of Being to 'the Gospel invitation to reject the Prince of this world', Calasso appears to incorporate much Orphic theology along with the pointlessness of Homer's radiance into his own comprehension of the mythic narrative of the Greeks and Romans. Consequently, we hear of Zeus swallowing Phanes Protogonus and such other gnostic notions like self-impregnation and the cosmic egg. Although Calasso's focus is foremost upon the brief age of heroes (Theseus, Heracles, Orpheus, Achilles, Pelops, Jason, the Dioscuri, Oedipus and Odysseus), his mythic figures – both human and divine – possess an Orphic and cruel colouring.

My own comprehension of the gods and their accompanying but tantalising labyrinth of mythology differs from Calasso's. Most enjoyably, he writes in a unique and supremely beautiful manner, and I remain in full agreement with his contention that for the wakefulness of both the self and the world, constant attention to the gods is what is necessary. In addition, I resonate with his reference to the Olympians' 'inextinguishable laughter' and their preference for a more colourful and playful life. Against the nihilistic poison of both Buddhism and Christianity, the fullness of life itself is named as the divine antidote. To this end, the hermeneutics of mythology – differing for each of us – provides a key to enchantment and the wondrousness of both nature and supernature. It is the very inconsistency and paradoxical variety in the legacy of myth that allows us individually to interpret the cultural heritage in the manners that become commensurate to our own individual needs and understandings. For me personally, the deities are more immediate, amiable, accessible and even compassionate. Perhaps this is a development that is as much a product of modernity and the difference of our times with those of a pre-Christian past. Calasso himself cites the dawning of a post-Olympian era as the most modern of dangers, and if, as he contends, our relationship with the gods has progressed through the successive stages of conviviality, rape and now indifference, perhaps it is time to complete the cycle and return once again to being mutually hospitable and jovial with deity. While the Greek gods impose no commandments, in resecuring the infatuation and intensity of divine awareness, we must delve further back than the time corresponding to Calasso's depiction of the gods of Olympus as unnatural and dissatisfied with nature and its cycles. Instead of a supposed preference for autonomy of spirit on the part of autochthonous gods, more relevant today – and certainly more vital – is to reclaim the seminal origins of resplendent divinity in the things of the earth and nature herself. This last is an aesthetic and ritual project coupled with a redeveloped mental acuity that can discern and navigate between the visible and invisible. Within the liminal and beyond but equally with the here-and-now and a cultivation of the imagination, the gods may be found to operate despite the current secularisation that has come to prevail along with our social, cultural and technological advances. The gods and legendary heroes of Greece from Zeus' precarious contest with Typhon and his endless amorous adventures to Apollo and Artemis' unexpected callous extinguishing of Niobe's children, Dionysus' viticultural dismemberment and rejuvenation (the god being Pindar's 'pure light of midsummer'), and the adventurous heroic defeats of various monsters and enemies constitute a veritable carnival of primal and irrational encounters. The mythic characters of the ancient Greeks and Romans all together, with their metaphorizations and fabulations of sexual, aggressive, ethereal and questing impulses, along with their ability to fly and live forever, still allow for the discerning an entry into an aesthetic realm of sublime enchantment.

And it is probably important to acknowledge that, as we ourselves should also be doing, the gods are not fixed and static but grow and develop. Though *areté* or the excellence of virtue is still a preeminent, while for the ancient Greeks enjoyment itself presumably was not, a major pagan affirmation today has become the celebration of pleasure. Aristotle considered that happiness is the universal human goal, and for many – and especially for many pagans of our day – this includes sensual pleasures as well. Besides the gods themselves (Zeus, Hades, Athena, Apollo, Dionysus, Demeter, Kore, etc.), Calasso has focused variously on Theseus as the strong man *par excellence*, fleet foot and furiously tempered Achilles (nature's *enfant gâté*), crafty Odysseus the thinker, Cadmus the wanderer and alphabet-bringer, Heracles as a beast of burden, unhappy and vulnerable but intelligent Oedipus, as well as the pivotal tale involving Pelops and the Pelopids, and the sordid narrative of Jason and Medea. For psychologist Julian Jaynes (*The Origin of Consciousness in the Breakdown of the Bicameral Mind*, 1976), the heroes of the *Iliad* represent the earlier stage of humanity before the development of consciousness – the mental state capable of verbal hallucinations. By contrast, it is the hero of the *Odyssey* who displays the conscious awareness and introspection now typical of modern man.

Perhaps surprisingly, there is only the scantiest mention in *The Marriage of Cadmus and Harmony* of either the heroes Bellerophon or Perseus. In a battle with Dionysus, Perseus with the severed head of Medusa turns Ariadne to stone. Ariadne herself, having been deserted by Theseus, becomes the wife of Dionysus, and Calasso mentions her as having also been killed by Dionysus as well as by Artemis. On the other hand, there are versions in which Ariadne is apotheosised as the consort of Dionysus. Most likely she is also the Sun Goddess of Arinna (Arinniti), the spouse of the Hittite Weather-God, Tarhunna. As this last is the 'Dios of Nesa', the god of the Nesians or Hittites, and imported by the Greeks as a second Zeus, that is, Dionysus, Ariadne apparently continues the chthonian associations of her Anatolian counterpart. Once again, we see the tangled complexity of myth and its narrative developments. This last appears even further with Calasso's discussions concerning the only mortal daughter of Zeus, that is, Helen of Troy, whose enchantment he names as the power of the phantom and simulacrum. But beside the egg-born, laughing and charismatic Helen, it is perhaps Ariadne ('the resplendent one') who is currently the most relevant goddess today – especially as the partner of Tarhunna and the immortalised spouse of Dionysus. White-armed Helen too achieves immortality, and Achilles becomes her fifth husband in their afterlife together on Leúkē (the Island of the Blest) at the mouth of the Ister. But the crown that Dionysus gives to Ariadne upon their marriage is subsequently placed in the heavens as the constellation Corona Borealis (the 'northern crown'). For Calasso, the 'crown is nothing less than the highest, most exposed level of existence'. He sees it as the forerunner of the magic circle, and the irony of Ariadne's celestial crown now reappearing as the coronavirus that plagues humanity during the pandemic of 2020 opens the possibility of intriguing speculations concerning this intersection of the divine with terrestrial imbalance. We might pause here to reflect on the climate changes of our planet and the reduction of wildlife separation from the accelerating expansions of human settlement.

Calasso's retelling of the Greek myths is certainly controversial, and he has his critics. Some of his book I find deeply annoying if not also incorrect while other parts strike me as brilliant and captivating. For the American-Italian freelance writer Piero Scaruffi, the writing is disorganised and convoluted – full of statements that are 'ridiculously meaningless.' In contrast, the English scholar Winifred Mary Beard reviews in the *Times Literary Supplement* Calasso's achievement as 'Greek myth in a late twentieth-century guise, Greek myth for a modern imagination'. While Scaruffi condemns the mix of sources 'from wildly different places and ages with widely different meanings', the multiplicity and variation of myth are seen by others, including myself, as a great strength rather than weakness. For Calasso, myths are not challenges concerning belief but rather enchantment as 'the human sense of overwhelming awe before the power of deity'. Perhaps the Dutch critic, Ivar Hagendoorn, sums this up best when he declares Calasso's book as

> the greatest encouragement to reread those myths yourself and recreate them in all their variations from the different sources that come to us. Not only books, but also operas, architecture, novels and ballets. The myths and the gods are not dead. They continue to live on in us.

As Calasso himself expresses this: beyond the single gesture in which mythical figures differ from the characters in novels and instead their many lives and deaths are all present simultaneously, it is 'Only when we become aware of a sudden consistency between incompatibles can we say we have crossed the threshold of myth'.

The mythological legacies that are available to us today include not only that of the Greco-Roman Classical tradition but also what we might variously glean from the *Mabinogion* and the *Tain Bó Cuailgne,* the Icelandic *Poetic* and *Prose Eddas,* the *Rigveda* as well as the *Ramayana* and *Mahābhārata* epics, and – even further afield – the Hittite and Mesopotamian cuneiform texts, the Pyramid Texts and the Egyptian Book of the Dead, the Shinto *Kojiki* and *Nihon-gi,* and the Chinese dynasty literature of the Chuci, Zhou, Han, Tang and Song dynasties and including the Confucian Classics. Each of these offers opportunities for exploration and insight respectively or more widely as in the case of reconstructing an understanding of Proto-Indo-European spirituality. All the same, none of these sources are 'holy books' in the sense that the Bible, Quran and Orphic literature (hymns, theogonies) are considered to be. For Hindus, the *Vedas* rank as sacred texts, but Hinduism is a later development than Vedism itself and whose Rigvedic hymns are for the most part telluric rather than brahmanic.

Within a pagan mythological universe, the pulsating dynamic is one of epiphany and imagination. Life itself has no intrinsic meaning. It is instead pure experience – which may be thought of as a gift of the gods, especially with the experience of ecstasy but also in our capacity for simply 'living easily'. For Christians, life's meaning involves serving their god and attaining heaven. For a pagan, by contrast, heaven would be nice, but it does not provide meaning for life itself. While we may contribute to the flow of things, even interacting with the wider world, this still only constitutes a part of the ongoing narrative but without some final goal being at the end of the road. Perhaps at best, it is through the *nexus rerum* – what in the East is referred to as Indra's Net – namely the connection of everything with everything else that we might find the freedom to create meaning ourselves.

In the past, a god could appear as the Unknown Guest or the Stranger, and this remains a possibility even today. For Calasso, a sudden intensity suggests one's being brought into a god's sphere of influence, but this may also relate to what we seek through ritual and worship, namely, the dazzling splendour of realisation. If the ordinary and everyday are divine, so too is excess and those epiphanies through which the 'divine overwhelms life'. Myth itself is enchantment – not a faith but a magical spell. A large part of mythology celebrates *megalophyía*, that is, 'the greatness of nature'. In Calasso's estimation, art becomes perfect only when it looks like nature, and nature is most obvious when it conceals art within itself. He explains the Hellenic speciality as a concealing with light. While Scaruffi laments that there is nothing to be learned from Calasso's book, one of the author's most riveting moments for me is his presentation of the Greek *gános* 'brightness, gladness' – a word that is cognate with 'joy', 'enjoy' and 'rejoice' and derives from a root signifying being happy along with feelings of religious awe. An invocation to Diktaian Zeus on the stele for the Palaikastro Kouros of Minoan Crete is *pankratēs gánous* which Calasso translates as 'sovereign of the liquid splendour'. The *Etymologicon Magnum* lexicon inventories *gános* as water, joy, light, brilliance, whiteness and shimmering sparkle. As Calasso explains further:

> *Gános* is a substance, a feeling, a radiance. Zeus is made of *gános*: the Twelve Olympians are made of *gános*. Zeus is the sovereign of the radiant material with which he shapes himself and with which the circle of the Twelve is shaped round about him. A reflection of that substance shone in the statue that Zeus fashioned to hide the heart of Zagreus.

Other cognates to *gános* are 'gaudy' and 'ganosis'. The latter refers to the process of toning down the glare of marble such as for the nude parts of classical sculptures. With the Cypriotes, *gános* is another word for paradise beside *parádeisos*. Through its range of qualities from flashing light and joyful brilliance to fluid magnificence and the awesome, we have a quasi-equivalent for *tellurique* that describes the invisible but concentrated magical emanation of earth that is precisely matter mattering, the divinely rapturous aura of the physical. The very treasure trove of mythology as art intersects with nature at the core of a pagan understanding.

The violence of the Greek Age of Heroes is almost astonishing until we reflect on history and the insurrections and terrorisms let alone the wars and governmental suppressions of today. In that brief period between the Age of Bronze and the Age of Iron, the celebrated deaths were those of combat, usually in a one-to-one confrontation, though there is also Medea's killing of Apsyrtes, Glauce, Alcimenes and Tisander, Agamemnon's sacrifice of Iphigeneia, Clytemnestra's murder of Agamemnon, and Orestes' matricide of Clytemnestra among many others. In 1960, I passed a wonderful summer school in Berkeley studying French and Philosophy. I frequently did my work in the UC Berkeley Library. One afternoon, I heard strange shooting-like sounds from the next room. I watched the librarian leave from her desk to enter the adjacent hall and then saw her rush back to grab the telephone. I then went myself to see what had happened. I found a group of people who were gathered near a young student who looked at first as if she were resting her head on her open books. She must have had a cold as an opened box of Kleenex sat on the table next to her work, but blood was pouring from her head from the bullets that had just been shot by a fellow she had rejected and had had a court order placed upon to stop him from pursuing her. She looked as if she was convulsively attempting to breathe. As the blood continued to cover the table, her body slithered to the floor where the murderer was also lying after having subsequently shot himself. When the emergency service arrived, they took him first since he was still alive and later recovered. I remember wanting them to take her instead. Back at my rooming house afterwards, my roommate asked what I had been doing. 'Watching people die in the Library', I replied. 'Oh, metaphorically?' he then said. 'No, literally', I answered. The next evening at the dinner table after the newspapers had reported the event, the other boarders asked why I hadn't said anything the night before, but I could not have at the time.

I have another memory from about six years later – this time in San Francisco. Nancy and I had just returned from visiting her sister in Santa Barbara. Nancy had already gone ahead to the North Beach flat near Grant Avenue. We had brought a huge amount of lemons that we had picked from Pat's trees in her garden in the south. As I was crossing the street on the slope of Telegraph Hill with the lemons, the paper bag ripped, and an avalanche of lemons began rolling all the way down the block and marching across Grant. Numerous Chinese people rushed out of their apartments and began catching the bouncing lemons – some waist-high. I found Nancy on the floor of the flat laughing in hysterics. She had not actually seen what had happened but had pictured it already in her mind. Later as we set out, 'There's one!' I exclaimed as I picked up a lemon caught behind a car's tyre.

Perhaps not the sublime to the ridiculous but the sorrowful to the humorous. How much of life encompasses both or all four possibilities? I think it was still my high school years; I was with my mother, brother and sister on the bus from Maplewood to downtown Newark. The traffic came to virtual standstill. We learned that the reason was a fatality ahead. A lorry carrying gigantic concrete sewer pipes had broken loose when the driver had stopped for a traffic light and rolled forward breaking his neck at the wheel of the vehicle. It was the first time I had seen a deceased person. My mother covered the eyes of my little sister with her hands, and then shortly later Mother fainted. In Germany, in the Grafing cemetery that I would frequently cut through when returning at night from München to my Goethe-Institut room, the chapel on occasion would have a corpse on display – a German custom. I saw a lot more in Munich itself when I visited a mausoleum – all on show as if in a zoo. I have seen my brother and my father in their coffins. Fortunately, I did not get to see my mother after her death. And during my extended visit to Acapulco in 1967, after a supremely amorous night, in the morning my *tryst d'amour* was informed that his grandfather had just died, and I remember seeing the man on display. I was with dear Donald with my hands on him when he passed. There was also Jacqueline's funeral in Amsterdam, but she did not look to be herself. I have always been grateful to Jackie concerning the purchase of the farm in Friesland. She knew that a Dutch contract becomes invalid if it contains a *verborgen gebreek,* a 'hidden flaw'. This is what saved us; the property had already been condemned. And in America (Boston I believe), I have been to Gunther von Hagens' Body Worlds exhibition before it came permanently to London. For me, once was enough. And, of course, I have seen Egyptian mummies as well as the video of the murder of George Floyd. At one point when I was much younger, I wanted to work for a while in a funeral home so that death and the dead body would become commonplace to me. That never happened, and I surmise that a corpse for me is still a numinous entity that evokes a strange and even unsettling mix of a person and a non-person.

My real encounter with the dead has occurred in Banaras. As Shiva's fire from which most pyres are lit is most likely the oldest continual fire that humanity has maintained, it always drew me as one of the city's three most sacred sites. The Gyan Vapi hill has itself been appropriated by Islam and no longer serves a ritual function for Hindus, but the Gyan Vapi or Well of Wisdom, adjacent to the equally sacred Vishvanath Temple that houses the Great Lord's phallus, is symbolically and metaphorically where the Primordial Male entered Mother Earth, and all creation ensued. These are all magical, numinous places – supreme concentrations of what Robert Corrington refers to as 'semiotic plenitude'. The Jalsain Burning Ghat of Shiva and its accompanying rituals are designed to insure for the departed the transition to whatever is to follow. As photographer Pete McBride expresses it, these funeral practices on the banks of the Ganges river are raw and transparent. Death here is celebrated as a part of life – an important part, yes, but nothing unusual. None of us get out of this alive. It's the one commonality so far that we all share until perhaps technology alters even that for a wealthy few.

If I were to recollect moments of sublimity in my life, there would be most likely more than I can remember. The first that come to mind, however, are my shamanic experiences with peyote and LSD – San Francisco, Amsterdam, the Provence, Rome, India, New Orleans and the American East Coast. The whole Haight-Ashbury phenomenon alone was an incredible and amazing whirlwind. With it, we had Woodstock, Tenino, the Isle of Wight – indescribable to today's mind that is preoccupied with maintaining the precarious balance between freedom and security. Our flower power duration through space and time was a collective smiling spirit that was both a supreme ecstasy and, at best, our legacy to those who come after us. I have known the joy of collective bonding with festival and Burning Man hordes, I have danced with Pan to the otherworldly melodies of an ethereal ancient Greece, I have walked wide-eyed through the kaleidoscopic but intimate slums of San Juan, I have watched the Turangalila moon set in the wee, wee hours of a Midi's summer night, I have worshipped in the Foro Romano and on the Palatine Hill, I have been endazzled by lightening dew drops along the banks of a Dutch canal, I have sat rapturously on the colourful strands of a cosmic cobweb, I have convulsed gleefully with emancipated abandon in the Bay Area, I have capered along the Kashi Coast in song, I have paid honour to Marie Laveau's place of rest and deeply inhaled the incomparable scents of Nola, I have laughed uncontrollably from a Manhattan lift, and I have indulged in extramundane delight while embraced by a Goulimine hot spring. If and when I think back, my high school days were purely ecstatic and much of my college days were as well. Travelling can be onerous and difficult at times, but overall the journeys have provided the thrill of discovery, adventure and euphoria. Teaching could be work but the actual encounter with learning faces and student exchange falls mostly to the realm of elation. And the times and meals and celebrations with friends and loved ones have constituted for me the relentless and continual rhythm of sublimity that has underpinned my life. What animates all these places and times of joy is that 'luminous splendour' of jouissance – virtually something quasi-physical and flowing. Perhaps this could be an accidental gift from Fortuna or of sheer chance, but I thank the gods themselves for the blissful gratitude that I have enjoyed for most of my life.

I kissed Marie-Hélène in Istanbul where we met. Her dream was to come to America, and when she sailed into New York, I had asked my parents if they could meet her. And bless them, they made a sign with her name on it, and she saw it when her ship arrived. Once arriving in California, she has lived in the state ever since. And recently she came across a letter I had written to her from Zeist on the 17th of April 1973 – just short of two years before Richard and I began our relationship. With Richard, our first four years were not easy. It was two independent souls attempting to adjust to the other, and it became a saga of one of us packing his bags and storming off – until we finally agreed to institute a truce. But before this, I wrote the following to Marie-Hélène:

> Where to begin? What to say? Your letter touched on so many issues – fundamental ones, but it was good in that it conveyed so much about you. Not that you are now any less a stranger, but perhaps a slightly better-known stranger as a result. I think we are all strangers and probably always remain such. If we're lucky, perhaps we develop an accustomedness with one or a few individual(s). And then we learn to accept the other's strangenesses and cope with them or even love them because of what they are and what there is of them we cannot know. I miss my brother. I knew him better than any other individual and he me. But he was tired of it all – or at least in the frantic race which has become twentieth century 'living', he had his understandable moments of being tired of it all. When he told me his plan, I could not argue with him. His defense was my own argument. Yet I'm still here. Why? I'm not really sure. When it had come right down to that moment, with no explanation I wanted to live – and still basically do. I hate it, yes – the endlessly accelerating syndrome, the inequalities, the waste and destruction, the increasing inability to find release and peace and rest and quiet. But still I go on.
>
> If I was not before, I have become a paradox. Moreover, I hate wanting what I cannot have and not wanting what I do have. I am rich in spite of

all the relativity involved with that term and my 'richness' is a direct product of that capitalistic system I abhor. But I do not look the gift horse in the mouth – or at least kick it in the mouth. I am an excellent rationalizer – that being perhaps my one great talent. I find that life has placed me in a completely unique [sic.] position. And so I live that position. I am weird and am reconciled to the realization that regardless of whatever age [in which] I may have lived, I would have been a total oddity within it. Wherever I go, people immediately sense my weirdness and react to it. Consequently, I am very much alone. But this is my life style – and as a product of the capitalistic system, I can simply be what I am, and that in itself would be enough to fight against the system – that in itself would be my part in the 'revolution'. Of course, I endeavor to do more, but I accept the comforts and pleasures I am fortunate enough to experience, and I utilize my relative freedom and mobility to acquire more information and insight leading toward that optimistic spot of sunlight through all the pessimistic mist and clouds.

I do not believe in a world of deprivation, but I also realize that payment must exist for the advancement of us all – even if that advancement belongs only to a minority now. Everything balances. The African may work 16 hours a day to die of hunger, but the Whitey lives 16+ neurotic hours a day to die of cancer or some other such disease as the product of his longer but infinitely more frenzied and frustrated life. And the really rich live in a constant state of fear or live the archetypal predicaments embodied in classical myth (e.g., Phaedra, Oedipus, Orestes, etc.)

Consequently and although I still (regardless of the paradox) believe very much in this life, I believe in something beyond or other than this life – embodied ubiquitously within it and recognized one way or another and often extremely subtly by various traditions of mankind. Whether it is what I see which makes me a social misfit or whether it is my being a social misfit which allows or enables me to see what I do see, what I am touching upon is 'shamanism'. Of course I do not live in (the so-called) primitive society, so what this becomes is (what I also feel is critically needed and that is) 'urban shamanism'. Consequently I can only fight my past to the degree it blocks the way toward the kind of life I see as of value, but I cannot fight my past to the degree it enables me to be in the position I am.

Perhaps as a brief statement though not as a complete resumé I can say that I am against:

Nixon
Pollution
Advertising
The expanding market and constantly-increasing-profits enterprise of Capitalism
Democracy – or especially democracy in the super-state
The Super State
The Nation-State

> The Levantine religions: Judaism, Christianity, Islam, and Parsiism
> and
> Violence
>
> I have a lukewarm respect for Buddhism but will not push it further, and possibly the same goes for LSD. I favor: aristocracy in the true sense of the word; royal families; grass, alcohol and abstinence in blended order; an occasional 'red'; and sunny days.
>
> I might add that I am not always as depressed as I currently am. I hope you are surviving America. It was good to hear from you. Hello to Rick.

What is surprising when I now read this letter I wrote almost a half-century ago is how little different my overall thought has continued to be. Perhaps I am not depressed, though I still find much too much of our present world depressing. I am unabashedly happy with my love and relationship with Richard. And my pagan affirmation is greatly stronger after living the greater part of my life in awareness of the earth's intrinsic enchantment, the beauty of myth and the power of sacred place and time. But the teacher's beheading in a north-western Paris suburb because of addressing the freedom of expression and the freedom to believe and not believe allows that the freedom of speech and belief are sacrosanct in French society and for the Western heritage of democratic rights. The former *Charlie Hebdo* journalist Maya Oppenheim circumscribes our problem the most succinctly when she says, 'We cannot win a war because it is an asymmetric war, between reason on one side and madness on the other side'. Christianity has at least progressed to some extent since the 'Burning Times' of the Middle Ages, but Israel's abuse of Palestinians and Islam's ISIL, Al Qaeda and jihadism continue a 'mad war' against any likelihood of humane global progress and effort toward a transcendence of divisive factionalism. While he espouses a form of paganism with which I am not in accord, Julius Evola has nevertheless predicted to Frank Gelli that 'What is repressed invariably returns. . . . the true father of the Turkish nation is Islam. Muhammed, if you like. Never mind how repressed such heritage may be in today's secular Turkey, within your lifetime things will change radically. . . . It will be so'. He saw the inevitable resurgence of Islam and the *Khilafa* or Caliphate. 'When the Islamic awakening comes, the Arabs will bounce back but not before'.

While Gelli argues in his *Julius Evola: The Sufi of Rome* (2012) that Evola, as part of his Malamatiyya sect of Islamic mysticism, sought deliberately to create a controversial and disreputable reputation, namely, the metaphysical mythology for which he has become known, he advocates a supra-rational intellectual intuition along the lines of Plato, Aquinas and Heidegger. Influenced by the traditionalist René Guénon, Evola developed his doctrine of 'two natures': the natural world and a primordial 'world of Being' – connected by the Neoplatonic 'great chain of Being' and imposing form and quality on what is referred to as 'lower matter'. Evola belonged to the *Gruppo di Ur* or 'Ur Group' that sought to revive ancient Roman religion by employing Buddhist, Tantric and Hermetic techniques. This may sound interesting and attractive to some, but the preference is a *Männerbund* founded upon a hypermasculine warrior ethos in which women's identity is to be found in total subjugation to men. This Traditionalist School which has adopted Nazi *völkisch* ideology seeks to separate aristocracy from 'commoners' along the lines of an allegedly organic but hierarchical and anti-democratic anti-individualism. This belief and practice are nonetheless to be found under the name of paganism, but they represent a much different expression than the predominant, and my preference for, an understanding of an immanent, horizontal spirituality that resists imperialism, fascism, racism, anti-semitsm and an anti-modernity *per se* for, instead, the values of freedom, human rights and a morality that encompasses a sense of universal enchantment. In short, a telluric materialism rather than gnostic escapism – natural growth in lieu of transcendent esoterica, this world even with all its flaws in place of the 'higher' and intellectually over-inflated. In pagan paganism, it becomes a love for tradition instead of the proclamation of Tradition with a capital T – Tradition and Transcendence.

Gelli's presentation of Evola ceaselessly refers to the vertical perspective of the 'higher'. The Pelasgic descendent is 'a defective, botched type of individual' whereas the true seeker after the beautiful allegedly 'moves from the lowest level of earthly drives and desires and ascends to [the] upper regions'. But even the actions of the far-right Norwegian terrorist, Anders Behring Breivik, are cited as illustrating Evola's destructive 'third aspect of the Transcendent.' The enemy is declared to be Western modernity and includes the Enlightenment, freemasonry, secularisation, relativism, republicanism, socialism, communism, Abu Bakr al-Razi, Gotthold Ephraim Lessing, Thomas Hobbes, the Utilitarians (Jeremy Bentham and J. S. Mill are mentioned along with Epicurus), Arthur Schopenhauer, Voltaire, Denis Diderot, Albert Camus, Jean-Paul Sartre, Umberto Eco, Gamal Abdel Nasser, the *Beat* generation and even Aleister Crowley. Evola is cited as saying that the 'biological is almost nothing' – what is of supreme importance is 'the non-material, the intangible, the soul, the spirit'. While I agree that American Neo-Cons and Leo Strauss are grotesque and that our task is indeed the restoration of the sacred, I do not subscribe to the idea that the French assertion of *liberté, égalité, fraternité* is an 'unholy trinity'. Perhaps the only other thing I might agree with Evola on is his belief that coitus is as much about ecstasy as it is about reproduction, and while I have my own criticisms of Schopenhauer, Sartre, Eco and Crowley as well as capitalism, I surmise that Evola's reputation as an ultra-fascist, racist and anti-Semitic chauvinist preclude any acceptance of him in the development and restoration of contemporary pagan thought. Gelli seeks to portray his youthful master as a professor of *Tasawwuf* or, more specifically, one who employs the 9th century *malamattiya* strategy of seeking purification and exaltation through blame and shame and who endeavours to develop oneself into a malevolent outcaste figure that can engender the scorn and hostility of others. Maybe so, and maybe Evola was employing a Sufi teaching method that uses only hints, allusions and suggestions rather than dogmatic assertion. He did predict, apparently correctly, the imminent resurgence of Islam and that the Uighurs would become China's nemesis. This becomes a threat, however, not only to Western values but also to the earth-centred pantheistic/polytheistic orientations of paganism as well. I am still much more firmly in accord with al-Razi's consideration of Moses, Jesus and Mohammed as the 'Three Imposters'.

Perhaps, thanks to Prudence Priest, the following Einsteinian understanding of Spinoza's pantheism says it best for telluric spirituality. I have pluralised 'God' into 'the gods', but the original idea remains the same:

> The gods would say:
>
> Stop praying. What we want you to do is go out into the world and enjoy your life. We want you to sing, have fun and enjoy everything we've made for you. Stop going into those dark, cold temples that you built yourself and saying they are our house. Our house is in the mountains, in the woods, rivers, lakes, beaches. That's where we live, and there we express our love for you.
>
> Stop blaming us for your miserable life; we never told you there was anything wrong with you or that you were a sinner, or that your sexuality was a bad thing. Sex is a gift we have given you and with which you can express your love, your ecstasy, your joy. So don't blame us for everything they made you believe.
>
> Stop reading alleged sacred scriptures that have nothing to do with us. If you can't read us in a sunrise, in a landscape, in the look of your friends, in your son's eyes... you will find us in no book!

Stop asking us 'will you tell me how to do my job?' Stop being so scared of us. We do not judge you or criticize you, nor get angry, or bothered. We are pure love.

Stop asking for forgiveness, there's nothing to forgive. If we made you... we filled you with passions, limitations, pleasures, feelings, needs, inconsistencies... free will. How can we blame you if you respond to something we put in you? How can we punish you for being the way you are, if we're the one who made you? Do you think we could create a place to burn all our children who behave badly for the rest of eternity? What kind of god would do that?

Respect your peers and don't do what you don't want for yourself. All we ask is that you pay attention in your life, that alertness is your guide.

Our beloved, this life is not a test, not a step on the way, not a rehearsal, nor a prelude to paradise. This life is the only thing here and now and it is all you need.

We have set you absolutely free, no prizes or punishments, no sins or virtues, no one carries a marker, no one keeps a record.

You are absolutely free to create in your life. Heaven or hell.

We can't tell you if there's anything after this life but we can give you a tip. Live as if there is not. As if this is your only chance to enjoy, to love, to exist.

So, if there's nothing after, then you will have enjoyed the opportunity we gave you. And if there is, rest assured that we won't ask if you behaved right or wrong, we'll ask. Did you like it? Did you have fun? What did you enjoy the most? What did you learn?...

Stop believing in us; believing is assuming, guessing, imagining. We don't want you to believe in us, we want you to believe in you. We want you to feel us in you when you kiss your beloved, when you tuck in your little girl, when you caress your dog, when you bathe in the sea.

Stop praising us, what kind of egomaniac gods do you think we are?

We're bored being praised. We're tired of being thanked. Feeling grateful? Prove it by taking care of yourself, your health, your relationships, the world. Express your joy! That's the way to praise us.

Stop complicating things and repeating as a parakeet what you've been taught about the godhead.

What do you need more miracles for? So many explanations?

The only thing for sure is that you are here, that you are alive, that this world is full of wonders.

So, whether one reads this textual insert in the wording of Einstein's humorous version depicting a personalised pantheistic God or as my emended polytheistic transcription, the pagan message of enjoyment, singing, fun, nature, sexuality, ecstasy, free will, lack of eternal punishment, the Golden Rule, mindful alertness, learning, self-belief, health, the here-and-now, freedom and the world's wondrousness is what is to be grasped here as telluric spirituality itself. Remembering Calasso, maybe the 'pure love' idea is pushing things too far. And for me at least, for expressing gratitude is why the gods as vehicles exist in the first place. But the intrinsic rejection of the one-eyed from Bentham's panopticon to Odin's non-dimensional vision is integral to the kind of organic liberation that I think most pagans are after.

Nevertheless, pagans tend to be as political as anyone else. Some of this spills into the likes of cancel culture, the Me Too movement, boycotts of artists, the culpability of colonialism and so forth. Much of current protest is valid and necessary for humanitarian progress. With the spiralling ascension of social media, however, public discourse often appears to become increasingly restricted. The bandwagon promotion of various ideologies is one consequence. Another is the distorted re-interpretation of our mythological and classical legacy. A recent example of this last is New York's Collect Pond Park erection of Luciano Garbati's *Medusa With The Head of Perseus*. As a Hellene and follower of ancient Greek religion, Chris Aldridge points out that apart for Ovid's version of the Gorgon's tale, in Greek myth itself from Hesiod on, 'There is not a single word of rape, a temple, or being unjustly punished for it'. He sees the statue as a promotion of a reverse sexism. For myself, Perseus is a fully honourable hero, and the only part of his mythic narrative I do not appreciate is Nonnus making him responsible for the death of Ariadne during a battle with Dionysus. Otherwise, his killing of Medusa serves as a prelude to his rescue of Andromeda ('ruler of men') from a monster. This compares with the St. George and the Dragon legend. Andromeda herself represents the possibility of black ethnicity and, through the etymology of her name, an ascendency of the female. Together, she and Perseus become the parents of seven sons and two daughters as well as the grandparents of Heracles. Consequently, for me, Garbati's creation is a violation of a significant ancient narrative that conforms simply to currently fashionable political thinking. But for all that, the Garbati piece probably functions little differently than the Charlie Hebdo cartoons of Mohammed. Offensive to some religious thought but expressions of the freedom of expression for which the French school teacher, Samuel Paty, has recently been martyred. Paganism is, verily, at the forefront of religion that does not entertain the possibility of blasphemy.

ADDENDUM

Upon further thought, however, my previously concluding statement that "Paganism is, verily, at the forefront of religion that does not entertain the possibility of blasphemy" is not completely true. The word *blasphemy* itself is Greek and signifies the 'speaking of evil'. As *The Oxford Dictionary of World Religions* elucidates, it refers to 'Impious or profane talk, especially against God; and in many [Western] legal systems, the offense of reviling God or Jesus Christ or an established church'. In this sense, my conclusion in reference to paganism is true. Scornful disparagement or verbal offense is inapplicable to pagan countenance. Essentially, however, what I have in mind is the expression from childhood that 'Sticks and stones may break my bones but words will never hurt me'. Likewise, one cannot blaspheme the other-world. Interestingly, the dictionary connects blasphemy only to Christianity, Judaism and Islam. But extending the written/speaking aspect of blasphemy, more broadly it concerns sacrilege, originally, 'the theft of sacred objects'. From a pagan perspective, sacrilege or blasphemy exists in the violation of the earth – including harming both humanity and the biotic communities. What is sacred from the earth religion perspective is both space and place, nature herself, and heedless pollution, the wanton destruction of the environment with its 'levelling' and contamination through pesticides and chemical fertilisers, human-engineered climate change, rainforest clearing and excessive artificial lighting let alone war, terrorism, dictatorship, Holocene extinction, racism, resource exploitation and avoidable inequity are all desecrations against the natural balance of Mother Earth and her inhabitants. So, while the blasphemous in its traditional sense is an obsolete and discardable concept for a pagan spirit, the parameters of the ecological remain sacrosanct. Their transgression is very much an operative instance of blasphemy.